# CONTEMPORARY LINGUISTIC ANALYSIS

## AN INTRODUCTION

### SIXTH EDITION

Edited by

## William O'Grady
University of Hawaii

and

## John Archibald
University of Calgary

PEARSON
Longman

Toronto

**Library and Archives Canada Cataloguing in Publication**

Contemporary linguistic analysis : an introduction / edited by William O'Grady and John Archibald.—6th ed.

Includes bibliographical references and index.
ISBN 978-0-321-47666-1

  1. Linguistics—Textbooks.  I. O'Grady, William D. (William Delaney), 1952–
II. Archibald, John, 1959–

P126.C66 2008     410     C2008-900174-5

ISBN-13: 978-0-321-47666-1
ISBN-10:    0-321-47666-2

Grateful acknowledgment is made to copyright holders for permission to reproduce copyright material.

Permission to reprint material from C.L. Baker's article in *Language 71* (1996):63–101 granted by the Linguistic Society of America.

Vice President, Editorial Director: Gary Bennett
Executive Acquisitions Editor: Christine Cozens
Sponsoring Editor: Carolin Sweig
Executive Marketing Manager: Judith Allen
Senior Developmental Editor: Jennifer Murray
Production Editor: Avivah Wargon
Copy Editor and Proofreader: Pam Erlichman
Production Coordinator: Avinash Chandra
Composition: Integra
Permissions Research: Leigh Bennett
Art Director: Julia Hall
Interior Design: Dave McKay
Cover Design: Kerrin Hands
Cover Image: Veer Incorporated

2 3 4 5    12 11 10 09

Printed and bound in United States of America.

PEARSON
Longman

*To the memory of our friend and colleague*
*Ewa Iwanicka*
*1950–1986*

*Convinced at once that, in order to break loose from the beaten paths of opinions and systems, it was necessary to proceed in my study of man and society by scientific methods, and in a rigorous manner, I devoted one year to philology and grammar; linguistics, or the natural history of speech, being, of all the sciences, that which best suited the researches which I was about to commence.*

PIERRE-JOSEPH PROUDHON, *WHAT IS PROPERTY?* (1840)

# Brief Contents

# Contents

# Preface

From its inception, the basic goal of *Contemporary Linguistic Analysis* has been to provide an up-to-date introduction to the discipline of linguistics while at the same time providing coverage of phenomena that are of special interest and relevance to the linguistic situation in Canada. (Indeed, *Contemporary Linguistic Analysis* was the first textbook to offer such a focus.)

These dual objectives have grown increasingly challenging in recent years, as work in the various subdisciplines of linguistics becomes more technical and far-reaching. As the size of the textbook increased in response to these trends, it has been necessary to search for new solutions to the problem of just how much an introductory textbook can and should cover. One innovation, adopted in the fifth edition and continued in this new edition, involves placing more advanced material on our Companion Website (**www.pearsoned.ca/ogrady**) rather than in the textbook itself. This allows instructors and students easy access to more challenging or detailed material, while keeping the size and complexity of the text within reasonable bounds.

It has often been difficult to decide where to draw the line between essential and advanced material, of course, and we now have some appreciation of what it feels like to be the Minister of Finance in tough economic times. The pressing need to reduce and restructure is constantly challenged by cries of "Don't cut there." After much experimentation and compromise (a Canadian virtue if ever there was one), we have arrived at a division of labour that we all—editors, referees, and publisher—feel reasonably comfortable with. We hope that this will still allow instructors the flexibility to create the kind of introductory course that they want for their students.

In the end, of course, no textbook can do everything. Nonetheless, we hope that our book will provide students not only with an initiation into the intricacies of scientific linguistic analysis, but also with a greater appreciation of the wonder of human language, the variety and complexity of its structure, and the subtlety of its use.

## New to This Edition

The sixth edition has been modified to reflect changes in the discipline as well as comments from faculty and students who used the fifth edition. Quite extensive revisions have been made to the following chapters:

- phonology,
- morphology,
- syntax, and
- language acquisition.

We are also happy to present **a completely rewritten chapter on sociolinguistics**. Throughout the text, we have reworked the writing style in an attempt to make it more accessible. In order to make way for these changes and for new "lighter" material of general interest (in the form of **Language Matters boxes**), we have moved the chapter on animal communication to the Companion Website.

# Acknowledgments

As has been the case since its inception, *Contemporary Linguistic Analysis* has benefited from the comments, advice, and assistance of many people. Since the early 1980s, when this project was first conceived, we have enjoyed extraordinary support from our publisher's executive team, first at Copp Clark, later at Addison Wesley Longman, and now at Pearson Education Canada. We would particularly like to acknowledge the pioneering efforts of Les Petriw, Brian Henderson, Jeff Miller, and the late Linda Scott and Steve Mills. Preparation of the current edition was made possible through the extraordinary efforts of the Pearson Education team, especially Jennifer Murray, Carolin Sweig, and Avivah Wargon.

Heartfelt thanks are also due to the many colleagues and students who have taken the time to offer their suggestions and corrections: (in alphabetical order) Jennifer Abel, Mark Aronoff, Howard Aronson, Peter Avery, Henry Bain, Keira Ballantyne, Byron Bender, Derek Bickerton, Chad Blecke, Didier Bloch, Vaiana Bloch, Robert Blust, Vit Bubenik, Patrick Burke, Ed Burstynsky, Gary Byma, Andrew Carnie, Steven Carey, Jack Chambers, Harold Chester, Shuji Chiba, Matthew Christian, Vanna Condax, Eung-Do Cook, Lynda Costello, John Davison, John DeFrancis, Denise Devenuto, Michael Dobrovolsky, Nicole Domingue, Elan Dresher, Matthew Dryer, Karine Dupuis, Carrie Dyck, Sheila Embleton, Evile Feleti, Robert Fisher, Laura Paterson Forbes, Michael Forman, Donald Frantz, Ali Al Ghail, Inge Genee, Donna Gerdts, Kevin Gregg, John Haiman, Alice Harris, Margaret Hayes, John Hewson, Joyce Hildebrand, Darin Howe, Robert Hsu, David Ingram, Ricky Jacobs, Kazue Kanno, Brian King, James Kirchner, Dawn Lee, Jinhwa Lee, Hsiu-chuan Liao, Gary Libben, Anatole Lyovin, Mary C. Marino, Barry Meislin, Yves-Charles Morin, Woody Mott, Robert Murray, Judith Nylvek, Michael O'Grady, George Patterson, Mary Pepper, David Peterson, Marilyn Philips, Terry Pratt and the students in his linguistics course at the University of Prince Edward Island, R. Radhakrishnan, Lawrence Reid, Keren Rice, Lorna Rowsell, Yutaka Sato, Coral Sayce, Albert Schütz, Carson Schütze, Peter Seyffert, Patricia Shaw, Ronald Southerland, Lois Stanford, Stanley Starosta, Leone Sveinson, Allison Teasdale, Alain Thomas, Charles Ulrich, Tim Vance, Theo Venneman, Douglas Walker, Lydia White, Norio Yamada, and Nava Zvaig.

Thanks are also due to the professors across Canada who read and commented on individual sixth-edition chapters and sections, including (in alphabetical order)

Cliff Burgess, Simon Fraser University
Annette Dominik, University College of the Cariboo
Inge Genee, University of Lethbridge
Sandra P. Kirkham, University of Victoria
Julia Peters, Grant MacEwan College
Nima Sadat-Tehrani, University of Manitoba
Eta Schneiderman, University of Ottawa
Magda Stroinska, McMaster University
Annette Teffeteller, Concordia University
Yanfeng Qu, Kwantlen University College
Gerard Van Herk, York University

Finally, we owe a special debt of gratitude to our superb copy editor, Pamela Erlichman, for advice and good cheer over the past years. Her dedication and talent (not to mention her willingness to sacrifice yet another Christmas vacation) have kept this project on course through five editions now and have contributed in countless substantial ways to its success.

## Supplements to the Text

*Contemporary Linguistic Analysis: An Introduction*, Sixth Edition, offers a number of supplements that will enrich both the professor's presentation of introductory linguistics and the student's understanding of it.

### Instructor Supplements

■ **Answer Key** (ISBN 978-0-321-55610-3). The Answer Key that accompanies *Contemporary Linguistic Analysis* contains solutions to the series of exercises found at the end of each chapter in the textbook.

### Student Supplements

■ **Study Guide** (ISBN 978-0-321-50281-0) Each Study Guide chapter lists the main topics and/or concepts discussed in the textbook and features a series of exercises designed to help you understand the core concepts.
■ **Companion Website (www.pearsoned.ca/ogrady)** Organized by textbook chapter number, the new website features advanced material relating to many topics covered in the textbook.

### New to the Website (www.pearsoned.ca/ogrady)

■ **Audio exercise files**
We have added sound files to accompany the textbook for the first time. This will be a resource primarily for the Phonetics chapter, but we plan on building this repository to provide support for other chapters. Students will be able to listen to exercises for transcription and hear pronunciations of the phonetic symbols used in the text.

■ **The chapter on animal communication**
Placing this more advanced content on the website, rather than in the textbook, allows instructors and students easy access to more challenging or detailed material, while keeping the size and complexity of the text within reasonable bounds.

# *About this book*

Thanks to the application of rigorous analysis to familiar subject matter, linguistics provides students with an ideal introduction to the kind of thinking we call "scientific." Such thinking proceeds from an appreciation of problems arising from bodies of data, to hypotheses that attempt to account for those problems, to the careful testing and extension of these hypotheses. But science is more than a formal activity. One of the great pleasures offered introductory students of linguistics is the discovery of the impressive body of subconscious knowledge that underlies language use. This book attempts to emphasize the extent of this knowledge as well as to introduce the scientific methodology used in linguistic analysis.

Although this is the first linguistics textbook designed primarily for a Canadian readership, we have tried to do much more than simply provide coverage of linguistic phenomena peculiar to Canada. As the title suggests, we have attempted an introduction to linguistic analysis as it is practised at this stage in the development of our discipline. While we do not ignore or reject other fruitful approaches to linguistics, we have taken the generative paradigm as basic for two reasons. First, generative linguistics provides a relatively coherent and integrated approach to basic linguistic phenomena. Phonetics, phonology, morphology, syntax, and semantics are viewed within this framework, as perhaps in no other, as fully integrated and interrelated. Second, the generative approach has been widely influential in its application to a broad range of other linguistic phenomena over the past twenty years.

The extent of our "contemporariness" has been limited by the inevitable compromise between the need to present basic concepts and the demands of sophisticated and competing recent approaches. In many cases, early versions of our chapters were judged "too contemporary" by instructors who were not specialists in the subfields in question. This led to substantial revisions and a somewhat more traditional approach to certain issues than was originally intended. Where possible, however, later sections of the chapters and our Companion Website present more contemporary material. In this way, we have attempted to provide what is promised by the title—an introductory text that provides a solid grounding in basic linguistic concepts, but one that also prepares the student to go on to current work in the discipline. To the extent possible, we have attempted to integrate the basic mechanisms outlined in the first five chapters of the book into our discussion of phenomena in later chapters. Thus, our discussion of semantics, historical linguistics, first and second language acquisition, psycholinguistics, and neurolinguistics draws to some degree on the notions presented in our introduction to generative grammar.

No textbook can be all things to all users. We hope that this book will provide students not only with a springboard to the realm of scientific linguistic analysis, but with a greater appreciation of the wonder of human language, the variety and complexity of its structure, and the subtlety of its use.

# List of technical abbreviations

| | | | |
|---|---|---|---|
| * | (in front of words or sentences) unacceptable | L2 | second language |
| # | word boundary | LN | last name |
| 1 | first person | Loc | locative case |
| 1 | primary stress | Loc | location |
| 2 | second person | M | mid tone |
| 2 | secondary stress | N | noun |
| 3 | third person | N | nucleus |
| A | adjective | Nom | nominative case |
| Abl | ablative case | NP | noun phrase |
| Abs | absolutive case | O | (direct) object |
| Acc | accusative case | O | onset |
| Adv | adverb | Obl | oblique |
| AdvP | adverb phrase | OE | Old English |
| Af | affix | P | preposition, postposition |
| ag | agent | Pass | passive |
| AP | adjective phrase | PCA | Principal Components Analysis |
| Aux | auxiliary verb | PET | Positron Emission Tomography |
| B | bound root | PIE | Proto-Indo-European |
| C | complementizer | pl | plural |
| C | consonant | PP | prepositional phrase |
| caus | cause | PR | phonetic representation |
| CG | constricted glottis | Prs | present tense |
| cmpl | completed action | Pst | past tense |
| $C_0$ | any number of consonants | R | rhyme |
| Co | coda | R | rounded |
| Com | comitative | RC | relative cause |
| CP | complementizer phrase | REA | right ear advantage |
| CT | computerized axial tomography | recip | recipient |
| DA | derivational affix | S | sentence |
| Dat | dative case | S | subject |
| Deg | degree word | σ | syllable |
| DR | delayed release | SES | socioeconomic status |
| EEG | electroencephalogram | SG | spread glottis |
| Erg | ergative case | sg | singular |
| ERP | event-related potentials | SLA | second language acquisition |
| ESL | English as a second language | th | theme |
| FN | first name | T | title alone |
| Fut | future tense | TLN | title + last name |
| Gen | genitive case | Top | topic |
| go | goal | UG | Universal Grammar |
| H | high tone | UR | underlying representation |
| IA | inflectional affix | UR | unrounded |
| indic | indicative | V | verb |
| IP | inflectional phrase (= S) | V | vowel |
| IPA | International Phonetic Alphabet | VP | verb phrase |
| L | low tone | W | woman |
| L1 | first language | Wd | word |

## A Great Way to Learn and Instruct Online

The Pearson Education Canada Companion Website is easy to navigate and is organized to correspond to the chapters in this textbook. Whether you are a student in the classroom or a distance learner you will discover helpful resources for in-depth study and research that empower you in your quest for greater knowledge and maximize your potential for success in the course.

Companion
Website

# [www.pearsoned.ca/ogrady]

Enter

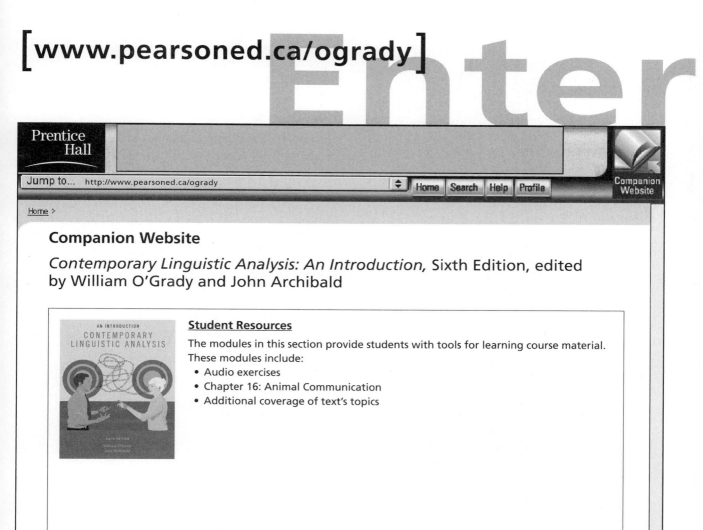

Prentice
Hall

Jump to...   http://www.pearsoned.ca/ogrady    ⬍   Home  Search  Help  Profile

Companion
Website

Home >

**Companion Website**

*Contemporary Linguistic Analysis: An Introduction,* Sixth Edition, edited by William O'Grady and John Archibald

### Student Resources

The modules in this section provide students with tools for learning course material. These modules include:

- Audio exercises
- Chapter 16: Animal Communication
- Additional coverage of text's topics

# Language: a preview

*The gift of language is the single human trait that marks us all genetically, setting us apart from the rest of life.*

LEWIS THOMAS, *THE LIVES OF A CELL*

Language is at the heart of all things human. We use it when we're talking, thinking, reading, writing, and listening. It's part of the social structure of our communities; it forges the emotional bond between parent and child; it's the vehicle for literature and poetry. Language is not just a part of us; language *defines* us. All normal human beings have at least one language, and it is difficult to imagine much significant social, intellectual, or artistic activity taking place without the opportunities for communication offered by language.

**Linguistics** is the study of how language works—how it is used, how it is acquired, how it changes over time, how it is represented in the brain, and so on. It is concerned not only with the properties of the world's languages (all 6912 of them), but also with the abilities and adaptations that have made it possible for our species to create and use language in the first place.

## 1.1 Specialization for language

Modern *homo sapiens* (our species) made its appearance 100 000 to 200 000 years ago, by many estimates. Early humans were anatomically like us—they had large brains and vocal tracts capable of producing speech. Archeological evidence (such as tools, carvings, and cave paintings) suggests that they also had the type of intellect that could support language.

---

**Language Matters   How Many Languages Are There in the World Today?**

That's not an easy question, since little is known about the linguistic situation in many parts of the world. The most complete compilation to date can be found at www.ethnologue.com, which lists 6912 languages.

But this is not the whole story. Many languages have only two or three hundred speakers (or fewer), and many others are in grave danger of demise as indigenous peoples throughout the world lose their traditional cultures and homelands. We discuss this in more detail in chapter 8. In the meantime, you can find out more by reading *Vanishing Voices: The Extinction of the World's Languages* by Daniel Nettles and Suzanne Romaine (New York: Oxford University Press, 2000), or by visiting www.terralingua.org.

Hundreds of thousands of years of evolution created a special capacity for language in humans that is not found in any other species. The evidence is literally inside us. For example, our speech organs (the lungs, larynx, tongue, teeth, lips, soft palate, and nasal passages) were—and still are—primarily concerned with breathing and eating. However, they have also all become highly specialized for use in language. Their structure and shape is unique to our species, as is the highly developed network of neural pathways that exercises control over them during speech production (see table 1.1).

| **Table 1.1** | Dual functions of the speech organs | |
|---|---|---|
| **Organ** | **Survival function** | **Speech function** |
| Lungs | to exchange carbon dioxide and oxygen | to supply air for speech |
| Vocal cords | to create seal over passage to lungs | to produce vibrations for speech sounds |
| Tongue | to move food to teeth and back into throat | to articulate vowels and consonants |
| Teeth | to break up food | to provide place of articulation for consonants |
| Lips | to seal oral cavity | to articulate vowels and consonants |
| Nose | to assist in breathing | to provide nasal resonance during speech |

Human beings are also especially equipped for the perception of speech. Newborns respond differently to human voices than to other types of sounds, and six-month-old infants are able to perceive subtle differences among sounds in languages that they have never heard before (this is discussed in more detail in chapter 10).

Of course, language is much more than just speech sounds and does not even have to be oral. In sign languages, meaning is conveyed via gestures, body posture, and facial expressions rather than through sounds. Moreover, much of what makes language special can be neither heard nor seen—it involves the way in which the human mind goes about forming words, building sentences, and interpreting meaning.

## Language Matters   **Sign Language**

There are many misconceptions about sign languages, the most prevalent being that they are just a way to 'spell out' an oral language. Although 'finger spelling' of words from an oral language is sometimes used (to indicate names or technical terms, for instance), sign languages are independent systems of communication, with their own vocabulary and grammatical rules. That's why British Sign Language and American Sign Language (ASL) are mutually unintelligible. And it's why Quebec Sign Language (Langue des signes québécoise) can be similar in many respects to American Sign Language, despite major differences between French and English. To find out more about ASL, go to http://facstaff.gallaudet.edu/harry.markowicz/asl/.

## 1.2 A creative system

What, precisely, is language? What does it mean to know a language? To answer these questions, it is first necessary to understand the resources that a language makes available to its **native speakers**, those who have acquired it as children in a natural setting (say, a home rather than a classroom).

The breadth and diversity of human thought and experience place great demands on language. Because there are always new things to say, new experiences to report, and new challenges to confront, language has to be **creative**, giving us the freedom to produce and understand new words and sentences as the need arises.

The creativity of language goes hand in hand with a second defining characteristic—the presence of systematic constraints that establish the boundaries within which innovation can occur. We can be innovative in our use of language, but there are rules to the game—and those rules are an integral part of our knowledge of language. As a preliminary illustration of this, consider the process that creates verbs from nouns in English as shown in table 1.2. (For now, you can think of verbs as words that name actions and nouns as words that name things.)

| **Table 1.2** Nouns used as verbs | |
|---|---|
| **Noun use** | **Verb use** |
| pull the boat onto the *beach* | *beach* the boat |
| keep the airplane on the *ground* | *ground* the airplane |
| tie a *knot* in the string | *knot* the string |
| put the wine in *bottles* | *bottle* the wine |
| catch the fish with a *spear* | *spear* the fish |
| clean the floor with a *mop* | *mop* the floor |

As the sentences in (1) show, there is a great deal of freedom to innovate in the formation of such verbs.

(1)  *a.* I *wristed* the ball over the net.
     *b.* He would try to *stiff-upper-lip* it through.
     *c.* She *Houdini'd* her way out of the locked closet.

However, there are also limits on this freedom. For instance, a new verb is rarely coined if a word with the intended meaning already exists. Although we say *jail the robber* to mean 'put the robber in jail', we do not say *prison the robber* to mean 'put the robber in prison'. This is because the well-established verb *imprison* already has the meaning that the new form would have.

There are also special constraints on the meaning and use of particular subclasses of these verbs. One such constraint involves verbs that are created from time expressions such as *summer, holiday,* and so on.

(2)  *a.* Julia *summered* in Paris.
     *b.* Harry *wintered* in Mexico.
     *c.* Bob *holidayed* in France.
     *d.* Harry and Julia *honeymooned* in Hawai'i.

Although the sentences in (2) are all natural-sounding, not all time expressions can be used in this way. (Throughout this book an asterisk is used to indicate that an utterance is unacceptable.)

(3) *a.* *Jerome *midnighted* in the streets.
    *b.* *Andrea *nooned* at the restaurant.
    *c.* *Philip *one o'clocked* at the airport.

These examples show that when a verb is created from a time expression, it must be given a very specific interpretation—roughly paraphrasable as 'to be somewhere for the period of time X'. Thus, *to summer in London* is 'to be in London for the summer', *to holiday in France* is 'to be in France for the holidays', and so on. Since *noon* and *midnight* express *points* in time rather than extended *periods* of time, they cannot be used to create new verbs of this type.[1]

Moreover, there are constraints on what verbs that are derived from nouns can mean. For instance, *winter in Hawaii* can only mean 'spend the winter in Hawaii', not 'make it snow in Hawaii' or 'stay in Hawaii until winter begins'. Without such constraints, creativity would run amok, undermining rather than enhancing communcation.

## Some other examples

Systematic rule-governed creativity is the hallmark of all aspects of language. For instance, consider the way in which sounds are combined to form words. Certain patterns of sounds, like the novel forms in (4), have the 'look' of English words—we recognize that they could become part of the language and be used as names for new products or scientific phenomena, for example.

(4) *a.* prasp
    *b.* flib
    *c.* traf

In contrast, the forms in (5) contain combinations of sounds that English just does not permit. As a result, they simply do not have the shape of English words.

(5) *a.* *psapr
    *b.* *bfli
    *c.* *ftra

Still other constraints determine how new words can be created from already existing forms with the help of special endings. Imagine, for example, that the word *soleme* entered the English language (used perhaps for a newly discovered atomic particle). As a speaker of English, you would then automatically know that something with the properties of a soleme could be called *solemic*. You would also know that to make something solemic is to *solemicize* it, and you would call this process *solemicization*. Further, you would know that the *c* is pronounced as *s* in *solemicize* but as *k* in *solemic*. Without hesitation, you would also recognize that *solemicize* is pronounced with the stress on the second syllable. (You would say *soLEmicize*, not *SOlemicize* or *solemiCIZE*.)

Nowhere is the ability to deal with novel utterances more obvious than in the production and comprehension of sentences. Apart from a few fixed expressions and greetings (*What's up?, How're things?, No way!*), much of what you say, hear, and read in the course of a day consists of sentences that are new to you. In conversations, lectures, newscasts, and textbooks, you are regularly exposed to novel combinations of words, unfamiliar ideas, and new information. Consider, for instance, the paragraph that you are currently reading. While each sentence is no doubt perfectly comprehensible to you, it is extremely unlikely that you have ever seen any of them before.

Not all new sentences are acceptable, however. For example, the words in (6) are all familiar, but they are simply not arranged in the right way to make a sentence of English.

(6)  *Frightened dog this the cat that chased mouse a.
     (cf. This dog frightened the cat that chased a mouse.)

As with other aspects of language, the ability to form and interpret sentences is subject to systematic limitations.

## 1.3  Grammar and linguistic competence

As we have just seen, speakers of a language are able to produce and understand an unlimited number of utterances, including many that are novel and unfamiliar. At the same time, they are able to recognize that certain utterances are not acceptable and simply do not belong in their language. This knowledge, which is often called **linguistic competence**, constitutes the central subject matter of linguistics and of this book.

In investigating linguistic competence, linguists focus on the mental system that allows human beings to form and interpret the sounds, words, and sentences of their language. Linguists call this system a **grammar** and often break it down into the components in table 1.3.

| **Table 1.3** | The components of a grammar |
| --- | --- |
| **Component** | **Domain** |
| Phonetics | the articulation and perception of speech sounds |
| Phonology | the patterning of speech sounds |
| Morphology | word formation |
| Syntax | sentence formation |
| Semantics | the interpretation of words and sentences |

As you can see, the term *grammar* is used in a special way within linguistics. A linguist's grammar is not a book and it is not concerned with just the form of words and sentences. Rather, it is an intricate system of knowledge that encompasses sound and meaning as well as form and structure. It contains the machinery needed to link a thought in the brain to movements of the tongue and lips, and vice versa—which, in the end, is what language is all about.

The study of grammar lies at the core of our attempts to understand what language is and what it means to know a language. Five simple points should help clarify why the investigation of grammatical systems is so important to contemporary linguistic analysis.

## 1.3.1  Generality: all languages have a grammar

One of the most fundamental claims of modern linguistic analysis is that all languages have a grammar. It could not be any other way. If a language is spoken, it must have a phonetic and phonological system; since it has words and sentences, it must also have a morphology and a syntax; and since these words and sentences have systematic meanings, there must obviously be semantic principles as well. In other words, each spoken language must have an intricate system of knowledge that encompasses sound and meaning as well as form and structure.

It is not unusual to hear the remark that some language—say, Acadian French, Cree, or Swahili—has no grammar. (This is especially common in the case of languages that are not written or are not taught in schools and universities.) Unfamiliar languages sometimes appear to an untrained observer to have no grammar simply because their grammatical systems are different from those of more frequently studied languages. In Walbiri (an indigenous language of Australia), for example, the relative ordering of words is so free that the English sentence *The two dogs now see several kangaroos* could be translated by the equivalent of any of the following sentences.

(7)  *a.* Dogs two now see kangaroos several.
    *b.* See now dogs two kangaroos several.
    *c.* See now kangaroos several dogs two.
    *d.* Kangaroos several now dogs two see.
    *e.* Kangaroos several now see dogs two.

Although Walbiri may not restrict the order of words in the way English does, its grammar imposes other types of requirements. For example, Walbiri speakers must place the ending *lu* on the word for 'dogs' to indicate that it names the animals that do the seeing rather than the animals that are seen. In English, by contrast, this information is conveyed by placing *two dogs* in front of the verb and *several kangaroos* after it.

Rather than showing that Walbiri has no grammar, such differences simply demonstrate that it has a grammar that is unlike the grammar of English in certain respects. This point holds across the board: although no two languages have exactly the same grammar, there are no languages without a grammar.

A similar point can be made about different varieties of the same language. Newfoundland English, Jamaican English, and Hawaiian English each have pronunciations, vocabulary items, and sentence patterns that may appear unusual to outsiders. But this does not mean that they have no grammar; it just means that their grammars differ from that of more familiar varieties of English in particular ways.

## Language Matters　**Regularization**

Why and how does the English spoken in one area end up being different from the English spoken in other places? One powerful force is *regularization*—the tendency to drive out exceptions by replacing them with a form that fits with a more general pattern.

With one exception, English verbs all have a single past tense form—*I just arrived, you just arrived, s/he just arrived*, and so on. The exception is the verb *be*, which has two forms—*was* and *were*: *I was there, you were there, s/he was there.*

Regularization has taken care of this anomaly in at least two varieties of English. In Yorkshire English (northern England), only *were* is used: *I were there, you were there, s/he were there.* In Appalachian English (West Virginia and parts of various nearby states), things have gone the other way, so that only *was* has been retained: *I was there, you was there, s/he was there.*

## 1.3.2　Parity: all grammars are equal

Contrary to popular belief, there is no such thing as a 'primitive' language, even in places untouched by modern science and technology. Indeed, some of the most complex linguistic phenomena we know about are found in societies that have neither writing nor electricity.

Moreover, there is no such thing as a 'good grammar' or a 'bad grammar'. In fact, all grammars do essentially the same thing: they tell speakers how to form and interpret the words and sentences of their language. The form and meaning of those words and sentences vary from language to language and even from community to community, of course, but there is no such thing as a language that doesn't work for its speakers.

Linguists sometimes clash over this point with people who are upset about the use of 'non-standard' varieties of English that permit sentences such as *I seen that, They was there, He didn't do nothing, He ain't here,* and so forth. Depending on where you live and who you talk to, speaking in this way can have negative consequences: it may be harder to win a scholarship, to get a job, to be accepted in certain social circles, and so forth. This is an undeniable fact about the social side of language and we'll return to it in chapter 14. From a purely linguistic point of view, however, there is absolutely nothing wrong with grammars that permit such structures. They work for their speakers, and they deserve to be studied in the same objective fashion as the varieties of English spoken by the rich and educated.

The bottom line for linguistics is that the analysis of language must reflect the way it is actually used, not someone's idealized vision of how it should be used. The linguist Steven Pinker offers the following illustration to make the same point.

> *Imagine that you are watching a nature documentary. The video shows the usual gorgeous footage of animals in their natural habitats. But the voiceover reports some troubling facts. Dolphins do not execute their swimming strokes properly. White-crowned sparrows carelessly debase their calls. Chickadees' nests are incorrectly constructed, pandas hold bamboo in the wrong paw, the song of the humpback whale contains several well-known errors, and the monkey's cries have been in a state of chaos and degeneration for hundreds of years. Your reaction would probably be, What on earth could it mean for the song of the humpback whale to contain an "error"? Isn't the song of the humpback whale whatever the humpback whale decides to sing? . . .*

As Pinker goes on to observe, language is like the song of the humpback whale. The way to determine whether a particular sentence is permissible is to find people who speak the language and observe how they use it.

In sum, linguists don't even think of trying to rate languages as good or bad, simple or complex. Rather, they investigate language in much the same way that other scientists study snails or stars—with a view to simply figuring out how it works. This same point is sometimes made by noting that linguistics is **descriptive**, not **prescriptive**. Its goal is to describe and explain the facts of languages, not to change them.

## 1.3.3    Universality: grammars are alike in basic ways

In considering how grammars can differ from each other, it is easy to lose sight of something even more intriguing and important—the existence of principles and properties shared by all human languages.

For example, all languages use a small set of contrastive sounds that help distinguish words from each other (like the *t* and *d* sounds that allow us to recognize *to* and *do* as different words). There are differences in precisely which sounds particular languages use, but there are also fundamental similarities. For instance, all languages have more consonant sounds (*p*, *t*, *d*, etc.) than vowel sounds (*a*, *e*, *i*); any language that has a *b* sound almost certainly has a *p* sound as well; and all languages have a vowel that sounds like the 'ah' in *father*. (For more on this, see chapter 8.)

There are also universal constraints on how words can be put together to form sentences. For example, no language can use the second of the sentences in (8) for a situation in which *he* refers to *Ned*.

(8)  *a.*  Ned lost his wallet.
     *b.*  He lost Ned's wallet.

Moreover, even when languages do differ from each other, there are often constraints on how much variation is possible. For example, some languages (like English) place question words at the beginning of the sentence.

---

**Language Matters    Don't End That Sentence in a Preposition**

One of the better-known prescriptive rules of English is 'Don't end a sentence with a preposition.' (In other words, say 'To whom were you talking?,' not 'Who were you talking to?') The problem with this rule is simply that people don't speak English that way. Prepositions often occur at the end of a sentence, and trying to prevent this from happening leads to all sorts of unnatural-sounding constructions, as Winston Churchill famously illustrated when he said, tongue in cheek, "This is something up with which I will not put."

Here's an extreme case of prepositions at the end of a sentence. A young girl, unhappy with the book that her father had brought upstairs for her bedtime story, was observed to say:

"What did you bring the book I didn't want to be read to out of up for?" There are five prepositions at the end of this sentence—an extreme case, admittedly, but it's still English!

(9)  What did Mary donate to the library?

Other languages, like Mandarin, make no such changes.

(10)  Mali juan shenme gei tushuguan?
      Mary donate what to library

But no language uniformly places question words at the end of the sentence in its basic word order.

In other cases, variation is constrained by strong tendencies rather than absolute prohibitions. Take three-word sentences such as *Canadians like hockey*, for instance. There are six logically possible orders for such sentences.

(11)  *a.* Canadians like hockey.
      *b.* Canadians hockey like.
      *c.* Like Canadians hockey.
      *d.* Like hockey Canadians.
      *e.* Hockey like Canadians.
      *f.* Hockey Canadians like.

All other things being equal, we would expect to find each order employed in about one-sixth of the world's languages. In fact, though, more than 95 percent of the world's languages adopt one of the first three orders for basic statements (and the vast majority of those use one or the other of the first two orders). Only a handful of languages use any of the last three orders as basic.

These are not isolated examples. As later chapters will show, languages are fundamentally alike in important ways.

## 1.3.4  Mutability: grammars change over time

The features of language that are not universal and fixed are subject to change over time. Indeed, within these limits, the grammars of all languages are constantly changing. Some of these changes are relatively minor and occur very quickly (for example, the addition of new words such as *blog, morphing, Internet, e-business, podcast,* and *cyberspace* to the vocabulary of English). Other changes have a more dramatic effect on the overall form of the language and typically take place over a long period of time. One such change involves the manner in which we negate sentences in English. Prior to 1200, English formed negative constructions by placing *ne* before the verb and a variant of *not* after it.

(12)  *a.* Ic *ne* seye *not*. ('I don't say.')
      *b.* He *ne* speketh *nawt*. ('He does not speak.')

By 1400 or thereabouts, *ne* was used infrequently and *not* (or *nawt*) typically occurred by itself after the verb.

(13)  *a.* I seye *not* the wordes.
      *b.* We saw *nawt* the knyghtes.

It was not until several centuries later that English adopted its current practice of allowing *not* to occur after only certain types of verbs (such as *do, have, will,* and so on).

> ## Language Matters   **Verbs Again**
>
> A thousand years ago, more than three hundred English verbs formed their past tense by making an internal change (*drive/drove*, *eat/ate*, etc.) rather than by adding a suffix (*walk/walked*, *dance/danced*). Today, there are about half as many verbs that do this. The past tense of *heave* used to be *hove*; now it is *heaved*. The past tense of *thrive* used to be *throve*; now it is *thrived*. The past tense of *chide* ('scold') used to be *chid*; now it is *chided*. And so on. These past tense forms have all been changed to comply with the more regular *-ed* pattern.
>
>      Then why aren't all verbs regular? One factor involves frequency: more frequent forms tend to resist regularization. That's why the most enduring irregular past tense forms in English (*was* and/or *were* for *be*, *had* for *have*, *went* for *go*, *came* for *come*, and so on) involve high-frequency verbs. To find out more, read *Words and Rules* by Steven Pinker (New York: Basic Books, 1999).

(14)   *a.* I will *not* say the words. (versus *I will say not the words.)

        *b.* He did *not* see the knights. (versus *He saw not the knights.)

These changes illustrate the extent to which grammars can be modified over time. The structures exemplified in (13) are archaic by today's standards and those in (12) sound completely foreign to speakers of modern English.

Through the centuries, those who believe that certain varieties of language are better than others have frequently expressed concern over what they perceive to be the deterioration of English. In 1710, for example, the writer Jonathan Swift (author of *Gulliver's Travels*) lamented 'the continual Corruption of our English Tongue.' Among the corruptions to which he objected were contractions such as *he's* for *he is*, although he had no objection to *Tis* for *It is*!

Similar concerns have been expressed about the state of English spoken in Canada. In 1857, members of the Canadian Institute in Toronto heard a speech describing Canadian English as 'a corrupt dialect growing up amongst our population.' The speaker objected to the use of words such as *lot* (for 'a division of land'), *boss* (for 'master'), *store* (for 'shop'), *fix* (for 'mend'), and *guess* (for 'think', as in *I guess I'll go*). Judging by current usage, he objected in vain.

Linguists reject the view that languages attain a state of perfection at some point in their history and that subsequent changes lead to deterioration and corruption. As noted above, there are simply no grounds for claiming that one language or variety of language is somehow superior to another.

## 1.3.5   Inaccessibility: grammatical knowledge is subconscious

Knowledge of a grammar differs in important ways from knowledge of arithmetic, traffic rules, and other subjects that are taught at home or in school: it is largely subconscious and not accessible to introspection (that is, you can't figure out how it works just by thinking about it). As an example of this, consider your pronunciation of the past tense suffix written as *ed* in the following words.

(15)   *a.* hunted

        *b.* slipped

        *c.* buzzed

You probably didn't notice it before, but the *ed* ending has a different pronunciation in each of these words. Whereas you say *id* in *hunted*, you say *t* in *slipped* and *d* in *buzzed*. Moreover, if you heard the new verb *flib*, you would form the past tense as *flibbed* and pronounce the ending as *d*. If you are a native speaker of English, you acquired the grammatical subsystem regulating this aspect of speech when you were a child and it now exists subconsciously in your mind, allowing you to automatically make the relevant contrasts.

The same is true for virtually everything else about language. Once we go beyond the most obvious things (such as whether words like *the* and *a* come before or after a noun), there is not much that the average person can say about how language works. For example, try explaining to someone who is not a native speaker of English why we can say *I went to school* but not *\*I went to supermarket*. Or try to figure out for yourself how the word *or* works. Matters are seemingly straightforward in a sentence such as the following, which means something like 'Either Mary drank tea, or she drank coffee—I don't know which.'

(16) Mary drank tea or coffee.

But *or* has a different interpretation in the next sentence.

(17) Mary didn't drink tea or coffee.

Now it seems to mean 'and'—'Mary didn't drink tea and she didn't drink coffee,' not 'Mary didn't drink tea or she didn't drink coffee—I don't know which.'

Being able to interpret these sentences is not the same thing as knowing *why* they have the particular meanings that they do. Speakers of a language know what sounds right and what doesn't sound right, but they are not sure how they know.

Because most of what we know about our language is subconscious, the analysis of human linguistic systems requires considerable effort and ingenuity. As is the case in all science, information about facts that can be observed (the pronunciation of words, the interpretation of sentences, and so on) must be used to draw inferences about the sometimes invisible mechanisms (atoms, cells, or grammars, as the case may be) that are ultimately responsible for these phenomena. A good deal of this book is concerned with the findings of this research and with what they tell us about the nature and use of human language and about how it is represented in the mind.

# Summing up

Human language is characterized by **creativity**. Speakers of a language have access to a **grammar**, a mental system that allows them to form and interpret both familiar and novel utterances. The grammar governs the articulation, perception, and patterning of speech sounds, the formation of words and sentences, and the interpretation of utterances. All languages have grammars that are equal in their expressive capacity, and all speakers of a language have (subconscious) knowledge of its grammar. The existence of such linguistic systems in humans is the product of unique anatomical and cognitive specialization not found in other species.

## Notes

[1] Not all nouns naming periods of time can be converted into verbs, however. Thus, for reasons that are not understood, the nouns *autumn* and *week* do not make very good verbs.

*They autumned/weeked in the Maritimes.

## Recommended reading

Bickerton, Derek. 1990. *Language and Species*. Chicago: University of Chicago Press.

Crystal, David. 1997. *The Cambridge Encyclopedia of the English Language*. New York: Cambridge University Press.

Pinker, Steven. 1994. *The Language Instinct: How the Human Mind Creates Language*. New York: Morrow.

## Exercises

**1.** The following sentences contain verbs created from nouns in accordance with the process described in section 1.2 of this chapter. Describe the meaning of each of these new verbs.
   a) We techno'd the night away.
   b) He dog-teamed his way across the Arctic.
   c) We MG'd to Oregon.
   d) They Concorded to London.
   e) He Crosby'd his way to the net.
   f) We Greyhounded to Toronto.
   g) We'll have to Ajax the sink.
   h) She Windexed the windows.
   i) You should Clairol your hair.
   j) Let's carton the eggs.

**2.** Using the examples in the preceding exercise as a model, create five new verbs from nouns. Build a sentence around each of these new verbs to show its meaning.

**3.** Which of the following forms are possible words of English? Show the words to an acquaintance and see if you agree on your judgments.

a) mbood    e) sproke

b) frall    f) flube

c) coofp    g) wordms

d) ktleem    h) bsarn

**4.** Imagine that you are an advertising executive and that your job involves inventing new names for products. Create four new forms that are possible words of English and four that are not.

**5.** Part of linguistic competence involves the ability to recognize whether novel utterances are acceptable. Consider the following sentences and determine which are possible sentences in English. For each unacceptable sentence, change the sentence to make it acceptable, and compare the two.

a) Jason's mother left himself with nothing to eat.

b) Miriam is eager to talk to.

c) This is the man who I took a picture of.

d) Colin made Jane a sandwich.

e) Is the dog sleeping the bone again?

f) Wayne prepared Zena a cake.

g) Max cleaned the garden up.

h) Max cleaned up the garden.

i) Max cleaned up it.

j) I desire you to leave.

k) That you likes liver surprises me.

**6.** Consider the following sentences, each of which is acceptable to some speakers of English. Try to identify the prescriptive rules that are violated in each case.

a) He don't know about the race.

b) You was out when I called.

c) There's twenty horses registered in the show.

d) That window's broke, so be careful.

e) Jim and me are gonna go campin' this weekend.

f) Who did you come with?

g) I seen the parade last week.

h) He been lost in the woods for ten days.

i) My car needs cleaned 'cause of all the rain.

j) Julie ain't got none.

k) Somebody left their book on the train.

l) Murray hurt hisself in the game.

What is the reaction of linguists to the claim that sentences of this sort are 'wrong'?

**7.** An interesting feature of the variety of English spoken in Hawaii involves the form of the 'possessive pronoun' that shows up in the following context.

That belongs to me. It's *mines*.

Make a list of other possessive pronoun forms in standard English by filling in the spaces below.

That belongs to you. It's _____.
That belongs to him. It's _____.
That belongs to her. It's _____.
That belongs to us. It's _____.
That belongs to them. It's _____.

What process in language change appears to be responsible for the form *mines*?

# CHAPTER Two

Michael Dobrovolsky

# Phonetics: the sounds of language

*Heavenly labials in a world of gutturals*

WALLACE STEVENS

We do not need to speak in order to use language. Language can be written, manually signed, mechanically reproduced, and even synthesized by computers with considerable success. Nevertheless, speech remains the primary way humans express themselves through language. Our species spoke long before we began to write and, as we saw in the first chapter of this book, this long history of spoken language is reflected in our anatomical specialization for it. Humans also appear to have specialized neural mechanisms for the perception of speech sounds. Because language and speech are so closely linked, we begin our study of language by examining the inventory and structure of the sounds of speech. This branch of linguistics is called **phonetics**.

Human languages display a wide variety of sounds, called **phones** (from Greek *phōnē* 'sound, voice') or **speech sounds**. There are a great many speech sounds, but not an infinite number of them. The class of possible speech sounds is finite, and a portion of the total set will be found in the inventory of any human language. Humans can also make sounds with the vocal tract that do not occur in speech, such as the sound made by inhaling through one corner of the mouth, or the 'raspberry' produced by sticking out the tongue and blowing hard across it. Nonetheless, a very wide range of sounds is found in human language (600 consonants and 200 vowels, according to one estimate), including such sounds as the click made by drawing the tongue hard away from the upper molars on one side of the mouth (imagine making a sound to get a horse to move), or the sound made by constricting the upper part of the throat as we breathe out. Any human, child or adult, can learn to produce any human speech sound.

There are two ways of approaching phonetics. One approach studies the physiological mechanisms of speech production. This is known as **articulatory phonetics**. The other, known as **acoustic phonetics**, is concerned with measuring and analyzing the physical properties of the sound waves we produce when we speak. Both approaches are indispensable to an understanding of speech. This chapter focuses on articulatory phonetics, but also makes some reference to the acoustic properties of sounds and to acoustic analysis.

## 2.1 Phonetic transcription

Since the sixteenth century, efforts have been made to devise a universal system for transcribing the sounds of speech. The best-known system, the **International Phonetic Alphabet (IPA)**, has been evolving since 1888. This system of transcription attempts to represent each sound of human speech with a single symbol. These symbols are enclosed in brackets [ ] to indicate that the transcription is phonetic and does not represent the spelling system of a particular language. For example, the sound spelled *th* in English <u>*th*</u>*is* is transcribed as [ð] (pronounced *eth*) as in *wea<u>th</u>er*. The IPA uses this symbol to represent the sound in whichever language it is heard, whether it is English, Spanish, or Turkmen (a Turkic language spoken in Central Asia and written in the Cyrillic alphabet), as shown in table 2.1.

**Table 2.1**    Use of [ð] in the International Phonetic Alphabet

| Language | Spelling | IPA | Meaning |
|---|---|---|---|
| English | <u>th</u>is | [ðɪs] | 'this' |
| Spanish | bo<u>d</u>a | [bɔða] | 'wedding' |
| Turkmen | a<u>д</u>ak | [aðak] | 'foot' |

### Language Matters **Sounds and Spelling**

Although the relationship between sound and symbol in IPA is one to one, things are very different in the writing system of English—as a quick look at the words *rough*, *through*, *bough*, *though*, and *cough* illustrates. All these words contain the sequence of symbols *ough*, yet we note two things: (1) the written symbols represent different sounds, and (2) the same four symbols may represent different numbers of sounds. In *rough* it represents two sounds, while in *through* it represents only one. There is no one-to-one correspondence between a symbol and a sound in English. This is also evident when we look at the pronunciation of the single symbol 'o', which is pronounced differently in *go*, *hot*, *women*, *more*, and *mutton*. Again, there is no one-to-one correspondence of sound and symbol in the English writing system.

George Bernard Shaw, the famous playwright who described himself as an "energetic, phonetic enthusiast", illustrated the problem in the following anecdote. Imagine a new word comes into the English language that is spelled *ghoti*. How would this word be pronounced? In an attempt to demonstrate what he felt were the inadequacies of the English spelling system, Shaw argued that the word could be pronounced as 'fish'. How so? Note the pronunciations of the italicized segments in the following words:

> enou*gh* → f
>
> w*o*men → i
>
> na*ti*on → sh

Shaw felt that any writing system that could possibly pronounce the string of letters *ghoti* as 'fish' was in desperate need of spelling reform.

The use of a standardized phonetic alphabet with a one-to-one correspondence between sound and symbol enables linguists to transcribe languages consistently and accurately. In North American (NA) usage, though, some phonetic symbols differ from those employed by IPA transcription. For example, the sound heard at the beginning of the English word _shark_ is transcribed as [ʃ] in IPA, but usually as [š] in North America. This book employs IPA transcription, but notes common North American symbols where relevant.

If you wish to start practising the phonetic transcription of English, turn to tables 2.16 and 2.17, pages 39–40, for examples.

## 2.1.1 Units of representation

Anyone who hears a language spoken for the first time finds it hard to break up the flow of speech into individual units. Even when hearing our own language spoken, we do not focus attention on individual sounds as much as we do on the meanings of words, phrases, and sentences. Many alphabets, including the IPA, represent speech in the form of **segments**—individual phones like [p], [s], or [m]. (Using segments, however, is only one way to represent speech. The **syllable**, presented in chapter 3, is also represented in some writing systems [see chapter 15, sections 15.1.2, 15.3.2, and 15.4.2]. In one type of Japanese writing, for example, signs such as か [ka], と [to], and み [mi] represent syllables without recourse to segmental transcription.)

Segments are produced by coordinating a number of individual articulatory gestures including jaw movement, lip shape, and tongue placement. Many of these individual activities are represented as smaller subunits called **features** that segments are made up of. Even though features are almost never represented in writing systems, they are important elements of linguistic representation. Features reflect individual aspects of articulatory control or acoustic effects produced by articulation. This chapter presents segmental transcription, since it is the most widely used way of representing speech. Features and syllables are introduced in the following chapter.

## 2.1.2 Segments

We have defined the **segment** as an individual speech sound (phone). There are several kinds of evidence that suggest that speakers are able to break down a stream of speech into sound segments.

Errors in speech production provide one kind of evidence for the existence of segments. Slips of the tongue such as _Kolacodor_ for _Kodacolor_ and _melcome wat_ for _welcome mat_ show segments shifting and reversing position within and across words. This suggests that segments are individual units of linguistic structure and can be represented individually in a system of transcription.

The relative invariance of speech sounds in human language also suggests that segmental phonetic transcription is a well-motivated way of transcribing speech. It is impossible to represent all variants of human speech sounds, since no one says the same sound in exactly the same way twice. Nonetheless, the sounds of speech remain invariant enough from language to language for us to transcribe them consistently. A _p_ sound is much the same in English, Russian, or Uzbek. The fact that when producing a _p_ sound, English speakers press

---

### Language Matters **An Interesting Phonetic Fact**

Words of two syllables are not necessarily longer than words of one syllable. If we measure the amount of time it takes us to say a word like *dad* we come up with a length of 520 milliseconds. The word *daddy*, though, which is two syllables long, takes only 420 milliseconds. Try it and see if you agree.

---

their lips together but Russian speakers draw theirs slightly inward does not make the sounds different enough to warrant separate symbols. But the sounds *p* and *t* are distinct enough from each other in languages the world over to be consistently transcribed with separate symbols.

## 2.2 The sound-producing system

Sound is produced when air is set in motion. Think of the speech production mechanism as consisting of an air supply, a sound source that sets the air in motion in ways specifically relevant to speech production, and a set of filters that modifies the sound in various ways (see figure 2.1). The air supply is provided by the lungs. The sound source is in the larynx, where a set of muscles called the **vocal folds** (or **vocal cords** [not *chords*]) is located. The filters

**Figure 2.1**
The sound-producing system

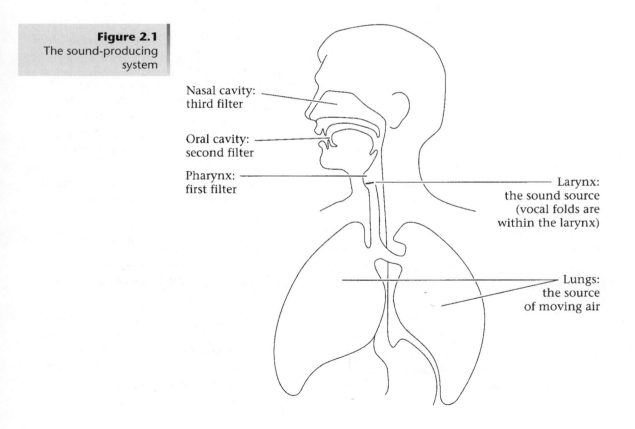

Nasal cavity:
third filter

Oral cavity:
second filter

Pharynx:
first filter

Larynx:
the sound source
(vocal folds are
within the larynx)

Lungs:
the source
of moving air

are the organs above the larynx: the tube of the throat between the larynx and the oral cavity, which is called the **pharynx**, the oral cavity, and the nasal cavity. These passages are collectively known as the **vocal tract**.

## 2.2.1 The lungs

In order to produce the majority of sounds in the world's languages, we take air into the lungs and expel it during speech. (A small number of phones are made with air as it flows *into* the vocal tract. Samples of these and other sounds can be heard on the Companion Website at **www.pearsoned.ca/ogrady**, chapter 2.) A certain level of air pressure is needed to keep the speech mechanism functioning steadily. The pressure is maintained by the action of various sets of muscles coming into play during the course of an utterance. The primary muscles are the **intercostals** (the muscles between the ribs) and the **diaphragm** (the large sheet of muscle separating the chest cavity from the abdomen). The intercostals raise the ribcage to allow air to flow into the lungs during inhalation, while the diaphragm helps to control the release of air during exhalation for speech so that we can speak for a reasonable period of time between breaths.

## 2.2.2 The larynx

As air flows out of the lungs up the **trachea** (windpipe), it passes through a box-like structure made of cartilage and muscle; this is the **larynx** (commonly known as the voice box or Adam's apple), as shown in figure 2.2. The main portion of the larynx is formed by the **thyroid cartilage**, which spreads outward at its front like the head of a plow. The thyroid cartilage rests on the ring-shaped **cricoid cartilage**. Fine sheets of muscle flare from the inner sides of the thyroid cartilage, forming the paired vocal folds. The inner edges of the vocal folds are attached to the vocal ligaments. The vocal folds can be pulled apart or drawn closer together, especially at their back or posterior ends, where each is attached to one of two small cartilages, the **arytenoids**. The arytenoids are opened, closed, and rotated by several pairs of small muscles (not shown in figure 2.2). As air passes through the space between the vocal folds, which is called the **glottis**, different glottal states are produced, depending on the positioning of the vocal folds.

**Figure 2.2**
The larynx: *a.* from the front; *b.* from the back; *c.* from above, with the vocal folds in open position. The striated lines in *c.* indicate muscles, a number of which have been eliminated from the drawings in order to show the cartilages more clearly.

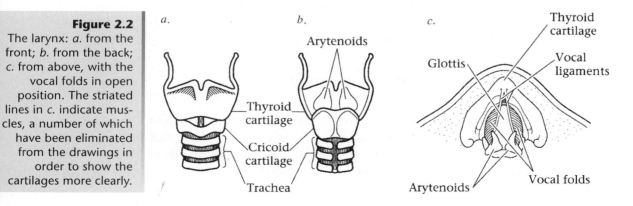

### 2.2.3  **Glottal states**

The vocal folds may be positioned in a number of ways to produce different glottal states. The first two glottal states presented in figure 2.3 are commonly encountered in most of the world's languages. The third diagram describes the glottal state that underlies a common speech phenomenon, and the fourth illustrates one of a number of glottal states not encountered in English.

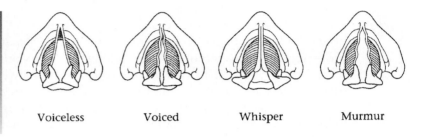

**Figure 2.3**
Four glottal states: the stylized drawing represents the vocal folds and glottis from above; the anterior portion at the larynx is towards the top. The small triangles represent the arytenoid cartilages, which help spread or close the vocal folds.

Voiceless    Voiced    Whisper    Murmur

## Voicelessness

When the vocal folds are pulled apart as illustrated in figure 2.3, air passes directly through the glottis without much interference. Any sound made with the vocal folds in this position is said to be **voiceless**. You can confirm a sound's voicelessness by touching your fingers to the larynx as you produce it. You will not feel any vibration from the vocal folds being transmitted to your fingertips. The initial sounds of *fish*, *sing*, and *house* are all voiceless. Voicelessness is a true speech state distinct from breathing; the vocal folds are not as far apart during speech voicelessness as they are in silent breathing.

## Voicing

When the vocal folds are brought close together, but not tightly closed, air passing between them causes them to vibrate, producing sounds that are said to be **voiced**. (See the second illustration in figure 2.3.) You can determine whether a sound is voiced in the same way you determined voicelessness. By lightly touching the fingers to the larynx as you produce an extended version of the initial sounds of the words *zip* or *vow*, or any vowel, you can sense the vibration of the vocal folds within the larynx. It can be helpful to contrast voiced versus voiceless sounds while resting your hand on your throat. Produce the following pairs of sounds and decide which are voiced and which are voiceless.

> [fffffffffffffffffffffffffvvvvvvvvvvvvvvvvvvvvvv]
> [ssssssssssssssssssssssssszzzzzzzzzzzzzzzzzzzzzzzz]

On which sounds did you feel vibration? Some people find it easier to hear this distinction in another way. Perform the same exercise as given above but this time with your fingers in your ears. You will feel much greater resonance on the sounds which are voiced. These techniques can be helpful as you try to hear which phones are voiced and which are voiceless.

## Whisper

Another glottal state produces a **whisper**. Whispering is voiceless, but, as shown in figure 2.3, the vocal folds are adjusted so that the anterior (front) portions are pulled close together, while the posterior (back) portions are apart.

## Murmur

Yet another glottal state produces a **murmur**, also known as **breathy voice**. Sounds produced with this glottal configuration are voiced, but the vocal folds are relaxed to allow enough air to escape to produce a simultaneous breathy effect. There are languages in the world that use breathy voice as an integral part of the sound system. Although it is difficult to generalize, sometimes when you see words or place names that have been borrowed into English with spellings such as 'bh' as in *Bhagavad-Gita*, 'dh' as in *dharma* or *dhal*, or 'gh' as in *ghee,* they can represent murmured sounds.

These four glottal states represent only some of the possibilities of sound production at the glottis. The total number of glottal states is still undecided, but there are more than a dozen. Combined with various articulations made above the larynx, they produce a wide range of phones. Before examining phones in more detail, we will first consider the three major classes of speech sound.

## 2.3 Sound classes

The sounds of language can be grouped into **classes** based on the phonetic properties that they share. You have already seen what some of these properties can be. All voiced sounds, for example, form a class, as do all voiceless sounds. The most basic division among sounds is into two major classes, **vowels** and **consonants**. Another class of sounds, the **glides**, shares properties of both vowels and consonants. Each class of sounds has a number of distinguishing features.

### 2.3.1 Vowels, consonants, and glides (syllabic and non-syllabic elements)

Vowels, consonants, and glides can be distinguished on the basis of differences in articulation, or by their acoustic properties. We can also distinguish among these elements with respect to whether they function as syllabic or non-syllabic elements.

## The articulatory difference

Consonantal sounds, which may be voiced ([v]) or voiceless ([f]), are made with either a complete closure ([p]) or a narrowing ([f]) of the vocal tract. The airflow is either blocked momentarily or restricted so much that noise is produced as air flows past the constriction. In contrast, vowels are produced with little obstruction in the vocal tract (you will note that for all vowels the tip of your tongue stays down by your lower front teeth) and are usually voiced.

## The acoustic difference

As a result of the difference in articulation, consonants and vowels differ in the way they sound. Vowels are more sonorous (acoustically powerful) than consonants, and so we perceive them as louder and longer lasting.

## Syllabic and non-syllabic sounds

The greater sonority of vowels allows them to form the basis of **syllables**. A syllable can be defined as a peak of sonority surrounded by less sonorous segments. For example, the words *a* and *go* each contain one syllable, the word *laughing* two syllables, and the word *telephone* three syllables. In counting the syllables in these words, we are in effect counting the vowels. A vowel is thus said to form the **nucleus** of a syllable. In section 2.5.7, we will see that certain types of consonants can form syllabic nuclei as well. It is a good idea, therefore, to think of vowels and consonants not simply as types of articulations, but as elements that may or may not be syllabic. In (1), the initial sounds of the words in the left column are all consonants; those on the right are all vowels.

(1)  take      above
     cart      at
     feel      eel
     jump      it
     think     ugly
     bell      open

Table 2.2 sums up the differences between consonants and vowels.

| **Table 2.2**    Major differences between syllabic and non-syllabic elements ||
| --- | --- |
| **Vowels (and other syllabic elements)** | **Consonants (non-syllabic elements)** |
| ■ are produced with relatively little obstruction in the vocal tract <br> ■ are more sonorous | ■ are produced with a complete closure or narrowing of the vocal tract <br> ■ are less sonorous |

## Glides

A type of sound that shows properties of both consonants and vowels is called a glide. Glides may be thought of as rapidly articulated vowels—this is the auditory impression they produce. Glides are produced with an articulation like that of a vowel. However, they move quickly to another articulation, as do the initial glides in *yet* or *wet*, or quickly terminate, as do the word-final glides in *boy* and *now*. You can feel how little movement is necessary to move from a vowel articulation to a glide articulation when you pronounce the following phrases:

     see you later
     who would do that

Make the vowel sound in the word *see* ([i]) and then make the glide in the word *you* ([j]). Now go back and forth from [i] to [j] and note that the small articulatory movement can cause us to perceive one sound as a vowel and the other as a glide. The same pattern emerges when you produce the vowel in *who* ([u]) and the glide in *would* ([w]).

Even though they are vowel-like in articulation, glides pattern as consonants. For example, glides can never form the nucleus of a syllable. Since glides show properties of both consonants and vowels, the terms *semivowel* and *semiconsonant* may be used interchangeably with the term *glide*.

## 2.4 Consonant articulation

Airflow is modified in the vocal tract by the placement of the tongue and the positioning of the lips. These modifications occur at specific **places** or **points of articulation**. The major places of articulation used in speech production are outlined in this section. Figure 2.4 provides a midsagittal section, or cutaway view, of the vocal tract on which each place of articulation has been indicated.

### 2.4.1 The tongue

The primary articulating organ is the tongue. It can be raised, lowered, thrust forward or retracted, and even rolled back. The sides of the tongue can also be raised or lowered.

**Figure 2.4**
The vocal tract

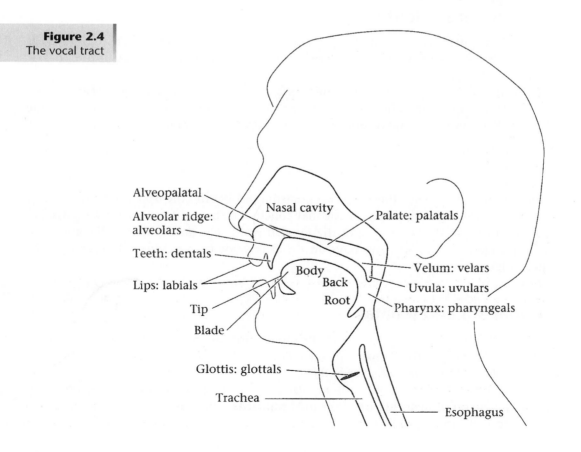

Phonetic description refers to five areas of the tongue. The **tip** is the narrow area at the front. Just behind the tip lies the **blade**. The main mass of the tongue is called the **body**, and the hindmost part of the tongue that lies in the mouth is called the **back**. The body and back of the tongue can also be referred to jointly as the **dorsum**. The **root** of the tongue is contained in the upper part of the throat (pharynx).

## 2.4.2  Places of articulation

Each point at which the airstream can be modified to produce a different sound is called a place of articulation. Places of articulation are found at the lips, within the oral cavity, in the pharynx, and at the glottis.

### Labial

Any sound made with closure or near-closure of the lips is said to be **labial**. Sounds involving both lips are termed *bilabial*; sounds involving the lower lip and upper teeth are called **labiodentals**. English includes the bilabials heard word-initially in *peer*, *bin*, and *month*, and the labiodentals heard initially in *fire* and *vow*.

### Dental and interdental

Some phones are produced with the tongue placed against or near the teeth. Sounds made in this way are called **dentals**. European French has dental sounds at the beginning of the words *temps*, *dire*, *sept*, and *zizi*.

If the tongue is placed between the teeth, the sound is said to be **interdental**. Interdentals in English include the initial consonants of the words *this* and *thing*. (Some English speakers produce *s* and *z* as dentals; see section 2.5.3 for more details.)

### Alveolar

Within the oral cavity, a small ridge protrudes from just behind the upper front teeth. This is called the **alveolar ridge**. The tongue may touch or be brought near this ridge. Alveolar sounds are heard at the beginning of the English words *top*, *deer*, *soap*, *zip*, *lip*, and *neck*. Some languages, such as Spanish, have an *r* that is made by touching the tongue to the alveolar ridge.

### Alveopalatal and palatal

Just behind the alveolar ridge, the roof of the mouth rises sharply. This area is known as the **alveopalatal** area (**palatoalveolar** in some books). Alveopalatal consonants are heard in the English words *show*, *measure*, *chip*, and *judge*.

The highest part of the roof of the mouth is called the **palate**, and sounds produced with the tongue on or near this area are called **palatals**. The word-initial phone in *yes* is a palatal glide.

### Velar

The soft area towards the rear of the roof of the mouth is called the **velum**. Sounds made with the tongue touching or near this position are called **velars**. Velars are heard in English at the beginning of the words <u>c</u>all and <u>g</u>uy, and at the end of the word *han<u>g</u>*. The glide heard word-initially in <u>w</u>et is called a **labiovelar**, since the tongue is raised near the velum and the lips are rounded at the same time. We refer to the velar aspect of the sound as its *primary* place of articulation while the labial aspect is a *secondary* place of articulation.

### Uvular

The small fleshy flap of tissue known as the **uvula** hangs down from the velum. Sounds made with the tongue near or touching this area are called **uvulars**. English has no uvulars, but the *r* sound of standard European French is uvular.

### Pharyngeal

The area of the throat between the uvula and the larynx is known as the pharynx. Sounds made through the modification of airflow in this region by retracting the tongue or constricting the pharynx are called **pharyngeals**. Pharyngeals can be found in many dialects of Arabic, but not in English.

### Glottal

Sounds produced using the vocal folds as primary articulators are called **glottals**. The sound at the beginning of the English words <u>h</u>eave and <u>h</u>og is made at the glottis. You can also hear a glottal sound in the Cockney English pronunciation of the 'tt' in words like *be<u>tt</u>er* or *bo<u>tt</u>le*.

## 2.5    Manners of articulation

The lips, tongue, velum, and glottis can be positioned in different ways to produce different sound types. These various configurations are called **manners of articulation**.

## 2.5.1    Oral versus nasal phones

A basic distinction in manner of articulation is between **oral** and **nasal** phones. When the velum is raised, cutting off the airflow through the nasal passages, oral sounds are produced. The velum can also be lowered to allow air to pass through the nasal passages, producing a sound that is nasal. Both consonants and vowels can be nasal, in which case they are generally voiced. (Unless otherwise noted, all nasals represented in this chapter are voiced.) The consonants at the end of the English words *su<u>n</u>, su<u>m</u>,* and *su<u>ng</u>* are nasal. For many speakers of English, the vowels of words such as *b<u>a</u>nk* and *w<u>i</u>nk* are also slightly nasal due to their proximity to nasal consonants.

## 2.5.2  Stops

**Stops** are made with a complete closure either in the oral cavity or at the glottis. In the world's languages, stops are found at bilabial, dental, alveolar, palatal, velar, uvular, and glottal points of articulation.

In English, bilabial, alveolar, and velar oral and nasal stops occur in the words shown in table 2.3. Note that [ŋ] does not occur word-initially in English though it can in other languages.

The glottal stop is commonly heard in English in the expression *uh-uh* [ʔʌʔʌ], meaning 'no'. The two vowels in this utterance are each preceded by a momentary closing of the airstream at the glottis. In some British dialects, the glottal stop is commonly heard in place of the [t] in a word like *bottle*. You may see this glottal stop spelled with an apostrophe *(bo'l)*.

| Table 2.3 | English stops and their transcription | |
|---|---|---|
| **Bilabial** | | **Transcription** |
| Voiceless | s<u>p</u>an | [p] |
| Voiced | <u>b</u>an | [b] |
| Nasal (Voiced) | <u>m</u>an | [m] |
| **Alveolar** | | |
| Voiceless | s<u>t</u>un | [t] |
| Voiced | <u>d</u>ot | [d] |
| Nasal (Voiced) | <u>n</u>ot | [n] |
| **Velar** | | |
| Voiceless | s<u>c</u>ar | [k] |
| Voiced | <u>g</u>ap | [g] |
| Nasal (Voiced) | wi<u>ng</u> | [ŋ] |
| **Glottal** | | |
| Voiceless | (see table 2.4) | [ʔ] |

## A grid for stops

Table 2.4 presents a grid on which the stop consonants of English are arranged horizontally according to point of articulation. As you can see, each stop, with one exception, has voiced

| Table 2.4 | English stop consonants | | | |
|---|---|---|---|---|
| | **Bilabial** | **Alveolar** | **Velar** | **Glottal** |
| Voiceless | [p] | [t] | [k] | [ʔ] |
| Voiced | [b] | [d] | [g] | |
| Nasal | [m] | [n] | [ŋ] | |

and voiceless counterparts. The glottal stop is always voiceless. It is produced with the vocal folds drawn firmly together and the arytenoids drawn forward; since no air can pass through the glottis, the vocal folds cannot be set in motion.

## 2.5.3 Fricatives

**Fricatives** are consonants produced with a continuous airflow through the mouth. They belong to a large class of sounds called **continuants** (a class that also includes vowels and glides), all of which share this property. The fricatives form a special class of continuants; during their production, they are accompanied by a continuous audible noise because the air used in their production passes through a very narrow opening either at the glottis or in the vocal tract.

### English fricatives

English has voiceless and voiced labiodental fricatives at the beginning of the words *fat* and *vat*, voiceless and voiced interdental fricatives word-initially in the words *thin* and *those*, alveolar fricatives word-initially in *sing* and *zip*, and a voiceless alveopalatal fricative word-initially in *ship*. The voiced alveopalatal fricative is rare in English. It is the first consonant in the word *azure*, and is also heard in the words *pleasure* and *rouge*. The voiceless glottal fricative of English is heard in *hotel* and *hat*. See the transcription of English fricatives in table 2.5.

Special note must be taken of the alveolar fricatives [s] and [z]. There are two ways that English speakers commonly produce these sounds. Some speakers raise the tongue tip to the alveolar ridge (or to just behind the upper front teeth) and allow the air to pass through a

| Table 2.5 | The transcription of English fricatives | |
|---|---|---|
| **Glottal state** | **Point of articulation** | **Transcription** |
| | *Labiodental* | |
| Voiceless | fan | [f] |
| Voiced | van | [v] |
| | *Interdental* | |
| Voiceless | thin | [θ] |
| Voiced | then | [ð] |
| | *Alveolar* | |
| Voiceless | sun | [s] |
| Voiced | zip | [z] |
| | *Alveopalatal* | |
| Voiceless | ship | [ʃ] |
| Voiced | azure | [ʒ] |
| | *Glottal* | |
| Voiceless | hat | [h] |

grooved channel in the tongue. Other speakers form this same channel using the blade of the tongue; the tip is placed behind the lower front teeth.

## A grid for fricatives

Table 2.6 presents a grid on which the fricative consonants of English are arranged according to point of articulation. As in table 2.5, dentals are not distinguished from alveolars, since most languages have sounds with either one point of articulation or the other, but not both. Note that IPA [ʃ] and [ʒ] correspond to North American [š] and [ž], respectively.

| Table 2.6 | English fricatives | | | | |
|---|---|---|---|---|---|
| | **Labiodental** | **Interdental** | **Alveolar** | **Alveopalatal** | **Glottal** |
| Voiceless | [f] | [θ] | [s] | [ʃ] | [h] |
| Voiced | [v] | [ð] | [z] | [ʒ] | |

## 2.5.4  Affricates

When a stop articulation is released, the tongue moves rapidly away from the point of articulation. However, some non-continuant consonants show a slow release of the closure; these sounds are called **affricates**. English has only two affricates, both of which are alveopalatal. They are heard word-initially in *church* and *jump,* and are transcribed as [tʃ] and [dʒ], respectively.

## A grid for affricates

Table 2.7 presents a grid showing the two English affricates. Note that IPA [tʃ] and [dʒ] correspond to North American [č] and [ǰ], respectively.

| Table 2.7 | English affricates |
|---|---|
| | **Alveopalatal (= IPA Palatoalveolar)** |
| Voiceless | [tʃ] |
| Voiced | [dʒ] |

## Stridents and sibilants

At the beginning of this chapter, it was noted that acoustic as well as articulatory criteria are sometimes used in describing speech sounds. An acoustic criterion comes into play to describe fricatives and affricates, which are subdivided into two types based on their relative loudness. The noisier fricatives and affricates are called **stridents** (see table 2.8). Their quieter counterparts, such as [θ] or [ð], which have the same or nearly the same place of articulation, are considered non-strident. Stridents are also known as **sibilants**.

| Table 2.8 | Strident fricatives and affricates in English | |
|---|---|---|
| **Place of articulation** | **Strident** | |
| | *Voiceless* | *Voiced* |
| Alveolar | [s] | [z] |
| Alveopalatal | [ʃ] | [ʒ] |
| | [tʃ] | [dʒ] |

## 2.5.5  Voice lag and aspiration

After the release of certain voiceless stops in English, you can hear a lag or brief delay before the voicing of a following vowel. Since the lag in the onset of vocalic voicing is accompanied by the release of air, the traditional term for this phenomenon is **aspiration**. It is transcribed with a small raised [ʰ] after the aspirated consonant. Table 2.9 provides some examples of aspirated and unaspirated consonants in English (some vowel symbols are introduced here as well). Notice that the sounds that have both aspirated and unaspirated varieties are all voiceless stops. In other languages, voiceless fricatives and affricates may also be aspirated or unaspirated.

| Table 2.9 | Aspirated and unaspirated consonants in English | | |
|---|---|---|---|
| **Aspirated** | | **Unaspirated** | |
| [pʰæt] | pat | [spæt] | spat |
| [tʰʌb] | tub | [stʌb] | stub |
| [kʰowp] | cope | [skowp] | scope |

Figure 2.5 shows how aspiration of a voiceless consonant takes place, using the aspirated consonant [pʰ] as an example. Though the sequence of articulations takes place continuously, the figure illustrates only certain moments.

**Figure 2.5**
Aspirated consonant production (English *pill*)

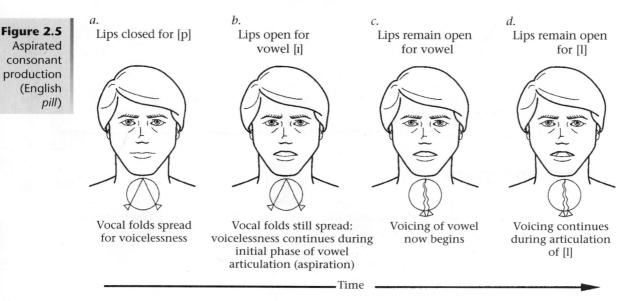

*a.*
Lips closed for [p]

*b.*
Lips open for vowel [ɪ]

*c.*
Lips remain open for vowel

*d.*
Lips remain open for [l]

Vocal folds spread for voicelessness

Vocal folds still spread: voicelessness continues during initial phase of vowel articulation (aspiration)

Voicing of vowel now begins

Voicing continues during articulation of [l]

— Time —

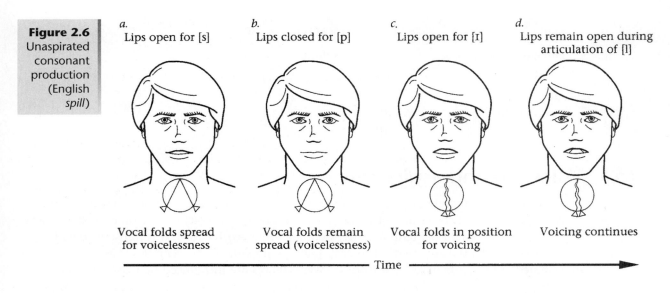

**Figure 2.6**
Unaspirated consonant production (English *spill*)

a. Lips open for [s]

b. Lips closed for [p]

c. Lips open for [ɪ]

d. Lips remain open during articulation of [l]

Vocal folds spread for voicelessness

Vocal folds remain spread (voicelessness)

Vocal folds in position for voicing

Voicing continues

Time

Figures 2.6 and 2.7 show the relation between articulation and voicing for unaspirated and voiced consonants. The unaspirated consonant, such as the [p] of English *spill*, shows voicing of the vowel starting very soon after release of the consonant closure. The voiced initial [b] of English *bill* shows voicing starting just before the release of the bilabial closure. In figure 2.7, note how voicing precedes the release of the labial articulators.

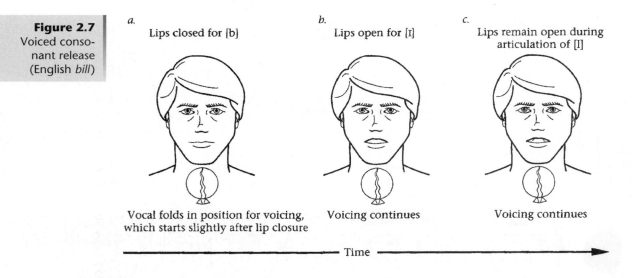

**Figure 2.7**
Voiced consonant release (English *bill*)

a. Lips closed for [b]

b. Lips open for [ɪ]

c. Lips remain open during articulation of [l]

Vocal folds in position for voicing, which starts slightly after lip closure

Voicing continues

Voicing continues

Time

## Unreleased Stops

Up to now in the chapter, we have described how stops may be either aspirated or unaspirated. Here we introduce a third variant: the *unreleased* stop. Pronounce the words in the following lists:

pave      cap
Tom       pot
king      back

The words in the first column have the stops ([pʰ], [tʰ], and [kʰ]) released into the following vowel. However, in the second column, it is quite common not to release these stops at all. When you pronounce the word *cap* you may well end with your lips closed. In *pot* and *back* your tongue stays on the roof of your mouth. The phonetic symbol for this is a raised [˺] as in [p˺].

## 2.5.6 Liquids

Among the sounds commonly found in the world's languages are *l* and *r* and their numerous variants. They form a special class of consonants known as *liquids*. Although there is a great deal of variation in the production of *l*s and *r*s in the languages of the world, they are grouped together in a single category because they often pattern together in phonology (more will be said about this in chapter 3).

### Laterals

Varieties of *l* are called **laterals**. As laterals are articulated, air escapes through the mouth along the lowered sides of the tongue. When the tongue tip is raised to the dental or alveolar position, the dental or alveolar laterals are produced. Both may be transcribed as [l].

Because laterals are generally voiced, the term *lateral* used alone usually means 'voiced lateral'. Still, there are instances of voiceless laterals in speech. The voiceless dental or alveolar lateral is written with an additional phonetic symbol, called a **diacritic**. In this case, the diacritic is a circle beneath the symbol: [l̥]. Voiceless laterals can be heard in the pronunciation of the English words p*l*ease and c*l*ear.

### English *rs*

Numerous varieties of *r* are also heard in the world's languages. This section describes the types found in English. The *r* of English as it is spoken in Canada and the United States is made either by curling the tongue tip back into the mouth or by bunching the tongue upward and back in the mouth. This *r*, which is known as a **retroflex** *r*, is heard in *ride* and c*ar*. IPA transcription favours [ɹ] for this sound, though it also offers the symbol [r] which we use in this book.

Another sound commonly identified with *r* is the **flap**. The flap is produced when the tongue tip strikes the alveolar ridge as it passes across it. It is heard in the North American

---

### Language Matters **Another Kind of *l***

Pronounce the words in the following two lists:

| | |
|---|---|
| leaf | fall |
| lie | milk |
| lawn | steal |

Notice that the *l* sounds are not pronounced in the same way. In the first column, the *l* is made with the tongue tip touching the alveolar ridge (as described in table 2.10 on the next page). In the second column, however, you will notice that the *l* sound is made with additional constriction further back in the mouth (at the velum). This type of *l* is known technically as a *velarized l* and more casually as a *dark l*. The phonetic symbol is [ɫ].

English pronunciation of *bitter* and *butter,* and in some British pronunciations of *very.* It is commonly transcribed as [ɾ] and is generally voiced. Table 2.10 presents the laterals *r, l,* and the flap of Canadian English.

| **Table 2.10** | **English liquids** | | |
|---|---|---|---|
| | | **Alveolar** | |
| Laterals | | voiced | [l] |
| | | voiceless | [l̥] |
| *r*s | retroflex | voiced | [r] |
| | | voiceless | [r̥] |
| | flap | | [ɾ] |

## 2.5.7  Syllabic liquids and nasals

Liquids and nasals are more sonorous than other consonants and in this respect are more like vowels than are the other consonants. In fact, they are so sonorous that they may function as syllabic nuclei. When they do so, they are called **syllabic liquids** and **syllabic nasals** (see table 2.11). Syllabic liquids and nasals are found in many of the world's languages, including English. In transcription, they are usually marked with a short diacritic line underneath.

| **Table 2.11** | **Syllabic liquids and nasals in English** | | |
|---|---|---|---|
| | **Syllabic** | | **Non-syllabic** |
| bottle | [bɑɾl̩] | lift | [lɪft] |
| funnel | [fʌnl̩] | pill | [pʰɪl] |
| bird | [bərd], [bɚd], or [br̩d] | rat | [ræt] |
| her | [hər], [hɚ], or [hr̩] | car | [kʰar] |
| button | [bʌtn̩] | now | [naw] |
| 'm-m' | [ʔm̩ʔm̩] (meaning 'no') | mat | [mæt] |

To be clear, then, the [n] in a word like *no* is not syllabic because it does not form the nucleus of the syllable. *No* is a one-syllable word and has one vowel. However, the [n] in a two-syllable word like *button* is syllabic. The second syllable has [n] as its nucleus. Therefore, whether a segment is syllabic or not is directly related to how it functions in the syllable. We will discuss this further in section 3.4 of chapter 3 on the syllable.

Unfortunately for beginning linguistics students, North American transcription is not always consistent here. The syllabic *r* sound heard in words like *bird* and *her* is often transcribed in North America as a vowel-*r* sequence: [ər]. (The vowel symbol is presented in section 2.6.2 of this chapter.) The IPA symbol for this sound is [ɚ]. For many linguists, the following transcriptions would be taken as notationally equivalent variants:

| | | |
|---|---|---|
| [bʌtən] | and | [bʌtn̩] |
| [bʌtər] | and | [bʌtr̩] |

## 2.5.8 Glides

Recall that a glide is a very rapidly articulated non-syllabic segment. The two glides of Canadian English are the jod (pronounced [jɑd]; NA 'y-glide') [j] of *yes* and *boy*, and the w-glide [w] of *wet* and *now*. The [j] in IPA transcription corresponds to the [y] of North American transcription.

The [j] is a palatal glide (sometimes described as alveopalatal as well) whose articulation is virtually identical to that of the vowel [i] of *see*. You can verify this by pronouncing a [j] in an extended manner; it will sound very close to an [i].

The glide [w] is made with the tongue raised and pulled back near the velum and with the lips protruding, or **rounded**. For this reason, it is sometimes called a labiovelar. The [w] corresponds closely in articulation to the vowel [u] of *who*. This can be verified by extending the pronunciation of a [w]. We will consider [w] a rounded velar glide for purposes of description. Some speakers of English also have a voiceless (labio)velar glide, transcribed [ʍ], in the words *when*, *where*, and *which* (but not in *witch*).

Table 2.12 provides a summary of the places and manners of articulation of English consonants.

| **Table 2.12** | English consonants: places and manners of articulation | | | | | | | |
|---|---|---|---|---|---|---|---|---|
| **Manner of articulation** | | **Place of articulation** | | | | | | |
| | | **Labial** | **Labiodental** | **Interdental** | **Alveolar** | **Alveopalatal** | **Velar** | **Glottal** |
| Stop | voiceless | p | | | t | | k | ʔ |
| | voiced | b | | | d | | g | |
| Fricative | voiceless | | f | θ | s | ʃ | | h |
| | voiced | | v | ð | z | ʒ | | |
| Affricate | voiceless | | | | | tʃ | | |
| | voiced | | | | | dʒ | | |
| Nasal | voiced | m | | | n | | ŋ | |
| Liquid | voiced lateral | | | | l | | | |
| | voiced retroflex | | | | r | | | |
| Glide | voiced | | | | | | j | w |
| | voiceless | | | | | | | ʍ |

---

### Language Matters **What's the World's Most Unusual Speech Sound?**

Pirahã, a language with a couple of hundred speakers in Brazil, has a sound that is produced as follows: the tongue tip first touches the alveolar ridge and then comes out of the mouth, almost touching the upper chin as the underblade of the tongue touches the lower lip.

Technically speaking, this is known as a 'voiced, lateralized apical-alveolar/sublaminal-labial double flap with egressive lung air'. (Fortunately, for all concerned, the sound is only used in 'certain special types of speech performance'.)

Source: *The Sounds of the World's Languages* by Peter Ladefoged and Ian Maddieson. Maldon, MA: Blackwell, 1996.

---

## 2.6  Vowels

Vowels are sonorous, syllabic sounds made with the vocal tract more open than it is for consonant and glide articulations. Different vowel sounds (also called vowel *qualities*) are produced by varying the placement of the body of the tongue (remember that for vowels your tongue tip is behind your lower front teeth) and shaping the lips. The shape of the vocal tract can be further altered by protruding the lips to produce rounded vowels, or by lowering the velum to produce a nasal vowel. Finally, vowels may be tense or lax, depending on the degree of vocal tract constriction during their articulation.

The following section on vowels introduces most of the basic vowels of English. Some phonetic detail is omitted that will be introduced in the following chapter.

### 2.6.1  Simple vowels and diphthongs

English vowels are divided into two major types, **simple vowels** and **diphthongs**. Simple vowels do not show a noticeable change in quality during their articulation. The vowels of *pit, set, cat, dog, but, put,* and the first vowel of *suppose* are all simple vowels.

Diphthongs are vowels that exhibit a change in quality within a single syllable. English diphthongs show changes in quality that are due to tongue movement away from the initial vowel articulation towards a glide position. In the diphthongs classified as *major* diphthongs, the change in articulation is quite extreme and, hence, easy to hear. Listen to the change in articulation in the following words: *buy* ([aj]), *boy* ([oj]), and *now* ([aw]). Each of these diphthongs starts in one position (e.g., [a]) and ends up in another position (e.g., [w]). There are also minor diphthongs in which the change in position of the articulators is less dramatic. If you listen carefully and note the change in your lip position as you pronounce the words *play* ([ej]) and *go* ([ow]), you will realize that in each of these diphthongs, too, the starting position is different from the ending position. The change is less easy to hear, and in fact is not made by all English speakers, in the vowels of words like *heed* and *lose,* and we will not transcribe these as diphthongs. Some instructors, however, may ask that you transcribe them in the diphthongized form. Table 2.13 presents the simple vowels and diphthongs of English. The diphthongs are transcribed as vowel-glide sequences. Although diphthongs are complex in an articulatory sense (in that they are transcribed as a vowel plus a glide), they still act as a single vowel in

> ### Language Matters **Cross-Dialectal Variation**
>
> One of the best ways to learn to appreciate some of these fine differences in vowel articulation is to think of some cross-dialectal variation in English. Let us first consider the question of the minor diphthongs in [ej] and [ow]. In Canadian English, these sounds are diphthongs (as reflected in our transcription) but this is not the case in *all* dialects of English. In Jamaican English words like *go* and *say* have simple vowels and would be transcribed as [go] and [se]. To listen to these sounds, please go to the website at **www.pearsoned.ca/ogrady** to note the difference.
>
> Comparison across dialects can also help us to understand why we have used the [a] symbol in the major diphthongs. In articulatory terms, the [a] sound is made at the front of the mouth a bit lower than [æ]. You can hear this sound in many Romance languages (like French or Spanish) in words like *la* or *gato*. However, you can also find that sound in Canadian English in words that have an [r] following the vowel. Say the following words as naturally as you can: *car, farm, heart.* Now try to say the same words, but stop before you pronounce the [r] sound. You will notice that the vowel in *car* ([a]) is not the same as the vowel in *saw* ([ɑ]). This [a] vowel is, in fact, where we start articulating our diphthongs. If you try to say words like *right* and *round* with an [ɑ] sound rather than an [a] you will find yourself speaking with one variety of a British accent. To hear these sound files, go to the website at **www.pearsoned.ca/ogrady.**

some respects. Our judgments tell us that both *pin* (simple vowel) and *pint* (diphthong) are single syllable words. Having a diphthong doesn't add a syllable to a word.

**Table 2.13**    Some simple vowels and diphthongs of Canadian English

| Simple vowels | | Minor diphthongs | | Major diphthongs | |
|---|---|---|---|---|---|
| p<u>i</u>t | [ɪ] | s<u>ay</u> | [ej] | m<u>y</u> | [aj] |
| s<u>e</u>t | [ɛ] | gr<u>ow</u> | [ow] | n<u>ow</u> | [aw] |
| p<u>u</u>t | [ʊ] | (h<u>ea</u>t | [ij]) | b<u>oy</u> | [oj] |
| c<u>u</u>t | [ʌ] | (l<u>o</u>se | [uw]) | | |
| m<u>a</u>t | [æ] | | | | |
| d<u>o</u>g | [ɑ] | | | | |
| h<u>ea</u>t | [i] | | | | |
| l<u>o</u>se | [u] | | | | |

## 2.6.2   Basic parameters for describing vowels

Vowel articulations are not as easy to feel at first as consonant articulations because the vocal tract is not narrowed as much. To become acquainted with vowel articulation, alternately pronounce the vowels of *he* and *awe*. You will feel the tongue move from a **high** front to a **low** back position. Once you feel this tongue movement, alternate between the vowels of *awe* and *at*. You will feel the tongue moving from the low **back** to low **front** position. Finally, alternate between the vowels of *he* and *who*. You will notice that in addition to a tongue movement between the high front and high back positions, you are also rounding your lips for the [u]. Figure 2.8 shows a midsagittal view of the tongue position for the vowels [i], [ɑ], and [u] based on X-ray studies of speech.

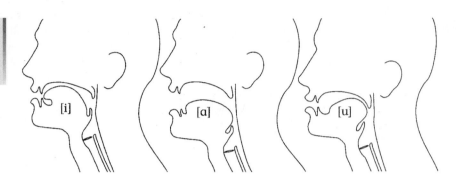

**Figure 2.8**
Tongue position and transcription for three English vowels

Vowels for which the tongue is neither raised nor lowered are called **mid vowels**. The front vowel of English *made* or *fame* is mid, front, and unrounded. The vowel of *code* and *soak* is mid, back, and rounded. In the case of diphthongs, the articulatory descriptions refer to the tongue position of the vowel nucleus, not the following glide. The vowels presented so far in this section are summed up in table 2.14. Note that in describing the vowels, the articulatory parameters are presented in the order *height, backness, rounding*.

| **Table 2.14** | Basic phonetic parameters for describing Canadian English vowels | |
|---|---|---|
| h<u>ea</u>t | [i] | high front unrounded |
| f<u>a</u>te | [ej] | mid front unrounded |
| m<u>a</u>d | [æ] | low front unrounded |
| S<u>ue</u> | [u] | high back rounded |
| b<u>oa</u>t | [ow] | mid back rounded |
| s<u>u</u>n | [ʌ] | mid back (central) unrounded |
| c<u>o</u>t, c<u>au</u>ght | [ɑ] | low back unrounded |

## Language Matters **More Cross-Dialectal Variation**

You will hear the [ɔ] sound in some dialects of English. If you know what speakers of certain New York dialects sound like when they say words like *coffee* or how speakers of certain British dialects say words like *saw*, you will know what this sounds like. Even in Canadian English, though, you will find the [ɔ] in some words. Say the word *more* as naturally as you can. Now say the same word but stop before you get to the [r]. You will find that you have said something like [mɔ] and not [mow]. While this can be transcribed as [o], note that you do not make a diphthong here. As with the [a] sound we looked at before, there is something special about vowels that occur before [r].

In standard Canadian English, there is no difference between the vowels of a pair of words like *cot* [ɑ] and *caught*, whose vowel is also [ɑ]. In some dialects of North American English, as well as in many other dialects of English worldwide, the vowel of *caught* (and certain other words such as *law*) is the mid back rounded lax vowel [ɔ].

Tongue positions for these vowels are illustrated in figure 2.9. The trapezoid corresponds roughly to the space within which the tongue moves, which is wider at the top of the oral cavity and more restricted at the bottom. Non-front vowels are traditionally divided into central and back vowels (see figures 2.9 and 2.10); often the term *back* alone is used for all non-front vowels.

**Figure 2.9**
Basic tongue positions for English vowels

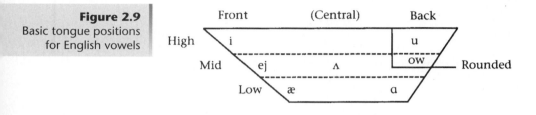

### 2.6.3 Tense and lax vowels

All the vowels illustrated in figure 2.9 except [æ] and [ʌ] are **tense**; they are produced with a placement of the tongue that results in greater vocal tract constriction than that of non-tense vowels; in addition, tense vowels are longer than non-tense vowels. Some vowels of English are made with roughly the same tongue position as the tense vowels, but with a less constricted articulation; they are called **lax**. The representation of vowels and their articulatory positions (figure 2.9) is expanded in figure 2.10 to include both tense and lax vowels.

**Figure 2.10**
Canadian English vowels (tense vowels are circled)

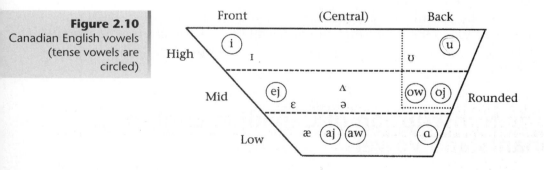

Table 2.15 provides examples from English comparing tense and lax vowels. Note that not all the vowels come in tense/lax pairs. The difference between two of the vowels illustrated in table 2.15 is often not easy to hear at first. Both the vowel [ʌ] in *cut, dud, pluck,* and *Hun,* and the vowel [ə] of *Canada, about, tomahawk,* and *sofa* are mid, back, unrounded,

| Table 2.15 | Tense and lax vowels in Canadian English | | |
|---|---|---|---|
| **Tense** | | **Lax** | |
| heat | [i] | hit | [ɪ] |
| mate | [ej] | met | [ɛ] |
| — | — | mat | [æ] |
| shoot | [u] | should | [ʊ] |
| coat | [ow] | (ought | [ɔ] in some dialects) |
| — | — | cut | [ʌ] |
| — | — | Canada | [ə] |
| lock | [ɑ] | — | — |
| lies | [aj] | | |
| loud | [aw] | | |
| boy | [oj] | | |

and lax. The vowel of the second set of examples, called **schwa**, is referred to as a **reduced vowel**. In addition to being lax, it has a very brief duration (briefer than that of any of the other vowels).

There is a simple test that helps determine whether vowels are tense or lax. In English, monosyllabic words spoken in isolation do not end in lax vowels. We find *see* [si], *say* [sej], *Sue* [su], *so* [sow], and *saw* [sɑ] in English, but not *s[ɪ], *s[ɛ], *s[æ], *s[ʊ], or *s[ʌ]. Schwa, however, frequently appears in unstressed position in polysyllabic words like *sof* [ə] and *Can*[ə]*d*[ə]. It should be pointed out—especially for those who think their ears are deceiving them—that many speakers produce the final vowel in the last two examples as [ʌ], and not as [ə].

This rather formidable crowd of vowels should not intimidate you. If you are a native speaker of English, you have been using these vowels (and others, some of which you will be introduced to in the next chapter) most of your life. Learning to hear them consciously and transcribe them is not a difficult task. If you are a non-native speaker of English, you have access to the sound files on our website to practise listening to these sounds. The next section provides more examples of the transcription of English consonants and vowels.

## 2.7 Phonetic transcription of Canadian English consonants and vowels

Tables 2.16 and 2.17 present the phonetic symbols for consonants and vowels commonly used to transcribe Canadian English. To illustrate how each symbol is used, one word is transcribed completely, and then some other words in which the same sound is found are given. You will notice that in the example words, the spelling of the sound may vary. Be careful of this when you transcribe words phonetically—the sound of a word, not its spelling, is what is transcribed!

| **Table 2.16** | Transcribing English consonants | | |
|---|---|---|---|
| **Symbol** | **Word** | **Transcription** | **More examples** |
| [pʰ] | pit | [pʰɪt] | pain, upon, apart |
| [p] | spit | [spɪt] | spar, crispy, upper, Yuppie, culprit, bumper |
| [tʰ] | tick | [tʰɪk] | tell, attire, terror, Tutu |
| [t] | stuck | [stʌk] | stem, hunter, nasty, mostly |
| [kʰ] | keep | [kʰip] | cow, kernel, recur |
| [k] | skip | [skɪp] | scatter, uncle, blacklist, likely |
| [tʃ] | chip | [tʃɪp] | lunch, lecher, ditch, belch |
| [dʒ] | judge | [dʒʌdʒ] | germ, journal, budgie, wedge |
| [b] | bib | [bɪb] | boat, liberate, rob, blast |
| [d] | dip | [dɪp] | dust, sled, draft |
| [ɾ] | butter | [bʌɾər] | madder, matter, hitting, writer, rider |
| [g] | get | [gɛt] | gape, mugger, twig, gleam |
| [f] | fit | [fɪt] | flash, coughing, proof, phlegmatic, gopher |
| [v] | vat | [væt] | vote, oven, prove |
| [θ] | thick | [θɪk] | thought, ether, teeth, three, bathroom |
| [ð] | though | [ðow] | then, bother, teethe, bathe |
| [s] | sip | [sɪp] | psychology, fasten, lunacy, bass, curse, science |
| [z] | zap | [zæp] | Xerox, scissors, desire, zipper, fuzzy |
| [ʃ] | ship | [ʃɪp] | shock, nation, mission, glacier, wish |
| [ʒ] | azure | [æʒər] | measure, rouge, visual, garage (for some speakers), Taj Mahal |
| [h] | hat | [hæt] | who, ahoy, forehead, behind |
| [j] | yet | [jɛt] | use, yes, cute |
| [w] | witch | [wɪtʃ] | wait, weird, queen, now |
| [ʍ] | which | [ʍɪtʃ] | what, where, when (only for some speakers) |
| [l] | leaf | [lif] | loose, lock, alive, hail |
| [l̩] | huddle | [hʌdl̩] | bottle, needle (for many speakers) |
| [r] | reef | [rif] | rod, arrive, tear |
| [r̩] | bird | [br̩d] [bɚd], [bərd] | early, hurt, stir, purr, doctor |
| [m] | moat | [mowt] | mind, humour, shimmer, sum, thumb |
| [m̩] | 'm-m' | [ʔm̩ʔm̩] | bottom, random |
| [n] | note | [nowt] | now, winner, angel, sign, wind |
| [n̩] | button | [bʌtn̩] | Jordan, batten |
| [ŋ] | sing | [sɪŋ] | singer, longer, bank, twinkle |

| Table 2.17 | Transcribing English vowels | | |
|---|---|---|---|
| **Symbol** | **Word** | **Transcription** | **More examples** |
| [i] | fee | [fi] | she, cream, believe, receive, serene, amoeba, highly |
| [ɪ] | fit | [fɪt] | hit, income, definition, been (for some speakers) |
| [ej] | fate | [fejt] | they, clay, grain, gauge, engage, great, sleigh |
| [ɛ] | let | [lɛt] | led, head, says, said, sever, guest |
| [æ] | bat | [bæt] | panic, racket, laugh, Vancouver |
| [u] | boot | [but] | to, two, loose, brew, Louise, Lucy, through |
| [ʊ] | book | [bʊk] | should, put, hood |
| [ow] | note | [nowt] | no, throat, though, slow, toe, oaf, O'Conner |
| [oj] | boy | [boj] | voice, boil, toy |
| [ɑ] | saw | [sɑ] | cot, caught, father, bought, across, Toronto |
| [ʌ] | shut | [ʃʌt] | other, udder, tough, lucky, was, flood |
| [ə] | roses | [rowzəz] | collide, hinted, telegraph, (to) suspect |
| [aw] | crowd | [krawd] | (to) house, plow, bough |
| [aj] | lies | [lajz] | my, tide, thigh, buy |

## 2.8    Suprasegmentals

All phones have certain inherent **suprasegmental** or **prosodic** properties that form part of their makeup no matter what their place or manner of articulation. These properties are **pitch**, **loudness**, and **length**.

All sounds give us a subjective impression of being relatively higher or lower in pitch. Pitch is the auditory property of a sound that enables us to place it on a scale that ranges from low to high. Pitch is especially noticeable in sonorous sounds like vowels, glides, liquids, and nasals. Even stop and fricative consonants convey different pitches. This is particularly noticeable among the fricatives, as you can hear by extending the pronunciation of [s] and then of [ʃ]; the [s] is clearly higher pitched. All sounds have some degree of intrinsic loudness as well or they could not be heard. Moreover, all sounds occupy a certain stretch of time—they give the subjective impression of length.

## 2.8.1    Pitch: tone and intonation

Speakers of any language have the ability to control the level of pitch in their speech. This is accomplished by controlling the tension of the vocal folds and the amount of air that passes through the glottis. The combination of tensed vocal folds and greater air pressure results in higher pitch on vowels and sonorant consonants, whereas less tense vocal folds and lower air pressure result in lower pitch. Two kinds of controlled pitch movement found in human language are called **tone** and **intonation**.

# Tone

A language is said to have tone or be a **tone language** when differences in word meaning are signalled by differences in pitch. Pitch on forms in tone languages functions very differently from the movement of pitch in a non-tone language. When a speaker of English says *a car?* with a rising pitch, the word *car* does not mean anything different from the same form pronounced on a different pitch level or with a different pitch contour. In contrast, when a speaker of a tone language such as Mandarin pronounces the form *ma* [mà] with a falling pitch, it means 'scold', but when the same form (*ma*) is pronounced with a rising pitch, as [má], the meaning is 'hemp' (see figure 2.13 opposite). There is no parallel to anything like this in non-tone languages such as English and French.

Unlike the preceding Mandarin falling or rising tone examples, some languages show only what are known as level tones. Tsúut'ína (or Sarcee), an Athabascan language spoken in Alberta, has high, mid, and low pitch level tones. In figure 2.11, the uppercase letters H, M, and L stand for high, mid, and low tones, respectively. An **association line** drawn from the letters to the vowel links the segments with their respective tones.

| H | M | L |
|---|---|---|
| \| | \| | \| |
| [miɬ] 'moth' | [miɬ] 'snare' | [miɬ] 'sleep' |

Level tones that signal meaning differences are called **register tones**: two or three register tones are the norm in most of the world's register tone languages, though four have been reported for Mazatec, a language spoken in Mexico.

A single tone may be associated with more than one syllabic element. In Mende, spoken in West Africa, certain polysyllabic forms show the same tone on each syllable (in table 2.18, the diacritic [´] indicates a high tone and the diacritic [`] indicates a low tone).

| Table 2.18 | High-tone and low-tone words in Mende |
|---|---|
| pélé | 'banana' |
| háwámá | 'waistline' |
| kpàkàlì | 'tripod chair' |

This notation allows us to represent the tone as characteristic of an entire form. The single underlying tone unit is associated with all vowels (see figure 2.12).

In some languages, tones can change pitch within a single syllabic element. Moving pitches that signal meaning differences are called **contour tones**. In Mandarin, both register and contour tones are heard. Contour tones are shown by pitch level notation lines that converge above the vowel, as shown in figure 2.13.

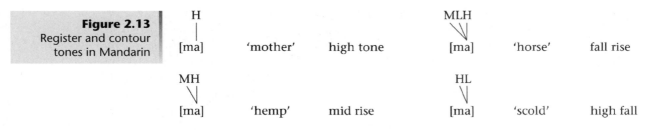

**Figure 2.13**
Register and contour
tones in Mandarin

In figure 2.13, there is one (high) register tone. The other tones are all contour tones.

In other languages, tone can have a grammatical function. In Bini, a language spoken in Nigeria, tone can signal differences in the tense of a verb (such as past versus present), as figure 2.14 shows.

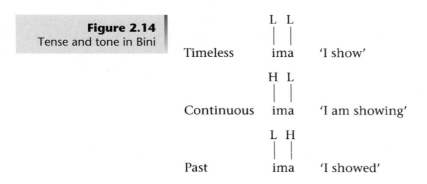

**Figure 2.14**
Tense and tone in Bini

Although tones may seem exotic to native speakers of Western European languages, they are very widespread. Tone languages are found throughout North and South America, sub-Saharan Africa, and the Far East.

## Intonation

Pitch movement in spoken utterances that is not related to differences in word meaning is called intonation. It makes no difference to the meaning of the word *seven*, for example, whether it is pronounced with a rising pitch or a falling pitch.

Intonation often does serve to convey information of a broadly meaningful nature, however. For example, the falling pitch we hear at the end of a statement in English such as *Fred parked the car* signals that the utterance is complete. For this reason, falling intonation at the end of an utterance is called a **terminal (intonation) contour**. Conversely, a rising or level intonation, called a **non-terminal (intonation) contour**, often signals incompleteness. Non-terminal contours are often heard in the non-final forms found in lists and telephone numbers.

In questions, final rising intonations also signal a kind of incompleteness in that they indicate that a conversational exchange is not finished: *Are you hungry?* However, English sentences that contain question words like *who, what, when,* and *how* (for example, *What did you buy?*) ordinarily do not have rising intonation. It is as if the question word itself is enough to indicate that an answer is expected.

Although intonation can be represented graphically as in figures 2.15 and 2.16, a more formal way of representing intonation is shown in figure 2.17. Here, as in tonal representation, L and H are relative terms for differences in pitch. The letters H and L are placed above the syllabic elements on which the pitch change occurs. The dotted lines indicate that the lowering pitch spreads across the remaining pitch-bearing elements.

**Figure 2.15**
Rising non-terminal intonations in a list and a telephone number

Sal<sup>ly</sup> Fr<sup>ed</sup>   He<sup>len and</sup> J<sub>oe</sub>

two eight f<sup>our</sup> two f<sup>ive</sup> <sup>one</sup> thr<sub>ee</sub>

**Figure 2.16**
Non-terminal intonation in a question

Did you <sup>have a</sup> <sup>nice</sup>      <sub>time</sub>

**Figure 2.17**
A terminal contour

L        H L

There's an elephant in here.

Rising intonation on names or requests is commonly heard in addressing people. Its use indicates that the speaker is opening a conversation or that some further action is expected from the addressee, as shown in figure 2.18.

**Figure 2.18**
Two non-terminal contours

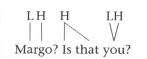

L H  H     L H
|  |   ∖     V
Margo? Is that you?

The complex use of intonation has just been touched on here. For example, rising intonation is often used to express politeness, as in *Please sit down*. Some linguists think that this is an extension of the 'open-ended mode' of intonation, and that since a rising intonation indicates that further response is expected (but not demanded) of the addressee, a sentence uttered with a rising intonation sounds less like an order and so is more polite.

## Intonation and tone

Tone and intonation are not mutually exclusive. Tone languages show intonation of all types. This is possible since tones are not absolute but relative pitches. For example, a tone is perceived as high if it is high relative to the pitches around it. As long as this relative difference is maintained, the pitch distinctions will also be maintained. This is shown graphically in figure 2.19, which represents the overall pitch of a declarative sentence in Igbo, a West African language with register tones. Note how an Igbo speaker clearly maintains the distinction among the pitch registers even as the overall pitch of the utterance falls. Each high tone is always lower than the preceding high tone, but higher than the low tone that immediately precedes it. This phenomenon is known as **downdrift**.

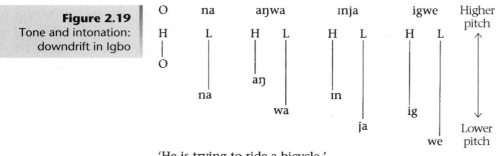

**Figure 2.19**
Tone and intonation: downdrift in Igbo

'He is trying to ride a bicycle.'

## 2.8.2 Length

In many languages there are both vowels and consonants whose articulation takes longer relative to that of other vowels and consonants. This phenomenon, known as length, is widespread in the world's languages. Length is indicated in phonetic transcription by the use of an IPA style colon [ː] (or simply a colon [:] in North American transcription) placed after the segment in question.

Hungarian, German, Cree, and Finnish are a few of the many languages that have long and short vowels. Yapese, a language spoken on the island of Yap in the Western Pacific, shows short and long vowels in pairs of words such as in table 2.19.

| Table 2.19 | Short and long vowels in Yapese | | |
|---|---|---|---|
| [θis] | 'to topple' | [θiːs] | '(a) post' |
| [pul] | 'to gather' | [puːl] | 'moon' |
| [ʔer] | 'near you' | [ʔeːr] | 'part of a lagoon' |

Italian has short and long consonants in pairs of words such as those shown in table 2.20. Long and short consonants are also found in many other languages, including Finnish, Turkish, and Hungarian.

| Table 2.20 | | Short and long consonants in Italian | | | |
|---|---|---|---|---|---|
| fato | [fatɔ] | 'fate' | fatto | [fatːɔ] | 'fact' |
| fano | [fanɔ] | 'grove' | fanno | [fanːɔ] | 'they do' |
| casa | [kasa] | 'house' | cassa | [kasːa] | 'box' |

## 2.8.3 Stress

In any utterance, some vowels are perceived as more prominent than others. In a word such as *banana* the second syllable is more prominent than the other two. In a word such as *telegraphic* [tʰɛləgrǽfɪk], the two vowel nuclei that are more prominent than the others are [ɛ] and [æ]. Syllabic segments perceived as relatively more prominent are stressed. Stress is a cover term for the combined effects of pitch, loudness, and length—the result of which is perceived prominence. In each language, the effect of these prosodic features varies. In general, English **stressed vowels** are higher in pitch, longer, and louder than unstressed ones. In some languages, the impression of vowel prominence results from a different interaction of the prosodic parameters than is found in English. In Modern Greek, for example, syllables tend to be of equal length. Stress, therefore, is manifested by a change only in pitch and loudness and not in syllable length. Tone languages do not change the pitch level or contour of tones to mark stress. In many of these languages, relative prominence is marked by exaggerating the vowel length or pitch contour.

There are various ways to mark stress in phonetic transcription. North American transcription commonly uses an acute accent [ ́] placed over the vowel nucleus in question to mark the most prominent or **primary** stress, and a grave accent [ ̀] to mark the second most prominent or **secondary** stress or stresses. (This should not be confused with the use of the same diacritics to mark tone in tone languages.) Stress can also be marked by placing numbers above the stressed vowels, usually [1] for a primary stress and [2] for a secondary stress. The word *telegraphic* can therefore be transcribed in either of the following ways:

(2)
$$[t^h\grave{\varepsilon}l\text{ə gr}\acute{æ}f\text{ɪk}] \quad \text{or} \quad [t^h\overset{2}{\varepsilon}l\text{ə gr}\overset{1}{æ}f\text{ɪk}]$$

The examples in table 2.21 illustrate some differences in English stress placement.

| Table 2.21 | Differing stress placement in English | | |
|---|---|---|---|
| (an) éxport | [ɛ́ksport] | (to) expórt | [ɛkspórt] |
| (a) présent | [prɛ́zənt] | (to) presént | [prəzɛ́nt] |
| télegràph | [tʰɛ́ləgræ̀f] | | |
| telégraphy | [tʰəlɛ́grəfì] | | |
| tèlegráphic | [tʰɛ̀ləgrǽfɪk] | | |

In the last four examples, you can also see that the quality of certain vowels varies depending on whether they are stressed or unstressed. This phenomenon is common in English, Russian, Palauan, and many other languages, but is not universal.

## 2.9 Speech production

Up to this point we have, for the most part, been describing phonetic segments as if they existed in isolation, and did not affect one another. However, speech production is not a series of isolated events. The phenomenon is a complex one, as the articulatory organs operate independently of each other (as we saw in section 2.5.5) and many fine adjustments are carried out very rapidly as we speak. As a consequence, speech production often results in the articulation of one sound affecting that of another sound.

### 2.9.1 Coarticulation

In order to articulate a sequence of phonetic segments, we have to plan a complex series of muscular movements. Due to the rapidity of speech (we can produce many segments in a second) and the design of the vocal tract, if our goal is to produce a [pl] sequence, we cannot first make the [p] and then make the [l]. Indeed, early speech synthesizers that produced speech in this way were practically unintelligible. Rather, as the sequence [pl] is produced, the tongue tip will start to move toward the alveolar ridge *before* the lips separate. The term **coarticulation** is used for situations such as this in which more than one articulator (here the lips and the tongue tip) is active. For more detailed information on this phenomenon, please see the website at **www.pearsoned.ca/ogrady**.

### 2.9.2 Processes

Articulatory adjustments that occur during the production of connected speech are called **processes**. Processes change the nature of the individual segment. Their cumulative effect often results in making words easier to articulate, and in this sense they are said to make speech more efficient. For example, when speakers of English nasalize the vowel of *bank*, they do not delay lowering the velum until the exact moment the nasal consonant articulation is reached. Instead, most English speakers begin lowering the velum for a nasal consonant almost as soon as they articulate the vowel that precedes it.

In a parallel manner, when speakers pronounce [k̟] as more palatal in a word such as *key*, they are speaking more efficiently from the point of view of articulation since they are making a less drastic adjustment in moving from the articulation of a more palatal [k̟] to that of a high front vowel than they would make in moving from a velar [k] to a high front vowel. Even more drastically, a speaker of English who says [pɹ̥ejd] for *parade* is making a major adjustment that results in a more efficient articulation: the two syllables of a careful pronunciation of *parade* are reduced to one by dropping the unstressed vowel of the first syllable; the tongue position for [r] can be anticipated during pronunciation of the [p]; and the voicelessness of the initial stop is carried on through the [ɹ̥].

Some processes appear to make articulation less, not more, efficient. For example, English speakers often lengthen consonants and vowels when they are asked to repeat a word that someone has not heard clearly. The following kind of exchange is typical.

**(3)**  "It's Fred."
"Did you say, 'It's red'?"
"No, I said, 'Fffreeed!'"

Lengthening segments results in a greater articulatory effort, but the process results in a more distinct form that is easier to perceive.

Another process that results in more easily perceivable speech adds a segment under certain conditions. When speaking slowly and carefully in a noisy environment, for example, English speakers often insert a vowel inside a group of consonants. This breaks up the sequence of consonants into separate syllables. To judge from the use people often make of this process when they wish to be clearly understood, it may well make words easier to perceive.

> **(4)** "Stop screaming!"
> "What? Stop dreaming?"
> "I said, 'Stop sc[ə]reaming!'"

These examples show that there are two basic reasons for the existence of articulatory processes. Some processes result in a *more efficient articulation* of a series of sounds in that the precise timing and coordination of speech is relaxed to various degrees. Other processes result in a *more distinct output*, which is easier to perceive than fluent or rapid everyday speech. Although these two types of processes might at first appear to be contradictory, each serves a particular end in speech production.

## 2.9.3　Some common articulatory processes

Only a finite number of processes operate in language, though their end result is a great deal of linguistic variability. In this section, we survey some of the most common of these processes.

### Assimilation

A number of different processes, collectively known as **assimilation**, result from the influence of one segment on another. Assimilation always results from a sound becoming more like another nearby sound in terms of one or more of its phonetic characteristics.

Nasalization of a vowel before a nasal consonant is caused by speakers anticipating the lowering of the velum in advance of a nasal segment. The result is that the preceding segment takes on the nasality of the following consonant as in [kʰæ̃nt] 'can't'. This type of assimilation is known as **regressive assimilation**, since the nasalization is, in effect, moving *backwards* to a preceding segment.

The nasalization of vowels following nasal consonants in Scots Gaelic is an example of **progressive assimilation**, since the nasality moves *forward* from the nasal consonant onto the vowel (see table 2.22). It results from not immediately raising the velum after the production of a nasal stop.

| **Table 2.22** | Progressive nasalization of vowels in Scots Gaelic |
|---|---|
| [mõːr] | 'big' |
| [nĩ] | 'cattle' |
| [mũ] | 'about' |
| [nẽːl] | 'cloud' |

**Voicing assimilation** is also widespread. For many speakers of English, voiceless liquids and glides occur after voiceless stops in words such as *please* [pl̥iz], *proud* [pr̥awd], and *pure* [pjuwr]. These sounds are said to be devoiced in this environment. **Devoicing** is a kind of assimilation since the vocal folds are not set in motion immediately after the release of the voiceless consonant closure. The opposite of devoicing is **voicing**. In Dutch, voiceless fricatives assimilate to the voicing of the stops that follow them, in anticipation of the voiced consonant. For example, the word *af* [ɑf] 'off, over' is pronounced with a [v] in the words *afbellen* 'to cancel' and *afdekken* 'to cover'.

Assimilation for place of articulation is also widespread in the world's languages. Nasal consonants are very likely to undergo this type of assimilation, as shown in table 2.23.

| **Table 2.23** | Assimilation for place of articulation in English |
|---|---|
| possible | i<u>m</u>possible |
| potent | i<u>m</u>potent |
| tolerable | i<u>n</u>tolerable |
| tangible | i<u>n</u>tangible |

The negative form of each of these words is made with either *im-* or *in-*. In both cases, the form shows a nasal consonant that has the same place of articulation as the stop consonant that follows it: labial in the case of *possible* and *potent*, and alveolar in the case of *tolerable* and *tangible*. In informal speech, many English speakers pronounce words like *inconsequential* and *inconsiderate* with an [ŋ] where the spelling shows *n*. Assimilation can also be heard in pronunciations such as *Va*[ŋ]*couver* and *Ba*[ɱ]*ff* (the symbol [ɱ] represents a labiodental nasal). Assimilation may even cross the boundary between words. In rapid speech, it is not uncommon to hear people pronounce phrases such as *in code* as [ɪŋkʰowd].

The preceding English example shows regressive assimilation for place of articulation. The following example, taken from German, shows progressive assimilation that again affects nasal consonants (see table 2.24). In careful speech, certain German verb forms are pronounced with a final [ən], as in *laden* 'to invite', *loben* 'to praise', and *backen* 'to bake'. In informal speech, the final [ən] is reduced to a syllabic nasal, which takes on the point of articulation of the preceding consonant. (Recall that the diacritic line under the phonetically transcribed nasals indicates that they are syllabic.)

| **Table 2.24** | Progressive assimilation in German | | |
|---|---|---|---|
| | **Careful speech** | **Informal speech** | |
| laden | [laːdən] | [laːdn̩] | 'to invite' |
| loben | [loːbən] | [loːbm̩] | 'to praise' |
| backen | [bakən] | [bakŋ̩] | 'to bake' |

**Flapping** is a process in which a dental or alveolar stop articulation changes to a flap [ɾ] articulation. In English, this process applies to both [t] and [d] when they occur between vowels, the first of which is generally stressed. Flaps are heard in the casual speech pronunciation of words such as *butter, writer, fatter, wader,* and *waiter,* and even in phrases such as *I bought it* [ajbárɪt]. The alveolar flap is always voiced. Flapping is considered a type of assimilation because it changes a non-continuant segment (a stop) to a continuant segment (flaps are classified as continuants) in the environment of other continuants (vowels). In addition, note that voicing assimilation also occurs in the change of the voiceless [t] to the voiced [ɾ].

## Dissimilation

**Dissimilation,** the opposite of assimilation, results in two sounds becoming less alike in articulatory or acoustic terms. The resulting sequence of sounds is easier to articulate and distinguish. It is a much rarer process than assimilation. One commonly heard example of dissimilation in English occurs in words ending with three consecutive fricatives, such as *fifths*. Many speakers dissimilate the final [fθs] sequence to [fts], apparently to break up the sequence of three fricatives with a stop.

## Deletion

**Deletion** is a process that removes a segment from certain phonetic contexts. Deletion occurs in everyday rapid speech in many languages. In English, a schwa [ə] is often deleted when the next vowel in the word is stressed, as shown in table 2.25.

| **Table 2.25** Deletion of [ə] in English | | |
|---|---|---|
| **Slow speech** | **Rapid speech** | |
| [pʰəréjd] | [pṛéjd] | parade |
| [kʰərówd] | [kṛówd] | corrode |
| [səpʰówz] | [spówz] | suppose |

Deletion also occurs as an alternative to dissimilation in words such as *fifths*. Many speakers delete the [θ] of the final consonant cluster and say [fɪfs]. In very rapid speech, both the second [f] and the [θ] are sometimes deleted, resulting in [fɪs].

## Epenthesis

**Epenthesis** is a process that inserts a syllabic or a non-syllabic segment within an existing string of segments. For example, in careful speech, the words *warmth* and *something* are pronounced [wormθ] and [sʌ̃məθɪ̃ŋ] (see table 2.26). It is common in casual speech for speakers to insert a [p] between the *m* and the *th* and pronounce the words [wormpθ] and [sʌ̃mpθɪ̃ŋ]. Consonant epenthesis of this type is another example of a coarticulation phenomenon. In English, the articulatory transition from a sonorant consonant to a non-sonorant appears to be eased by the insertion of a consonant that shares properties of both segments. Notice that the epenthesized consonants are all non-sonorant, have the same place of articulation as the sonorant consonant to their left, and have the same voicing as the non-sonorant consonant to their right.

**Table 2.26**    Some examples of English consonant epenthesis

| Word | Non-epenthesized pronunciation | Epenthesized pronunciation |
|---|---|---|
| *something* | [sãmθĭŋ] | [sãmpθĭŋ] |
| *warmth* | [wormθ] | [wormpθ] |
| *length* | [lẽŋθ] | [lẽŋkθ] |
| *prince* | [prĭns] | [prĭnts] |
| *tenth* | [tẽnθ] | [tẽntθ] |

Vowels may also be inserted epenthetically. In Turkish, a word may not begin with two consonants. When words are borrowed into Turkish, an epenthetic vowel is inserted between certain sequences of two initial consonants, creating a new and permissible sequence (see table 2.27). (The reason for the differences among the vowels need not concern us here; note, though, that the vowel is always high; see section 2.10 for further presentation of these and other unfamiliar symbols.)

**Table 2.27**    Vowel epenthesis in Turkish

| Source word | Turkish form |
|---|---|
| *train* | t<u>i</u>ren |
| *club* | ky<u>l</u>ʏp |
| *sport* | s<u>ɯ</u>por |

## Metathesis

**Metathesis** is a process that reorders a sequence of segments. This often results in a sequence of phones that is easier to articulate. It is common to hear metathesis in the speech of children, who often cannot pronounce all the consonant sequences that adults can. For example, some English-speaking children pronounce *spaghetti* as *pesghetti* [pəskɛɾi]. In this form, the initial sequence [spə], which is often difficult for children to pronounce, is metathesized to [pəs].

The pronunciations of *prescribe* and *prescription* as *perscribe* and *perscription* are often-cited examples of metathesis in adult speech. In these cases, metathesis appears to facilitate the pronunciation of two successive consonant-*r* sequences in each word.

## Vowel reduction

In many languages, the articulation of vowels may move to a more central position when the vowels are unstressed. This process is known as **(vowel) reduction**. Typically, the outcome of vowel reduction is a schwa [ə]; this can be observed in pairs of related words that show different stress placement such as *Canada* [kʰǽnədə] versus *Canadian* [kʰənéjdiən]. Note that the first vowel in *Ca<u>na</u>da* is [æ] when stressed but schwa when unstressed (compare the pronunciation of the first vowel in *Canadian*), whereas the second vowel of the word *Ca<u>na</u>dian* is [ej] when stressed but a schwa when unstressed (compare the pronunciation of the second vowel in *Canada*). Since we cannot predict what vowel a schwa may 'turn into' when it is stressed, we assume that [æ] and [ej] are basic to the words in question and are reduced in unstressed position.

## 2.10 Other Vowels and Consonants

So far, this chapter has described only the vowels and consonants of English. Many, but not all, of these sounds are found in other languages. Moreover, many of the sounds found in other languages do not occur in English. Tables 2.28 and 2.29 introduce a number of novel vowels and consonants that are relevant to the discussion and problems throughout this book. Once the basic articulatory parameters have been understood, it's not a big jump to describe and to pronounce new and unfamiliar sounds.

Remember that phonetic descriptions are universal—they apply to the sounds of any human language. If you encounter the description 'voiced velar fricative', you know that the sound is a voiced continuant consonant made at the velum (i.e., the same place as the stop [g]). If you want to make this sound, the articulatory description can guide you: make a near closure at the velum and allow airflow to pass though. If you come across the description 'high front rounded vowel', and want to produce this sound, make the high front unrounded vowel [i] and then round the lips to produce the high front rounded vowel [y].

 For detailed descriptions and examples of the sounds presented in tables 2.28 and 2.29, go to the website at **www.pearsoned.ca/ogrady**.

---

**Table 2.28**　Modified IPA chart for vowels, including the sounds of English (circled) and many of those found in other languages. All vowels can be nasalized.

|  | Front | | (Central) | | Back | |
|---|---|---|---|---|---|---|
|  | **UR** | **R** | **UR** | **R** | **UR** | **R** |
| High | ⓘ | y |  |  | ɯ | ⓤ tense |
|  | ⓘ (lax) | ʏ (lax) |  |  |  | ⓤ lax |
| Mid | ⓔ | ø | ⓐ (reduced/lax) |  |  | ⓞ tense |
|  | ⓔ (lax) | œ (lax) | ⓐ (lax) |  |  | ⓞ lax |
| Low | ⓐ (lax) |  |  |  | ⓐ (tense) |  |

---

**Table 2.29**　Modified IPA chart for consonants, including the sounds of English (circled) and many of those found in other languages. Voiceless phones are always on the left of pairs with the same place of articulation.

|  | Bilabial | Labiodental | Dental | Alveolar | Alveopalatal | Retroflex | Palatal | Velar | Uvular | Pharyngeal | Glottal |
|---|---|---|---|---|---|---|---|---|---|---|---|
| Stop | ⓟⓑ |  | ⓣⓓ |  |  | ʈ ɖ | c ɟ | ⓚⓖ | q ɢ |  | ⓠ |
| Fricative | ɸ β | ⓕⓥ | ⓗⓓ | ⓢⓩ | ⓙ ʒ | ʂ ʐ | ç ʝ | x ɣ |  | ħ ʕ | ⓗ ɦ |
| Nasal | ⓜ ⓜ |  | ⓝ |  |  | ɳ | ɲ | ⓝ |  |  |  |
| Trill |  |  | r̃ |  |  |  |  |  | R |  |  |
| Flap |  |  | ⓡ |  |  |  |  |  |  |  |  |
| Approximant |  |  | ⓡ |  |  | ɻ | ɥ/ⓙ ⓦ |  |  |  |  |
| Lateral Approximant |  |  | ⓛⓛ |  |  |  | ʎ ʎ |  |  |  |  |
| Lateral Fricative |  |  | ɬ ɮ |  |  |  |  |  |  |  |  |

# Summing up

The study of the sounds of human language is called *phonetics*. These sounds are widely transcribed by means of the **International Phonetic Alphabet**.

The sounds of language are commonly described in **articulatory** and **acoustic** terms, and fall into two major types: syllabic sounds (**vowels, syllabic liquids**, and **syllabic nasals**) and non-syllabic sounds (**consonants** and **glides**). Sounds may be **voiced** or **voiceless**, and **oral** or **nasal**. Consonants are produced at various places of articulation: labial, dental, alveolar, alveopalatal, palatal, velar, uvular, glottal, and pharyngeal. At the places of articulation, the airstream is modified by different **manners of articulation** and the resulting sounds are **stops, fricatives, affricates,** or **liquids**. Vowels are produced with less drastic closure and are described with reference to tongue position (**high, low, back,** and **front**), tension (**tense** or **lax**), and lip rounding (**rounded** or **unrounded**). Language also exhibits **suprasegmental** phenomena such as **tone, intonation,** and **stress**.

## Notes

[1] There is still a great deal of discussion among linguists on the subject of diphthongs. English vowels that show a change in quality are considered diphthongs as long as the change in quality *follows* the vowel nucleus. Words such as *yes* and *wet* are considered to begin with a glide that is not an integral part of the vocalic nucleus. However, in transcribing other languages (Finnish, for example), sounds like [jɛ] and [wo] are considered to be diphthongs. For now, treat the diphthongs presented in table 2.1.3 as unit vowels, and the initial two sounds of words like *yes* and *wet* as distinct segments. This approach will be revised somewhat in chapter 3.

## Recommended reading

Catford, J.C. 2001. *A Practical Introduction to Phonetics*. 2nd ed. New York, NY: Oxford University Press.

Kent, R.D., and C. Read. 1993. *The Acoustic Analysis of Speech*. San Diego, CA: Singular Publishing Group.

Ladefoged, P. 2001. *A Course in Phonetics*. 4th ed. Toronto: Harcourt College Publishers.

Ladefoged, P., and I. Maddieson. 1995. *The Sounds of the World's Languages*. Cambridge, MA: Blackwell.

Pullum, G.K., and W.A. Ladusaw. 1986. *Phonetic Symbol Guide*. Chicago: University of Chicago Press.

Rogers, H. 1991. *Theoretical and Practical Phonetics*. Toronto: Copp Clark Pitman.

Shearer, William M. 1968. *Illustrated Speech Anatomy*. Springfield, IL: Charles C. Thomas.

Walker, Douglas C. 1984. *The Pronunciation of Canadian French*. Ottawa: University of Ottawa Press.

Go to http://psyc.queensu.ca/~munhallk/05_database.htm for ultrasound and X-ray images.

# Exercises

1. In order to become more aware of the differences between spelling and pronunciation, answer the following questions about English spelling.
   a) Find four words that show four alternative spellings of the sound [f].
   b) Find six words that have the letter 'a' pronounced differently.
   c) Find four words in which different groups of letters represent only one sound.
   d) Find two words in which two different sounds are pronounced but not spelled out.

2. How many segments are there in the following words?
   a) at              e) psychology
   b) math            f) knowledge
   c) cure            g) mailbox
   d) hopping         h) awesome

3. Is the first sound in each of the following words voiced or voiceless?
   a) though    e) zoom    i) huge    m) when (*may vary*)
   b) thought   f) silk    j) choose  n) ghetto
   c) form      g) pan     k) judge   o) pneumatic
   d) view      h) boat    l) buns    p) winced

4. Using the words presented in question 3, state whether the last sound of each word is voiced or voiceless.

5. For each of the following pairs of sounds, state whether they have the same or a different place of articulation. Then identify the place of articulation for each sound.
   a) [s] : [l]       e) [m] : [n]       i) [b] : [f]
   b) [k] : [ŋ]       f) [dʒ] : [ʃ]      j) [tʃ] : [dʒ]
   c) [p] : [g]       g) [f] : [h]       k) [s] : [v]
   d) [l] : [r]       h) [w] : [j]       l) [θ] : [t]

6. For each of the following pairs of sounds, state whether they have the same or different manners of articulation. Then identify the manner of articulation for each sound.
   a) [s] : [θ]       e) [l] : [t]       i) [r] : [w]
   b) [k] : [g]       f) [ð] : [v]       j) [tʃ] : [dʒ]
   c) [w] : [j]       g) [tʃ] : [s]      k) [h] : [ʔ]
   d) [f] : [ʃ]       h) [m] : [ŋ]       l) [z] : [dʒ]

7. After each of the following articulatory descriptions, write the sound described in phonetic brackets.
   a) voiceless velar stop              e) voiced velar nasal
   b) voiced labiodental fricative      f) voiceless interdental fricative
   c) voiced alveopalatal affricate     g) high back rounded lax vowel
   d) voiced palatal glide              h) low front unrounded vowel

**8.** Which of the following pairs of words show the same vowel quality? Mark each pair as *same* or *different*. Then transcribe the vowels of each word.

a) back      sat          h) hide      height
b) cot       caught       i) least     heed
c) bid       key          j) drug      cook
d) luck      flick        k) sink      fit
e) ooze      deuce        l) oak       own
f) cot       court        m) pour      port
g) fell      fail         n) mouse     cow

**9.** Using descriptive terms like sibilant, fricative, and so on, provide a single phonetic characteristic that all the segments in each group share. Try to avoid over-obvious answers such as 'consonant' or 'vowel'.
*Example:* [b d g u m j] are all voiced.

a) [p t k g ʔ]         e) [ʌ ə ʊ a]          i) [l r m n ŋ j w]
b) [i e ɛ æ]           f) [h ʔ]              j) [t d l r n s z]
c) [tʃ ʒ ʃ dʒ]         g) [u o]
d) [p b m f v]         h) [s z tʃ dʒ ʃ ʒ]

**10.** Transcribe the following sets of words. You may use these words to practise transcribing aspiration.

a) tog        i) peel       q) spell
b) kid        j) stun       r) cord
c) attain     k) Oscar      s) accord
d) despise    l) cooler     t) astound
e) elbow      m) sigh       u) pure
f) haul       n) hulk       v) wheeze
g) juice      o) explode    w) remove
h) thimble    p) tube       x) clinical

**11.** Using H, L, and association lines, transcribe the intonation of the following English phrases. Compare your results with the transcriptions of several classmates. Are they the same? If they aren't, discuss what aspects of intonation (such as emotion or speech context) might account for the differences in transcription.
a) 'Hi, Alice.'
b) 'Three people got off the bus at the last stop.'
c) 'My uncle likes to mountain climb.'

**12.** Mark primary and (where present) secondary stresses on the following words. It is not necessary to transcribe them.

a) sunny          f) arrive        k) secret
b) banana         g) defy          l) exceed
c) blackboard     h) summary       m) summery
d) Canada         i) Canadian      n) Canadianize
e) (to) reject    j) (a) reject    o) difficult

**13.** Find a fluent speaker of a language other than English and transcribe phonetically ten words of that language. If you encounter any sounds for which symbols are not found in this chapter, attempt to describe them in phonetic terms and then invent diacritics to help you transcribe them.

**14.** Provide coarticulation diagrams (see **www.pearsoned.ca/ogrady**) for the following words. Be sure that your diagrams capture the movement of the lips, tongue, velum, and glottis as in the model.

a) had

b) snap

c) please

d) dome

**15.** Compare the careful speech and rapid speech pronunciations of the following English words and phrases. Then, name the process or processes that make the rapid speech pronunciation different from the careful speech. (Stress is omitted here.)

|  | *Careful speech* | *Rapid speech* |
|---|---|---|
| a) in my room | [ɪn maj rum] | [ɪm maj rum] |
| b) I see them | [aj si ðɛm] | [aj siəm] |
| c) I see him | [aj si hɪm] | [aj siəm] |
| d) within | [wɪθɪn] | [wɪðɪn] |
| e) balloons | [bəlunz] | [blunz] |
| f) popsicle | [pʰɑpsɪkəl] | [pʰɑpskəl] |
| g) sit down | [sɪt dawn] | [sɪɾawn] |
| h) my advice | [maj ədvʌjs] | [maj əvʌjs] |
| i) Scotch tape | [skɑtʃ tʰejp] | [kʰɑtʃ stejp] |
| j) protection | [pɹowtʰɛkʃən] | [pərtʰɛkʃən] |
| k) hand me that | [hænd mi ðæt] | [hæmiðæt] |
| l) Pam will miss you | [pæm wɪl mɪs juw] | [pæml̩mɪʃjə] |

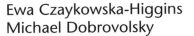

Ewa Czaykowska-Higgins
Michael Dobrovolsky

# CHAPTER *Three*

# Phonology: the function and patterning of sounds

*A person's tongue is a twisty thing, there are plenty of words there of every kind, and the range of words is wide, and their variation.*

HOMER, *THE ILIAD*, 20

We saw in chapter 2 that human beings can produce and perceive a large number of speech sounds. No human language exploits *all* of these phonetic possibilities. Instead, every language makes its own particular selection from the range of all possible speech sounds and organizes them into a system. The component of grammar that determines the selection of speech sounds and that governs both the sound patterns and the systematic phonetic variation found in language is known as **phonology**. While phonetics is primarily concerned with the concrete physical properties of language sounds, phonology investigates how sound and meaning are connected.

Speakers have some subconscious knowledge of the phonetic patterns that make up phonological systems. For example, as we saw in chapter 1, speakers of English recognize without being taught that certain combinations of consonants are acceptable in English, even if those combinations occur in forms that are not real words, while other combinations are not acceptable; thus, *slish* [slɪʃ] and *screnk* [skrɛŋk] are acceptable to English speakers, while *srish* [srɪʃ] and *screpk* [skrɛpk] are not. In fact, speakers can do more than recognize that certain forms are unnatural in their system; they can even correct unnatural forms to make them conform to the patterns that are acceptable in their own language. Without knowing exactly why, most English speakers would pronounce a form like *srish* as [sərɪʃ] breaking up the unacceptable consonant combination with a vowel, rather than, say, deleting one of the consonants to form [sɪʃ] or [rɪʃ] (something that children learning English as a first language or adults learning English as a second language might do). The task of phonologists, then, is (1) to discover and describe the systematic phonetic patterns found in individual languages and (2) to discover the general principles that underlie the patterning of sounds across all human languages. In doing this, phonologists hope to uncover the largely subconscious knowledge that speakers have of sound patterns. We want to answer the question *what do you know when you know the phonology of your language?*

It turns out that phonological knowledge can be characterized as knowledge of structures at different levels. In this chapter, we will examine three major phonological units: the **feature**, the **segment**, and the **syllable**.

We are already acquainted with the idea that the flow of speech can be divided into segments (as reflected in the phonetic transcription of a word like [sɛgmɛntəl]) and that segments are characterized by specific phonetic properties (voicing, nasality, etc.). In this chapter we will investigate the types of patterned, predictable phonetic variation that segments exhibit in individual languages and cross-linguistically. We will also demonstrate that segments are composed of smaller structural units known as *features*.

Features correspond to articulatory or acoustic categories such as [voice] or [strident]. They are the smallest building blocks of phonological structure, and, as we will see, the types of phonological patterns found in language are directly related to the properties of the features that make up segments. Finally, we will learn about the ways in which segments combine to form into larger structural units known as *syllables*. Syllables consist of a syllabic element—usually a vowel—and any preceding or following segments that are associated with it. As the representation of the word *segment* in figure 3.1 illustrates, features, segments, and syllables are organized into hierarchical levels, where each level is composed of units from the level beneath it. In figure 3.1, *segment* is a word-level unit represented by the abbreviation *Wd*. This word in turn consists of two syllables, each of which is represented by the Greek letter σ (sigma). Each syllable itself consists of several segments. Finally, each segment is composed of features. (For purposes of illustration, only a few features are provided for each segment. The internal hierarchical structure of syllables and segments is not represented; these are treated below, in sections 3.4, 3.5.2, and 3.5.3, respectively.)

**Figure 3.1**
Partial phonological representation of *segment*

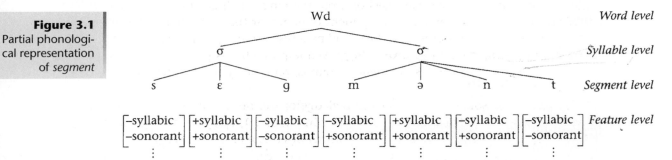

As units of phonological structure, syllables, segments, and features play major roles in the processes we investigated in the previous chapter, and, in combination with certain general principles of phonology, produce the sound patterns of language that characterize our phonological knowledge. In the next sections we examine these sound patterns and the phonological knowledge that enables speakers to distinguish among forms and to deal with the systematic phonetic variation found in the pronunciation of speech sounds. We begin by looking at how sound changes can lead to meaning changes.

# 3.1  Segments in contrast

All speakers know which segments of their language **contrast** and which do not. Segments are said to contrast (or to be *distinctive* or be in *opposition*) in a particular language when their presence alone may result in a change of meaning. For instance, the phonetically distinct segments [s] and [z] contrast in the English words *s̲ip* and *z̲ip*, as do the vowels in the words *h̲i̲t*, *h̲a̲te*, and *h̲o̲t*. In these examples, when we change the sound, we also change the meaning.

In this section we will consider how to determine which segments contrast in a language. In section 3.2 we will consider the systematic patterns associated with phonetically similar segments when they do not contrast.

## 3.1.1  Minimal pairs

Since knowledge of segmental contrasts is fundamental to knowing any language, the first step in an analysis of the phonology of a language is to establish which sounds in that language are in contrast with each other. In order to establish contrasts, it is necessary to examine the distribution of sounds in words and to compare word meanings. The most straightforward way to accomplish this examination is by way of the **minimal pair** test.

A minimal pair consists of two forms with distinct meanings that differ by only one segment found in the same position in each form (for example, at the beginning or end of a word). Thus, the examples [sɪp] *sip* and [zɪp] *zip* form a minimal pair (changing the sound at the beginning of the word) which shows that the sounds [s] and [z] contrast in English. The words [lus] *loose* and [luz] *lose* are also minimal pairs (changing the sound at the end of the word).

A number of minimal pairs that demonstrate consonant contrasts for English are given in table 3.1. It is important to remember that it is on the basis of *sound* and not spelling that minimal pairs are established. For purposes of analysis, contrasting words are often placed along the horizontal axis with respect to their place of articulation, reading from left to right (labial, alveolar, and so on), and vertically with respect to manner of articulation, in order to show which places and manners of articulation are relevant to the language in question.[1]

| **Table 3.1** | Contrasts among consonants in English | | | | | | | | | | |
|---|---|---|---|---|---|---|---|---|---|---|---|
| **Stops and affricates (non-continuants)** | | | | | | | | | | | |
| *Labial* | | *Interdental* | | *Alveolar* | | *Alveopalatal* | | *Velar* | | *Glottal* | |
| tap | [p] | | | pat | [t] | batch | [tʃ] | pick | [k] | | |
| tab | [b] | | | pad | [d] | badge | [dʒ] | pig | [g] | | |
| **Continuants** | | | | | | | | | | | |
| leaf | [f] | thigh | [θ] | sip | [s] | mesher | [ʃ] | | | hip | [h] |
| leave | [v] | thy | [ð] | zip | [z] | measure | [ʒ] | | | | |
| **Nasals** | | | | | | | | | | | |
| sum | [m] | | | sun | [n] | | | sung | [ŋ] | | |
| **Liquids and glides** | | | | | | | | | | | |
| | | | | | | yet | [j] | wet [w] | | | |
| | | | | leer | [l] | | | | | | |
| | | | | rear | [r] | | | | | | |

The phonetic context in which a sound occurs is called its **environment**. Examples of environments include *at the beginning of a word*, or *after a nasal*. Pairs of words that have segments in *nearly* identical environments (sometimes languages don't give the linguist a perfect data set for analysis), such as *assure* [əʃʊ́r]/*azure* [ǽʒər], which contrast [ʃ] and [ʒ], or *author* [áθər]/*either* [íðər], which contrast [θ] and [ð], are called **near-minimal pairs**. They can be used to establish contrasts if no minimal pairs for a particular set of segments can be found.

Once you have established the existence of a minimal or a near-minimal pair for a set of two segments, you may assume that those two segments contrast—or are *distinctive*—in that language. Segments that contrast with each other in a particular language are said to belong to separate **phonemes** of that language. Phonemes then are contrastive phonological units. When you know the phonology of a language, you know which sounds are capable of producing a change in meaning. Whereas *phones* come out of your mouth, *phonemes* are in your head. Notationally, this is captured by using square brackets for phones like [i] and slash brackets for phonemes like /i/. All the consonants in table 3.1 belong to separate phonemes in English, since all of them are contrastive in the language.

When looking for the contrastive sounds of a language, it is rare to find minimal pairs for all possible pairs of sounds, since some sounds are used more frequently than others, and some do not occur in particular environments. For example, you will find no minimal pairs involving [h] and [ŋ] in word-initial or word-final position in English, because there are no words that begin with [ŋ] or end in [h]. It is also difficult to find minimal pairs in English that have the phone [ʒ], which occurs for the most part in words borrowed from French such as *azure* and *mirage*. *Leash* and *liege* are one pair. See if you can come up with any more.

## Vowel contrasts in English

Vowel contrasts in English can be established with a few sets of examples. We assume in table 3.2 that English vowel-glide sequences like [ej] and [ow] are single vowels. You can think of these sounds as being phonetically complex but acting phonologically as simple

---

### Language Matters **Tongue Twisters**

Although some tongue twisters are difficult because of repeated sound combinations (e.g., The Leath police dismisseth us), others are tricky because of the phonemic contrasts they require you to make (e.g., She sees cheese). For more tongue twisters, go to www.vehersetzung.at/twister/.

Try these tongue twisters from other languages:

**Yiddish**

Fir Funr Forn Firn Korn, Barg Arup un Barg Arip.
('Four wagons are driving carrying wheat, up hill and down hill.')

**Swedish**

I åa ä e ö å i öa ä e å.
('In the stream there is an island and in the island there is a stream.')

**Greek**

Kala Kaka a Kali Kaki ne Kanma Kahyu Ke Kando Kapi Kachumber Kar.
('Uncle Kala whispered to Aunti Kali to prepare a salad by cutting the onion.')

**Italian**

Il papá pesa al pepe a Pisa. A Pisa pesa il pepe al papá. ('The father weighs the pepper in Pisa. In Pisa, the pepper is weighed by the father.')

| Table 3.2 | Vowel contrasts in Canadian English | |
|---|---|---|
| beet | [bit] | [i] |
| bit | [bɪt] | [ɪ] |
| bait | [bejt] | [ej] |
| bet | [bɛt] | [ɛ] |
| bat | [bæt] | [æ] |
| cooed | [kʰud] | [u] |
| could | [kʰʊd] | [ʊ] |
| code | [kʰowd] | [ow] |
| cod | [kʰɑd] | [ɑ]² |
| cud | [kʰʌd] | [ʌ] |
| lewd | [lud] | [u] |
| loud | [lawd] | [aw] |
| lied | [lajd] | [aj] |
| Lloyd | [lojd] | [oj] |

sounds. (Note that English does not have a phonological contrast between a word like /bej/ and a word like /be/.) For the purposes of phonemic analysis, diphthongs are treated as single segments.

## 3.1.2  Language-specific contrasts

Whether segments contrast with each other is determined on a language-particular basis. In other words, two sounds can be phonetically distinct without necessarily being phonologically distinct or contrastive. Moreover, sounds that are contrastive in one language may not necessarily be contrastive in another. For example, the difference between the vowels [ɛ] and [æ] is crucial to English, as we can see from minimal pairs like *Ben* [bɛn] and *ban* [bæn] (see table 3.3). But in Turkish, this difference in pronunciation is not distinctive. A Turkish speaker may pronounce the word for 'I' as [bɛn] or [bæn], and it will make no difference to the meaning.

| Table 3.3 | Language-specific vowel contrasts: English versus Turkish | | |
|---|---|---|---|
| **English** | | **Turkish** | |
| [bɛn] | 'Ben' | [bɛn] | 'I' |
| [bæn] | 'ban' | [bæn] | 'I' |

Conversely, sounds that do not contrast in English, such as long and short vowels, may be distinctive in another language. There are no minimal pairs of the type [hæt]:[hæːt] or [lus]:[luːs] in English. But in Japanese and Finnish, short and long vowels contrast, as the examples in table 3.4 show.

Establishing the contrasting segments in a language is a first step in phonological analysis. However, in any language, there are also many sounds that never contrast. The following section deals with this aspect of phonology.

| Table 3.4 | Short/long vowel contrasts in Japanese and Finnish | | |
|---|---|---|---|
| **Japanese** | | | |
| [tori] | 'bird' | [toriː] | 'shrine gate' |
| [kibo] | 'scale' | [kiboː] | 'hope' |
| **Finnish** | | | |
| [tuli] | 'fire' | [tuːli] | 'wind' |
| [hætæ] | 'distress' | [hæːtæː] | 'to evict' |

## 3.2 Phonetically conditioned variation: phonemes and allophones

Everyday speech contains a great deal of phonetic variation that speakers pay little or no attention to. Some of this variation arises from non-linguistic factors such as fatigue, excitement, orthodontic work, gum chewing, and the like. This kind of variation is not part of the domain of phonology as it is unpredicatable or random. You may stumble over some words or sounds when you're excited but this is more a property of your motoric system than something represented in your phonological grammar. Yet there is much phonetic variation that is systematic. It occurs most often among phonetically similar segments and is conditioned by the phonetic context or environment in which the segments are found. This variation occurs because segments are affected and altered by the phonetic characteristics of neighbouring elements or by the larger phonological context in which they occur. We saw this in chapter 2 when we discussed assimilation. Speakers and listeners of any language tend to factor out this type of variation in order to focus on the contrasts that affect meaning, which is why you may never have noticed it. In this section we will consider the patterns of variation exhibited by non-contrastive sounds, how to analyze these patterns, and the conclusions that can be drawn from them.

### 3.2.1 Complementary distribution

When first learning phonetic transcription, English speakers are often surprised that all *l*s are not identical. In table 3.5, the *l*s in column A are voiced, while those in column B are voiceless (indicated here by the subscript ̥ ). Many speakers of English are unaware that they routinely produce this difference, which can be heard clearly when the words in column B are

| Table 3.5 | Voiced and voiceless /l/ in English | | |
|---|---|---|---|
| **A** | | **B** | |
| blue | [blu] | plow | [pl̥aw] |
| gleam | [glim] | clap | [kl̥æp] |
| slip | [slɪp] | clear | [kl̥ir] |
| flog | [flɑg] | play | [pl̥ej] |
| leaf | [lif] | | |

pronounced slowly. Say each of the words in table 3.5 and try to extend the '*l* sound' and stop before you get to the vowel.

The two *l*s never contrast in English: there are no minimal pairs like [plej] and [pl̥ej] in which the phonetic difference between [l] and [l̥] functions to indicate a difference in meaning.

Moreover, when one examines the distribution of the two *l*s in English it becomes apparent that voiced and voiceless *l*s vary systematically: all of the voiceless [l̥]s occur after the class of voiceless stops, while the voiced [l]s never occur after voiceless stops. The voicelessness of the *l*s in column B is thus a consequence of their phonetic environment. So, it is unlike examples of free variation (where you might sometimes say "[i]conomics" and sometimes "[ɛ]conomics". It is a predictable property of the phonology of English, in the sense that in English only voiceless [l̥]s occur after voiceless stops. Since no voiced [l] ever occurs in the same phonetic environment as a voiceless one (and vice versa), we say that the two variants of *l* are in **complementary distribution**.

---

### Language Matters **Definitions from *The Canadian Oxford Dictionary***

*Complement*: Noun. **a** something that completes; **b** one of a pair, or one of two things that go together. Verb. Form a complement to.
E.g., His tie complements his jacket. Their skills complement each other nicely.

*Complementary*: Adjective. Completing; forming a complement.
E.g., Their skills are complementary. Their phonetic environments are complementary.

Contrast:
*Compliment*: Noun. A spoken or written expression of praise.
E.g., Thank you for your compliment.

*Complimentary*: Adjective. Expressing a compliment.
E.g., The students were complimentary.

Courtesy of: Oxford University Press Canada

---

In the data in table 3.5, voiced [l] occurs in a greater number of phonetic environments (after voiced stops, voiceless fricatives, and in word-initial position) than does voiceless [l̥]. Moreover, the various environments in which voiced [l] occurs cannot be easily described, as they do not naturally fall together as a class. Therefore, when two (or more) segments are in complementary distribution, the term *elsewhere* is used, as in table 3.6, to indicate the kind of wider distribution exhibited by [l] in table 3.5. Specifically, we find [l̥] after voiceless stops, and [l] elsewhere.

| **Table 3.6** | Complementary distribution of [l] and [l̥] in English | |
| --- | --- | --- |
| | [l] | [l̥] |
| After voiceless stops | no | yes |
| Elsewhere | yes | no |

One way to think about this is to paraphrase the distribution as follows: usually the phoneme /l/ will be realized as [l] but under certain circumstances (in certain well-defined phonetic environments) it will be realized as [l̥]. In spite of these differences in phonetic environment, native speakers of English consider the two *l*s to be instances of the same segment, since they are not contrastive, and are similar phonetically (they are both types of *l*s). The differences between them are systematic and predictable. We can sum up the relationship that the two *l*s bear to each other by stating that the two *l*s are *phonetically* distinct but that because of their phonetic similarity, predictable distribution, and non-contrastiveness, they are *phonologically* the same in the sound system of English.

## 3.2.2 Phonemes and allophones

When two (or more) segments are phonetically distinct, but phonologically the same, they are referred to as **allophones** (predictable variants) of one **phoneme** (contrastive phonological unit). The ability to group phonetically distinct sounds into phonemes is shared by all speakers of all languages. Phonologists represent this phonological knowledge formally by distinguishing two levels of representation: the **phonetic representation** that consists of predictable variants or allophones, and the **phonemic** (or phonological) **representation** that consists of the phonemes to which the allophones belong. A representation of the relationship between phonemes and their allophones is given in figure 3.2.

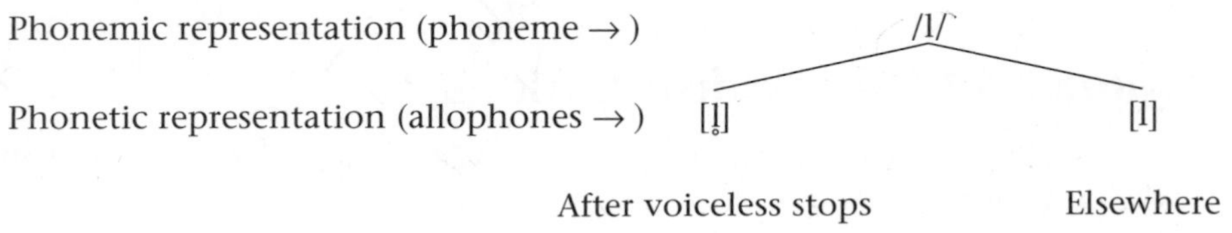

**Figure 3.2**
The phoneme /l/ and its allophones [l̥] and [l] in English

Phonemic representation (phoneme → )  /l/

Phonetic representation (allophones → )  [l̥]        [l]

After voiceless stops        Elsewhere

In figure 3.2 the symbols for allophones are enclosed in square brackets, while the symbol for the phoneme is placed between slashes. Notice that the phoneme /l/ in figure 3.2 is the same as its voiced allophone [l]. In most cases, the elsewhere variant or allophone of a phoneme can be chosen to represent the phoneme itself.

In thinking of the difference between phonemic and phonetic representations, remember the following. Phonemes are mental representations: the way in which sounds are stored in the mind. When you learn a word, you need to remember the phonemes because they make a difference when it comes to the meaning of a word. Allophones, on the other hand, are not part of what you remember when you store a word in your mind. We have a phonological system that automatically produces the appropriate variant of a particular phoneme when you pronounce a word. As we have said before, phonemes (like /l/) are in your head, but allophones (like [l] and [l̥]) come out of your mouth.

As we have seen, segments that can be considered allophones of one phoneme are phonetically similar and occur in phonetically predictable environments. In fact, it is frequently the case that allophones of one phoneme are in complementary distribution with each other. (That is, they never occur in the same environment.) Consequently, we can use the fact that allophones occur in complementary distribution as a way of testing whether or not two (or more) segments should be considered to be allophones of one phoneme.

> ## Language Matters  **Can You Predict the Variation?**
>
> Here is an example that may help you to understand the notion of predictable versus unpredictable variation. Consider the sounds [p] and [b] in English. In the following phonetic environment, can you predict whether you will get a [p] or a [b]?
>
> [ ___ aj]
>
> You can't predict, as both *pie* [paj] and *buy* [baj] are possible words. This is unpredictable variation, which means that [p] and [b] are contrastive and hence that /p/ and /b/ are phonemes. Now consider the sounds [l] and [l̥] in English. In the following phonetic environment, can you predict whether you will get an [l] or an [l̥]?
>
> [ ___ aj]
>
> In this case you can predict that you will get [l] because the voiceless allophone never occurs at the beginning of a word. This is predictable variation, which means that [l] and [l̥] are not contrastive in English and hence that they are not phonemes but rather allophones.

Allophonic variation is found throughout language. In fact, every speech sound we utter is an allophone of some phoneme. An important part of phonological analysis thus deals with discovering inventories of the phonemes of languages and accounting for allophonic variation.

## Some problematic distributions

At this point, some other considerations in determining phonemes and allophones must be taken into account. So far, we have seen that a minimal pair test is a quick and direct way of establishing that two sounds belong to separate phonemes in a language. If the sounds contrast, they are members of different phonemes. We have also seen that if certain sounds are non-contrastive and in complementary distribution, they may be considered allophones of a single phoneme. In some cases, however, we must go beyond these procedures to discover the phonemic inventory of a language.

As noted in section 3.1.1, certain patterns of distribution prevent some sounds in a language from ever contrasting with each other. In cases like these, we can establish the phonemic status of a sound by default. If the sound cannot be grouped together with any other phonetically similar sounds as an allophone of a phoneme, we may assume that it has phonemic status itself. The following data from English help to illustrate this point.

(1)  *[ŋowp]    (does not exist)    [howp]    'hope'
     *[ŋejt]    (does not exist)    [hejt]    'hate'

We can see here that [h] and [ŋ] do not contrast in initial position in English. The following examples show that they do not contrast in final position either.

(2)  [laŋ]     'long'    *[lah]     (does not exist)
     [sɪŋ]     'sing'    *[sɪh]     (does not exist)
     [kl̥æŋ]    'clang'   *[kl̥æh]    (does not exist)

These lists could be extended for pages, but a minimal pair involving [h] and [ŋ] could never be found in English. Additionally, as (1) and (2) have shown, [h] and [ŋ] are in complementary distribution. Do these facts taken together not lead us to conclude that [h] and [ŋ] are allophones of one phoneme? No. Since [h] and [ŋ] are so distinct phonetically, we assume that each one is a member of a separate phoneme and that the pattern of distribution is of secondary importance in this instance.

Minimal pairs or near-minimal pairs help us establish which sounds contrast in a language; phonetic similarity and complementary distribution help us decide which sounds are allophones of a particular phoneme. But not all examples of variation among sounds can be dealt with through these approaches.

In some cases, phonetically similar sounds are neither in complementary distribution nor are they found to contrast. It is still possible, nevertheless, to determine which phonemes these sounds belong to. A case in point is the variation in English voiceless stops when they are found in word-final position, as in the word *stop*. Sometimes an English speaker releases the articulation of these sounds rather forcefully. Let us represent this with a diacritic sign [!]. At other times, as we saw in chapter 2, the same speaker may keep the articulators closed for a moment before releasing the final stop consonant; the diacritic [ ˺ ] represents this extended closure. Some speakers may even coarticulate a glottal closure (represented here with the raised symbol for a glottal stop following the consonant in question) and produce the word as [stɑpˀ]. Thus, we can find at least three pronunciations of *stop*: [stɑp!], [stɑp˺], and [stɑpˀ]. Since there is no difference in the meaning of these forms and since the final consonants are phonetically similar, we say that these sounds are in **free variation**, and that they are all allophones of the phoneme /p/. The same pattern holds for the other voiceless stops of English.

## 3.2.3 Classes and generalization in phonology

Phonological analysis permits us to account for the great amount of phonetic variation in everyday speech. This variation, which is usually systematic, is found throughout language. Evidence of its systematic nature comes from the fact that allophones in languages pattern according to their membership in phonetic classes. This point is illustrated in tables 3.7 and 3.8 by comparing the patterns of distribution of *r*s and glides in English to the patterning of *l*s that was illustrated earlier in table 3.5.

| **Table 3.7** | Voiced and voiceless allophones of English /r/ | | |
|---|---|---|---|
| **A** | | **B** | |
| brew | [bru] | prow | [pr̥aw] |
| green | [grin] | trip | [tr̥ɪp] |
| drip | [drɪp] | creep | [kr̥ip] |
| frog | [frɑg] | pray | [pr̥ej] |
| shrimp | [ʃrɪmp] | | |

The data in table 3.7 show that in English, voiceless [r̥] occurs after voiceless stops, while voiced [r] occurs elsewhere. Based on this information we can conclude that there is an /r/ phoneme in English with (at least) two allophones—one voiced, the other voiceless—and that the allophones of English /r/ thus pattern like those of /l/. But if we were to stop there, we would overlook an important point. The phonemes /r/ and /l/ belong to the same class of sounds: both are *liquids*. By taking this information into account, we can state a general fact about English.

(3) In English, liquids have voiceless allophones after voiceless stops and voiced allophones elsewhere.

Now examine the data in table 3.8.

| Table 3.8 | Voiced and voiceless allophones of English glides | | |
|---|---|---|---|
| **A** | | **B** | |
| beauty | [bjuɾi] | putrid | [pjutr̥ɪd] |
| Duane | [dwejn] | twin | [tw̥ɪn] |
| Gwen | [gwɛn] | quick | [kw̥ɪk] |
| view | [vju] | cute | [kj̥ut] |
| swim | [swɪm] | | |
| thwack | [θwæk] | | |

These forms demonstrate that the contrasting glides /j/ and /w/ pattern like the liquids. We can now extend our general statement even further.

(4) In English, liquids and glides have voiceless allophones after voiceless stops, and voiced allophones elsewhere.

When we consider the fact that liquids and glides all belong to the same phonetic class—namely, the class of non-nasal **sonorant** consonants—we can understand why the allophones of liquids and glides pattern similarly. One of the major goals of phonological description is the discovery of such broad patterns of variation, and the formulation of the most general statements possible to describe them.

## 3.2.4 Canadian Raising

Another example of allophonic variation comes from English. In most Canadian and some American dialects, pronunciations like those illustrated in table 3.9 are common.

| Table 3.9 | Low and mid central vowel allophones in Canadian English | | |
|---|---|---|---|
| [ajz] | eyes | [ʌjs] | ice |
| [lajz] | lies | [lʌjs] | lice |
| [tr̥ajd] | tried | [tr̥ʌjt] | trite |
| [tr̥ajb] | tribe | [tr̥ʌjp] | tripe |
| [hawz] | (to) house (verb) | [hʌws] | house (noun) |
| [lawd] | loud | [lʌwt] | lout |
| [kaw] | cow | [skʌwt] | scout |
| [flaj] | fly | [flʌjt] | flight |

In table 3.9, the vowels [aj] and [ʌj] are in complementary distribution. The [aj] occurs before the class of voiced consonants or in word-final position (i.e., elsewhere), and the [ʌj] occurs before the class of voiceless consonants. The two are allophones of a single phoneme /aj/. The same relationship holds between the vowels [aw] and [ʌw], which are allophones of /aw/ (see figure 3.3).

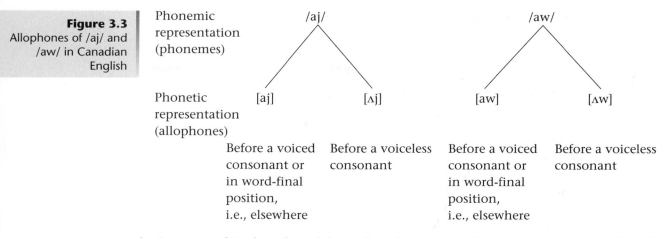

**Figure 3.3**
Allophones of /aj/ and /aw/ in Canadian English

Phonemic representation (phonemes)

/aj/                     /aw/

Phonetic representation (allophones)

[aj]          [ʌj]          [aw]          [ʌw]

Before a voiced consonant or in word-final position, i.e., elsewhere

Before a voiceless consonant

Before a voiced consonant or in word-final position, i.e., elsewhere

Before a voiceless consonant

Again, we see this phonological fact reflected in everyday language use. Most speakers of Canadian English find it difficult to distinguish between these allophones, even when the difference is pointed out to them. This is because the difference is not contrastive. On the other hand, many people who speak varieties of English that do not have the [ʌj] or [ʌw] allophones are very much aware of their presence in Canadian English. To them, a Canadian speaker sounds markedly different, even though they may be confused about what causes the difference. This phenomenon is sometimes referred to as Canadian Raising, since the allophones [ʌj] and [ʌw] have higher vowel components than the elsewhere variants [aj] and [aw].

---

### Language Matters  **Canadian Raising**

*I don't agree he was an American . . . . Where all other English-speaking people pronounce OU as a diphthong, the Canadian . . . makes a separate sound for each letter. The word* about, *for instance, he pronounces as* ab-oh-oot.

—Philip MacDonald, *The List of Adrian Messenger*

---

## 3.2.5  English mid vowels and glides

The vowels that exhibit the Canadian Raising alternation are the central (unreduced) vowels of Canadian English; the two mid allophones [ʌj] and [ʌw] both occur before voiceless consonants, while the two low allophones [aj] and [aw] both occur elsewhere. Just as in the

---

### Language Matters  **Canajun, eh?**

*Townsman:* Say—you must be a Canadian.
*Davis* (delighted)*:* I am. How'd you know?
*Townsman:* Say 'house' [haws].
*Davis:* House [hʌws].
*Townsman:* Say 'about' [əbawt].
*Davis:* About [əbʌwt].
*Townsman:* I knew it.

Source: Rick Salutin and Theatre Passe Muraille, *1837: The Farmers' Revolt.*

case of the liquid and glide patterns seen in section 3.2.3, the allophones that participate in the Canadian Raising pattern are distributed according to their membership in phonetic classes. A final example of predictable variation that refers to classes of segments but that differs crucially from examples seen so far also comes from English.

Table 3.2 showed contrasts among English vowels. In most dialects of English, the mid, tense vowels [ej] and [ow] are always diphthongized and thus end in the glide [j] or [w].[3] Significantly, the non-back (i.e., front) vowel [e] is always followed by the palatal glide [j], which is a non-back unrounded segment, while the back rounded vowel [o] is always followed by the labiovelar glide [w], which is a back rounded segment. These facts are summed up in table 3.10.

| **Table 3.10** | Tense vowel-glide combinations in English | | | | | | |
|---|---|---|---|---|---|---|---|
| **Vowel** | **Glide** | | | **Vowel** | **Glide** | | |
| **(both non-back and unrounded)** | | | | **(both back and rounded)** | | | |
| e | j | [fejt] | fate | o | w | [bowt] | boat |
| | | [kejn] | cane | | | [kown] | cone |

In other words, the occurrence of the glides following the mid tense vowels is predictable. The following generalization states the distribution of the two glides.

(5) The mid tense vowels of English are predictably followed by a glide that has the same backness and roundness as the vowel.

The data in table 3.10 show parallels with the allophonic distribution we have considered so far in the sense that certain elements in it are predictable under certain phonetic conditions. However, there is a difference between allophonic distribution and the kind of distribution exhibited by the glides. Specifically, in table 3.10, instead of a number of variants of one phoneme, we have two segments, [ej] and [ow], which share a predictable phonetic characteristic: these mid tense vowels of English are always followed by glides of the same backness and roundness. We have seen that when certain sounds are found predictably in a given environment, they are not included in phonemic representations. Thus, although the phonetic representations of English mid vowels include the glides, the corresponding phonemic representations do not (see figure 3.4).

| **Figure 3.4** Two representations of mid vowels in English | Phonemic representation | /e/ | /o/ |
|---|---|---|---|
| | | \| | \| |
| | Phonetic representation | [ej] | [ow] |

This is consistent with something we have said before: the phonemic representation includes information that is not predictable. Phonetic detail—whether it is about voiceless sonorants or which glide follows a mid vowel—of this type is predictable.

## 3.2.6 Language-specific patterns

The phenomenon of allophonic variation is universal. However, just as the phonemic contrasts found in each language are specific to that language, the actual patterning of phonemes and allophones is also language-specific. Thus, whatever distribution we discover for one language may not hold true for another.

## Language-specific variation in allophonic nasalization

Some languages have nasal as well as oral vowels and glides. It is usual in such languages for nasal vowel (and nasal glide) allophones to occur near nasal consonants, but, as tables 3.11 and 3.12 illustrate, the details of the patterning may vary from language to language.

In Scots Gaelic, for instance, whenever a nasal consonant occurs in a word, the vowel adjacent to it is nasalized. Glides do not get nasalized, however.

| **Table 3.11** | Nasal and oral vowels in Scots Gaelic |
|---|---|
| [mõːr] | 'big' |
| [nĩ] | 'cattle' |
| [nẽːl] | 'cloud' |
| [mũ] | 'about' |
| [rũːn] | 'secret' |
| [ʃalak] | 'hunting' |

The generalization governing the distribution of nasal vowels in Scots Gaelic is stated as follows.

(6)  Vowels are nasal in Scots Gaelic when preceded or followed by a nasal consonant.

Malay, a language spoken in Malaysia and Singapore, has both nasalized vowels and glides. In Malay, all vowels and glides following a nasal are predictably nasalized until an obstruent, liquid, or glottal ([h], [ʔ]) is reached.

| **Table 3.12** | Nasalization in Malay |
|---|---|
| [mẽw̃ãh] | 'luxurious' |
| [mãj̃ãn] | 'stalk' |
| [mãrah] | 'scold' |
| [nãẽʔ] | 'ascend' |
| [mə̃laraŋ] | 'forbid' |
| [mãkan] | 'eat' |
| [rumãh] | 'house' |
| [kəreta] | 'car' |

For Malay, then, the generalization governing nasalization is different from the Scots Gaelic case both in the direction and the targets of nasalization.

(7)  In Malay, all vowels and glides following a nasal consonant and not separated from it by a non-nasal consonant are nasalized.

## Language-specific variation in allophonic distribution

In section 3.1.2 we saw that a phonemic contrast in one language may not prove to be a phonemic contrast in another. This means that the relationship of phonemes to allophones may vary. A comparison of the contrasts among stops in English and Khmer (Cambodian) in table 3.13 illustrates this point. In both languages, aspirated and unaspirated phones can be heard.

| Table 3.13 | Stop phones in English and Khmer | | |
|---|---|---|---|
| **English** | | **Khmer** | |
| [p] | [pʰ] | [p] | [pʰ] |
| [t] | [tʰ] | [t] | [tʰ] |
| [k] | [kʰ] | [k] | [kʰ] |

In English, aspirated and unaspirated stops are allophones of their respective phonemes (the distribution is explained in section 3.4.5 of this chapter); there are no contrasting forms like [pɪk] and [pʰɪk]. In Khmer, though, unaspirated and aspirated voiceless stops contrast (see table 3.14).

| Table 3.14 | Khmer contrastive voiceless stops | | |
|---|---|---|---|
| [pɔːŋ] | 'to wish' | [pʰɔːŋ] | 'also' |
| [tɔp] | 'to support' | [tʰɔp] | 'be suffocated' |
| [kat] | 'to cut' | [kʰat] | 'to polish' |

The phonological contrasts of the two languages are different, even though the phones are not (see figure 3.5). These distributions are the same for the other voiceless stops in both languages.

**Figure 3.5**
English and Khmer voiceless bilabial stop phonemes and allophones

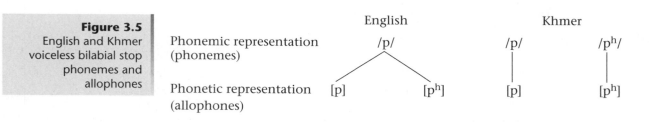

The phonological contrasts of the two languages are different, even though the phones are not (see figure 3.5). These distributions are the same for the other voiceless stops in both languages.

## 3.3 Phonetic and phonemic transcription

We have seen so far that each language has a set of contrastive phonemes (which can be established largely by means of the minimal pair test) and that phonemes themselves can have predictable variants or allophones (which are usually in complementary distribution with each other). We have also seen that there are two distinct levels of representation:

the phonemic (or phonological) and the phonetic. We can now illustrate more clearly the types of transcription used at each level of representation.

The phonetic level of representation includes both predictable and unpredictable phonetic information. In contrast, the phonemic level includes all and only those aspects of a representation that are unpredictable; all predictable information is excluded. The examples in table 3.15 show this difference for the classes of sounds in English that we have examined so far.

| Table 3.15 | Phonetic and phonemic transcription of English | | |
|---|---|---|---|
| **Phonetic transcription** | **Phonemic transcription** | **Word** | **Predictable property(s) not represented in phonemic transcription** |
| [pl̥aw] | /plaw/ | plow | voicelessness of liquid |
| [kr̥ip] | /krip/ | creep | voicelessness of liquid |
| [kw̥ɪk] | /kwɪk/ | quick | voicelessness of glide |
| [lejt] | /let/ | late | glide after mid tense vowel |
| [lɛt] | /lɛt/ | let | – |
| [tʰajd] | /tajd/ | tied | aspiration |
| [tʰʌjt] | /tajt/ | tight | aspiration; Canadian Raising |

In the phonemic transcriptions in table 3.15 the words are transcribed using only phonemes; in the phonetic transcriptions, however, the allophones of each phoneme are transcribed (in the environments in which they predictably occur). There is thus more phonetic information in the phonetic transcriptions than in the phonemic ones. If one compares the two transcriptions of *tight*, for instance, one sees that the phonetic transcription indicates the aspiration of the initial *t*, and the raised pronunciation of the vowel. In the corresponding phonemic transcription, the aspiration is left out, because its occurrence is predictable, and the [ʌj] allophone of /aj/ is replaced by its phoneme.

The contrast between phonetic and phonemic representation is even more striking for the Malay forms given earlier, as shown in table 3.16.

| Table 3.16 | Phonetic and phonemic transcription of Malay nasal vowels | | |
|---|---|---|---|
| **Phonetic transcription** | **Phonemic transcription** | **Word** | **Predictable property(s) not represented in phonemic transcription** |
| [mẽw̃ãh] | /mewah/ | 'luxurious' | nasalization |
| [mãj̃ãn] | /majan/ | 'stalk' | nasalization |
| [nãɛ̃ʔ] | /naɛʔ/ | 'ascend' | nasalization |

Here, nasalization on all vowel and glide segments is predictable and is therefore omitted from the phonemic representation.

## 3.3.1  Phonetic and phonemic inventories

All languages have both a phonetic level of representation and a phonemic one. The phonetic level represents the allophones of a language. The phonemic level represents the language's phonemes. What this means is that each language has two inventories of sounds: one for the allophones of the language, which is used to transcribe phonetically; the other inventory is of the phonemes of the language and this inventory is used to transcribe phonemically. Since every language has more allophones of phonemes than it has phonemes, phonetic inventories of sounds are always larger than phonemic ones. Table 3.17 illustrates a partial phonetic inventory and the phonemic inventory for the vowels of English. Only those allophones that we have discussed so far in this chapter are listed (the phonetic inventory is thus obviously incomplete). Phonetically, vowels are described as either *front*, *central* or *back*, but phonologically (as we will see in section 3.5) only the features *front* and *back* are necessary.

| Table 3.17 | Phonetic and phonemic inventories of the vowels of English | | | | |
|---|---|---|---|---|---|
| **Phonetic inventory** | | | **Phonemic inventory** | | |
| **Front** | **Central** | **Back** | **Front** | **(Central)** | **Back** |
| i |  | u | i |  | u |
| ɪ |  | ʊ | ɪ |  | ʊ |
| ej |  | ow | e |  | o |
| ɛ | ʌ  ʌj | oj | ɛ | ʌ | oj |
|  | ʌw |  |  | ə |  |
|  | ə |  | æ | aj | ɑ |
| æ | aj | ɑ |  | aw |  |
|  | aw |  |  |  |  |

Table 3.18 illustrates a phonetic inventory (again based on allophones discussed so far) and the phonemic inventory of English consonants.

| Table 3.18 | Phonetic and phonemic inventories of the consonants of English[4] | | | | | | | | |
|---|---|---|---|---|---|---|---|---|---|
| **Phonetic inventory** | | | | | **Phonemic inventory** | | | | |
| p |  | t | k | ʔ | p |  | t | k |  |
| pʰ |  | tʰ | kʰ |  |  |  |  |  |  |
| b |  | d | g |  | b |  | d | g |  |
|  |  | tʃ |  |  |  |  | tʃ |  |  |
|  |  | dʒ |  |  |  |  | dʒ |  |  |
|  | f θ | s | ʃ |  | h | f θ | s | ʃ | h |
|  | v ð | z | ʒ |  |  | v ð | z | ʒ |  |
| m |  | n | ŋ |  | m |  | n | ŋ |  |
|  |  | l | j w |  |  |  | l | j w |  |
|  |  | l̥ | j̥ w̥ |  |  |  |  |  |  |
|  |  | r |  |  |  |  | r |  |  |
|  |  | r̥ |  |  |  |  |  |  |  |

Since there are two levels of representation—the phonetic and the phonemic—one obvious question to ask is how they are related to each other. In section 3.6 we consider in detail the nature of the relationship between phonetic and phonemic levels and inventories and discuss how this relationship can be represented formally. Before we get to that, though, let us consider another level of representation.

## 3.4 Above the segment: syllables

So far we have been discussing the distributional properties of segments, and have established the existence of the segmental units of phonological analysis known as phonemes and their allophones. We have also seen that allophonic variation may be conditioned by neighbouring segments. We turn now to a different unit of phonological representation, namely, the **syllable**. We will see that syllables are composed of segments, and thus impose an organization on segments; in this sense, syllables are what are known as **suprasegmental** (that is to say, *above the segment*) units. We will also see that the shapes of syllables are governed by both universal and language-specific constraints. Finally, we will examine examples of allophonic variation that is conditioned by syllable structure, rather than by neighbouring segments.

### 3.4.1 Defining the syllable

As we saw in chapter 2, vowels, glides, liquids, and nasals are sonorant (singable) sounds, while **obstruents** (stops, fricatives, and affricates) are not; of the sonorant sounds, vowels are most sonorous, and glides, liquids, and nasals are correspondingly less sonorous. A syllable consists of a sonorous element and its associated non-syllabic (less sonorous) segments. Since vowels are the most sonorous sounds, syllables usually have a vowel nucleus at their core. Less sonorous sounds may appear on either side of a nucleus. Thus the word *telegraph* has three syllables because it has three vowels that serve as syllable nuclei. [Note how in the word *plant*, the vowel is in the middle, with a liquid and a nasal on either side, and stops at the edges.]

Native speakers of a language demonstrate their awareness of the sonority values of segments and of the syllable as a unit of phonological structure whenever they count syllables in a word. No English speaker would hesitate to say that the words *telegraph* and *accident* have three syllables, and most speakers would feel confident that the words could be broken up into the syllables [tɛ.lə.græf] and [æk.sə.dənt] (the '.' marks syllable divisions informally).

Speakers also know that syllables have internal subsyllabic structure as well. This internal organization of the syllable unit is shown in figure 3.6 for the monosyllabic English word *sprint*. As you can see, syllables consist of an **onset** and a **rhyme**; the rhyme, in turn, consists of the **nucleus** or syllable core, and a **coda**.

**Figure 3.6**
Internal structure of a syllable

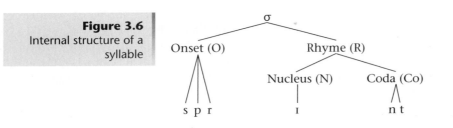

## Language Matters **Ever Wonder Where Rhymes in Poetry Come From?**

Draw the internal structure of the final syllables in each line of the following poems and see what patterns you observe.

> All that is gold does not glitter,
> Not all those who wander are lost,
> The old that is strong does not wither,
> Deep roots are not reached by frost.
>            —J.R.R. Tolkien, *The Lord of the Rings*

> My candle burns at both ends;
> It will not last the night;
> But, ah, my foes, and, oh, my friends—
> It gives a lovely light.
>            —Edna St. Vincent Millay, "First Fig" from *A Few Figs from Thistles*

What constituents are most important in the creation of rhyming?

We will see later on in this chapter that some allophonic variation makes reference to internal subsyllabic structure such as the coda.

In addition, one version of the English language game known as Pig Latin is played by displacing the onset of the first syllable of a word to the end of the word and then tacking on the rhyme *ay* [ej]: thus *strong* becomes *ong-str-ay,* and *swivel* become *ivel-sw-ay.* Speakers can do this because they have knowledge of the internal structure of syllables.

Furthermore, when speakers are asked to syllabify words, they are able to do so in ways that are neither random nor variable. The word *extreme* /ɛkstrim/ would never be syllabified as /ɛ.kstrim/, for example. Instead, syllables comply with certain constraints that prohibit them from beginning with a sequence like *kstr* and thus result in the actual syllabification /ɛk.strim/. The examples in table 3.19 are all from English, but similar kinds of evidence for the existence of subsyllabic constituents can be found in many other languages as well.

| Table 3.19 | Some examples of English syllables |
|---|---|
| /ə.plɑd/ | applaud |
| /di.klajn/ | decline |
| /ɛk.splen/ | explain |
| /ɪm.prə.vajz/ | improvise |

All languages have syllables. The shapes of these syllables are governed by various kinds of constraints, but certain universal tendencies are observable: (1) syllable nuclei usually consist of one vowel (V); (2) syllables usually begin with onsets; (3) syllables often end with codas; (4) onsets and codas usually consist of one consonant (C). Putting these tendencies together, we find that the most common types of syllables found in languages throughout the world take the shapes CV and CVC. These are general tendencies, not absolute laws, and languages may, and often do, violate them. But even when a language violates the universal tendencies, the types of syllables that do occur are governed by other constraints on the shapes of the subsyllabic units O, N, and Co. To illustrate this, we turn to the constraints that govern the phonological shape of consonant sequences in onsets in English.

## 3.4.2 Onset constraints and phonotactics

Native speakers of any language intuitively know that certain words from other languages sound unusual, and they often adjust the segment sequences of these words to conform with the pronunciation requirements of their own language. These intuitions are based on a tacit knowledge of the permissible syllable structures of the speaker's own language. For example, English-speaking students learning Russian often have difficulty pronouncing a word like *vprog* /fprɔk/ 'value, good', since the sequence /fpr/ is never found in English onsets. Since speakers typically adjust an impermissible sequence by altering it to a permissible one, many English speakers would pronounce the Russian word [fprɔk] as [fəprɔk], or even delete the initial /f/ and say [prɔk] in order to adjust the impermissible sequence /fpr/ to a permissible English onset. **Phonotactics**—the set of constraints on how sequences of segments pattern—forms part of a speaker's knowledge of the phonology of his or her language.

### Some English onsets

English is a language that allows onsets to contain more than one consonant; in this sense, English permits syllables that are more complex than those found in many languages. Nevertheless, there are very strict phonotactic constraints on the shapes of English onsets. Table 3.20 contains examples of the possible syllable-initial consonant sequences of English that contain a voiceless stop consonant. These sequences are all illustrated in word-initial position to make them easier to pick out. (Stress marking and phonetic details such as liquid-glide devoicing that are not relevant to the present discussion are omitted here.)

| **Table 3.20** | Initial consonant clusters in English containing a voiceless stop | | | | |
|---|---|---|---|---|---|
| **Labial + sonorant** | | **Alveolar + sonorant** | | **Velar + sonorant** | |
| [pl] | please | [tl] | – | [kl] | clean |
| [pr] | proud | [tr] | trade | [kr] | cream |
| [pw] | – | [tw] | twin | [kw] | queen |
| [pj] | pure | [tj] | tune (British) | [kj] | cute |
| [spl] | splat | [stl] | – | [skl] | sclerosis |
| [spr] | spring | [str] | strip | [skr] | scrap |
| [spw] | – | [stw] | – | [skw] | squeak |
| [spj] | spew | [stj] | stew (British) | [skj] | skewer |

The examples in table 3.20 show that the first segment of a word-initial three-consonant cluster in English is always *s*; the second consonant in the series is always a voiceless stop, and the third is either a liquid or a glide. These sound patterns can be formally represented as follows:

$$\sigma \ [s \left\{ \begin{array}{l} p \\ t \\ k \end{array} \right. \quad \left\{ \begin{array}{l} (l) \\ r \\ (w) \\ j \end{array} \right.$$

In this formalization, σ indicates the boundary of a syllable and the curly braces designate 'either/or'. The sounds in parentheses are not found in all combinations. An important observation about the types of onsets that are allowed in English is that the consonant combinations are not random: in fact, (1) the consonant combinations are dependent primarily on the manners of articulation of the consonants and (2) sonorant consonants (here liquids and glides) are closer to the nucleus than are stops and fricatives. Both these phonotactic constraints reflect universal restrictions on consonant combinations, and are found in other languages that allow complex onsets.

### 3.4.3  Accidental and systematic gaps

Although there are twenty-four possible two- and three-consonant syllable-initial sequences in English containing a voiceless stop, not all of these combinations are exploited in the vocabulary of the language.

Some gaps in the inventory of possible English words include *snool, splick, sklop, flis, trok,* and *krif,* although none of these forms violates any constraints on onset combinations found in English. Gaps in a language's vocabulary that correspond to non-occurring but possible forms are called **accidental gaps**. Occasionally, an accidental gap will be filled by the invention of a new word. The word *Kodak* is one such invented word; its shape conforms to the phonotactic constraints of English, but it only became part of English vocabulary in the twentieth century. Borrowed words such as *perestroika* (from Russian), *taco* (from Spanish), and *Zen* (from Japanese) are readily accepted into English because their syllable structures conform to the phonotactic patterns of the language.

Table 3.20 has shown which syllable-initial consonant clusters involving voiceless stops are permissible in English. Gaps in the syllable structures of a language that result not by accident, but from the exclusion of certain sequences are called **systematic gaps**. Certain onset sequences like /bz/, /pt/, and /fp/ are systematic gaps in the pattern of English. They are outright unacceptable to English speakers, and never occur in spoken English. Instead, such sequences will be adjusted phonologically when they are pronounced in spontaneous speech. This can be seen in the case of borrowings from other languages into English. Many Greek words beginning with *ps-* and *pt-* have been absorbed into English, as the spellings of *psychology, psoriasis,* and *pterodactyl* attest. In all of them the impermissible syllable-initial clusters *\*ps-* and *\*pt-* have been reduced to *s-* or *t-* in onsets of spoken English. However, when these same forms occur word-internally, where their syllabification is different, the 'lost' segments may resurface. For example, the *pter* of *pterodactyl* means 'wing'; both consonants are heard in the word *helicopter,* where English syllabification has resulted in a structure *he.li.cop.ter* in which the members of the cluster *pt* belong to different syllables.

Other words that violate phonotactic constraints commonly appear in spoken English, including *pueblo* [pwɛblow], and *Tlingit* [tlɪŋɪt]. The fact that such words and pronunciations occur in spoken English even though they violate phonotactic constraints is due to the fact that phonotactic constraints vary in their strength. Thus, the sequences *\*ps-, \*pt-,* and *\*bz-* are excluded from the initial position of English syllables because English has a very strong and absolute constraint against allowing stop-stop or stop-fricative clusters in onsets. In contrast, the restriction against sequences like *\*pw-* and *\*tl-* in English onsets is due to a weaker and violable constraint on stop-sonorant onset sequences with the same place of articulation. Thus, a labiovelar glide is not usually permitted to occur after a labial consonant, and an alveolar stop such as /t/ is not usually permitted to precede an alveolar /l/ in English words, but as our examples show, this constraint is violable.

## Language-specific phonotactics

It is important to emphasize again that certain aspects of the particular constraints discussed in the previous section are universal whereas others are language-specific. An onset like *pl-* is found in many languages besides English (for example, in Russian, Thai, and French), while an onset sequence like *lp-* is never found. We may therefore say that no restrictions against an onset like *pl-* appear to exist as part of universal linguistic knowledge, whereas the non-existence of onsets like *\*lp-* suggest that something in their phonetic makeup disqualifies them from occurring in language. Language-specific constraints, on the other hand, hold true for individual languages such as English, but they may or may not be found in other languages. Each language has its own set of restrictions on the phonological shapes of its syllable constituents. Speakers of Russian, for example, are quite accustomed to pronouncing onset sequences such as *ps-, fsl-,* and *mgl-,* which are not found in English (see table 3.21).

| **Table 3.21** | Some onset sequences in Russian |
|---|---|
| [psa] | 'dog's' |
| [fslux] | 'aloud' |
| [mgla] | 'fog' |

Phonotactic constraints of the kind that we have seen for English represent one kind of phonological knowledge. You might, however, wonder what prevents English words like *extreme, applaud, decline, explain,* and *improvise* from being syllabified as the incorrect *\*/ɛks.trim/, \*/ʌp.lɑd/, \*/dik.lajn/, \*/ɛks.plen/,* and *\*/ɪmp.rəv.ajz/,* instead of the correct /ɛk.strim/, /ʌ.plɑd/, /di.klajn/, /ɛk.splen/, and /ɪm.prə.vajz/. In the incorrect syllabifications, the syllable divisions do not violate any phonotactic constraints, raising the question of why the syllabifications are nevertheless incorrect. The answer is that such syllabifications are prevented by a universal constraint on general syllable shapes, rather than by a phonotactic constraint on segment sequences. As mentioned in section 3.4.1, there is a universal syllable-shape constraint that encourages languages to make syllables with onsets; as a result, onsets in languages tend to be as large as possible. The next section illustrates how this universal constraint works by providing a procedure for establishing the association of consonants and vowels within syllables.

## 3.4.4  Setting up syllables

Each language defines its own syllable structure through the interaction of universal and language-specific constraints. The process for setting up syllables in a given language has three steps: (1) nucleus-formation, (2) onset-formation, and (3) coda-formation. Then the resulting syllables are incorporated into word-level units. The first step reflects the universal tendency for syllables to have a sonorant core, the second step reflects the tendency for syllables to have onsets, and the third step reflects the tendency for syllables to have codas. Ordering onset-formation before coda-formation reflects a cross-linguistic tendency of *Onsets before codas* (in a sequence of VCV, the consonant C will always be syllabified as an onset rather than a coda), and ensures that onsets gather up as many consonants as possible before any codas are formed.

- **Step a** *Nucleus-formation:* Since the syllable nucleus is the only obligatory constituent of a syllable, it is constructed first. Each vowel segment in a word makes up a syllabic **nucleus**. To represent this, link a vowel to an N symbol above it by drawing an association line. Above each nucleus symbol, place an R symbol (for **rhyme**—in section 3.4.1 we saw that the rhyme consists of the nucleus plus the coda), which is filled out in step c below. Above each R, place a σ symbol; link all with association lines (see figure 3.7).

**Figure 3.7**

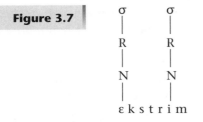

- **Step b** *Onset-formation:* The longest sequence of consonants to the left of each nucleus that does not violate the phonotactic constraints of the language in question is the **onset** of the syllable. Link these consonants to an O symbol and join it to the same syllable as the vowel to the right (see figure 3.8). Note that there is no onset in the first syllable of *extreme*.

**Figure 3.8**

σ    σ
|    /|
R   /R
|   / |
N  O N
|  /\\ |
ɛ k s t r i m

- **Step c** *Coda-formation:* Any remaining unassociated consonants to the right of each nucleus form the **coda**, and are linked to a Co symbol above them. This Co is associated with the syllable nucleus to its left in the rhyme (see figure 3.9). A syllable with a coda is called a **closed syllable**; a syllable without a coda is called **open**.

**Figure 3.9**

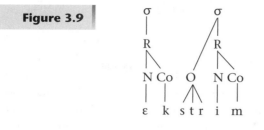

- **Step d** *Word-level construction:* Syllables that make up a single form (usually a word) branch out from the representation *Wd* as in figure 3.10 (this step is frequently omitted from phonological representations to save space; the complete representation is understood even when *Wd* is not written out).

**Figure 3.10**

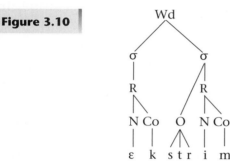

The steps in the procedure just outlined reflect universal constraints on syllable shapes. These interact with universal and language-specific phonotactic constraints. Given the procedure and the phonotactic constraints, we can now explain why words such as *applaud* and *explain* are syllabified as /ʌ.plɑd/ and /ɛk.splen/ (see figure 3.11). In accordance with step b, onset-formation, all the consonants in the clusters between the two vowel nuclei in each word (*pl* and *kspl*, respectively) are considered for syllabification as onsets of the second syllable. Thus *pl* is a possible candidate for an onset. According to the phonotactic constraints that are active in English, it is also a permissible onset, so both consonants are syllabified as part of the second syllable onset. In contrast, *kspl* is not a permissible onset in English; *spl* is a permissible onset, however, so the last three consonants of *kspl* are syllabified as part of the second syllable onset, and the first consonant *k* is left to be syllabified as a coda to the preceding syllable.

**Figure 3.11**
Syllabification: onsets before codas and phonotactic constraints

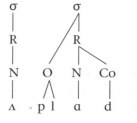
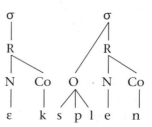

For a more advanced discussion of these issues, go to the Companion Website at **www.pearsoned.ca/ogrady**, chapter 3.

## 3.4.5  Syllabic phonology

One reason that syllables are treated as units of phonological structure is that they are relevant to stating generalizations about the distribution of allophonic features. The next sections provide examples of the role of syllables and subsyllabic constituents in phonological patterns. The fact that syllables and their internal constituents have such a role is thus evidence that they are part of the knowledge that speakers have of the phonology of their language.

### Aspiration in English

As table 3.22 shows, the voiceless stops of English each have an aspirated and an unaspirated allophone.[5]

| Table 3.22 | English aspiration | | | | |
|---|---|---|---|---|---|
| **A** | | **B** | | **C** | |
| [pʰǽn] | pan | [spǽn] | span | [slǽp] | slap |
| [pʰéjn] | pain | [spéjn] | Spain | [slát] | slot |
| [pʰówk] | poke | [spówk] | spoke | [blák] | block |
| [tʰówn] | tone | [stówn] | stone | | |
| [kʰín] | kin | [skín] | skin | | |
| [pʰərspájr] | perspire | [splǽt] | splat | | |
| [tʰəméjɾow] | tomato | [ʌpsét] | upset | | |
| [kʰənú] | canoe | | | | |
| [əpʰán] | upon | | | | |
| [ətʰǽk] | attack | | | | |
| [tʰəkʰílə] | tequila | | | | |

The distribution of aspiration can be stated generally by referring to syllable structure, and, in the case of the distribution of unaspirated stops, by referring to the subsyllabic onset and coda units (see table 3.23).

| Table 3.23 | Distribution of aspirated stops in English |
|---|---|
| **Aspirated stops** | **Unaspirated stops** |
| ■ syllable-initially | Elsewhere<br>■ in a syllable onset preceded by *s* (whether another C follows or not)<br>■ in a coda |

## Language Matters  **A Syllabic Game**

Many cultures have language games that attempt to create 'secret' languages. One such game in English is known (with some dialect variation) as *Ubbi Dubbi*. The game works like this. Start with a one-syllable word like *John* ([dʒɑn]) and insert the nonsense syllable [ʌb] after the onset. Try it. This will now be pronounced as [dʒʌbɑn]. This may seem pretty easy. Now try a two-syllable word like *Peter* [pitər]. Insert the nonsense syllable after both onsets. This is a bit harder, right? [pʌbitʌbər]. And it's probably getting a bit harder to understand. Try words of more syllables and build up to a sentence. [jʌbu wʌbɪl fʌbajnd ðʌbæt prʌbæktʌbɪs ʌbɪz hʌbɛlpfʌbəl].

The phonemic representations of the three English stops are unaspirated, since aspiration is predictable. The environments where aspiration occurs can be stated very generally by referring to syllable structure.

(8)  English voiceless stops are aspirated syllable-initially.

This statement accounts for all the data in column A of table 3.22, where voiceless stops appear syllable-initially. No aspiration is found in the forms in columns B and C since the voiceless stops appear either as the second member of the syllable onset (in *span*, *Spain*, *spoke*, *stone*, and *skin*), or in a coda, as in *upset*.[6]

## Phonetic length in English vowels

English offers a second example of the phonological relevance of syllables. Phonetic length is predictable in English vowels, as the examples in table 3.24 show.

| **Table 3.24** | Phonetic length in English: long vowels before voiced coda consonants | | |
|---|---|---|---|
| **A** | | **B** | |
| bad | [bæːd] | bat | [bæt] |
| Abe | [eːjb] | ape | [ejp] |
| phase | [feːjz] | face | [fejs] |
| leave | [liːv] | leaf | [lif] |
| tag | [tʰæːg] | tack | [tʰæk] |
| brogue | [broːwg] | broke | [browk] |
| | | tame | [tʰẽjm] |
| | | meal | [mil] |
| | | soar | [sor] |
| | | show | [ʃow] |

English vowels, whether or not they are diphthongs, are shorter before voiceless consonants, before sonorant consonants, and in word-final position; they are longer before voiced non-sonorant consonants provided these non-sonorant consonants are in coda position in the same syllable. As the next examples show, if vowels are followed by non-sonorant consonants that are onsets of the following syllable, the vowels are short. Thus, in table 3.25 the vowels in the first syllable all precede a voiced, non-sonorant consonant, but they are short since the voiced consonant is in the following syllable.

| Table 3.25 | Short vowels before voiced onset consonants in English | |
|---|---|---|
| obey | [ow.bej] | /obe/ |
| redo | [ri.du] | /ridu/ |
| regard | [ri.gard] | /rigard/ |
| ogre | [ow.gər] | /ogər/ |
| Odin | [ow.dɪn] | /odin/ |

Compare your vowel length in the following pairs where one item has a closed syllable (lengthened vowel) and the other has an open syllable (shortened vowel).

> robe/obey
> brogue/ogre
> rode/Odin

In order for an English vowel to be long, it must be followed by a voiced obstruent in the same syllable. The following generalization can now be made.

(9) English vowels are long when followed by a voiced obstruent in the coda position of the same syllable.

As the analyses of the distribution of aspiration and vowel length in English have shown, the use of syllabic representations in phonology permits us to make more general statements about certain allophonic patterns in language than if we use only statements that do not make reference to syllable structure.

For more discussion of syllables and stress in English, go to **www.pearsoned.ca/ ogrady**.

Now we return to some of the fine phonetic detail we introduced at the end of chapter 2. We looked at the production of two different kinds of 'l' sound as found in the following words:

> leaf      fall
> lie       milk
> lawn      steal

Can you see how to analyze this now in terms of syllable structure? Notice that we find the clear 'l' in onset position, and the dark 'l' in coda position.

We also saw the difference between two types of stop (released and unreleased) as found in:

> pave      cap
> Tom       pot
> king      back

Is this distribution amenable to a syllable structure analysis? Notice that the unreleased stops are always in coda position while the released stops are in onset position.

## 3.5    Features

In the previous section, we saw the role that syllable structure plays in verse, language games, and especially in allophonic variation. We also saw that universal and language-specific constraints govern the ways in which segment units combine to form the suprasegmental units of structure known as syllables. In this section we will discover that segments themselves are composed of even smaller, subsegmental, phonological units known as **features**. In fact, features are like atoms: they are the smallest units of phonology and as such are the basic building blocks of human speech sounds.

## 3.5.1  Why we use features

There are a number of reasons why linguists consider features to be the most basic units of the phonology.

### Features as independent and coordinated phonetic elements

We have already seen in chapter 2 that speech is produced by a number of independent but coordinated articulatory activities such as voicing, tongue position, lip rounding, and so on. For example, when we produce the voiceless bilabial stop [p], the vocal cords in the larynx are open and not vibrating (hence the sound is voiceless), and the lips are pressed together to form a complete constriction (hence the sound is a labial stop). Each sound is thus the result of the coordinated articulatory activity of the larynx—and the various articulators such as the tongue body, the tongue blade, the lips, and the velum—found in the oral and nasal cavities of the vocal tract. By assuming that segments are composed of features, we are able to model this phonetic reality.

Features reflect the articulatory basis of speech in the sense that each feature encodes one of the independently controllable aspects of speech production. For example, in the case of [p], the feature [−voice] reflects laryngeal activity; the feature [LABIAL] reflects the activity of the lips; and the feature [−continuant] reflects the stop manner of articulation (note that features are written in square brackets; the use of '+' and '−' signs and upper versus lower case letters is explained below). As a further example, consider the sound [ɑ]. This sound is produced with a low, back, and tense tongue body (dorsal) position, with no rounding of the lips (therefore no labial activity) and little constriction. It is a vowel, and therefore is voiced and sonorant as well. All these phonetic properties are represented in terms of separate features in figure 3.12. An 'o' before a feature indicates that the articulator is active or in use.

In this representation the features of the segment are listed in an array called a **matrix**. This is a common way of presenting sets of features.

**Figure 3.12**
Feature representation for the English vowel /ɑ/

[ɑ]

| | |
|---|---|
| −consonantal<br>+syllabic<br>+sonorant | These features define the segment as vowel, consonant, or glide (here a vowel) |
| +voice | This feature defines laryngeal states (phonation) |
| oDORSAL | This feature defines articulation (here dorsal, since vowels are produced with tongue body activity) |
| −high<br>+low<br>+back | These features specify the exact position of the articulator (here the dorsum is low and back) |
| +tense | This feature defines tenseness/laxness (here tense) |

## Features and natural classes

A second reason for viewing segments as composed of features is that doing so gives us an economical way of characterizing natural classes. **Natural classes** are classes of sounds that share a feature or features and that pattern together in sound systems.

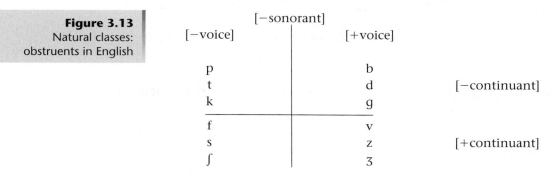

**Figure 3.13**
Natural classes:
obstruents in English

To see what is meant by this, consider the set of English sounds /p/, /t/, /k/, /f/, /s/, /ʃ/, and /b/, /d/, /g/, /v/, /z/, /ʒ/ given in figure 3.13. All these sounds belong to the class of obstruents (/tʃ/, /dʒ/, /θ/ and /ð/ are also obstruents, but we will ignore them for now). In order to capture this fact, we can say that they are all [−sonorant] (the '−' means 'not' in this context; definitions of the features are given in section 3.5.2). In addition, a subset of the members of this [−sonorant] class, namely /p/, /t/, /k/, /f/, /s/, /ʃ/, all of which differ in place and (in part) in manner of articulation, can be readily distinguished from the subset, /b/, /d/, /g/, /v/, /z/, /ʒ/, by the single feature [voice]. Finally a third feature, [continuant] (which refers to whether or not a sound is produced with continuous, free airflow), can distinguish all the (non-continuous) stops in the obstruent class, /p/, /t/, /k/, /b/,/d/, /g/ from all the (continuous) fricatives, /f/, /s/, /ʃ/, /v/, /z/, /ʒ/. Thus by using three features we are able to capture nine different natural classes of sounds; these are given in table 3.26.

| **Table 3.26** | Nine natural classes: obstruents in English | | | | | | | |
|---|---|---|---|---|---|---|---|---|
| [−sonorant] | [−sonorant −continuant] | [−sonorant +continuant] | [−sonorant −voice] | [−sonorant +voice] | [−sonorant −continuant −voice] | [−sonorant −continuant +voice] | [−sonorant +continuant −voice] | [−sonorant +continuant +voice] |
| p t k | p t k | f s ʃ | p t k | b d g | p t k | b d g | f s ʃ | v z ʒ |
| b d g | b d g | v z ʒ | f s ʃ | v z ʒ | | | | |
| f s ʃ | | | | | | | | |
| v z ʒ | | | | | | | | |

Any natural class requires fewer features to define it than to define any one of its members. In table 3.26 the largest class, that of the obstruents, is defined by only one feature, while the four classes containing three segments each are defined by three features each.

Every set of sounds that constitutes a natural class has the potential to pattern together in some way in the phonology of a language. For instance, we saw above that aspiration in English affects /p/, /t/, and /k/, the [−sonorant, −continuant, −voice] sounds of the language. All and only these sounds are affected by the aspiration process. An interesting point about features is that their use allows us to exclude sounds from (as well as to include them in) natural classes.

Thus, because /b/ is [+voice], it does not belong to the same class in English as /p/, /t/, and /k/. As a result /b/ is not affected by aspiration.

Table 3.27 provides an additional illustration of the use of features to distinguish natural classes—in this case, the class of front and back vowels in English. Again we see that fewer features are needed to define the larger class of English front vowels than to capture the vowel /æ/ alone.

| **Table 3.27** | Two natural classes: front and back vowels in English |
|---|---|

$$
\begin{bmatrix}
-\text{consonantal} \\
+\text{syllabic} \\
+\text{sonorant} \\
0\text{DORSAL} \\
-\text{back}
\end{bmatrix}
\quad
\begin{bmatrix}
-\text{consonantal} \\
+\text{syllabic} \\
+\text{sonorant} \\
0\text{DORSAL} \\
+\text{back}
\end{bmatrix}
\quad
\begin{bmatrix}
-\text{consonantal} \\
+\text{syllabic} \\
+\text{sonorant} \\
0\text{DORSAL} \\
-\text{back} \\
-\text{high} \\
+\text{low} \\
-\text{tense} \\
-\text{reduced}
\end{bmatrix}
$$

| *Front vowels* | *Back vowels* | |
|---|---|---|
| /i/ | /u/ | /æ/ |
| /ɪ/ | /ʊ/ | |
| /e/ | /o/ | |
| /ɛ/ | /ʌ/ | |
| /æ/ | /ɑ/ | |

In preceding sections we listed those segments of English that contrast, and that therefore make up the phonemes of English. Because features define natural classes, it is not just individual phonemes such as /p/, /b/, /k/, and /g/ that contrast in English; in fact, the entire class of voiced stops contrasts with the class of voiceless stops. All the contrasts found in the English sound system (and in the sound system of any language) can be defined in terms of the features that make up those phonemes. Thus, the distinctions between /p/ and /b/, /t/ and /d/, and /k/ and /g/ all reside in the feature [voice]. In addition, words like *pit* and *bit*, which constitute a minimal pair, contrast in the segments /p/ and /b/, and /p/ and /b/ themselves contrast in the feature [voice]. What these examples show us, then, is that features as well as segments can be contrastive. When a feature is the source of phonemic contrasts in a language, we say that it is a **distinctive feature** in the language. Thus, [voice] is a distinctive feature in English.

Other features provide for other contrasts. For example, we can capture the contrast between /t/ and /s/ in English with the feature [continuant]. Both /t/ and /s/ are voiceless and have an alveolar point of articulation. By viewing the relevant distinctive feature as [continuant], we can use the same feature to distinguish between /p/ and /f/, /b/ and /v/, and /d/ and /z/ (see table 3.28).

| **Table 3.28** | Stop-fricative contrasts as a feature |
|---|---|

| [−continuant] | [+continuant] |
|---|---|
| p | f |
| b | v |
| t | s |
| d | z |

By systematically examining the phonemic contrasts of a language, we can extract the distinctive features and use these irreducible linguistic elements to describe the phonemic inventory.

## Features, processes, and allophonic variation

A third reason for using features is that reference to features enables us to understand the nature of allophonic variation more exactly. Viewed from the perspective of features, allophonic variation is seen to be not simply the substitution of one allophone for another, but rather the environmentally conditioned change or specification of a feature or features. The liquid-glide devoicing that occurs in English words like *tree* and *twinkle*, for example, is a change in the value of the feature [voice] from [+voice] to [−voice] after voiceless (i.e., [−voice]) stop consonants. Similarly, the vowel and glide nasalization that occurs in Malay forms like /mewah/ [mẽw̃ãh] 'luxurious' is a change in the value of the feature [nasal] from [−nasal] to [+nasal] following a nasal (i.e., [+nasal]) consonant (see (7) in section 3.2.6).

We saw above that features reflect the fact that speech is produced by a number of independent but coordinated articulatory activities. Certain features, however, reflect classes of sounds that are not always recognized in the traditional descriptive terminology of phonetics that was introduced in chapter 2, but that are nevertheless relevant to phonological patterning. For example, the feature [CORONAL] (the use of upper case as opposed to lower case letters here reflects a difference in feature type which will be clarified below) refers to the class of sounds made with the tongue tip or blade raised: this class includes sounds made with interdental, alveolar, and alveopalatal places of articulation. It turns out that just this feature is required to state a constraint on the selection of consonant sequences in coda position in English: according to this constraint, when a vowel is tense and followed by two consonants (*pint* [pajnt]), or when a vowel is lax and followed by three consonants (*next* [nɛkst]), the final consonant in the coda must always be [CORONAL] (t, d, s, z, θ, ð, ʃ, ʒ, tʃ, or dʒ). Although the feature [CORONAL] does not reflect a traditional phonetic term, it plays a very important role in the phonologies of many languages. This fact shows us that features reflect articulatory reality in a way that involves more than just presenting traditional phonetic descriptions in a different guise.

## 3.5.2   Feature representations

We have seen that segments are composed of subsegmental units or features and that features reflect phonetic reality. Since features are considered to be the basic building blocks of speech sounds, and thus of phonology, linguists have attempted to state all possible phonological facts about language with the fewest number of features possible. Only a limited number of features—currently around twenty-four—have been proposed. Features thus constitute an important part of a theory of what is possible (and what is not possible) in the phonological behaviour of human beings. In this section we present and define features that are needed to characterize the sounds of English, as well as of many other languages.

## Defining the features of English

Most features have labels that reflect traditional articulatory terms such as [voice], [consonantal], and [nasal]. These features require little further description. A few features have less familiar labels, such as [CORONAL] and [anterior]. From this point on, features will be used to describe classes of sounds. At the same time, we will continue throughout the book to use terms such as *consonant, glide,* and *obstruent* (a fricative, affricate, or non-nasal stop) in phonetic description. This traditional terminology will be maintained because it is still widely used in phonetic description.

Features are organized into groups that reflect natural classes. The following headings indicate what these classes are and how the features represent them. Most of the features given below are written in lower case and are **binary**; in other words, they can have one of two values, '+' or '−', each of which defines a particular class of sounds. For example, [+voice] sounds involve vibration or voicing in the larynx, while [−voice] sounds involve an open glottis and therefore no vibration or voicing. Three of the features ([LABIAL], [CORONAL], and [DORSAL]) are written in upper case and have only one value. These features classify the places of articulation in the mouth in terms of the articulators that are used to produce them. Thus [LABIAL] represents sounds made using the lips, [CORONAL] represents sounds made with the tongue tip or tongue blade, and [DORSAL] represents sounds made with the tongue body/back.

- **Major class features** *features that represent the classes consonant, obstruent, and sonorant (nasal, liquid, glide, vowel)*

  **[±consonantal]** Sounds that are [+consonantal] are produced with a major obstruction in the vocal tract. All non-sonorant consonants (except the glottals [h] and [ʔ]), as well as liquids and nasals are [+consonantal]. Glides and vowels are [−consonantal].

  **[±syllabic]** Sounds that can act as syllable nuclei are [+syllabic]; this includes vowels, and syllabic liquids or syllabic nasals. All other sounds are [−syllabic].

  **[±sonorant]** All and only those sounds that are 'singable' are [+sonorant]; this includes vowels, glides, liquids, and nasals (even if the [+sonorant] sounds are voiceless). All non-singable sounds (obstruents) are [−sonorant].

Table 3.29 illustrates how the major class features are used to divide sounds into classes. Note that nasals and liquids have the same values for the three major class features; to distinguish these two classes from each, other additional (manner) features are therefore needed.

| **Table 3.29** Use of major class features | | | | | |
|---|---|---|---|---|---|
| | **Obstruents** | **Nasals** | **Liquids** | **Glides** | **Vowels** |
| [±consonantal] | + | + | + | − | − |
| [±syllabic] | − | − | − | − | + |
| [±sonorant] | − | + | + | + | + |
| Examples: | p d v tʃ | m n | l r | j w | i a |

The manner features given next represent manners of articulation. Their use is particularly important in distinguishing the following classes: stops/affricates as opposed to fricatives ([±continuant]); affricates as opposed to stops ([±delayed release]); nasals from non-nasals ([±nasal]); and laterals from non-laterals ([±lateral]).

- **Manner features** *features that represent manner of articulation*

  **[±continuant]** Sounds produced with free or nearly free airflow through the centre of the oral cavity are [+continuant]; these include vowels, glides, liquids, and fricatives. All other sounds are [−continuant]; these include nasal and oral stops.

**[±delayed release] ([±DR])** In the stop portion [t] of an affricate sound such as [tʃ], the tongue is slower in leaving the roof of the mouth than when a stop like [t] is produced on its own. Hence affricates are said to be produced with 'delayed release'. All and only affricates such as [tʃ] and [dʒ] are [+delayed release]. All other sounds are [−delayed release].

**[±nasal]** Sounds produced with a lowered velum are [+nasal]; this includes nasal stops and all nasalized sounds. Sounds that are oral, and thus produced with a raised velum, are [−nasal].

**[±lateral]** All and only varieties of *l* are [+lateral]. All other sounds are [−lateral].

Voicing, aspiration, and glottal constriction are all the result of laryngeal activity. To represent different laryngeal states, we use the features [±voice], [±spread glottis], and [±constricted glottis].

- **Laryngeal features** *features that represent laryngeal activity*

  **[±voice]** All voiced sounds are [+voice]; all voiceless sounds are [−voice].

  **[±spread glottis] ([±SG])** All aspirated consonants are [+SG]; all others are [−SG].

  **[±constricted glottis] ([±CG])** All sounds made with a closed glottis are [+CG]; all others are [−CG]. In English only the glottal stop [ʔ] is [+CG].

The next set of features is used to represent the supralaryngeal (above the larynx) articulatory activity, which determines place of articulation. So far, all the features that we have discussed have been binary, and have therefore had either '+' or '−' values. Articulatory features, however, are of two types.

The first type includes the features [LABIAL], [CORONAL], and [DORSAL] that, as noted above, are used specifically to represent and to distinguish the *articulators* that are active in executing (producing) particular places of articulation. For instance, the sound [k] is produced when the dorsum or body of the tongue touches the velum (soft palate) to form a constriction. Thus [k] has a *velar* place of articulation that is executed (produced) by moving the DORSAL (tongue body) articulator. The sound [k] therefore has the feature [DORSAL] in its feature representation.

In addition, when [k] is pronounced, the tongue body is always positioned high and back in the oral cavity. In this respect, [k] is different from [j]. Like [k], [j] is [DORSAL]. However, unlike [k], [j] is pronounced with the tongue body positioned high and front. In order to indicate that the LABIAL, CORONAL, and DORSAL articulators can occur in different positions, we use binary features such as [±high], [±back], [±round], etc., in addition to the articulator features. For instance, since [k] is pronounced with a high, back tongue body position, it is represented as being [+high] and [+back] as well as being [DORSAL]; in contrast, [j] is [+high] and [−back] in addition to being [DORSAL].

- **Place of articulation features** *features that represent supralaryngeal activity*

  **[LABIAL]** This feature represents the labial articulator: any sound that is produced with involvement of one or both of the lips is [LABIAL].

  **[±round]** A sound produced with the labial articulator may be produced by protruding the lips; such sounds are [+round]; labial sounds made with no lip protrusion are [−round]. [+round] labial sounds are rounded vowels and the rounded labiovelar glide [w]. [−round] labial sounds include [p, b, f, v].

**[CORONAL]** This feature represents the coronal articulator: any sound that is produced with involvement of the tongue tip or blade raised is [CORONAL].

**[±anterior]** All coronal sounds articulated in front of the alveopalatal region (interdentals and alveolars) are [+anterior]; coronal sounds articulated at or behind the alveopalatal region (alveopalatals) are [−anterior].

**[±strident]** All 'noisy' coronal fricatives and affricates ([s z ʃ ʒ tʃ dʒ]) are [+strident]; all other coronal fricatives and affricates ([θ, ð]) are [−strident].

**[DORSAL]** This feature represents the dorsal articulator: any sound that is produced with involvement of the body of the tongue is [DORSAL].

**[±high]** Dorsal consonants (velars or palatals) or vowels produced with the tongue body raised from a central position in the oral cavity are [+high]. Sounds produced with a neutral or lowered tongue body are [−high].

**[±low]** Vowels produced with the tongue body lowered from a central position in the oral cavity are [+low]. All other vowels are [−low]. [low] is not needed for consonants in English, although it may be used in languages that have uvular or pharyngeal consonants.

**[±back]** Dorsal consonants or vowels produced with the tongue body behind the palatal region (hard palate) in the oral cavity are [+back]. Sounds produced with the tongue body at the palatal region are [−back].

**[±tense]** Vowels that are tense are [+tense]; vowels that are lax are [−tense].

**[±reduced]** The vowel schwa ([ə]) is a lax and exceptionally brief vowel and is therefore [+reduced]; all other vowels are [−reduced].

To set the articulator features apart from other features, they are written with capitals. They do not have '+' and '−' values associated with them because if they are not being used to execute an articulation, they are simply inactive and are therefore absent from a representation. In other words, if a sound is a velar [k], it is produced with the tongue body, and neither the lips nor the tongue blade/tip are actively involved in the production of the sound. Consequently, the feature representation for [k] does not include the articulator features [LABIAL] and [CORONAL]; it only includes the feature [DORSAL].

It is important to remember that the binary articulatory features like [±round], [±anterior], or [±high] are specific to individual articulators. In other words, only the tongue body DORSAL articulator can be in [±high] or [±back] positions. The LABIAL articulator, the lips, can be rounded or unrounded, namely, [±round], but lips do not have high or back positions, and therefore DORSAL features like [±high] and [±back] are irrelevant to sounds made exclusively with the lips. Conversely, the tongue body never manifests roundness. Therefore, the feature [±round] is relevant only to the LABIAL articulator. Thus the binary articulatory features are used only to distinguish sounds produced by specific articulators. For instance, only [DORSAL] sounds like [k] that are produced with the tongue body may be [±high], [±low], or [±back]. Sounds made with other articulators are *not* represented with values for these features.

To see exactly how the articulator features are used to represent the various places of articulation of the consonants found in English, let us look at table 3.30. In the feature representations, 'o' indicates that the relevant articulator is active in the production of a sound. Where no 'o' is present, the articulator is inactive.

The feature representations in table 3.30 can be understood as follows:

■ [p] is produced with the lips in an unrounded state. It is therefore a [LABIAL], [−round] sound. The tongue blade and the tongue body are not used in the production of [p] and therefore it has no feature specifications for the coronal and dorsal articulators or for [CORONAL] or [DORSAL] features.

| **Table 3.30** | Use of place of articulation features in representing some English consonants | | | | | | |
|---|---|---|---|---|---|---|---|
| | **Labials** | | **Dentals** | **Alveolars** | **Alveopalatals**[7] | **Palatals** | **Velars** |
| | p | w | θ | s | ʃ | j | k |
| LABIAL | o | o | | | | | |
| [±round] | − | + | | | | | |
| CORONAL | | | o | o | o | | |
| [±anterior] | | | + | + | − | | |
| [±strident] | | | − | + | + | | |
| DORSAL | o | | | | | o | o |
| [±high] | + | | | | | + | + |
| [±back] | + | | | | | − | + |

■ [θ s ʃ] are all [CORONAL] sounds because they are produced with the tongue blade. [θ s] are produced with the tongue blade before or at the alveolar ridge and are therefore [+anterior], while [ʃ] is produced with the tongue blade behind the alveolar ridge and is therefore [−anterior]. [θ] is produced with a quiet airflow and so is [−strident], while [s ʃ] are produced with noisy airflow and so are [+strident]. Since neither the lips nor the tongue body are used to produce these sounds, they have no specifications for the labial and dorsal articulators or for [LABIAL] or [DORSAL] features. (For further discussion of the representation of [ʃ] and other alveopalatal sounds, see Note 7 at the end of the chapter.)

■ [j k] are both produced with the tongue body and are therefore [DORSAL] sounds. Both have a raised tongue body so are [+high], but [j] is pronounced with the tongue body at the hard palate, so is [−back]. In contrast, [k] is pronounced with the tongue body behind the hard palate, so it is [+back]. Finally, since neither the lips nor the tongue blade are used to produce these sounds, they have no specifications for the labial and coronal articulators or for [LABIAL] or [CORONAL] features.

■ [w] is a labiovelar sound and is thus coarticulated: it is produced with both a tongue body that is raised and behind the hard palate, *and* with lip rounding. This means that both the dorsum and the lips are used to produce [w], so it is executed with two articulators acting simultaneously. It is therefore both [LABIAL] and [DORSAL]; as a [LABIAL] sound it is [+round], and as a [DORSAL] sound it is [+high, +back]. Since the tongue blade is not used to produce this sound, it has no specifications for the [CORONAL] articulator or for coronal features.

Table 3.31 exemplifies how the place of articulation features are used to represent vowels in English. All the vowels in the table are produced with an active tongue body and therefore are [DORSAL]; this is true of all vowels, in English and in all other languages. Vowels that involve lip rounding are also produced with the [LABIAL] articulator. [CORONAL] is never used in the feature representations of vowels. All vowels except schwa are unreduced and therefore specified as [−reduced].

| **Table 3.31** | Use of place of articulation features in representing some English vowels | | | |
|---|---|---|---|---|
| | u | ɛ | ə | ɑ |
| LABIAL | o | | | |
| [±round] | + | | | |
| DORSAL | o | o | o | o |
| [±high] | + | − | − | − |
| [±low] | − | − | − | + |
| [±back] | + | − | + | + |
| [±tense] | + | − | − | + |
| [±reduced] | − | − | + | − |

- [u] is a high, back, tense vowel, and is therefore specified as [+high], [+back], and [+tense]. Since it is round, it is [LABIAL, +round] in addition to being [DORSAL]. Since it is [+high], it is also [−low] (since the tongue body cannot be both raised and lowered at the same time, all [+high] vowels are also [−low]).

- [ɛ] is a mid, front (non-back), lax, unrounded vowel. Since it is unrounded, it does not use the labial articulator. As a mid vowel, it has neither a raised nor a lowered tongue body, so it is [DORSAL] and specified as both [−high] and [−low]. As a front vowel, it is [−back] and as a lax vowel, it is [−tense].

- [ə] is a mid, central, unrounded, lax, and reduced vowel. As a mid vowel, it is [DORSAL, −high] and [−low]. As a central and therefore non-front vowel, it is [+back] (all central vowels are always [+back] in feature representations). Being unrounded, it does not involve the labial articulator. Because it is a lax reduced vowel, it is [−tense] and [+reduced].

- [ɑ] is a low, back, unrounded, tense vowel. Since it is produced with a lowered tongue body it is [DORSAL, +low]; because a lowered tongue body cannot be simultaneously raised, it is also [−high]. Since it is back, it is [+back]. Being tense, it is [+tense], and being unrounded, it has no labial specifications.

Feature notation does not provide a convenient way to distinguish diphthongs such as [aj], [aw], and [oj] from the other vowels. These diphthongs may be treated as vowel-glide sequences when using features.

For more advanced information on determining feature representations, please go to **www.pearsoned.ca/ogrady**.

Tables 3.32 and 3.33 provide the feature representations for all the consonants and vowels of English. As you go through these tables, notice that for every sound features are listed in the following order: major class features, manner features, laryngeal features, and place of articulation features. To remind yourselves of what a feature matrix for a segment looks like, go back to figure 3.12, which illustrates the matrix for the segment [ɑ].

Further discussion of how to determine feature representations is provided in the materials in the website at **www.pearsoned.ca/ogrady**.

**Table 3.32**    Feature matrix for English consonants

| | | p | pʰ | b | t | tʰ | d | k | kʰ | g | f | v | s | z | θ | ð | ʃ | ʒ | tʃ | dʒ | m | n | ŋ | l | r | j | w | ʍ | h | ʔ |
|---|---|---|---|---|---|---|---|---|---|---|---|---|---|---|---|---|---|---|---|---|---|---|---|---|---|---|---|---|---|---|
| *Major class features* | [consonantal] | + | + | + | + | + | + | + | + | + | + | + | + | + | + | + | + | + | + | + | + | + | + | + | + | − | − | − | − | − |
| | [sonorant] | − | − | − | − | − | − | − | − | − | − | − | − | − | − | − | − | − | − | − | + | + | + | + | + | + | + | + | − | − |
| | [syllabic] | − | − | − | − | − | − | − | − | − | − | − | − | − | − | − | − | − | − | − | − | − | − | − | − | − | − | − | − | − |
| *Manner features* | [nasal] | − | − | − | − | − | − | − | − | − | − | − | − | − | − | − | − | − | − | − | + | + | + | − | − | − | − | − | − | − |
| | [continuant] | − | − | − | − | − | − | − | − | − | + | + | + | + | + | + | + | + | − | − | − | − | − | − | + | + | + | + | + | − |
| | [lateral] | − | − | − | − | − | − | − | − | − | − | − | − | − | − | − | − | − | − | − | − | − | − | + | − | − | − | − | − | − |
| | [delayed release] | − | − | − | − | − | − | − | − | − | − | − | − | − | − | − | − | − | + | + | − | − | − | − | − | − | − | − | − | − |
| *Laryngeal features* | [voice] | − | − | + | − | − | + | − | − | + | − | + | − | + | − | + | − | + | − | + | + | + | + | + | + | + | + | − | − | − |
| | [CG] | − | − | − | − | − | − | − | − | − | − | − | − | − | − | − | − | − | − | − | − | − | − | − | − | − | − | − | − | + |
| | [SG] | − | + | − | − | + | − | − | + | − | − | − | − | − | − | − | − | − | − | − | − | − | − | − | − | − | − | − | + | − |
| *Place of articulation features* | LABIAL | o | o | o | | | | | | | o | o | | | | | | | | | o | | | | | | o | o | | |
| | [round] | − | − | − | | | | | | | − | − | | | | | | | | | − | | | | | | + | + | | |
| | CORONAL | | | | o | o | o | | | | | | o | o | o | o | o | o | o | o | | o | | o | o | | | | | |
| | [anterior] | | | | + | + | + | | | | | | + | + | + | + | − | − | − | − | | + | | + | − | | | | | |
| | [strident] | | | | − | − | − | | | | | | + | + | − | − | + | + | + | + | | − | | − | − | | | | | |
| | DORSAL | | | | | | | o | o | o | | | | | | | | | | | | | o | | | o | o | | | |
| | [high] | | | | | | | + | + | + | | | | | | | | | | | | | + | | | + | + | | | |
| | [back] | | | | | | | + | + | + | | | | | | | | | | | | | + | | | − | + | | | |

*Note:* [low], [tense], and [reduced] are not used for English consonants.

| Table 3.33 | Feature matrix for English vowels | | | | | | | | | | |
|---|---|---|---|---|---|---|---|---|---|---|---|---|
| | | i | ɪ | e | ɛ | æ | ʌ | ə | ɑ/a* | u | ʊ | o |
| *Major class features* | [consonantal] | − | − | − | − | − | − | − | − | − | − | − |
| | [sonorant] | + | + | + | + | + | + | + | + | + | + | + |
| | [syllabic] | + | + | + | + | + | + | + | + | + | + | + |
| *Manner feature* | [continuant] | + | + | + | + | + | + | + | + | + | + | + |
| *Laryngeal feature* | [voice] | + | + | + | + | + | + | + | + | + | + | + |
| *Place of articulation features* | LABIAL | | | | | | | | | o | o | o |
| | [round] | | | | | | | | | + | + | + |
| | DORSAL | o | o | o | o | o | o | o | o | o | o | o |
| | [high] | + | + | − | − | − | − | − | − | + | + | − |
| | [low] | − | − | − | − | + | − | − | + | − | − | − |
| | [back] | − | − | − | − | − | + | + | + | + | + | + |
| | [tense] | + | − | + | − | − | − | − | + | + | − | + |
| | [reduced] | − | − | − | − | − | − | + | − | − | − | − |

*Note: While [a] and [ɑ] are phonetically different, in English they have the same phonological features because they are not contrastive—and remember, central vowels (like [a]) are [+back]. For languages in which they contrast phonemically, the two sounds would have distinct feature specifications.

For more advanced discussion of features go to **www.pearsoned.ca/ogrady**.

## 3.6    Derivations and rules

To this point we have established the existence of related levels of phonological structure. In this model, phonological units from a lower level of structure are organized and grouped into higher-level structural units. Thus, *features* are grouped into *segments*, which in turn are organized into *syllables*. We have established that segments can be contrastive and hence belong to separate *phonemes*, or non-contrastive and hence function as predictable *allophonic variants* of phonemes. We have also seen that general statements referring to natural classes and to syllable structure can account for the patterning of non-contrastive elements. Finally, we have seen that there are two levels of representation associated with the difference between contrastive and non-contrastive segments: the *phonemic* level represents unpredictable, phonemic properties and units of a language, while the *phonetic* level represents predictable, allophonic properties and units. In this section we will explore the relationship between the phonemic and phonetic levels of representation and illustrate how this relationship is formalized.

Phonologists assume that phonemic representations are equivalent to the mental representations that speakers have of the words in their language, while phonetic representations are equivalent to the actual phonetic outputs that are produced in the course of speech. In this sense, phonemic representations are understood to be the basic representations of units such as the word. The unpredictable phonological information represented in a phonemic representation thus underlies all actual phonetic forms; for this reason, phonemic representations are also called **underlying representations** (or forms) while phonetic representations are also called **surface representations** (or forms).

Phonemic representations become phonetic representations as a result of being acted upon by *phonological processes* such as the devoicing of liquids and glides that follow voiceless stops in English, the aspiration of voiceless stops at the beginning of syllables in English, the lengthening of English vowels preceding voiced coda obstruents, and so on. Thus we say that phonetic or surface forms are **derived** from phonemic or underlying forms by means of phonological processes. These phonological processes are formalized as **phonological rules** (formalized statements of phonological processes). In this section, we focus on understanding how rules act in derivations and how they should be formalized.

## 3.6.1  Derivations

Underlying representations are composed of phonemes (which are composed of distinctive features). Phonetic forms are derived by allowing phonological processes—formalized as rules—to operate on underlying representations in those contexts where the processes are relevant.

The derivation of three phonetic representations (PRs) from underlying representations (URs) is illustrated in figure 3.14. Here, the underlying representation is on the top line (the cross hatch # symbolizes a word boundary); reading downwards, each rule applies in sequence, and the underlying representation is adjusted as required. Where a rule fails to apply, the form remains unchanged; this information is conveyed by dashes. The resulting output then serves as the input to the following rule. Finally, when all rules relevant to the derivation in question have applied, a phonetic representation is formed. The two rules presented in the following example are aspiration and vowel lengthening (see section 3.4.5).

| | UR | #slæp# | 'slap' | #tæp# | 'tap' | #pæd# | 'pad' |
|---|---|---|---|---|---|---|---|
| Aspiration | | – | | #tʰæp# | | #pʰæd# | |
| V-length | | – | | – | | #pʰæːd# | |
| | PR | [slæp] | | [tʰæp] | | [pʰæːd] | |

**Figure 3.14** The phonological derivation of three English words

In this example, two rules have applied (since the words being derived are all monosyllabic, the syllable boundaries are equivalent to word boundaries and so are not indicated here). The first accounts for aspiration. Since the initial consonants of the URs #tæp# and #pæd# are voiceless stops found in onset position, they fulfill the conditions under which English stops become aspirated. We therefore indicate that aspiration occurs by providing an intermediate form on a new line.

We have also seen that in English, vowels are predictably long when they occur before a voiced stop in the same syllable. In figure 3.14, the /æ/s of *slap* and *tap* occur before voiceless stops and so are not lengthened. The vowel of *pad*, however, occurs in just the environment associated with long vowels and so is predictably lengthened.

The use of such derivations underscores the fact that allophonic variation is the result of processes that apply in the course of language use. Underlying representations capture the knowledge that speakers have about the nature of their phonological system, rules reflect the application of allophonic processes, and the phonetic representation reflects the speech output. The relationship between phonemic or underlying representations and phonetic or surface representations is the result of the action of phonological processes.

## 3.6.2 Rule application

We have seen that more than one rule may be employed in a derivation. Consequently, we must now ask how several rules are applied to a given underlying form when these rules interact.

### Rule ordering

In figure 3.14 we examined the application of the rules of English aspiration and vowel lengthening, which apply to voiceless stops and vowels, respectively. Note that the environments in which each of these rules apply (onset and pre-coda position, respectively) are entirely different. Therefore, these rules do not interact or affect each other in any way; the order in which they are applied makes no difference to the outcome of the derivation. As figure 3.15 shows, there is no difference in the outcome when the same rules are applied in reverse order.

| | UR | #slæp# | 'slap' | #tæp# | 'tap' | #pæd# | 'pad' |
|---|---|---|---|---|---|---|---|
| | V-length | – | | – | | #pæːd# | |
| | Aspiration | – | | #tʰæp# | | #pʰæːd# | |
| | PR | [slæp] | | [tʰæp] | | [pʰæːd] | |

**Figure 3.15** Unordered rule application

We therefore say that the rules of aspiration and vowel lengthening are *unordered* with respect to each other. There are cases, however, in which two rules have to be ordered with respect to each other. For example, in some instances, the application of one rule creates an environment that makes possible the application of another rule. A case of ordered rules is illustrated in figure 3.16. In casual speech, the word *parade* in English is pronounced [pɾ̥éːjd]: there is initially a schwa between *p* and *r* which gets deleted by means of a rule of schwa-deletion because it is unstressed.

| | UR | #pəred# | 'parade' |
|---|---|---|---|
| | Stress | #pəréd# | |
| | Schwa deletion | #préd# | |
| | Liquid-glide devoicing | #pɾ̥éd# | |
| | Diphthongization | #pɾ̥éjd# | |
| | Vowel lengthening | #pɾ̥éːjd# | |
| | PR | [pɾ̥éːjd] | |

**Figure 3.16** Rule order in a derivation

After the schwa is deleted, the liquid *r* that follows the schwa in the underlying representation gets positioned directly after a voiceless stop. As a result, the *r* becomes subject to the rule of liquid-glide devoicing (given in example (4) in section 3.2.3), and is therefore devoiced.

In figure 3.16 the arrow, which is not normally written in derivations, indicates that the schwa deletion rule must apply before liquid-glide devoicing. Notice also that a rule that assigns stress to the final vowel applies before schwa-deletion. In addition, notice that if liquid-glide devoicing applied before schwa-deletion, the devoicing of *r* would not be able to take place because *r* would not be positioned right after the voiceless *p* and therefore would not get devoiced. What is clear, then, is that to get the correct surface form [pré:jd], schwa-deletion must be ordered before liquid-glide devoicing.

## 3.6.3  The form and notation of rules

General statements about allophonic distribution are formalized as rules, which are written so as to reflect the dynamic nature of processes (see chapter 2, section 2.9.3).

### Rules

Rules take the following form.

(10)  A → B / X ___ Y

In this notation, *A* stands for an element in a representation, *B* for the change it undergoes or for the output of the rule, and *X* and *Y* for the conditioning environment. Either *X* or *Y* may be absent (null) if the conditioning environment is found only on one side of the allophone. The __ (focus bar) indicates the position of the segment undergoing the rule. The slash separates the statement of the change from the statement of the conditioning environment, and can be thought of as meaning 'in the environment of'. This rule is therefore read as *A becomes B in the environment between X and Y*.

As an example of rule writing, we return to the distribution of liquid-glide devoicing in English (section 3.2.4): liquids and glides have voiceless allophones after syllable-initial voiceless stops (and voiced allophones elsewhere). The rule statement treats the voiced allophones of liquids and glides as basic (underlying) and changes the feature [+voice] to [−voice] in the appropriate environment (see figure 3.17).

**Figure 3.17**
Liquid-glide devoicing in English expressed as a rule

$$\begin{bmatrix} \text{−syllabic} \\ \text{+sonorant} \\ \text{+voice} \\ \text{−nasal} \end{bmatrix} \rightarrow [\text{−voice}] \,/\, \sigma \begin{bmatrix} \text{−syllabic} \\ \text{+consonantal} \\ \text{−sonorant} \\ \text{−continuant} \\ \text{−voice} \\ \text{−delayed release} \end{bmatrix} \underline{\qquad}$$

The rule in figure 3.17 is a rule to describe the prose statement given in (11).

(11)  Liquids and glides become voiceless after syllable-initial voiceless stops.

The use of features in figure 3.17 expresses the fact that liquids and glides form a natural class of sounds: specifically, they are the non-nasal sonorant consonants of

English. It also formally represents the fact that the process is phonetically based. For example, the devoicing of liquids and glides in English is a typical process of assimilation. The rule notation in figure 3.17 explicitly shows this by indicating that the [+voice] feature of sonorant consonants changes to [−voice] following the class of voiceless stops, sounds that are themselves [−voice].

## Deletion and epenthesis as rules

We have already seen that English speakers (optionally) drop a schwa [ə] in an open syllable when it is followed by a stressed syllable, as in *police* [pl̩ís] and *parade* [pr̩éjd]. The rule can be formalized as in figure 3.18. Here, $C_0$ is an abbreviation for any number of successive consonants from zero on up and the σ represents a syllable boundary.[8]

| | |
|---|---|
| **Figure 3.18**<br>Schwa deletion in English | $[\text{ə}] \rightarrow \varnothing \; / \; C_0 \underline{\quad}_\sigma C_0 \quad\quad V$<br>$\qquad\qquad\qquad [+\text{stress}]$ |

All deletion rules are written in the same way as the schwa-deletion rule in figure 3.18: the rule output (the part replacing B in the rule formalization in (10)) is always written as a null sign (Ø). Conversely, in the case of rules of epenthesis, the null sign is always included in the rule input (the part replacing A in the rule formalization in (10)).

An example of epenthesis in English involves the insertion of a vowel that is frequently triggered when an impermissible phonotactic structure is encountered in a borrowed word, as in the English pronunciation of the name *Dmitri*. It is also the case that in some dialects of English, a coda consisting of *l* and another consonant is not permitted. In these dialects, *milk* is pronounced [mɪlək] and *film* [fɪləm]. This latter change can be represented in rule format as in figure 3.19. It should be noted, however, that this rule applies for only a small number of words.

| | |
|---|---|
| **Figure 3.19**<br>Schwa epenthesis in English as a rule | $\varnothing \; \rightarrow \; [\text{ə}] \; / \; [+\text{lateral}] \underline{\quad\quad} \begin{bmatrix} -\text{syllabic} \\ +\text{consonantal} \end{bmatrix} \; \sigma$ |

For more on the rules of epenthesis, go to **www.pearsoned.ca/ogrady**.

## Rules that refer to syllable structure

The epenthesis rule in figure 3.19 refers to syllable structure. Notice that there is a syllable boundary marker [σ] at the end of the rule statement; this marker is used to indicate that the schwa is inserted between a lateral and another consonant at the end of a syllable. Although the rule formulated in figure 3.19 does not explicitly state this, the insertion of the schwa actually changes the syllable structure of the input word. In other words, a word such as *film*, which constitutes one syllable initially, becomes two syllables after epenthesis. This change in syllable structure is illustrated in figure 3.20.

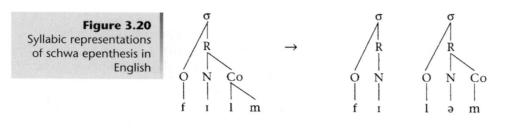

**Figure 3.20**
Syllabic representations of schwa epenthesis in English

Many other rules in English and in other languages make reference to syllable structure. One of these is the rule of vowel lengthening in English. Remember the data from table 3.24 that showed the differences in vowel length in words such as *phase* versus *face*?

(12)  English vowels are long when followed by a voiced obstruent consonant in the same syllable.

The corresponding rule (in figure 3.21) states that an underlying short vowel is lengthened in the appropriate context. As in the case of the epenthesis rule, the boundary of the syllable is represented by a syllable marker σ. Notice that the onset of the syllable is irrelevant to the statement of the rule and so is not included in the formalization.

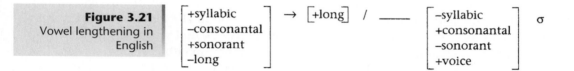

**Figure 3.21**
Vowel lengthening in English

For an advanced discussion of the nature and structure of phonological representations, go to **www.pearsoned.ca/ogrady**.

### 3.6.4  Processes and rules: a last word

The combined use of features and processes in phonological description reflects the dynamic nature of linguistic behaviour. First, the use of features reflects a basic level of phonological activity—contrasts take place on the feature level, not on the level where segments are represented. Secondly, the use of process notation and formalization with rules reflects the realities of linguistic production, in which sounds are affected by the context in which they are pronounced as we speak. Overall, the patterning of phonological units follows from the interaction of a universal set of features, universal and language-specific phonotactic constraints and syllabification procedures, and the use of rules. This current theory of phonology is based on principles that are applicable to the study of any human language.

# Summing up

Phonology deals with the sequential and phonetically conditioned patterning of sounds in language. To account for this patterning, three units of phonological representation have been established: the **feature**, the **phoneme**, and the **syllable**. Phonemes are contrastive segmental units composed of distinctive features. Phonetically conditioned variants of phonemes are called **allophones**.

Phonology makes use of **underlying forms**, **derivations**, and **phonological rules** in its formal notation. Some rules are ordered with respect to each other.

## Notes

1   Of course, words can differ in meaning without contrasting phonetically. In every language, there are words (called *homophones*) that are identical in pronunciation but that differ in meaning, such as English *well* 'spring' and *well* 'all right'. The following French words provide a more dramatic example of homophones.

| | | |
|---|---|---|
| vert | [vɛ:r] | 'green' |
| vers | [vɛ:r] | 'towards' |
| vers | [vɛ:r] | 'verse' |
| verre | [vɛ:r] | 'glass' |
| ver | [vɛ:r] | 'worm' |

2   In some dialects of English there is also a contrast between [ɑ] and the mid back rounded lax vowel [ɔ] in words like *cot* [kʰɑt] and *caught* [kʰɔt]. In Canadian English, these words and other analogous ones are both pronounced [kʰɑt].

3   In some dialects of English the high tense vowels /i/ and /u/ are pronounced with strong off-glides—[ij] and [uw], respectively. In other dialects, these off-glides are very weak, and, in still other dialects, they are not present at all. Since there is less variability in the pronunciation of the mid vowels with off-glides, we focus on the mid vowels in this section. To account for dialects with [ij, ej, uw, ow], the generalization given in (5) that follows can be restated as: the non-low (high and mid) tense vowels of English are predictably followed by a glide that has the same backness and roundness as the vowel.

4   The sounds [w] and [ʍ] are labiovelar sounds, but in representations of inventories they are usually listed in the same column as velar sounds.

5   Perhaps you have noticed that voiceless·sonorant allophones occur in the same context as aspiration: in syllable onsets. Both types of voicelessness are indeed a manifestation of voice lag. It would not be inappropriate to represent aspiration as [pɪ̥n] 'pin' or liquid-glide devoicing as [pʰl̥ʌk]. This book, however, will stick to the traditional representations.

6   Some English words, such as *upper, happy,* and *walking,* do not show aspiration where it is expected, given that the syllabification procedure results in the following:

/ʌ.pər/, /hæ.pi/, and /wɑ.kɪŋ/. This fact is accounted for by assuming that the voiceless stops in these forms are simultaneously in both syllables, a phenomenon that is known as **ambisyllabicity**:

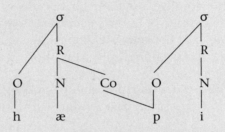

We will not address the details and motivations of ambisyllabicity here.

[7] Alveopalatals may pattern together with high front vowels and glides for purposes of some rules. In such cases, we can assume they are specified with the features [oDORSAL, +high, −back] as well as [oCORONAL, −anterior, +strident]. In other words, in such cases, alveopalatals have two articulators.

[8] The English schwa-deletion rule interacts with the constraint on possible consonant sequences, automatically failing to apply when an impermissible sequence would result. Since σ[ptʰ and σ[dl are impermissible onsets in English, there are no forms like *[ptʰéjɾow] *potato* or *[dlít] *delete* (except in very, very fast speech).

## Recommended reading

Anderson, Stephen R. 1985. *Phonology in the Twentieth Century.* Chicago: University of Chicago Press.

Blevins, Juliette. 2004. *Evolutionary Phonology: The Emergence of Sound Patterns.* Cambridge: Cambridge University Press.

Burton-Roberts, Noel, Philip Carr, and Gerard Docherty. 2000. *Phonological Knowledge: Conceptual and Empirical Issues.* Oxford: Oxford University Press.

Carr, Philip. 1993. *Phonology.* London: Macmillan.

Goldsmith, John. 1990. *Autosegmental and Metrical Phonology.* Cambridge, MA: Blackwell.

Goldsmith, John, ed. 1995. *The Handbook of Phonological Theory.* Cambridge, MA: Blackwell.

Keating, Patricia. 1988. *The Phonology-Phonetics Interface.* In *Linguistics: The Cambridge Survey.* Vol. 1. Edited by F. Newmeyer, 281–302. London: Cambridge University Press.

Kenstowicz, Michael. 1994. *Phonology in Generative Grammar.* Cambridge, MA: Blackwell.

Silverman, Daniel Doron. 2006. *A Critical Introduction to Phonology: Of Sound, Mind and Body.* London: Continuum Publishing.

Stampe, David. 1980. *A Dissertation on Natural Phonology.* New York: Garland.

## Appendix: hints for solving phonology problems

The task of solving a phonology problem is made easier if certain facts presented in this chapter and summarized here are kept in mind. The data that we consider below are taken from Tagalog (Filipino), a language spoken in the Philippines.

**1.** In the following data, consider the phones [h] and [ʔ] and determine whether they contrast, or whether they are allophones of one phoneme.

| | | | | |
|---|---|---|---|---|
| a) kahon | 'box' | d) ʔari | 'property' |
| b) hariʔ | 'king' | e) kaʔon | 'to fetch' |
| c) ʔumagos | 'to flow' | f) humagos | 'to paint' |

In order to determine whether the phones contrast, we begin by looking for minimal pairs. These establish which segments are contrastive. For example, in the data in a) through f), minimal pairs occur in items a–e and c–f; b–d is a near-minimal pair. The existence of minimal and near-minimal pairs of words indicates that [h] and [ʔ] contrast. Therefore, we can conclude that /h/ and /ʔ/ are separate phonemes.

**2.** Now consider the following data, and determine whether the two sounds [d] and [r] contrast or whether they are allophones of one phoneme.

| | | | |
|---|---|---|---|
| a) datiŋ | 'to arrive' | f) daraʔiŋ | 'will complain' |
| b) dami | 'amount' | g) marumi | 'dirty' |
| c) dumi | 'dirt' | h) marami | 'many' |
| d) daratiŋ | 'will arrive' | i) daʔiŋ | 'to complain' |
| e) mandurukot | 'pickpocket' | j) mandukot | 'to go pickpocketing' |

Since there are no minimal pairs in the data which contrast [d] and [r], we proceed to check whether the two sounds are in complementary distribution. Normally, when two sounds are in complementary distribution and therefore allophones of one phoneme, they must be phonetically similar. In Tagalog, [d] and [r] are both voiced alveolar segments; thus, they are sufficiently similar phonetically to be viewed as potential allophones of one phoneme.

To check whether two (or more) sounds are in complementary distribution, the best thing to do is to list the environments in which the sounds occur:

| [d] occurs: | [r] occurs: |
|---|---|
| –word-initially (e.g., *dami*) | –between two vowels (e.g., *marami*) |
| –following a nasal (e.g., *mandukot*) | |

[d] never occurs between two vowels, and [r] never occurs word-initially or following a nasal. Since the two sounds never occur in identical environments, they are in complementary distribution and their distributions are predictable.

**3.** If two potential allophones of one phoneme are in complementary distribution, we can be reasonably sure that they are allophones of one phoneme. We can therefore make a general statement about their distribution, in terms of some natural phonological class. For example: Tagalog [d] and [r] are in complementary distribution and are allophones of one phoneme. The allophone [r] occurs between vowels; [d] occurs elsewhere—here, word-initially, as in items a), b), c), f), and so on, and after nasal consonants, as in items e) and j).

**4.** Once we have determined that two sounds are allophones of one phoneme, we need to determine what the phoneme that they are both derived from is. Usually this can be done by selecting one of the allophones as basic. In most cases, the allophone chosen to represent the phoneme is the one with the widest distribution (the elsewhere variant). In the Tagalog case, the elsewhere variant is [d], so we posit the phoneme /d/, which has two allophones, [d] and [ɾ]. It may be helpful to set up a traditional phoneme-allophone diagram to illustrate this (see figure 3.2).

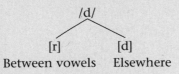

5. Now that we know that [d] and [ɾ] are allophones of the phoneme /d/, we need to determine the phonological rule that accounts for the predictable features of the other allophones. Our rule is probably correct if it describes a common linguistic process (such as assimilation) in terms of natural classes of sounds interacting with neighbouring segments and/or syllable structure.

For example, for the above: d → ɾ / V___V

The process at work here is a form of assimilation, in that an underlying voiced stop consonant becomes a continuant when found between two continuants (vowels).

6. We can assume that segments are phonemic if there are no minimal pairs for them but they cannot be shown to be allophones of one phoneme. In such a case, we can conclude that the data simply did not provide minimal pairs.

## Exercises

Assume phonetic transcription of the data in all exercises.

1. *Inuktitut* (Eastern) (Native Canadian)

| | | | | |
|---|---|---|---|---|
| a) iglumut | 'to a house' | h) | pinna | 'that one up there' |
| b) ukiaq | 'late fall' | i) | ani | 'female's brother' |
| c) aiviq | 'walrus' | j) | iglu | '(snow)house' |
| d) aniguvit | 'if you leave' | k) | panna | 'that place up there' |
| e) aglu | 'seal's breathing hole' | l) | aivuq | 'she goes home' |
| f) iglumit | 'from a house' | m) | ini | 'place, spot' |
| g) anigavit | 'because you leave' | n) | ukiuq | 'winter' |

**i)** List all the minimal pairs in this data. Based on the minimal pairs you have found, list all the contrastive pairs of vowels.

**ii)** Using the vowel charts in figures 2.9 and 2.10 as your models, make a chart of Inuktitut vowel phonemes.

**iii)** Now consider the data again; here it is transcribed in more phonetic detail. In it, there are phonetically similar segments that are in complementary distribution. Look for them and then answer the question that follows the data.

| | | | | |
|---|---|---|---|---|
| aa) iglumut | 'to a house' | hh) | pinna | 'that one up there' |
| bb) ukiaq | 'late fall' | ii) | anɪ | 'female's brother' |
| cc) aivɪq | 'walrus' | jj) | iglʊ | '(snow)house' |
| dd) aniguvit | 'if you leave' | kk) | panna | 'that place up there' |
| ee) aglʊ | 'seal's breathing hole' | ll) | aivʊq | 'she goes home' |
| ff) iglumit | 'from a house' | mm) | inɪ | 'place, spot' |
| gg) anigavit | 'because you leave' | nn) | ukiʊq | 'winter' |

**iv)** List the phonetically similar segments that are in complementary distribution. State their distribution in words.

2. *Hindi* (Hindi is a language of the Indo-European family spoken in India)
Consider the segments [b] and [b̤] in the data below and answer the questions that follow. The segment transcribed [b̤] is a murmured voiced stop.

| a) [bara] | 'large' | f) [b̤ɛd] | 'disagreement' |
|---|---|---|---|
| b) [b̤ari] | 'heavy' | g) [bais] | 'twenty-two' |
| c) [bina] | 'without' | h) [b̤əs] | 'buffalo' |
| d) [b̤ir] | 'crowd' | i) [bap] | 'father' |
| e) [bori] | 'sackcloth' | j) [b̤ag] | 'part' |

**i)** Are the segments [b] and [b̤] allophones of the same phoneme or do they belong to separate phonemes? If you believe they belong to separate phonemes, give evidence from the data to support your analysis. If you believe they are allophones of the same phoneme, list the conditioning environments.

3. *Mokilese* (Mokilese is an Austronesian language of the South Pacific)
Examine the following data from Mokilese carefully, taking note of where voiceless vowels occur.

| a) pi̥san | 'full of leaves' | g) uduk | 'flesh' |
|---|---|---|---|
| b) tu̥pu̥kta | 'bought' | h) kaskas | 'to throw' |
| c) pu̥ko | 'basket' | i) poki | 'to strike something' |
| d) ki̥sa | 'we two' | j) pil | 'water' |
| e) su̥pwo | 'firewood' | k) apid | 'outrigger support' |
| f) kamwɔki̥ti | 'to move' | l) ludʒuk | 'to tackle' |

**i)** The vowel phonemes of Mokilese are /i e ɛ u o ɔ a/. In Mokilese, [i̥] is an allophone of /i/, and [u̥] is an allophone of /u/. No other vowels have voiceless allophones. State in words the conditioning factors that account for this distribution. Be as general as possible in referring to classes of sounds.

**ii)** If you have completed the section on rule formalization, write a rule (using features) that accounts for the derived allophones.

4. *Gascon* (Gascon is spoken in southwest France)
The phones [b], [β], [d], [ð], [g], and [ɣ] are all found in Gascon, as the following examples show. The phone [β] is a voiced bilabial fricative; [ɣ] is a voiced velar fricative.

| a) brẽn | 'endanger' | n) gat | 'cat' |
|---|---|---|---|
| b) bako | 'cow' | o) lũŋg | 'long' |
| c) ũmbro | 'shadow' | p) saliβo | 'saliva' |
| d) krãmbo | 'room' | q) noβi | 'husband' |
| e) dilys | 'Monday' | r) aβe | 'to have' |
| f) dũŋko | 'until' | s) ʃiβaw | 'horse' |
| g) duso | 'sweet' | t) byðɛt | 'gut' |
| h) taldepãn | 'leftover bread' | u) eʃaðo | 'hoe' |
| i) pũnde | 'to lay eggs' | v) biɣar | 'mosquito' |
| j) dudze | 'twelve' | w) riɣut | 'he laughed' |
| k) guteʒa | 'flow' | x) agro | 'sour' |
| l) ẽŋgwãn | 'this year' | y) ʒuɣɛt | 'he played' |
| m) puðe | 'to be able' | | |

**i)** Which pairs among the phones [b], [β], [d], [ð], [g], and [ɣ] are the most phonetically similar? Support your claim with phonetic descriptions of the similar pairs.

**ii)** List the environments in which the phones [b], [β], [d], [ð], [g], and [ɣ] are found.

**iii)** Is there any evidence for grouping the pairs of sounds into phonemes? State the evidence for each pair.

**iv)** Make a general statement about the patterning of the phonemes you have established.

**v)** Following your analysis, write the following forms in phonemic transcription.

  a) [puɣo]        b) [deðat]        c) [ʃiβaw]        d) [krãmbo]

5. *Swampy Cree* (Swampy Cree is a Native Canadian language of the Algonquian family) The following data from Swampy Cree shows a number of different voiced and voiceless consonantal segments.

| | | | |
|---|---|---|---|
| a) niska | 'goose' | l) nisto | 'three' |
| b) kodak | 'another' | m) tʃiːgahigan | 'axe' |
| c) asabaːp | 'thread' | n) adim | 'dog' |
| d) waskoːw | 'cloud' | o) miːbit | 'tooth' |
| e) paskwaːw | 'prairie' | p) pimiː | 'lard' |
| f) niːgi | 'my house' | q) mide | 'heart' |
| g) koːgoːs | 'pig' | r) oːgik | 'these' |
| h) tahki | 'often' | s) tʃiːmaːn | 'canoe' |
| i) namwaːtʃ | 'not at all' | t) waːbos | 'rabbit' |
| j) ospwaːgan | 'pipe' | u) naːbeːw | 'man' |
| k) midʒihtʃij | 'hand' | v) miːdʒiwin | 'food' |

**i)** Do [p] and [b] belong to separate phonemes, or are they allophones of one phoneme? If you think they belong to separate phonemes, list data to support your case. If you think they are allophones, first state the conditioning factors in words, and then, using features, write a rule that accounts for their distribution.

**ii)** Do the same for [t] and [d], [k] and [g], and [tʃ] and [dʒ].

**iii)** Can you make a general statement about the relationship among all the consonantal pairs whose distribution you have examined?

**iv)** Using figure 3.14 as your model, provide complete derivations of the forms for k) *hand*, m) *axe*, and o) *tooth*.

6. There are a number of natural classes in the vowel and consonant data below. Circle three natural classes in each set of data. Indicate which feature or features define the class, as in the example. The phone [x] is a voiceless velar fricative.

*Example:*   [+voice]———( b   d ) tʃ ( k ) h ———[–continuant]

a)  i        u              b)  p            tʃ    k

   e        o                               dʒ

      a                           f    θ    ʃ    x

                    m                    ŋ

**7.** Name the single feature that distinguishes the following pairs of sounds.

| | | |
|---|---|---|
| a) [θ] : [ð] | e) [b] : [m] | i) [ʌ] : [ə] |
| b) [p] : [f] | f) [s] : [ʃ] | j) [s] : [θ] |
| c) [u] : [ʊ] | g) [i] : [ɪ] | k) [e] : [ɛ] |
| d) [i] : [e] | h) [k] : [g] | l) [u] : [o] |

**8.** Complete the feature matrix for each of the sounds indicated. The V abbreviates the features [+syllabic, −consonantal], and the C abbreviates the features [−syllabic, +consonantal].

a)  [e]        V
$$\begin{bmatrix} +\text{sonorant} \\ \text{oDORSAL} \\ -\text{high} \\ -\text{low} \end{bmatrix}$$

b)  [ʃ]        C
$$\begin{bmatrix} -\text{sonorant} \\ -\text{voice} \\ -\text{nasal} \end{bmatrix}$$

c)  [m]        C
$$\begin{bmatrix} +\text{sonorant} \\ \text{oLABIAL} \end{bmatrix}$$

d)  [s]        C
$$\begin{bmatrix} -\text{sonorant} \\ \text{oCORONAL} \\ +\text{strident} \end{bmatrix}$$

e)  [g]        C
$$\begin{bmatrix} -\text{sonorant} \\ \text{oDORSAL} \\ +\text{high} \end{bmatrix}$$

f)  [j]
$$\begin{bmatrix} -\text{syllabic} \\ -\text{consonantal} \end{bmatrix}$$

**9.** *English/Korean*
As we have seen, phonological adaptation of loan words may reflect facts about syllable structure. Recently, the Korean automobile name Hyundai has been adapted into English in various ways, one of which follows. Give the Korean form and the English adaptation provided, state two reasons based on syllable structure conditions that explain why the English form is pronounced the way it is.

| *Korean form* | | *English form* |
|---|---|---|
| /hjʌndæ/ | → | /hʌnde/ [hʌndej] |

**10.** *English*
Many speakers of English have two variants of [l]. One, called *clear l*, is transcribed as [l] in the following data. The other, called *dark l*, is transcribed with [ɫ]. Examine the data, and answer the questions that follow.

| | | | |
|---|---|---|---|
| a) [lʌjf] | 'life' | g) [pʰɪɫ] | 'pill' |
| b) [lip] | 'leap' | h) [fiɫ] | 'feel' |
| c) [luːz] | 'lose' | i) [hɛɫp] | 'help' |
| d) [ilowp] | 'elope' | j) [bʌɫk] | 'bulk' |
| e) [dilʌjt] | 'delight' | k) [sowɫd] | 'sold' |
| f) [slip] | 'sleep' | l) [fʊɫ] | 'full' |

Do [l] and [ɫ] belong to separate phonemes or are they allophones of the same phoneme? If you think they belong to separate phonemes, answer question **i)**. If you think they are allophones of the same phoneme, answer question **ii)**.

i)   List the evidence that makes your case for considering [l] and [ɫ] as separate phonemes.

ii)  State the distribution of [l] and [ɫ] in words.
     Which variant makes the best underlying form? Why?
     Can you make reference to syllable structure in your distribution statement? If you can, do so in rule form.

11. *Canadian French*
    For the purposes of this problem, you may assume that syllables in Canadian French have the following structure:

    ■ Maximum number of consonants in an onset: 2. Where there are two onset consonants, the first must be an obstruent, the second a sonorant or a fricative.
    ■ Each vowel forms a syllable nucleus.
    ■ Maximum number of consonants in a coda: 2.

    With these stipulations in mind, syllabify the following forms:
    a) bukan 'smoke'        b) erite 'to inherit'     c) pudrəri 'snowstorm'
    d) plie 'to fold'

    In the following data from Canadian French, each pair of phones is in complementary distribution.
    [i] and [ɪ]     are allophones of one phoneme
    [y] and [ʏ]     are allophones of a second phoneme
    [u] and [ʊ]     are allophones of a third phoneme

    It is possible to make a general statement about the distribution of the vowel allophones that accounts for all three phonemes. [y] is a high, front, rounded, tense vowel while [ʏ] is a high, front, rounded, lax vowel.

    Examine the data and answer the questions that follow.

| | | | | | |
|---|---|---|---|---|---|
| a) | pilʏl | 'pill' | o) | fini | 'finished' |
| b) | griʃe | 'to crunch' | p) | fɪj | 'girl' |
| c) | grɪʃ | 'it crunches' | q) | dzʏr | 'hard' |
| d) | pətsi | 'little (masc.)' | r) | tryke | 'to fake' |
| e) | pətsɪt | 'little (fem.)' | s) | fʊl | '(a) crowd' |
| f) | vitamɪn | 'vitamin' | t) | plʏs | 'more' |
| g) | saly | 'hi' | u) | ru | 'wheel' |
| h) | ʒʏp | 'skirt' | v) | rʊt | 'road' |
| i) | fyme | 'smoke' | w) | suvã | 'often' |
| j) | lynɛt | 'glasses' | x) | trupo | 'herd' |
| k) | tɔrdzy | 'twisted" | y) | sʊp | 'flexible' |
| l) | lʏn | 'moon' | z) | tʊʃ | 'touch' |
| m) | pɪp | 'pipe' | aa) | fu | 'crazy (masc.)' |
| n) | grimas | 'grimace' | bb) | trʏk | '(a) trick' |

**i)** Provide a statement of the distribution of [i] and [ɪ], [y] and [ʏ], [u] and [ʊ] in words. Make your statement as general as possible, but be precise!

**ii)** If you have completed the section on rule formalization, write a single rule that derives the allophones of each phoneme from the underlying form. Use features! Be sure to give your rule a name; use this name in the answer to question **iii)**.

**iii)** Provide derivations for the following underlying forms.

| UR | # | # | 'vitamin' | # | # | 'glasses' |
|----|---|---|-----------|---|---|-----------|
|    |   |   |           |   |   |           |
| PR | [vitamɪn] | | | [lynɛt] | | |

**12.** *English*

The following data contains both careful speech and fast speech forms. Note the differences and answer the questions that follow. Some phonetic detail irrelevant to the question has been omitted from the transcription. Remember that an asterisk before a form indicates that it is not acceptable to (most) native speakers.

| *Careful speech* | | *Fast speech* | *Spelled form* |
|------------------|--|---------------|----------------|
| a) [ǽspərən] | k) | [ǽsprən] | aspirin |
| b) [pɔ́rsələn] | l) | [pɔ́rslən] | porcelain |
| c) [nǽʃənəlàjz] | m) | [nǽʃnəlàjz] | nationalize |
| d) [rízənəbl̩] | n) | [ríznəbl̩] | reasonable |
| e) [ɪmǽdʒənətɪv] | o) | [ɪmǽdʒnətɪv] | imaginative |
| f) [sèpərəbílɪɾi] | p) | [sèprəbílɪɾi] | separability |
| g) [méθəd] | q) | [méθəd] *[méθd] | method |
| h) [féjməs] | r) | [féjməs] *[féjms] | famous |
| i) [méməràjz] | s) | [méməràjz] *[mémràjz] | memorize |
| j) [kʰənsìdəréjʃən] | t) | [kʰənsìdəréjʃən] *[kʰənsìdréjʃən] | consideration |

**i)** The schwa deletion between the careful speech forms and the rapid speech forms in items a–f is systematic. State in words the phonetic conditions that account for the deletion.

**ii)** The same pattern that occurs between the careful speech forms and the rapid speech forms in items a–f does not occur in items g–j. State in words the phonetic difference between these sets of forms that accounts for the lack of schwa deletion.

**iii)** Now that you have taken items g–j into account, will you have to change your original statement of the phonetic conditions governing schwa deletion in the fast speech forms? If so, do this in words.

**iv)** If you have completed the section on rule formalization, convert your statement in **iii)** into formal notation.

**13.** Change the following statements into rule notation. Be sure to name the process in question for each case.

a) Voiceless stops become corresponding fricatives between vowels.

b) A schwa is inserted between a voiced stop and a word-final voiced fricative.

c) Low unrounded vowels become rounded before *m*.

**14.** State each of the following rules in English, making reference to natural classes and common linguistic processes.

*Example:*
$$\begin{bmatrix} -\text{syllabic} \\ +\text{consonantal} \\ -\text{sonorant} \end{bmatrix} \rightarrow \varnothing / \underline{\quad} \# \text{ (an obstruent is deleted word-finally)}$$

a) $\varnothing \rightarrow \begin{bmatrix} +\text{syllabic} \\ -\text{consonantal} \\ +\text{sonorant} \\ o\text{DORSAL} \\ -\text{high} \\ -\text{low} \\ -\text{back} \\ +\text{tense} \end{bmatrix} / \# \underline{\quad} \begin{bmatrix} -\text{syllabic} \\ +\text{consonantal} \\ -\text{sonorant} \end{bmatrix} \begin{bmatrix} -\text{syllabic} \\ +\text{consonantal} \\ -\text{sonorant} \end{bmatrix}$

b) $\begin{bmatrix} -\text{syllabic} \\ +\text{consonantal} \\ -\text{sonorant} \\ -\text{nasal} \\ -\text{continuant} \\ -\text{delayed release} \\ +\text{voice} \\ o\text{CORONAL} \\ +\text{anterior} \end{bmatrix} \rightarrow [+\text{nasal}] / \underline{\quad} \begin{bmatrix} -\text{syllabic} \\ +\text{consonantal} \\ +\text{sonorant} \\ +\text{nasal} \end{bmatrix}$

c) $\begin{bmatrix} +\text{syllabic} \\ -\text{consonantal} \\ +\text{sonorant} \end{bmatrix} \rightarrow [+\text{round}] / \begin{bmatrix} -\text{syllabic} \\ +\text{consonantal} \\ o\text{LABIAL} \end{bmatrix} \underline{\quad\quad\quad} \begin{bmatrix} -\text{syllabic} \\ +\text{consonantal} \\ o\text{LABIAL} \end{bmatrix}$

**15.** *Tamil* (Tamil is a Dravidian language spoken in South India and Sri Lanka)
In the following Tamil data, some words begin with glides while others do not. The symbol [ḍ] represents a voiced retroflex stop and the diacritic [ ̪ ] indicates dentals.

| *Initial j-glide* | | *Initial w-glide* | | *No initial glide* | |
|---|---|---|---|---|---|
| a) jeli | 'rat' | f) woḍi | 'break' | k) arivu | 'knowledge' |
| b) jiː | 'fly' | g) woːlaj | 'palm leaf' | l) ain̪tu | 'five' |
| c) jilaj | 'leaf' | h) wuːsi | 'needle' | m) aːsaj | 'desire' |
| d) jeŋgeː | 'where' | i) wujir | 'life' | n) aːru | 'river' |
| e) jiḍuppu | 'waist' | j) woːram | 'edge' | o) aːḍi | 'origin' |

**i)** The occurrence of these glides is predictable. Using your knowledge of natural classes, make a general statement about the distribution of the glides.

**ii)** Assuming the glides are not present in the underlying representations, name the process that accounts for their presence in the phonetic forms.

# *Four*

William O'Grady
Videa de Guzman

# Morphology: the analysis of word structure

*Carve every word before you let it fall.*

OLIVER WENDELL HOLMES, SR.

Nothing is more important to language than words. Unlike phonemes and syllables, which are simply elements of sound, words carry meaning. And unlike sentences, which are made up as needed and then discarded, words are permanently stored in a speaker's mental dictionary or **lexicon**. They are arguably the fundamental building blocks of communication.

The average high school student knows about sixty thousand basic words—items such as *read*, *language*, *on*, *cold*, and *if*, whose form and meaning cannot be predicted from anything else. Countless other words can be constructed and comprehended by the application of general rules to these and other elements. For example, any speaker of English who knows the verb *phish* ('fraudulently obtain sensitive information via email') recognizes *phished* as its past tense form, and can construct and interpret words such as *phisher*, *phishing*, and *unphishable*.

Linguists use the term **morphology** to refer to the part of the grammar that is concerned with words and word formation. As we will see, the study of morphology offers important insights into how language works, revealing the need for different categories of words, the presence of word-internal structure, and the existence of operations that create and modify words in various ways.

## Language Matters  How Many Words Are There in English?

*The Oxford English Dictionary* (20 volumes), which "attempts to record all known uses and variants of a word in all varieties of English, worldwide, past and present," contains a total of 616 500 word forms. But no dictionary can ever be up to date, because new words and new uses of old words are being added to the language all the time. The online *Urban Dictionary* (www.urbandictionary.com) adds hundreds of new definitions EVERY DAY!

## 4.1  Words and word structure

As speakers of English, we rarely have difficulty segmenting a stream of speech sounds into words or deciding where to leave spaces when writing a sentence. What, though, is a word?

Linguists define the **word** as the smallest **free form** found in language. A free form is simply an element that does not have to occur in a fixed position with respect to neighbouring elements; in many cases, it can even appear in isolation. Consider, for instance, the following sentence.

(1)  Dinosaurs are extinct.

We all share the intuition that *dinosaurs* is a word here, and that the plural marker -*s* is not. But why? The key observation is that -*s* is not a free form: it never occurs in isolation and cannot be separated from the noun to which it belongs. (Elements that must be attached to another category are written here with a hyphen.)

(2)  *Dinosaur are -s extinct.

In contrast, *dinosaurs* is a word because it can occur both in isolation, as in the following example, and in different positions within sentences.

(3)  *Speaker A*: What creatures do children find most fascinating?
     *Speaker B*: Dinosaurs.

(4)  *a.* Paleontologists study *dinosaurs*.
     *b.* *Dinosaurs* are studied by paleontologists.
     *c.* It's *dinosaurs* that paleontologists study.

Some words—like *are*—normally do not occur in isolation. However, they are still free forms because their positioning with respect to neighbouring words is not entirely fixed. As shown by the following example, *are* can occur at the beginning of a sentence when a question is called for.

(5)  *Are* dinosaurs extinct? (Compare: Dinosaurs are extinct.)

### 4.1.1  Morphemes

Like syllables and sentences, words have an internal structure consisting of smaller units organized with respect to each other in a particular way. The most important component of word structure is the **morpheme**, the smallest unit of language that carries information about meaning or function. The word *builder*, for example, consists of two morphemes: *build* (with the meaning 'construct') and -*er* (which indicates that the entire word functions as a noun with the meaning 'one who builds'). Similarly, the word *houses* is made up of the morphemes *house* (with the meaning of 'dwelling') and -*s* (with the meaning 'more than one').

Some words consist of a single morpheme. For example, the word *train* cannot be divided into smaller parts (say, *tr* and *ain* or *t* and *rain*) that carry information about its meaning or function. Such words are said to be **simple** and are distinguished from **complex** words, which contain two or more morphemes (see table 4.1).

| Table 4.1 | Words consisting of one or more morphemes | | |
|-----------|-----------------|-----------|-----------------|
| **One** | **Two** | **Three** | **More than three** |
| and | | | |
| couple | couple-s | | |
| hunt | hunt-er | hunt-er-s | |
| act | act-ive | act-iv-ate | re-act-iv-ate |

## Free and bound morphemes

A morpheme that can be a word by itself is called **free**, whereas a morpheme that must be attached to another element is **bound**. The morpheme *boy*, for example, is free because it can be used as a word on its own; plural *-s*, on the other hand, is bound.

Concepts that are expressed by free morphemes in English do not necessarily have the same status in other languages. For example, in Hare (an Athabascan language spoken in Canada's Northwest Territories), morphemes that indicate body parts must always be attached to a morpheme designating a possessor as shown in table 4.2. (The diacritic ´ marks a high tone.)

| Table 4.2 | Some body part names in Hare | | |
|-----------|---------|------|--------------------------|
| **Without a possessor** | | **With a possessor** | |
| *fí | 'head' | sefí | 'my head' |
| *bé | 'belly' | nebé | 'your belly' |
| *dzé | 'heart' | ʔedzé | 'someone's heart/a heart' |

In English, of course, body part names are free morphemes and do not have to be attached to another element.

Conversely, there are also some bound forms in English whose counterparts in other languages are free. For example, the notion 'past' or 'completed' is expressed by the bound morpheme *-ed* in English (as in *I wash<u>ed</u> the car*, or *a wash<u>ed</u> car*), but by the free morpheme *lɛɛw* in Thai. As the following sentence shows, this morpheme can even be separated from the verb by an intervening word. (Tone is not marked here.)

(6)  Boon thaan khaaw lɛɛw.
     Boon eat   rice   past
     'Boon ate rice.'

## Allomorphs

The variant forms of a morpheme are called its **allomorphs**. The morpheme used to express indefiniteness in English has two allomorphs—*an* before a word that begins with a vowel sound and *a* before a word that begins with a consonant sound.

(7) an orange        a building
    an accent        a car
    an eel           a girl

Notice, by the way, that the choice of *an* or *a* is determined on the basis of pronunciation, not spelling, which is why we say <u>*an*</u> *M.A. degree* and <u>*a*</u> *U.S. dollar*.

Another example of allomorphic variation is found in the pronunciation of the plural morpheme *-s* in the following words.

(8) cats
    dogs
    judges

Whereas the plural is /s/ in the first case, it is /z/ in the second, and /əz/ in the third. Here again, selection of the proper allomorph is dependent on phonological facts. (For more on this, see section 4.6.)

Yet another case of allomorphic variation is found in pairs of words such as *permit/permiss-ive*, *include/inclus-ive*, *electric/electric-ity*, *impress/impress-ion*, and so on. As you will see if you say these words aloud, the pronunciation of the final consonant in the first morpheme changes when a suffix is added.

It is important not to confuse spelling changes with allomorphic variation. For example, the final *e* in the spelling of *create* and *ride* is dropped in *creat-ive* and *rid-ing*, but this is not allomorphic variation because there is no change in pronunciation. On the other hand, there is allomorphic variation in *electric/electric-ity* and *impress/impress-ion*, where the pronunciation of the first morpheme changes even though its spelling remains the same.

## 4.1.2 Analyzing word structure

In order to represent the internal structure of words, it is necessary not only to identify each of the component morphemes but also to classify them in terms of their contribution to the meaning and function of the larger word.

### Roots and affixes

Complex words typically consist of a **root** morpheme and one or more **affixes**. The root constitutes the core of the word and carries the major component of its meaning. Roots typically belong to a **lexical category**, such as noun (N), verb (V), adjective (A), or preposition (P).

---

### Language Matters **Having Trouble Figuring Out a Word's Category?**

Here are some rules of thumb:

- Nouns typically refer to people and things (*citizen, tree, intelligence*, etc.)
- Verbs tend to denote actions, sensations, and states (*depart, teach, melt, remain*, etc.)
- Adjectives usually name properties (*nice, red, tall*, etc.)
- Prepositions generally encode spatial relations (*in, near, under*, etc.)

We will consider these categories in more detail in chapter 5, section 5.1.1.

Unlike roots, affixes do not belong to a lexical category and are always bound morphemes. For example, the affix *-er* is a bound morpheme that combines with a verb such as *teach*, giving a noun with the meaning 'one who teaches'. The internal structure of this word can be represented in figure 4.1. (The symbol 'Af' stands for affix.)

**Figure 4.1**
The internal structure of the word *teacher*

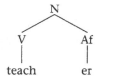

Figure 4.2 provides some additional examples of word structure.

**Figure 4.2**
Some other words with an internal structure consisting of a root and an affix

The structural diagrams in figures 4.1 and 4.2 are often called **trees**. The information they depict can also be represented by using labelled bracketing—[A [Af un] [A kind]] for *unkind* and [N [N book] [Af s]] for *books*. (This is somewhat harder to read, though, and we will generally use tree structures in this chapter.) Where the details of a word's structure are irrelevant to the point being considered, it is traditional to use a much simpler system of representation that indicates only the location of the morpheme boundaries: *un-kind*, *book-s*, and so on.

## Bases

A **base** is the form to which an affix is added. In many cases, the base is also the root. In *books*, for example, the element to which the affix *-s* is added corresponds to the word's root. In other cases, however, the base can be larger than a root, which is always just a single morpheme. This happens in words such as *blackened*, in which the past tense affix *-ed* is added to the verbal base *blacken*—a unit consisting of the root morpheme *black* and the suffix *-en*.

**Figure 4.3**
A word illustrating the difference between a root and a base

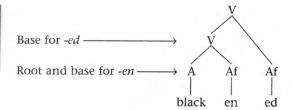

In this case, *black* is not only the root for the entire word but also the base for *-en*. The unit *blacken*, on the other hand, is simply the base for *-ed*.

## Types of affixes

An affix that is attached to the front of its base is called a **prefix**, whereas an affix that is attached to the end of its base is termed a **suffix**. Both types of affix occur in English, as shown in table 4.3.

| Table 4.3 | Some English prefixes and suffixes |
|-----------|------------------------------------|
| **Prefixes** | **Suffixes** |
| *de*-activate | faith-*ful* |
| *re*-play | govern-*ment* |
| *il*-legal | hunt-*er* |
| *in*-accurate | kind-*ness* |

We will consider the nature and properties of English affixes in more detail in sections 4.2.1 and 4.4.1.

Far less common than prefixes and suffixes are **infixes**, a type of affix that occurs within another morpheme. The data in table 4.4 from the Philippine language Tagalog contains examples of the infix *-in-*, which is inserted after the first consonant of the root to mark a completed event.

| Table 4.4 | Some examples of the Tagalog infix *-in-* | | |
|-----------|-------|-------------------|---------|
| **Base** | | **Infixed form** | |
| bili | 'buy' | b-*in*-ili | 'bought' |
| basa | 'read' | b-*in*-asa | 'read' |
| sulat | 'write' | s-*in*-ulat | 'wrote' |

Beginning students sometimes think that a morpheme such as *-ish* in *boy-ish-ness* is an infix since it occurs between two other morphemes (*boy* and *-ness*), but this is not right. To be an infix, an affix must occur inside another morpheme (as when *-in-* in Tagalog occurs inside *sulat* 'write'). Nothing of this sort happens in the case of *-ish*, which simply occurs between two morphemes.

A very special type of infixing system is found in Arabic and other Semitic languages, in which a typical root consists simply of three consonants. Various combinations of vowels are then added, including some between the consonants, to express a range of grammatical contrasts. (In the examples that follow, the segments of the root are written in boldface.)

(9) **k**a**t**a**b**a       **k**u**t**i**b**              a**k**tu**b**
    'wrote'       'has been written'       'am writing'

One way to represent the structure of such words is as follows, with the root and affixal vowels assigned to different **tiers**, or levels of structure, that are intercalated in the actual pronunciation of the word (see figure 4.4).

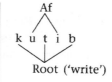

**Figure 4.4**
Two tiers are used to represent the structure of infixed words in Arabic

## Problematic cases

The majority of complex words in English are built from roots that are free morphemes. In the words *re-do* and *treat-ment*, for example, the root (*do* and *treat*, respectively) can itself be used as a word. Because most complex words work this way in English, English morphology is said to be **word-based**.

Not all languages have this type of word-building system, however. In Japanese and Spanish, for instance, verbal roots are always bound and can therefore not stand alone: *camin* is not a word in Spanish, *arui* is not a word in Japanese, and so on.

(10)  *a.* Spanish:

| **camin**-ó | **escuch**-ó | **limpi**-ó |
|---|---|---|
| walk-Pst | listen-Pst | wipe-Pst |

*b.* Japanese

| **arui**-ta | **kii**-ta | **hui**-ta |
|---|---|---|
| walk-Pst | listen-Pst | wipe-Pst |

English too has a sizeable number of bound roots. For example, the word *unkempt* seems to consist of the prefix *un-* (with the meaning 'not') and the root *kempt* (meaning 'groomed'), even though *kempt* cannot be used by itself. There was once a word *kempt* in English (with the meaning 'combed'), and it was to this base that the affix *un-* was originally attached. However, *kempt* later disappeared from the language, leaving behind the word *unkempt* in which an affix appears with a bound root.

Still other words with bound roots were borrowed into English as whole words. *Inept*, for instance, comes from Latin *ineptus* 'unsuited'. Its relationship to the word *apt* may have been evident at one time, but it now seems to consist of a prefix and a bound root.

---

### Language Matters  **Word Play**

The following excerpt from the humorous essay "How I Met My Wife" by Jack Winter plays on the fact that certain English roots are bound and cannot be used as words:

I was **furling** my **wieldy** umbrella for the coat check when I saw her standing alone in the corner. She was a **descript** person, a woman in a state of total **array**. Her hair was **kempt**, her clothing **shevelled**, and she moved in a **gainly** way. (From *The New Yorker*, July 25, 1994).

Another class of words that are problematic for morphological analysis includes items such as *receive*, *deceive*, *conceive*, and *perceive* or *permit*, *submit*, and *commit*. These items were borrowed into English from Latin (usually via French) as whole words and their component syllables have no identifiable meaning of their own. The *re* of *receive*, for instance, does not have the sense of 'again' that it does in *redo*, and no specific meaning can be assigned to *-ceive* or *-mit*. For this reason, we will not treat these word parts as morphemes, even though they do sometimes behave like structural units (the *ceive* in *receive* and *deceive* becomes *cept* in *receptive* and *deceptive* while the *mit* in *submit* and *permit* becomes *miss* in *submissive* and *permissive*).

## 4.2 Derivation

**Derivation** is an affixational process that forms a word with a meaning and/or category distinct from that of its base. One of the most common derivational affixes in English is the suffix *-er*, which combines with a verb to form a noun with the meaning 'one who does X' as shown in table 4.5. (Do not confuse this suffix with the *-er* that applies to a noun in cases such as *Quebecer* and *islander* or the *-er* that combines with an adjective in cases such as *taller* and *smarter*.)

| **Table 4.5** | The *-er* affix |
| --- | --- |
| **Verb base** | **Resulting noun** |
| sell | sell-er |
| write | writ-er |
| teach | teach-er |
| sing | sing-er |
| discover | discover-er |

Words formed by derivation exhibit the type of internal structure illustrated in figure 4.5.

**Figure 4.5**
Some words formed by derivation

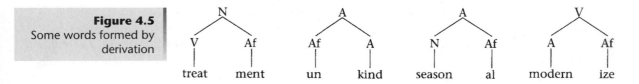

In each of these structures, a suffix or prefix combines with a base of a particular type to give a new word. In the case of *seller*, for instance, the suffix *-er* combines with the verb *sell* to give the noun *seller*; in the case of *unkind*, the prefix *un-* combines with the adjective *kind* to give a new adjective with a different meaning; and so on.

Once formed, derived words become independent lexical items that receive their own entry in a speaker's mental dictionary. As time goes by, they often take on special senses that are not predictable from the component morphemes. The word *writer*, for example, is often used not just for someone who can write but rather for someone who writes for a living (e.g., *He's a writer*); *comparable* (with stress on the first syllable) means 'similar' rather than 'able to be compared'; *profession* usually denotes a career rather than the act of professing; and so on.

## 4.2.1 Some English derivational affixes

Table 4.6 provides a partial list of English derivational affixes, along with information about the category of their usual base (ignoring bound roots) and of the resulting new word. The

| Table 4.6 | Some English derivational affixes | |
| --- | --- | --- |
| **Affix** | **Change** | **Examples** |
| *Suffixes* | | |
| -able | V → A | fix-able, do-able, understand-able |
| -al | V → N | refus-al, dispos-al, recit-al |
| -ant | V → N | claim-ant, defend-ant |
| -(at)ion | V → N | realiz-ation, assert-ion, protect-ion |
| -er | V → N | teach-er, work-er |
| -ing$_1$ | V → N | the shoot-ing, the danc-ing |
| -ing$_2$ | V → A | the sleep-ing giant, a blaz-ing fire |
| -ive | V → A | assert-ive, impress-ive, restrict-ive |
| -ment | V → N | adjourn-ment, treat-ment, amaze-ment |
| -dom | N → N | king-dom, fief-dom |
| -ful | N → A | faith-ful, hope-ful, dread-ful |
| -(i)al | N → A | president-ial, nation-al |
| -(i)an | N → A | Arab-ian, Einstein-ian, Albert-an |
| -ic | N → A | cub-ic, optimist-ic, moron-ic |
| -ize$_1$ | N → V | hospital-ize, crystal-ize |
| -less | N → A | penni-less, brain-less |
| -ous | N → A | poison-ous, lecher-ous |
| -ish | A → A | green-ish, tall-ish |
| -ate | A → V | activ-ate, captiv-ate |
| -en | A → V | dead-en, black-en, hard-en |
| -ity | A → N | stupid-ity, prior-ity |
| -ize$_2$ | A → V | modern-ize, national-ize |
| -ly | A → Adv | quiet-ly, slow-ly, careful-ly |
| -ness | A → N | happi-ness, sad-ness |
| *Prefixes* | | |
| anti- | N → N | anti-abortion, anti-pollution |
| ex- | N → N | ex-president, ex-wife, ex-friend |
| de- | V → V | de-activate, de-mystify |
| dis- | V → V | dis-continue, dis-obey |
| mis- | V → V | mis-identify, mis-place |
| re- | V → V | re-think, re-do, re-state |
| un$_1$- | V → V | un-tie, un-lock, un-do |
| in- | A → A | in-competent, in-complete |
| un$_2$- | A → A | un-happy, un-fair, un-intelligent |
| Note: Unlike suffixes, English prefixes do not change the category of the base. | | |

first entry states that the affix *-able* applies to a verb base and converts it into an adjective. Thus, if we add the affix *-able* to the verb *fix*, we get an adjective (with the meaning 'able to be fixed').

It is sometimes difficult to determine the category of the base to which an affix is added. In the case of *worker*, for instance, the base (*work*) is sometimes used as a verb (as in *they work hard*) and sometimes as a noun (as in *the work is time-consuming*). How can we know which of these forms serves as the base for *-er*? The key is to find words such as *teacher* and *writer*, in which the category of the base can be unequivocally determined. Because *teach* and *write* can only be verbs, we can infer that the base with which *-er* combines in the word *worker* is also a verb.

## Complex derivations

Since derivation can apply more than once, it is possible to create multiple levels of word structure, as in the following example.

**Figure 4.6**
A word with a multilayered internal structure

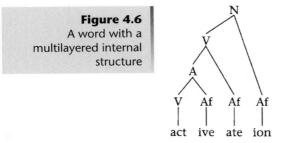

The word *activation* contains several layers of structure, each of which reflects the attachment of an affix to a base of the appropriate type. In the first layer, the affix *-ive* combines with the verbal base *act* to give an adjective. (As noted in table 4.6, *-ive* is the type of affix that converts a verb into an adjective.) In the next layer, the affix *-ate* combines with this adjective and converts it into a verb (*activate*). At this point, the affix *-ion* is added, converting the verb into a noun and giving the word *activation*.

In some cases, the internal structure of a complex word is not so obvious. The word *unhappiness*, for instance, could apparently be analyzed in either of the ways indicated in figure 4.7. However, by considering the properties of the affixes *un-* and *-ness*, it is possible to find an argument that favours figure 4.7a over 4.7b. The key observation is that the prefix *un-* combines quite freely with adjectives but not with nouns, as shown in table 4.7.

**Figure 4.7**
Two possible structures for the word *unhappiness*

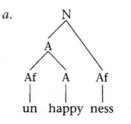
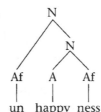

| Table 4.7 | The prefix *un-* |
|-----------|------------------|
| ***un* + A** | ***un* + N** |
| unable | *unknowledge |
| unkind | *unhealth |
| unhurt | *uninjury |

This suggests that *un-* must combine with the adjective *happy* before it is converted into a noun by the suffix *-ness*, exactly as depicted in figure 4.7a.

By contrast, in a word such as *unhealthy*, the prefix *un-* can be attached only AFTER the suffix has been added to the root. That is because *-y* turns nouns into adjectives, creating the category of word with which *un-* can combine (see figure 4.8).

**Figure 4.8**
The internal structure of the word *unhealthy*

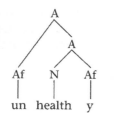

## Constraints on derivation

Derivation is often subject to special constraints and restrictions. For instance, the suffix *-ant* (see table 4.6) can combine with bases of Latin origin such as *assist* and *combat*, but not those of native English origin such as *help* and *fight*. Thus, we find words such as *assistant* and *combatant*, but not *\*helpant* and *\*fightant*.

Sometimes, a derivational affix is able to attach only to bases with particular phonological properties. A good example of this involves the suffix *-en*, which can combine with some adjectives to create verbs with a causative meaning as shown in table 4.8 (*whiten* means roughly 'cause to become white').

| Table 4.8 | Restrictions on the use of *-en* |
|-----------|----------------------------------|
| **Acceptable** | **Unacceptable** |
| whiten | *abstracten |
| soften | *bluen |
| madden | *angryen |
| quicken | *slowen |
| liven | *greenen |

The contrasts illustrated here reflect the fact that *-en* can only combine with a monosyllabic base that ends in an obstruent (a stop, affricate, or fricative). Thus, it can be added to *white*, which is both monosyllabic and ends in an obstruent. But it cannot be added to *abstract*, which has two syllables, or to *blue*, which does not end in an obstruent.

## 4.2.2   Two classes of derivational affixes

It is common to distinguish between two types of derivational affixes in English. **Class 1 affixes** often trigger changes in the consonant or vowel segments of the base and may affect stress placement. In addition, they often combine with bound roots, as in the last of the following examples in table 4.9.

| Table 4.9 | Typical effects of Class 1 affixes | |
|---|---|---|
| **Affix** | **Sample word** | **Change triggered by affix** |
| -ity | san-ity | vowel in the base changes from /e/ to /æ/ (cf. *sane*) |
| | public-ity | final consonant of the base changes from /k/ to /s/, stress shifts to second syllable (cf. *públic* vs. *publícity*) |
| -y | democrac-y | final consonant of the base changes from /t/ to /s/ stress shifts to second syllable (cf. *démocrat* vs. *demócracy*) |
| -ive | product-ive | stress shifts to second syllable (cf. *próduct* vs. *prodúctive*) |
| -(i)al | part-ial | final consonant of the base changes from /t/ to /ʃ/ (cf. *part*) |
| -ize | public-ize | final consonant of the base changes from /k/ to /s/ (cf. *public*) |
| -ion | nat-ion | final consonant of the base changes from /t/ to /ʃ/ (cf. *native*) |

In contrast, **Class 2 affixes** tend to be phonologically neutral, having no effect on the segmental makeup of the base or on stress placement (see table 4.10).

| Table 4.10 | Some typical Class 2 affixes | |
|---|---|---|
| **Affix** | **Sample word** | **Change triggered by affix** |
| -ness | prompt-ness | None |
| -less | hair-less | None |
| -ful | hope-ful | None |
| -ly | quiet-ly | None |
| -er | defend-er | None |
| -ish | self-ish | None |

As the following examples help illustrate, a Class 2 affix usually cannot intervene between the root and a Class 1 affix.

(11)   relat-ion-al         divis-ive-ness        *fear-less-ity        fear-less-ness
       ROOT 1  1            ROOT 1  2            ROOT 2  1            ROOT 2  2

Notice that all combinations of Class 1 and Class 2 affixes are found in English words, except one—a Class 2 suffix followed by a Class 1 suffix.

## 4.3   Compounding

Another common technique for word building in English involves **compounding**, the combination of two already existent words (see figure 4.9). With very few exceptions, the resulting compound word is a noun, a verb, or an adjective. (Possible examples of compound prepositions include the words *into* and *onto*.)

**Figure 4.9**
Some English
compounds

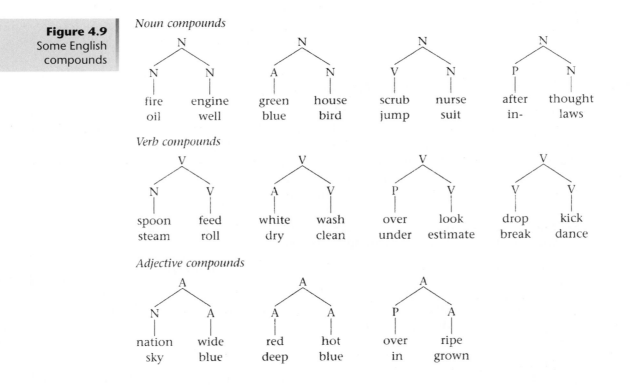

In these and most other compounds of this type, the rightmost morpheme determines the category of the entire word. Thus, *greenhouse* is a noun because its rightmost component is a noun, *spoonfeed* is a verb because *feed* also belongs to this category, and *nationwide* is an adjective just as *wide* is. The morpheme that determines the category of the entire word is called the **head**.

Once formed, compounds can be combined with other words to create still larger compounds, as the examples in figure 4.10 show.

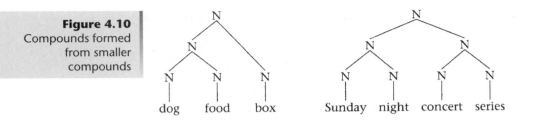

**Figure 4.10**
Compounds formed from smaller compounds

In addition, compounding can interact with derivation, yielding forms such as *election date*, in which the first word in the compound is the result of derivation, as shown in figure 4.11.

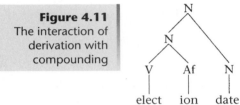

**Figure 4.11**
The interaction of derivation with compounding

## 4.3.1 Properties of compounds

English orthography is not consistent in representing compounds, which are sometimes written as single words, sometimes with a hyphen, and sometimes as separate words. In terms of pronunciation, however, there is an important generalization to be made (see table 4.11). In particular, adjective–noun compounds are characterized by more prominent stress on their first component. In non-compounds consisting of an adjective and a noun, in contrast, the second element is generally stressed.

| **Table 4.11** Compounds versus non-compounds | | | |
|---|---|---|---|
| **Compound word** | | **Non-compound expressions** | |
| greénhouse | 'a glass-enclosed garden' | green hoúse | 'a house painted green' |
| bláckboard | 'a chalkboard' | black boárd | 'a board that is black' |
| wét suit | 'a diver's costume' | wet suít | 'a suit that is wet' |

A second distinguishing feature of compounds in English is that tense and plural markers can typically not be attached to the first element, although they can be added to the compound as a whole. (There are some exceptions, however, such as *swordsman* and *parks supervisor*.)

(12)  *The player [dropped kick] the ball through the goal posts.

The player [drop kick]ed the ball through the goal posts.

(13)  *The [foxes hunter] didn't have a licence.

The [fox hunter]s didn't have a licence.

## 4.3.2  Endocentric and exocentric compounds

Compounds are used to express a wide range of meaning relationships in English. Table 4.12 contains examples of some of the semantic patterns found in noun–noun compounds.

| Table 4.12 | Some noun–noun compounds |
|---|---|
| **Example** | **Meaning** |
| steamboat | 'a boat powered by steam' |
| airplane | 'a conveyance that travels through the air' |
| air hose | 'a hose that carries air' |
| air field | 'a field where airplanes land' |
| fire truck | 'a vehicle used to put out fires' |
| fire drill | 'a practice in the event of a fire' |
| bath tub | 'a place in which to bathe' |
| bath towel | 'a towel used after bathing' |

In most cases, a compound denotes a sub-type of the concept denoted by its head (the rightmost component). Thus *dog food* is a type of food, a *cave man* is a type of man, *sky-blue* is a type of blue, and so on. Such compounds, including all the examples in table 4.12, are called **endocentric**. In a smaller number of cases, however, the meaning of the compound does not follow from the meanings of its parts in this way. Thus, a *redhead* is not a type of head; rather, it is a person with red hair. Similarly, a *redneck* is a person and not a type of neck. Such compounds are said to be **exocentric**.

A very striking difference between English endocentric and exocentric compounds sometimes shows up in cases where the head is a word like *tooth* or *foot*, which has an irregular plural form. Consider in this regard the examples in table 4.13.

| Table 4.13 | Pluralization in English compounds |
|---|---|
| **In endocentric compounds** | **In exocentric compounds** |
| wisdom t<u>ee</u>th | saber t<u>ooth</u>s (extinct species of carnivore) |
| club f<u>ee</u>t | big<u>foot</u>s (mythical creatures; 'Sasquatch') |
| police<u>me</u>n | Watchm<u>an</u>s (a type of portable TV) |
| oak lea<u>ve</u>s | Maple Lea<u>fs</u> (Toronto's NHL hockey team) |

Notice that whereas the endocentric compounds employ the usual irregular plural (*teeth, feet*, etc.), the exocentric compounds permit the plural suffix *-s* for words such as *tooth, foot*, and *man*.

## 4.3.3  Compounds in other languages

The practice of combining words (especially nouns) to build a more complex word is very widespread in the languages of the world. With the exception of Tagalog, in which compounds are left-headed, the languages exemplified in table 4.14 all have compounds in which the rightmost element is the head.

| **Table 4.14** | Noun compounds in various languages | |
|---|---|---|
| **Korean** | | |
| kot elum | isul pi | nwun mwul |
| straight ice | dew rain | eye water |
| 'icicle' | 'drizzle' | 'tears' |
| **Tagalog** | | |
| balat sibuyas | basag ulo | anak araw |
| skin onion | break head | child sun |
| 'thin skinned' | 'a fight/brawl' | 'albino' |
| **German** | | |
| gast-hof | Wort-bedeutungs-lehre | Fern-seher |
| guest-inn | word-meaning-theory | far-seer |
| 'hotel' | 'semantics' | 'television' |
| **Finnish** | | |
| lammas-nahka-turkki | elin-keino-tulo-vero-laki | |
| sheep-skin-coat | life's-means-income-tax-law | |
| 'sheepskin coat' | 'income tax law' | |
| **Tzotzil** | | |
| piʃ-xól | méʔ-k'ínobal | ʔóra-tʃón |
| wrap-head | mother-mist | rightaway-snake |
| 'hat' | 'rainbow' | 'deadly viper' |

## 4.4 Inflection

Virtually all languages have contrasts such as singular versus plural and present versus past. Such contrasts are often marked with the help of **inflection**, the modification of a word's form to indicate grammatical information of various sorts. (The base to which an inflectional affix is added is sometimes called a **stem**.)

### 4.4.1 Inflection in English

Inflection is most often expressed via affixation, and many languages (e.g., Japanese, Swahili, Inuktitut, and Finnish) have dozens of inflectional affixes. With only eight inflectional affixes (all suffixes), English is not a highly inflected language. Table 4.15 lists the inflectional affixes of English.[1]

| **Table 4.15**    English inflectional affixes | |
| --- | --- |
| **Nouns** | |
| Plural -*s* <br> Possessive (genitive) -*'s* | the book<u>s</u> <br> John<u>'s</u> book |
| **Verbs** | |
| 3rd person sing. non-past -*s* <br> Progressive -*ing* <br> Past tense -*ed* <br> Past participle -*en/-ed* | He read<u>s</u> well. <br> He is work<u>ing</u>. <br> He work<u>ed</u>. <br> He has eat<u>en</u> /stud<u>ied</u>. |
| **Adjectives** | |
| Comparative -*er* <br> Superlative -*est* | the small<u>er</u> one <br> the small<u>est</u> one |

Although most inflection in English involves affixation, some words mark inflectional contrasts in other ways. This is most obvious in the case of verbs, a number of which indicate past tense by substituting one form with another (as in *am-was* or *go-went*) or by internal changes of various sorts (*come-came*, *see-saw*, *fall-fell*, *eat-ate*). We will consider these processes in more detail in section 4.5.

## 4.4.2 Inflection versus derivation

Because inflection and derivation are both commonly marked by affixation, the distinction between the two can be subtle and it is sometimes unclear which function a particular affix has. Four criteria are commonly used to help distinguish between inflectional and derivational affixes.

### Category change

First, inflection does not change either the grammatical category or the type of meaning found in the word to which it applies, as shown in figure 4.12.

**Figure 4.12** The output of inflection: there is no change in either the category of the base or the type of meaning it denotes.

The form produced by adding the plural suffix -*s* in figure 4.12a is still a noun and has the same type of meaning as the base. Even though *hearts* differs from *heart* in referring to several things rather than just one, the type of thing(s) to which it refers remains the same.

Similarly, a past tense suffix such as the one in figure 4.12b indicates that the action took place in the past, but the word remains a verb and it continues to denote an action.

In contrast, derivational suffixes characteristically change the category and/or the type of meaning of the form to which they apply. Consider the examples of derivation given in figure 4.13.

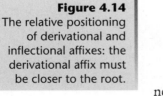

**Figure 4.13**
The output of derivation: there can be a change in the category of the base and/or the type of meaning it denotes.

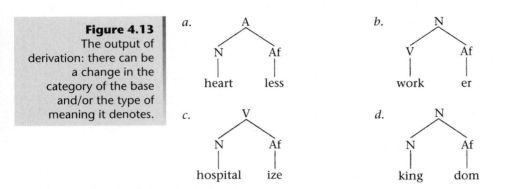

As figure 4.13a shows, *-less* makes an adjective out of a noun, changing the type of meaning it expresses from a thing (*heart*) to a property (*heartless*). Parallel changes in category and type of meaning are brought about by *-er* (V to N) and *-ize* (N to V). Matters are a little different in the case of *-dom*, which does not bring about a category change in the word *kingdom* since both the base and the resulting word are nouns. However, *-dom* does modify the type of meaning from 'person' (for *king*) to 'place' (for *kingdom*).

## Order

A second property of inflectional affixes has to do with the order in which they are combined with a base relative to derivational affixes. As figure 4.14 illustrates, a derivational affix must combine with the base before an inflectional affix does (IA = inflectional affix; DA = derivational affix).

**Figure 4.14**
The relative positioning of derivational and inflectional affixes: the derivational affix must be closer to the root.

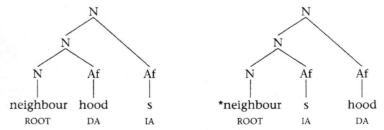

The positioning of inflectional affixes outside derivational affixes in these examples reflects the fact that inflection applies to the output of derivation.

## Productivity

A third criterion for distinguishing between inflectional and derivational affixes has to do with **productivity**, the relative freedom with which they can combine with bases of the appropriate category. Inflectional affixes typically have relatively few exceptions. The suffix *-s*, for example, can combine with virtually any noun that allows a plural form (aside from a few exceptions such as *oxen* and *feet*). In contrast, derivational affixes characteristically apply to restricted classes of bases. Thus, *-ize* can combine with only certain adjectives to form a verb.

(14) modern-ize        *new-ize
      legal-ize         *lawful-ize
      final-ize         *permanent-ize

In the case of verbs, matters are somewhat more complicated, since many English verbs have irregular past tense forms (*saw*, *left*, *went*, and so on). Nonetheless, the inflectional affix *-ed* is much more generally applicable than a derivational affix such as *-ment*. For example, all the verbs in table 4.16 can take the regular past tense ending, but only those in the top three rows are able to take the *-ment* suffix.

| **Table 4.16** | Compatibility of verb bases with inflectional *-ed* and derivational *-ment* | |
| --- | --- | --- |
| **Verb** | **With *-ed*** | **With *-ment*** |
| confine | confined | confinement |
| align | aligned | alignment |
| treat | treated | treatment |
| arrest | arrested | *arrestment |
| straighten | straightened | *straightenment |
| cure | cured | *curement |

## Semantic transparency

Finally, the contribution of an inflectional affix to the word's meaning is usually completely transparent and consistent. Adding a plural suffix gives the meaning 'more than one' (*cat-cats*, *tree-trees*), adding a past tense suffix gives the meaning 'prior to the present' (*walk-walked*, *play-played*), and so forth.

Things are not always so straightforward in the case of derivation, where it is often not possible to predict the word's meaning from its parts. An *actor* is someone who acts, but a *professor* is not someone who professes. The word *teacher* often refers to someone who holds a teaching job, but no such implication is associated with *walker*. *Government* can be used to refer either to an institution (as in 'the government's agenda') or the act of governing (as in 'government by the people'), but *treatment* lacks the first type of meaning.

## 4.4.3  Other inflectional phenomena

Inflection is a very widely used morphological process and its effects can be seen in far more phenomena than can be discussed here. Nonetheless, two additional phenomena are worth mentioning, however briefly, because of their importance and frequency in languages of the world.

**Case** involves a change in a word's form to indicate its grammatical role (subject, direct object, and so on). A very simple example of this can be seen in English, where the pronoun form *he* is used for subjects and the form *him* is employed for direct objects. There is a comparable contrast between *I* and *me*, *she* and *her*, *we* and *us*, and *they* and *them*.

(15)  He met the new professor.          The new professor met him.
        ↑                                                          ↑
        subject                                                direct object

**Agreement** takes place when one word is inflected to match certain grammatical properties of another word. Especially common is agreement for number (singular vs. plural) and for person (first person—speaker, second person—addressee, third person—anyone else). Here again English offers a simple example: the suffix *-s* appears on a present tense verb when the subject is third person singular.

(16)  That man speaks French.

(Compare: *I speak French* or *They speak French*, with no *-s* suffix.)

For a more detailed discussion of these and other inflectional phenomena, go to the Companion Website at **www.pearsoned.ca/ogrady**, chapter 4 and chapter 5.

## 4.5   Other morphological phenomena

No introductory textbook can hope to offer a full survey of the processes that contribute to word formation in human language. The preceding sections have touched upon many of the most common and central processes, but a number of others merit consideration as well. We will divide these into two groups—those that pertain primarily to inflection and those that involve other sorts of phenomena.

## 4.5.1   Processes primarily related to inflection

### Internal change

**Internal change** is a process that substitutes one non-morphemic segment for another to mark a grammatical contrast, as illustrated in the following pairs of words in table 4.17.

| Table 4.17    Internal change in English | |
| --- | --- |
| sing (present) | sang (past) |
| sink (present) | sank (past) |
| drive (present) | drove (past) |
| foot (singular) | feet (plural) |
| goose (singular) | geese (plural) |

Verbs such as *sing*, *sink*, and *drive* form their past tense by changing the vowel (e.g., from *i* to *a* in the first two examples). The term **ablaut** is often used for vowel alternations that mark grammatical contrasts in this way.

Some internal changes reflect phonologically conditioned alternations from an earlier stage in the language's history. The irregular plurals *geese* and *feet* came about in this way: the original vowel in the words *goose* and *foot* was fronted under the influence of the front vowel in the old plural suffix /i/, which was subsequently dropped. This type of change in English and other Germanic languages is known as **umlaut**.

(17)  Old singular form of *goose*:      /gos/
      Old plural form:      /gos-i/
      Umlaut:      /gœs-i/
      Loss of the plural suffix:      /gœs/
      Other changes (see chapter 7)      /ges/ and then /gis/ 'geese'

Internal change differs from infixing in important ways. As shown by the Tagalog examples in table 4.4 (see page 114), the base into which a real infix is inserted typically exists as a separate form elsewhere in the language (compare *sulat* 'write' with *s-in-ulat* 'wrote'). Matters are quite different in the case of alternations such as *foot/feet* or *sing/sang* in English, since we have no form *ft* meaning 'lower extremity of the leg' or *sng* meaning 'produce words in a musical tone'. Moreover, in contrast to the situation in Tagalog, the segments that alternate when there is internal change are not systematically associated with a particular meaning and therefore do not count as morphemes: the *a* of *ran* and the *o* of *drove* do not in general carry the meaning 'past' in English any more than the *ee* of *geese* normally carries the meaning 'plural'.

The existence of internal change and of infixing (section 4.1.2) illustrates an important point about word structure: morphology is not always **concatenative**. That is, not all word structure is built by assembling morphemes in an additive, linear fashion.

## Suppletion

**Suppletion** replaces a morpheme with an entirely different morpheme in order to indicate a grammatical contrast. Examples of this phenomenon in English include the use of *went* as the past tense form of the verb *go* and *was* and *were* as the past tense forms of *be* (see table 4.18 for suppletion in some other European languages).

| **Table 4.18**  Suppletion in some European languages | | |
| --- | --- | --- |
| **Language** | **Basic form** | **Suppletive form** |
| French | *avoir* 'to have' | *eu* 'had' |
| Spanish | *ir* 'to go' | *fue* '(s/he) went' |
| German | *ist* 'is' | *sind* 'are' |
| Russian | *xoroʃo* 'good' | *lutʃʃe* 'better' ('more good') |

In some cases, it is hard to distinguish between suppletion and internal change. For example, is the past tense of *think* (*thought*) and *seek* (*sought*) an instance of suppletion or internal change? This type of alternation is often treated as an extreme form of internal change, but the term **partial suppletion** is also used by some linguists.

## Reduplication

A common morphological process in some languages involves **reduplication**, which marks a grammatical or semantic contrast by repeating all or part of the base to which it applies. Repetition of the entire base yields **full reduplication**, as in the data from Turkish and Indonesian given in table 4.19.

| Table 4.19 | Some examples of full reduplication | | |
|---|---|---|---|
| **Base** | | **Reduplicated form** | |
| *Turkish* | | | |
| tʃabuk | 'quickly' | tʃabuk tʃabuk | 'very quickly' |
| javaʃ | 'slowly' | javaʃ javaʃ | 'very slowly' |
| iji | 'well' | iji iji | 'very well' |
| gyzel | 'beautifully' | gyzel gyzel | 'very beautifully' |
| *Indonesian* | | | |
| oraŋ | 'man' | oraŋ oraŋ | 'men' |
| anak | 'child' | anak anak | 'children' |
| maŋga | 'mango' | maŋga maŋga | 'mangoes' |

In contrast, **partial reduplication** copies only part of the base. In the data from Tagalog in table 4.20, for instance, reduplication affects only the first consonant-vowel sequence.

| Table 4.20 | Reduplication in Tagalog | | |
|---|---|---|---|
| **Base** | | **Reduplicated form** | |
| takbo | 'run' | tatakbo | 'will run' |
| lakad | 'walk' | lalakad | 'will walk' |
| piliʔ | 'choose' | pipiliʔ | 'will choose' |

English makes limited use of partial reduplication in diminutive expressions such as *teeny-weeny* and *itsy-bitsy*, but this is not general enough to be counted as an inflectional contrast.

## Tone placement

In Mono-Bili (spoken in the Congo), tone is used to make the distinction between past and future tense. (A high tone is marked by ´ and a low tone by ` in table 4.21.)

| Table 4.21 | | Past versus future in Mono-Bili | |
|---|---|---|---|
| **Past** | | **Future** | |
| dá | 'spanked' | dà | 'will spank' |
| zí | 'ate' | zì | 'will eat' |
| wó | 'killed' | wò | 'will kill' |

## 4.5.2  Other processes

### Cliticization

Some morphemes behave like words in terms of their meaning and function, but are unable to stand alone as independent forms for phonological reasons. Called **clitics**, these elements must always be pronounced with another word (known as a **host**). A good example of this can be found in English, where certain verb forms have reduced variants (*'m* for *am*, *'s* for *is*, and *'re* for *are*) that cannot stand alone because they no longer constitute a syllable. Cliticization occurs, attaching these elements to the preceding word.

(18)   *a.*  I*'m* leaving now.
      *b.*  Mary*'s* going to succeed.
      *c.*  They*'re* here now.

Cliticization is also common in French, which has a set of unstressed clitic object pronouns that must be attached to the verb. The two are then pronounced as if they formed a single word.

(19)  Jean *t'*aime.     Suzanne *les* voit.
      John you-likes     Suzanne them-sees
      'John likes you.'     'Suzanne sees them.'

Clitics that attach to the end of their host (as in the English examples) are called **enclitics**; those that attach to the beginning of their host (as in the French example) are known as **proclitics**.

The effects of cliticization can bear a superficial resemblance to affixation because, in both cases, an element that cannot stand alone is attached to a base. The key difference is that—unlike affixes—clitics are members of a lexical category such as verb, noun (or pronoun), or preposition.

### Conversion

**Conversion** is a process that assigns an already existing word to a new syntactic category. Even though it does not add an affix, conversion is often considered to be a type of derivation because of the change in category and meaning that it brings about. For this reason, it is sometimes called **zero derivation**. Table 4.22 contains examples of the three most common types of conversion in English.

Less common types of conversion can yield a noun from an adjective (*the poor*, *gays*) and even a verb from a preposition (*down a beer*, *up the price*).

| Table 4.22 | Some examples of conversion | |
|---|---|---|
| **V derived from N** | **N derived from V** | **V derived from A** |
| ink (a contract) | (a long) run | dirty (a shirt) |
| butter (the bread) | (a hot) drink | empty (the box) |
| ship (the package) | (a pleasant) drive | better (the old score) |
| nail (the door shut) | (a brief) report | right (a wrong) |
| button (the shirt) | (an important) call | total (a car) |

Conversion is usually restricted to words containing a single morpheme, although there are some exceptions such as *refer-ee* (noun to verb) and *dirt-y* (adjective to verb).

Conversion in two-syllable words is often accompanied by stress shift in English. As the examples in table 4.23 show, the verb has stress on the final syllable while the corresponding noun is stressed on the first syllable. (Stress is represented here by ´.)

| Table 4.23 | Stress placement in English |
|---|---|
| **Verb** | **Noun** |
| implánt | ímplant |
| impórt | ímport |
| presént | présent |
| subjéct | súbject |
| contést | cóntest |

# Clipping

**Clipping** is a process that shortens a polysyllabic word by deleting one or more syllables. Some of the most common products of clipping are names—*Liz, Ron, Rob, Sue*, and so on. Clipping is especially popular in casual speech, where it has yielded forms like *prof* for *professor*, *psych* for *psychology*, *flu* for *influenza*, *doc* for *doctor*, and *burger* for *hamburger*. However, many clipped forms have also been accepted in general usage: *ad, auto, lab, sub, deli, porn, demo*, and *condo*.

**Language Matters Some Cases of Clipping That Might Surprise You**

zoo < zoological garden
fax < facsimile
fan (as in sports) < fanatic
van < caravan
vegan < vegetarian
mob < mobile crowd (according to some suggestions)

An interesting recent clip is *blog*, from *Web log*—a personal website-based log of events, comments, and links. Once formed, *blog* quickly appeared in compounds (*blog archive*, *blog template*) and has undergone conversion to a verb (as in 'things to blog about'). The verb in turn has undergone derivation, resulting in the noun *blogger*. No wonder that *blog* was voted the new word most likely to succeed at the 2003 meeting of the American Dialect Society!

## Blends

**Blends** are words that are created from non-morphemic parts of two already existing items, usually the first part of one and the final part of the other. Familiar examples include *brunch* from *breakfast* and *lunch*, *smog* from *smoke* and *fog*, *motel* from *motor* and *hotel*, *telethon* from *telephone* and *marathon*, *aerobicise* from *aerobics* and *exercise*, *chunnel* (for the underwater link between Britain and mainland Europe) from *channel* and *tunnel*, and *infomercial* from *information* and *commercial*. In July 2007, the dictionary-maker Merriam Webster announced that it would be adding a new blend to its next edition—*ginormous*, from *gigantic* and *enormous*.

In Japanese, Korean, and Mandarin, blending is commonly used for names of universities.

(**20**)  *a.*  Korea Tayhakkyo > Kotay
Korea University

     *b.*  Tōkyō Daigakku > Tōdai
Tokyo University

     *c.*  Beijing Da Xue > Bei Da
Beijing University

Sometimes, a word is formed by a process that is on the borderline between compounding and blending in that it combines all of one word with part of another. Examples of this in English include *email*, *perma-press*, *workaholic*, *medicare*, *guesstimate*, and *threepeat* (used by sports fans to refer to the winning of a championship in three successive years). Even *blog* has managed to participate in this process—*blogma* is a blend of *blog* and *dogma*.

## Backformation

**Backformation** is a process that creates a new word by removing a real or supposed affix from another word in the language. *Resurrect* was originally formed in this way from

---

### Language Matters  **Some Other Words That Originated as Blends—Unbeknownst to Many Speakers!**

bit (unit of information in computer science) < binary + digit
modem < modulator + demodulator
napalm < naphthenic + palmitic
quasar < quasi + stellar
chortle < chuckle + snort
spam (the sandwich meat) < spiced + ham

*resurrection*. Other backformations in English include *enthuse* from *enthusiasm*, *donate* from *donation*, *orient* or *orientate* from *orientation*, and *self-destruct* from *self-destruction*.

Sometimes, backformation involves an incorrect assumption about a word's form: for example, the word *pea* was derived from the singular noun *pease*, whose final /z/ was incorrectly interpreted as the plural suffix.

Words that end in *-or* or *-er* have proven very susceptible to backformation in English. Because hundreds of such words are the result of affixation (*runner, walker, singer*, etc.), any word with this shape is likely to be perceived as a verb + *er* combination. The words *editor, peddler*, and *swindler* were (mis)analyzed in just this way, resulting in the creation of the verbs *edit, peddle*, and *swindle*, as shown in table 4.24.

| **Table 4.24**     Some examples of backformation | | |
|---|---|---|
| **Original word** | **Misanalysis** | **Verb formed by backformation** |
| editor | edit + or | edit |
| peddler | peddle + er | peddle |
| swindler | swindle + er | swindle |

A more recent backformation of this type is the verb *lase*, produced by backformation from *laser*, which itself had an unusual origin (see below).

Backformation continues to produce new words in modern English—*aggress* (from *aggression*), *allegate* (from *allegation*), *liase* (from *liason*), *administrate* (from *administration*), and *liposuct* (from *liposuction*) have all recently been brought to our attention.

## Acronyms and Initialisms

**Acronyms** are formed by taking the initial letters of (some or all) the words in a phrase or title and pronouncing them as a word. This type of word formation is especially common in names of organizations and in military and scientific terminology. Common examples include UNICEF for United Nations International Children's Emergency Fund, CIDA for Canadian International Development Agency, NATO for North Atlantic Treaty Organization, and AIDS for acquired immune deficiency syndrome.

Acronyms are to be distinguished from **initialisms** such as PEI for Prince Edward Island or USA for United States of America, which are pronounced as a series of letters rather than a word. An intermediate case is *CD-ROM*, consisting of the initialism *CD* (*compact disc*) and the acronym *ROM* (*read-only memory*).

In some cases, speakers may not know that a word in their vocabulary originated as an acronym. Three commonly used words of this type are *radar* (from *radio detecting and ranging*), *scuba* (*self-contained underwater breathing apparatus*), and *laser* (*light amplification by stimulated emission of radiation*).

## Onomatopoeia

All languages have some words that have been created to sound like the thing that they name. Examples of such **onomatopoeic** words in English include *buzz, hiss, sizzle*, and *cuckoo*. Since onomatopoeic words are not exact phonetic copies of noises, their form can differ from language to language as shown in table 4.25.

| **Table 4.25** | Onomatopoeia across languages | |
|---|---|---|
| **English** | **Japanese** | **Tagalog** |
| cock-a-doodle-doo | kokekokko | kuk-kukaok |
| meow | nyaa | ngiyaw |
| chirp | pii-pii | tiririt |
| bow-wow | wan-wan | aw-aw |

English does not always have an equivalent for the onomatopoeic words found in other languages. The Athabascan language Slavey, for instance, has the onomatopoeic word *sah sah sah* for 'the sound of a bear walking unseen not far from camp', *ðik* for 'the sound of a knife hitting a tree', and *tɬóòtʃ* for 'the sound of an egg splattering'.

## Other sources of new words

Sometimes, a word may be created from scratch. Called **word manufacture** or **coinage**, this phenomenon is especially common in the case of product names, including *Kodak*, *Dacron*, *Orlon*, and *Teflon*. (Notice how the *-on* of the final three words makes them more scientific-sounding, perhaps because an affix of this form occurs in words of Greek origin such as *phenomenon* and *automaton*.)

New words can also sometimes be created from names, including those listed in table 4.26. Words created in this way are called **eponyms**.

| **Table 4.26** | Some English words created from names |
|---|---|
| **Word** | **Name of the person** |
| watt | James Watt (late 19th-century scientist) |
| curie | Marie and Pierre Curie (early 20th-century scientists) |
| fahrenheit | Gabriel Fahrenheit (18th-century scientist) |
| boycott | Charles Boycott (19th-century land agent in Ireland, who was ostracized for refusing to lower rents) |

In still other cases, brand names can become so widely known that they are accepted as generic terms for the product with which they are associated. The words *Kleenex* for 'facial tissue' and *Xerox* for 'photocopy' are two obvious examples of this.

Finally, as we will see in more detail in chapter 7, languages frequently look to other languages for new words. English has always been open to borrowing of this sort, and the language continues to absorb new words from many different sources—*latte* from Italian, *feng shui* from Chinese, *al-qaeda* from Arabic, and so forth.

---

**Language Matters  A Trivia Question—What's the Longest Word in English?**

Is it:

>    ANTIDISESTABLISHMENTARIANISM (28 letters)
>    (*the belief that opposes removing the tie between church and state*)?

Or is it:

>    SUPERCALIFRAGILISTICEXPIALIDOCIOUS (34 letters)
>    (*'extremely wonderful'* from the Disney movie *Mary Poppins*)?

Neither! The longest English word in any dictionary is:

PNEUMONOULTRAMICROSCOPICSILICOVOLCANOCONIOSIS
(45 letters; also spelled '. . . koniosis') (*a lung disease caused by breathing in particles of siliceous volcanic dust*).

---

## 4.6  Morphophonemics

As we saw in chapter 3, a word's pronunciation is often sensitive to the particular phonetic context in which phonemes occur. For instance, an /æ/ that occurs in front of a nasal consonant is nasalized (e.g., [kæ̃nt] 'can't' vs. [kæt] 'cat'), an /æ/ that occurs before a voiced consonant is longer than one that occurs before a voiceless consonant (e.g., [hæ:d] 'had' vs. [hæt] 'hat'), and so on. Pronunciation can also be sensitive to morphological factors, including a word's internal structure. The study of this phenomenon is known as **morphophonemics** (or **morphophonology**).

Morphophonemic phenomena are extremely common in language. A famous example from English involves the way that we pronounce the plural suffix *-s*. As first noted in chapter 1, the morpheme can be pronounced as [s], [z], or [əz].

**(21)**  lip[s]
         pill[z]
         judg[əz]

There are good reasons for this alternation: voiceless -[s] occurs after voiceless sounds (such as [p]), voiced -[z] occurs after voiced sounds (such as [l]), and the -[əz] form shows up only when a vowel is needed to break up an otherwise illegal consonant cluster (no English syllable ends with the coda [dʒz]). The key point for now, though, has to do with the conditions under which all of this happens. This is a classic example of a morphophonemic alternation for two reasons.

First, it occurs at a morpheme boundary, where a suffix of a particular type is attached to its base. It is perfectly possible to pronounce an [s] sound after an [l] in English when they are both in the same morpheme—as in a word like *else*. Yet, the plural morpheme *-s* has to be pronounced as [z] when it attaches to a base that ends in [l], as happens in *pill*-[z].

Second, the alternation involves sounds that are associated with separate phonemes—/s/ and /z/. In this, it differs from the alternations considered in the preceding chapter, which involved allophones of the same phoneme.

For a more detailed discussion of morphophonemics, go to **www.pearsoned.ca/ogrady**.

# Summing up

This chapter has focused on the structure and formation of **words** in human language. Many words consist of smaller formative elements, called **morphemes**. These elements can be classified in a variety of ways (**free** versus **bound**, **root** versus **affix**, **prefix** versus **suffix**) and can be combined and modified under various conditions to build words.

The two basic types of word formation in English are **derivation** and **compounding**. **Inflection**, a change in the form of a word to convey grammatical information such as plurality or tense, can be expressed via **affixation**, **internal change**, **reduplication**, **and tone placement**. Other important morphological phenomena include **cliticization**, **conversion**, **clipping**, **blends**, and **backformation**.

## Notes

[1]  There are three *-ing* affixes in English, one inflectional and two derivational. Inflectional *-ing* combines with a verb to give another verb, as in *He is breathing*. One derivational *-ing* combines with a verb to give a noun (*The breathing of the runners*) and the other converts a verb into an adjective (*the sleeping giant*)—see table 4.6. There are also two types of *-en/-ed* suffix, one inflectional, as noted in table 4.15, and the other derivational. The latter converts verbs into adjectives so that they can appear in structures such as the following.

a  The *stolen* money
b  The *escaped* convict

## Recommended reading

Anderson, Stephen. 1988. "Morphological Theory." In *Linguistics: The Cambridge Survey*. Vol. 1. Edited by F. Newmeyer, 146–91. New York: Cambridge University Press.
Bauer, Laurie. 1983. *English Word-Formation*. New York: Cambridge University Press.
Gleason, Henry Allan. 1955/1961. *An Introduction to Descriptive Linguistics*. New York: Holt, Rinehart and Winston.
Jensen, John. 1990. *Morphology: Word Structure in Generative Grammar*. Amsterdam: John Benjamins Publishing.
Katamba, Francis. 1993. *Morphology*. London: Macmillan.
Pinker, Steven. 1999. *Words and Rules*. New York: Basic Books.
Spencer, Andrew. 1991. *Morphological Theory*. Cambridge, MA: Blackwell.

## Appendix: how to identify morphemes in unfamiliar languages

An important part of morphological analysis involves identifying morphemes in unfamiliar languages and determining the nature of the information that they carry. (A number of the problems in the set of exercises that follow this chapter will give you an opportunity to practise this type of analysis.) The key procedure to follow in working on this sort of problem can be stated simply as follows:

- Identify recurring strings of sounds and match them with recurring meanings.

Consider in this regard the following small sample of data in table 4.27 from Turkish, consisting of four words along with their English translations. (A more realistic data sample would not only be much larger, but would also include sentences in which it might well be unclear where the word boundaries should be placed.)

**Table 4.27**    Some Turkish words

| | |
|---|---|
| /mumlar/ | 'candles' |
| /toplar/ | 'guns' |
| /adamlar/ | 'men' |
| /kitaplar/ | 'books' |

As you can probably see, the syllable /lar/ occurs in all four items in our sample. From the translations of these items, you can see that a particular feature of meaning—namely, plurality—is present in all four cases as well. Using the procedure just stated, we therefore hypothesize that /lar/ is the morpheme marking plurality in Turkish. Once this has been determined, we can then infer that /mum/ in /mumlar/ is also a morpheme (with the meaning 'candle'), that /top/ in /toplar/ is a morpheme (with the meaning 'gun'), and so on. A larger sampling of Turkish data would confirm the correctness of these inferences.

In doing morphological analysis in unfamiliar languages, there are a number of pitfalls to avoid. For the type of data normally investigated at the introductory level, the following guidelines are especially important.

- Do not assume that the morpheme order in the language you are analyzing is the same as in English. In Korean, for example, morphemes indicating location (the rough equivalent of 'at', 'in', and so forth) follow rather than precede the noun (*hakkyo-eyse* 'at school' is literally 'school at').

- Do not assume that every semantic contrast expressed in English will also be manifested in the language you are analyzing. In Turkish, for instance, there is no equivalent for English *the* and *a*. In Mandarin Chinese, the same pronoun form can be used to refer to a male or a female (there is no *he-she* distinction).

- Do not assume that every contrast expressed in the language you are analyzing is manifested in English. For example, as discussed at **www.pearsoned.ca/ogrady**, some languages distinguish more than two number categories (Inuktitut distinguishes singular, dual and plural); and some languages make multiple tense contrasts (ChiBemba has an eight-way distinction).

- Remember that a morpheme can have more than one form (allomorph). For example, further study of Turkish would reveal that the plural suffix in this language can also be realized as /ler/, depending on the vowel in the base to which the suffix is attached.

# Exercises

1. Consider the following words and answer the questions below.

| | | | |
|---|---|---|---|
| a) fly | f) reuse | k) spiteful | p) preplan |
| b) desks | g) triumphed | l) suite | q) optionality |
| c) untie | h) delight | m) fastest | r) prettier |
| d) tree | i) justly | n) deform | s) mistreat |
| e) dislike | j) payment | o) disobey | t) premature |

   **i)** For each word, determine whether it is simple or complex.

   **ii)** Circle all the bound morphemes. Underline all the roots.

2. Consider the following data from Zapotec, an indigenous language of Mexico.

| | | | |
|---|---|---|---|
| pizaanaya | 'my sister' | pizaannoo | 'our sister' |
| pizaanalo | 'your (sg) sister' | pizaannatoo | 'your (pl) sister' |
| pizaannani | 'his/her sister' | pizaannani | 'their sister' |

   **i)** Match each of the following notions with a Zapotec morpheme:

   sister _____

   my _____          our _____

   your (sg) _____   your (pl) _____

   his/her _____     their _____

   **ii)** If 'brother' is *beiran*, how would you say each of the following?

   my brother _____

   our brother _____

   their brother _____

   (Data from *Gramática de la lengua zapoteca*, by an anonymous author. Mexico: Oficina Tip. de la Secretaría de Formento, 1897, p. 4.)

3. Consider the following data from Kwakum, a Bantu language spoken in Cameroun.

| | |
|---|---|
| sɛbɔmmɛ | 'We bought (a long time ago).' |
| sɛbɔmko | 'We bought (recently).' |
| sɛbɔmkowɛɛ | 'We did not buy (recently).' |
| nyebɔmmɛ | 'I bought (a long time ago).' |
| ɔbɔmmɛ | 'You (sg) bought (a long time ago).' |
| yebɔmko | 'They bought (recently).' |
| nɛbɔmko | 'You (pl) bought (recently).' |
| abɔmmɛwɛɛ | 'S/he did not buy (a long time ago).' |

   **i)** What are the Kwakum morphemes for each of the following concepts?

   'I' ___                      'we' ___

   'you (sg)' ___               'you (pl)' ___

   's/he' ___                   'they' ___

   'buy' ____

   'negation (not)' ___

   'recent past (recently)' ____

   'remote past (a long time ago)' ___

**ii)** How do you say the following in Kwakum?
I bought (recently).
I didn't buy (recently).
They bought (a long time ago).

(Data from *The Bantu languages of Western Equatorial Africa* by M. Guthrie. Oxford: Oxford University Press, 1953.)

**4.** All the following Persian words consist of two or more morphemes. (*Note*: *xar* means 'buy' and *-id* designates the past tense.)

a)  xaridam          'I bought'
b)  xaridi           'you (sg) bought'
c)  xarid            '(he) bought'
d)  naxaridam        'I did not buy'
e)  namixaridand     'they were not buying'
f)  naxaridim        'we did not buy'
g)  mixarid          '(he) was buying'
h)  mixaridid        'you (pl) were buying'

**i)** Match each of the following notions with a morpheme in the Persian data.

a)  I _____                    e)  they _____
b)  you (sg) _____             f)  not _____
c)  we _____                   g)  was/were + -ing (continuous) _____
d)  you (pl) _____

**ii)** How would you say the following in Persian?
a)  They were buying.
b)  You (sg) did not buy.
c)  You (sg) were buying.

**5.** Consider the following data from Zapotec, an indigenous language of Mexico.

| racañeea | 'I help' | racañeetonoo | 'we help' |
|---|---|---|---|
| racañeelo | 'you (sg) help' | racañeetoo | 'you (pl) help' |
| racañeeni | 's/he helps' | racañeeni | 'they help' |
| cocañeea | 'I helped' | cocañeetonoo | 'we helped' |
| cocañeelo | 'you (sg) helped' | cocañeetoo | 'you (pl) helped' |
| cocañeeni | 's/he helped' | cocañeeni | 'they helped' |
| cacañeea | 'I will help' | cacañeetonoo | 'we will help' |
| cacañeelo | 'you (sg) will help' | cacañeetoo | 'you (pl) will help' |
| cacañeeni | 's/he will help' | cacañeeni | 'they will help.' |

Match each of the following notions with a Zapotec morpheme.
help _____
Present _____
Past _____
Future _____

I _____                     we _____
you (sg) _____              you (pl) _____
he/she/they _____

(Data from *Gramática de la lengua zapoteca*, by an anonymous author. Mexico: Oficina Tip. de la Secretaría de Formento, 1897, p. 8.)

**6.** Consider the following data from Turkish.

| | | | | |
|---|---|---|---|---|
| a) | lokanta | 'a restaurant' | lokantada | 'in/at a restaurant' |
| b) | kapɨ | 'a door' | kapɨda | 'in/at a door' |
| c) | randevu | 'an appointment' | randevuda | 'in/at an appointment' |
| d) | baʃ | 'a head' | baʃta | 'in/at a head' |
| e) | kitap | 'a book' | kitapta | 'in/at a book' |
| f) | koltuk | 'an armchair' | koltukta | 'in/at an armchair' |
| g) | taraf | 'a side' | tarafta | 'in/at a side' |

**i)** Does the Turkish morpheme meaning 'in/at' have more than one allomorph?

**ii)** If so, what are the allomorphs? Describe their distribution as generally as possible.

**7.** Consider the following words.

| | | | |
|---|---|---|---|
| a) desks | e) triumphed | i) prearrange (V) | m) optionality |
| b) untie | f) ageless | j) smartest | n) prettier |
| c) insincere | g) loser | k) redistribute | o) mistreat |
| d) disprove | h) payment | l) disobey | p) resell |

**i)** Draw a tree structure for each word.

**ii)** For the word *optionality*, what is the base for the affix *-ion*? What is the base for the suffix *-ity*? Are either of these bases also the root for the entire word? If so, which one?

**8.** The following data from Agta (spoken in the Philippines) illustrates a specific type of affix.

| | | | | |
|---|---|---|---|---|
| a) dakal | 'big' | | dumakal | 'grow big, grow up' |
| b) darág | 'red' | | dumarág | 'redden' |
| c) furáw | 'white' | | fumuráw | 'become white' |

**i)** What is the affix in Agta meaning 'become X'?

**ii)** What type of affix is it?

**9.** In this chapter, an argument was presented in favour of the following structure for the word *unhappiness*.

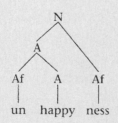

Using the same type of argument, justify tree structures for the words *inexpensive*, *redisposal*, and *disinvestment*. (*Hint:* This will involve determining the type of syntactic category with which the affixes in these words can combine; see table 4.6.)

**10.** In English, the suffix *-er* can be added to a place name. Examine the words in the two columns below.

| Column 1 | Column 2 |
|---|---|
| Long Islander | *Denverer |
| Vermonter | *Philadelphiaer |
| New Yorker | *Vancouverer |
| Newfoundlander | *Torontoer |
| Londoner | *Miamier |

    **i)**   In general terms, what does the suffix *-er* mean in these words?
    **ii)**  How is this *-er* different in meaning from the *-er* found in the words *skater* and *walker*?
    **iii)** State the constraint on the distribution of *-er* illustrated in this data.
    **iv)** Does this constraint also apply to the type of *-er* used in the word *skater*? (*Hint*: What would you call 'one who discovers' or 'one who plows'?)

**11.** The following words have all been formed by compounding. Draw a tree structure for each word. If you are in doubt as to the lexical category of the compound, remember that the category of the head determines the category of the word.

| | | |
|---|---|---|
| a) football | i) tree trunk | q) hockey match |
| b) billboard | j) lead free | r) coffee table |
| c) sunspot | k) home plate | s) flower child |
| d) in-crowd | l) girlfriend | t) blueprint |
| e) fast food | m) city centre | u) Greenpeace |
| f) softball | n) failsafe | v) space ship |
| g) freeze-dry | o) potato peel | w) brain dead |
| h) oversee | p) bittersweet | x) kill-joy |

**12.** Examine the following compounds and answer the questions below.

| Column 1 | Column 2 |
|---|---|
| a) loudmouth | h) cutthroat |
| b) skinhead | i) pickpocket |
| c) kill-joy | j) spoilsport |
| d) bath towel | k) crybaby |
| e) death blow | l) brain dead |
| f) airhead | m) blow-dry |
| g) Walkman | n) armchair |

    **i)**  For each of the compounds in column 1, determine whether it is endocentric or exocentric.
    **ii)** How do you form the plural of *Walkman* (a portable radio) and *loudmouth*? (*Hint*: See table 4.13. Also, pay special attention to the pronunciation of *mouth*. Is it any different here than when it is an independent word?)

**13.** Indicate whether the words in each of the following groups are related to one another by processes of inflection or derivation.
    a) go, goes, going, gone
    b) discover, discovery, discoverer, discoverable, discoverability

   c) lovely, lovelier, loveliest
   d) inventor, inventor's, inventors, inventors'
   e) democracy, democrat, democratic, democratize

**14.** The following sentences contain both derivational and inflectional affixes. Underline all of the derivational affixes and circle the inflectional affixes.

   a) The farmer's cows escaped.
   b) It was raining.
   c) Those socks are inexpensive.
   d) Jim needs the newer copy.
   e) The strongest rower continued.
   f) The pitbull has bitten the cyclist.
   g) She quickly closed the book.
   h) The alphabetization went well.

**15.** Each of the following columns illustrates a different type of inflection.

| Column 1 | Column 2 | Column 3 |
|---|---|---|
| a) mouse/mice | f) go/went | k) record/recorded |
| b) dive/dove | g) is/was | l) arrive/arrived |
| c) take/took | h) good/better | m) start/started |
| d) man/men | i) she/her | n) discuss/discussed |
| e) eat/ate | j) am/are | o) try/tried |

   **i)** How is inflection expressed in column 1? column 2? column 3?
   **ii)** Think of at least one more English example to add to each column.

**16.** Consider the following data from Samoan.

| | | | |
|---|---|---|---|
| a) | mate | 'he dies' | mamate | 'they die' |
| b) | nofo | 'he stays' | nonofo | 'they stay' |
| c) | galue | 'he works' | galulue | 'they work' |
| d) | tanu | 'he buries' | tatanu | 'they bury' |
| e) | alofa | 'he loves' | alolofa | 'they love' |
| f) | taʔoto | 'he lies' | taʔoʔoto | 'they lie' |
| g) | atamaʔi | 'he is intelligent' | atamamaʔi | 'they are intelligent' |

   **i)** What morphological process is used to express the inflectional contrast between singular and plural here?
   **ii)** Describe how it works in your own words.
   **iii)** If 'he is strong' in Samoan is *malosi*, how would you say 'they are strong'?

**17.** The following words from Chamorro, spoken in Guam and the Mariana Islands, all involve derivation. (Data are presented in the orthography of Chamorro, not in phonetic transcription.)

| *I. Root* | | *Derived word* | |
|---|---|---|---|
| a) adda | 'mimic' | aadda | 'mimicker' |
| b) kanno | 'eat' | kakanno | 'eater' |
| c) tuge | 'write' | tutuge | 'writer' |

| *II. Root* | | *Derived word* | |
|---|---|---|---|
| d) atan | 'look at' | atanon | 'nice to look at' |
| e) sangan | 'tell' | sanganon | 'tellable' |
| f) guaiya | 'love' | guaiyayon | 'lovable' |
| g) tulaika | 'exchange' | tulaikayon | 'exchangeable' |
| h) chalek | 'laugh' | chalekon | 'laughable' |
| i) ngangas | 'chew' | ngangason | 'chewable' |

*III. Root*                                         *Derived word*

| | | | | |
|---|---|---|---|---|
| j) | nalang | 'hungry' | nalalalang | 'very hungry' |
| k) | dankolo | 'big' | dankololo | 'very big' |
| l) | metgot | 'strong' | metgogot | 'very strong' |
| m) | bunita | 'pretty' | bunitata | 'very pretty' |

Like inflection, derivation can be expressed in a variety of ways—including by affixation of various types (prefixation, suffixation, infixation) and by reduplication.

**i)**  What morphological process is manifested in I? in II? in III?

**ii)**  Formulate a general statement as to how the derived words in I are formed. Do the same for II and III.

**iii)**  One of these derivational processes consists of affixation involving allomorphs. What is the distribution of the allomorphs?

**18.** The following words can be either nouns or verbs.

| | | | | | |
|---|---|---|---|---|---|
| a) | record | f) | outline | k) | report |
| b) | journey | g) | convict | l) | assault |
| c) | exchange | h) | imprint | m) | answer |
| d) | remark | i) | reply | n) | import |
| e) | surprise | j) | retreat | o) | cripple |

**i)**  For each word, determine whether stress placement can be used to make the distinction between noun and verb.

**ii)**  Think of two more English examples illustrating the process of stress shift to mark a category distinction.

**19.** Indicate the morphological phenomenon illustrated by the items in column 2.

| | *Column 1* | *Column 2* |
|---|---|---|
| a) | automation | → automate |
| b) | humid | → humidifier |
| c) | information, entertainment | → infotainment |
| d) | love, seat | → loveseat |
| e) | prógress | → progréss |
| f) | typographical error | → typo |
| g) | aerobics, marathon | → aerobathon |
| h) | act | → deactivate |
| i) | curve, ball | → curve ball |
| j) | perambulator | → pram |
| k) | (the) comb | → comb (your hair) |
| l) | beef, buffalo | → beefalo |
| m) | random access memory | → RAM |
| n) | megabyte | → meg |
| o) | teleprinter, exchange | → telex |
| p) | influenza | → flu |
| q) | They have finished | → They've finished |
| r) | GST | → Goods and Services Tax |

**20.** Here are five instances where a new word is needed. Create a word for each of these definitions in the manner indicated. Fill in the blanks with your new words.

    a) Use an acronym . . . for your uncle's second oldest brother.
       "We visited my _____ at Christmas."

    b) Use onomatopoeia . . . for the sound of a coffee percolator at work.
       "I can't concentrate because my perc is _____ing."

    c) Use conversion . . . for wrapping something breakable in bubbles.
       "You'd better _____ that ornament or else it might break."

    d) Use a compound . . . for the annoying string of cheese stretching from a slice of hot pizza to one's mouth.
       "As the _____ hung precariously from my lips, our eyes met!"

    e) Use backformation . . . for the action of backformation.
       "We had to _____ words in Linguistics today."

**21.** Create new words for each of the following situations.

    a) Use a product name . . . for the act of scrubbing with Ajax.
       "I _____ed the tub after giving Fido a bath."

    b) Use a proper name . . . for the act of breaking dishes, which Jonathan does regularly.
       "He's going to _____ all of my best dishes."

    c) Use clipping . . . for a course in ovinology (the study of sheep).
       "Have you done your _____ assignment yet?"

    d) Use derivation . . . for being able to be contacted.
       "The counsellor is not very _____."

    e) Use a blend . . . for a hot drink made with chocolate and ginseng.
       "I'll have a _____ and two peanut butter cookies, please."

William O'Grady

# Syntax: the analysis of sentence structure

*. . . the game is to say something new with old words*

RALPH WALDO EMERSON, *JOURNALS*, 1849

Not much can be said with a single word. If language is to express complex thoughts and ideas, it has to have a way to combine words into sentences. In this chapter, we will consider how this is done, focusing on the component of the grammar that linguists call **syntax**.

As noted in chapter 1, speakers of a language are able to combine words in novel ways, forming sentences that they have neither heard nor seen before. However, not just any combination of words will give a well-formed sentence. English speakers recognize that the pattern in (1) is not permissible even though the same words can be combined in a different way to form the acceptable sentence in (2).

(1) *House painted student a the.

(2) A student painted the house.

We say that an utterance is **grammatical** if native speakers judge it to be a possible sentence of their language.

The study of syntax lies very close to the heart of contemporary linguistic analysis and work in this area is notorious both for its diversity and for its complexity. New ideas are constantly being put forward, and there is considerable controversy over how the properties of sentence structure should be described and explained.

This chapter will introduce a simple version of **transformational** (or **generative**) **grammar**. Although many linguists disagree with various features of this approach, it is very widely used in linguistics and other disciplines concerned with language (especially cognitive science). For this reason, it is the usual point of departure for introductions to the study of sentence structure.

An intriguing aspect of work within transformational syntax is the emphasis on **Universal Grammar (UG)**, the system of categories, operations, and principles that are shared by all languages. The key idea is that despite the many superficial differences among languages, there are certain commonalities with respect to the manner in which sentences are formed.

As things now stand, it is widely believed that the syntactic component of any grammar must include at least two subcomponents. The first of these is a **lexicon**, or mental dictionary, that provides a list of the language's words along with information about their pronunciation, their category, and their meaning.

George Bernard Shaw wrote one that was 110 words long. William Faulkner's novel *Absalom, Absalom!* includes a 1300-word sentence. James Joyce managed to produce a 4391-word sentence (that goes on for 40 pages) in *Ulysses*. But even that's not the longest known sentence—*The Rotter's Club* by Jonathon Coe contains a sentence that is 13 955 words long!

The bottom line is that there's no such thing as the world's longest sentence—any sentence can be made longer. That's because the words and structure-building operations involved in sentence formation can be used over and over again, without limit.

a man . . . and a woman
a man . . . and a woman . . . and a child
a man . . . and a woman . . . and a child . . . and a dog
a book . . . on a table . . . near the bed . . . in the room . . . at the back . . . of the house . . . on the tree-lined street . . .

The possibility of applying operations in this way to create an ever more complex structure is called **recursivity**, and it's a very essential part of our ability to build sentences.

The second subcomponent consists of what can be called a **computational system**, by which we simply mean operations that combine and arrange words in particular ways. As we will see a little later in this chapter, the two principal structure-building operations made available by Universal Grammar are **Merge** (which combines elements to create phrases and sentences) and **Move** (which transports an element to a new position within a particular structure).

We will begin our discussion of these matters in section 5.1 by introducing some of the most common categories of words found in language and by investigating how they can be combined into larger structural units.

# 5.1 Categories and structure

A fundamental fact about words in all human languages is that they can be grouped together into a relatively small number of classes called **syntactic categories**. This classification reflects a variety of factors, including the type of meaning that words express, the type of affixes that they take, and the type of structures in which they can occur.

## 5.1.1 Categories of words

Table 5.1 on page 148 provides examples of the word-level categories that are most central to the study of syntax. The four most studied syntactic categories are **noun (N)**, **verb (V)**, **adjective (A)**, and **preposition (P)**. These elements, which are often called **lexical categories**, play a very important role in sentence formation, as we will soon see. A fifth and less studied lexical category consists of **adverbs (Adv)**, most of which are derived from adjectives.

Languages may also contain **non-lexical** or **functional categories**, including **determiner (Det)**, **auxiliary verb (Aux)**, **conjunction (Con)**, and **degree word (Deg)**. Such elements generally have meanings that are harder to define and paraphrase

| Table 5.1 | Syntactic categories |
|---|---|
| **Lexical categories** ('content words') | **Examples** |
| Noun (N) | Harry, boy, wheat, policy, moisture, bravery |
| Verb (V) | arrive, discuss, melt, hear, remain, dislike |
| Adjective (A) | good, tall, old, intelligent, beautiful, fond |
| Preposition (P) | to, in, on, near, at, by |
| Adverb (Adv) | slowly, quietly, now, always, perhaps |
| **Non-lexical categories** ('function words') | **Examples** |
| Determiner (Det) | the, a, this, these, no (as in *no books*) |
| Degree word (Deg) | too, so, very, more, quite |
| Auxiliary (Aux) | |
|    Modal | will, would, can, could, may, must, should |
|    Non-modal | be, have, do |
| Conjunction (Con) | and, or, but |

than those of lexical categories. For example, the meaning of a determiner such as *the* or an auxiliary such as *would* is more difficult to describe than the meaning of a noun such as *hill* or *vehicle*.

A potential source of confusion in the area of word classification stems from the fact that some items can belong to more than one category.

(3) *comb* used as a noun:
The woman found a comb.

*comb* used as a verb:
The boy should comb his hair.

(4) *near* used as a preposition:
The child stood near the fence.

*near* used as a verb:
The runners neared the finish line.

*near* used as an adjective:
The end is nearer than you might think.

How then can we determine a word's category?

## Meaning

One criterion involves meaning. For instance, nouns typically name entities ('people and things'), including individuals (*Harry, Sue*) and objects (*book, desk*). Verbs, on the other hand, characteristically designate actions (*run, jump*), sensations (*feel, hurt*), and states (*be, remain*).

Consistent with these tendencies, *comb* in (3) refers to an object when used as a noun but to an action when used as a verb.

The typical function of an adjective is to designate a property or attribute of the entities denoted by nouns. Thus, when we say *that tall building*, we are attributing the property 'tall' to the building designated by the noun.

In a parallel way, adverbs typically denote properties and attributes of the actions, sensations, and states designated by verbs. In the following sentences, for example, the adverb *quickly* indicates the manner of Janet's leaving and the adverb *early* specifies its time.

(5) Janet left quickly.
   Janet left early.

A word's category membership does not always bear such a straightforward relationship to its meaning, however. For example, there are nouns such as *difficulty*, *truth*, and *likelihood* which do not name entities in the strict sense. Moreover, even though words that name actions tend to be verbs, nouns may also denote actions (*push* is a noun in *give someone a push*).

Matters are further complicated by the fact that in some cases, words with very similar meanings belong to different categories. For instance, the words *like* and *fond* are very similar in meaning (as in *Mice like/are fond of cheese*), yet *like* is a verb and *fond* an adjective.

## Inflection

Most linguists believe that meaning is only one of several criteria that enter into determining a word's category. As shown in table 5.2, inflection can also be very useful for distinguishing among different categories of words. (For a discussion of inflection, see chapter 4, section 4.4.)

**Table 5.2**   Lexical categories and their inflectional affixes

| Category | Inflectional affix | Examples |
|---|---|---|
| N | plural -*s* <br> possessive -*'s* | books, chairs, doctors <br> John's, (the) man's |
| V | past tense -*ed* <br> progressive -*ing* <br> third person singular -*s* | arrived, melted, hopped <br> arriving, melting, hopping <br> arrives, melts, hops |
| A | comparative -*er* <br> superlative -*est* | taller, faster, smarter <br> tallest, fastest, smartest |

However, even inflection does not always provide the information needed to determine a word's category. In English, for example, not all adjectives can take the comparative and superlative affixes (*\*intelligenter*, *\*beautifulest*) and some nouns cannot be pluralized (*moisture*, *bravery*, *knowledge*).

# Distribution

A third and often more reliable criterion for determining a word's category involves the type of elements (especially functional categories) with which it can co-occur (its **distribution**). For example, nouns can typically appear with a determiner, verbs with an auxiliary, and adjectives with a degree word in the sort of patterns illustrated in table 5.3.

| Table 5.3 | Distributional properties of nouns, verbs, and adjectives | |
|---|---|---|
| **Category** | **Distributional property** | **Examples** |
| Noun | occurrence with a determiner | a car, the wheat |
| Verb | occurrence with an auxiliary | has gone, will stay |
| Adjective | occurrence with a degree word | very rich, too big |

Of course, a verb cannot occur with a determiner or degree word in these sorts of patterns, and a noun cannot occur with an auxiliary.

(6) a verb with a determiner:
   *the destroy

   a verb with a degree word:
   *very arrive

   a noun with an auxiliary:
   *will destruction

Distributional tests for category membership are simple and highly reliable. They can be used with confidence when it is necessary to categorize unfamiliar words.

## Language Matters  A Poem That Syntacticians Love

Thanks to distributional and inflectional clues, it's often possible to identify a word's category without knowing its meaning. The poem "Jabberwocky," by Lewis Carroll, illustrates this point in a particularly brilliant way—it's interpretable precisely because readers are able to figure out that *gyre* is a verb (note the auxiliary verb to its left), that *borogroves* is a noun (it's preceded by a determiner and takes the plural ending), and so on.

   'Twas brillig, and the slithy toves
   Did gyre and gimble in the wabe;
   All mimsy were the borogoves,
   And the mome raths outgrabe.

   'Beware the Jabberwock, my son!
   The jaws that bite, the claws that catch!
   Beware the Jubjub bird, and shun
   The frumious Bandersnatch!'

## 5.1.2    Phrase structure

Sentences are not formed by simply stringing words together like beads on a necklace. Rather, they have a hierarchical design in which words are grouped together into larger structural units called **phrases**. In the sentence *The doctor arrived quickly*, for example, the words *the* and *doctor* form a phrase, and *arrived* and *quickly* make up another.

(7) [The doctor] [arrived quickly].

Similarly, in the following sentence, *those* and *students* are grouped together, as are *ride* and *bicycles*.

(8) [Those students] [ride bicycles].

In traditional syntactic analysis, *the doctor* and *those students* are identified as the subject of the sentence, while *arrived quickly* and *ride bicycles* make up the predicate. Further analysis reveals that the verb *ride* is **transitive**, since it takes a direct object (*bicycles*), whereas *arrive* is **intransitive** since it has no direct object.

Terms such as 'subject' and 'direct object' are very useful tools for syntactic description, and you can find out more about them at our Companion Website at **www.pearsoned. ca/ogrady**, chapter 5. For the purposes of this chapter, however, we will present a different (and more popular) system of syntactic description that focuses on a sentence's internal 'geometry'.

### The blueprint

As a first approximation, it is often suggested that a typical phrase can be broken down into three parts—a head, a specifier, and a complement—arranged in accordance with the blueprint or 'schema' shown in figure 5.1 (X' is pronounced 'X-bar').

**Figure 5.1**
The X' schema

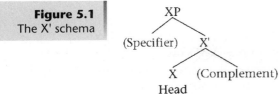

Such structures, which are often called (inverted) 'trees', capture the hierarchical organization of phrases and sentences. In particular, the X' schema captures four generalizations:

1. All phrases have a three-level structure (X, X', and XP).
2. All phrases contain a head, X.
3. If there is a complement, it is attached at the intermediate X' level, as a 'sister' of the head.
4. If there is a specifier, it is attached at the XP level.

Let us consider each part of a phrase's architecture in turn.

## Heads

The head is the obligatory nucleus around which a phrase is built. For now, we will focus on four categories that can function as the **head** of a phrase—nouns, verbs, adjectives, and prepositions. Thus, to start out, the X in the X' schema can be N, V, A, or P.

Although phrases usually consist of two or more words, a head may form a phrase all by itself as shown in the examples in figure 5.2. When this happens, the resulting structure has a single straight 'branch' from which only the head hangs.

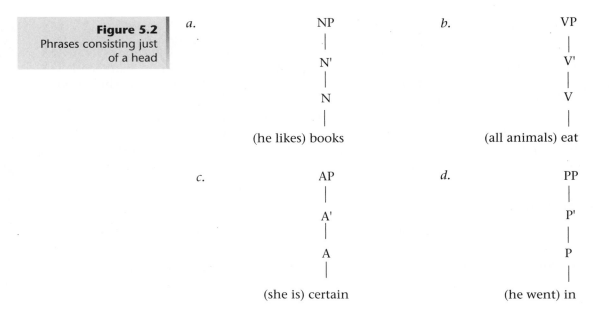

**Figure 5.2**
Phrases consisting just of a head

## Specifiers

The type of specifier that appears in a particular phrase depends on the category of the head. Determiners serve as the specifiers of Ns, while preverbal adverbs typically function as the specifiers of Vs and degree words as the specifiers of As and (some) Ps (see table 5.4).

| Table 5.4 | Some specifiers | |
|---|---|---|
| **Category** | **Typical function** | **Examples** |
| Determiner (Det) | specifier of N | the, a, this, those, no |
| Adverb (Adv) | specifier of V | never, perhaps, often, always |
| Degree word (Deg) | specifier of A or P | very, quite, more, almost |

When a specifier is present, it attaches to XP, in accordance with the X' schema. This gives structures such as the ones shown in figure 5.3.

Syntactically, specifiers typically mark a phrase boundary. In English, specifiers occur at the left boundary (the beginning) of their respective phrases. Semantically, specifiers help to make the meaning of the head more precise. Hence, the determiner (Det) *the* in *a*) indicates that the speaker has in mind specific books, the adverb *never* in *b*) indicates non-occurrence of the event, and the degree words (Deg) *quite* and *almost* in *c*) and *d*) indicate the extent to which a particular property or relation is manifested.

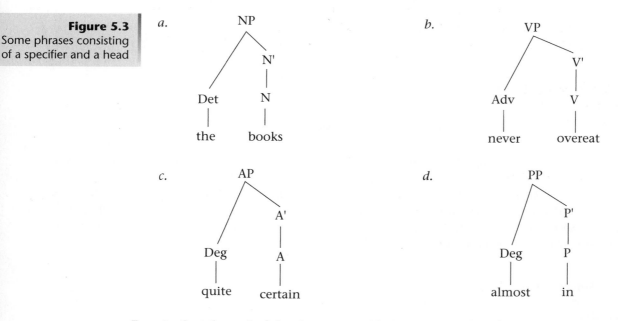

**Figure 5.3**
Some phrases consisting of a specifier and a head

Exercise 3 at the end of the chapter provides practice in identifying specifiers and heads.

## Complements

Consider now some examples of slightly more complex phrases.

(9)  *a.* [NP a <u>picture</u> of the ocean]
      *b.* [VP never <u>trust</u> a rumour]
      *c.* [AP quite <u>certain</u> about Mary]
      *d.* [PP almost <u>in</u> the house]

In addition to a specifier and the underlined head, the phrases in (9) also contain a **complement**. These elements, which are themselves phrases, provide information about entities and locations whose existence is implied by the meaning of the head. For example, the meaning of *trust* implies something that is trusted, the meaning of *in* implies a location, and so on.

(10)  A vegetarian would never eat [a hamburger].
                                    ↑              ↑
                                  *head*    *complement naming the thing eaten*

(11)  in    [the house]
       ↑         ↑
     *head*    *complement naming a location*

Figure 5.4 shows the structure of a phrase consisting of a specifier, a head, and a complement. (The NP serving as complement of a V corresponds to the sentence's **direct object**.)

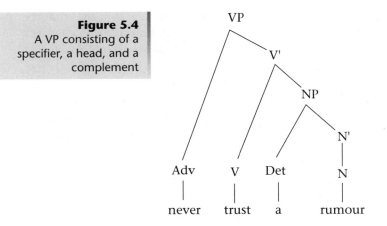

**Figure 5.4**
A VP consisting of a specifier, a head, and a complement

As noted on page 153, complements are themselves phrases. Thus, the complement of the V *trust* is an NP that itself consists of a determiner (*a*) and a head (*rumour*).

NPs, APs, and PPs have a parallel internal structure, as the examples in figure 5.5 illustrate. (In order to save space, we do not depict the internal structure of the complement phrases in these examples. The full structure of any tree abbreviated in this way can be found at **www.pearsoned.ca/ogrady**.)

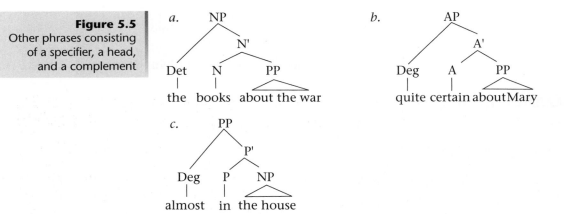

**Figure 5.5**
Other phrases consisting of a specifier, a head, and a complement

Of course, it is also possible to have phrases that consist of just a head and a complement, with no specifier. This results in the type of 'bottom-heavy' structures depicted in figure 5.6. Exercise 4 at the end of the chapter provides practice in identifying complements.

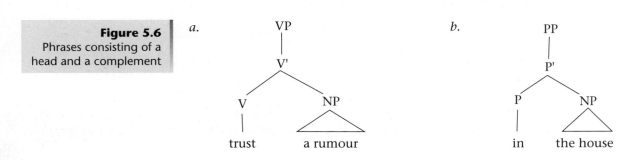

**Figure 5.6**
Phrases consisting of a head and a complement

# The Merge operation

We can now formulate the following operation for sentence building.

(12)    *Merge*
           Combine words in a manner compatible with the X' schema.

The Merge operation is able to take a determiner such as *the* and combine it with an N' consisting of the N *house* to form the NP *the house*. It is then able to take a head such as the preposition *in* and combine it with the NP *the house* to form the P' and PP *in the house* (see figure 5.7).

**Figure 5.7**
The Merge operation in action

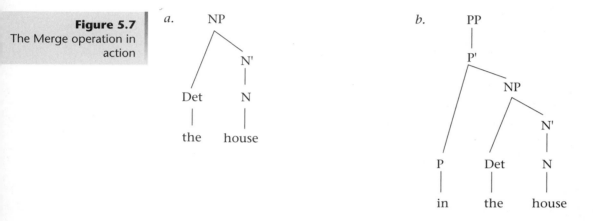

Continued application of the Merge operation to additional words can lead to the formation of phrases and sentences of unlimited complexity.

## Language Matters  **The Mirror Image**

Many languages have a phrase structure whose X' level is the mirror image of the one found in English—the complement occurs on the left side of the head, rather than on the right side. (In both types of language, the specifier appears on the left side of the head.) Japanese works that way: the V occurs at the end of the VP, the P at the end of the PP, and the N at the end of the NP.

| NP + V | NP + P | PP + N |
|---|---|---|
| [sono hon] yonda | [sono gakko]-ni | [Mary-no] shashin |
| that book read (Pst) | that school at | Mary of picture |
| 'read that book' | 'at that school' | '(a) picture of Mary' |

The version the X' schema needed for these languages looks like this—with the head to the right of its complement:

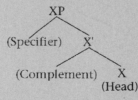

About half of the world's languages use this version of the X' schema.

## 5.1.3   Sentences

The largest unit of syntactic analysis is the sentence. Sentences typically consist of a subject (typically an NP) and a VP, which are linked together by an abstract category dubbed 'I' or 'Infl' (for 'inflection') that indicates the sentence's tense. As illustrated in figure 5.8, I serves as head of the sentence, taking the VP as its complement and the subject as its specifier[1] (Pst = Past).

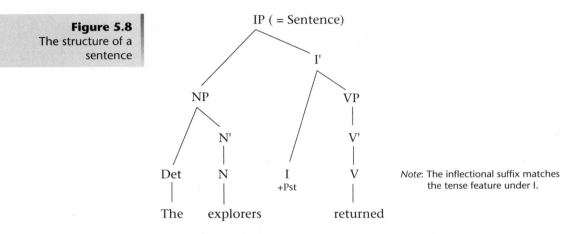

**Figure 5.8**
The structure of a sentence

*Note*: The inflectional suffix matches the tense feature under I.

The tense feature in I must be compatible with the form of the verb. So a sentence like the one above whose head contains the feature +Pst must contain a verb marked for the past tense.

Although somewhat abstract, this analysis has the advantage of giving sentences the same internal structure as other phrases (with a specifier, a head, and a complement), making them consistent with the X' schema. Moreover, because I, like all heads, is obligatory, we also account for the fact that all sentences have tense (i.e., they are all past or non-past).

The structure in figure 5.8 also provides us with a natural place to locate modal auxiliaries such as *can*, *will*, and *must*, most of which are inherently non-past, as shown by their incompatibility with time adverbs such as *yesterday*—e.g., *\*He can/will/must work yesterday*. (The auxiliaries *could* and *would* can be either past or non-past—e.g., *He could swim tomorrow/He could swim when he was three*.) Although traditionally analyzed as auxiliary verbs, these words are treated as instances of the I category in contemporary linguistic analysis, as depicted in figure 5.9. (We will discuss the status of non-modal auxiliaries such as *have* and *be* in section 5.3.3.)

**Figure 5.9**
An IP with an auxiliary in the I position

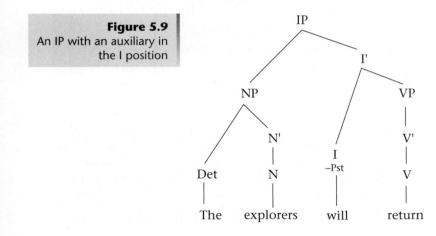

This neatly accounts not only for the fact that modals have an inherent tense, but also for their occurrence between the subject (the specifier) and the VP (the complement)—in the position reserved for the head of the sentence. (It must be admitted, however, that the use of the term *inflection* by syntacticians to include free morphemes is unfortunate.)

The appendix at the end of the chapter outlines a procedure that should help you assign sentences an appropriate structure. Exercise 5 provides an opportunity to practise this procedure.

## 5.1.4  Tests for phrase structure

How can linguists be sure that they have grouped words together into phrases in the right way? The existence of the syntactic units, or **constituents**, found in tree structures can be independently verified with the help of special tests. We will consider three such tests here as they apply to XP-level constituents. (Not every test is applicable to every constituent, though.)

### The substitution test

Evidence that phrases are syntactic units comes from the fact that they can often be replaced by an element such as *they*, *it*, or *do so*. This is illustrated in (13), where *they* replaces the NP *the children* and *do so* replaces the VP *stop at the corner*. (This is called a **substitution test**.)

(13)  [$_\text{NP}$The children] will [$_\text{VP}$ stop at the corner] if *they* see us *do so*.
      (*they* = the children; *do so* = stop at the corner)

The substitution test also confirms that a PP such as *at the corner* is a unit since it can be replaced by a single word in a sentence such as (14).

(14)  The children stopped [$_\text{PP}$ at the corner] and we stopped *there* too.
      (*there* = at the corner)

Elements that do not form a constituent cannot be replaced in this way. Thus, there is no word in English that we can use to replace *children stopped,* for example, or *at the*.

### The movement test

A second indication that *at the corner* forms a constituent is that it can be moved as a single unit to a different position within the sentence. (This is called a **movement test**.) In (15), for instance, *at the corner* can be moved from a position after the verb to the beginning of the sentence.

(15)  They stopped [$_\text{PP}$ at the corner] → [$_\text{PP}$ At the corner], they stopped.

Of course, *at the*, which is not a syntactic unit, cannot be fronted in this manner (\**At the, they stopped corner*).

### The coordination test

Finally, we can conclude that a group of words forms a constituent if it can be joined to another group of words by a conjunction such as *and*, *or*, or *but*. (This is known as the **coordination test** since patterns built around a conjunction are called **coordinate structures**.) The sentence in (16) illustrates how coordination can be used to help establish that *stopped at the corner* is a constituent.

(16)  The children [$_\text{VP}$ stopped at the corner] but [$_\text{VP}$ didn't look both ways].

## 5.2  Complement options

How can we be sure that individual words will occur with a complement of the right type in the syntactic structures that we have been building? Information about the complements permitted by a particular head is included in its entry in a speaker's lexicon. For instance, the lexicon for English includes an entry for *devour* that indicates its syntactic category (V), its phonological representation, its meaning, and the fact that it takes an NP complement.

(17) *devour*:  category: V
         phonological representation: /dəvawər/
         meaning: EAT HUNGRILY
         complement: NP

The term **subcategorization** is used to refer to information about a word's complement options.

Subcategorization information helps ensure that lexical items appear in the appropriate types of tree structures. For example, because *devour* belongs to the subcategory of verbs that require an NP complement, it can occur in patterns such as (18a), but not (18b).

(18) *a. devour* with an NP complement:
        The child devoured [NP the sandwich].

     *b. devour* without an NP complement:
        *The child devoured.

## 5.2.1  Complement options for verbs

Table 5.5 illustrates some of the more common complement options for verbs in English. The subscripted prepositions indicate subtypes of PP complements, where this is relevant. *Loc* stands for any preposition expressing a location (such as *near*, *on*, and *under*).

The verbs in the first line of table 5.5 (*vanish*, *arrive*, and *die*) occur without any complement, those in the second line occur with an NP complement, and so on.

| **Table 5.5**    Some examples of verb complements | | |
|---|---|---|
| **Complement option** | **Sample heads** | **Example** |
| Ø | vanish, arrive, die | The rabbit vanished __. |
| NP | devour, cut, prove | The professor proved [NP *the theorem*]. |
| AP | be, become | The man became [AP *very angry*]. |
| PP$_{to}$ | dash, talk, refer | The dog dashed [PP *to the door*]. |
| NP NP | spare, hand, give | We handed [NP *the man*] [NP *a map*]. |
| NP PP$_{to}$ | hand, give, send | He gave [NP *a diploma*] [PP *to the student*]. |
| NP PP$_{for}$ | buy, cook, reserve | We bought [NP *a hat*] [PP *for Andy*]. |
| NP PP$_{loc}$ | put, place, stand | He put [NP *the muffler*] [PP *on the car*]. |
| PP$_{to}$ PP$_{about}$ | talk, speak | I talked [PP *to a doctor*] [PP *about Sue*]. |
| NP PP$_{for}$ PP$_{with}$ | open, fix | We opened [NP *the door*] [PP *for Andy*] [PP *with a crowbar*]. |

A word can belong to more than one subcategory. The verb *eat*, for example, can occur either with or without an NP complement and therefore belongs to both of the first two subcategories in our table.

(19)  After getting home, they ate (the sandwiches).

Of course, not all verbs exhibit this flexibility. As we have already seen, *devour*—although similar in meaning to *eat*—requires an NP complement and therefore belongs only to the second subcategory in our table.

As the examples in table 5.5 also show, some heads can take more than one complement. The verb *put* is a case in point, since it requires both an NP complement and a PP complement (or a locative adverb such as *there*).

(20)  *put* with an NP complement and a PP complement:
      The librarian put [<sub>NP</sub> the book] [<sub>PP</sub> on the shelf].

(21)  *put* without an NP complement:
      *The librarian put [<sub>PP</sub> on the shelf].

(22)  *put* without a PP complement:
      *The librarian put [<sub>NP</sub> the book].

The VP *put the book on the shelf* has the structure in figure 5.10, in which the V' consists of the head *put* and its two complements—the NP *the book* and the PP *on the shelf*.

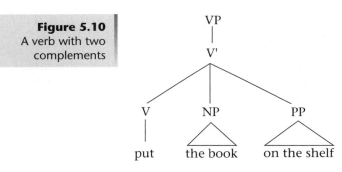

**Figure 5.10**
A verb with two complements

## 5.2.2  Complement options for other categories

Various complement options are also available for Ns, As, and Ps. Tables 5.6, 5.7, and 5.8 provide examples of just some of the possibilities.

| Table 5.6 | Some examples of noun complements | |
|---|---|---|
| **Complement option** | **Sample heads** | **Example** |
| Ø | car, boy, electricity | the car __ |
| PP<sub>of</sub> | memory, failure, death | the memory [<sub>PP</sub> *of a friend*] |
| PP<sub>of</sub> PP<sub>to</sub> | presentation, description, donation | the presentation [<sub>PP</sub> *of a medal*] [<sub>PP</sub> *to the winner*] |
| PP<sub>with</sub> PP<sub>about</sub> | argument, discussion, conversation | an argument [<sub>PP</sub> *with Stella*] [<sub>PP</sub> *about politics*] |

| Table 5.7 | Some examples of adjective complements | |
|---|---|---|
| **Complement option** | **Sample heads** | **Example** |
| Ø | tall, green, smart | very tall __ |
| PP$_{about}$ | curious, glad, angry | curious [$_{PP}$ *about China*] |
| PP$_{to}$ | apparent, obvious | obvious [$_{PP}$ *to the student*] |
| PP$_{of}$ | fond, full, tired | fond [$_{PP}$ *of chocolate*] |

| Table 5.8 | Some examples of preposition complements | |
|---|---|---|
| **Complement option** | **Sample heads** | **Example** |
| Ø | near, away, down | (he got) down __ |
| NP | in, on, by, near | in [$_{NP}$ *the house*] |
| PP | down, up, out | down [$_{PP}$ *into the cellar*] |

Here again, subcategorization ensures that particular heads can appear in tree structures only if there is an appropriate type of complement. Thus, the adjective *sick* takes an '*of*-PP' as its complement, while the adjective *satisfied* takes a '*with*-PP'.

(23)  *a.* sick [$_{PP}$ of cafeteria food] (compare: *sick with cafeteria food)
       *b.* satisfied [$_{PP}$ with cafeteria food] (compare: *satisfied of cafeteria food)

A good deal of what we know about our language consists of information about words and the type of complements with which they can appear. Much of this information must be stored in the lexicon, since it cannot be predicted from a word's meaning.

## 5.2.3 Complement clauses

All human languages allow sentence-like constructions to function as complements. A simple example of this from English is given in (24).

(24)                         ⌒ complement clause ⌒
     [The coach knows [that/whether/if the team will win]].
     ⌣———————————— matrix clause ————————————⌣

The smaller bracketed phrase in (24) is called a **complement clause**; the larger phrase in which it occurs is called the **matrix clause**.

Words such as *that*, *whether*, and *if* are known as **complementizers** (**C**s). They take an IP complement, forming the CP (complementizer phrase) depicted in figure 5.11.

Given our X' schema, we must also ask about a possible specifier position for CP. As we will see in section 5.3.2, there is even a type of element that can occur in the specifier position under CP.

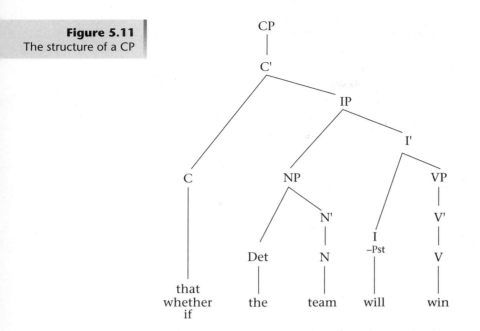

**Figure 5.11**
The structure of a CP

When a CP occurs in a sentence such as (24), in which it serves as complement of the verb *know*, the entire sentence has the structure in figure 5.12.

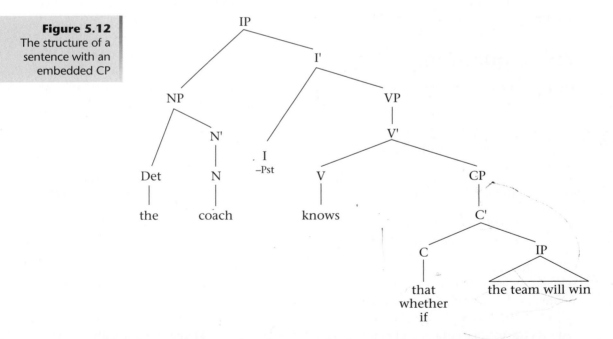

**Figure 5.12**
The structure of a sentence with an embedded CP

Table 5.9 provides examples of some verbs that are often found with a CP complement.

There is no limit on the number of embedded clauses that can occur in a sentence, as (25) helps show.

**(25)** A man thought [$_{CP}$ that a woman said [$_{CP}$ that Sue reported [$_{CP}$ that . . .

| Table 5.9 | Some verbs permitting CP complements | |
|---|---|---|
| **Complement(s)** | **Sample heads** | **Example** |
| CP | believe, know, think, remember | They believe [$_{CP}$ *that Eric left*]. |
| NP CP | persuade, tell, convince, promise | They told [$_{NP}$ *Mary*] [$_{CP}$ *that Eric had left*]. |
| PP$_{to}$ CP | concede, admit | They admitted [$_{PP}$ *to Mary*] [$_{CP}$ *that Eric had left*]. |

This structure is made possible by the fact that any CP can contain a verb that itself takes a complement CP. The first clause contains the verb *think*, whose complement clause contains the verb *say*, whose complement clause contains *report*, and so on.

## 5.3 Move

As we have seen, it is possible to build a very large number of different sentences by allowing the Merge operation to combine words and phrases in accordance with the X' schema and the subcategorization properties of individual words. Nonetheless, there are still many sentences that we cannot build. This section considers two such patterns and discusses the sentence-building operation needed to accommodate them.

### 5.3.1 *Yes-no* questions

To begin, let us consider the question sentences exemplified in (26). (Such structures are called *yes-no* **questions** because the expected response is usually 'yes' or 'no'.)

(26)  a. *Should* that guy go?
     b. *Can* the cat climb this tree?

A curious feature of these sentences is that the auxiliary verb occurs at the beginning of the sentence rather than in its more usual position to the right of the subject, as illustrated in (27).

(27)  a. That guy *should* go.
     b. The cat *can* climb this tree.

Given that auxiliary verbs such as *should* and *can* are instances of the I category, the X' schema dictates that they should occur between the subject NP and the VP, as depicted in figure 5.13 on page 163.

How, then, does the word order in (26) come about? The formation of question structures requires the use of a structure-building operation that we can call **Move**. Traditionally known as a **transformation** because it transforms an existing structure, Move transports the auxiliary verb in the I position to a new position to the left of the subject.

(28)  Should that guy _ go?

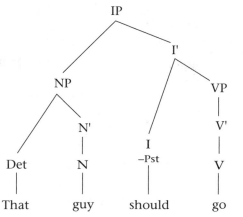

**Figure 5.13**
*Should* occurring in
the head position
between the subject
(its specifier) and the
VP (its complement)

The transformational analysis has at least two advantages. First, it allows us to avoid positing two types of auxiliary verbs in English: one that occurs between the subject and the VP and one that occurs to the left of the subject. Under the transformational analysis, there is just one type of auxiliary. Auxiliaries that occur to the left of the subject simply undergo an 'extra' process—the Move operation that transports the I category to the left of the subject in order to signal a question.

Second, the transformational analysis automatically captures the fact that the sentence *Should that guy go?* is the question structure corresponding to *That guy should go*. According to the analysis presented here, both sentences initially have the same basic structure. They differ only in that the Move operation has applied to the I category in the question structure.

## A landing site for I

In what position does the auxiliary verb 'land' when it is moved to the left of the subject? This question can be answered if we assume that IPs occur within larger CPs, as depicted in figure 5.14.

By adopting this structure, we take the position that all IPs occur within a CP, whether they are embedded or not. It may help to think of the CP category as a 'shell' that forms an

**Figure 5.14**
An IP inside a CP 'shell'

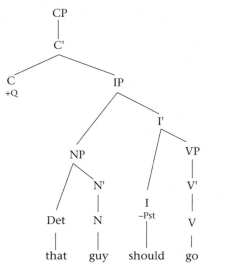

outer layer of structure around an IP. When embedded within a larger sentence, the CP can contain an overt complementizer such as *that* or *whether*. Elsewhere, the C position simply contains information about whether the sentence is a statement or a question. For the sake of illustration, we use the symbol '+Q' to indicate a question; sentences with no such symbol in their C position will be interpreted as statements.

In some languages, the Q feature is 'spelled out' as a separate morpheme (see page 165). In languages like English, where there is no such morpheme, the feature must attract another element to its position. The auxiliary verb in the I position is that element. This is illustrated in figure 5.15, where the Q feature in the C position attracts the auxiliary verb in the I position, causing it to move to the beginning of the sentence.

**Figure 5.15**
Movement of an auxiliary from the I position to C

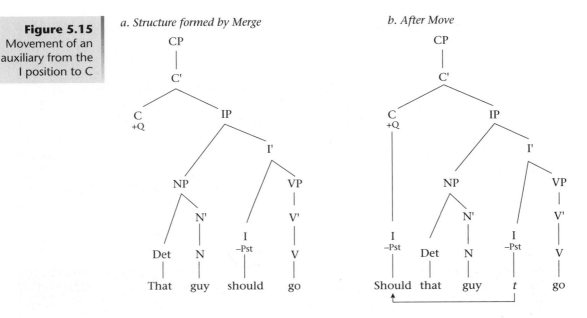

A transformation (i.e., a Move operation) can do no more than change an element's position. It does not change the categories of any words and it cannot eliminate any part of the structure created by the Merge operation. Thus, *should* retains its I label even though it is moved into the C position, and the position that it formerly occupied remains in the tree structure. Called a **trace** and marked by the symbol *t*, it records the fact that the moved element comes from the head position within IP.

The Move operation used for *yes-no* questions is often informally called **Inversion** and is formulated as follows.

(29)  Inversion:
      Move I to C.

Is there any way to be sure that this idea is on the right track and that the auxiliary verb in the I position really does move to the C position? Some interesting evidence comes from the analysis of the embedded CPs in sentences such as the following.

(30)  He asked [₍CP₎ whether we would return].

Notice that the C position in the embedded clause is occupied by the complementizer *whether*. Assuming that no more than one word can occur in a particular position, we predict that Inversion should not be able to apply in the embedded clause since there is nowhere for the moved auxiliary verb to land. The ungrammaticality of (31) shows that this is correct.

(31)    Inversion in an embedded CP that includes a complementizer:
      *He asked [<sub>CP</sub> whether would we *t* return].

Interestingly, the acceptability of Inversion improves quite dramatically when there is no complementizer and the C position is therefore open to receive the moved auxiliary. (In fact, such sentences are perfectly acceptable in Appalachian English. For other English speakers, they may sound most natural when the embedded clause is interpreted as a sort of quote.)

(32)    Inversion in an embedded CP that does not have a complementizer:
      He asked [<sub>CP</sub> would we *t* return].

Although some speakers prefer not to apply Inversion in embedded clauses at all (especially in formal speech), most speakers of English find (32) to be much more natural than (31). This is just what we would expect if Inversion moves the auxiliary to an empty C position, as required by our analysis.

To summarize before continuing, we have introduced two changes into the system of syntactic analysis used until now. First, we assume that all IPs occur inside CPs. Second, we assume that the Inversion transformation moves the auxiliary from the I position to an empty C position to the left of the subject NP. This not only gives the correct word order for question structures, it also helps explain why inversion sounds so unnatural when the C position is already filled by another element, as in (31).

## Language Matters  **Another Way to Ask a *Yes-No* Question**

Although inversion is a widely used question-marking strategy in the world's language, many languages go about things in an entirely different way. Instead of moving a verb to the C position, they place a special question morpheme there to begin with. Japanese and Tamil (a Dravidian language of India) work that way. (The diacritic ˌ indicates a dental point of articulation; the diacritic ˉ marks a long vowel; ḷ is a retroflex liquid.)

| Japanese | Tamil |
|---|---|
| Hiro-ga kimasu-ka? | Muṭṭu paḷam parittān-ā. |
| Hiro-Nom come-Ques | Muttu    fruit picked-Ques |
| Did Hiro come? | 'Did Muttu pick the fruit?' |

The C position in both languages occurs at the end of the sentence, since they employ the 'mirror-image' X' scheme discussed in section 5.1.2.

## 5.3.2 **Deep structure and surface structure**

The preceding examples show that at least some sentences must be analyzed with the help of two distinct types of mechanisms. The first of these is the Merge operation, which creates tree structures by combining categories in a manner consistent with their subcategorization properties and the X' schema. The second is the Move operation, which can modify these tree structures by moving an element from one position to another. The process whereby a syntactic structure is formed by these operations is called a **derivation**.

In traditional work in transformational syntax, all instances of the Merge operation take place before any instances of the Move operation. As a result, the derivation for a sentence typically yields two distinct levels of syntactic structure, as shown in figure 5.16. The first, called **deep structure** (or **D-structure**), is formed by the Merge operation in accordance with the X' schema and the subcategorization properties of the individual words making up the sentence. As we will see in the chapter on semantics, deep structure plays a special role in the interpretation of sentences.

The second level of syntactic structure corresponds to the final syntactic form of the sentence. Called **surface structure** (or **S-structure**), it results from applying whatever other operations are appropriate for the sentence in question.

| | |
|---|---|
| **Figure 5.16**<br>How a derivation works | Merge     (in accordance with the X'<br>↓     schema and subcategorization)<br>DEEP STRUCTURE<br>↓<br>Move<br>↓<br>SURFACE STRUCTURE |

## 5.3.3 *Do* Insertion

As we have just seen, formation of *yes-no* questions in English involves moving the I category, and the auxiliary verb that it contains, to the C position. How, then, do we form the questions corresponding to sentences such as those in (33), which contain no auxiliary verb?

(33) *a.* The students liked the movie.
    *b.* Those birds sing.

Since the I category in these sentences contains only an abstract tense marker (see figure 5.17a), applying the Inversion transformation would have no visible effect and there would be no indication that the sentence was being used as a question. English circumvents this problem by adding the special auxiliary verb *do*.

(34) *a. Did* the students like the movie?
    *b. Do* those birds sing?

As these examples show, *do* is inserted into sentences that do not already have an auxiliary verb, thereby making Inversion possible. We can capture this fact by formulating an **insertion rule** that adds an element to a tree structure.

(35) *Do* Insertion

Insert interrogative *do* into an empty I position.

The sentence in (34b) can now be analyzed as shown in figure 5.17b.

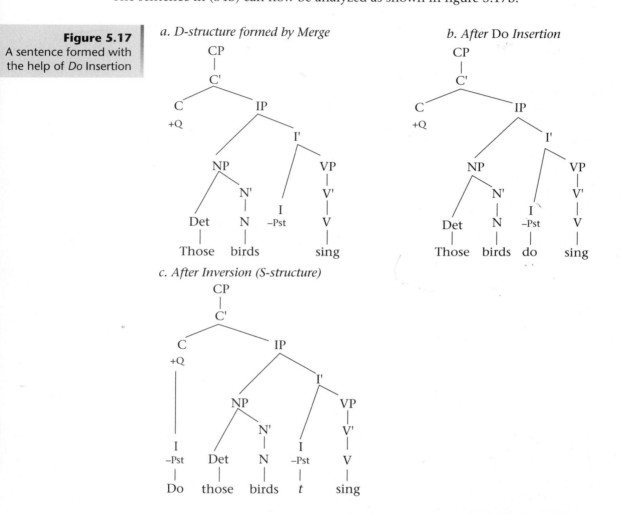

**Figure 5.17**
A sentence formed with the help of *Do* Insertion

*a. D-structure formed by Merge*

*b. After* Do *Insertion*

*c. After Inversion (S-structure)*

As these tree structures show, the sentence *Do those birds sing?* is built in three steps. In the initial step, the Merge operation interacts with the X' schema to give the D-structure in figure 5.17a, which contains no auxiliary verb in the I position. The *Do* Insertion rule then adds the special interrogative auxiliary *do*, creating an intermediate level of structure in figure 5.17b. The Move operation then moves I to the C position, creating the sentence's S-structure in figure 5.17c.

## 5.3.4 *Wh* Movement

Consider now the set of question constructions exemplified in (36). These sentences are called **wh questions** because of the presence of a question word beginning with *wh*.

(36) *a.* Which languages could Aristotle speak?

*b.* What can the child sit on?

There is reason to believe that the *wh* elements at the beginning of these sentences have been moved there from the positions indicated in figure 5.18. (We take the question word *which* to be a determiner and *what* to be a noun in these sentences.)

**Figure 5.18**
D-structures depicting the original positions of the *wh* expressions in (36)

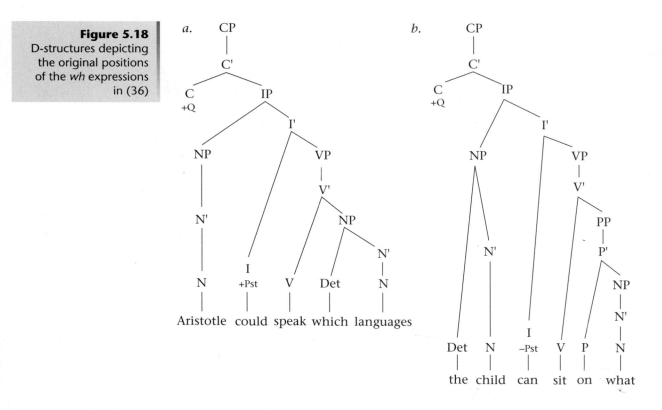

Notice that *which languages* occurs as complement of the verb *speak* while *what* appears as complement of the preposition *on*, in accordance with the subcategorization requirements of these words. As the sentences in (37) show, both *speak* and *on* commonly occur with an NP complement.

(37)  *a.* Aristotle could speak *Greek*.
      *b.* The child can sit on *the bench*.

The structures in figure 5.18 capture this fact by treating the *wh* phrase as complement of the verb in the first pattern and complement of the preposition in the second.

How then do the *wh* phrases end up at the beginning of the sentence? The answer is that they are attracted there by the Q feature, which results in the application of a second Move operation. (Recall that we have already posited one Move operation, which we have been calling Inversion.)

(38)  Which languages could Aristotle *t* speak *t*?

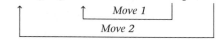

Application of the same two transformations to the structure in figure 5.18b yields the *wh* question in (39).

(39) Movement of the NP *what*:
[_NP_ What] can the child *t* sit on *t*?

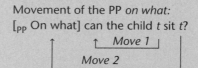

---

## Language Matters **Pied Piping**

In more formal varieties of English, there is a second possibility—the *wh* word can take the preposition with it when it moves.

Movement of the PP *on what:*
[_PP_ On what] can the child *t* sit *t*?

*Move 1*
*Move 2*

This phenomenon is known as 'pied-piping', a whimsical reference to *The Pied Piper of Hamelin* folk tale, in which (in the words of Robert Browning) "the Piper advanced and the children followed."

## A landing site for *wh* words

As the examples in (38) and (39) help illustrate, the Move operation carries the *wh* phrase to the beginning of the sentence, to the left even of the fronted auxiliary. But where precisely does the *wh* phrase land?

Given that the moved auxiliary is located in the C position (see figure 5.15 above, for example), it seems reasonable to conclude that the fronted *wh* phrase ends up in the specifier position of CP. Not only is this the only position in syntactic structure to the left of the C, it is empty prior to the application of the Move operation.

We can make this idea precise by formulating the Move operation that applies to *wh* phrases as follows.

(40) ***Wh* Movement:**
Move a *wh* phrase to the specifier position under CP.

The sentence *Which languages could Aristotle speak?* can now be analyzed in steps, the first of which involves formation of the structure in figure 5.19 on page 170 by the Merge operation. Consistent with our earlier assumption, the IP here occurs within a CP shell. *Wh* Movement and Inversion then apply to this structure, yielding the structure in figure 5.20.

Like other transformations, *Wh* Movement cannot eliminate any part of the previously formed structure. The position initially occupied by the *wh* phrase is therefore not lost. Rather, it remains as a trace (an empty category), indicating that the moved element corresponds to the complement of the verb *speak*.

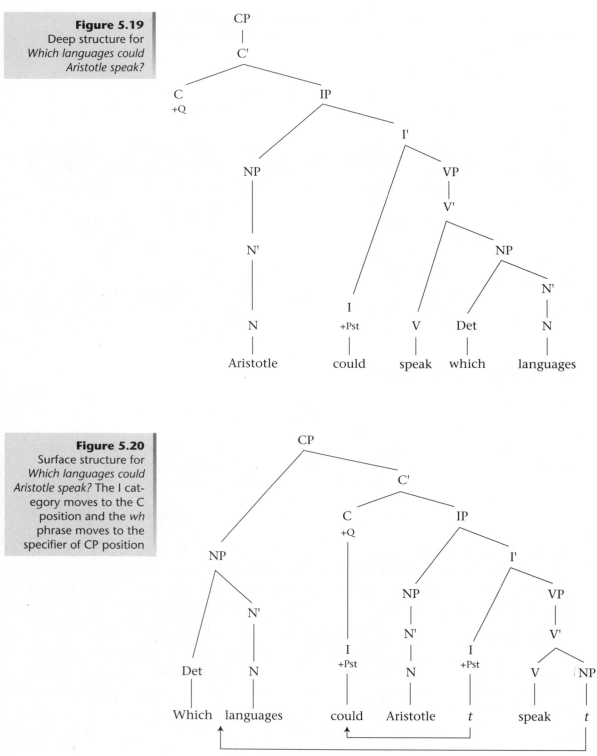

In the examples considered so far, the *wh* word originates as the complement of a verb or preposition. In sentences such as the following, however, the *wh* word asks about the subject (the person who does the criticizing).

**(41)** Who criticized Maxwell?

In such patterns, the *wh* word originates in the subject position and subsequently moves to the specifier position within CP even though the actual order of the words in the sentence does not change as a result of this movement (see figure 5.21). (For reasons that are not fully understood, there is no *Do* Insertion in this type of question structure, except for purposes of emphasis, as in *Who DID criticize Maxwell?*)

**Figure 5.21**
Movement of a subject *wh* word. Since there is nothing for the *wh* word to move over in such cases, there is no visible change in word order.

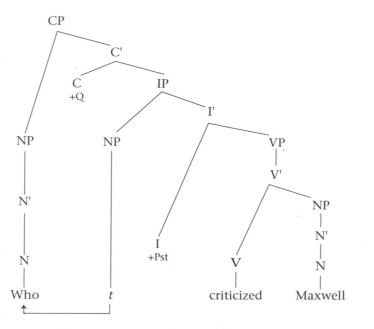

 For more about Move, and particularly about limits on its operation, go to **www. pearsoned.ca/ogrady**.

---

### Language Matters *Wh* Questions without Movement

In many languages, *wh* words are ambiguous between an interrogative sense ('who', 'what', 'when', etc.) and an indefinite sense ('someone/anyone', 'something/anything', 'sometime/anytime', etc.) Mandarin Chinese works that way—*shei* can mean either 'who' or 'anyone', *shenme* can mean either 'what' or 'anything', and so on. Many languages of this type do not make use of *wh* movement. The *wh* word remains in its 'original' position; instead, intonation is used to signal that the sentence is intended as a *wh* question.

| Ni | mai-le | **shenme?** | Wo | bu | xiang | mai | **shenme** |
|----|--------|-------------|-----|-----|-------|-----|------------|
| you | buy-Asp | what | I | not | want | buy | anything |
| 'What did you buy?' | | | 'I don't want to buy anything.' | | | | |

## 5.4 ▮ Universal grammar and parametric variation

Thus far, our discussion has focused on English. Before looking at any further phenomena in this language, it is important to extend the scope of our analysis to other languages.

As noted at the beginning of this chapter, recent work on Universal Grammar suggests that all languages are fundamentally alike with respect to the basics of syntax. For instance, all languages use the Merge operation to combine words on the basis of their syntactic category and subcategorization properties, creating phrases that comply with the X' schema.

This does not mean that languages must be alike in all respects, though. Universal Grammar leaves room for variation, allowing individual languages to differ with respect to certain **parameters**. (You can think of a parameter as the set of options that UG permits for a particular phenomenon.) The next section presents an example of this that involves the Move operation. Some additional instances of cross-linguistic differences in syntax are considered at **www.pearsoned.ca/ogrady** and in section 9.2.3 of chapter 9.

### 5.4.1   Verb Raising

Consider the contrast between the following two English sentences.

> (42)  *a.*  Paul always works.
>        *b.*  *Paul works always.

The ungrammaticality of the second sentence is expected since the preverbal adverb *always* functions as specifier of the verb and therefore should occur to its left, as in (42a). Surprisingly, however, the equivalent adverb must follow the verb in French, even though specifiers in French normally precede the head, just as they do in English.

> (43)  *a.*  The adverb precedes the verb; the sentence is ungrammatical:
>             *Paul toujours travaille. (= English (42a))
>             Paul always work.
>             'Paul always works.'
>
>        *b.*  The adverb follows the verb; the sentence is grammatical:
>             Paul travaille toujours. (= English (42b))
>             Paul work always
>             'Paul always works.'

Why should this be? One possibility is that the tense feature in the I category attracts the verb to that position in French, just as the Q feature can attract verbs to the C position in some languages. As a result, French has the Verb Raising transformation outlined in (44). (It's called 'Raising' because the verb moves upward in the tree.)

> (44)  *Verb Raising*
>        Move V to I.

This Move operation brings about the change depicted in figure 5.22.

An important piece of independent evidence for the existence of Verb Raising in French comes from the operation of the Inversion transformation. As we have already seen

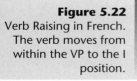

**Figure 5.22**
Verb Raising in French. The verb moves from within the VP to the I position.

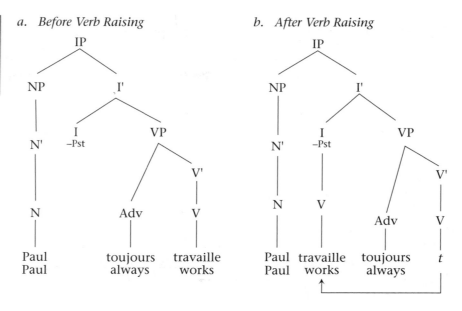

(section 5.3.1), this transformation moves the I category to the C position. In English only auxiliary verbs occur in the I position, which explains why only they can undergo Inversion.

(45)   *a.*   Inversion of an auxiliary verb in English:

Will you  *t*  stay for supper?

*b.*   Inversion of a non-auxiliary verb in English:

*Stay you  *t*  for supper?

In French, however, regular verbs can occur in the I position, thanks to the Verb Raising transformation. This predicts that Inversion should be able to apply to these Vs in French as well as to auxiliaries. This is correct. Like English, French can form a question by moving an auxiliary leftward, as (46) illustrates.

(46)   Inversion of an auxiliary:

As-tu  *t*  essayé?

'Have you tried?'

However, unlike English, French also allows inversion of non-auxiliary Vs.

(47)   Inversion of a non-auxiliary verb:

Vois-tu *t*  le livre?

see  you the book
'Do you see the book?'

Figure 5.23 depicts the interaction between Verb Raising and Inversion needed to form this sentence. As you can see, the V first raises to the I position, and the I category then moves to the C position. (We treat the pronoun *tu* 'you' as a type of N.)

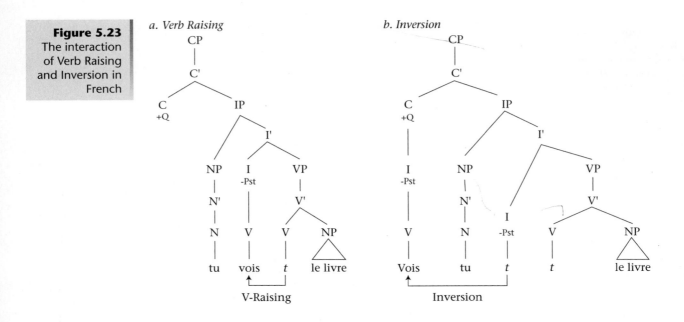

**Figure 5.23**
The interaction of Verb Raising and Inversion in French

## Verb Raising in English

At this point, it might seem that there is a simple Verb Raising parameter with two options—raising (as in French) and no raising (as in English). This neatly accounts for the facts that we have considered so far, but matters are not so simple. As we'll see next, Verb Raising can apply in English, but only to *have* and *be*.

To begin, consider the sentences in (48), which contain two auxiliaries—one modal and one non-modal.

(48)  *a.* The children should have waited.
      *b.* Those guys could be sleeping.

As we have already seen, the modal auxiliary occurs under I, but what of the non-modal auxiliary? As depicted in figure 5.24 opposite, it is considered to be a special type of V that takes a VP complement.

As expected, only the modal auxiliary can undergo inversion in this structure.

(49)  *a.* The modal auxiliary verb moves to the C position:
         [_CP Should [_IP the children *t* have waited]]

      *b.* The non-modal auxiliary moves to the C position:
         *[_CP Have [_IP the children should *t* waited]]

Crucially, however, a non-modal auxiliary can undergo Inversion when there is no modal auxiliary in the sentence.

(50)  *a.* Have the children *t* waited for two hours?

         (from: The children have waited for two hours)

      *b.* Is the dog *t* sleeping?

         (from: The dog is sleeping)

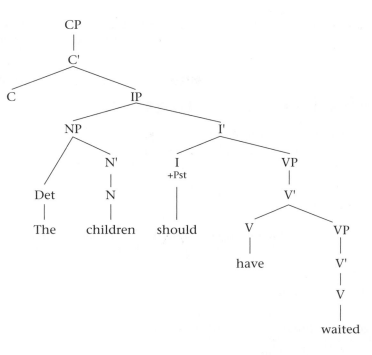

**Figure 5.24**
A structure containing two auxiliary verbs. The modal auxiliary is treated as an instance of the I category, which takes the VP headed by *have* as its complement. *Have* in turn is a V that takes the VP headed by *wait* as its complement.

Since Inversion involves movement from I to C, the auxiliary in (50a, b) must have moved to the I position, as depicted in figure 5.25—an instance of the same V Raising operation that is used more generally in French. Once in the I position, it can undergo inversion (I-to-C movement), giving the question structure.

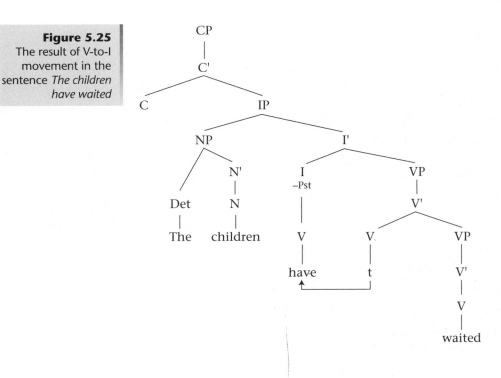

**Figure 5.25**
The result of V-to-I movement in the sentence *The children have waited*

In sum, then, it appears that the two options permitted by the Verb Raising parameter are: (a) any type of verb raises (the case in French), and (b) only auxiliary verbs raise (the case in English).

## 5.5 Some additional structures

Now that we have in place a basic system for forming sentences, it is possible to extend it to encompass various other syntactic phenomena. We will consider three such phenomena here.

## 5.5.1 Coordination

A common syntactic phenomenon in English and other languages involves **coordination**—the grouping together of two or more categories with the help of a conjunction such as *and* or *or*.

(51) coordination involving NPs:
[$_{NP}$ the man] and [$_{NP}$ a child]

(52) coordination involving VPs:
[$_{VP}$ go to the library] and [$_{VP}$ read a book]

(53) coordination involving PPs:
[$_{PP}$ down the stairs] and [$_{PP}$ out the door]

Coordination exhibits several important properties, three of which will be considered here. First, a category at any level (a head, an X', or an entire XP) can be coordinated. The preceding examples illustrate coordination of XPs; following are examples involving word-level and X'-level categories.

(54) coordination involving Ps:
[$_{P}$ up] and [$_{P}$ down] the stairs

(55) coordination involving Vs:
[$_{V}$ repair] and [$_{V}$ paint] the deck.

(56) coordination involving V's:
never [$_{V'}$ drink alcohol] and [$_{V'}$ drive a car]

Second, the category of the coordinate structure must be identical to the category of the elements being conjoined. Hence, if NPs are conjoined, the coordinate structure is an NP; if V's are conjoined, the coordinate structure is a V'; if Ps are conjoined, the coordinate structure is a P; and so on (see figure 5.26).

Third, conjoined categories are usually of the same type—they must both be NPs, or V's, or Ps; and so on. As (57) shows, coordination that involves different categories generally gives a quite unnatural result.

(57) *a.* coordination involving an NP and a PP:
*He read [$_{NP}$ the book] and [$_{PP}$ in the library]

*b.* coordination involving an NP and an AP:
*He left [$_{NP}$ the house] and [$_{AP}$ very angry]

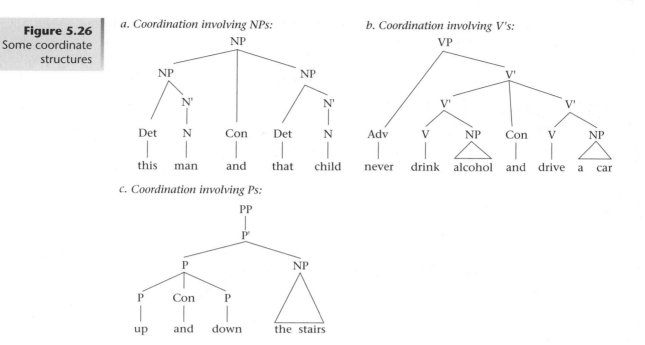

**Figure 5.26**
Some coordinate
structures

We can accommodate these facts if we assume that the X' schema is supplemented by the coordination schema depicted in figure 5.27.

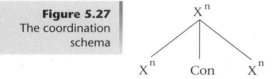

**Figure 5.27**
The coordination
schema

The superscripted symbol $^n$ stands for a category at any structural level, indicating that a coordinate structure can involve Xs, X's, or XPs. Moreover, because the same symbol (X) is used both for the categories that are conjoined and for the larger resulting phrase, we also neatly capture the fact that the conjoined elements and the resulting phrase must all be of the same type.

## 5.5.2  Modifiers

Another important syntactic phenomenon involves the use of **modifiers**—words and phrases that denote properties of heads. For example, adjective phrases (APs) commonly serve as modifiers of Ns, while adverb phrases (AdvPs) modify Vs.

(58)  *a.* The [$_{AP}$ very tall] man walked into the room.
    *b.* The guests left [$_{AdvP}$ rather quickly].

The AP *very tall* denotes a property of the man, while the AdvP describes the manner in which the guests left.

How do modifiers fit into phrase structure? For the purposes of this introduction to syntax, we will attach modifiers at the XP level of phrase structure, as sister of X'. As illustrated in figure 5.28, adjectival phrases occur on the left side of the head, while most adverbial phrases occur on the right side.

<table>
<tr><td>

**Figure 5.28**
Phrases containing modifiers

</td><td>

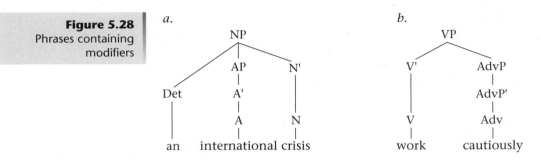

</td></tr>
</table>

Where there is a complement, a modifier that occurs after the head will normally occur to the right of the complement as well. This is to be expected: as illustrated in figure 5.29, the head and the complement are grouped together within the X' constituent, leaving no room for a modifier, which attaches at a higher level, to intervene between them.

<table>
<tr><td>

**Figure 5.29**
A phrase in which both the complement and the modifier occur after the head. In such cases, the modifier occurs after the complement.

</td><td>

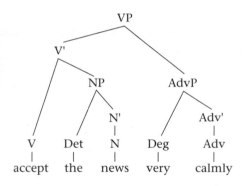

</td></tr>
</table>

## 5.5.3  Passives

Another important syntactic phenomenon involves the relationship between particular types of sentences. A famous example of this involves sentences such as the following. (The first type of sentence is called **active** because the subject denotes the 'agent' or 'instigator' of the action denoted by the verb, while the second type is called **passive**.)

(59)  *a.* A thief stole the painting. (active sentence)
       *b.* The painting was stolen (by a thief). (passive sentence)

We will focus here on three key properties of passive constructions.

First, passive constructions involve a major reduction in the importance of the agent. Indeed, whereas the agent serves as subject of an active clause, it is not expressed at all in the vast majority of passive sentences in English.

(60)  The painting was stolen.

When it does appear, as in (59b), it is relegated to a position inside a PP at or near the end of the sentence.

Second, some other NP—usually the direct object of the corresponding active sentence—functions as subject in the passive sentence. This can be seen in example (59) on page 178, where the NP *the painting* serves as direct object in the active sentence and as subject in the passive sentence.

Third, and related to the second point, verbs that cannot occur with a direct object NP in an active sentence typically cannot occur in a passive sentence. Take the verb *arrive*, for instance. It cannot be used with an NP complement in an active sentence, nor can it occur in a passive sentence.

(61)  *a. Arrive* with an NP complement in an active sentence:
　　　　　　 *The waiter arrived the dinner.

　　  *b. Arrive* in a passive sentence:
　　　　　　 *The dinner was arrived (by the waiter).

The D-structure for a passive sentence such as *The painting was stolen* is depicted in figure 5.30. (Note that the auxiliary *be* is treated as a V that takes a VP complement. To save space, we drop the CP level here. We include an empty specifier position under IP to capture the fact that all sentences require a subject.)

**Figure 5.30**
D-structure for *The painting was stolen (by the thief)*

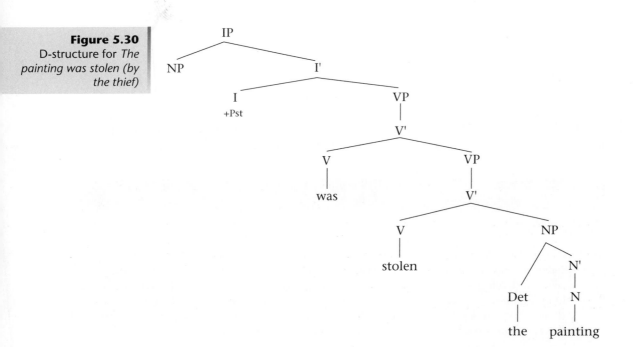

This D-structure is admittedly abstract—it does not sound like any sentence that we actually utter. However, it does neatly capture the first and third properties of passive constructions: the agent is not expressed, and the verb occurs with a direct object. (When the agent is expressed as a PP (e.g., *by a thief* ), it is attached to the V' headed by *stolen*.)

This leaves just the second property to be accounted for—the NP that functions as direct object in the active sentence becomes the subject in the passive. This is accomplished by moving the direct object NP to the subject position. The Move operation needed to bring about this result can be stated as follows.

**(62)** *NP Movement*
  Move NP into the subject position.

This gives the S-structure depicted in figure 5.31. (Note that *be* also raises to I for the reasons discussed in section 5.4.1.)

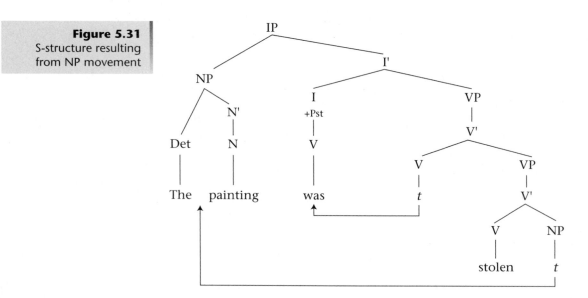

**Figure 5.31**
S-structure resulting from NP movement

  The website provides additional information about passives and how other approaches to syntax deal with them; go to **www.pearsoned.ca/ogrady**.

---

# *Summing up*

**Universal Grammar** provides all languages with the same general type of syntactic mechanisms. As we have seen, this includes a **Merge** operation that combines words in accordance with their **syntactic category** and their **subcategorization** properties, creating a representation called **deep structure**. Deep structure must comply with the X' schema, which stipulates the place of **heads**, **specifiers**, and **complements** in phrase structure. **Move** operations (**transformations**) can modify deep structure by moving words and phrases in particular ways to produce a **surface structure**.

Although the form of sentences can vary considerably from language to language, such differences can for the most part be attributed to a small set of **parameters**, each of which makes available a variety of alternatives from which individual languages may choose.

## Notes

1   In order to abbreviate and simplify, linguists sometimes use tree structures such as the following in which the X' level has been eliminated, so that specifiers, heads, and complements are all attached at the XP level. Your instructor will decide whether this is appropriate in your class.

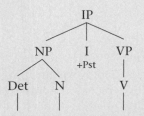

**Figure i**   A simplified sentence structure

## Recommended reading

Carnie, Andrew. 2006. *Syntax: A Generative Introduction*. 2nd ed. Cambridge, MA: Blackwell.
Haegeman, Liliane. 1994. *Introduction to Government and Binding Theory*. 2nd ed. Cambridge, MA: Blackwell.
Palmer, F.R. 1994. *Grammatical Roles and Relations*. New York: Cambridge University Press.
Payne, Thomas. 1997. *Describing Morphosyntax: A Guide for Field Linguists*. New York: Cambridge University Press.
Radford, Andrew. 1997. *Syntax: A Minimalist Introduction*. New York: Cambridge University Press.

## Appendix: how to build tree structures

In building a tree structure from scratch for a phrase or sentence that you are analyzing, you will probably find it easiest to proceed in steps, working from the bottom up and from right to left. As an illustration, let us first consider the phrase *near the door*.

The first step involves assigning each word to the appropriate category, as depicted in figure 5.32.

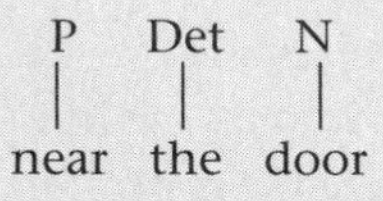

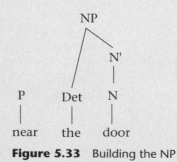

```
P    Det   N
|     |    |
near the  door
```

**Figure 5.32**   The first step: determining the word-level categories

Then, working from right to left, the appropriate phrasal structure (X' and XP) is built above each head. Thus, we first build an N' and an NP above the N *door*. There is clearly no complement here, but there is a specifier (the determiner *the*), which combines with the N' in accordance with the X' schema.

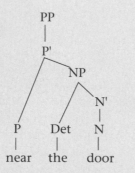

**Figure 5.33**   Building the NP

Next, we carry out the same procedure for the P *near*. The NP to the right of the P clearly functions as its complement, since it names the location entailed by the meaning of *near*. We therefore combine the P and the NP, forming the P' and PP depicted in figure 5.34.

**Figure 5.34**   The complete PP

## A sentential example

Consider now how we proceed in the case of a complete sentence such as *The dog might bite that man*. Assignment of each word to the appropriate category gives the structure depicted in figure 5.35.

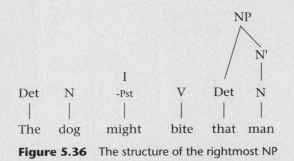

**Figure 5.35**   The categories for each word in the sentence

Working from right to left, it is easy to see that the noun *man* heads an NP that contains a specifier but no complement as depicted in figure 5.36.

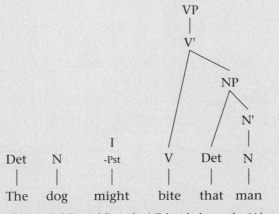

**Figure 5.36**   The structure of the rightmost NP

Next, we focus on the V *bite*, combining it with the complement NP *that man* and building the required V' and VP as depicted in figure 5.37.

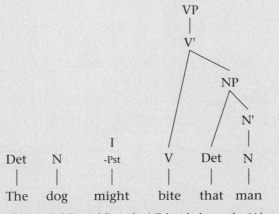

**Figure 5.37**   Adding the VP level above the V head

As an instance of the I category, the modal auxiliary *might* is the head of IP, with the VP to the right serving as its complement and the NP to the left functioning as its specifier. This yields the complete sentence illustrated in figure 5.38, which includes the CP 'shell'.

## Transformations

As explained in section 5.3, the syntactic analysis of some sentences involves the Move operation in addition to Merge. Recognizing that one of the transformations used in this

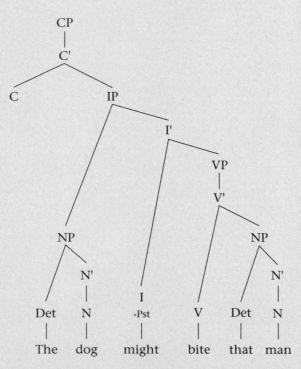

**Figure 5.38**   The sentence embedded in a CP shell

---

### Some things to remember!

- Every sentence contains a verb, so every tree you draw must have a VP.
- Every VP must be a complement of I, so every tree must have an I.
- The I position will be filled by a modal auxiliary (if there is one) and/or ± Pst.
- Every I will have an NP (the subject) in its specifier position.
- Every IP occurs inside a CP shell.

---

chapter has applied is relatively simple: if a sentence contains an auxiliary verb to the left of the subject, then Inversion has applied; if it begins with a *wh* word, then *Wh* Movement has applied. In the sentence *What should the farmers plant?*, then, both of these transformations have applied.

In order to determine the deep structure, we must 'return' the auxiliary verb to its position under I and we must determine the position from which the *wh* word has been moved. Since the *wh* word in the sentence *What should the farmers plant?* asks about the complement of the verb (the thing that is planted), we place *what* in the complement position within VP in deep structure. This gives the deep structure depicted in figure 5.39.

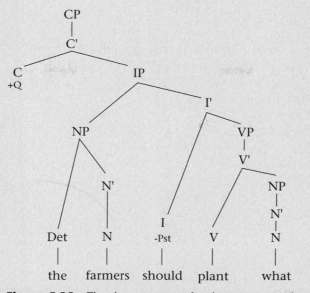

**Figure 5.39**   The deep structure for the sentence *What should the farmers plant?*

Attracted by the +Q feature, the auxiliary *should* then moves to the C position (Inversion) and *what* moves to the specifier position under CP (*Wh* Movement), yielding the complete surface structure depicted in figure 5.40.

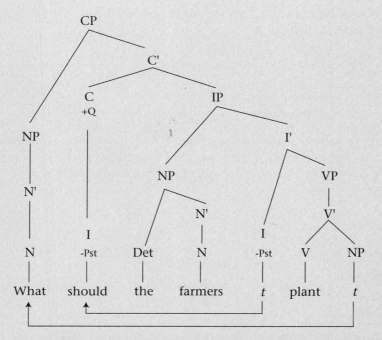

**Figure 5.40**   The surface structure for *What should the farmers plant?*

## Exercises

1. Place an asterisk next to any of the sentences that are ungrammatical for you. Can you figure out what makes these sentences ungrammatical?
   a) The instructor told the students to study.
   b) The instructor suggested the students to study.
   c) The customer asked for a cold beer.
   d) The customer requested for a cold beer.
   e) He gave the Red Cross some money.
   f) He donated the Red Cross some money.
   g) The pilot landed the jet.
   h) The jet landed.
   i) A journalist wrote the article.
   j) The article wrote.
   k) Jerome is satisfied of his job.
   l) Jerome is tired of his job.

2. Indicate the category of each word in the following sentences. (It may help to refer back to section 5.1.1.)
   a) That glass broke.
   b) A jogger ran toward the end of the lane.
   c) These tall trees are blocking the road.
   d) The detective looked through the records.
   e) The peaches never appear quite ripe.
   f) Jeremy will play the trumpet and the drums in the orchestra.

3. Each of the following phrases consists of a specifier and a head. Build a tree structure for each example that complies with the X' schema.
   a) the zoo            f) this house
   b) always try         g) very competent
   c) so witty           h) quite cheap
   d) perhaps pass       i) never surrender
   e) less bleak         j) those books

4. The following phrases include a head, a complement, and (in some cases) a specifier. Build a tree structure for each example that complies with the X' schema. For now, there is no need to depict the internal structure of complements. (See the tree diagrams in figure 5.5 in the chapter.)
   a) into the house
   b) fixed the telephone
   c) full of mistakes
   d) more towards the window
   e) a film about pollution
   f) always study this material
   g) perhaps earn the money
   h) that argument with Owen
   i) the success of the program

**5.** Drawing on the X' schema, create trees for each of the following sentences.
   a) Those guests should leave.
   b) Maria never ate a brownie.
   c) That shelf will fall.
   d) The glass broke.
   e) The student lost the debate.
   f) The manager may offer a raise.
   g) The judge often jails shoplifters.
   h) The teacher often organized a discussion.
   i) A psychic will speak to this group.
   j) Marianne could become quite fond of Larry.

**6.** Apply the substitution test to determine which of the bracketed sequences in the following sentences form constituents.
   a) [The news] upset the entire family.
   b) They hid [in the cave].
   c) The [computer was very] expensive.
   d) [The houses] will be rebuilt.
   e) Jane will [leave town].
   f) The goslings [swam across] the lake.

**7.** Apply the movement test to determine which of the bracketed sequences in the following sentences form constituents.
   a) We ate our lunch [near the river bank].
   b) Steve looked [up the number] in the book.
   c) The [island has been] flooded.
   d) I love [peanut butter and bacon sandwiches].
   e) The environmental [movement is gaining momentum].

**8.** Lexical categories are divided into subcategories on the basis of their complements. For each of the following words, two potential complement options are given. For each of the words:

   **i)** Determine which one of the two options better matches its subcategorization requirements.

   **ii)** Justify your choice by creating a sentence using that complement option.

| Verb | Options | | Verb | Options |
|------|---------|---|------|---------|
| a) expire | Ø *or* NP NP | | e) clean | NP $PP_{for}$ *or* NP NP |
| b) destroy | NP *or* Ø | | f) mumble | NP *or* NP NP |
| c) observe | NP *or* $PP_{to}$ $PP_{about}$ | | g) throw | Ø *or* NP $PP_{loc}$ |
| d) discuss | NP *or* Ø | | h) paint | NP $PP_{to}$ *or* NP $PP_{for}$ |

| Noun | Options |
|------|---------|
| i) debate | $PP_{of}$ $PP_{to}$ *or* $PP_{with}$ $PP_{about}$ |
| j) hammer | Ø *or* $PP_{with}$ $PP_{about}$ |
| k) success | $PP_{of}$ $PP_{to}$ *or* $PP_{of}$ |
| l) transfer | $PP_{with}$ $PP_{about}$ *or* $PP_{of}$ $PP_{to}$ |
| m) sickness | Ø *or* $PP_{with}$ $PP_{about}$ |

|              *Adjective*       | *Options*                              |
|--------------------------------|----------------------------------------|
| n) strong                      | Ø *or* $PP_{about}$                    |
| o) sick                        | NP *or* $PP_{of}$                      |
| p) bored                       | $PP_{with}$ *or* $PP_{of}$             |
| q) knowledgeable               | $PP_{to}$ *or* $PP_{about}$            |
| r) small                       | $PP_{of}$ *or* Ø                       |

**9.** The following sentences all contain embedded clauses that function as complements of a verb. Draw a tree structure for each sentence.
   a) The reporter said that an accident injured a woman.
   b) The fishermen think that the company polluted the bay.
   c) Bill reported that a student asked whether the eclipse would occur.

**10.** The derivations of the following sentences involve the Inversion transformation. Give the deep structure and the surface structure for each sentence.
   a) Will the boss hire Hillary?
   b) Can the dog fetch the frisbee?
   c) Should the student report the incident?
   d) Must the musicians play that sonata?
   e) Might that player leave the team?

**11.** The following sentences involve the rules of *Wh* Movement and Inversion. Draw the trees to show the deep structure and the surface structure for each of these sentences.
   a) Who should the director call?
   b) Who should call the director?
   c) What can Joanne eat?
   d) Who will the visitors stay with?
   e) What might Terry bake?
   f) What could Anne bring to the gathering?
   g) What did the lightning hit?

**12.** The following data illustrates the formation of *yes-no* questions in German.
   a) Das Kind wird die Schwester lehren.
      the child will the sister teach
      'The child will teach the sister.'
   b) Wird das Kind die Schwester lehren?
      will the child the sister teach
      'Will the child teach the sister?'
   c) Der Mann liebt die Frau.
      the man loves the woman
      'The man loves the woman.'
   d) Liebt der Mann die Frau?
      loves the man the woman
      'Does the man love the woman?'

Assuming that German makes uses of the same Inversion transformation as English (i.e., 'Move I to the C position'), does the above data tell us whether German employs the Verb Raising transformation?

**13.** The following sentences all contain coordinate phrases. Draw a tree structure for each sentence.

a) The cyclist drank a gallon of water and a litre of cola.

b) The airplane will land at the airport and taxi to the terminal.

c) The dog ran down the stairs and out the door.

d) Jill should recycle that book and magazine.

e) Hillary knows that spring will come and that the snow will melt.

f) Mary is fond of dogs but tired of the fleas.

William O'Grady

# CHAPTER Six

# *Semantics: the analysis of meaning*

*. . . in every object there is inexhaustible meaning.*

THOMAS CARLYLE

U p to now, this book has focused on the *form* of utterances—their sound pattern, morphological structure, and syntactic organization. But there is more to language than just form. In order for language to fulfill its communicative function, utterances must also convey a message; they must have content. Speaking very generally, we can refer to an utterance's content as its **meaning**.

This chapter is concerned with **semantics**, the study of meaning in human language. Because some work in this complicated area of linguistic analysis presupposes considerable knowledge of other disciplines (particularly logic, mathematics, and philosophy), not all aspects of contemporary semantics are suitable for presentation in an introductory linguistics textbook. We will restrict our attention here to four major topics in semantics: (1) the nature of meaning, (2) some of the properties of the conceptual system underlying meaning, (3) the contribution of syntactic structure to the interpretation of sentences, and (4) the role of non-grammatical factors in the understanding of utterances.

## 6.1 The nature of meaning

Long before linguistics existed as a discipline, thinkers were speculating about the nature of meaning. For thousands of years, this question has been considered central to philosophy; more recently, it has come to be important in other disciplines as well, including of course linguistics and psychology. Contributions to semantics have come from a diverse group of scholars, ranging from Plato and Aristotle in ancient Greece to Bertrand Russell in the twentieth century. Our goal in this section will be to consider in a very general way what this research has revealed about meaning in human language. We will begin by considering some of the basic analytic notions used in evaluating the meanings of words and sentences.

### 6.1.1 Semantic relations among words

Words and phrases can enter into a variety of semantic relations with each other. Because these relations help identify those aspects of meaning relevant to linguistic analysis, they constitute a good starting point for this chapter.

# Synonymy

**Synonyms** are words or expressions that have the same meaning in some or all contexts. The following pairs of words in table 6.1 provide plausible examples of synonymy in English.

| **Table 6.1** | Some synonyms in English |
|---|---|
| vacation | holidays |
| youth | adolescent |
| automobile | car |
| remember | recall |
| purchase | buy |
| big | large |

Because it would be inefficient for a language to have two words or phrases with absolutely identical meanings, perfect synonymy is rare, if not impossible. Words such as *vacation* and *holidays* may be interchangeable in particular contexts *(I spent my vacation/holidays in the Maritimes)*, but their meanings are not always identical. For example, Christmas and Canada Day are holidays, but they are not necessarily part of one's vacation. Similarly, although *youth* and *adolescent* both refer to people of about the same age, only the latter word can be used to imply immaturity—as in *What adolescent behaviour!*

# Antonymy

**Antonyms** are words or phrases that are opposites with respect to some component of their meaning. The pairs of words in table 6.2 provide examples of antonymy.

| **Table 6.2** | Some antonyms in English |
|---|---|
| dark | light |
| boy | girl |
| hot | cold |
| up | down |
| in | out |
| come | go |

In each of these pairs, the two words contrast with respect to at least one aspect of their meaning. For instance, the meanings of *boy* and *girl* are opposites with respect to gender, although they are alike in other respects (both are human). Similarly, *come* and *go* are opposites with respect to direction, although both involve the concept of movement.

> **Language Matters** **Hypernyms and Related Relations**
>
> There are also various less-known relations among words—such as the relationship between the word *dog* and the words for various types of dogs (*spaniel, collie, beagle,* etc.) The word for the general class (here, *dog*) is called the *hypernym*, whereas the words for the members of that class are its *hyponyms*. Of course, *dog* has a hypernym too—*animal*.
>
> *Meronyms* designate the parts of a whole, and a *holonym* is the whole to which parts belong. Meronyms for *dog* include *head, nose, paws, tail,* and so forth. Conversely, *dog* is the holonym for those parts.
>
> You can find a large online database of these relations at http://wordnet.princeton.edu.

## Polysemy and homophony

**Polysemy** occurs where a word has two or more related meanings. Table 6.3 contains some examples of polysemous words in English.

| **Table 6.3** | Some polysemy in English | |
|---|---|---|
| **Word** | **Meaning *a*** | **Meaning *b*** |
| bright | 'shining' | 'intelligent' |
| to glare | 'to shine intensely' | 'to stare angrily' |
| a deposit | 'minerals in the earth' | 'money in the bank' |

If you consult a reasonably comprehensive dictionary for any language, you will find numerous examples of polysemy. For example, my dictionary lists several related meanings for the word *mark*.

(1) Polysemy in the meaning of *mark*
   - a visible trace or impression on something (*The tires left a mark on the road.*)
   - a written or printed symbol (*You need a punctuation mark here.*)
   - a grade, as in school (*He got a good mark on the math test.*)
   - a target (*She hit the mark every time.*)
   - an indication of some quality or property (*The mark of a good diplomat is the ability to negotiate.*)

**Homophony** exists where a single form has two or more entirely distinct meanings (see table 6.4). In such cases, it is assumed that there are separate words with the same pronunciation rather than a single word with different meanings.

| **Table 6.4** | Some homophones in English | |
|---|---|---|
| **Word** | **Meaning *a*** | **Meaning *b*** |
| light | 'not heavy' | 'illumination' |
| bank | 'a financial institution' | 'a small cliff at the edge of a river' |
| club | 'a social organization' | 'a blunt weapon' |
| pen | 'a writing instrument' | 'a small cage' |

---

### Language Matters  **Similar in Other Ways**

Different words with the same spelling are called **homographs**. The examples in table 6.4 are therefore homographs as well as homophones, whereas *write* and *right* are just homophones. In contrast, the *bow* that means 'weapon for shooting arrows' and the *bow* that means 'bend at the waist' are homographs but not homophones since they have different pronunciations—[bow] and [baw], respectively. Words that are both homophones and homographs are commonly called **homonyms**.

---

Homophones need not have identical spellings—*write* and *right* are homophones, as are *piece* and *peace*.

Polysemy and homophony create **lexical ambiguity,** in that a single form has two or more meanings. Thus, a sentence such as (2) could mean either that Liz purchased an instrument to write with or that she bought a small cage.

(2)  Liz bought a pen.

Of course, in actual speech the surrounding words and sentences usually make the intended meaning clear. The potential lexical ambiguity in sentences such as the following therefore normally goes unnoticed.

(3)  He got a loan from the *bank*.

(4)  Because Liz needed a place to keep her guinea pig, she went downtown and bought a *pen* for $20.

---

### Language Matters  **The Pinnacle of Polysemy**

The most ambiguous word in English may well be the verb *set*. In an entry that extends over 19 pages, the *Oxford English Dictionary* lists more than 150 meanings and uses.

---

## 6.1.2  Semantic relations involving sentences

Like words, sentences have meanings that can be analyzed in terms of their relation to other meanings. Three such relations—paraphrase, entailment, and contradiction—are particularly important.

### Paraphrase

Two sentences that can have the same meaning are said to be **paraphrases** of each other. The following pairs of sentences provide examples of paraphrase.

(5)  *a.* The police chased the burglar.
    *b.* The burglar was chased by the police.

(6)  *a.* I gave the summons to Erin.
    *b.* I gave Erin the summons.

## Language Matters **Sometimes a Paraphrase, and Sometimes Not**

In fact, active and passive sentences aren't always paraphrases. Things get tricky if the sentence contains a quantifier such as *everyone* and a pronoun—the paraphase relation is lost.

Everyone admires his parents.
His parents are admired by everyone.

Notice that the active sentence is ambiguous: it can mean either that everyone admires his own parents, or (less obviously) that everyone admires the parents of some particular person not mentioned in the sentence. In contrast, the passive sentence can only have the second meaning.

(7) *a.* It is unfortunate that the team lost.
　　*b.* Unfortunately, the team lost.

(8) *a.* Paul bought a car from Sue.
　　*b.* Sue sold a car to Paul.

(9) *a.* The game will begin at 3:00 p.m.
　　*b.* At 3:00 p.m., the game will begin.

The (a) and (b) sentences in each of the above pairs are obviously very similar in meaning. Indeed, it would be impossible for one sentence to be true without the other also being true. Thus, if it is true that the police chased the burglar, it must also be true that the burglar was chased by the police. (Sentences whose meanings are related to each other in this way are said to have the same **truth conditions**—that is, they are true under the same circumstances.)

For some linguists, this is enough to justify saying that the two sentences have the same meaning. However, you may notice that there are subtle differences in emphasis between the (a) and (b) sentences in (5) to (9). For instance, it is natural to interpret (5a) as a statement about what the police did and (5b) as a statement about what happened to the burglar. Similarly, (9b) seems to place more emphasis on the starting time of the game than (9a) does. As is the case with synonymy, many linguists feel that languages do not permit two or more structures to have absolutely identical meanings and that paraphrases are therefore never perfect.

## Entailment

When the truth of one sentence guarantees the truth of another sentence, we say that there is a relation of **entailment**. This relation is mutual in the case of examples (5) to (9) since the truth of either sentence in the pair guarantees the truth of the other. In examples such as the following, however, entailment is asymmetrical.

(10) *a.* The park wardens killed the bear.
　　 *b.* The bear is dead.

(11) *a.* Prince is a dog.
　　 *b.* Prince is an animal.

If it is true that the park wardens killed the bear, then it must also be true that the bear is dead. However, the reverse does not follow since the bear could be dead without the park wardens having killed it. Similarly, if it is true that Prince is a dog, then it is also true that Prince is an animal. Once again though, the reverse does not hold: even if we know that Prince is an animal, we cannot conclude that he is a dog rather than, say, a horse or a cat.

## Contradiction

Sometimes, it turns out that if one sentence is true, then another sentence must be false. This is the case with the examples in (12).

(12) *a.* Charles is a bachelor.
  *b.* Charles is married.

If it is true that Charles is a bachelor, then it cannot be true that he is married. When two sentences cannot both be true, we say that there is a **contradiction**.

## 6.1.3  What is meaning?

Although it is relatively easy to determine whether two words or sentences have identical or different meanings, it is much more difficult to determine precisely what meaning is in the first place. In fact, despite many centuries of study, we still know very little about the nature of meaning or how it is represented in the human mind. Nonetheless, it is worthwhile to review briefly some of the better-known proposals and the problems that they encounter.

### Connotation

One notion that is closely linked with the concept of meaning is **connotation**, the set of associations that a word's use can evoke. For most Canadians, for example, the word *winter* evokes thoughts of snow, bitter cold, short days, frozen fingertips, and the like. These associations make up the word's connotation, but they cannot be its meaning (or at least not its entire meaning). The word *winter* does not become meaningless just because it is a mild year or because one moves to Florida in November. We must therefore look beyond connotation for our understanding of what meaning is.

### Denotation

One well-known approach to semantics attempts to equate the meaning of a word or phrase with the entities to which it refers—its **denotation** or **referents**. The denotation of the word *winter*, for example, corresponds to the season between the winter solstice and the spring equinox (regardless of whether it is cold and unpleasant). Similarly, the denotation of the word *dog* corresponds to the set of canines, and so on.

Although a word's denotation is clearly connected to its meaning in some way, they cannot be one and the same thing. This is because there are words such as *unicorn* and phrases such as *the present king of France* which have no referents in the real world even though they are far from meaningless.

A problem of a different sort arises with expressions such as *the Prime Minister of Canada* and *the leader of the Conservative Party*, both of which refer (in 2007, at least) to Stephen

Harper. Although these two expressions may have the same referent, it seems wrong to say that they mean the same thing. Thus, we would not say that the phrase *Prime Minister of Canada* is defined as 'the leader of the Conservative Party' or that the definition of the phrase *leader of the Conservative Party* is 'Prime Minister of Canada'.

## Extension and intension

The impossibility of equating an element's meaning with its referents has led to a distinction between **extension** and **intension**. Whereas an expression's extension corresponds to the set of entities that it picks out in the world (its referents), its intension corresponds to its inherent sense, the concepts that it evokes. Thus, the extension of *woman* is a set of real world entities (women) while its intension involves notions like 'female' and 'human'. Similarly, the phrase *Prime Minister of Canada* has as its extension an individual (Stephen Harper), but its intension involves the concept 'leader of the governing party' (see table 6.5).

| **Table 6.5**   Extension versus intension | | |
|---|---|---|
| **Phrase** | **Extension** | **Intension** |
| Prime Minister of Canada | Stephen Harper | leader of the governing party |
| Stanley Cup champions (2007) | Anaheim Ducks | winners of the NHL championship |
| Capital of Manitoba | Winnipeg | city containing the provincial legislature |

The distinction between intension and extension does not allow us to resolve the question of what meaning is. It simply permits us to pose it in a new way: what are intensions?

One suggestion is that intensions correspond to mental images. This is an obvious improvement over the referential theory since it is possible to have a mental image of a unicorn or even of the king of France, although there are no such entities in the real world. However, problems arise with the meanings of words such as *dog*, which can be used to refer to animals of many different sizes, shapes, and colours. If the meaning of this word corresponds to a mental image, that image would have to be general enough to include Chihuahuas and St. Bernards, yet still exclude foxes and wolves. If you try to draw a picture that satisfies these requirements, you will see just how hard it is to construct an image for meanings of this sort.

## Componential analysis

Still another approach to meaning tries to represent a word's intension by breaking it down into smaller semantic components. Sometimes known as **componential analysis** or **semantic decomposition**, this approach has often been used to analyze the meaning of

## Language Matters **Images Are Real**

Images may not work for everything, but we do construct images of various sorts as we interpret sentences. In an elegant experiment, people were shown a picture of a nail and asked whether the corresponding word had appeared in a sentence such as *The man hammered the nail into the wall.*

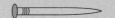

It took less time to answer the experimenter's question when the picture provided a horizontal depiction of the nail (as above) than when it provided a vertical depiction. (The reverse was true for the sentence *The man hammered the nail into the floor.*) This can only mean that the participants in the experiment had constructed a mental image of a horizontally oriented nail as they heard 'into the wall', making it easier to recognize the object in the picture as something that had been named in the sentence.

Source: R. Stanfield and R. Zwan, "The Effect of Implied Orientation Derived from Verbal Context on Picture Recognition," *Psychological Science* 12 (2001):153–56.

certain types of nouns in terms of **semantic features**. The analysis in figure 6.1 for the words *man*, *woman*, *boy*, and *girl* illustrates how this works. (Nothing depends on the choice of feature names here; the analysis would work just as well with the feature ±female as ±male.)

**Figure 6.1**
Semantic feature composition for *man, woman, boy, girl*

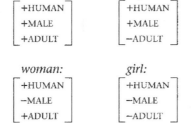

An obvious advantage of this approach is that it allows us to group entities into natural classes (much as we do in phonology). Hence, *man* and *boy* could be grouped together as [+human, +male] while *man* and *woman* could be put in a class defined by the features [+human, +adult].

This in turn can be useful for stating generalizations of various sorts. For instance, there are certain verbs, such as *marry*, *argue*, and the like, that we expect to find only with subjects that are [+human]. Moreover, within the English pronoun system, *he* is used to refer to [+human] entities that are [+male] while *she* is used for [+human] entities that are [–male].

There are limits on the insights into word meaning offered by componential analysis. What value, for example, is there in characterizing the meaning of *dog* as [+animal, +canine] as long as there is no further analysis of these features? Similarly, do we say that the meaning of *blue* consists of the feature [+colour] and something else? If so, what is that other thing? Isn't it blueness? If so, then we have not really broken the meaning of *blue* into smaller components, and we are back where we started.

To date, componential analysis has given its most impressive results in the study of verb meaning. A typical component of verb meaning is the concept GO, which is associated with change of various sorts. (The components of verb meaning tend not to be binary features. We use uppercase letters to represent a semantic concept.)

(13)  manifestations of the concept GO:
    *a.* positional change:
        Harvey went from Toronto to Winnipeg.

    *b.* possessional change:
        The inheritance went to Marla.

    *c.* identificational change:
        Max went from being a rational gentleman to being a stark raving maniac.

Despite their somewhat different senses, all three uses of the verb *go* have something in common that can be traced to the GO component of their meaning—they typically occur with a phrase that denotes the entity undergoing change (e.g., the subject in these examples) and with a phrase expressing the endpoint of that change (the *to* complements).

The GO concept is manifested in the meaning of verbs other than just *go*. For instance, positional GO is present in the meaning of *fly* ('go through the air'), *walk* ('go on foot'), *crawl* ('go on hands and knees'), and so forth. Possessional GO is manifested in the meaning of *give*, *buy*, and *inherit*, all of which involve a change of possession, while identificational GO shows up in *become* and *turn into*. Because these verbs all share the abstract GO meaning, they are all typically used with a phrase denoting the entity undergoing the change (marked below by a single underline) and a phrase denoting the endpoint of that change (marked by a double underline).

(14)  *a.* positional Go:
       The bird flew <u>to its nest</u>.

    *b.* possessional Go:
       The coach gave <u>a new ball</u> <u>to the children</u>.

    *c.* identificational Go:
       The caterpillar turned into a <u>butterfly</u>.

## Verb meaning and subcategorization

Sometimes, quite surprising features of verb meaning can be relevant to the choice of accompanying phrases. Consider, for instance, the contrast between the verbs in list *a*, which can occur with two NP complements, and the verbs in list *b*, which cannot.

(15)  *a.* throw [$_{NP}$ the boy] [$_{NP}$ a ball]     *b.* *push [$_{NP}$ the boy] [$_{NP}$ the package]
       toss                                  *pull
       kick                                  *lift
       fling                                 *haul

Can you see the semantic difference? The verbs in list *a* all denote ballistic motion that results from the instantaneous application of force to an object at its point of origin. (When we throw something, for example, we thrust it forward and then release it.) In contrast, the verbs in list *b* all denote motion that is accompanied by the continuous application of force to the object as it moves from one point to another. (For instance, pulling typically involves the extended use of force as the object moves, rather than a single quick motion.)

> ## Language Matters **Meaning and the Body**
>
> There is reason to think that the meanings of many words are tightly integrated with physical experience. That is why exposure to verbs denoting various physical actions triggered involuntary activation of the part of the brain responsible for controlling those actions. Seeing the word *chew* leads to activation of the part of the brain that controls movement of the mouth, seeing *kick* stimulates the part of the brain associated with leg movements, and so on.
>
> Sources: F. Pulvermüller, M. Haerle, and F. Hummel, "Walking or Talking? Behavioral and Neurophysiological Correlates of Action Verb Processing," *Brain and Language* 78 (2001):143–68.
>
> O. Hauk, I. Johnsrude, and F. Pulvermüller, "Somatopic Representation of Action Words in Human Motor and Premotor Cortex," *Neuron* 41 (2004):301–7.

Now think about the contrast between the following two sets of verbs.

(16)  *a.*  fax [NP Helen] [NP the news]      *b.*  *murmur [NP Helen] [NP the news]
          radio                                  *mumble
          wire                                    *mutter
          phone                                 *shriek

Once again, componential analysis reveals a subtle semantic contrast. The first group of verbs (*phone*, *radio*, etc.) have meanings that include the means by which a message was communicated (by phone, by radio, and so on). In contrast, the verbs in the second group all have meanings that describe the type of voice that was used to communicate the message (murmuring, mumbling, shrieking, etc.). For reasons that are not yet fully understood, meaning differences like these help determine the type of complements that particular verbs can select.

## 6.2 The conceptual system

Underlying the use of words and sentences to express meaning in human language is a conceptual system capable of organizing and classifying every imaginable aspect of our experience, from inner feelings and perceptions, to cultural and social phenomena, to the physical world that surrounds us. This section focuses on what the study of this conceptual system reveals about how meaning is expressed through language. We will begin by considering some examples that illustrate the way in which these concepts are structured, extended, and interrelated.

## 6.2.1 Fuzzy concepts

We tend to think that the concepts expressed by the words and phrases of our language have precise definitions with clear-cut boundaries. Some concepts may indeed be like this. For example, the concept expressed by the phrase *Member of Parliament* seems to have a clear-cut definition: one is a Member of Parliament if and only if one is duly elected to a particular legislative body; no other person can be truthfully called a Member of Parliament.

But are all concepts so straightforward? Consider the concept associated with the word *rich*. How much does a person have to be worth to be called rich? Five hundred thousand dollars? Eight hundred thousand? A million? Is there any figure that we can give that would be so precise that a person who is short by just five cents would not be called rich? It seems not. While one could miss out on being a Member of Parliament by five votes, it does not seem possible to miss out on being rich by just five cents. Moreover, whereas some people clearly qualify as rich and others uncontroversially do not, an indefinitely large number of people fall into the unclear area at the borderline of the concept, and it is just not possible to say definitively whether or not they count as rich. This is because the notion of 'richness' does not have clear-cut boundaries; it is what we call a **fuzzy concept**.

This type of fuzziness pervades the human conceptual system. With only a little effort, you should be able to think of many everyday concepts whose boundaries are fuzzy—*tall, old, playboy, strong, grey-haired, genius, clean,* and *bargain* are just a few examples.

## Graded membership

A second important fact about concepts is that their members can be graded in terms of their typicality. Consider first a fuzzy concept such as 'hockey star'. Of the people who we can agree are hockey stars, some provide better examples of this concept than others. At the time of writing, for instance, Sidney Crosby is a better example of a hockey star than is Dany Heatley. Although hockey fans agree that both players are stars, Sidney Crosby scored more points in the 2006/07 season, received more media attention, won the Most Valuable Player award, and so on. This makes him a better example of a star than Dany Heatley.

Even concepts whose boundaries can be scientifically defined exhibit this type of graded membership. A good example of this involves the concept 'bird' as shown in figure 6.2. Even assuming that all English speakers think of birds as 'warm-blooded, egg-laying, feathered vertebrates with forelimbs modified to form wings' (the dictionary definition), they still feel that some of these creatures are more birdlike than others. For instance, robins and magpies are intuitively better examples of birds than are hummingbirds, ostriches, or penguins. Examples

**Figure 6.2**
Internal structure of
the concept 'bird'

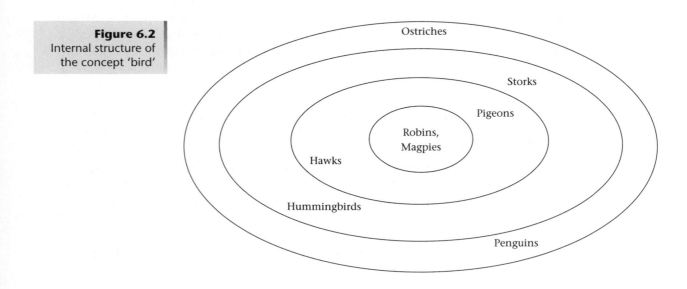

like these suggest that concepts have an internal structure, with the best or **prototypical** exemplars (Sidney Crosby in the case of 'hockey stars', robins in the case of 'birds') close to the core and less typical members arranged in successively more peripheral regions.

The existence of fuzzy concepts and of graded membership provides important insights into the nature of the human conceptual system. In particular, it seems that many (perhaps even most) concepts expressed in language are not rigid all-or-nothing notions with precise and clear-cut boundaries. Rather, they exhibit degrees of typicality and fuzzy boundaries that sometimes overlap with those of other concepts.

## 6.2.2   Metaphor

The concepts expressed by language make up a giant network, with many interconnections and associations. A good example of these interconnections involves **metaphor**, the understanding of one concept in terms of another.

Many people think of metaphor as a literary device reserved for the use of authors and poets. In fact, however, it has a prominent place in the conceptual system shared by all human beings. This can be seen in the way that we use language to talk about even commonplace notions such as time.

The dominant metaphor for talking about time involves treating it as if it were a concrete commodity that can be saved, wasted, and invested just like other valuable things.

(17)  *a.* You're *wasting* my time.
  *b.* This gadget will *save* you hours.
  *c.* How do you *spend* your time these days?
  *d.* I have *invested* a lot of time in that project.
  *e.* You need to *budget* your time.
  *f.* Is that *worth* your while?
  *g.* He's living on *borrowed* time.
  *h.* You don't use your time *profitably*.

What is the basis for this metaphor? There is apparently no objective, inherent similarity between time and commodities such as gold or money. What brings these concepts together is the *perception*, based in part on culture and in part on feelings that human beings share, that time is like a valuable commodity that can be gained and lost.

### A spatial metaphor

Another very prevalent metaphor in our language involves the use of words that are primarily associated with spatial orientation to talk about physical and psychological states (see table 6.6 on page 202).

The basis for these metaphors appears to lie in our physical experience. Unhappiness and ill health tend to be associated with lethargy and inactivity, which often involve being on one's back (physically down). In contrast, happiness and good health are often correlated with energy and movement, which involve being on one's feet (physically up).

These few examples illustrate the point that the concepts expressed through language are interrelated in special and intriguing ways. By investigating phenomena such

| **Table 6.6** | Metaphorical use of spatial terms |
|---|---|
| **Emotions: *happy* is up; *sad* is down** | |

| | |
|---|---|
| I'm feeling *up*. | I'm feeling *down*. |
| That *boosted* my spirits. | He *fell* into a depression. |
| My spirits *rose*. | Her spirits *sank*. |
| You're in *high* spirits. | He's feeling *low*. |
| the *height* of ecstasy | the *depths* of depression |
| That gave me a *lift*. | |

| **Physical health: *health* and *life* are up; *sickness* and *death* are down** | |
|---|---|
| He's at the *peak* of health. | He's *sinking* fast. |
| Lazarus *rose* from the dead. | He *fell* ill. |
| He's in *top* shape. | He came *down* with the flu. |
| | Her health is *declining*. |
| | She's feeling *under* the weather. |

as the use of metaphor to represent abstract concepts in terms of more basic physical and cultural experience, we can gain valuable insights into how language is used to communicate meaning.  ✗

## 6.2.3  The lexicalization of concepts

Do all human beings share the same conceptual system? Do all languages express concepts in the same way? These are questions that have fascinated and puzzled researchers for many decades. At the present time, there is no reason to believe that human beings in different linguistic communities have different conceptual systems. But there is ample evidence that languages can differ from each other in terms of how they express particular concepts.

### Lexicalization

A notorious example of how languages can supposedly differ from each other in the expression of concepts involves the number of words for snow in Inuktitut. Sometimes estimated to be in the hundreds, the number is actually much, much smaller. In fact, one dictionary gives only the four items in table 6.7 (although other dictionaries give a few more, at least for some varieties of Inuktitut).

| **Table 6.7** | Words for 'snow' in Inuktitut |
|---|---|
| *aput* | 'snow on the ground' |
| *qana* | 'falling snow' |
| *piqsirpoq* | 'drifting snow' |
| *qimuqsuq* | 'snow drift' |

As you can see, there is nothing particularly startling about this list of words. In fact, even in English there is more than just one word to describe snow in its various forms—*snow*, *slush*, *blizzard*, and *sleet* come to mind.

These examples illustrate the phenomenon of **lexicalization**, the process whereby concepts are encoded in the words of a language. Inuktitut lexicalizes the concepts 'falling' and 'snow' in a single word (*qana*) while English uses two separate words. While some lexicalization differences may correlate with cultural factors (the relative importance of types of snow in traditional Inuit culture), this is not always so. For example, English has an unusually rich set of vocabulary items pertaining to the perception of light (see table 6.8).

| **Table 6.8** | Some verbs pertaining to light in English |
| --- | --- |
| glimmer | glisten |
| gleam | glow |
| glitter | flicker |
| shimmer | shine |
| flare | glare |
| flash | sparkle |

Although English speakers know and use the words in this list, it is hard to see how the richness in this particular area of vocabulary can be correlated with any significant feature of culture.

As we have tried to emphasize throughout this book, linguistic analysis focuses on the *system* of knowledge that makes it possible to speak and understand a language. The fact that a particular language has more words pertaining to snow or light does not in and of itself provide any insight into the nature of the human linguistic system, and therefore does not merit special attention. However, as we will see in the next subsection, certain lexicalization differences do shed light on how language expresses meaning.

## Motion verbs

All languages have words that can describe motion through space (English has *come*, *go*, and *move*, among many others). However, there are systematic differences in terms of how languages express motion and the concepts related to it. In English, for example, there are many verbs that simultaneously express both the concept of motion and the manner in which the motion occurs (see table 6.9).

| **Table 6.9** | Some verbs expressing motion and manner in English |
| --- | --- |
| The rock *rolled* down the hill. | |
| The puck *slid* across the ice. | |
| She *limped* through the house. | |
| The smoke *swirled* through the opening. | |

Notice how each of these verbs expresses both the fact that something moved and the manner in which it moved (by rolling, sliding, limping, and so on). We describe this fact by saying that English lexicalization includes a **conflation pattern** that combines manner and motion into a single verb meaning.

Interestingly, Romance languages (descendants of Latin) generally don't express motion events in this way. Thus, while French has a verb *rouler* with the meaning 'to roll', it does not use this verb to simultaneously express both manner and motion as English does.

(18)  *La bouteille a roulé dans la caverne.
       'The bottle rolled into the cave.'

Instead, the motion and its manner have to be expressed separately.

(19)  La bouteille est entrée dans la caverne en roulant.
       'The bottle entered the cave, rolling.'

Although French does not have the motion + manner conflation pattern, it does have verbs whose meaning brings together the concepts of motion and path (see table 6.10). As the English translations show, French verbs of motion express both the concept of movement and the direction of its path—down, up, back, across, out, and so forth. (English too has verbs that can express both motion and path—*descend, ascend, return,* and so on—but these words are not part of its native vocabulary. Rather, they were borrowed into English from Latinate sources, usually through French.)

| **Table 6.10**    Some verbs expressing motion and path in French |
| --- |
| L'enfant *monte* l'escalier.<br>'The child goes up the stairs.' |
| L'enfant *descend* l'escalier.<br>'The child goes down the stairs.' |
| Les passagers *retournent* à l'aéroport.<br>'The passengers go back to the airport.' |
| Le bateau *traverse* l'océan.<br>'The ship goes across the ocean.' |
| La bouteille *sort* de la caverne.<br>'The bottle comes out of the cave.' |

Yet another conflation pattern is found in the Amerindian language Atsugewi, in which verbs can express both motion and the type of thing that moves (see table 6.11).

We learn two things from these facts. First, the concept of motion is associated with a number of other concepts, including 'path', 'manner of movement', and 'moving thing'. Second, the way in which these concepts are combined for the purposes of lexicalization can differ systematically from language to language. Languages such as English have verbs that conflate motion and manner while other languages have verbs that conflate motion and path (French) or motion and the type of thing that moves (Atsugewi).

| **Table 6.11** | Some verb roots expressing motion and the thing moving in Atsugewi |
|---|---|
| *lup* | for movement of a small, shiny spherical object (a hailstone) |
| *t* | for movement of a smallish, flat object that can be attached to another (a stamp, a clothing patch, a shingle) |
| *caq* | for movement of a slimy, lumpish object (a toad, a cow dropping) |
| *swal* | for movement of a limp linear object, suspended by one end (a shirt on a clothesline, a hanging dead rabbit) |
| *qput* | for movement of loose, dry dirt |
| *staq* | for movement of runny, unpleasant material (manure, guts, chewed gum, rotten tomatoes) |

The general picture that is emerging from this type of work is consistent with the key idea underlying componential analysis (section 6.1.3). In particular, it seems that at least within certain semantic domains, there may be a small universal set of concepts (motion, manner, path, thing that moves, and so on) and a small set of options for how these concepts can be combined for purposes of lexicalization (see figure 6.3).

**Figure 6.3**
Systematic differences in conflation patterns

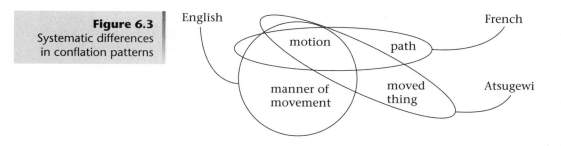

Unlike the lexicalization differences involving snow and light discussed earlier, these differences appear to be highly systematic and to reveal some general tendencies about the organization of the human conceptual system and the way in which meaning is expressed in language.

## 6.2.4 Grammatical concepts

Of the indefinitely large set of concepts expressible in human language, a relatively small subset is grammaticalized—they are used to express the grammatical contrasts that are expressed as affixes and non-lexical (functional) categories. Some of the concepts that are treated this way in English are listed in table 6.12 on page 206.

Some concepts, such as negation, tense, and number, are grammaticalized in a very large number of languages. On the other hand, contrasts involving **evidentiality** (the source of a speaker's evidence for a statement) are less commonly treated in this way. As illustrated in table 6.13, a refined set of grammaticalized evidentiality contrasts is found in Hidatsa (a Siouan language spoken in North Dakota).

**Table 6.12** Some concepts associated with affixes and non-lexical categories in English

| Concept | Affix |
|---|---|
| Past | *-ed* |
| More than one | *-s* |
| Again | *re-* |
| Negation | *in-*, *un-* |

| Concept | Non-lexical category |
|---|---|
| Obligation | *must* |
| Possibility | *may* |
| Definite, specific | *the* |
| Indefinite, non-specific | *a* |
| Disjunction | *or* |
| Negation | *not* |
| Conjunction | *and* |

Choice of the appropriate sentence-ender is extremely important in Hidatsa. Speakers who utter a false sentence marked by the morpheme *-ski* are considered to be liars. Had they used the morpheme *-c*, on the other hand, it would be assumed that they simply made a mistake. While English has ways of indicating these contrasts (by using expressions such as *perhaps*, *I heard that*, and *I guess*), it does not have a grammatical system of morphemes to encode this information.

**Table 6.13** Evidentiality morphemes in Hidatsa

*ski* THE SPEAKER IS CERTAIN OF THE STATEMENT'S TRUTH
Waceo iikipi kure heo -<u>ski</u>.
'The man (definitely) carried the pipe.'

*c* THE SPEAKER BELIEVES THE STATEMENT TO BE TRUE
Waceo iikipi kure heo -<u>c</u>.
'The man (supposedly) carried the pipe.'

*wareac* THE SPEAKER REGARDS THE STATEMENT TO BE COMMON KNOWLEDGE
Waceo iikipi kure heo -<u>wareac</u>.
'The man carried the pipe (they say).'

*rahe* THE STATEMENT IS BASED ON AN UNVERIFIED REPORT FROM SOMEONE ELSE
Waceo wiira rakci heo -<u>rahe</u>.
'The man roasted the goose (it is rumoured).'

*toak* THE TRUTH OF THE STATEMENT IS UNKNOWN TO BOTH SPEAKER AND LISTENER
Waceo cihpa rakci heo -<u>toak</u>.
'The man roasted the prairie dog (perhaps).'

---

**Language Matters** **Where Do Grammaticalized Forms Come From?**

In many cases, the forms expressing grammatical concepts were originally ordinary nouns and verbs. Over time, and through frequent use, their form was reduced and their meaning was modified to express a related grammatical notion.

A good example of this can be found in English, where the verb *going*, whose literal meaning involves directional motion, has come to be used (with the pronunciation 'gonna') as a future marker—something that was not possible in Shakespeare's time.

I'm going to (*gonna) school now. (directional motion)
The snow is going to (gonna) melt. (future time)

The two principal sources of future tense markers in languages of the world are verbs of motion and verbs of wanting. English provides a good illustration of the second case as well: the auxiliary *will* evolved from the verb *willan*, which meant 'to want'.

---

Source: Joan Bybee, "Cognitive Processes in Grammaticalization," in M. Tomasello (ed.), *The New Psychology of Language*, Vol. 2 (Mahwah, NJ: Lawrence Erlbaum Associates, 2003), pp. 145–67.

## 6.3 Syntax and sentence interpretation

The two preceding sections have focused on the meaning conveyed by the individual words and phrases that make up a sentence. In this section, we turn to the problem of sentence interpretation, with an emphasis on how the positioning of words and phrases in syntactic structure helps determine the meaning of the entire sentence, consistent with the following principle.

> **(20)** *The Principle of Compositionality*
> The meaning of a sentence is determined by the meaning of its component parts and the manner in which they are arranged in syntactic structure.

Syntactic structure is relevant to meaning in a variety of ways. For purposes of illustration, we will consider four aspects of its contribution to the interpretation of sentences—constructional meaning, the representation of structural ambiguity, the assignment of thematic roles, and the interpretation of pronouns.

## 6.3.1 Constructional meaning

There is reason to believe that structural patterns are themselves capable of carrying meaning above and beyond the meaning of their component parts. One example of this **constructional meaning** can be seen in 'the caused-motion construction' exemplified in (21).

> **(21)** *a.* Seymour pushed the truck off the table.
> *b.* Mabel moved the car into the garage.
> *c.* Perry pulled the dog into the swimming pool.

As these examples help illustrate, the 'caused-motion construction' consists of a structural pattern (NP V NP PP) that is used to express the meaning 'X causes Y to go somewhere'. Thus, the first sentence describes a situation in which Seymour causes the truck to go off the table by pushing it; the second sentence is used for situations in which Mabel causes the car to go into the garage; and so on.

(22) *The caused-motion construction*
Form:　　　NP　V　　NP　PP
Meaning:　'X　causes　Y　to go somewhere'

Evidence for the existence of a constructional meaning comes from sentences such as the following.

(23) *a.* Boris sneezed the handkerchief right across the room.
　　 *b.* The judges laughed the poor guy off the stage.
　　 *c.* Morley squeezed the shirt into the suitcase.

There is clearly nothing in the meaning of verbs such as *sneeze*, *laugh*, and *squeeze* that implies caused motion. Yet, when they occur in the NP V NP PP pattern, the resulting sentence has a meaning in which X causes Y to go somewhere. Thus, sentence (23a) means that Boris caused the handkerchief to fly across the room by sneezing; (23b) means that the judges forced someone off the stage by laughing at him; and so on.

How can this be? It seems that part of the meaning of these sentences comes from the construction itself: in (23a), the verb *sneeze* provides the meaning 'involuntarily expel air from the mouth and nose', while the structural pattern tells us that this action caused the handkerchief to be propelled across the room. Without both types of information, the sentence could not mean what it does.

Another example of constructional meaning can be found in patterns such as the following.

(24) *a.* Jerry sent Lou a present.
　　 *b.* The company gave its employees a bonus.
　　 *c.* The secretary handed Mary a message.
　　 *d.* Marvin threw Harry the ball.

---

## Language Matters　**What's This Fly Doing in My Soup?**

A defining feature of constructions is that at least some aspect of their meaning cannot be determined from the meaning of their parts. A good example of this involves sentences of the type 'What's X doing . . . ?'

What's this scratch doing on my new car?
What's this hotel room doing without a decent bed?
What's my wallet doing in your pocket?

Even though the verb *do* normally denotes an activity (as in, 'What are you doing?'), these sentences are used to demand an explanation for an unexpected and inappropriate situation that doesn't even involve an activity—the construction has taken on a special meaning of its own. An old and famous joke plays on this fact.

*Diner*: Waiter, what's this fly doing in my soup? [special construction-based meaning intended]
*Waiter*: Madam, I believe that's the backstroke. [pretending to get only the literal meaning]

Source: P. Kay and C. Fillmore, "Grammatical Constructions and Linguistic Generalizations: The *What's X Doing Y* Construction," *Language* 75 (1999):1–33. Reprinted with permission.

These sentences are instances of the so-called ditransitive construction that is typically associated with the meaning 'X causes Y to have Z'. Thus (24a) describes a situation in which Jerry causes Lou to have a present by sending it to him.

(25) *The Ditransitive Construction*
        Form:           NP    V          NP    NP
        Meaning:     'X     causes   Y      to have Z'

An indication that the structure itself contributes part of the meaning associated with ditransitive constructions comes from sentences such as *Jerry baked Lou a cake*. This sentence describes a situation in which Lou ends up with a cake, even though there is clearly nothing in the meaning of *bake* that implies that one person causes another person to have something. This part of the sentence's meaning comes from the structure itself—another example of constructional meaning.

## 6.3.2  Structural ambiguity

Some sentences are **structurally ambiguous** in that their component words can be combined in more than one way. A simple example of this is found in the phrase *wealthy men and women*, where 'wealthy' can be seen as a property of both the men and the women or of just the men alone. These two interpretations or **readings** are depicted in figure 6.4 (Con = conjunction; see chapter 5, section 5.5.1).

**Figure 6.4**
An ambiguous phrase. The structure on the left indicates that both the men and the women are wealthy; the structure on the right indicates that only the men are wealthy.

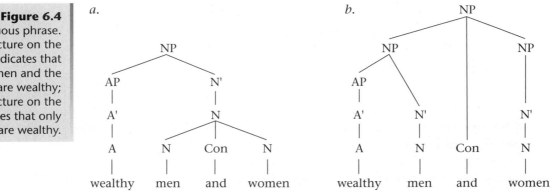

Figure 6.4a corresponds to the reading in which *wealthy* modifies both *men* and *women*. This is shown by having the adjective combine with a category that includes both nouns. In figure 6.4b, on the other hand, the adjective combines only with the N *men*. This structure corresponds to the reading in which 'wealthy' applies only to the men.

Another case of structural ambiguity is found in sentences such as the following.

(26) Nicole saw people with binoculars.

In one interpretation of (26), the people had binoculars when Nicole noticed them (the phrase *with binoculars* modifies the noun *people*) while in the other interpretation Nicole saw the people by using the binoculars (the PP modifies the verb). These two readings are represented in figure 6.5.

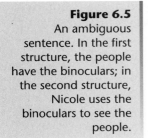

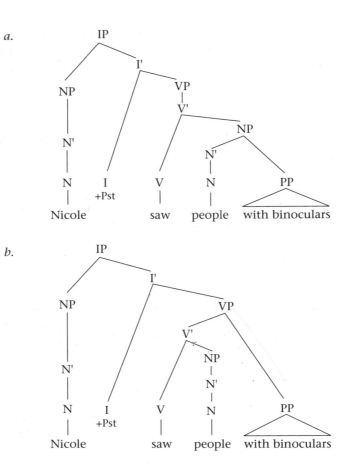

In figure 6.5a, the PP *with binoculars* occurs inside the NP headed by the N *people*, reflecting the first reading for this sentence. In figure 6.5b, on the other hand, the PP is part of the VP headed by the verb *saw*. This corresponds to the interpretation in which *with binoculars* describes how Nicole saw the people.

In sum, the manner in which words are grouped together in syntactic structure reflects the way in which their meanings are combined. Sometimes, as in the examples we have just considered, identical strings of words can be combined in either of two ways, creating structural ambiguity that can be neatly captured with the help of tree structures.

## 6.3.3  Thematic roles

Another aspect of semantic interpretation involves determining the role that the referents of NPs play in the situations described by sentences. Consider in this regard the sentence in (27).

(27)  The courier carried the document from Halifax to Vancouver.

It would be impossible to understand this sentence if we could not identify the courier as the person who is responsible for carrying something, the document as the thing that is carried,

Halifax as the point of origin, and Vancouver as the destination. Linguists often use **thematic roles** to categorize the relation between a sentence's parts and the event that it describes. In most linguistic analyses, at least the following thematic roles are recognized (see table 6.14).

| **Table 6.14** | Thematic roles |
|---|---|
| Agent | the entity that performs an action |
| Theme | the entity undergoing an action or a movement |
| Source | the starting point for a movement |
| Goal | the end point for a movement |
| Location | the place where an action occurs |

Examples of these thematic roles can be seen in sentences such as the following.

(28)  *a.* The courier carried the document from Halifax to Vancouver.
       *agent*         *theme*       *source*     *goal*

     *b.* The athletes practised in the Saddledome.
       *agent*           *location*

The notion of movement used in the definition of theme, source, and goal is intended to involve not only actual physical motion, but also changes in possession, as in (29), and identity, as in (30).

(29)  Terry gave the skis to Mary.
    *agent*        *theme* *goal*

(30)  The magician changed the ball into a rabbit.
       *agent*        *theme*    *goal*

As you may recall, we observed a similar set of contrasts in the manifestation of the GO concept discussed in section 6.1.3. This is no coincidence. Thematic roles can be traced to particular aspects of word meaning, and the presence of GO in a verb's meaning is specifically linked to the presence of a theme role and a goal role.

## Thematic role assignment

How does the grammar ensure that the appropriate thematic role is associated with each NP in a sentence? As we have just seen, thematic roles originate in word meaning. Thus, if the sentence *Marvin purchased a pen at the bookstore* contains an agent and a theme, it is because the verb *purchase* has the type of meaning that implies an entity that does the purchasing (an agent) and an entity that gets purchased (a theme). Similarly, *the bookstore* is taken to denote the location of the action because of the meaning of the preposition *at*.

Information about the thematic roles assigned by a particular lexical item is recorded in a **thematic grid**, as depicted in table 6.15 on p. 212.

| Table 6.15 | Some words and the thematic roles implied by their meanings |
|---|---|
| *purchase* | <agent, theme> |
| *walk* | <agent> |
| *to* | <goal> |
| *from* | <source> |
| *at* | <location> |

The thematic roles implied by the meanings of lexical items are assigned to NPs based on their position in syntactic structure, with each NP receiving a single role. As a first example of this, let us consider the complement of a preposition. In such cases, the process of thematic role assignment can be summarized as follows:

(31)  A P assigns a thematic role to its complement NP.

The operation of this convention is illustrated in figure 6.6.

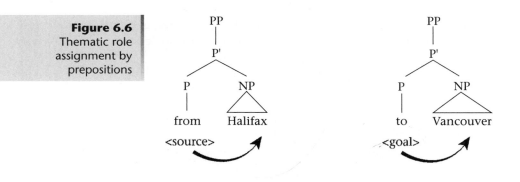

**Figure 6.6**
Thematic role assignment by prepositions

Matters are slightly more complicated in the case of Vs. Here we must distinguish between the theme role, which is assigned to the verb's complement, and the agent role, which is assigned to its subject.

(32)  A V assigns a theme role (if it has one) to its complement NP.
A V assigns an agent role (if it has one) to its subject NP.

This is exemplified in the structures in figure 6.7 (next page). In accordance with (32), the theme role is assigned to the V's NP complement while the agent role is assigned to the subject.

The structure in figure 6.8 (next page) illustrates the assignment of thematic roles in a sentence that contains a P in addition to a V. Here, the P *at* assigns its location role to its complement NP (*the bookstore*) while the verb *purchase* assigns its theme role to the complement *a pencil* and its agent role to the subject *Marvin*.

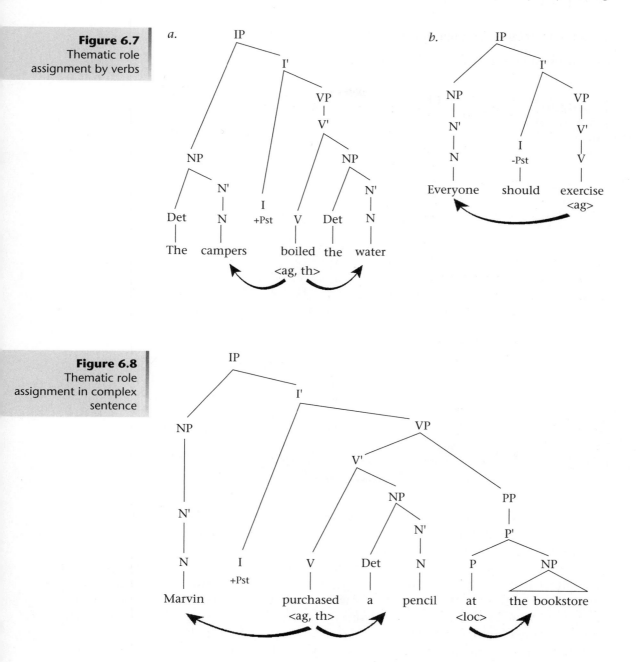

**Figure 6.7**
Thematic role assignment by verbs

**Figure 6.8**
Thematic role assignment in complex sentence

## Deep structure and thematic roles

In the examples considered to this point, it is unclear whether an NP receives its thematic role on the basis of its position in deep structure or surface structure. This is because our example sentences are all formed without the help of the Move operation, so that each NP occupies the same position in both deep structure and surface structure. But now consider a sentence such as (33), which is formed with the help of *Wh* Movement.

(33)  Which book should the students read?

This sentence has the deep structure depicted in figure 6.9.

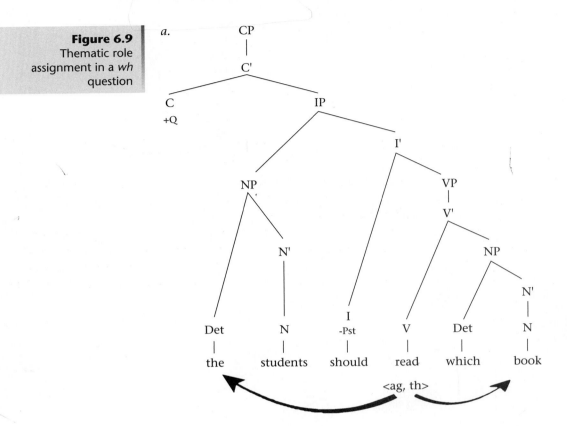

**Figure 6.9**
Thematic role assignment in a *wh* question

Since the theme role is assigned to the complement of V, it follows that the NP *which book* in the above example receives this role by virtue of its position in deep structure, not surface structure (where it occurs in the specifier of CP position).

In sum, an NP's initial position in syntactic structure (the result of the Merge operation) determines its thematic role. The Move operation may subsequently transport the NP to another position (as is the case with *wh* words), but the original thematic role remains unchanged. The relationship between syntactic structure and the part of a sentence's meaning represented by thematic roles is thus very intricate, reflecting the structural relations manifested in deep structure rather than position in surface structure.

## 6.3.4  The interpretation of pronouns

Syntactic structure also has an important role to play in the interpretation of **pronouns**, including **pronominals** such as *he, him, she,* and *her* and **reflexive pronouns** such as *himself* and *herself* (see table 6.16 on p. 215).

A defining property of pronouns is that their interpretation can be determined by another element, called the **antecedent**. As the following sentences help show, pronominals and reflexive pronouns differ in terms of where their antecedents occur.

| **Table 6.16** | Subject and object pronouns in English | | | |
|---|---|---|---|---|
| | **Pronominals** | | **Reflexives** | |
| | *Sg* | *Pl* | *Sg* | *Pl* |
| 1st person | I, me | we, us | myself | ourselves |
| 2nd person | you | you | yourself | yourselves |
| 3rd person | he, him | | himself | |
| | she, her | they | herself | themselves |
| | it | | itself | |

(34) *a.* [$_{IP}$ Claire knew that [$_{IP}$ Alexis trusted *her*]].
   *b.* [$_{IP}$ Claire knew that [$_{IP}$ Alexis trusted *herself* ]].

Notice that *her* can refer either to Claire or to someone not mentioned in the sentence, but that *herself* refers only to Alexis. This reflects the fact that a reflexive pronoun typically must have an antecedent in the smallest IP containing it.

A somewhat more abstract feature of syntactic structure enters into the interpretation of the reflexive pronoun in a sentence such as (35), which has the tree structure in figure 6.10. (Pronouns are treated as N-type categories that head NPs; to save space, some word-level category labels are omitted. Possessor NPs occur in the specifier position within a larger NP.)

(35) That boy's teacher admires himself.

**Figure 6.10**
Structure containing a reflexive pronoun

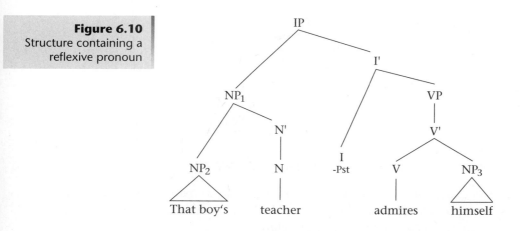

Although there are two NPs in the same IP as *himself* (namely, *that boy* and *that boy's teacher*), only one (*that boy's teacher*) can serve as antecedent for the reflexive pronoun. Thus, the person who is admired in (35) must have been the boy's teacher, not the boy.

## Principles A and B

The principle needed to ensure this interpretation makes use of the notion **c-command**, which is defined as follows.

(36) NP$_a$ c-commands NP$_b$ if the first category above NP$_a$ contains NP$_b$.

Although c-command might appear to be a rather technical notion, the underlying idea is very simple. Figure 6.11 on page 216 illustrates the type of configuration in which c-command occurs. When trying to determine c-command relations, you can use either the definition in (36) or the template in figure 6.11.

**Figure 6.11**
The c-command
configuration

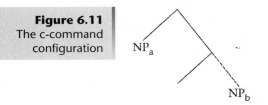

We can now formulate the constraint on the interpretation of reflexives, called **Principle A**, as follows. (The 'minimal IP' is just the smallest IP containing the pronoun.)

(37) *Principle A*

A reflexive pronoun must have an antecedent that c-commands it in the same minimal IP.

When using Principle A, the key step involves determining whether a potential antecedent c-commands the reflexive pronoun. Compare in this regard the status of the NPs *that boy* and *that boy's teacher* in figure 6.12.

**Figure 6.12**
Structure illustrating
c-command relations.
NP₁ c-commands NP₃
but NP₂ does not.

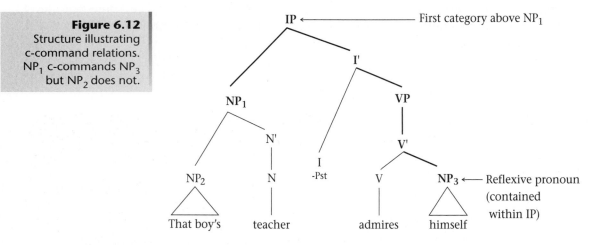

Since the first category above the NP *that boy's teacher* (namely, IP) contains the reflexive, this NP c-commands *himself* according to our definition and can therefore serve as its antecedent. As we have already seen, the sentence has this interpretation.

Now let us consider the interpretation of pronominals. As the following example in (38) shows, the interpretation of the pronominal *him* contrasts sharply with that of the reflexive *himself* in the structure that we have been considering. Thus, *him* can refer to the boy, but not to the boy's teacher—the opposite of what we observed for *himself*.

(38) That boy's teacher admires him.

How are we to account for these facts? The relevant constraint, called **Principle B**, is stated in (39).

(39) *Principle B*

A pronominal must not have an antecedent that c-commands it in the same minimal IP.

To see how this principle works, consider the structure in figure 6.13 on page 217.

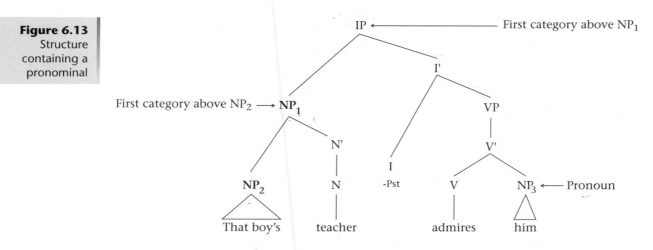

**Figure 6.13** Structure containing a pronominal

In this structure, NP$_1$ (*that boy's teacher*) c-commands *him* since the first category above it (namely, IP) also contains *him*. Principle B therefore prevents NP$_1$ from serving as antecedent for *him*. In contrast, NP$_2$ (*the boy*) does not c-command *him* since the first category above it (namely, NP$_1$) does not contain the pronoun. Thus, nothing prevents the interpretation in which *him* and *that boy* refer to the same person.

There is much more that can and should be said about the interpretation of pronouns. However, the examples we have just considered suffice to illustrate the crucial point in all of this, which is that syntactic structure plays an important role in the interpretation of both pronominals and reflexive pronouns. For more on this subject, go to the Companion Website at **www.pearsoned.ca/ogrady**, chapter 6.

---

## Language Matters  **It Wasn't Always That Way**

In earlier varieties of English, simple pronouns could be used in positions where today we must use a reflexive.

> . . . hweðer *he hine* gefreclsian wolde (from the Old English *Blickling Homilies*, c. 971).
> . . . whether he him set-free would
> '. . . whether he would set himself free'

> *Every wight* out at the dore *him* dighte (from the Middle English poem *Troilus and Criseyde* by Geoffrey Chaucer, c. 1385).

> Every man out at the door him threw
> 'Every man threw himself out the door.'

'Pronoun-*self* forms' existed in Old and Middle English, but were used primarily for emphasis or contrast, even when the antecedent was not in the same clause. This practice continued well into the nineteenth century, as shown in the following examples from the writing of Jane Austen:

> If *Cassandra* has filled my bed with fleas, I am sure they must bite *herself* (from a letter written in 1814).

> But *Marianne* . . . could easily trace it to whatever cause best pleased *herself* (*Sense and Sensibility*, p. 247, published in 1811).

Sources: C.L. Baker, "Contrast, Discourse Prominence, and Intensification, with Special Reference to Locally Free Reflexives in British English," *Language* 71 (1996): 63–101.

E. Keenan, *Creating Anaphors: The History of Reflexive Pronouns in English* (Cambridge, MA: MIT Press, 2001).

## 6.4    Other factors in sentence interpretation

Syntactic structure provides only some of the information needed to interpret a sentence. Other necessary information comes from **pragmatics**, which includes the speaker's and addressee's background attitudes and beliefs, their understanding of the context in which a sentence is uttered, and their knowledge of how language can be used to inform, to persuade, to mislead, and so forth. This section focuses on the role of pragmatics in sentence interpretation.

### 6.4.1    The role of beliefs and attitudes

As we saw in the preceding section, the grammar includes a structural principle (Principle B) that regulates the interpretation of pronominals such as *he* and *they*. However, as the following sentences show, non-linguistic knowledge and beliefs can also play an important role in selecting the antecedent for a pronominal.

(40)  *a.* The judge denied the prisoner's request because he was cautious.
      *b.* The judge denied the prisoner's request because he was dangerous.

These two sentences have identical syntactic structures, differing only in the choice of the adjective in the second clause (*cautious* in the first sentence versus *dangerous* in the second). Yet, most people feel that *he* refers to the judge in (40a) but to the prisoner in (40b). Why should this be?

The crucial factor involves our beliefs about people in our society and their likely characteristics and behaviour. All other things being equal, we are more likely to believe that a judge is cautious and a prisoner dangerous than vice versa. This in turn leads us to interpret the pronoun as referring to the judge in the first sentence in (40) but to the prisoner in the second.

#### Presupposition

There are many other ways in which a speaker's beliefs can be reflected in language use. Compare in this regard the following two sentences.

(41)  *a.* Have you stopped exercising regularly?
      *b.* Have you tried exercising regularly?

Use of the verb *stop* implies a belief on the part of the speaker that the listener has been exercising regularly. No such assumption is associated with the verb *try*.

The assumption or belief implied by the use of a particular word or structure is called a **presupposition**. The following two sentences provide another example of this.

(42)  *a.* Nick admitted that the team had lost.
      *b.* Nick said that the team had lost.

Choice of the verb *admit* in (42a) indicates that the speaker is presupposing the truth of the claim that the team lost. No such presupposition is associated with choice of the verb *say* in (42b), where the speaker is simply reporting Nick's statement without taking a position on its accuracy.

Still another type of presupposition is illustrated in (43).

(43)  *a.* D'Arcy McGee was assassinated in 1868.
      *b.* D'Arcy McGee was murdered in 1868.

Notice that use of the verb *assassinate* in (43a) involves the assumption that D'Arcy McGee was a prominent person, but that no such presupposition is associated with the verb *murder*.

## 6.4.2　Setting

As noted at the beginning of this section, the pragmatic factors relevant to sentence interpretation can include knowledge of the context in which a sentence is uttered, including its physical environment or setting.

All languages have forms whose use and interpretation depend on the location of the speaker and/or hearer within a particular setting. Called spatial **deictics**, these forms are exemplified in English by words such as *this* and *here* (proximity to the speaker) versus *that* and *there* (proximity to the hearer and/or distance from the speaker). Thus, if Steve and Brian are sitting across from each other at a table, each would refer to a plate directly in front of him as *this plate* and to a plate in front of the other or a plate distant from both as *that plate*. Without an understanding of how the setting in which a sentence is uttered can influence the choice of words such as *this* and *that*, it would be impossible for speakers of English to use or interpret these forms correctly.

As the preceding examples show, English makes a two-way distinction in its expression of deictic contrasts. However, many languages have a three-way system that may be sensitive to distance from the speaker, the addressee, or both (depending on the language) (see table 6.17).

| **Table 6.17**　Languages with a three-way deictic distinction | | | |
|---|---|---|---|
| **Language** | **'this'** | **'that'** | **'that over there'** |
| Spanish | este | ese | aquel |
| Japanese | kono | sono | ano |
| Korean | i | ku | ce |
| Palauan (the Pacific islands of Palau and Guam) | tia | tilęcha | se |
| Turkish | bu | ʃu | o |

An even more complex system is found in the Amerindian language Tlingit (spoken in British Columbia and Alaska), which makes a four-way distinction: *yáa* 'this one right here', *héi* 'this one nearby', *wée* 'that one over there', and *yóo* 'that one far off'.

Determiners are not the only type of element whose use and interpretation require reference to features of the setting. Deictic contrasts are also crucial to the understanding of such commonly used verbs as *come* and *go*. Notice in this regard the striking difference in perspective found in the following two sentences.

(**44**)　*a.* The bear is coming into the tent!
　　　*b.* The bear is going into the tent!

Whereas *come* with a third person subject implies movement towards the speaker (hence we can infer that the person who utters (44a) is in the tent), *go* with the same type of subject suggests movement away from the speaker.

## 6.4.3  Discourse

An additional source of contextual information relevant to sentence interpretation can be found in **discourse**, the connected series of utterances produced during a conversation, a lecture, a story, or other speech act. The importance of discourse stems from the fact that individual sentences commonly include elements whose interpretation can only be determined with the help of information in preceding utterances. For instance, each of the italicized words in the following passage relies for its interpretation on information encoded in a preceding sentence.

> (45)  A little girl went for a walk in the park. While *there*, *she* saw a rabbit. Since *it* was injured, *she* took *it* home.

We interpret *there* with reference to *in the park*, *she* with reference to *a little girl*, and *it* with reference to *a rabbit*.

One of the most important contrasts in the study of discourse involves the distinction between new and old information. **Old** (or **given**) **information** consists of the knowledge that the speaker assumes is available to the addressee at the time of the utterance, either because it is obvious or because it has been previously mentioned in the discourse. In contrast, **new information** involves knowledge that is introduced into the discourse for the first time. Consider the contrast between the following two sentences.

> (46)  *a.* The man is at the front door.
> *b.* A man is at the front door.

The choice of *the* as the determiner for *man* in (46a) suggests that the referent of the phrase is someone who has already been mentioned in the discourse and is therefore known to the addressee (old information). In contrast, the choice of the determiner *a* in (46b) implies that the referent is being introduced into the discourse for the first time (new information).

Notice that both sentences in (46) use *the* as the determiner for *front door* and that the indefinite determiner *a* would not be natural in this context. This is because the setting for the conversation is likely to include only one front door. Since this information is presumably known to both the speaker and the addressee (i.e., it is old information), *the* is the right determiner to use in this context.

### Topics

Another important notion for the study of discourse is that of **topic**, which corresponds to what a sentence or a portion of the discourse is about. Consider the following passage:

> (47)  Once upon a time there was a merchant with two sons. The older son wanted to be a scholar. He spent his time reading and studying. As for the younger son, he preferred to travel and see the world.

The first sentence in this passage introduces a merchant and his two sons as new information. A topic (the older son) is selected in the second sentence and maintained in the third, in which *he* refers back to the older son. The final sentence then switches to a new topic (the younger son), providing some information about him. This switch is facilitated by the expression *as for*, which can be used in English to mark new topics.

There is a strong tendency in language to encode the topic as subject of a sentence. This is why (as mentioned in section 6.1.2) it is natural to interpret the active sentence in (48a) as being about the police and the passive sentence in (b) as being about the burglar (see also section 5.6 of chapter 5).

**(48)**　*a.* The police chased the burglar.
　　　*b.* The burglar was chased by the police.

In some languages, a special affix is used to identify the topic. The following sentences from Japanese illustrate this phenomenon (Nom = nominative, the subject marker; Top = topic marker; Ques = question marker).

**(49)** *Speaker A:*　　Dare-ga kimasita-ka?
　　　　　　　　　　Who-Nom came-Ques?

　　　　*Speaker B:*　　John-ga kimasita.
　　　　　　　　　　John-Nom came.

　　　　*Speaker A:*　　John-wa dare-to kimasita-ka?
　　　　　　　　　　John-Top who-with came-Ques?
　　　　　　　　　　'Who did John come with?'

The topic marker in Japanese (the suffix *-wa*) is distinguished from the subject marker (*-ga*) by its use to mark old or background information. This is why speaker B responds to A's first question by using the subject marker on the NP *John*, which provides new information (in answer to A's question). And it is why the second use of the NP *John*, which is now associated with previously established information, is accompanied by the topic suffix *-wa*.

## 6.4.4　Conversational maxims

In addition to background beliefs, the setting, and the discourse, there is at least one other major type of information that enters into the interpretation of utterances. This information has to do with the 'rules for conversation'—our understanding of how language is used in particular situations to convey a message. For example, if I ask you, *'Would you like to go to a movie tonight?'* and you respond by saying, *'I have to study for an exam'*, I know that you are declining my invitation even though there is nothing in the literal meaning of the sentence that says so. Moreover, I recognize that this is a perfectly appropriate way to respond. (Notice that the same could not be said of a response like *'I have to scratch my arm'* or *'It's a bit warm in here'*.)

As speakers of a language, we are able to draw inferences about what is meant but not actually said. Information that is conveyed in this way is called **conversational implicature**. The ease with which we recognize and interpret implicature stems from our knowledge of how people in our linguistic community use language to communicate with each other.

The general overarching guideline for conversational interactions is often called the **Cooperative Principle**.

(50) *The Cooperative Principle*
   Make your contribution appropriate to the conversation.

More specific maxims or guidelines ensure that conversational interactions actually satisfy the Cooperative Principle as shown in table 6.18. These maxims are responsible for regulating normal conversation but, as we will see, each can be suspended under certain circumstances to create particular effects.

| **Table 6.18**   Some conversational maxims |
| --- |
| **The Maxim of Relevance**<br>Be relevant. |
| **The Maxim of Quality**<br>Try to make your contribution one that is true. (Do not say things that are false or for which you lack adequate evidence.) |
| **The Maxim of Quantity**<br>Do not make your contribution more or less informative than required. |
| **The Maxim of Manner**<br>Avoid ambiguity and obscurity; be brief and orderly. |

## Relevance

The Maxim of Relevance gives listeners a 'bottom line' for inferring the intent of other speakers. It is because of this maxim that we are able to interpret the utterance *'I have to study for an exam'* (in response to the question *'Would you like to go to a movie?'*) as a 'no'.

   Failure to respect the Maxim of Relevance creates a peculiar effect. For example, if someone asks you, *'Have you finished that term paper yet?'*, and you respond, *'It's been raining a lot lately, hasn't it?'*, you violate the Maxim of Relevance by not responding in a relevant way. But by giving this response, you signal that you want to change the topic of conversation.

## Quality

The Maxim of Quality requires that the statements used in conversations have some factual basis. If, for example, I ask, *'What's the weather like?'* and someone responds, *'It's snowing'*, I will normally assume that this statement provides reliable information about the current weather.

   In order to achieve irony or sarcasm, however, it is sometimes possible to abandon the Maxim of Quality and say something that one knows to be false. Thus, if two people live in the middle of a sweltering desert and one person insists on asking every morning, *'What's the weather like?'*, it might be appropriate for the other person to respond sarcastically, *'Oh, today it's snowing, as usual'*, perhaps with a particular facial expression or intonation to indicate that the statement was not intended as a true report of the facts.

   Considerations of politeness can also justify suspension of the Maxim of Quality. For instance, in order to avoid hurt feelings, you might congratulate a fellow student on a presentation, even though you were not impressed by it.

## Quantity

The Maxim of Quantity introduces some very subtle guidelines into a conversation. Imagine, for example, that someone asks me where a famous Canadian author lives. The nature of my response will depend in large part on how much information I believe to be appropriate for that point in the conversation. If I know that the other person is simply curious about which part of the country the author lives in, it might suffice to respond *'in Manitoba'*. On the other hand, if I know that the person wants to visit the author, then much more specific information (perhaps even an address) is appropriate.

## Manner

The Maxim of Manner imposes several constraints on language use, two of which will be exemplified here. First, imagine that I refer to a particular person as *the man who Mary lives with*. A listener would be justified in concluding that the man in question is not Mary's husband. This is because, by the Maxim of Manner, a briefer and less obscure description, *Mary's husband*, would have been used if it could have correctly described Mary's companion.

   Second, imagine that an employer asks me about a former student of mine who has applied for a job and I say, with some sarcasm, *"You will be fortunate indeed if you can get him to work for you."* By using a sentence that can be interpreted in two very different ways (*"You will be glad to have him on your staff"* versus *"It is not easy to get him to do any work"*), I violate the Maxim of Manner by using an ambiguous structure. Since the maxims are violated only for specific purposes, the employer would be justified in doubting the sincerity of my recommendation.

# *Summing up*

The study of **semantics** is concerned with a broad range of phenomena, including the nature of **meaning**, the role of syntactic structure in the interpretation of sentences, and the effect of **pragmatics** on the understanding of utterances. Although much remains to be done in each of these areas, work in recent years has at least begun to identify the type of relations, mechanisms, and principles involved in the understanding of language. These include the notions of **extension** and **intension** in the case of word meaning, **thematic roles** in the case of NPs, and **c-command** in the case of pronouns. Other factors known to be involved in an utterance's interpretation include **constructional meaning**, the speaker's and hearer's background beliefs (as manifested, for example, in **presuppositions**), the context provided by the setting and the **discourse**, and the **maxims** associated with the **Cooperative Principle**.

## Recommended reading

Chierchia, Gennaro, and Sally McConnell-Ginet. 1990. *Meaning and Grammar*. Cambridge, MA: MIT Press.

Horn, Laurence. 1988. "Pragmatic Theory." In *Linguistics: The Cambridge Survey*. Vol. 1. Edited by F. Newmeyer, 113–45. New York: Cambridge University Press.

Ladusaw, William. 1988. "Semantic Theory." In *Linguistics: The Cambridge Survey*. Vol. 1. Edited by F. Newmeyer, 89–112. New York: Cambridge University Press.

Lakoff, George, and Mark Johnson. 1982. *Metaphors We Live By*. Chicago: University of Chicago Press.

Lappin, Shalom (ed.). 1997. *The Handbook of Contemporary Semantic Theory*. Boston: Blackwell.

McCawley, James. 1993. *Everything That Linguists Have Always Wanted to Know About Logic*. 2nd ed. Chicago: University of Chicago Press.

Prince, Ellen. 1988. "Discourse Analysis: A Part of the Study of Linguistic Competence." In *Linguistics: The Cambridge Survey*. Vol. 2. Edited by F. Newmeyer, 164–82. New York: Cambridge University Press.

Saeed, John. 1996. *Semantics*. Boston: Blackwell.

Schiffrin, Deborah. 1993. *Approaches to Discourse: Language as Social Interaction*. Boston: Blackwell.

## Exercises

1. Two relations involving word meanings are antonymy and synonymy. Which relation is illustrated in each of the pairs of words below?

    a) flourish-thrive
    b) intelligent-stupid
    c) casual-informal
    d) young-old
    e) uncle-aunt
    f) intelligent-smart
    g) flog-whip
    h) drunk-sober

2. It was noted in this chapter that a single form can have two or more meanings. Depending on whether these meanings are related to each other, this phenomenon involves polysemy or homophony. Which of these two relations is exemplified by the forms below?

    a) *grass:* herbage used for grazing animals; marijuana
    b) *leech:* a bloodsucking worm; a hanger-on who seeks advantage
    c) *range:* a cooking stove; a series of mountains
    d) *key:* an instrument used to apply to a lock; an answer sheet for a test or assignment
    e) *steal/steel*: rob; a type of metal
    f) *race:* the act of running competitively; people belonging to the same genetic grouping
    g) *flower/flour:* a type of plant; finely ground wheat

3. Three semantic relations among sentences were covered in this chapter: paraphrase, entailment, and contradiction. Which of these relations is exemplified in each of the following pairs of sentences?

    a) I saw Timothy at the anniversary party.
       It was Timothy that I saw at the anniversary party.
    b) Jules is Mary's husband.
       Mary is married.
    c) My pet cobra likes the taste of chocolate fudge.
       My pet cobra finds chocolate fudge tasty.

d) Vera is an only child.
   Olga is Vera's sister.
e) It is fifty kilometres to the nearest service station.
   The nearest service station is fifty kilometres away.
f) My cousin Bryan teaches at the community college for a living.
   My cousin Bryan is a teacher.

**4.** In discussing the nature of meaning, we noted that it is necessary to distinguish between intension and extension. Describe the intensions and the extensions of each of these phrases.

a) the President of the United States
b) the Queen of England
c) the capital of Canada
d) women who have walked on the moon
e) my linguistics professor

**5.** In our discussion of semantic decomposition, we noted that at least some words have meanings that can be represented in terms of smaller semantic features. Four such words are *dog*, *puppy*, *cat*, and *kitten*.

**i)**   Attempt to provide semantic features associated with each of these words.
**ii)**  How are the pairs *dog-puppy* and *cat-kitten* different from *man-boy* and *woman-girl*?
**iii)** Try to provide semantic features for the words *circle*, *triangle*, and *quadrangle*. What problems do you encounter?

**6.** Each of the following words is associated with a concept.

a) island            e) food
b) soft              f) husband
c) white             g) baseball bat
d) wristwatch        h) mountain

**i)**  Determine which of these examples involve fuzzy concepts.
**ii)** Choose one of the fuzzy concepts above. Name one prototypical member of that concept and one member that is closer to the concept boundary.

**7.** Draw a diagram for the concept 'dwelling' similar to that of figure 6.2 in this chapter. Do the same for the concept 'vehicle'.

**8.** Examine the following sets of sentences.

a) She gave him an icy stare.
   He gave her the cold shoulder.
   He exudes a lot of warmth towards people.
   They got into a heated argument.
b) He drops a lot of hints.
   The committee picked up on the issue.
   She dumps all her problems on her friends.
   Although he disagreed, he let it go.

c) the eye of a needle
   the foot of the bed
   the hands of the clock
   the arm of a chair
   the table legs
d) This lecture is easy to digest.
   He just eats up the lecturer's words.
   Chew on this thought for a while.
   Listen to this juicy piece of gossip.

For each set of sentences:

**i)**   Identify the words or phrases that are used metaphorically in each sentence.
**ii)**  Determine the basis for each of these metaphor sets.
Use the pattern: 'The metaphors in (x) describe _____ in terms of _____.'
*Example*: The metaphors in (a) describe human relationships in terms of temperature.

9. The section on lexicalization of concepts discussed how some languages simultaneously express motion and path, motion and manner, and/or motion and thing moving in motion verbs. Can you change the sentence *He moved the goods by truck to the warehouse* so that both the movement and the vehicle used for the move are lexicalized in one verb? Can you think of another verb that expresses a similar combination of concepts?

10. Consider the following Fijian pronouns.

| | |
|---|---|
| *au* | 1st person singular 'me' |
| *iko* | 2nd person singular 'you' |
| *koya* | 3rd person singular 'him/her/it' |
| *kedaru* | 1st person dual 'you and me' |
| *keirau* | 1st person dual 'one other (not you) and me' |
| *kemudrau* | 2nd person dual 'you two' |
| *rau* | 3rd person dual 'those two' |
| *kedatou* | 1st person trial 'two others (including you) and me' |
| *keitou* | 1st person trial 'two others (excluding you) and me' |
| *kemudou* | 2nd person trial 'you three' |
| *iratou* | 3rd person trial 'those three' |
| *keda* | 1st person plural 'us' (more than three, including you) |
| *keimami* | 1st person plural 'us' (more than three, excluding you) |
| *kemuni:* | 2nd person plural 'you' (more than three) |
| *ira* | 3rd person plural 'them' (more than three) |

**i)**   Some concepts are grammaticalized in the Fijian pronoun system that are not grammaticalized in the English pronoun system. Can you identify them?
**ii)**  Which concept is grammaticalized in the English pronoun system but not in the Fijian system?

11. A well-known joke goes something like this: 'I just shot an elephant in my pyjamas. How he got in my pyjamas, I don't know.' With the help of tree structures, explain how being able to recognize structural ambiguity is essential to 'getting' the joke.

**12.** Each NP in the following sentences has a thematic role that represents the part that its referent plays in the situation described by the sentence.

a) The man chased the intruder.
b) The cat jumped from the chair onto the table.
c) Aaron wrote a letter to Marilyn.
d) The premier entertained the guests in the lounge.
e) Henry mailed the manuscript from Edmonton.

Using the terms described in this chapter, label the thematic role of each NP in these sentences and identify the assigner for each thematic role.

*Example*: <u>Bill</u> wrote <u>a novel</u> in <u>the park</u>

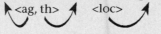

**13.** Each of the following sentences has undergone a movement transformation.

a) What should Larry give to the bride?
b) Who will Liane kiss?
c) Which house will the group leave from?
d) What might Marvin forget on the bus?

Write out the deep structure string for each of these sentences and mark all thematic roles and thematic role assigners.

*Example*: a) <u>Larry</u> should give <u>what</u> to <u>the bride</u>

&lt;ag,th&gt; &lt;goal&gt;

**14.** It is often suggested that *each other* (a so-called reciprocal pronoun) behaves like reflexive pronouns in obeying Principle A. How does this idea explain the acceptable and unacceptable uses of *each other* illustrated in the following sentences?

i) *The men* admire *each other*.
ii) **The men's* boss admires *each other*.
iii) **The men* think that [$_{IP}$ the boss admires *each other*].

**15.** In the following sentence, the pronoun *she* could, according to Principle B, refer to either *the architect* or *the secretary*.

The architect gave the secretary a raise after she typed the report.

i)   Which interpretation for *she* comes to mind first?
ii)  Why?
iii) What happens to the pronoun's interpretation if you change the word *secretary* to *janitor*?

**16.** In each of the following pairs of sentences, one of the sentences contains a presupposition relating to the truth of the complement clause.

a) John regrets that Maria went to the graduation ceremony.
   John believes that Maria went to the graduation ceremony.
b) The captain thought that the ship was in danger.
   The captain realized that the ship was in danger.
c) It is significant that the criminal was sentenced.
   It is likely that the criminal was sentenced.

For each pair:

i)   Identify the sentence that contains the presupposition.

ii)  Locate the word that is responsible for the presupposition.

**17.** The syntactic construction *It was _____ that _____* is called a 'cleft construction' and is used in certain discourse contexts. Consider the following conversations involving cleft constructions.

a) *A*:  Did Sally claim that she saw a flying saucer last night?
   *B*:  No, it was <u>a meteorite</u> that <u>Sally claimed she saw last night</u>.
b) *A*:  Did Sally claim that she saw a flying saucer last night?
   *B*:  No, it was <u>Sally</u> that <u>claimed she saw a meteorite last night</u>.
c) *A*:  Did Sally claim that she saw a flying saucer last night?
   *B*:  No, it was <u>last week</u> that <u>Sally claimed she saw a flying saucer</u>.

i)   In which example is B's response inappropriate?

ii)  Focus first on contexts in which B's response is appropriate. How do the underlined parts correspond to new and old information?

iii) Can you now explain why the cleft construction is unacceptable in one of the examples?

**18.** Each of the following examples contains a conversational implicature.

a) *A*:  Have you washed the floor and done the dishes?
   *B*:  I've washed the floor.
b) *A*:  Did you get hold of Carl yet?
   *B*:  I tried to call him yesterday.
c) *A*:  What did you think of the movie?
   *B*:  Well, the supporting actor was great.
d) *A*:  Do you have any pets?
   *B*:  Yes, I have two cats.

What is the implicature for each example?

# *Seven*

Robert W. Murray

# *Historical linguistics: the study of language change*

*Many men sayn that in sweveninges*
*Ther nys but fables and lesynges;*
*But men may some swevenes sene*
*Whiche hardely that false ne bene,*
*But afterwarde ben apparaunt.*

CHAUCER, *THE ROMANCE OF THE ROSE* (c. 1370)

Language change is both obvious and rather mysterious. The English of the late fourteenth century, for example, is so different from Modern English that without special training it is difficult to understand the opening lines to *The Romance of the Rose* cited above. Not only would these sentences have a foreign sound, but words and structures such as *sweveninges*, *lesynges*, and *false ne bene* are unfamiliar.[1] The existence of such differences between early and later variants of the same language raises questions as to how and why languages change over time.

**Historical linguistics** is concerned with both the description and explanation of language change. In this chapter we examine the nature and causes of language change and survey phonological, morphological, syntactic, lexical, and semantic change. We also explore techniques used to reconstruct linguistic pre-history and briefly discuss related research into language acquisition and linguistic universals.

## 7.1 The nature of language change

All languages undergo change over time. English has undergone continuous and dramatic change throughout its three major periods: Old English (roughly from 450 to 1100), Middle English (from 1100 to 1500), and Modern English (from 1500 to the present). Although Chaucer's Middle English is at least partially comprehensible today, Old English looks like a completely foreign language. The following is an extract from an eighth-century Old English

---

**Language Matters** **What Did Old English and Middle English Sound Like?**

Thanks to the efforts of linguists and literary scholars, a great deal has been learned about what Old English and Middle English sounded like, and trained readers often recite literary works from those periods. For a sample of Old English, go to www.tha-engliscan-gesithas.org.uk/readings/readings. html. For Middle English, go to http://academics.vmi.edu/english/audio/audio_index.html. Want to learn to write and communicate in Old English? Go to www.rochester.edu/englisc/.

---

document, a translation of Bede's Latin history of England. (The letter /þ/, called 'thorn', represented the phoneme /θ/ in Old English; here and elsewhere in this chapter ‾ marks a long vowel in the orthography.)

(1)  and Seaxan þā sige geslōgan.
and Saxons the victory won
'And the Saxons won the victory.'

þā sendan hī hām ǣrenddracan.
then sent they home messenger
'Then they sent home a messenger.'

These Old English sentences differ from their Modern English counterparts in many respects. In terms of pronunciation, for instance, the Old English word *hām* [hɑːm] 'home' in the second sentence became [hɔːm] in Middle English, and then [howm] in Modern English. In its morphology, Old English differed significantly from Modern English. The suffix *-an* on the Old English word for 'sent' indicates both past tense and plurality of the subject (*hī* 'they'). Differences in word order are also readily apparent, with the verb following both the subject and the direct object in the first sentence and preceding both the subject and the direct object in the second. Neither of these word orders would be acceptable in the Modern English forms of these sentences.

In addition, some Old English words have disappeared from use, as the unfamiliar *ǣrenddracan* 'messenger' and *sige* 'victory' indicate. Still other words have been maintained, but with a change in meaning. For example, the Old English word *geslōgan* (which we translated as 'won') is the past tense of the verb *slēan*, the Old English predecessor of our word *slay*. Although the Modern English meaning of this word in normal usage is restricted to the act of killing, the Old English verb could also mean 'to strike, beat, coin (money), and forge (weapons)'. As these examples imply, all components of the grammar from meaning (semantics) to individual sounds (phonology) are subject to change.

## 7.1.1  Systematicity of language change

A striking fact about language change in general is its regularity and systematicity. For example, the development of a fixed subject-verb-direct object (SVO) word order in English did not affect just a few verbs; all verbs in Modern English appear before rather than after the direct object. Similarly, the changes affecting the vowel in the word *hām* did not occur in that word only; they represent the regular development of the Old English vowel *ā* ([ɑː]). (See table 7.1.)

| Table 7.1 | Changes affecting Old English [ɑː] | | |
|---|---|---|---|
| **Old English** | **Middle English** | **Modern English** | |
| [bɑːt] | [bɔːt] | [bowt] | 'boat' |
| [ɑːθ] | [ɔːθ] | [owθ] | 'oath' |
| [stɑːn] | [stɔːn] | [stown] | 'stone' |

## 7.1.2 Causes of language change

The inevitability of language change is guaranteed by the way in which language is passed on from one generation to the next. Children do not begin with an intact grammar of the language being acquired but rather must construct a grammar on the basis of the available data (see chapter 10). In such a situation it is hardly surprising that differences arise, even if only subtle ones, from one generation to the next. Moreover, since all children draw on the same physiological and cognitive endowment in learning language, it is to be expected that the same patterns of change will be consistently and repeatedly manifested in all languages. Following is a brief overview of the principal causes of language change.

### Articulatory simplification

As might be expected, most sound changes have a physiological basis. Since such sound changes typically result in **articulatory simplification**, they have traditionally been related to the idea of 'ease of articulation'. Although this notion is difficult to define precisely, we can readily identify cases of articulatory simplification in our everyday speech, such as the deletion of a consonant in a complex cluster or, in some dialects, the insertion of a vowel to break up a complex cluster (see table 7.2).

| Table 7.2 | Simplification of complex clusters | | |
|---|---|---|---|
| **Deletion of a consonant** | | | |
| [fɪfθs] | → | [fɪfs] | 'fifths' |
| **Insertion of a vowel** | | | |
| [æθlit] | → | [æθəlit] | 'athlete' |

### Spelling pronunciation

Not all changes in pronunciation have a physiological motivation. A minor, but nevertheless important, source of change in English and other languages is **spelling pronunciation**. Since the written form of a word can differ significantly from the way it is pronounced, a new pronunciation can arise that seems to reflect more closely the spelling of the word. A case in point is the word *often*. Although this word was pronounced with a [t] in earlier

English, the voiceless stop was subsequently lost, resulting in the pronunciation [ɑfən] (compare *soften*). However, since the letter *t* was retained in the spelling, [t] has been reintroduced into many speakers' pronunciation of this word.

Another case in point is the pronunciation of [s] in words such as *assume* and *consume*. Although in earlier English such words were pronounced with [s], sound change resulted in a pronunciation with [ʃ] (as in *assure*). Similar to the case of *often* above, a pronunciation with [s] has been reintroduced into many dialects on the basis of the spelling (which remained unchanged even after the sound change took place). Since spelling tends to remain stable even though sound changes have occurred (English spelling began stabilizing more than three hundred years ago), spelling pronunciation can reintroduce a pronunciation that was earlier altered through sound change.

## Analogy and reanalysis

Cognitive factors also play a role in change in all components of the grammar. Two sources of change having a cognitive basis are **analogy** and **reanalysis**. Analogy reflects the preference of speakers for regular patterns over irregular ones. It typically involves the extension or generalization of a regularity on the basis of the inference that if elements are alike in some respects, they should be alike in others as well. Both phonological and semantic characteristics can serve as a basis for analogy. For example, on the basis of its phonological similarity with verbs such as *sting/stung* and *swing/swung*, in some dialects *bring* has developed a form *brung*, as in *I brung it into the house*. The effects of analogy can also be observed in the speech of children, who often generalize the regular *-ed* past tense form to produce forms such as *goed* and *knowed* (see chapter 10). As we will see shortly, analogy plays a very important role in morphological change as well.

Reanalysis is particularly common in morphological change. Morphological reanalysis typically involves an attempt to attribute a compound or root + affix structure to a word that formerly was not broken down into component morphemes. A classic example in English is the word *hamburger*, which originally referred to a type of meat patty deriving its name from the city of Hamburg in Germany. This word has been reanalyzed as consisting of two components, *ham* + *burger*. The latter morpheme has since appeared in many new forms including *fishburger*, *chickenburger*, and even as a free morpheme *burger*. Note that the reanalysis need not be correct. (There is usually no ham in a burger—especially a *veggie burger!*)

## Language contact

Another cause of language change is **language contact**. Language contact refers to the situation where speakers of a language frequently interact with the speakers of another language or dialect. As a consequence, extensive **borrowing** can occur, particularly where there are significant numbers of bilinguals or multilinguals. Although borrowing can affect all components of the grammar, the lexicon is typically most affected. English, for example, has borrowed many Aboriginal words including *Canada, moccasin, totem, tomahawk, chinook, moose,* and *skunk*.

Among the effects that borrowing can have on the sound system are the introduction of new phonemes or allophones and changes in their distribution. For example, some English speakers pronounce the name of the classical composer *Bach* with the final velar fricative [x] found in the German pronunciation. If there are a significant number of borrowings from another language, the borrowed foreign segment can eventually become a new phoneme. In the early Middle English period, the London dialect had [f] but not [v] in word-initial position. The [v] was later introduced as a result of contact with other English dialects and with French, in which it did occur word-initially. This contact was a likely factor in the development of a contrast between /f/ and /v/ word-initially, as found in Modern English pairs such as *file* and *vile*.

Language (as well as dialect) contact also results in another minor but nevertheless important source of language change, **hypercorrection**. Hypercorrection occurs when a speaker who is attempting to speak another dialect or language overgeneralizes particular rules. For example, most Canadians speak a dialect in which no distinction is made between intervocalic [t] and [d] so that words such as *latter* and *ladder* are both pronounced with an intervocalic flap [ɾ] (see chapter 2). If a speaker from such a dialect attempts to emulate the pronunciation of a speaker from another dialect who does distinguish the two stops intervocalically, hypercorrection could result in the use of intervocalic [t] in words where [d] should be used; for example, the pronunciation *pro*[t]*igy* for *pro<u>d</u>igy*.

Another example of hypercorrection is the use of *I* in constructions such as *He saw John and I*. This usage is an overgeneralization of the rule that only *I* should be used in subject position, never *me*. According to this rule, *John and I are going* is correct but *John and me/me and John are going* is incorrect. For some speakers, hypercorrection has resulted in the inference that all coordinate phrases containing *me* (such as *John and me*) are incorrect even when they serve as direct object (complement) of the verb. Note that even a person who says *He saw John and I* would not say *He saw I*.

## 7.2  Sound change

Although all components of the grammar are susceptible to change over time, some types of change yield more obvious results than others. Variation and change are particularly noticeable in the phonology of a language. Several common types of sound change can be distinguished.

Most sound changes begin as subtle alterations in the sound pattern of a language in particular phonetic environments. The linguistic processes underlying such **phonetically conditioned** change are identical to the ones found in the phonology of currently spoken languages (see chapter 2, section 2.2). The application of such processes usually brings about an articulatory simplification, and over time significant changes in the phonology of a language can result.

Although all aspects of a language's phonology (e.g., tone, stress, and syllable structure) are subject to change over time, we will restrict our attention here to change involving segments. Since most sound changes involve sequences of segments, the main focus will be on **sequential change**. However, we will also discuss one common type of **segmental** change, involving the simplification of an affricate. In addition, in order to demonstrate that more than just articulatory factors play a role in sound change, we will discuss a case of sound change based on auditory factors. All important sound changes discussed in this section and referred to in this chapter are found in the catalogue of sound changes in table 7.3.

| Table 7.3     Catalogue of sound changes | |
|---|---|
| **Sequential change** | Consonants |
| |     Degemination |
| Assimilation |     Voicing |
|     Place and/or manner of articulation |     Frication |
|     Palatalization/affrication |     Rhotacism |
|     Nasalization |     Deletion |
|     Umlaut | Consonant strengthening |
| Dissimilation |     Glide strengthening |
| Epenthesis (segment addition) | |
| Metathesis (segment movement) | **Segmental change** |
| Weakening and deletion | |
|     Vowels | Deaffrication |
|         Vowel reduction | **Auditorily based change** |
|         Syncope | |
|         Apocope | Substitution |

## 7.2.1  Sequential change

### Assimilation

The most common type of sequential change is **assimilation**, which has the effect of increasing the efficiency of articulation through a simplification of articulatory movements. We will focus here on the four main types indicated in the catalogue.

Partial assimilation involving **place or manner of articulation** is a very common change that, over time, can result in total assimilation. In the Spanish and Latin examples in table 7.4, the nasal assimilated in place of articulation to the following consonant.

| Table 7.4     Assimilation (place of articulation) in Spanish and Latin[2] | | | | |
|---|---|---|---|---|
| Old Spanish | se<u>md</u>a | Modern Spanish | se<u>nd</u>a | 'path' |
| Early Latin | i<u>np</u>ossibilis | Later Latin | i<u>mp</u>ossibilis | 'impossible |

The first of the Old English examples in table 7.5 shows voicing assimilation and the second shows the assimilation of nasality.

| Table 7.5     Assimilation in manner of articulation in Old English | | |
|---|---|---|
| **Early Old English** | **Later Old English** | |
| slæ<u>pd</u>e | slæ<u>pt</u>e | 'slept' |
| ste<u>fn</u> | ste<u>mn</u> | 'stem (of a plant)' |

In the Italian examples in table 7.6, a stop assimilates totally to a following stop.

| Table 7.6 | Total assimilation in Italian | |
|---|---|---|
| **Latin** | **Italian** | |
| o<u>ct</u>o (*c* = [k]) | o<u>tt</u>o | 'eight' |
| se<u>pt</u>em | se<u>tt</u>e | 'seven' |
| da<u>mn</u>um | da<u>nn</u>o | 'damage |

Another type of assimilation is **palatalization**—the effect that front vowels and the palatal glide [j] typically have on velar, alveolar, and dental stops, making their place of articulation more palatal. If you compare your pronunciation of *keep* as opposed to *cot*, you will notice that the pronunciation of [k] in the former is much more palatal than in the latter due to the influence of [i]. Palatalization is often the first step in **affrication**, a change in which palatalized stops become affricates, either [ts] or [tʃ] if the original stop was voiceless or [dz] or [dʒ] if the original stop was voiced (see table 7.7).

| Table 7.7 | Palatalization/affrication induced by front vowels and [j] |
|---|---|

| **Examples from the Romance languages** | | | | |
|---|---|---|---|---|
| Latin | <u>c</u>entum [k] | Old French | <u>c</u>ent | [ts] | 'one hundred' |
| Latin | <u>c</u>entum [k] | Italian | <u>c</u>ento | [tʃ] | 'one hundred' |
| Latin | me<u>d</u>ius [d] | Italian | me<u>zz</u>o | [dz] | 'half' |
| Latin | <u>g</u>entem [g] | Old French | <u>g</u>ent | [dʒ] | 'people' |

**Nasalization** refers to the nasalizing effect that a nasal consonant can have on an adjacent vowel. This change occurred in both French and Portuguese, with the subsequent loss of the nasal consonant. (The pronunciation of the vowels in the examples in table 7.8 underwent additional changes in height and backness in French.)

| Table 7.8 | Nasalization in Portuguese and French | |
|---|---|---|
| **Latin** | **Portuguese** | **French** | |
| bon- | bom [bõ] | bon [bɔ̃] | 'good' |
| un- | um [ũ] | un [œ̃] | 'one' |

Although assimilation is probably most common in the case of adjacent segments, it can also apply at a distance. A case in point is **umlaut**, the effect a vowel or sometimes a glide in one syllable can have on the vowel of another syllable, usually a preceding one. Umlaut (resulting in the front rounded vowels [y] and [ø]) played an important role in Old English and is the source of irregular plurals such as *goose/geese* and *mouse/mice* in Modern English. For example, the plural of the pre-Old English words *gōs* 'goose' and *mūs* 'mouse' was formed by adding a suffix -[i]. As a result, umlaut of the vowel in the preceding syllable occurred in the plural forms (see pre-Old English stages 1 and 2) but not in the singular forms. By early Old English, the suffix -[i] had been lost in a separate change leaving the umlauted vowel as the marker of the plural form. (Subsequent changes included the derounding of the umlauted vowels [ȳ] and [ø̄] yielding [ī] and [ē] respectively by Middle English, and the Great Vowel Shift as described in section 7.2.4; see table 7.9.)

| Table 7.9 | | Umlaut in English Plurals | | | | | |
|-----------|---|---------------------------|---|----------|---|---------------------|---|
| **Pre-Old English 1** | | **Pre-OE 2** | | **Early OE** | | **Subsequent changes** | |
| [gōs] | > | [gōs] | > | [gōs] | > | [gus] | 'goose' |
| [gōsi] | > | [gø̄si] | > | [gø̄s] | > | [gis] | 'geese' |
| [mūs] | > | [mūs] | > | [mūs] | > | [maws] | 'mouse' |
| [mūsi] | > | [mȳsi] | > | [mȳs] | > | [majs] | 'mice' |

*Note*: It is traditional in historical linguistics to use the sign > to mean 'changed into'.

## Dissimilation

**Dissimilation**, the process whereby one segment is made less like another segment in its environment, is much less frequent than assimilation. This type of change typically occurs when it would be difficult to articulate or perceive two similar sounds in close proximity. The word *anma* 'soul' in Late Latin, for example, was modified to *alma* in Spanish, thereby avoiding two consecutive nasal consonants. Like assimilation, dissimilation can also operate at a distance to affect non-adjacent segments. For instance, the Latin word *arbor* 'tree' became *arbol* in Spanish and *albero* in Italian, thereby avoiding two instances of *r* in adjacent syllables. (By contrast, dissimilation did not occur in French where *arbre* has retained both instances of *r*.)

## Epenthesis

Another common sound change, **epenthesis**, involves the insertion of a consonant or vowel into a particular environment (see table 7.10). In some cases, epenthesis results from the anticipation of an upcoming sound.

| Table 7.10 | Epenthesis in Old English | | | | |
|------------|---------------------------|---|--------|------------|---------|
| **Earlier form** | **Change** | | | **Later form** | |
| ganra | VnrV | > | VndrV | gandra | 'gander' |
| simle | VmlV | > | VmblV | simble | 'always' |
| ǣmtig | VmtV | > | VmptV | ǣmptig | 'empty' |

In these examples, the epenthetic [b], [d], or [p] has the place of articulation of the preceding nasal but agrees with the following segment in terms of voice and nasality. The epenthetic segment therefore serves as a bridge for the transition between the segments on either side.

| **Table 7.11** | The nature of epenthesis | | | | |
|---|---|---|---|---|---|
| [m] | [b] | [l] | [m] | [p] | [t] |
| labial | labial | non-labial | labial | labial | non-labial |
| nasal | non-nasal | non-nasal | nasal | non-nasal | non-nasal |
| voiced | voiced | voiced | voiced | voiceless | voiceless |

In other cases, vowel epenthesis serves to break up a sequence of sounds that would otherwise be difficult to pronounce or even inconsistent with the phonotactic patterns of the language. As mentioned above, some English speakers avoid [θl] clusters by inserting an epenthetic [ə] in their pronunciation of words such as *athlete* as *ath*[ə]*lete*. In the history of Spanish, word-initial [sk] clusters were avoided by inserting a vowel (see table 7.12).

| **Table 7.12** | Examples of epenthesis | | | | |
|---|---|---|---|---|---|
| Latin | schola [sk] | Spanish | escuela [esk] | 'school' | |
| Latin | scrībere [sk] | Spanish | escribir [esk] | 'write' | |

## Metathesis

**Metathesis** involves a change in the relative positioning of segments. This change, like assimilation and dissimilation, can affect adjacent segments or segments at a distance (see table 7.13).

| **Table 7.13** | Metathesis of adjacent segments in Old English | |
|---|---|---|
| **Earlier form** | **Later form** | |
| wæps | wæsp | 'wasp' |
| þridda | þirdda | 'third' |

Metathesis at a distance is found in the change from Latin *mīrāculum* 'miracle' to Spanish *milagro*, in which [r] and [l] have changed places although they were not adjacent (see figure 7.1).

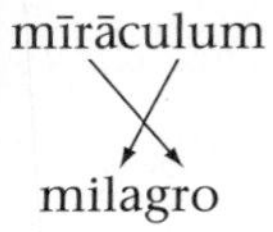

**Figure 7.1**
Metathesis of non-adjacent segments in Spanish

mīrāculum

milagro

Although users of signed languages do not use their oral articulators to produce speech sounds, they do, nonetheless, *articulate*. The difference is that they use the shape, position, and orientation of the hands to create meaning. These gestures are subject to processes very much like the ones we have been talking about. For example, the sign for *deaf* in American Sign Language was originally made by touching the jaw beside the ear with the index finger, and then touching the cheek beside the mouth. Over time, the movement changed from ear-to-jaw to jaw-to-ear, especially when following a sign that ended near the jaw. Today, both versions are acceptable.

## Weakening and deletion

Both vowels and consonants are also susceptible to outright **deletion** as well as to various **weakening** processes. We will first treat the effects of these processes on vowels and then turn to their effects on consonants.

Vowel deletion commonly involves a word-final vowel (**apocope**) or a word-internal vowel (**syncope**) (see table 7.14). A vowel in an unstressed syllable is particularly susceptible to deletion, especially when a nearby neighbouring syllable is stressed.

| **Table 7.14**   Vowel deletion in French | | |
|---|---|---|
| **Apocope** | | |
| *Latin* | *French* | |
| cū́ra | cure [kyʁ] | 'cure' |
| ōrnā́re | orner | 'decorate' |
| **Syncope** | | |
| *Latin* | *French* | |
| pḗrdere | perdre | 'lose' |
| vī́vere | vivre | 'live' |

The effects of syncope are also apparent in the loss of the medial vowel in Modern English words such as *vegetable*, *interest*, and *family*, which are frequently pronounced as [védʒtəbl̩], [íntrɪst], and [fǽmli].

More frequent words are, in general, more likely to have a shortened pronunciation than are less common words. That's why the middle vowel in *every* is far more likely to be dropped than the middle vowel in *summery* (in the sense of 'summerlike'). Words such as *memory* and *family*, which are intermediate in frequency, permit more variation in terms of whether the middle vowel is lost or retained.

Vowel deletion is commonly preceded diachronically by **vowel reduction**, in which a full vowel is reduced to a schwa-like vowel (i.e., short, lax, central [ə]). Vowel reduction typically affects short vowels in unstressed syllables and may affect all or only a subset of the full vowels (see figure 7.2).

**Figure 7.2**
Vowel reduction

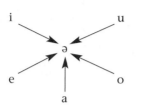

Vowel reduction with subsequent deletion (syncope and apocope) occurred in Middle English and Early Modern English as shown in table 7.15.

| **Table 7.15** | Vowel reduction and deletion in English | |
|---|---|---|
| **Syncope** | | |
| ***Old English*** | ***Middle English*** *(vowel reduction)* | ***Early Modern English*** *(vowel deletion)* |
| stān<u>as</u> [a] | ston<u>es</u> [ə] | ston<u>es</u>  Ø |
| stān<u>es</u> [e] | ston<u>es</u> [ə] | ston<u>e</u>'s  Ø |
| **Apocope** | | |
| ***Old English*** | ***Middle English*** *(vowel reduction)* | ***Early Modern English*** *(apocope)* |
| nam<u>a</u> [a] | nam<u>e</u>  [ə] | nam<u>e</u>  Ø |
| tal<u>u</u>  [u] | tal<u>e</u>  [ə] | tal<u>e</u>  Ø |

**Consonant deletion** is also a very common sound change. For example, the word-initial cluster [kn] was found in Old and Middle English, as the spelling of such words as *knight*, *knit*, *knot*, and *knee* implies, but the [k] was subsequently lost, giving us our modern pronunciation. The loss of word-final consonants has played a major role in the evolution of Modern French. The final letters in the written forms of the words in table 7.16 reflect consonants that were actually pronounced at an earlier stage of the language.

| **Table 7.16** | Consonant loss in French | |
|---|---|---|
| **French spelling** **(masculine form)** | **Current pronunciation** | |
| gros | [gro] | 'large' |
| chaud | [ʃo] | 'warm' |
| vert | [vɛr] | 'green' |

Just as vowel reduction can be identified as a weakening process since it represents an intermediate step on the pathway from a full vowel to deletion of the vowel, so too can pathways of **consonant weakening** be identified. The scale of **consonantal strength** in figure 7.3 can be helpful in identifying cases of weakening.

|  |  |
|---|---|
| **Figure 7.3**<br>Scale of consonantal<br>strength | Consonantal strength<br>stronger ▲ voiceless stops<br>            voiceless fricatives, voiced stops<br>            voiced fricatives<br>            nasals<br>            liquids<br>weaker ▼ glides |

(*Note:* Geminate consonants are stronger than their non-geminate counterparts.)

Accordingly, geminates weaken to non-geminates (**degemination**), stops weaken to fricatives (**frication**), and voiceless stops or voiceless fricatives weaken to voiced stops or voiced fricatives respectively (**voicing**).[3] Weakening can ultimately result in the deletion of the consonant. Figure 7.4 is a typical pathway of weakening.

**Figure 7.4**
Typical pathway of
consonant weakening

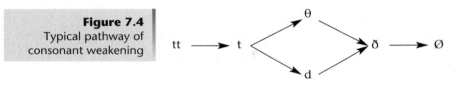

Consonants are particularly subject to weakening in an intervocalic environment. Parts of the pathway of consonantal weakening are exemplified with developments from the Romance languages shown in table 7.17.

| **Table 7.17** | Consonantal weakening in Romance | | | | | |
|---|---|---|---|---|---|---|
| Degemination (tt > t): | Latin | mi̱ṯtere | Spanish | meṯer | 'to put' | |
| Voicing (t > d): | Latin | mātūrus | Old Spanish | maḏuro | 'ripe' | |
| Frication (d > ð): | Old Spanish | maḏuro | Spanish | maḏuro [ð] | 'ripe' | |
| Deletion (ð > Ø): | Old French | [maðyr] | French | mûr | 'ripe' | |

**Rhotacism** is a relatively common type of weakening that typically involves the change of [z] to [r]. Often rhotacism is preceded by a stage involving the voicing of [s] to [z]. Within the Germanic family of languages, for instance, [s] first became [z] in a particular intervocalic environment. This [z] remained in Gothic but became [r] in other Germanic languages such as in English, German, and Swedish. The effects of the latter part of this change can be seen in the standard spellings of the words in table 7.18 on p. 241.

In Modern English, rhotacism is the source of the alternation between [z] and [r] in *was* and *were*. The [r] resulted from earlier [z], which was originally intervocalic.

| Table 7.18 | Rhotacism in English, German, and Swedish | | |
|---|---|---|---|
| **Gothic** | **English** | **German** | **Swedish** |
| maiza | more | mehr | mera |
| diuzam | deer | Tier | djur |
| huzd | hoard | Hort | — |

## Consonantal strengthening

Just as consonants weaken, they can also strengthen. **Glide strengthening** (the strengthening of a glide to an affricate) is particularly common, especially in word-initial position. In the Italian examples in table 7.19, the glide [j] has been strengthened to [dʒ].

| Table 7.19 | Glide strengthening in Italian | | | | | |
|---|---|---|---|---|---|---|
| Latin | iūdicium | [j] | Italian | giudizio | [dʒ] | 'justice' |
| Latin | iuvenis | [j] | Italian | giovane | [dʒ] | 'young' |

## 7.2.2 Segmental change

Segments such as affricates are considered phonologically complex because they represent the fusing of a stop plus a fricative into a single segment, e.g., [dʒ] or [ts]. Such complex segments are commonly subject to simplification. A very common type of segmental simplification is **deaffrication**, which has the effect of turning affricates into fricatives by eliminating the stop portion of the affricate (see table 7.20).

| Table 7.20 | Deaffrication in French | | | | | |
|---|---|---|---|---|---|---|
| Old French | cent | [ts] | French | cent | [s] | 'one hundred' |
| Old French | gent | [dʒ] | French | gent | [ʒ] | 'people, tribe' |

Since deaffrication of [tʃ] (as well as of [dʒ]) has not occurred in English, early borrowings from French maintain the affricate, while later borrowings have a fricative (see table 7.21).

| Table 7.21 | Borrowing from French |
|---|---|
| **Early borrowing (before deaffrication occurred in French)** | |

| *Old French* [tʃ] | *English* [tʃ] |
|---|---|
| chaiere | chair |
| chaine | chain |

(*Note*: Compare Modern French [ʃ] in *chaire* 'throne, seat' and *chaîne* 'chain'.)

(*continued*)

| **Table 7.21 (continued)**   Borrowing from French | |
|---|---|
| **Later borrowings (after deaffrication occurred in French)** | |
| *Modern French* [ʃ] | *English* [ʃ] |
| <u>ch</u>andelier | <u>ch</u>andelier |
| <u>ch</u>auffeur | <u>ch</u>auffeur |

## 7.2.3  Auditorily based change

Although articulatory factors (particularly relating to 'ease of articulation') are of central importance in sound change as indicated in the discussion above, auditory factors also play a role. **Substitution** is a type of auditorily based change involving the replacement of one segment with another similar-sounding segment. A common type of substitution involves [f] replacing either [x] (a voiceless, velar fricative) or [θ]. Earlier in the history of English, [f] replaced [x] in some words in standard varieties of English while [f] replaced [θ] in Cockney, a non-standard dialect spoken in London (see table 7.22).

| **Table 7.22**   Auditorily based substitution | | | | |
|---|---|---|---|---|
| [x] > [f] | Middle English | lau<u>gh</u> [x] | English | lau<u>gh</u> [f] |
| [θ] > [f] | English | <u>th</u>in [θ] | Cockney | [fɪn] |

So far we have treated sound changes without consideration of their effect on the sound pattern of the particular language as a whole. All the foregoing sound changes can lead both to new types of allophonic variation and to the addition or loss of phonemic contrasts. Examples of such cases are presented in the next section.

## 7.2.4  Phonetic versus phonological change

The sound changes outlined in the previous sections can affect the overall sound pattern (phonology) of a language in different ways. Commonly, the first stage of a sound change results in the creation of a new allophone of an already existing phoneme. The term **phonetic sound change** can be used to refer to this stage.

A good example of phonetic sound change involves the laxing of short high vowels that has developed in Canadian French (see table 7.23). This change can be seen in closed word-final syllables, among other environments.

Whereas Canadian French has the lax vowels [ɪ] and [ʊ] in closed final syllables, European French has kept the tense vowels [i] and [u]. Both dialects of French retain [i] and [u] in open syllables. This suggests that Canadian French has developed the rule in figure 7.5.

**Figure 7.5**
Vowel laxing rule in
Canadian French

$$\begin{bmatrix} V \\ +\text{high} \\ -\text{long} \end{bmatrix} \rightarrow [-\text{tense}] \ / \ \_\_\_ \ C \ (C) \ \#$$

| Table 7.23 Vowel laxing in Canadian French | | |
| --- | --- | --- |
| **European French** | **Canadian French** | |
| ***Closed syllable*** | | |
| [vit] | [vɪt] | 'quick' |
| [libʁ] | [lɪb] | 'free' |
| [ekut] | [ekʊt] | 'listen' |
| [pus] | [pʊs] | 'thumb' |
| ***Open Syllable*** | | |
| [vi] | [vi] | 'life' |
| [li] | [li] | 'bed' |
| [vu] | [vu] | 'you' |
| [lu] | [lu] | 'wolf' |

Although this rule did introduce an allophone not present in European French, it did not create any new phonemes because there was no contrast between lax vowels and their tense counterparts in Canadian French.[4]

## Splits

Sometimes sound change can lead to changes in a language's phonological system by adding, eliminating, or rearranging phonemes. Such **phonological change** can involve **splits**, **mergers**, or **shifts**.

In a phonological split, allophones of the same phoneme come to contrast with each other due to the loss of the conditioning environment, with the result that one or more new phonemes are created. The English phoneme /ŋ/ was the result of a phonological split (see table 7.24). Originally, [ŋ] was simply the allophone of /n/ that appeared before a velar consonant. During Middle English, consonant deletion resulted in the loss of [g] in word-final position after a nasal consonant, leaving [ŋ] as the final sound in words such as *sing*.

| Table 7.24 Phonological split resulting in /ŋ/ | |
| --- | --- |
| Original phonemic form | /sɪŋg/ |
| Original phonetic form | [sɪŋg] |
| Deletion of [g] | [sɪŋg] > [sɪŋ] |
| New phonemic form | /sɪŋ/ |

The loss of the final [g] in words created minimal pairs such as *sin* (/sɪn/) and *sing* (/sɪŋ/), in which there is a contrast between /n/ and /ŋ/. This example represents a typical phonological split. When the conditioning environment of an allophonic variant of a phoneme is lost through sound change, the allophone is no longer predictable and thus becomes contrastive (i.e., phonemic). The original phoneme (in figure 7.6, /n/) splits into two phonemes (/n/ and /ŋ/).

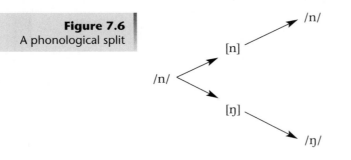

**Figure 7.6**
A phonological split

## Mergers

In a phonological merger, two or more phonemes collapse into a single one, thereby reducing the number of phonemes in the language. The case of auditorily based substitution discussed above has this effect in Cockney English, where all instances of the interdental fricative /θ/ have become /f/ (see figure 7.7). Consequently, the phonemes /θ/ and /f/ have merged into /f/ and words such as *thin* and *fin* have the same phonological form (/fɪn/). Similarly, /v/ and /ð/ have merged (e.g., /smuv/ for *smooth*).

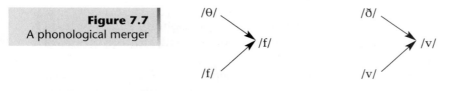

**Figure 7.7**
A phonological merger

## Shifts

A phonological shift is a change in which a series of phonemes is systematically modified so that their organization with respect to each other is altered. A well-known example of such a change is called the Great English Vowel Shift. Beginning in the Middle English period and continuing into the eighteenth century, the language underwent a series of modifications to its long vowels (see table 7.25).

**Table 7.25**    The Great English Vowel Shift

| Middle English | Great Vowel Shift | | Modern English | |
| --- | --- | --- | --- | --- |
| [tiːd] | [iː] | > [aj] | /tajd/ | 'tide' |
| [luːd] | [uː] | > [aw] | /lawd/ | 'loud' |
| [geːs] | [eː] | > [iː] | /gis/ | 'geese' |
| [sɛː] | [ɛː] | > [iː] | /si/ | 'sea' |
| [goːs] | [oː] | > [uː] | /gus/ | 'goose' |
| [brɔːkən] | [ɔː] | > [oː] | /brokən/ | 'broken' |
| [naːmə] | [aː] | > [eː] | /nem/ | 'name' |

Figure 7.8 illustrates the changes that gradually affected the English long vowels.

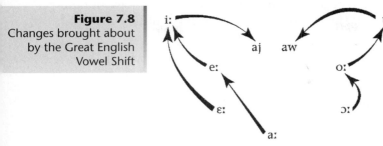

**Figure 7.8**
Changes brought about by the Great English Vowel Shift

Another well-known shift, Grimm's Law, is discussed later in section 7.7.4.

## 7.2.5  Explaining phonological shift

The causes and even the details of the Great English Vowel Shift still remain unclear. In fact, the causes of phonological shift in general are not well understood. A possible motivation in some cases may involve the notion of phonological space. Although the vowel systems of languages can be arranged in various ways (see chapter 8), there is a tendency for languages to maximize the use of space in the vowel quadrangle (i.e., the oral cavity). Accordingly, if a language has only three vowels, they will likely be [i], [a], and [o] or [u], not (for example) [i], [e], [ɛ]. Similarly, if a language has five vowels, they will be distributed throughout the phonological space typically as [i], [e], [a], [o], [u] rather than [u], [ʊ], [a], [o], [ɔ], for example (see figure 7.9).

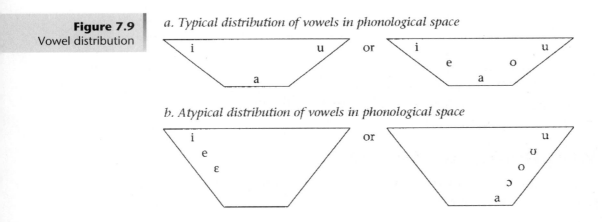

**Figure 7.9**
Vowel distribution

*a. Typical distribution of vowels in phonological space*

*b. Atypical distribution of vowels in phonological space*

Languages with seven (or more) vowels (e.g., English at the starting point of the Great English Vowel Shift in figure 7.8) often undergo **diphthongization**. This can be seen as a reaction to the overcrowding of the phonological space since the effect of the diphthongization of a pair of vowels is to reduce a seven-vowel system to a five-vowel system. (Think of the two diphthongs as not infringing on the space of the simple vowels.)

### 7.2.6  Sound change and rule ordering

In describing language change, it is often crucial to identify the relative chronology, or times at which different changes have occurred. Three important changes in the history of English can be given as the following (somewhat simplified) rules in figure 7.10.

**Figure 7.10**
Three rules in the history of English

1) Voicing
   C → [+voice] / [+voice] ___ [+voice]

2) Syncope
   V → Ø / ___ C #
   [−stress]

3) Assimilation
   C → [+voice] / C ___ [+voice]

These changes have played an important role in the evolution of English plural forms such as *hooves* (versus *hoof*) and *wolves* (versus *wolf*). Of the possible orderings of these three rules, only one will derive the contemporary pronunciation from the earlier (Old English) phonemic form. Two of the possible orderings are given in table 7.26.

**Table 7.26**    Rule ordering in the history of English

| Hypothesis A | | Hypothesis B | |
|---|---|---|---|
| Original phonemic form | /wulfas/ | Original phonemic form | /wulfas/ |
| Voicing | wulvas | Voicing | wulvas |
| Syncope | wulvs | Assimilation | (cannot apply) |
| Assimilation | wulvz | Syncope | wulvs (incorrect) |

If we assume hypothesis A with the ordering voicing, syncope, and assimilation, we can account for the [vz] in the modern pronunciation of a word such as *wolves*. By contrast, the ordering proposed in hypothesis B would not account for the present pronunciation.

## 7.3  Morphological change

In this section we discuss morphological changes resulting from analogy and reanalysis as well as changes involving the addition or loss of affixes.

### 7.3.1  Addition of affixes

Borrowing has been a very important source of new affixes in English. During the Middle English period, many French words containing the suffix *-ment* (e.g., *accomplishment, commencement*) made their way into the language. Eventually, *-ment* established itself as a productive suffix in

English and was used with bases that were not of French origin (e.g., *acknowledgement, merriment*). The ending *-able*, which converts a verb into an adjective (e.g., *readable, lovable*, etc.), followed a similar pattern. Although words with this ending (e.g., *favourable, conceivable*) were initially borrowed into English as whole units, eventually the suffix became productive and was used with new bases.

Not all new affixes are the result of borrowing. Lexical forms can become grammatical forms over time through a process called **grammaticalization**. Grammaticalized forms often undergo dramatic phonological reduction, as well as semantic change in which they can lose much of their original content; for example, the Latin word *habeō* '(I) have, hold, grasp' is the source of the Italian future suffix *ō*. In the first stage of grammaticalization, *habeō* remained an independent word but underwent semantic reduction and functioned as an auxiliary verb indicating future tense; for example, *amāre habeō* 'I will love'. In the case where two words are frequently adjacent, over time they can become fused together to form a single unit consisting of a base and an affix. **Fusion** refers to this specific type of grammaticalization where words develop into affixes (either prefixes or suffixes) (see table 7.27).

| **Table 7.27** | Fusion | | |
|---|---|---|---|
| word word | > | base + affix (suffixation) | |
| word word | > | affix + base (prefixation) | |

A number of Modern English suffixes are derived from earlier words by means of fusion (see table 7.28).

| **Table 7.28** | English suffixes resulting from fusion | |
|---|---|---|
| **Suffix** | **Old English word** | |
| -hood (childhood) | hād | 'state, condition, rank' |
| -dom (freedom) | dōm | 'condition, power' |
| -ly (fatherly) | (ge-)līc | 'similar, equal, like' |

Fusion is also the source of the future tense suffixes in Italian, which are derived from various forms of the Latin word *habere* 'to have' (see table 7.29).

| **Table 7.29** | Fusion resulting in a future tense suffix in Italian | |
|---|---|---|
| **Latin** | **Italian** | |
| amāre habeō̱ | amerò̱ | 'I will love' |
| amāre habē̱mus | amere̱mo | 'we will love' |

## 7.3.2  Loss of affixes

Just as affixes can be added to the grammar, they can also be lost. Sometimes affixes simply fall into disuse for no apparent reason. For example, a number of Old English derivational affixes, including *-bǣre* and *-bora*, are no longer used (see table 7.30).

| **Table 7.30**   Affixes no longer found in English |
| --- |
| N + bǣre  →  A (e.g., *lustbǣre* 'pleasant, agreeable' from *lust* 'pleasure'; *-bǣre* 'bearing') |
| N + bora  →  N (e.g., *mundbora* 'protector' from *mund* 'protection'; *-bora* 'rules') |

It is also very common for affixes to be lost through sound change. For example, Old English had a complex system of affixes marking case and gender. Nouns were divided into three gender classes—masculine, neuter, and feminine. Assignment to a class was not based on sex (natural gender) but on grammatical gender; for example, the word for *stone* (Old English *stān*) and even a word for *woman* (*wīfmann*) were masculine, the word for *sun* (*sunne*) was feminine, and another word for *woman* (*wīf*) was neuter. Each gender class was associated with a different set of case endings (see table 7.31).

| **Table 7.31**   Old English case affixes | | | |
| --- | --- | --- | --- |
| | **Masculine** | **Neuter** | **Feminine** |
| ***Singular*** | | | |
| | hund 'dog' | dēor 'animal' | gief 'gift' |
| Nominative | hund | dēor | gief-u |
| Accusative | hund | dēor | gief-e |
| Genitive | hund-es | dēor-es | gief-e |
| Dative | hund-e | dēor-e | gief-e |
| ***Plural*** | | | |
| Nominative | hund-as | dēor | gief-a |
| Accusative | hund-as | dēor | gief-a |
| Genitive | hund-a | dēor-a | gief-a |
| Dative | hund-um | dēor-um | gief-um |

The following Old English sentence contains all four case categories.

(2)  Se cniht          geaf     gief-e        þæs hierd-es          sun-e.
    the youth-Nom   gave     gift-Acc      the shepherd-Gen      son-Dat
    'The youth gave a gift to the shepherd's son.'

By the fifteenth century, English case endings had changed radically. Consonant deletion resulted in the loss of the earlier [m] of the dative plural suffix and through vowel reduction all the unstressed vowels of the case endings were reduced to the short, lax vowel [ə] (which was later lost through vowel deletion). Consequently, many of the earlier case and gender distinctions were obliterated. (The examples in table 7.32 also include changes to the stem-internal vowels as the result of various processes, including the Great English Vowel Shift.)

| **Table 7.32** The loss of case affixes through sound change (in English *hound*) | | | |
|---|---|---|---|
| | **Old English** | **Middle English (e = [ə])** | **Modern English** |
| ***Singular*** | | | |
| Nominative | hund | hund | hound |
| Accusative | hund | hund | hound |
| Genitive | hund-es | hund-(e)s | hound's |
| Dative | hund-e | hund-(e) | hound |
| | | | |
| ***Plural*** | | | |
| Nominative | hund-as | hund-(e)s | hounds |
| Accusative | hund-as | hund-(e)s | hounds |
| Genitive | hund-a | hund-(e) | hounds' |
| Dative | hund-um | hund-(e) | hounds |

Whereas Old English had five distinct suffixes for cases, Middle English had only two suffixes, -*e* and -*es,* which, with the loss of schwa, were ultimately reduced to a single suffix -*s,* still used in Modern English for the plural and the possessive. This represents a typical example of how sound change can result in modification to the morphological component of the grammar.

## 7.3.3 From synthetic to analytic to synthetic

Since languages vary greatly in the complexity of their morphology, linguists often make a distinction between analytic and synthetic languages (see chapter 8). Whereas analytic languages have very few inflectional affixes (e.g., Modern English), synthetic languages have many (e.g., Latin, Old English).

Even in the absence of borrowing, sound change and fusion ensure that there is an endless transition in the morphology of a language over time. As we have seen, due to the loss of case endings through sound change, English has developed from a synthetic language with many inflectional affixes to a more analytic one with very few, as the above discussion of nouns such as *hound* indicates.

By contrast, fusion ensures the rise of new synthetic forms. Fusion can be observed in some Modern English dialects in forms such as *coulda* (e.g., *I coulda won*), which represents the fusion of *could* and *have*. For many speakers, the -*a* is treated as a suffix that is no longer related to *have*, as evident in spellings such as *coulda* which result from confusion over how to represent the pronunciation of the fused form in written English. Through fusion, a language with an analytic morphology can become more synthetic over time.

## 7.3.4 Analogy

The drastic effects that sound change can have on the morphology of a language are often alleviated through analogy. For example, the plural of Old English *hand* 'hand' was *handa*. Vowel reduction and apocope applying to *handa* would have yielded a Modern English plural form identical to the singular form, namely *hand* (see table 7.33).

| **Table 7.33**  Sound changes applied to Old English *handa* 'hands' | |
| --- | --- |
| handa | |
| handə | vowel reduction |
| hand | apocope |

Obviously, then, the Modern English plural *hands* cannot be the consequence of sound change. Rather, it is the result of earlier analogy with words such as Middle English *hund* 'hound' (see table 7.32), which did form the plural with the suffix *-s*. This suffix, whose earlier form *-as* was predominant even in Old English, was extended by analogy to all English nouns with a few exceptions (*oxen*, *men*, *geese*, etc.). Other plural forms besides *hands* that were created on the basis of analogy include *eyes* (*eyen* in Middle English) and *shoes* (formerly *shooen*).

Continuing analogy along these lines is responsible for the development of the plural form *youse* (from *you*) in some English dialects. Each generation of English-speaking children temporarily extends the analogy still further by producing forms such as *sheeps*, *gooses*, and *mouses*. To date, however, these particular innovations have not been accepted by adult speakers of Standard English and are eventually abandoned by young language learners.

## 7.3.5 Reanalysis

As mentioned in section 7.1.2, reanalysis can result in a new morphological structure for a word. It can affect both borrowed words and, particularly in cases where the morphological structure of the word is no longer transparent, native words. Reanalysis can result in new productive patterns (as in the case of *(-)burger*) or it can remain quite isolated, affecting perhaps only one word. Since the type of reanalysis exemplified by *hamburger* is not based on a correct analysis of a word (at least from a historical perspective) and does not usually involve a conscious or detailed study of the word on the part of the speaker, it is often called **folk etymology** (see table 7.34).

| **Table 7.34**   Folk etymology in English (native words and borrowings) | |
| --- | --- |
| **Modern word** | **Source** |
| belfry | Middle English *berfrey* 'bell tower' (unrelated to *bell*) |
| bridegroom | Middle English *bridegome* (unrelated to *groom*)(compare Old English *brȳd* 'bride' and *guma* 'man') |
| muskrat | Algonquian *musquash* (unrelated to either *musk* or *rat*) |
| woodchuck | Algonquian *otchek* (unrelated to either *wood* or *chuck*) |

In the case of *hamburger*, the only evidence of folk etymology is the productive use of *(-)burger* as an independent word and in compounds like *fishburger*. However, in other cases, folk etymology commonly involves changes in pronunciation that reflect the new morphological analysis. For example, our word *earwig* derives from Old English *ēarwicga* [ǽərwidʒa], a compound consisting of 'ear' and 'insect'. Taking into consideration sound change alone, the expected Modern English pronunciation of this word would be *earwidge* [irwɪdʒ]. However, the second part of the compound was lost as an independent word by Middle English, so speakers could no longer associate it with the meaning of 'insect'. Subsequently, reanalysis related the second part of the compound to the verb 'wiggle' resulting in Middle English *arwygyll* (literally 'ear + wiggle'). The end result is Modern English *-wig* and not *-widge*.

Although reanalysis of individual words is common, affixes can also be affected, sometimes with new productive morphological rules developing as a result. This is the case of the Modern English adverbial suffix *-ly* (from Old English *-lic(e)*). In Old English, adjectives could be derived from nouns by adding the suffix *-lic*. Adverbs, in turn, could be derived by adding the suffix *-e* to adjectives (including those derived with *-lic*) (see table 7.35). At some point, the entire complex suffix *-lic+e* was reanalyzed as an adverbial suffix (rather than as an adjectival suffix *-lic* plus an adverbial suffix *-e*). It was then used by analogy to derive adverbs from adjectives in forms where it was not used before, resulting in Modern English *deeply* and other such words.

| **Table 7.35**   The derivation of Old English adjectives and adverbs |
| --- |
| **Formation of an adjective from a noun** |
| [dæg]$_N$    + lic    →    [dæglic]$_A$    'daily' (e.g., as in 'daily schedule') |
| **Formation of an adverb from an adjective** |
| [dēop]$_A$    + e    →    [dēope]$_{Adv}$    'deeply' |
| **Formation of an adverb from a derived adjective with *-lic*** |
| [dæg+lic]$_A$    + e    →    [dæglice]$_{Adv}$    'daily' (e.g., as in 'she ran daily') |

# 7.4  Syntactic change

Like other components of the grammar, syntax is also subject to change over time. Syntactic changes can involve modifications to phrase structure (such as word order) and to transformations, as the following examples illustrate.

## 7.4.1  Word order

All languages make a distinction between the subject and direct object. This contrast is typically represented through case marking or word order. Since Old English had an extensive system of case marking, it is not surprising that its word order was somewhat more variable than that of Modern English. In unembedded clauses, Old English placed the verb in second position (much like Modern German). Thus we find subject-verb-object order in simple transitive sentences such as the following.

(3) S         V          O
    Hē     geseah   þone mann.
    'He      saw       the man.'

When the clause began with an element such as *þa* 'then' or *ne* 'not', the verb preceded the subject as in the following example.

(4)            V          S             O
    þa       sende    sē cyning    þone disc
    then     sent      the king      the dish
    'Then the king sent the dish.'

Although this word order is still found in Modern English, its use is very limited and subject to special restrictions, unlike the situation in Old English.

(5)            V  S                    O
    Rarely has he ever deceived me.

When the direct object was a pronoun, the subject-object-verb order was typical.

(6) S         O          V
    Hēo     hine      lǣrde.
    She      him       advised
    'She advised him.'

The subject-object-verb order also prevailed in embedded clauses, even when the direct object was not a pronoun.

(7)            S          O          V
    þa       hē       þone cyning    sōhte,      hē bēotode.
    when    he       the king         visited,     he boasted
    'When he visited the king, he boasted.'

After case markings were lost during the Middle English period through sound change, fixed subject-verb-object order became the means of marking grammatical relations. As table 7.36 shows, a major change in word order took place between 1300 and 1400, with the verb-object order becoming dominant.

| **Table 7.36** Word order patterns in Middle English | | | | | |
|---|---|---|---|---|---|
| **Year** | 1000 | 1200 | 1300 | 1400 | 1500 |
| Direct object before the verb (%) | 53 | 53 | 40 | 14 | 2 |
| Direct object after the verb (%) | 47 | 47 | 60 | 86 | 98 |

## From SOV to SVO

Just as languages can be classified in terms of their morphology, languages can also be grouped on the basis of the relative order of subject (S), object (O), and verb (V) in basic sentences. Almost all languages of the world fall into one of three types: SOV, SVO, or VSO, with the majority of languages being one of the first two types. Just as languages change through time from one morphological type to another, they can also change from one syntactic type to another. A case in point is found in the history of English, which shows the development from SOV to SVO syntax.

Evidence indicates that the earliest form of Germanic from which English descended was an SOV language. One of the earliest recorded Germanic sentences, for example, has this word order. The sentence in (8) was inscribed on a golden horn (now called the Golden Horn of Gallehus) about 1600 years ago.

(8) Horn of Gallehus

| S | | | O | V |
|---|---|---|---|---|
| ek | HlewagastiR | HoltijaR | horna | tawido |
| I | Hlewagastir | of Holt | horn | made |

'I, Hlewagastir of Holt, made the horn.'

Another type of evidence for an earlier SOV order is found in morphological fusion (see section 7.3.1). Since fusion depends on frequently occurring syntactic patterns, it can sometimes serve as an indicator of earlier syntax. The OV compound, very common in Old English (as well as in Modern English), likely reflects an earlier stage of OV word order (see table 7.37).

| **Table 7.37** | Old English compounds with OV structure | |
|---|---|---|
| manslæht | 'man' + 'strike' | 'manslaughter, murder' |
| æppelbǣre | 'apple' + 'bear' | 'apple-bearing' |

If the earliest Germanic was SOV and Modern English is firmly SVO, then Old English represents a transitional syntactic type. In developing from SOV syntax to SVO syntax, languages seem to follow similar pathways. For example, Modern German, which developed from the same Germanic SOV source as English, shares two of Old English's distinguishing characteristics. First, the verb is typically placed in the second position of the sentence in main clauses, preceded by the subject or some other element (such as an adverb). Secondly, the SOV order is employed for embedded clauses.

(9) Modern German word order

   *a.* Verb in second position in unembedded clauses
      (Compare the Old English sentence in (4).)

| | V | S | | O |
|---|---|---|---|---|
| Gestern | hatte | ich | keine | Zeit. |
| yesterday | had | I | no | time |

'I had no time yesterday.'

   *b.* SOV in embedded clauses
      (Compare the Old English sentence in (7).)

| | S | O | V |
|---|---|---|---|
| Als | er | den Mann | sah . . . |
| when | he | the man | saw |

'When he saw the man . . .'

The change from SOV to SVO is not restricted to English and other Germanic languages. The same change is evident, for example, in completely unrelated languages such as those of the Bantu family of Africa. Since linguists are still not sure why languages change from one syntactic type to another, the causes of such change will undoubtedly remain an important area of investigation, especially since the relative order of verb and object (OV versus VO) has been closely linked with other word order patterns (see chapter 8).

## 7.4.2    Inversion in the history of English

In Old and Middle English the inversion transformation (see chapter 5) involved in the formation of *yes-no* questions could apply to all verbs, not just auxiliaries, yielding forms that would be unacceptable in Modern English.

> (10)  Speak they the truth?

During the sixteenth and seventeenth centuries, the Inversion rule was changed to apply solely to auxiliary verbs.

> (11) *Inversion    (old form)*
>       The V moves to the left of the subject
>       They speak → Speak they?
>       They can speak → Can they speak?
>
> *Inversion    (new form)*
>       The Aux moves to the left of subject
>       They speak → *Speak they?
>       They can speak → Can they speak?

With this change, structures such as *Speak they the truth?* were no longer possible. The corresponding question came to be formed with the auxiliary *do* as in *Do they speak the truth?*[5]

## 7.5    Lexical and semantic change

Another obvious type of language change involves modifications to the lexicon. Since we have already dealt with some changes relating to derivational and inflectional morphology in section 7.3, the main focus here will be on lexical change involving entire words. Simply stated, there are two possible types of lexical change: addition and loss. The addition or loss of words often reflects cultural changes that introduce novel objects and notions, and that eliminate outmoded ones.

## 7.5.1    Addition of lexical items

Addition is frequently the result of technological innovations or contact with other cultures. Such developments result in **lexical gaps** that can be filled by adding new words to the lexicon. New words are added either through the word formation processes available to the language or through borrowing.

# Word formation

The most important word formation processes are compounding and derivation, although other types, including conversion, blends, backformation, clipping, and acronyms (see chapter 4), can play a significant role.

Compounding and derivation have always been available to English speakers for the creation of new words. In fact, much of the compounding and derivation in Old English seems very familiar (see table 7.38).

| **Table 7.38** | Compounding and derivation in Old English | | |
|---|---|---|---|
| **Noun compounds** | | | |
| N + N | sunbēam | 'sunbeam' | |
| A + N | middelniht | 'midnight' | |
| **Adjective compounds** | | | |
| N + A | blōdrēad | 'blood-red' | |
| A + A | dēadboren | 'stillborn' | |
| **Derived nouns** | | | |
| [bæc]$_V$ + ere | → | bæcere | 'baker' |
| [frēond]$_N$ + scipe | → | frēondscipe | 'friendship' |
| **Derived adjectives** | | | |
| [wundor]$_N$ + full | → | wundorfull | 'wonderful' |
| [cild]$_N$ + isc | → | cildisc | 'childish' |

Just as speakers of Modern English can use compounding and derivational rules to create new words (e.g., the N + N compound *airhead*), so could Old English speakers create new words such as the poetic N + N compound *hwælweg*, literally 'whale' + 'path' to mean 'sea'.

## Language Matters  **Dictionaries as Historical Records**

There are some dictionaries, such as the *Oxford English Dictionary*, that provide us with a window on language change. A lexical entry includes not only definitions of the word, but also examples of how the word has been used in written documents over many years. Consider the citations for the word *linguist*:

> 1591. Shakespeare, *Two Gentlemen of Verona*. "Seeing you are beautiful, with goodly shape; and by your owne report A Linguist."
>
> 1695. Edwards. *Perfect Script*. "Here linguists and philologists may find that which is to be found no where else."

*The Oxford English Dictionary* (Second Edition) © Oxford University Press 1989.

Note however that even though many Old English compounding and derivational patterns have been maintained in Modern English, words that were acceptable in Old English are not necessarily still in use in Modern English, even though many of them are quite understandable (see table 7.39).

| **Table 7.39** Old English compound and derived forms that are no longer used | | | |
|---|---|---|---|
| **Noun compounds** | | | |
| N + N | bōccræft ('book' + 'craft') | | 'literature' (compare *witchcraft*) |
| A + N | dimhūs ('dim' + 'house') | | 'prison' |
| **Adjective compounds** | | | |
| N + A | ælfscīene ('elf' + 'beautiful') | | 'beautiful as a fairy' |
| A + A | eallgōd ('all' + 'good') | | 'perfectly good' |
| **Derived nouns** | | | |
| [sēam]$_V$ + ere | $\rightarrow$ | sēamere | 'tailor' (compare *seamster*, *seamstress*) |
| [man]$_N$ + scipe | $\rightarrow$ | manscipe | 'humanity' (compare *friendship*) |
| **Derived adjectives** | | | |
| [word]$_N$ + full | $\rightarrow$ | wordfull | 'wordy' (compare *wonderful*) |
| [heofon]$_N$ + isc | $\rightarrow$ | heofonisc | 'heavenly' (compare *childish*) |

However, not all word formation processes available to Modern English speakers were found in Old English. For example, conversion (as in Modern English [summer]$_N$ → [summer]$_V$) was not possible in Old English. In fact, conversion is typically not available to (synthetic) inflectional languages such as Old English since change in a word category in such languages is usually indicated morphologically and conversion, by definition, does not involve the use of affixes.

## Borrowing

As discussed in section 7.1.2, language contact over time can result in an important source of new words: borrowing. Depending on the cultural relationship holding between languages, three types of influence of one language on the other are traditionally identified: **substratum**, **adstratum**, and **superstratum** influence.

Substratum influence is the effect of a politically or culturally non-dominant language on a dominant language in the area. Both Canadian and American English and Canadian French, for instance, have borrowed vocabulary items from Aboriginal languages (see examples in section 7.1.2). From a much earlier period in the history of English, the influence of a Celtic substratum is also evident, particularly in place names such as *Thames*, *London*, and *Dover*. Substratum influence does not usually have a major impact on the lexicon of the borrowing language. Borrowed words are usually restricted to place names and unfamiliar items or concepts. This situation reflects the fact that it is usually the speakers of the substratum language who inhabited the area first.

Superstratum influence is the effect of a politically or culturally dominant language on another language or languages in the area. For example, the Athapaskan language Gwich'in (Loucheux) (spoken in Canada's Northwest Territories) has borrowed a number of governmental terms and expressions from English, including *bureaucratic, constituents, program, business, development,* and *political.*

In the case of English, Norman French had a superstratum influence. The major impact of French on the vocabulary of English is related to a historical event—the conquest of England by French-speaking Normans in 1066. As the conquerors and their descendants gradually learned English over the next decades, they retained French terms for political, judicial, and cultural notions (see table 7.40). These words were in turn borrowed by native English speakers who, in trying to gain a place in the upper middle class, were eager to imitate the speech of their social superiors. Not surprisingly, borrowing was especially heavy in the vocabulary areas pertaining to officialdom: government, the judiciary, and religion. Other areas of heavy borrowing include science, culture, and warfare.

**Table 7.40**    Some French loan words in English

| | |
|---|---|
| Government | tax, revenue, government, royal, state, parliament, authority, prince, duke, slave, peasant |
| Religion | prayer, sermon, religion, chaplain, friar |
| Judiciary | judge, defendant, jury, evidence, jail, verdict, crime |
| Science | medicine, physician |
| Culture | art, sculpture, fashion, satin, fur, ruby |
| Warfare | army, navy, battle, soldier, enemy, captain |

## Language Matters  Getting Rid of French

The following whimsical piece, from the March 14, 2003, *Christian Science Monitor*, gives you an idea what English would be like without the influence of French.

The Franco-American ~~dispute~~ *falling out* over the best ~~approach~~ *way* to ~~disarming Iraq~~ *take away Iraq's weapons* has resulted in perhaps the highest ~~level of~~ anti-French feeling in the United ~~States~~ *Lands* since 1763.

A French-owned ~~hotel~~ *innkeeping* firm, Accor, has taken down the ~~tricolor~~ *three-hued flag*. In the House of ~~Representatives~~ *Burghers*, the ~~chairman~~ *leader* of the ~~Committee~~ *Body* on ~~Administration~~ *Running Things* has ~~renamed~~ *named anew* French fries "freedom fries" and French toast "freedom toast" in House ~~restaurants~~ *eating rooms*.

It is time for English-speaking ~~peoples~~ *folk* to throw off this cultural ~~imperialism~~ *lording-it-over-others* and ~~declare~~ *say* our linguistic freedom. It is time to ~~purify~~ *clean* the English ~~language~~ *tongue*. It will take some ~~sacrifices~~ *hardship* on everyone's part to get used to the new ~~parlance~~ *speech*. But think of the ~~satisfaction~~ *warm feeling inside* on the day we are all ~~able to~~ *can* all stare the *Académie Française* in the eye and say without fear of ~~reprisal~~ *injury*: "Sumer is icumen in . . ."

Reproduced with permission from the March 14, 2003 issue of the *Christian Science Monitor* (www.csmonitor.com)

## Language Matters  **Multiple Borrowings**

Languages have been known to re-borrow their own words. For example, the French word *biftek* comes from the English word *beefsteak*. However, earlier, English borrowed the French word *boeuf* as *beef*.

In some cases, French loan words were used in conjunction with native English words to convey distinctions of various sorts. For a minor crime, for example, the English word *theft* was employed, but for a more serious breach of the law the French word *larceny* was used. The English also kept their own words for domesticated animals, but adopted the French words for the meat from those creatures (see table 7.41).

**Table 7.41**    French loan words used in conjunction with native English words

| English origin | French origin |
|---|---|
| cow | beef |
| calf | veal |
| sheep | mutton |
| pig | pork |

Adstratum influence refers to the situation where two languages are in contact and neither one is clearly politically or culturally dominant. In a city such as Montreal, with its large number of bilingual speakers, English and French inevitably influence each other (see table 7.42).

**Table 7.42**    French influence on Montreal English

| Montreal English | |
|---|---|
| subvention | 'subsidy' |
| metro | 'subway' |
| autoroute | 'highway' |

Earlier in the history of English, when the Scandinavians settled part of England beginning in AD 800, there was substantial contact between the speakers of English and Scandinavian, resulting in an adstratum relationship. As evident in the examples in tables 7.42 and 7.43, adstratum contact usually results in the borrowing of common, everyday words. In fact, without consulting a dictionary, most English speakers could not distinguish between borrowings from Scandinavian and native English words.

**Table 7.43**    Some loan words from Scandinavian

anger, cake, call, egg, fellow, gear, get, hit, husband, low, lump, raise, root, score, seat, skill, skin, take, their, they, thrust, ugly, window, wing

Borrowed words from many other languages attest to various types of cultural contact and serve often to fill the lexical gaps such contact inevitably brings (see table 7.44).

| Table 7.44 | Some lexical borrowings into English |
| --- | --- |
| Italian | motto, artichoke, balcony, casino, mafia, malaria |
| Spanish | comrade, tornado, cannibal, mosquito, banana, guitar, vigilante, marijuana |
| German | poodle, kindergarten, seminar, noodle, pretzel |
| Dutch | sloop, cole slaw, smuggle, gin, cookie, boom |
| Slavic languages | czar, tundra, polka, intelligentsia, robot |
| Aboriginal languages | toboggan, opossum, wigwam, chipmunk, Ottawa, Toronto |
| Hindi | thug, punch (drink), shampoo, chintz |

Although borrowing has been a very rich source of new words in English, it is noteworthy that loan words are least common among the most frequently used vocabulary items. This reflects a general tendency for highly frequent words to be relatively resistant to loss or substitution (see table 7.45).

| Table 7.45 | Origin of the 5000 most frequent words in English | | | |
| --- | --- | --- | --- | --- |
| **Degree of frequency** | **Source language (%)** | | | |
| | *English* | *French* | *Latin* | *Other* |
| First 1000 | 83 | 11 | 2 | 4 |
| Second 1000 | 34 | 46 | 11 | 9 |
| Third 1000 | 29 | 46 | 14 | 11 |
| Fourth 1000 | 27 | 45 | 17 | 11 |
| Fifth 1000 | 27 | 47 | 17 | 9 |

## 7.5.2 Loss of lexical items

Just as words can be added to the lexicon, they can also be lost. Changes in society play an important role in the loss of words since words often fall into disuse because the object or notion they refer to has become obsolete (see table 7.46).

| Table 7.46 | Some Old English words lost through cultural change |
| --- | --- |
| dolgbōt | 'compensation for wounding' |
| þeox | 'hunting spear' |
| eafor | 'tenant obligation to the king to convey goods' |
| flȳtme | 'a blood-letting instrument' |

> ## Language Matters **Borrowing Phrases**
>
> Sometimes languages borrow simple phrases or expressions and translate them word-for-word. The following are all examples of common English phrases that came from another language.
>
> | *English phrase* | *Source phrase* |
> | --- | --- |
> | brainwashing | Chinese *xiù naùo* |
> | flea market | French *marché aux puces* |
> | antibody | German *Antikörper* |
> | moment of truth | Spanish *el momento de la verdad* |

## 7.5.3  Semantic change

Although changes in word meaning take place continually in all languages, words rarely jump from one meaning to an unrelated one. Typically, the changes are step by step and involve one of the following phenomena.

**Semantic broadening** is the process in which the meaning of a word becomes more general or more inclusive than its historically earlier form (see table 7.47).

| **Table 7.47** | Semantic broadening | |
| --- | --- | --- |
| **Word** | **Old meaning** | **New meaning** |
| bird | 'small fowl' | 'any winged creature' |
| barn | 'place to store barley' | 'farm building for storage and shelter' |
| aunt | 'father's sister' | 'father or mother's sister' |

**Semantic narrowing** is the process in which the meaning of a word becomes less general or less inclusive than its historically earlier meaning (see table 7.48).

| **Table 7.48** | Semantic narrowing | |
| --- | --- | --- |
| **Word** | **Old meaning** | **New meaning** |
| hound | 'any dog' | 'a hunting breed' |
| meat | 'any type of food' | 'flesh of an animal' |
| fowl | 'any bird' | 'a domesticated bird' |
| disease | 'any unfavourable state' | 'an illness' |

> ## Language Matters **Dictionaries Help Track Meaning Changes**
>
> The word *girl* in Middle English was used to refer to a child of either sex. Note the following definition from the *Oxford English Dictionary*:
>
> Girl. A child or young person of either sex; a youth or maiden.
> 1290. "And gret prece of gurles and men comen hire."
> ('And a great throng of children and men came here.')

In **amelioration**, the meaning of a word becomes more positive or favourable. The opposite change, **pejoration**, also occurs (see tables 7.49 and 7.50).

| **Table 7.49** | Amelioration | |
|---|---|---|
| **Word** | **Old meaning** | **New meaning** |
| pretty | 'tricky, sly, cunning' | 'attractive' |
| knight | 'boy' | 'a special title or position' |

| **Table 7.50** | Pejoration | |
|---|---|---|
| **Word** | **Old meaning** | **New meaning** |
| silly | 'happy, prosperous' | 'foolish' |
| wench | 'girl' | 'wanton woman, prostitute' |

Given the propensity of human beings to exaggerate, it is not surprising that the **weakening** of meaning frequently occurs. For example, our word *soon* used to mean 'immediately' but now simply means 'in the near future'. Other examples are included in table 7.51.

| **Table 7.51** | Weakening | |
|---|---|---|
| **Word** | **Old meaning** | **New meaning** |
| wreak | 'avenge, punish' | 'to cause, inflict' |
| quell | 'kill, murder' | 'to put down, pacify' |

**Semantic shift** is a process in which a word loses its former meaning and takes on a new, but often related, meaning (see table 7.52).

| **Table 7.52** | Semantic shift | |
|---|---|---|
| **Word** | **Old meaning** | **New meaning** |
| immoral | 'not customary' | 'unethical' |
| bead | 'prayer' | 'prayer bead, bead' |

Sometimes a series of semantic shifts occurs over an extended period of time, resulting in a meaning that is completely unrelated to the original sense of a word. The word *hearse*, for example, originally referred to a triangular harrow. Later, it denoted a triangular frame for church candles and later still was used to refer to the device that held candles over a coffin. In a subsequent shift, it came to refer to the framework on which curtains were hung over a coffin or tomb. Still later, *hearse* was used to refer to the coffin itself before finally taking on its current sense of the vehicle used to transport a coffin.

More recently the word *gay* has undergone a dramatic and unusually rapid set of shifts. Just a few generations ago this word was typically used in the sense of 'lively, happy'. It then came to designate 'homosexual', and a phrase such as 'a gay film' would be interpreted in this sense. However, for many younger speakers today the primary meaning of *gay* is simply 'bad', as in 'the game is gay'.

One of the most striking types of semantic change is triggered by **metaphor**, a figure of speech based on a perceived similarity between distinct objects or actions. (See chapter 6 for a discussion of metaphor.) Metaphorical change usually involves a word with a concrete meaning taking on a more abstract sense, although the word's original meaning is

## Language Matters **A Surprising Dictionary Employee**

In 1896, in a small village in England, one of the most remarkable conversations in literary history took place. Perhaps it is apocryphal, but we can enjoy it anyway. One of the people was Dr. James Murray, editor of the *Oxford English Dictionary* (OED). Murray had travelled to Crowthorne from Oxford to meet Dr. W.C. Minor. Dr. Minor was one of the legion of volunteers whose work made the OED possible. He looked for illustrative quotations that the dictionary used in its definitions. For more than twenty years, the men had corresponded but had never met. Murray had invited him to come to Oxford, but Minor was never willing to leave Crowthorne. Finally, Murray decided that he would make the trip in order to thank the man who had done so much for the OED.

Murray telegraphed that he would be taking the train, and Minor wired back that he would be most welcome. When Murray arrived, he was met at the station by a coach and driven to a red-brick mansion. He was shown into a book-lined study where a man stood behind a mahogany desk. Murray began the speech he had rehearsed:

"A very good afternoon to you, sir. I am Dr. James Murray of the London Philological Society, and the editor of the *Oxford English Dictionary*. It is indeed an honour and a pleasure to make your acquaintance—for you must be, kind sir, my most assiduous helpmeet, Dr. W.C. Minor?"

There was a brief pause, and then the man behind the desk, spoke:

"I regret, kind sir, that I am not. It is not at all as you suppose. I am in fact the Governor of the Broadmoor Criminal Lunatic Asylum. Dr. Minor is most certainly here. But he is an inmate. He has been a patient here for more than twenty years. He is our longest-staying resident."

William Chester Minor was a former U.S. army officer. He was thirty-seven years old when he was arrested for murdering a man named George Merrett. He admitted to the shooting but said that he did so "in error." During his trial, it became clear that he was, in fact, insane, and had an overriding fear that militant Irish nationalists were trying to kill him. On the day in question, he had woken in the night convinced that someone was in his room. He ran outside and shot a man. At his trial, he was ruled to be held in permanent custody as a "certified criminal lunatic."

He had his books shipped from America and set up quite a library in the asylum. Somehow, he saw a flyer that Murray had sent out asking for volunteer readers to read either specific books or from specific time periods to look for examples of word usage. Minor did this assiduously.

Over the years, he provided between 10 000 and 12 000 quotations to the OED. After thirty years in Broadmoor he was transferred to an asylum in Washington, to be closer to his family. He died on March 26, 1920.

— Summarized from *The Professor and the Madman* by Simon Winchester (New York: HarperCollins, 1998).

not lost. The meanings of many English words have been extended through metaphor (see table 7.53).

| Table 7.53 | Some examples of metaphor in English |
|---|---|
| **Word** | **Metaphorical meaning** |
| grasp | 'understand' |
| yarn | 'story' |
| high | 'on drugs' |

##  The spread of change

Up to this point, we have been concerned with the causes and description of linguistic change. Still to be dealt with is the question of how linguistic innovations spread. This section focuses on two types of spread, one involving the way in which an innovation is extended through the vocabulary of a language and the other the way in which it spreads through the population.

### 7.6.1  Diffusion through the language

Some linguistic change first manifests itself in a few words and then gradually spreads through the vocabulary of the language. This type of change is called **lexical diffusion**. A well-attested example in English involves an ongoing change in the stress pattern of words such as *convert*, which can be used as either a noun or a verb. Although the stress originally fell on the second syllable regardless of lexical category, in the latter half of the sixteenth century three such words, *rebel*, *outlaw*, and *record*, came to be pronounced with the stress on the first syllable when used as nouns. As figure 7.11 illustrates, this stress shift was extended to an increasing number of words over the next decades.

**Figure 7.11**
Diffusion of stress shift in English

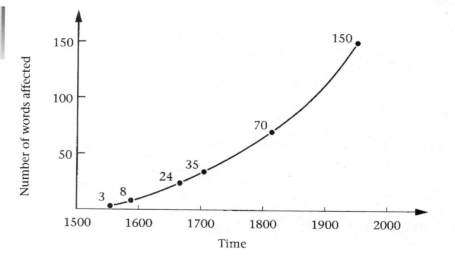

This change still has not diffused through the entire vocabulary of English. There are about a thousand nouns of the relevant sort that still place the stress on the second syllable (e.g., *report*, *mistake*, and *support*). Table 7.54 illustrates the spread of this change to date.

| **Table 7.54** | Stress shift in English (nouns) | | |
|---|---|---|---|
| **Before the 16th century** | **During the 16th century** | **During the 18th century** | **Today** |
| rebél | rébel | rébel | rébel |
| affíx | affíx | áffix | áffix |
| recéss | recéss | recéss | récess |
| mistáke | mistáke | mistáke | mistáke |

This ongoing change can be observed in progress today. The noun *address*, for example, is pronounced by many people with stress on the first syllable as [ǽdrɛs], although the older pronunciation [ǝdrés] is still heard. Some speakers alternate between the two pronunciations. This change may continue to work its way through the language until all nouns in the class we have been considering are stressed on the first syllable.

The changes discussed in the section on analogy also spread word by word. For example, the transition of strong (irregular) verbs (the *sing/sang/sung* type) to the weak verb class (regular verbs with past tense *-ed*) is an ongoing change. Both strong and weak past tense forms of original strong verbs such as *dive* and *shine* are heard in current English: *dove/dived* and *shone/shined*.

However, not all linguistic change involves gradual diffusion through the vocabulary of a language. Sound changes typically affect all instances of the segment(s) involved. For example, in some dialects of Spanish (such as Cuban) the consonantal weakening of [s] to [h] in syllable-final position affects all instances of *s* in those positions. The relevant rule can be stated as in figure 7.12.

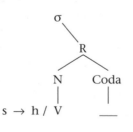

This rule has resulted in changes such as those exemplified in table 7.55.

| **Table 7.55** | The effects of the [s] to [h] change in Spanish dialects | |
|---|---|---|
| **Standard pronunciation** | **New pronunciation** | |
| [felismente] | [felihmente] | 'happily' |
| [estilo] | [ehtilo] | 'type' |
| [espaɲa] | [ehpaɲa] | 'Spain' |

This change is entirely regular, affecting all instances of syllable-final [s] in the speech of individuals who adopt it.

Accordingly, two types of language change can be identified. One, exemplified by the stress shifts in bisyllabic English nouns of the type we have discussed, affects individual words one at a time and gradually spreads through the vocabulary of the language. The other, exemplified by the consonant weakening of syllable-final [s] to [h] in some dialects of Spanish, involves an across-the-board change that applies without exception to all words.

## 7.6.2 Spread through the population

For a language change to take place, the particular innovation must be accepted by the linguistic community as a whole. For example, although children acquiring English typically form the past tense of *go* as *goed* instead of *went*, *goed* has never received widespread acceptance. Doubtless the verb form in *he throve on fame* would be equally unacceptable to most speakers today. In earlier English, however, *throve* was the past tense form of *thrive* (compare *drive/drove*). At some point in the past then, the novel form *thrived* did receive general acceptance. It's no coincidence the irregular form that survived is from a frequent verb, and the one that was lost is from a verb that is less commonly used. The frequency with which irregular forms are heard and used is a major determinant of their longevity.

Just as change sometimes begins with a small number of words, the effects of a change often appear first in the speech of only a small number of people. Social pressures often play an important role in whether a particular innovation will spread through the entire linguistic community. Since speakers can consciously or subconsciously alter the way they speak to approximate what they perceive to be a more prestigious or socially desirable variety of speech, once a change has taken hold in the speech of a particular group it may gradually spread to other speakers and ultimately affect the entire linguistic community.

There have been numerous examples of this in the history of English, notably the loss of postvocalic [r] along the east coast of the United States. This change, which led to an 'r-less' pronunciation of words such as *far* as [faː], originated in parts of England in the seventeenth and eighteenth centuries. At that time, postvocalic [r] was still pronounced throughout English-speaking settlements in North America. Two factors accounted for its loss in parts of this continent. First, the children of the New England gentry picked up the new pronunciation in British schools and subsequently brought it back to the colony. Second, the speech of newly arrived immigrants, including colonial administrators and church officials who enjoyed high social status in the colony, typically lacked the postvocalic [r]. As a result, the innovation was widely imitated and ultimately spread along much of the east coast and into the south.

Social pressures were also involved in limiting the spread of this innovation. It did not penetrate Pennsylvania or the other midland states since the most prestigious group of settlers there were Quakers from northern England, an area that retained the postvocalic [r]. Similarly, in Canada, the influence of Scottish and Irish settlers, whose dialects did not undergo the change in question, helped ensure the survival of postvocalic [r] in all but a few areas where contact with New England was strongest, most notably Lunenburg County in Nova Scotia and Grand Manan Island in New Brunswick. More recently the 'r-less' pronunciation has become stigmatized in some areas, even where it was previously firmly entrenched, and we now see a trend to restoration of [r] in environments where it had been deleted.

## 7.7 Language reconstruction

When we compare the vocabulary items of various languages, we cannot help but notice the strong resemblance certain words bear to each other. By systematically comparing languages, we can establish whether two or more languages descended from a common parent and are therefore **genetically related** (see chapter 8). The **comparative method** refers to the procedure of reconstructing earlier forms on the basis of a comparison of later forms. By means of such comparative reconstruction we can reconstruct properties of the parent language with a great degree of certainty.

### 7.7.1 Comparative reconstruction

The most reliable sign of family relationships is the existence of **systematic phonetic correspondences** in the vocabulary items of different languages. Many such correspondences can be found in the sample of vocabulary items in table 7.56 from English, Dutch, German, Danish, and Swedish, all of which are members of the Germanic family of languages.

Since the relationship between the phonological form of a word and its meaning is mostly arbitrary, the existence of systematic phonetic correspondences in the forms of two or more languages must point towards a common source. Conversely, where languages are not related, their vocabulary items fail to show systematic similarities. This can be seen by comparing words from Turkish, which is not related to the Germanic languages, with their counterparts in the languages cited in table 7.57.

Words that have descended from a common source (as shown by systematic phonetic correspondences and, usually, semantic similarities) are called **cognates**. Cognates are not always as obvious as the Germanic examples in table 7.56. Where languages from the same family are only distantly related, the systematic correspondences may be considerably less

| **Table 7.56** | Some Germanic cognates | | | |
|---|---|---|---|---|
| **English** | **Dutch** | **German** | **Danish** | **Swedish** |
| man | man | Mann | mand | man |
| hand | hand | Hand | hånd | hand |
| foot | voet | Fuß (β = [s]) | fod | fot |
| bring | brengen | bringen | bringe | bringa |
| summer | zomer | Sommer | sommer | sommar |

| **Table 7.57** | Some words in Turkish, a non-Germanic language (phonemic transcription) |
|---|---|
| adam | 'man' |
| el | 'hand' |
| ajak | 'foot' |
| getir | 'bring' |
| jaz | 'summer' |

striking. This is exemplified in the data in table 7.58 from English, Russian, and Hindi, all of which are distantly related to each other. Forms from the unrelated Turkish are included to emphasize the similarities among the first three languages.

| Table 7.58 | Some distantly related cognates compared to non-related Turkish | | |
|---|---|---|---|
| **English** | **Russian** | **Hindi** | **Turkish (phonemic transcription)** |
| two | dva | dō | iki |
| three | tri | tīn | ytʃ |
| brother | brat | bhāī | kardeʃ |
| nose | nos | nahī̃ | burun |

Once the existence of a relationship between two or more languages has been established, an attempt can be made to reconstruct the common source. This reconstructed language, or **proto-language**, is made up of **proto-forms**, which are written with a preceding * (e.g., *hand) to indicate their hypothetical character as reconstructions of earlier forms that have not been recorded or are not directly observable.

## 7.7.2 Techniques of reconstruction

Reconstruction can be undertaken with some confidence because (as discussed in the previous sections) the processes underlying language change are systematic. Once the processes are uncovered by linguists, they can be reversed, allowing us to infer earlier forms of the language. Although it is possible to reconstruct all components of a proto-language (its phonology, morphology, syntax, lexicon, and semantics), we will focus in the following on phonological reconstruction, the area in which linguists have made the most progress.

### Reconstruction strategies

Reconstruction of a proto-form makes use of two general strategies. The most important one is the **phonetic plausibility strategy**, which requires that any changes posited to account for differences between the proto-forms and later forms must be phonetically plausible. Secondarily, the **majority rules strategy** stipulates that if no phonetically plausible change can account for the observed differences, then the segment found in the majority of cognates should be assumed. It is important to note that the first strategy always takes precedence over the second; the second strategy is a last resort.

Consider the cognates in table 7.59 (somewhat simplified) from members of the Romance family.

| Table 7.59 | Romance cognates | | | |
|---|---|---|---|---|
| **French** | **Italian** | **Romanian** | **Spanish** | |
| si | si | ʃi | si | 'yes' |

The data exemplify a correspondence between [s] and [ʃ] before the vowel [i]. To account for this, we could assume either that Romanian underwent a change that converted [s] to [ʃ] before [i] or that the other three languages underwent a change converting [ʃ] to [s] before [i] as shown in figure 7.13.

<table>
<tr><td>Figure 7.13<br>Romance cognates</td><td>

*Hypothesis A*<br>
Proto-form                  *si<br>
Sound change (Romanian only)    *s > ʃ / ___ i

*Hypothesis B*<br>
Proto-form                  *ʃi<br>
Sound change (French, Italian, and Spanish)    *ʃ > s / ___ i

</td></tr>
</table>

Both reconstruction strategies favour hypothesis A. Most importantly, the phonetic change needed to account for the Romanian pronunciation involves palatalization before [i]. Since palatalization in this context is a very common phenomenon in human language, it is reasonable to assume that it occurred in Romanian. It would be much more difficult to argue that the proto-language contained [ʃ] before [i] and that three languages underwent the change posited by Hypothesis B, since depalatalization before [i] would be an unusual phonetic process. (The reconstructed *s posited in hypothesis A is also compatible with the majority rules strategy since three of the four languages in the data have [s] before [i].)

## Reconstruction and the catalogue of sound changes

Although there are factors that can confound our attempt to determine the relative plausibility of various sound changes, the changes listed in the catalogue in table 7.3 can generally be considered highly plausible. Table 7.60 lists some plausible versus less plausible or even implausible changes based on that catalogue.

| **Table 7.60** | Different rules in terms of their plausibility based on the catalogue |
|---|---|
| **Rule** | **Name of sound change in catalogue** |
| *High probability* | |
| t > tʃ / __ i | palatalization/affrication |
| n > m / __ b | assimilation (place of articulation) |
| t > d / V __ V | voicing |
| k > Ø / V __ st | consonant deletion (cluster simplification) |
| *Low probability* | |
| tʃ > t / __ i | (does not correspond to any listed change) |
| m > n / __ b | (does not correspond to any listed change) |
| d > t / V __ V | (does not correspond to any listed change) |
| Ø > k / V __ st | (does not correspond to any listed change) |

# Reconstructing Proto-Romance

Consider now the slightly more complex example in table 7.61 involving data from several languages of the Romance family.

**Table 7.61**  Some Romance cognates

| Spanish | Sardinian | French | Portuguese | Romanian | Original meaning |
|---|---|---|---|---|---|
| riba [β] | ripa | rive [ʁiv] | riba | rîpă | 'embankment' |
| amiga [ɣ] | amica | amie [ami] | amiga | – | 'female friend' |
| copa | cuppa | coupe [kup] | copa | cupă | 'cup, goblet' |
| gota | gutta | goutte [gut] | gota | gută | 'drop' |

*Note*: Orthographic *c* represents [k] in all the above examples. Romanian ă and î represent the central vowels [ə] and [ɨ], respectively. [β] is a voiced bilabial fricative and [ɣ] a voiced velar fricative. Some details of vowel quality have been ignored.

Our goal here is to reconstruct the proto-forms for these words in Proto-Romance, the parent language of the Modern Romance languages, which stands very close to Latin.

Let us first consider the reconstruction of the Proto-Romance form for 'embankment'. Since the first two segments are the same in all the cognate languages, we can reconstruct Proto-Romance *r and *i on the basis of the majority rules strategy. In the case of the second consonant, however, there are differences between the cognates (see table 7.62).

**Table 7.62**  Systematic correspondences in the cognates for 'embankment'

| Spanish | Sardinian | French | Portuguese | Romanian |
|---|---|---|---|---|
| -β- | -p- | -v- | -b- | -p- |

It is most important that we first think in terms of phonetic plausibility. In the absence of evidence to the contrary, we will assume that one of the segments found in the cognates ([p], [b], [v], or [β]) should be reconstructed for Proto-Romance. Logically possible changes ranked with respect to their phonetic plausibility are found in table 7.63.

**Table 7.63**  Changes based on phonetic plausibility

| Change in V__V | Name of change based on catalogue | Phonetic plausibility |
|---|---|---|
| p > b | voicing | high |
| p > v | voicing (p > b) and frication (b > v) | high |
| p > β | voicing (p > b) and frication (b > β) | high |
| b > p | – | low |
| β > p | – | low |
| v > p | – | low |

In terms of plausibility, the only possible reconstruction for Proto-Romance is *p*. Proto-Romance *p* underwent no change in Sardinian and Romanian, but in Portuguese it underwent intervocalic voicing and in Spanish it underwent both voicing and frication (that is, weakening) (see table 7.64). (We assume that voicing preceded frication since Portuguese shows voicing but no frication.) If we assume that the final vowel of the proto-form was still present in French when the consonant changes took place, we can conclude that voicing and frication occurred in this language as well. (In its written form, *rive* retains a sign of the earlier reduced vowel [ə].) These changes are phonetically plausible and thus expected.

| **Table 7.64** | **Summary of the changes affecting Proto-Romance *p*** |
|---|---|
| *p > p / V__V | no change in Sardinian or Romanian |
| *p > b / V__V | voicing in Portuguese |
| *p > b > β / V__V | voicing and frication in Spanish |
| *p > b > v / V__V | voicing and frication in French |

Turning now to the final vowel, we note that three languages have full vowels, Romanian has [ə], and French has no vowel (see table 7.65). Since vowel reduction and apocope are identified as phonetically plausible changes in the catalogue, it is appropriate to posit a full vowel for the proto-language. Furthermore, since the three languages with a full vowel all have [a], we can posit this vowel on the basis of the majority rules strategy. Accordingly, the reconstructed proto-form is *ripa*.

| **Table 7.65** | **Summary of the changes affecting Proto-Romance *a*** | |
|---|---|---|
| **Language** | **Change (word final)** | **Name of change(s)** |
| Romanian | *a > ə | vowel reduction |
| French | *a > ə > Ø | vowel reduction and deletion |

We can now outline the evolution of this word in French, which has the most complicated development of the six languages (see table 7.66).

| **Table 7.66** | **Evolution of French *rive* from *ripa*** | |
|---|---|---|
| **Change** | ***ripa** | **Name of change** |
| p > b / V__ V | riba | voicing |
| b > v / V __ V | riva | frication |
| a > ə / __ # | rivə | vowel reduction |
| ə > Ø / __ # | riv | apocope |

In the case of the cognates for 'female friend' (the second row of table 7.61), the first three segments are the same in all the languages in the data. According to the majority rules strategy we can reconstruct them as *ami-. In the reconstruction of the second consonant, however, we must appeal to our strategy of phonetic plausibility (see table 7.67).

| **Table 7.67** | Systematic correspondences in the second consonant of the cognates for 'female friend' | | | |
|---|---|---|---|---|
| **Spanish** | **Sardinian** | **French** | **Portuguese** | **Romanian** |
| -ɣ- | -k- | -Ø | -g- | – |

Once again, since intervocalic voicing, frication, and deletion are phonetically plausible changes, it is most appropriate to posit *k for the proto-form (see table 7.68).

| **Table 7.68** | Summary of the changes affecting Proto-Romance *k | |
|---|---|---|
| **Language** | **Change (in V_V)** | **Name of change(s)** |
| Portuguese | *k > g | voicing |
| Spanish | *k > g > ɣ | voicing and frication |
| French | *k > g > ɣ > Ø | voicing, frication, and deletion |

In the case of the final vowel, we have the same situation we had in the previous form. The full vowel is found in Spanish, Sardinian, and Portuguese but there is no vowel in French. We can therefore assume the full vowel *a for the proto-form, with subsequent vowel reduction and apocope in French. Consequently, we arrive at the proto-form *amika.

Finally, applying the same procedure to the cognates in the final two rows of table 7.61 yields the proto-forms *kuppa 'cup' and *gutta 'drop'. All the languages in the data retain the initial consonant of both proto-forms. The vowel *u is reconstructed on the basis of the majority rules strategy, since we have no phonetic grounds for choosing either [u] or [o] as the older vowel.[6] The systematic correspondences involving the intervocalic consonants are given in table 7.69.

| **Table 7.69** | Systematic correspondences of the medial consonants of *kuppa and *gutta | | | |
|---|---|---|---|---|
| **Spanish** | **Sardinian** | **French** | **Portuguese** | **Romanian** |
| -p- | -pp- | -p | -p- | -p- |
| -t- | -tt- | -t | -t- | -t- |

Regardless of whether we are dealing with original *pp or *tt, the same pattern is evident in the case of both geminate types. There is a geminate stop consonant in Sardinian and a single consonant in Spanish, French, Portuguese, and Romanian. Since degemination is an expected sound change (see the catalogue in table 7.3), we assume that the proto-forms contained geminate consonants that underwent degemination except in Sardinian. This is an example of a case where the phonetic plausibility strategy overrules the majority rules strategy (since four of the five languages have [p]/[t] whereas only one language has [pp]/[tt]). As far as the final vowels are concerned, the same pattern found in the previous examples is once again evident. Proto-Romance *a* was retained in Spanish, Sardinian, and Portuguese, reduced to [ə] in Romanian, and deleted in French (see table 7.65).

Of the languages exemplified here, Sardinian is considered the most conservative since it has retained more of the earlier consonants and vowels. (In fact, the Sardinian words in the examples happen to be identical with the proto-forms, but this degree of resemblance would not be maintained in a broader range of data.) In the case of the other Romance languages and changes we have discussed, the most to least conservative are: Portuguese (degemination and voicing) and Romanian (degemination and vowel reduction); Spanish (degemination, voicing, and frication); and French (degemination, voicing, frication, consonant deletion, vowel reduction, and apocope).

Although Proto-Romance is not identical with Classical Latin, close similarity is expected.[7] Accordingly, the fact that our reconstructions are so close to the Latin words gives us confidence in our methods of reconstruction (see table 7.70).

| **Table 7.70**  Comparison of Latin and Proto-Romance forms | |
| --- | --- |
| **Latin** | **Proto-Romance form** |
| rīpa | *ripa |
| amīca (c = [k]) | *amika |
| cuppa | *kuppa |
| gutta | *gutta |

Notice that it is sometimes not possible to reconstruct all the characteristics of the proto-language. For example, on the basis of our data we were not able to reconstruct vowel length (Latin had a distinction between long and short vowels) since there was no evidence of this characteristic in the cognate forms.

It is also worth noting that we are not always so fortunate as to have written records of a language we expect to be very close to our reconstructed language. In the case of the Germanic languages, for example, there is no ancient written language equivalent to Latin. We must rely completely on our reconstruction of Proto-Germanic to determine the properties of the language from which the modern-day Germanic languages descended. Furthermore, for many languages of the world we have no written historical records at all and for other languages, such as the Aboriginal languages of North America, it is only very recently that we have written records.

In summary, when the forms of two or more languages appear to be related, we can, through a consideration of systematic phonetic correspondences among cognates, reconstruct the common form from which all the forms can be derived by means of phonetically plausible sound changes. The reconstructed forms are proto-forms, and a reconstructed language, a proto-language.

## 7.7.3 Internal reconstruction

Sometimes it is possible to reconstruct the earlier form of a language even without reference to comparative data. This technique, known as **internal reconstruction**, relies on the analysis of morphophonemic variation within a single language. The key point is that the sound changes that create allomorphic and allophonic variation can be identified and then used to infer an earlier form of the morpheme. The data in table 7.71 are from French; because of borrowing, English exhibits a parallel set of contrasts involving [k] and [ʃ].

| **Table 7.71** | [k] / [s] correspondence in French | | |
|---|---|---|---|
| maʒik | 'magic' | maʒis-jẽ | 'magician' |
| lɔʒik | 'logic' | lɔʒis-jẽ | 'logician' |
| myzik | 'music' | myzis-jẽ | 'musician' |

The root morpheme in each row exhibits two forms, one ending in [k], the other ending in [s]. The same methods and principles used in comparative reconstruction can be applied here to reconstruct the historically earlier form of the root morpheme. If a root ending in *s is posited, no phonetically plausible change can account for the [k] in the left-hand column. By contrast, if a root-final *k is posited, the [s] can be accounted for by assuming that the *k was fronted under the influence of the high front vowel of the suffix (palatalization) and became an affricate [ts] (affrication) which was later simplified to a fricative [s] (deaffrication). All of these changes are phonetically plausible and listed in the catalogue in table 7.3. Accordingly, internal reconstruction indicates that at an earlier point in the development of French, the root morphemes in table 7.71 contained the consonant *k.

## 7.7.4 The discovery of Indo-European

The late eighteenth-century discovery that Sanskrit (an ancient language of India) was related to Latin, Greek, Germanic, and Celtic revolutionized European linguistic studies. Sir William Jones, a British judge and scholar working in India, summed up the nature and implications of the findings in his 1786 address to the Royal Asiatic Society, a part of which follows:

> *The Sanskrit language, whatever be its antiquity, is of a wonderful structure; more perfect than the Greek, more copious [having more cases] than the Latin, and more exquisitely refined than either, yet bearing to both of them a stronger affinity, both in the roots of the verbs and in the forms of the grammar, than could possibly have been produced by accident; so strong indeed, that no philologer could examine them all three, without believing them to have sprung from some common source, which, perhaps, no longer exists; there is a similar reason . . . for supposing that both the Gothic and the Celtic . . . had the same origin with the Sanskrit; and the old Persian might be added to the same family. . . .*

This discovery led to several decades of intensive historical-comparative work and to important advances in historical linguistics during the nineteenth century. By studying phonetic correspondences from an ever-increasing number of languages, linguists eventually ascertained that most of the languages of Europe, Persia (Iran), and the northern part of India belong to a single family, now called Indo-European. By applying the techniques of the comparative method, they began reconstructing the grammar of the proto-language from which these languages evolved, **Proto-Indo-European (PIE)**.

A number of individuals advanced this research. In 1814, the Danish linguist Rasmus Rask carefully documented the relationships among cognates in a number of Indo-European languages, and at the same time established the methods that would govern the emerging science of historical-comparative linguistics. He wrote:

> *When agreement is found in [the most essential] words in two languages, and so frequently that rules may be drawn up for the shift in letters [sounds] from one to the other, then there is a fundamental relationship between the two languages; especially when similarities in the inflectional system and in the general make-up of the languages correspond with them.*

Rask worked without access to Sanskrit. The first comparative linguistic analysis of Sanskrit, Greek, Persian, and the Germanic languages was done by the German scholar Franz Bopp in 1816. In 1822 another German, Jacob Grimm, extended Rask's observations and became the first person to explain the relationships among the cognates noted by Rask in terms of a **sound shift**, the systematic modification of a series of phonemes. Some of the correspondences on which he based his work are given in table 7.72.

| Table 7.72    Some Indo-European phonetic correspondences | | |
|---|---|---|
| **Greek** | **Latin** | **English** |
| patér | pater | father |
| treîs | trēs | three |
| hekatón | centum [k] | hundred |

The crucial observation is that where English has [f], [θ], and [h] (here, in word-initial position), Greek and Latin have [p], [t], and [k]. Grimm tabulated a series of consonant shifts for Proto-Germanic that differentiated it from other Indo-European languages. **Grimm's Law** is the name given to the consonant shifts that took place between Proto-Indo-European and Proto-Germanic (see table 7.73).

| Table 7.73    The sound shifts underlying Grimm's Law | | | | | | | | | |
|---|---|---|---|---|---|---|---|---|---|
| Proto-Indo-European | p | t | k | b | d | g | bh | dh | gh |
| Germanic | f | θ | x | p | t | k | b | d | g |

*Note:* [x] undergoes a subsequent change to [h].

## Language Matters  **The Brothers Grimm**

Jacob Grimm is, of course, well known for the collection of fairy tales and songs that he compiled with his brother Wilhelm. Stories such as "Snow White" and "Sleeping Beauty" were first written down by the Brothers Grimm. However, the two siblings were also scholars. Wilhelm focused on literary studies and Jacob was a philologist, who developed Grimm's Law.

Some additional examples of the relationships captured by these shifts follow in table 7.74. The Proto-Indo-European consonants were either maintained in Sanskrit, Greek, and Latin or, in some cases, underwent changes different from those found in Germanic (represented here by English).

**Table 7.74**  Some examples of the consonant shifts underlying Grimm's Law

| Shift in Germanic | | | Sanskrit | Greek | Latin | English |
|---|---|---|---|---|---|---|
| p | > | f | pād- | pod- | ped- | foot |
| t | > | θ | tanu- | tanaós | tenuis | thin |
| k | > | x | çatam | hekatón | centum | hundred |
| b | > | p | – | – | lūbricus | slippery |
| d | > | t | daça | déka | decem | ten |
| g | > | k | ajras | agrós | ager | acre |
| bh | > | b | bhrātā | phrátēr | frāter | brother |
| dh | > | d | vidhavā | ēítheos | vidua | widow |
| gh | > | g | hansas | khḗn | (h)ānser | goose |

*Note*: [x] undergoes a subsequent change to [h].

It should also be noted here that borrowing is an important factor that must be taken into consideration in comparative reconstruction. For example, English has many words that do not show the effects of Grimm's Law (see table 7.75).

**Table 7.75**  English words not showing the effects of Grimm's Law

| Expected by Grimm's Law | Latin | English |
|---|---|---|
| p > f | ped- | pedestrian |
| t > θ | tenuis | tenuous |
| k > x (> h) | canalis | canal |

The apparent failure of Grimm's Law here stems from the fact that the English words were borrowed directly from Latin or French many centuries after the sound shifts described by Grimm's Law had taken place. The task of reconstruction can often be complicated by such borrowings.

## Subsequent developments

By the middle of the nineteenth century, the study of language had made great strides, especially in the field of phonetics, which opened the way for the detailed comparison of linguistic forms. One influential hypothesis at that time was that sound laws operated without exception. A group of linguists known as the Neogrammarians adopted this idea and made many important contributions to the fledgling science of linguistics by applying it to new and more complicated data. Although such factors as lexical diffusion and social

---

**Language Matters  Reviving Indo-European**

A non-profit organization in Europe, the Dnghu Association, is devoted to reviving Indo-European and promoting its use as the main official language of the European Union and as the second language of all its citizens (*dnghu* is the reconstructed Indo-European word for 'tongue' or 'language'.) To read more about this project, go to the association's website at http://dnghu.org/en/, which also includes a proposed grammar and dictionary of Indo-European.

---

pressures were more or less ignored by the Neogrammarians, their hypothesis represented an important and daring advance in the scientific study of language.

The nineteenth century also saw major advances in the classification of languages. A German scholar, August Schleicher, developed a classification for the Indo-European languages in the form of a genealogical tree. This type of genetic classification is discussed in more detail in the chapter on language typology that follows.

Work in comparative reconstruction is far from finished. In particular, linguists are now considering the possibility of superfamilies. One such proposed family is Nostratic, which includes Indo-European, Afro-Asiatic (e.g., Arabic, Hebrew), Altaic (e.g., Japanese, Korean, Turkic), and Uralic (e.g., Finnish, Hungarian). (See chapter 8 for further discussion.) Comparative reconstruction is also playing an important role in determining the genetic relationships of the hundreds of North American indigenous languages, a topic that still remains highly controversial.

## 7.7.5  Reconstruction and typology

Since the 1800s, when the reconstruction of Proto-Indo-European was carried out, linguists have accumulated vast amounts of information on thousands of languages. This is in part due to the explosion of studies in the field of linguistic typology, which is concerned with the investigation of structural similarities among languages that are not genetically related. Even languages that do not belong to the same family can have striking similarities. For example, in addition to shared word order patterns, SOV languages commonly exhibit a strong tendency towards agglutinating morphology (a type of complex affixation; see chapter 8). Typological studies play an important role in the linguist's search for universals of language—statements that are true for all languages.

The extensive information on the languages of the world available to modern linguists was, of course, not available at the time the original reconstruction of Proto-Indo-European was undertaken. Modern linguists involved in comparative reconstruction now take a keen interest in typological studies and the role of **typological plausibility** in reconstruction has become an important topic. For example, a linguist would be very reluctant to propose a reconstruction that violated a universal property of language or that had no parallel in any known language.

Some linguists have argued that the traditional reconstruction of the PIE consonant system (given in table 7.76) should be rejected on the basis of typological plausibility.

| Table 7.76 | The traditional reconstruction of the Proto-Indo-European consonants | | | | |
|---|---|---|---|---|---|
| p | t | ḱ [c] | k | kʷ | (voiceless stops) |
| (b) | d | ǵ [ɟ] | g | gʷ | (voiced stops) |
| bh | dh | ǵh | gh | gʷh | (voiced aspirated stops) |
|  | s |  |  |  |  |

*Note*: ḱ, ǵ, and ǵh are palatal stops and ʷ indicates a labialized consonant.

This reconstruction is typologically questionable in at least two respects. First, reconstructed forms with PIE *b are extremely rare, almost as if there were a gap in the labial system. Such a gap is very uncommon in the languages of the world. Typically if there is a missing labial stop, it is the voiceless stop that is missing, not the voiced counterpart. Second, the traditional reconstruction posits a series of voiced aspirated stops but no corresponding series of voiceless aspirated stops, even though some typologists have argued that all languages that have a voiced series also have the voiceless one.

Such facts have led some linguists to propose what they believe is a more typologically plausible reconstruction of Proto-Indo-European involving a voiceless stop series, an ejective series, and a voiced stop series (as well as *s as in the traditional reconstruction) (see table 7.77).[8]

| Table 7.77 | A recent reconstruction of the Proto-Indo-European consonants | | | | |
|---|---|---|---|---|---|
| p | t | ḱ | k | kʷ | (voiceless stops) |
| (p') | t' | ḱ' | k' | k'ʷ | (ejectives) |
| b | d | ǵ | g | gʷ | (voiced stops) |
|  | s |  |  |  |  |

Not only does this reconstruction avoid the problem with aspirates, it is also common for languages with an ejective series to lack the labial. From this perspective, this reconstruction seems much more plausible than the traditional one.

Both reconstructions have their supporters, and it is difficult to come to a definitive decision on the basis of typological considerations since it is common for a proposed universal to have exceptions. For example, a few languages have been found with the characteristics attributed to Proto-Indo-European by the traditional reconstruction. These languages have labial gaps in the voiced series (e.g., Aboriginal languages of the Athabaskan and Caddoan families) and a voiced aspirate series but no voiceless counterpart (Madurese, an Indonesian language). Accordingly, as long as the traditional reconstruction is linguistically possible, it would not seem possible to reject it simply because the phonological system proposed would be a rare one.

Typological plausibility will likely continue to play a secondary role in reconstruction until linguists can draw a clear line between what is linguistically possible and what is not possible. Nevertheless, as our knowledge and understanding of language universals continues to improve, it is certain that linguists involved in the reconstruction of proto-languages will maintain an interest in typological plausibility.

# 7.8 Language change and naturalness

A striking fact about language change is that the same patterns of change occur repeatedly, not only within a particular language at different periods in its history but also across languages. Both the similarity of changes across languages as well as the directionality of language change suggest that some changes are more natural than others. This notion of **naturalness** is implicit in the phonetic plausibility strategy introduced in the section on comparative reconstruction.

If naturalness is a factor in language change, its manifestations should also be found in language acquisition and in language universals. This does seem to be the case. As a specific example, let us consider the frequently made claim that the CV syllable is the most natural of all syllable types. At least three different kinds of evidence can be brought forth in support of this claim.

First, in terms of universals, all languages of the world have CV syllables in their syllable type inventory, and some languages only have CV syllables. Second, a variety of sound changes have the effect of reducing less natural syllable types to the more natural CV type (see table 7.78).

**Table 7.78**   Sound changes yielding CV syllables

**Deletion**

| CCV | > | CV | Old English | cnēow | English | knee | /ni/ |
|-----|---|-----|-------------|-------|---------|------|------|
| CVC | > | CV | Old Spanish | non | Spanish | no | |

**Vowel epenthesis**

| CCVCV | > | CVCVCV | Italian | croce | Sicilian | kiruci | 'cross' |
|-------|---|--------|---------|-------|----------|--------|---------|

By contrast, note that such changes rarely, if ever, apply to a CV syllable to yield a different syllable type. Deletion of the C in a word-initial CV syllable is extremely rare, as is vowel epenthesis in a CV syllable or a sequence of CVCV syllables.

Third, in terms of language acquisition, the CV syllable type is one of the first syllable types to be acquired and many phonetic processes found in child language have the effect of yielding CV syllables, just like the sound changes listed above (see chapter 10 on language acquisition; see table 7.79).

**Table 7.79**   Phonetic processes in language acquisition yielding CV syllables

| CCV → CV | tree → [ti] | (simplification of consonant clusters) |
|----------|-------------|----------------------------------------|
| CVC → CV | dog → [dɑ] | (deletion of final consonants) |

The precise effects of linguistic naturalness are not yet fully understood. For example, some sound changes actually do produce less natural syllables. Thus, syncope has the effect of reducing a sequence of CVCVCV syllables to the less natural CVCCV. Usually in such cases, a different motivation can be identified, such as the preference for shorter phonological forms over longer forms. But given the complexity of human language, not to mention human behaviour in general, it should not be surprising that there are many different parameters of linguistic naturalness and that these can, in turn, lead to apparently conflicting changes in language over time. It remains an important task of the linguist to identify, rank, and ultimately explain relations of linguistic naturalness. The study of language change will continue to make an important contribution to this area.

# Summing up

Historical linguistics studies the nature and causes of language change. The causes of language change find their roots in the physiological and cognitive makeup of human beings. Sound changes usually involve articulatory simplification, as in the case of the most common type, **assimilation**. **Analogy** and **reanalysis** are particularly important factors in morphological change. **Language contact** resulting in **borrowing** is another important source of language change. All components of the grammar, from phonology to semantics, are subject to change over time. A change can simultaneously affect all instances of a particular sound or form, or it can spread through the language word by word by means of **lexical diffusion**. Sociological factors can play an important role in determining whether or not a linguistic innovation is ultimately adopted by the linguistic community at large. Since language change is systematic, it is possible, by identifying the changes that a particular language or dialect has undergone, to reconstruct linguistic history and thereby posit the earlier forms from which later forms have evolved. Using sets of **cognates**, **comparative reconstruction** allows us to reconstruct the properties of the parent or **proto-language** on the basis of **systematic phonetic correspondences**.

Studies in historical linguistics can provide valuable insights into relationships among languages and shed light on prehistoric developments. Furthermore, historical studies of language are of great importance to our understanding of human linguistic competence. In fact, it has often been stated that language change provides one of the most direct windows into the workings of the human mind. Furthermore, the study of language change contributes to our understanding of how social, cultural, and psychological factors interact to shape language. Finally, the integration of studies on language change, language acquisition, and language universals remains one of the most important challenges facing linguists today.

## Notes

[1]  The translation for the passage is as follows:
Many men say that in dreams
There is nothing but talk and lies
But men may see some dreams
Which are scarcely false
But afterward come true.

2   In these and other examples throughout this chapter, orthographic forms are given where these clearly reflect the sound change(s) in question. If required, partial or full phonetic transcriptions are provided.

3   Since voicing commonly occurs between voiced segments, it can also be considered a type of assimilation. It is treated here as a weakening since it is often part of a larger pattern of change involving various weakening processes.

4   A fully phonemic contrast between lax and tense vowels appears to be developing in Canadian French. Borrowings from English are contributing to this development (e.g., *poule* 'hen' versus *pool*).

5   We have simplified here in two respects. First, we ignore the fact that the verbs *be* and *have* can undergo Inversion even when they do not function as auxiliaries.
    *Are they here?*
    *Have you no sense?*
    Second, we have not traced the emergence of the auxiliary verb *do* in the formation of questions.

6   In fact, the assumption of umlaut would be a very good working hypothesis; that is, *\*u* became [o] in Spanish and Portuguese due to the lowering influence of the word-final low vowel *\*a*. However, a larger dataset would show that this type of umlaut did not occur in these languages.

7   Classical Latin was the literary language of ancient Rome, whereas Proto-Romance represents an attempt to reconstruct the spoken language spread throughout Europe that was the source of the various Romance languages.

8   Ejectives are produced by a closing of the glottis and raising of the larynx.

## Recommended reading

Anttila, Raimo. 1989. *Historical and Comparative Linguistics*. 2nd ed. Amsterdam: John Benjamins.

Brinton, Laurel J., and Leslie K. Arnovick. 2006. *The English Language: A Linguistic History*. Oxford: Oxford University Press.

*The Cambridge History of the English Language, 1992–2001*. Six volumes. Cambridge, UK: Cambridge University Press.

Campbell, Lyle. 2004. *Historical Linguistics. An Introduction*. 2nd ed. Cambridge, MA: MIT Press.

Gelderen, Elly van. 2006. *A History of the English Language*. Amsterdam: John Benjamins.

Hock, Hans Henrich. 1992. *Principles of Historical Linguistics*. 2nd ed. Amsterdam: Mouton de Gruyter.

Hock, Hans Henrich, and Brian D. Joseph. 1996. *Language History, Language Change, and Language Relationship: An Introduction to Historical and Comparative Linguistics*. New York: Mouton de Gruyter.

Hopper, Paul J., and Elizabeth Closs Traugott. 2003. *Grammaticalization*. 2nd ed. Cambridge, UK: Cambridge University Press.

Joseph, Brian D., and Richard Janda, eds. 2003. *The Handbook of Historical Linguistics*. Oxford: Blackwell.

Koerner, E.F., and R.E. Asher, eds. 1995. *Concise History of the Language Sciences: From the Sumerians to the Cognitivists*. New York: Pergamon.

Labov, William. 1994. *Principles of Linguistic Change,* Vol. 1: *Internal Factors*. Oxford: Blackwell.

Labov, William. 2001. *Principles of Linguistic Change,* Vol. 2: *Social Factors*. Oxford: Blackwell.

Lass, Roger. 1997. *Historical Linguistics and Language Change*. Cambridge, UK: Cambridge University Press.

Lehmann, Winfred P. 1992. *Historical Linguistics*. 3rd ed. New York: Routledge.

McMahon, April M.S. 1994. *Understanding Language Change*. Cambridge, UK: Cambridge University Press.

Trask, R.L. 2007. *Historical Linguistics*. 2nd ed. London: Arnold.

## Exercises

1. Identify the following sound changes with reference to the catalogue of sound changes provided in table 7.3. In each pair of examples, focus on the segment(s) in bold only. The form on the left indicates the original segment(s) before the change and the form on the right indicates the segment(s) after the change.

| | | | | | |
|---|---|---|---|---|---|
| a) | Sanskrit | **sn**eha | Pali | **sin**eha | 'friendship' |
| b) | Old English | **hl**āf | English | **l**oaf | |
| c) | Latin | **i**uvenis [j] | Italian | **gi**ovane [dʒ] | 'young' |
| d) | English | tria**thl**on | dialect | triath**[ə]l**on | |
| e) | Latin | vi**du**a [dw] | Spanish | vi**ud**a [wd] | 'widow' |
| f) | Sanskrit | sa**pt**a | Pali | sa**tt**a | 'seven' |
| g) | Latin | tur**tur** | English | tur**tle** | |
| h) | Pre-Spanish | *ve**nr**é | Spanish | ve**ndr**é | 'I will come' |
| i) | Italian | mu**nd**o | Sicilian | mu**nn**u | 'world' |
| j) | Old French | **c**ire [ts] | French | **c**ire [s] | 'wax' |
| k) | Latin | p**ān**- | French | p**ain** [ɛ̃] | 'bread' |
| l) | Latin | **m**ulgēre | Italian | **m**ungere | 'to milk' |
| m) | Latin | pa**c**are [k] | Italian | pa**g**are | 'to pay' |
| n) | Old Spanish | ni**d**o | Spanish | ni**d**o [ð] | 'nest' |
| o) | Latin | pe**cc**ātum [kk] | Spanish | pe**c**ado [k] | 'sin' |
| p) | Pre-Latin | *honō**s**is | Latin | honō**r**is | 'honor (gen sg)' |
| q) | English | ra**ge** | French | ra**ge** [ʒ] | 'rage' |
| r) | English | cof**f**ee | Chipewyan | [ka**θ**i] | |
| s) | Latin | mar**e** | Portuguese | mar | 'sea' |
| t) | Latin | vīcīn**it**ās | Spanish | vecindad | 'neighbourhood' |
| u) | Gothic | **þ**liuan [θ] | English | **f**lee | |
| v) | Old English | (ic) sing**e** | English | (I) sing | |
| w) | Latin | su**mm**a | Spanish | su**m**a | 'sum, gist' |
| x) | Latin | ōrn**ā**mentum | Old French | orn**e**ment [ə] | 'ornament' |
| y) | Pre–Old English | *l**ū**si | Old English | l**ȳ**s [yː] | 'lice' |

**2.** a) Describe the difference between the two French dialects in the following data. Assume that the data are in phonetic transcription.

b) What sound change would you posit here? Why?

c) State the sound change in the form of a rule.

|      | *European French* | *Acadian French* |           |
|------|-------------------|------------------|-----------|
| *i)* | okyn              | otʃyn            | 'none'    |
| *ii)* | kør              | tʃør             | 'heart'   |
| *iii)* | ke              | tʃe              | 'wharf'   |
| *iv)* | kɛ̃:z            | tʃɛ̃:z           | 'fifteen' |
| *v)* | akyze             | atʃyze           | 'accuse'  |
| *vi)* | ki               | tʃĩ              | 'who'     |
| *vii)* | kav             | kav              | 'cave'    |
| *viii)* | kɔr            | kɔr              | 'body'    |
| *ix)* | kurir            | kurir            | 'run'     |
| *x)* | ɑ̃kɔ:r            | ɑ̃kɔ:r           | 'again"   |

**3.** a) What sound changes differentiate Guaraní from its parent language, Proto-Tupí-Guaraní, in the following data?

b) State these changes in rule form.

|      | *Proto-Tupí-Guaraní* | *Guaraní* |           |
|------|----------------------|-----------|-----------|
| *i)* | jukɨr                | jukɨ      | 'salt'    |
| *ii)* | moajan              | moajã     | 'push'    |
| *iii)* | puʔam              | puʔã      | 'wet'     |
| *iv)* | meʔeŋ               | meʔẽ      | 'give'    |
| *v)* | tiŋ                  | tʃĩ       | 'white'   |
| *vi)* | potiʔa              | potʃiʔa   | 'chest'   |
| *vii)* | tatatiŋ            | tatatʃĩ   | 'smoke'   |
| *viii)* | kɨb               | kɨ        | 'louse'   |
| *ix)* | men                  | mẽ        | 'husband' |

**4.** a) Describe the three changes that took place between Proto-Slavic and Bulgarian in the following data. (The symbol ˘ over a vowel indicates that it is short.)

b) State these changes as rules and indicate, as far as possible, the order in which they must have applied.

c) Apply these rules to the Proto-Slavic word for 'adroit' to show how the Bulgarian form evolved.

|      | *Proto-Slavic* | *Bulgarian* |            |
|------|----------------|-------------|------------|
| *i)* | gladŭka        | glatkə      | 'smooth'   |
| *ii)* | kratŭka        | kratkə      | 'short'    |
| *iii)* | blizŭka       | bliskə      | 'near'     |
| *iv)* | ʒeʒĭka        | ʒeʃkə       | 'scorching'|
| *v)* | lovŭka         | lofkə       | 'adroit'   |
| *vi)* | gorĭka         | gorkə       | 'bitter'   |

**5.** Determine all the sound changes required to derive the later form from the proto-form. Where necessary, give the chronology of the sound changes.

a) *feminam    Old French    femme (final e = [ə])    'woman'
b) *lumine     Spanish       lumbre                   'fire'
c) *tremulare  Spanish       temblar                  'tremble'
d) *stuppam    Spanish       estopa                   'tow'
e) *populu     Romanian      plop                     'poplar'

6. Taking into consideration the Great Vowel Shift, give all the changes necessary to derive the Modern English forms from the Old English forms. (*Note:* Assume, simplifying somewhat, that the Old English forms were pronounced as they are written.)

   *Old English*          *Modern English*
   a) brōde (SG ACC)      brood [brud]
   b) cnotta (c = [k])    knot [nɑt]
   c) wīse                wise [wajz]
   d) hlǣfdige            lady[lejdi]

7. Place names are often subject to spelling pronunciation. Transcribe your pronunciation of the following words and then compare your pronunciation with that recommended by a good dictionary. Do you think any of your pronunciations qualify as spelling pronunciations?

   a) Worcestershire
   b) Thames
   c) Edinburgh (Scotland; compare Edinburgh, Texas)
   d) Cannes (France)
   e) Newfoundland

8. Compare the Old English singular and plural forms:

   *Singular*    *Plural*
   bōc           bēc         'book(s)'
   āc            ǣc          'oak(s)'

   Although the Old English words have an umlaut plural (as in Old English gōs/gēs 'goose/geese'), the Modern English forms do not. Explain how the change in plural formation could have come about.

9. As evident in the following sentence, Shona, a modern Bantu language, has SVO word order. (*Note*: The morpheme *ano-* marks present tense.)

   mwana      anotengesa     miriwo
   child      sells          vegetables
   'The child sells vegetables'.

   By contrast, Shona's morphology reflects a different pattern as evident in the following examples.

   mwana      ano**mu**ona
   child      **him**+see
   'The child sees him'.
   mukadzi    ano**va**batsira
   woman      **them**+help
   'The woman helps them'.

   What do these examples indicate about earlier Shona or Proto-Bantu word order?

10. All of the following English words at one time had meanings that are quite different from their current ones. Identify each of these semantic changes as an instance of narrowing, broadening, amelioration, pejoration, weakening, or shift.

| Word | Earlier meaning |
|---|---|
| a) moody | 'brave' |
| b) uncouth | 'unknown' |
| c) aunt | 'father's sister' |
| d) butcher | 'one who slaughters goats' |
| e) witch | 'male or female sorcerer' |
| f) sly | 'skilful' |
| g) accident | 'an event' |
| h) argue | 'make clear' |
| i) carry | 'transport by cart' |
| j) grumble | 'murmur, make low sounds' |
| k) shrewd | 'depraved, wicked' |
| l) praise | 'set a value on' |
| m) ordeal | 'trial by torture' |
| n) picture | 'a painted likeness' |
| o) seduce | 'persuade someone to desert his or her duty' |
| p) box | 'a small container made of boxwood' |
| q) baggage | 'a worthless person' |
| r) virtue | 'qualities one expected of a man' |
| s) myth | 'story' |
| t) undertaker | 'one who undertakes' |
| u) hussy | 'housewife' |
| v) astonish | 'strike by thunder' |
| w) write | 'scratch' |
| x) quell | 'kill' |

11. Look up the following words in a good dictionary. Discuss any semantic changes that have affected the underscored portions since Old English. Do you think speakers of Modern English have reanalyzed any of these forms in terms of folk etymology?
    a) wed<u>lock</u>
    b) witch<u>craft</u>
    c) stead<u>fast</u>
    d) after<u>ward</u>

12. The following line is from *Troilus and Criseyde V* by Geoffrey Chaucer.
    His lighte goost ful blisfully is went.
    [hɪs liçtə gɔːst fʊl blɪsfʊlli ɪs wɛnt] ([ç] is a voiceless palatal fricative.)
    His light spirit has gone very blissfully.
    a) How has the meaning of the word *ghost* changed since Chaucer's time?
    b) Describe the changes that have taken place in the pronunciation of *light* and *ghost*.

13. Consider the following lyrics from the Middle English song "Sumer is i-cumen in." Compare the Middle English lyrics with the Modern English translation and answer the questions that follow.

| Original text | Transcription |
|---|---|
| Sumer is i-cumen in; | [sʊmər ɪs ɪkʊmən ɪn |
| Lhude sing, cuccu! | luːdə sɪŋg kʊkku |

Grōweþ sēd, and blōweþ mēd,          grɔ:wəθ se:d and blɔ:wəθ me:d
And springþ þe wude nū.              and springθ ðə wʊdə nu:]

*Translation*
'Summer has come in;
Loudly sing, cuckoo!
Seed grows and meadow blooms
And the wood grows now.'

a)  What affix converted the adjective *loud* into an adverb in Middle English?
b)  What accounts for the difference between the Middle English and Modern English pronunciation of the vowel in *loud*?
c)  What other words in this poem reflect this general shift?
d)  How has the relative ordering of the subject and verb changed since this was written?
e)  How has the third person singular present tense suffix changed since Middle English?

14. The following words found in various Cree dialects were borrowed from French as the result of contact between the two groups on the Canadian prairies. (Notice that the French determiner was not treated as a separate morpheme and was carried along with the borrowed word.) What types of considerations could one plausibly assume played a role in the borrowing of these words into Cree?

| *Cree* | *French* | |
|--------|----------|---|
| a) labutōn | le bouton | 'button' |
| b) lībot | les bottes | 'boots' |
| c) lamilās | la mélasse | 'molasses' |
| d) lapwīl | la poêle | 'frying pan' |
| e) litī | le thé | 'tea' |

15. The following Latin roots are found in words that have been borrowed into English. Since these words were borrowed after Grimm's Law had applied, they do not show its effects. All of these roots, however, do have Germanic cognates that did undergo Grimm's Law. On the basis of your knowledge of this law and the meaning of the borrowing, try to determine the Modern English (Germanic) cognate for each root. Consult a good dictionary if you need help. (*Note:* Focus on the portion of the Latin word in bold only; vowel changes must also be taken into consideration.)

| *Latin root* | *Related borrowing* | *English cognate* |
|--------------|---------------------|-------------------|
| a) **ped**is | pedestrian | <u>foot</u> |
| b) **nep**os | nepotism | _____ |
| c) **pisc**es | piṣcine | _____ |
| d) **ten**uis | tenuous | _____ |
| e) **córn**u | cornucopia | _____ |
| f) **ḍuo** | dual | _____ |
| g) **ed**ere | edible | _____ |
| h) **gen**us | genocide | _____ |
| i) **ager** | agriculture | _____ |

**16.** Attempt to reconstruct the Proto-Germanic form for each pair of cognates. Focusing on the vowels, describe the changes that affected the Old English forms. (*Note*: y = [y], œ = [ø], c = [k], and j = [j]).

| | Gothic | Old English | |
|---|---|---|---|
| a) | kuni | cyn | 'kin' |
| b) | badi | bed | 'bed' |
| c) | dōmjan | dœman | 'to judge' |
| d) | sōkjan | sœcan | 'to seek' |
| e) | bugjan | bycgan | 'to buy' |
| f) | nati | net | 'net' |

**17.** Reconstruct the Proto-Romance form for each set of cognates. Give all the changes necessary to derive each of the modern forms from the proto-forms. If you are not sure how to proceed, return to section 7.7. (*Note*: The Spanish and Romanian spelling 'ie' represents the sequence /je/, and the Romanian spelling 'ia' represents the sequence /ja/.)

| | Spanish | Sardinian | Romanian | |
|---|---|---|---|---|
| a) | vida | bita | vită (ă = [ə]) | 'life' |
| b) | sí | si | și (ș = [ʃ]) | 'yes' |
| c) | riso | rizu | rîs | 'laugh' |
| d) | miel | mele | miere | 'honey' |
| e) | hierro | ferru | fier | 'iron' |
| f) | piedra | pedra | piatră (ă = [ə]) | 'stone' |
| g) | hierba | erva | iarbă (ă = [ə]) | 'grass' |
| h) | oso | ursu | urs | 'bear' |
| i) | roto | ruttu | rupt | 'broken' |
| j) | lecho | lettu | – | 'bed' |

# Eight

Aleksandra Steinbergs

# The classification of languages

*Everything it is possible for us to analyze
depends on a clear method which distinguishes
the similar from the not similar.*

LINNEUS, *GENERA PLANTARUM* (1754)

In the world today there are almost 7000 different languages, each with its own sound patterns, syntax, and vocabulary. But underlying these differences are similarities of various sorts that allow linguists to arrange languages into groups based on shared features. This chapter describes the methods of classification linguists use, and some of the findings that have resulted from this type of research.

## 8.1 Some preliminaries

We will begin by considering two topics—the problem of distinguishing between a language and a dialect, and the chief methods of language classification used in linguistics today.

### 8.1.1 Dialect and language

It is often difficult to determine whether two linguistic communities speak different languages or merely different dialects of the same language. One test that linguists use to decide this involves the criterion of **mutual intelligibility**. Mutually intelligible varieties of the same language can be understood by speakers of each variety. According to this criterion, the English of Toronto, the English of Milwaukee, and the English of London qualify as dialects of the same language. On the other hand, if two speakers cannot understand one another, then linguists normally conclude that they are speaking different languages. The Italian of Florence and the French of Paris are examples of varieties of speech that are not mutually intelligible.

Political, cultural, social, historical, and religious factors frequently interfere when determining linguistic boundaries. (In fact, it is sometimes said that a language is just a dialect with an army and a navy!) For example, Serbs and Croats, with their different histories, cultures, and religions, often claim that they speak different languages. However, even though they use different alphabets, Serbian and Croatian are actually mutually intelligible dialects of the same language, which linguists call Serbo-Croatian. In contrast, we often speak of Chinese as if it were a single language, even though it is actually a number of individual, mutually unintelligible languages (Mandarin, Cantonese, Taiwanese, Wu, and so on), each with a multitude of dialects of its own.

In addition to the problems presented by these non-linguistic considerations, complications also arise when we try to divide a continuum of mutually intelligible dialects whose two endpoints are not intelligible. Dutch and German, for example, are mutually intelligible around the border area between Germany and the Netherlands; however, the Dutch of Amsterdam and the German of Munich are not. Similarly, Palestinian Arabic and Syrian Arabic are mutually intelligible, but Moroccan Arabic and Saudi Arabian Arabic are not.

## The threat to human linguistic diversity

Taking these considerations into account, how many languages are there in the world today? The best available estimate, from the Ethnologue organization (www.ethnologue.com), places the figure at about 6900, with the following geographic distribution (see table 8.1).

| Table 8.1 | The geographical distribution of the world's living languages | |
|---|---|---|
| **Region** | **Number of languages** | **% of the total** |
| The Americas | 1 002 | 14.5 |
| Africa | 2 092 | 30.3 |
| Europe | 239 | 3.5 |
| Asia | 2 269 | 32.8 |
| The Pacific | 1 310 | 19.0 |
| Total | 6 912 | |

Source: www.ethnologue.com

Table 8.2 presents the estimated speaker populations for the world's twenty most-spoken languages. (Except where otherwise indicated, estimates include only native speakers; L2 = second language.) These are large numbers, but they are not typical—most languages have fewer than 10 000 speakers and many are at risk of disappearing altogether.

Ask the average person to name a dead language, and he or she is likely to mention Latin. In fact, Latin did not really die; rather, it evolved over a period of centuries into French, Spanish, Italian, Portuguese, Romanian, and the other modern-day Romance languages (see section 8.3.1).

Contrast this with the situation of Manx, a Celtic language indigenous to the Isle of Man, a small island midway between Ireland and Great Britain. Its last speaker, Ned Madrell, died in 1974. Just one hundred years earlier, 12 000 people had spoken Manx. Now no one does. Manx didn't just change over time; it eventually ceased to be spoken.

This sort of language death is increasingly common in the contemporary world, accelerating a process that has been underway for several centuries. Indeed, according to some estimates, 60 percent of the world's languages are currently at risk, with few, if any, children learning them. The situation is grim in many different areas of the world. Just four of the sixty

| Table 8.2 | The world's twenty most spoken languages and estimated number of speakers |
|---|---|
| Mandarin | 873 014 000 [+178 000 000 L2 speakers] |
| Spanish | 322 029 000 [+60 000 000 L2 speakers] |
| English | 309 352 000 [+200 000 000 L2 speakers] |
| Hindi | 180 764 000 |
| Portuguese | 177 457 000 |
| Bengali (Bangladesh, India) | 171 070 000 |
| Russian | 145 031 000 [+110 000 000 L2 speakers] |
| Japanese | 122 434 000 |
| German | 95 393 000 |
| Wu (China) | 77 175 000 |
| Javanese (Indonesia) | 75 508 000 |
| Telugu (India) | 69 688 000 |
| Marathi (India) | 68 049 000 |
| Vietnamese | 67 439 000 |
| Korean | 67 019 000 |
| Tamil (India, Sri Lanka) | 66 020 000 |
| French | 64 858 000 [+50 000 000 L2 speakers] |
| Urdu (India, Pakistan) | 60 503 000 |
| Yue (China) | 54 810 000 |
| Turkish | 50 625 000 |

Source: www.ethnologue.com.

indigenous languages once spoken in Canada—Cree, Ojibwe, Inuktitut, and Dëne Su̱łiné—have large enough speaker populations to have a good chance of surviving over the long term (see chapter 9 for details). Of the 300 languages spoken in the area corresponding to the United States at the time of Columbus, there are now just 175—many of which are on the verge of disappearing. Ninety percent of Australia's 250 Aboriginal languages are near extinction.

The death of languages is lamentable for a variety of reasons. From a purely linguistic perspective, the loss of linguistic diversity means that we have much less information about how language works and about the different forms that it can take. For example, when the last speaker of Ubykh (a North Caucasian language spoken in Turkey) died in 1992, linguists lost the opportunity to study a very unusual phonological system—Ubykh had eighty-one consonants and just three vowels. (In contrast, a typical variety of Canadian English has twenty-four consonants and around sixteen vowels and diphthongs—see chapter 3.)

Just as serious is the loss of cultural knowledge that accompanies language death. A language's vocabulary encodes much of a community's cultural and scientific knowledge, including the distinctions that it makes among the plants and animals in its environment. This knowledge, accumulated over centuries, is not insignificant: many indigenous languages distinguish among thousands of species of plants, fish, and animals based on their appearance, behaviour, edibility, and even medicinal properties.

How and why do languages die? In some cases, they die because the people who speak them perish as the result of war or disease. Indeed, according to some estimates, up to 95 percent of the Native population of North America died from diseases brought to their continent by European colonists.

More commonly these days, however, languages die because their speakers gradually use them less and less in favour of a language that appears to offer greater economic or educational opportunities. English, Spanish, and French are obvious examples of international languages that acquire new speakers in this way, but many other languages are dominant on a more local scale: Thai, Bahasa Indonesia, Swahili, and Filipino (among others) are all threats to smaller languages in their respective territories.

The classic pattern of language loss involves three generations: the parents are monolingual, their children become bilingual by adopting a new language, and their children's children grow up monolingual in the new language. They end up unable to speak to their own grandparents.

With almost 7000 languages in the world today and only about 200 countries, the vast majority of the world's languages do not have the protection of a national government. Nor are smaller language communities well equipped to compete with the larger languages that surround them, tempting their young people to abandon their linguistic heritage.

This ongoing pervasive threat to the world's linguistic diversity is of great concern to linguists, many of whom are actively involved in studying and documenting languages on the verge of extinction. Where feasible, linguists are also seeking ways to improve the prospects for endangered languages by participating in linguistic, social, and educational programs designed to promote and protect the use of indigenous languages.

## 8.1.2    Types of classification

Within the field of linguistics, three different approaches to language classification are used.

**Genetic classification** categorizes languages according to their descent. Languages that developed historically from the same ancestor language are grouped together and are said to be **genetically related**. This ancestor may be attested (that is, texts written in this language have been discovered or preserved, as in the case of Latin), or it may be a reconstructed proto-language for which no original texts exist (as is the case for Indo-European; see chapter 7, section 7.7.4). Section 8.3 of this chapter and our Companion Website present an overview of a few hundred languages and the families to which they belong (see **www.pearsoned.ca/ogrady**, chapter 8).

---

**Language Matters  Language Immersion to the Rescue?**

In the 1960s a group of Canadian parents and educators launched "French immersion"—a wildly successful program that made French the language of instruction for English-speaking schoolchildren—taking advantage of the fact that children are naturally successful language learners.

This same idea underlies a series of exciting immersion initiatives whose goal is the survival of indigenous languages. Following the pioneering effort of the Maori in New Zealand in the early 1980s, immersion programs have been implemented with varying degrees of success for many endangered languages, including Hawaiian, Blackfoot, and Mohawk.

Sources: L. Hinton and K. Hale, eds., *The Green Book of Language Revitalization in Practice* (San Diego: Academic Press, 2001). www.ahapunanaleo.org/(website for Hawaiian immersion); www.indiancountry.com/content.cfm?id=1096413577 (information on Mohawk language immersion); www.kohanga.ac.nz/(website for Maori immersion).

Although genetically related languages often share structural characteristics, they do not necessarily bear a close structural resemblance. For example, Latvian and English are genetically related (both are descended from Indo-European), but their morphological structure is quite different. An English sentence like *It has to be figured out* can be expressed in Latvian by the single word *ja-izgudro*. Of course, Latvian and English are very distantly related, and languages that are more closely related typically manifest greater similarity.

At the same time, however, even languages that are totally unrelated may be similar in some respects. For example, English, Thai, and Swahili, which are unrelated to each other, all employ subject-verb-object word order in simple declarative sentences.

(1) *Swahili*
Maria anapenda Anna.
Maria likes        Anna.
'Maria likes Anna.'

(2) *Thai*
roudbuntuk  ding  roud.
truck            push car.
'Trucks push cars.'

For this reason, another approach to language classification is useful. Known as **linguistic typology**, it classifies languages according to their structural characteristics, without regard for genetic relationships. Thus, typologists might group together languages with similar sound patterns or, alternatively, those with similar grammatical structures. Typological studies also endeavour to identify **linguistic universals**, that is, structural characteristics that occur in all or most languages. We discuss linguistic typology further in section 8.2.

Finally, **areal classification** identifies characteristics shared by languages that are in geographical contact. Languages in contact often borrow words, sounds, morphemes, and even syntactic patterns from one another. As a result, neighbouring languages can come to resemble each other, even though they may not be genetically related. Because of space considerations, this chapter will not deal with areal classification specifically; however, borrowing is discussed in sections 7.1.2 and 7.5.1 of chapter 7.

## 8.2 Typological classification

As just noted, the classification of languages according to their structural characteristics is known as linguistic typology. Typological studies group together languages on the basis of similarities in their syntactic patterns, morphological structure, and/or phonological systems. An important area of research within the study of linguistic typology is the search for linguistic universals. Structural patterns and traits that occur in all languages are called **absolute universals**, while those that simply occur in most languages are known as **universal tendencies**.

Many typological generalizations involve **implicational universals**, which specify that the presence of one trait implies the presence of another (but not vice versa). For instance, languages with fricative phonemes (such as /f/ and /s/) also have stop phonemes (such as /p/ and /t/), although the reverse is not necessarily true.

Another way to analyze linguistic universals is through **markedness theory**. **Marked traits** are considered to be more complex and/or universally rarer than **unmarked** characteristics. In addition, a marked trait is usually found in a particular language only if its unmarked counterpart also occurs.

A simple example of markedness and its relevance to implicational universals involves vowels and nasality. Nasal vowel phonemes are more complex than oral vowel phonemes, since they allow the airstream to exit through both the nose and the mouth, rather than just the mouth. Cross-linguistically, we find that all languages have oral vowels, but that only some have nasal vowels. (Moreover, even in languages that have both, there are usually far fewer nasal vowels than oral vowels.) Thus, oral vowels are unmarked—they are both more common and phonologically less complex than nasal vowels, which are marked. We can represent this fact with the help of the following markedness hierarchy, in which '>' can be read as 'less marked than' or 'is implied by'.

(3)  oral vowel > nasal vowel

This, in turn, means that we make the distinction outlined in table 8.3 between possible and impossible vowel systems in human language.

| **Table 8.3**  Oral and nasal vowels | | |
| --- | --- | --- |
| **Oral vowels** | **Nasal vowels** | |
| yes | no | possible |
| yes | yes | possible |
| no | yes | **impossible** |

The following sections present some of the typological generalizations and universals that have been proposed in the areas of phonology, morphology, and syntax.

## 8.2.1  Phonology

In this section, we represent all vowel and consonant systems phonemically. This simplifies their presentation; note, however, that the exact phonetic realization of these systems may vary in the individual languages.

### Vowel systems

Languages are often classified according to the size and pattern of their vowel systems. The most common vowel system has five phonemes—two high vowels, two mid vowels, and one low vowel (see figure 8.1). The front vowels are unrounded, as is the low vowel, and the back vowels are rounded. About half the world's languages, including Basque, Hawaiian, Japanese, Spanish, and Swahili, have such a system.

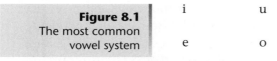

**Figure 8.1**
The most common
vowel system

i            u

e           o

a

The majority of the world's other languages have vowel systems with three, four, six, seven, eight, or nine different vowels (disregarding contrasts based on length or nasalization, which can double or triple the number of vowel phonemes). Languages with fewer than three, or more than nine distinctive vowels are rare. Some typical vowel systems are presented in figure 8.2.

**Figure 8.2**
Common vowel systems

| i | u | i | | i | | u |
|---|---|---|---|---|---|---|
| | | e | o | e | ʌ | o |
| a | | a | | | ə | |
| | | | | | a | |

Three-vowel system
Gudanji (Australia)

Four-vowel system
Navajo (Arizona)

Seven-vowel system
Geez (Ethiopia)

Analysis of many languages has led to the discovery of a number of universal tendencies pertaining to vowel systems. Some of these tendencies are listed here, along with a description of the most commonly occurring vowels.

- The most commonly occurring vowel phoneme is /a/, which is found in almost all the languages of the world. The vowels /i/ and /u/ are almost as common as /a/.
- Front vowel phonemes (e.g., /i, e, ɛ, æ/) are generally unrounded, while non-low back vowel phonemes (e.g., /ɔ, o, u/) are generally rounded.
- Low vowels (e.g., /æ, a, ɑ/) are generally unrounded.

Although English has an above-average number of vowels, they all conform to the above tendencies. Thus, English has only front unrounded vowels, all the low vowel phonemes are unrounded, and all of the back, non-low vowels are rounded. The vowel system of Canadian English is represented in figure 8.3.

**Figure 8.3**
The vowel system of
Canadian English

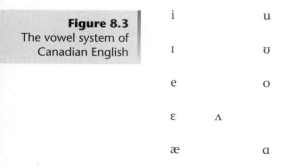

The relationship between contrasting vowel types (such as oral versus nasal, and long versus short) can also be expressed in terms of implicational universals, since the presence of one vowel phoneme type implies the presence of another (but not vice versa).

- As already noted, if a language has contrastive nasal vowels, then it will also have contrastive oral vowels. For example, French contrasts different nasal vowels—as in *long* /lɔ̃/ 'long' versus *lent* /lã/ 'slow'. And it contrasts oral vowels with nasal vowels, as in *las* /la/ 'weary' versus *lent* /lã/ 'slow'). Predictably, French also contrasts different oral vowels, as in *clos* /klo/ 'shut' versus *clou* /klu/ 'nail'. English shows contrasts among oral vowels but does not contrast nasal vowels with oral vowels. There are no contrasts in English like /bɑt/ 'bought' and */bãt/.

- If a language has contrasting long vowels, then it will also have contrasting short vowels. For example, Finnish has contrasting long vowels, and, predictably, contrasting short vowels (see table 8.4).

| **Table 8.4** | Finnish vowel contrasts | |
|---|---|---|
| Long versus long | /viːli/ 'junket' | /vaːli/ 'election' |
| Short versus short | /suka/ 'bristle' | /suku/ 'family' |
| Short versus long | /tuli/ 'fire' | /tuːli/ 'wind' |

The reverse is not necessarily the case. While English has contrasts based on vowel quality (e.g., *meet* vs. *mate*), it has no long vowel phonemes because length is predictable. Its vowels are therefore all considered to be typologically short (see table 8.5).

| **Table 8.5** | Long and short vowels: short vowels > long vowels | |
|---|---|---|
| **Contrasting short vowels** | **Contrasting long vowels** | |
| yes | no | possible (English) |
| yes | yes | possible (Finnish) |
| no | yes | **impossible** |

## Consonant systems

It is not particularly useful to classify languages according to the number of consonants that they contain, since languages may have as few as six consonant phonemes (as in Rotokas, spoken in Papua New Guinea), or more than ninety. (!Kung, a language spoken in Namibia, has ninety-six consonant phonemes.) Nevertheless, typological analysis of consonant systems has produced a number of well-substantiated universals:

- All languages have stops.
- The most common stop phonemes are /p, t, k/. Very few languages lack any one of these, and there are no languages that lack all three. If any one of these three stops is missing, it will probably be /p/; for example, Aleut, Nubian, and Wichita have no /p/ phoneme. The most commonly occurring phoneme of the three is /t/.
- The most commonly occurring fricative phoneme is /s/. If a language has only one fricative, it is most likely to be /s/. It is the only fricative found in Nandi (a language of Kenya) and Weri (a language of New Guinea). The next most common fricative is /f/.
- The vast majority of languages have at least one nasal phoneme. In cases where a language has only one nasal phoneme, that phoneme is usually /n/ (as in Arapaho, spoken in Wyoming). If there are two contrasting nasals, they are normally /m/ and /n/.

- Most languages have at least one phonemic liquid. However, a relatively small number of languages have none at all; for example, Blackfoot, Dakota, Efik (spoken in Nigeria), and Siona (found in Ecuador). English, of course, has two: /l/ and /r/.

Consonant phonemes are also subject to various implicational universals:

- If a language has voiced obstruent phonemes (stops, fricatives, or affricates), then it will also have voiceless obstruent phonemes (see table 8.6). The reverse is not necessarily true; for example, Ainu (a language of northern Japan) has only voiceless obstruent phonemes: /p, t, k, tʃ, s/.

**Table 8.6** Obstruent voicing: voiceless obstruents > voiced obstruents

| Voiceless obstruents | Voiced obstruents | |
|---|---|---|
| yes | no | possible (Ainu) |
| yes | yes | possible (English) |
| no | yes | **impossible** |

- Sonorant consonants are generally voiced. Very few languages have voiceless sonorants; those that do always have voiced sonorants as well (see table 8.7). For example, Burmese contrasts voiced and voiceless nasals and laterals.

**Table 8.7** Sonorants: voiced sonorants > voiceless sonorants

| Voiced sonorants | Voiceless sonorants | |
|---|---|---|
| yes | no | possible (English) |
| yes | yes | possible (Burmese) |
| no | yes | **impossible** |

- If a language has fricative phonemes, then it will also have stop phonemes (see table 8.8). There are no languages that lack stops; however, there are some languages that lack fricatives. For example, Gilbertese (Gilbert Islands), Kitabal (eastern Australia), and Nuer (southeastern Sudan) have no fricatives.

**Table 8.8** Stops and fricatives: stops > fricatives

| Stops | Fricatives | |
|---|---|---|
| yes | no | possible (Nuer) |
| yes | yes | possible (English) |
| no | yes | **impossible** |

- Languages that have affricates will also have fricatives and stops (see table 8.9). This is not surprising, since an affricate is, in essence, a sequence of a stop followed by a fricative. However, many languages lack affricates altogether. For example, French has fricative and stop phonemes, but no affricate phonemes. In contrast, English has all three consonant types.

| **Table 8.9** | Types of obstruents: stops > fricatives > affricates | | |
|---|---|---|---|
| **Stops** | **Fricatives** | **Affricates** | |
| yes | yes | yes | possible (English) |
| yes | yes | no | possible (French) |
| yes | no | no | possible (Kitabal) |
| no | yes | yes | **impossible** |
| no | yes | no | **impossible** |
| no | no | yes | **impossible** |

## Language Matters  Record-Breaking Languages

There are no official records within linguistics, but it's natural to wonder about languages that are 'extreme' in some way. Here are some languages that are frequently mentioned for the unusual size (large or small) of their phonological inventory.

- *Fewest consonants*: Rotokas has just 6 consonant phonemes. (A Papuan language, Rotokas has about 4300 speakers in Papua New Guinea.)
- *Fewest vowels*: Some dialects of Abkhaz have just 2 vowel phonemes. (This North Caucasian language has approximately 106 000 speakers, mostly in the Republic of Georgia.)
- *Fewest overall number of phonemes*: Rotokas again (11).
- *Greatest overall number of phonemes*: By some counts !Xóõ has 77 consonant phonemes, including dozens of clicks, and 31 vowel phonemes. (You can hear a brief sample of !Xóõ, which is spoken by about 4000 people in Botswana, at www.phonetics.ucla.edu/vowels/chapter14/_xoo.html.)

## Suprasegmental systems

Languages can also be classified according to their suprasegmental (or prosodic) type. Languages that use pitch to make meaning distinctions between words are called **tone languages**. (The phonetics and phonology of tone were introduced in chapters 2 and 3.) As illustrated in table 8.10, Mandarin has four contrastive tones.

| **Table 8.10** | Tone contrasts in Mandarin | |
|---|---|---|
| High tone | dā | 'build' |
| Low rising tone | dá | 'achieve' |
| Falling rising tone | dǎ | 'hit' |
| High falling tone | dà | 'big' |

The other Chinese languages, as well as many languages of Southeast Asia, Africa, and the Americas, are also tone languages. A few tone languages are also found in Europe; for example, one of the dialects of Latvian makes a three-way tonal distinction (see table 8.11).

| Table 8.11 | Tone contrasts in Latvian | | | |
|------------|------|----------|---------------|
| Falling tone | loks | [lùoks] | 'arch, bow' |
| Level (high) tone | loks | [lūoks ] | 'green onion' |
| Rising-falling (broken) tone | loks | [lûoks ] | 'window'' |

As noted in the chapter on phonetics, there are two types of tones: level tones and contour tones. Tone languages most often contrast only two tone levels (usually high and low). However, contrasts involving three tone levels (such as high, low, and mid tones) are also relatively common. Five or more levels of tonal contrast are practically unknown.

Tone systems, too, exhibit various universal tendencies:

- If a language has contour tones (such as rising tone or falling tone), then it will also have level tones (such as high, mid, or low tone) as outlined in table 8.12. Burmese, Crow, Latvian, and Mandarin are examples of languages that fit this pattern. The reverse pattern (languages with contour tones but no level tones) is extremely rare; Dafla, spoken in northern India, has such a system.

| Table 8.12 | Tones: level tones > contour tones | |
|------------|---------------|---------------------|
| **Level tones** | **Contour tones** | |
| yes | no | possible (Sarcee) |
| yes | yes | possible (Mandarin) |
| no | yes | **very rare** (Dafla) |

- If a language has complex contour tones (such as rising-falling, or falling-rising), then it will also have simple contour tones (like rising or falling) as summarized in table 8.13. Both the Mandarin and Latvian examples fit this pattern.

| Table 8.13 | Contour tones: simple contour tones > complex contour tones | |
|------------|---------------|---------------------|
| **Simple contour tones** | **Complex contour tones** | |
| yes | no | possible (Hausa) |
| yes | yes | possible (Mandarin) |
| no | yes | **impossible** |

Differences in stress are also useful in classifying languages. **Fixed stress** languages are those in which the position of stress on a word is predictable. For example, in Modern Hebrew and K'iché (a Mayan language), stress always falls on the last syllable of a word; in Polish, Swahili, and Samoan, stress falls on the penultimate (second-to-last) syllable of words, while in Czech, Finnish, and Hungarian, the stressed syllable is always the first syllable of a word. In **free stress** languages, the position of stress is not predictable and must be learned for each word. Free stress is also called phonemic stress because of its role in distinguishing between words. Russian is an example of a language with free stress, as shown in table 8.14.

| **Table 8.14** | Stress contrasts in Russian | | |
|---|---|---|---|
| múka | 'torture' | muká | 'flour' |
| zámok | 'castle' | zamók | 'lock' |
| rúki | 'hands' | rukí | 'hand's' (genitive singular) |

---

**Language Matters  How to Say "Merry Christmas" in Hawaiian**

Differences in syllable structure constraints can have interesting consequences when languages come in contact. For example, in Hawaiian only V and CV syllables are permitted. Thus, when a word is borrowed from a language like English, which allows more complicated syllable structures, vowels are inserted to produce the allowed syllable structures. For example, when the phrase *Merry Christmas* was borrowed into Hawaiian, it was reformulated as *mele kalikimaka*. (Of course, some consonant changes were made as well, since Hawaiian lacks /r/ and /s/ phonemes.)

## Syllable structure

The CV and V syllable types are unmarked. They are simpler than other syllable types (CVC, VCC, and so on), are found in all languages, and are learned first by children (see chapter 10, section 10.2.3).

In any given language, onsets may be structured differently from codas. For example, in English, a nasal + stop sequence is permitted in the coda (in a word like *hand*), but not in the onset (there are no English words that begin with the sequence *nd*). However, Swahili has precisely the opposite restrictions: the *nd* sequence is permitted in onset position (in words like *ndizi* 'banana'), but not in coda position. In fact, Swahili syllables are coda-less—they can only end in vowels.

Two examples of implicational universals for syllable structure are presented below. Both deal with the structure of onsets as opposed to codas.

- If a language permits sequences of consonants in the onset, then it will also permit syllables with single consonant onsets (see table 8.15).

| **Table 8.15** | Onsets: single consonant onsets > multiple consonant onsets | |
|---|---|---|
| **Single C onsets** | **Multiple C onsets** | |
| yes | no | possible (Hawaiian) |
| yes | yes | possible (English) |
| no | yes | **impossible** |

- If a language permits sequences of consonants in the coda, then it will also permit syllables with single consonant codas and syllables with no coda at all (see table 8.16).

| **Table 8.16** Onsets: single consonant codas/no codas > multiple consonant codas | | |
|---|---|---|
| **Single C codas/no codas** | **Multiple C codas** | |
| yes | no | possible (Cantonese) |
| yes | yes | possible (English) |
| no | yes | **impossible** |

## 8.2.2 Morphology

Both words and morphemes are found in all languages. However, there are clear differences in the ways in which individual languages combine morphemes to form words. Four types of systems can be distinguished.

### The isolating type

A language that is purely **isolating** or **analytic** would contain only words that consist of a single (root) morpheme. In such a language there would be no affixes, and categories such as number and tense would therefore have to be expressed by a separate word. In Mandarin, which is primarily an isolating language, the morpheme *le* is often used to indicate a past or completed action. Although this morpheme is thus semantically similar to a past tense, it acts just like an independent word, since its position in the sentence may vary:

(4) *a.* Ta chi fan    le.
　　　 he eat meal past
　　　 'He ate the meal.'

　　 *b.* Ta chi le    fan.
　　　 he eat past meal
　　　 'He ate the meal.'

Other languages that are primarily isolating include Cantonese, Vietnamese, Laotian, and Khmer (Cambodian).

### The polysynthetic type

In a **polysynthetic** language, single words can consist of long strings of roots and affixes that often express meanings that are associated with entire sentences in other languages. The following word from Inuktitut illustrates this.

(5) Qasuiirsarvigssarsingitluinarnarpuq.
　　 Qasu -iir -sar    -vig  -ssar  -si -ngit-luinar    -nar  -puq
　　 tired not cause-to-be place-for suitable find not completely someone 3.SG.
　　 'Someone did not find a completely suitable resting place.'

Polysynthesis is common in many Aboriginal languages of North America, including Inuktitut, Cree, and Sarcee, to name but a few.

The terms *isolating* and *polysynthetic* refer to two extremes: words consisting only of a single morpheme versus words that can be complete sentences. Few if any languages are either purely isolating or purely polysynthetic. Instead, the vast majority of languages are **synthetic**, in that they permit at least some multimorphemic words with non-sentential meanings. There are two types of synthetic languages.

## The agglutinating type

An **agglutinating** language has words that can contain several morphemes, but the words are easily divided into their component parts (normally a root and affixes). In such languages, each affix is clearly identifiable and typically represents only a single grammatical category or meaning. The following examples are from Turkish.

(6)  *a.* köj
     'village'

   *b.* köj-ler
     village-PL
     'villages'

   *c.* köj-ler-in
     village-PL-GEN
     'of the villages'

Turkish words can have a complex morphological structure, but each morpheme typically has a single, clearly identifiable function. In (6c), for instance, *-ler* marks plurality and *-in* marks the genitive case, giving the meaning 'of the villages'.

## The fusional type

Words in a **fusional** or **inflectional language** can also consist of root + affix combinations. However, in contrast to agglutinating systems, the affixes in fusional languages often mark several grammatical categories simultaneously. In Russian, for example, a single inflectional affix simultaneously marks the noun's gender class (masculine, feminine, or neuter), its number (singular or plural), and its grammatical role (subject, direct object, and so on). This is illustrated in (7) for the suffix *-u*.

(7)  mi  vid^jim ruk-u
    we  see    hand-FEM.SG.ACC
    'We see a/the hand.'

The distinction between agglutinating and fusional is sensitive to the number of semantic 'bits' of information normally packed into an affix. In an agglutinating language, each affix normally contains only one element of grammatical or lexical meaning, while in a fusional language, affixes often denote several such bits of information.

## Mixed types

Many (perhaps most) languages do not belong exclusively to any of the four categories just outlined. For example, English employs isolating patterns in many verbal constructions, where each notion is expressed by a separate word. The future, for instance, is indicated by the independent word *will* (rather than by an affix) in structures such as *I will leave.* On the other hand, English also exhibits considerable agglutination in derived words, such as *re-en-act-ment*, which consist of a series of clearly identifiable morphemes, each with its own unique meaning and function. However, the English pronoun system is largely fusional, since a single form can be used to indicate person, number, gender, and case. The word *him*, for instance, is used to express a third person, singular, masculine direct object.

Since many, if not most, of the world's languages exhibit mixed patterns of this type, it has been suggested that terms like *isolating*, *agglutinating*, and *fusional* should be used to refer not to a language as a whole, but to particular structures within a language.

It is also important to recognize that these classifications do not take into consideration morphological processes such as compounding (e.g., English *greenhouse*), reduplication (e.g., Tagalog *sulat* 'write' versus *susulat* 'will write'), grammatical use of stress or tone (e.g., the noun *présent* versus the verb *presént* in English), and internal word change (e.g., vowel ablaut, as in English *run* versus *ran*).

## Implicational universals: morphology

A variety of generalizations can be made about word structure in human language.

- If a language has inflectional affixes, it will also have derivational affixes (see chapter 4, section 4.4.2). For example, English not only has inflectional affixes such as the past tense *-ed* and plural *-s*, but it also contains derivational affixes like *un-* (*unhappy*, *unwanted*) and *-ly* (*quickly*, *slowly*).
- If a word has both a derivational and an inflectional affix, the derivational affix is closer to the root (DA = derivational affix; IA = inflectional affix) (see table 8.17).
- If a language has only suffixes, it will also have only postpositions. (As noted in chapter 5, postpositions are the equivalent of prepositions in languages that place the head at the end of the phrase.) Turkish, for example, has only suffixes; as expected, it also has postpositions rather than prepositions. This is illustrated in the following sentence.

(8) Ahmet Ajʃe    itʃin kitab-ɨ      al-dɨ.
    Ahmet Ayshe for    book-ACC  buy-PST
    'Ahmet bought a book for Ayshe.''

---

**Table 8.17** The ordering of derivational and inflectional affixes

**English**

| friend-ship-s | | | *friend-s  -ship | | |
|---|---|---|---|---|---|
| Root | DA | IA | Root | IA | DA |

**Turkish**

| iʃ | -tʃi | -ler | *iʃ | -ler | -tʃi |
|---|---|---|---|---|---|
| work | -er | -pl | work | -pl | -er |
| Root | DA | IA | Root | IA | DA |

## 8.2.3  Syntax

Because we lack detailed descriptions for most of the world's languages, much of the work on syntactic universals has been restricted to the study of word order in simple declarative sentences such as *The men built the house*. Preliminary classification focuses on the relative order of the subject (S), direct object (O), and verb (V). The three most common word orders (in descending order of frequency) are SOV, SVO, and VSO. Over 95 percent of the world's languages use one of these patterns as their basic word order.

(9) SOV (Turkish):
Hasan öküz-ü al-dɪ.
Hasan ox-ACC bought
'Hasan bought the OX.'

(10) SVO (English):
The athlete broke the record.

(11) VSO (Welsh):
Lladdodd y   ddraig y   dyn.
killed    the dragon the man
'The dragon killed the man.'

SOV, SVO, and VSO patterns all have one trait in common: the subject appears before the direct object. The prevalence of the S-O pattern may be due to the fact that the subject usually coincides with the topic of the sentence (i.e., what the sentence is about; see chapter 6, section 6.4.3), and therefore is more useful at an early point in the utterance.

While an overwhelming majority of the world's languages place the subject to the left of the direct object in their basic word order, this pattern is not universal. There are a small number of VOS languages, of which the best-known example is Malagasy.

(12) VOS (Malagasy):
Nahita ny   mpianatra ny   vehivavy.
saw     the student      the woman
'The woman saw the student.'

As well, there are a very few OVS or OSV languages, all of which seem to be spoken in South America:

(13) OVS (Hixkaryana):
Kana    janɪmno    bɪrjekomo
fish     caught       boy
'The boy caught a fish'

(14) OSV (Apuriña)
Anana         nota    apa
pineapple    I         fetch
'I fetch a pineapple'

## Word order universals

Sometimes, the order of elements within one kind of structure has implications for the order of elements in other structures. Many of these implications concern the relationship between the verb and its (direct) object.

- If a language has VO word order, then it will have prepositions rather than postpositions. Languages of this type include Berber (spoken in Morocco), Hebrew, Maori (spoken in New Zealand), Maasai (spoken in Kenya), Welsh, and Irish Gaelic.

(15) *Irish Gaelic*
  a. VSO pattern:
     Chonaic  mé  mo  mháthair
     saw       I   my  mother
     'I saw my mother.'

  b. Preposition pattern:
     sa teach
     in house
     'in the house'

- If a language has OV word order, then it will probably have postpositions rather than prepositions. Languages with this structural pattern include Basque, Burmese, Hindi, Japanese, Korean, Quechua, Turkish, and Guugu Yimidhirr, an Aboriginal language of Australia (ERG = ergative, a case used for the subject of a transitive verb).

(16) *Guugu Yimidhirr*
  a. SOV pattern:
     Gudaa-ngun  yarrga  dyindaj
     dog-ERG      boy     bit
     'The dog bit the boy'

  b. Postposition pattern:
     yuwaal  nganh
     beach   from
     'from the beach'

- PPs almost always precede the verb in OV languages, and usually follow the verb in VO languages.

(17) *Japanese*
  a. SOV pattern:
     Gakusei-ga      hon-o        yonda
     student-NOM     book-ACC     read
     'The student read a book'

  b. PP precedes verb:
     Taroo-ga [$_{PP}$ nitiyoobi ni] tsuita.
     Taroo-NOM    Sunday  on   arrived
     'Taroo arrived on Sunday.'

(18) *English*
  a. SVO pattern:
     I like candy.

  b. PP follows verb:
     George left [$_{PP}$ on Sunday].

■ Manner adverbs overwhelmingly precede the verb in OV languages and generally
follow the verb in VO languages.

(19) *Japanese* (SOV pattern, as seen in (17a)):
Manner adverb precedes verb:
joozu hasiru
well   run
'(He) runs well.'

(20) *English* (SVO pattern, as seen in (18a)):
Manner adverb follows verb:
John runs well.

■ With respect to possessive structures, there is an overwhelming preference
for Genitive + N order in OV languages, and a (somewhat weaker) preference
for N + Genitive order in VO languages.

(21) *Japanese* (SOV pattern, as seen in (17a)):
Genitive structure precedes head N:
Taroo-no     hon
Taroo-GEN    book
'Taroo's book'

(22) *French*
a. SVO pattern:
Pierre   aime    Marie.
'Pierre  likes   Marie.'

b. Genitive structure follows head N:
la     maison  de          Marie
the    house   of (GEN)    Marie
'Marie's house'

English, although an SVO language, exhibits both Genitive + N and N + Genitive patterns:

(23) a. Genitive + N pattern:
the country's laws

b. N + Genitive pattern:
the laws of the country

## Grammatical hierarchies

Implicational universals are often stated in terms of hierarchies of categories or relations. One
of the most important hierarchies of this type refers to the grammatical relations of subject
and direct object.

(24) The grammatical relation hierarchy
subject > direct object > other

According to this hierarchy, a process that applies only to subjects is less marked than a
process that applies to direct objects, and so on. In other words, if a particular phenomenon

applies to direct objects, it should also apply to subjects. In contrast, it would not be surprising to find a process that applies to subjects but not direct objects.

Among the many typological phenomena that conform to this hierarchy is verb agreement, first mentioned in chapter 4 (section 4.4.3). As the following examples show, there are languages in which the verb agrees only with the subject, and there are languages in which it agrees with both the subject and the direct object (3 = 3rd person; SG = singular; PL = plural).

(25) Agreement with subject only (Spanish):

     *Subject*
     Juan       parti-ó
     Juan       leave-3SG.PST
     'Juan left.'

(26) Agreement with subject and direct object (Swahili):

     *Subject*       *Direct object*
     Juma   a- li-wa-piga  watoto
     Juma   3SG.PST-3PL-hit  children
     'Juma hit the children.'

However, as predicted by the hierarchy, there are no languages in which the verb agrees only with the direct object.

## 8.2.4   Explaining universals

Linguists are still uncertain about how to explain the existence of many linguistic universals. Nonetheless, a number of interesting proposals have been made, and it is worthwhile to consider some of them here.

---

### Language Matters  **The Ergative Way**

In some languages, the verb agrees with the subject of an intransitive verb and the direct object of a transitive verb, but not with the subject of a transitive verb. The following example (provided by Farooq Babrakzai) is from Pashto, one of the major languages of Afghanistan.

   a. *Agreement with the 3rd person subject of an intransitive verb:*
      **xəza**     də-daftar -na    raɣ-**a**.
      woman   POSS-office-from  came-3FS*
      'The woman came from the office.'
   b. *Agreement with the 3rd person direct object of a transitive verb:*
      ma **xəza**   wəlid-**a**.
      I   woman saw-3FS
      'I saw the woman.'

A grammatical rule that treats the subject of an intransitive verb and the direct object of a transitive verb alike is said to be ergative. The existence of such rules calls into question the universality of the traditional grammatical hierarchy.

*3FS = third person feminine singular.

## Phonology

Perceptual factors play a role in shaping phonological universals. For example, the fact that /s/ is the most commonly occurring fricative may have to do with its acoustic prominence: varieties of /s/ are inherently louder and more strident (chapter 2, section 2.5.4) than other kinds of fricatives.

Vowel systems (discussed in section 8.2.1) develop so as to keep vowel phonemes as different from each other as possible. A three-vowel system such as the one in figure 8.4 allows for plenty of 'space' around each vowel, which probably makes each vowel easier to distinguish from the others.

| | | |
|---|---|---|
| **Figure 8.4** | i | u |
| A three-vowel system | | |
| | a | |

The same holds true for the distribution of stop phonemes. It may be that /p/, /t/, and /k/ are the three most common stops because they occur at three maximally distant places of articulation within the supralaryngeal vocal tract. These three stops are much easier to distinguish perceptually than a sequence of dental, alveolar, and palatal stops, for example, all of which are produced in the central region of the oral cavity.

It has been suggested that consonant systems in general respond to the articulatory pressures that give rise to unmarked sounds and systems. Articulatorily basic obstruents such as [p], [t], and [k] are found much more commonly than more complex articulations such as [tɬ] and [qw]. Table 8.18 presents the set of obstruents that is most widely used across human languages.

| **Table 8.18** | Obstruents most often found cross-linguistically | | |
|---|---|---|---|
| p | t | k | ʔ |
| b | d | g | |
| f | s | | h |
| | tʃ | | |

Languages tend to have consonant systems that consist of about 70 percent obstruents and 30 percent sonorants, no matter what the total size of their consonant inventories may be. These figures reflect the articulatory possibilities available for contrast: more distinctions can be made among obstruents than among sonorants. There are, for example, no nasal fricative sonorants, because the air pressure needed to force air through a narrow opening (which is necessary for the production of fricatives) cannot be built up when so much air is flowing through the nasal passage at the same time. For reasons such as this, the number of obstruent consonants in any language is potentially much larger than the number of possible sonorant consonants. This is just one example of how considerations involving articulation can play a role in the shaping of consonant systems.

## Morphology

Other types of explanations are appropriate for morphological universals. For example, the fact that languages with suffixes but no prefixes always have postpositions (section 8.2.2) may have a historical explanation. In these languages, some postpositions became attached to a preceding word and were thereby converted into suffixes. Because suffixes in such languages evolved from postpositions, the link between the two elements can be traced to their common origin.

An example of this very phenomenon can be seen in the closely related languages Finnish and Estonian. Their ancestor language (Proto-Baltic-Finnic) contained a postposition *kanssa* 'with', which is still evident in Standard Finnish, but has evolved into the suffix -*ga* in Estonian (see table 8.19) (COM = comitative, a case expressing accompaniment).

| **Table 8.19** Proto-Baltic-Finnic postposition *kanssa* becomes suffix -*ga* |
| --- |

Standard Finnish: postposition *kanssa* 'with'

| poja | 'boy' | poja-n | kanssa | 'with the boy' |
| --- | --- | --- | --- | --- |
| | | boy-GEN | with | |

Estonian: case suffix -*ga*

| poja | 'boy' | poja-ga | | 'with the boy' |
| --- | --- | --- | --- | --- |
| | | boy-COM | | |

The requirement that derivational affixes occur closer to the root than inflectional affixes has another type of explanation. As noted in the morphology chapter, derivation typically forms new words, while inflection marks the subclass (for example, plural for Ns, past tense for Vs) to which a word belongs. Given that a word must be formed before its subclass can be determined, it follows that derivational processes will precede inflection. This is reflected in word structure, where derivational affixes appear closer to the root than inflectional markers. In figure 8.5, for instance, the verbal root *treat* is converted into a noun by the affix -*ment* before the plural inflectional marker is added.

**Figure 8.5**
The structure of a word containing a derivational affix and an inflectional affix

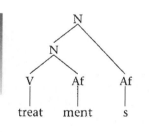

## Syntax

At least some syntactic universals may be explained in terms of the way that the human brain processes sentence structure. Consider the summary of word order patterns in table 8.20, which is based on the implicational universals discussed in section 8.2.3.

| **Table 8.20** Word order patterns | | |
| --- | --- | --- |
| **Constituents** | **Order in VO language** | **Order in OV language** |
| P & NP | preposition-NP | NP-postposition |
| V & PP | verb-PP | PP-verb |
| V & manner Adv | verb-manner Adv | manner Adv-verb |
| Gen & N | noun-genitive | genitive-noun |

One explanation as to why the word order properties in the second and third columns cluster together involves the contrast between right-branching and left-branching languages. In right-branching languages, the more elaborate part of a phrase's structure occurs on its right branch; in left-branching languages, it occurs on the left. Thus, a verb-object pattern is right-branching since a phrasal constituent (an XP) appears on its right branch, but an object-verb pattern is left-branching, as shown in figure 8.6.

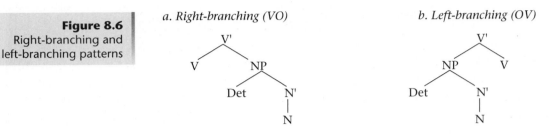

**Figure 8.6**
Right-branching and
left-branching patterns

*a. Right-branching (VO)*

*b. Left-branching (OV)*

As you can easily determine for yourselves, the P-NP, V-PP, V-Adv, and N-Gen patterns commonly associated with VO languages are also all right-branching (both genitives and adverbials are a type of phrase). In contrast, the NP-P, PP-V, Adv-V, and Gen-N patterns typically found in OV languages are all left-branching. In other words, it seems that languages are fairly consistent in using one or the other type of branching structure. This sort of uniformity may make it easier for speakers and hearers to process syntactic structure. Thus, just as some human beings are right-handed and others left-handed, it appears that some languages prefer to use consistently right-branching systems, while others prefer consistently left-branching systems.

## 8.3    Genetic classification

The goal of genetic classification is to group languages into families based on evidence of a common origin established through use of the comparative method (chapter 7, section 7.7). This work is difficult and challenging for a variety of reasons.

Perhaps the biggest problem is simply the amount of data that must be collected before linguists can be confident about the status of a group of languages. It is only in the last two or three decades, for example, that enough information has been accumulated to propose a detailed classification of the languages of Africa. Moreover, many of the languages of South America, New Guinea, and Australia are still relatively unknown.

Matters are further complicated by the fact that entirely unrelated languages may be similar in various ways. This is particularly likely if the languages have been in contact long enough to have borrowed a large number of words, sounds, morphemes, or syntactic structures from one another.

Moreover, even languages that are related may not look that similar. The more distant the genetic relationship between languages, the less likely that a large number of obvious similarities will be found, especially since sound changes can obscure relationships between cognate words. English and Latin are related (though distantly), but the similarity between cognates like Latin *unda* 'wave' and English *water* is certainly not striking.

Research is also made difficult by the fact that words that may be excellent indicators of a genetic relationship can drop out of the lexicon. For example, Old English had a word *leax* 'salmon' (which was cognate with German *Lachs* and Yiddish *lox*), but this lexical item has since been lost from the native English lexicon. (*Lox* has been borrowed back into some varieties of English as the name for a popular delicatessen food.)

Since word loss is a common historical event, linguists prefer to use the oldest available form of a language for their research. Thus, our knowledge of Proto-Indo-European is drawn from the study of Old English, Sanskrit, Latin, etc., rather than English, Hindi-Urdu, French, and their other modern descendants.

Some language families contain many hundreds of languages. In other cases, only one language may remain to represent a family. In still other cases, families have become extinct. The following section summarizes some of what we know about the Indo-European family of languages. Although it might appear to be overly 'Eurocentric' to focus on this particular family, you will see that the homelands of the various Indo-European languages extend well beyond Europe into the Middle East and India. It is also worth noting that a number of languages spoken in Europe (Finnish, Hungarian, and Basque, to name three) do not belong to the Indo-European family.

## 8.3.1 The Indo-European family

If we consider only living languages, the Indo-European family currently has nine branches, which are listed in table 8.21.

| **Table 8.21** Main branches of the Indo-European family | | |
|---|---|---|
| Germanic | Hellenic | Baltic |
| Celtic | Albanian | Slavic |
| Italic | Armenian | Indo-Iranian |

## Germanic

The Germanic branch of Indo-European can be divided into three sub-branches: East, North, and West. The East Germanic branch included Gothic, the oldest Germanic language for which written texts exist (dating from the fourth century AD). Gothic and any other languages belonging to this branch of Germanic have long been extinct.

The North Germanic (or Scandinavian) branch originally included Old Norse (also known as Old Icelandic), which was the language of the Vikings and the ancestor of modern Icelandic, Norwegian, and Faroese (spoken on the Faroe islands, north of Scotland). Swedish and Danish are two other familiar North Germanic languages.

The West Germanic branch includes English, German, Yiddish, Dutch, Frisian, and Afrikaans. Afrikaans is descended from the Dutch spoken by seventeenth-century settlers (known as Boers) in South Africa.

Frisian is the language most closely related to English. It is spoken on the north coast of Holland, and on the Frisian Islands just off the coast, as well as on the northwestern coast of Germany. English descended from the speech of the Angles, Saxons, and Jutes—Germanic tribes who lived in northern Germany and southern Denmark (in an area just east of the Frisians) before invading England in AD 449 and settling there.

The organization of the Germanic family of languages is illustrated in table 8.22. (In this and other tables, parentheses are used to indicate languages that no longer have any native speakers. The tables are intended to illustrate the membership and organization of the families; they do not necessarily provide a complete list of the languages in each family.)

| **Table 8.22**    The Germanic family | | |
| --- | --- | --- |
| **(East Germanic)** | **North Germanic** | **West Germanic** |
| (Gothic) | Icelandic | English |
| | Faroese | German |
| | Norwegian | Dutch |
| | Danish | Frisian |
| | Swedish | Afrikaans |
| | | Yiddish |

Although we use tables to represent family groupings in this book, trees of the sort illustrated in figure 8.7 are widely used as well.

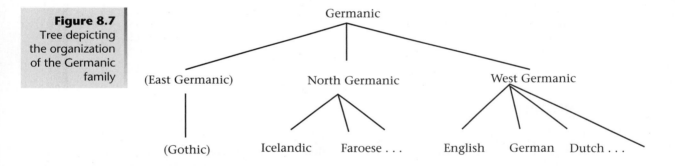

**Figure 8.7** Tree depicting the organization of the Germanic family

## Celtic

The Celtic branch of Indo-European (see table 8.23) has two main sub-branches: Insular and Continental (now extinct). Gaulish, a member of the Continental branch, was once spoken in France (the Gauls were the tribe Julius Caesar defeated), but it has long been extinct.

The Insular sub-branch can be subdivided into two groups of languages: Brythonic or British (also called P-Celtic) and Goidelic or Gaelic (also called Q-Celtic). Brythonic languages include Welsh and Breton (which is spoken in northwestern France) as well as Cornish, which was formerly spoken in southwest Britain but no longer has any native speakers. The Goidelic branch contains Irish (or Irish Gaelic), which is still spoken natively in the western parts of Ireland, the now extinct Manx, and Scots Gaelic, which is spoken in parts of northwestern Scotland (especially the Hebrides Islands) and, to a lesser extent, Cape Breton Island in Nova Scotia.

| Table 8.23 | The Celtic family | | |
|---|---|---|---|
| **Insular** | | | **Continental** |
| ***Brythonic*** | ***Goidelic*** | | |
| Welsh | Irish [= Irish Gaelic] | (Gaulish) | |
| Breton | Scots Gaelic | | |
| (Cornish) | (Manx) | | |

## Italic

The Italic family originally had a number of branches, which included several now-extinct languages spoken in the area corresponding roughly to modern-day Italy. However, the only Italic languages that are presently spoken are all descended from Latin, the language of the Roman Empire (hence the term 'Romance languages').

These languages are commonly divided into four groups. Ibero-Romance includes Portuguese and Spanish, while Gallo-Romance contains French, Catalan (spoken in north-eastern Spain, around Barcelona), and Romansch (one of the four official languages of Switzerland). The Italo-Romance branch includes Italian and Sardinian; Romanian is the best-known language in the Balkano-Romance group (see table 8.24).

| Table 8.24 | The Romance family | | |
|---|---|---|---|
| **Ibero-Romance** | **Gallo-Romance** | **Italo-Romance** | **Balkano-Romance** |
| Spanish | French | Italian | Romanian |
| Portuguese | Catalan | Sardinian | |
| | Romansch | | |

## Hellenic

The Hellenic branch of Indo-European has only one living member, Greek. All modern Greek dialects are descended from the classical dialect known as Attic Greek, which was the speech of Athens during the Golden Age of Greek culture (approximately 500 to 300 BC).

Hellenic Greek, which was used in subsequent centuries, was the language of commerce throughout the Middle East. (Hellenic Greek was also Cleopatra's native language; she was descended from one of Alexander the Great's generals and Egyptian was long extinct by her time.)

## Albanian

The Albanian branch of Indo-European has only one member, Albanian, which is spoken not only in Albania, but also in parts of the former Yugoslavia, Greece, and Italy.

## Armenian

The Armenian branch also has only one member, Armenian. This language is centred in the Republic of Armenia (formerly part of the USSR), but is also spoken in Turkey, Iran, Syria, Lebanon, and Egypt.

# Baltic

The Baltic branch contains only two surviving languages, Latvian (or Lettish) and Lithuanian. They are spoken in Latvia and Lithuania (located just west of Russia and northeast of Poland). Lithuanian has an elaborate case system, which resembles the one proposed for Proto-Indo-European.

# Slavic

The Slavic branch of Indo-European can be divided into three sub-branches: East, West, and South. The East Slavic branch is made up of Russian (also called Great Russian), Ukrainian, and Byelorussian (or White Russian). The latter is spoken in Belorussia (Belarus), which is just east of northern Poland. The West Slavic branch includes Czech, Slovak, and Polish.

The South Slavic branch consists of Bulgarian, Macedonian, Serbo-Croatian, and Slovene (or Slovenian). The latter three languages are all spoken in the former Yugoslavia. Note that although Alexander the Great was king of Macedonia, he spoke Greek, not (Slavic) Macedonian; Slavic-speaking tribes did not move into that area until several centuries later.

The organization of the Slavic group of languages is represented in table 8.25.

| **Table 8.25**  The Slavic family | | |
|---|---|---|
| **East Slavic** | **South Slavic** | **West Slavic** |
| Russian | Serbo-Croatian | Polish |
| Ukrainian | Bulgarian | Czech |
| Byelorussian | Macedonian | Slovak |
| | Slovene | |

# Indo-Iranian

The Indo-Iranian branch of Indo-European is divided into the Iranian and Indic sub-branches. The Iranian sub-branch contains about two dozen different languages, including Modern Persian (also called Parsi or Farsi, spoken in Iran), Pashto (the principal language of Afghanistan), and Kurdish (found in Iran, Iraq, Turkey, and Syria). Other Iranian languages are spoken in Pakistan, southern parts of the former USSR, and China.

There are about thirty-five different Indic languages. Most of the languages spoken in northern India, Pakistan, and Bangladesh belong to this branch of Indo-European. Some of the most widespread (in terms of number of speakers) are Hindi-Urdu, Bengali, Marathi, and Gujarati. Although Hindi and Urdu are two dialects of the same language, they have totally different writing systems and are associated with different cultures; Urdu is spoken principally in Pakistan by Muslims while Hindi is spoken primarily in India by Hindus. For this reason, we listed them as separate languages in table 8.2 on page 289.

Less well known as an Indic language is Romany, or Gypsy. It is now believed that the Gypsies (or Roma) fled to Turkey from northwestern India during the Middle Ages, after being defeated by Islamic invaders. Subsequently they spread throughout Europe: gypsies are found as far west as Ireland, and as far east as Russia. Many now also live in North America. Romany contains many borrowed words—particularly from Greek, which was widely spoken in Turkey during the Middle Ages.

Table 8.26 depicts the organization of Indo-Iranian.

| **Table 8.26** The Indo-Iranian family | |
| --- | --- |
| **Iranian** | **Indic** |
| Persian [= Farsi] | Hindi-Urdu |
| Pashto | Bengali |
| Kurdish | Marathi |
| | Gujarati |
| | Romany [= Gypsy] |

The map in figure 8.8 on page 314 illustrates the geographic location of the Indo-European families identified in this chapter.

## 8.3.2 Some other families

Although no introductory text could hope to present a complete survey of all of the world's language families, you can find additional information on this topic at our website—go to **www.pearsoned.ca/ogrady**. Among the families discussed there are Uralic (which includes Finnish and Hungarian), Altaic (Turkish, and possibly Japanese and Korean as well), Austronesian (Samoan, Fijian, Filipino, and Indonesian), Austroasiatic (Vietnamese and Khmer), Afroasiatic (Arabic and Hebrew), and Niger-Congo (Swahili), in addition to the dozens of languages families indigenous to the Americas. Chapter 9 deals with the Aboriginal languages of Canada.

Not all of the world's languages have been placed in families at this point in time. Languages with no known relatives are called **isolates**. Basque (spoken in northern Spain and southwestern France), Ainu (northern Japan), Burushaski (Pakistan), Kutenai (British Columbia), Gilyak (Siberia), Taraskan (California), and Yukagir (Siberia) are among the languages that are widely considered to be isolates.

## 8.3.3 Language phyla

In recent years attempts have been made to place many of the world's language families in even larger groupings called **phyla** (singular phylum), **stocks**, or macrofamilies.

One of the best known of the proposed phyla is Nostratic (also called Eurasiatic). Supposedly dating back 20 000 years, this hypothetical phylum includes Indo-European, Uralic, Altaic, and (depending on the proposal) various other languages and language families as well. This proposal is controversial, however, and most linguists remain very skeptical about the evidence and conclusions associated with comparative research

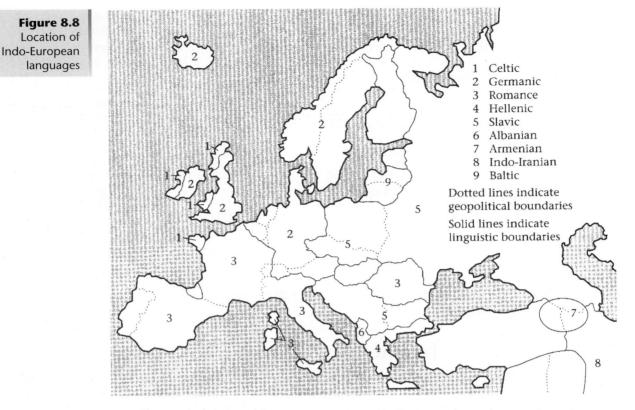

**Figure 8.8**
Location of
Indo-European
languages

1 Celtic
2 Germanic
3 Romance
4 Hellenic
5 Slavic
6 Albanian
7 Armenian
8 Indo-Iranian
9 Baltic

Dotted lines indicate
geopolitical boundaries

Solid lines indicate
linguistic boundaries

Source: Adapted from *Problems in The Origins and Development of the English Language*, 2nd ed., by Algeo (New York: Harcourt Brace Jovanovich, 1972), p. 84. © 1972. Reprinted with permission of Heinle, a division of Thomson Learning, www.thomsonrights.com. Fax 800-730-2215.

involving a time depth greater than eight or ten thousand years because phonetic changes over longer periods obscure the similarities needed for meaningful comparative work.

## Language Matters  Could All Languages Be Related?

Some linguists have even gone so far as to begin reconstructing a single, common ancestor for all human languages. Called Proto-World, or Proto-Sapiens, it is assumed to have been spoken approximately 60 000 to 70 000 years ago. Here is a proposed reconstruction:

**Proto-World** *\*mena* **'to think (about)'** Possible cognates: Latin *men(s)* 'mind', Basque *munak* (pl) 'brains', Hungarian *mon(-d)* 'say', Telugu *manavi* 'prayer, humble request', Shawnee *menw* 'prefer, like', Bambara *mɛ* 'know', Tumale *aiman* 'think', Songhai *ma* 'understand', Masa *min* 'wish'.

Work along these lines is both intriguing and entertaining, but its validity is not currently accepted by most professional linguists.

For more reading:
Wright, Robert. 1991. "Quest for the Mother Tongue," *The Atlantic Monthly*, April. Available at www.exploratorium.edu/exploring/language/.

# Summing up

The focus of this chapter is on the criteria that linguists use to classify languages, and on the enormous variety of languages found throughout the world. Linguists sometimes attempt to classify languages solely in terms of their structural similarities and differences (that is, in terms of their **linguistic typology**). Analysis of cross-linguistic data has identified a number of linguistic **universals**, indicating the most common characteristics of human language. The other major type of classificatory work in linguistics is concerned with **genetic relationships**—establishing language families such as Indo-European whose members are descended from a common ancestor. While research in this area is hampered both by the large number of languages involved and the scarcity of the available data, a sizable portion of the world's several thousand languages have been placed in families.

## Recommended reading

Comrie, Bernard. 1989. *Language Universals and Linguistic Typology*. 2nd ed. Oxford: Blackwell.

Croft, William. 2003. *Typology and Universals*. 2nd ed. New York: Cambridge University Press.

Greenberg, Joseph, ed. 1966. *Universals of Language*. 2nd ed. Cambridge, MA: MIT Press.

Haspelmath, Martin, Matthew Dryer, David Gil, and Bernard Comrie, eds. 2005. *The World Atlas of Language Structures* (with interactive CD-ROM), sample available at www.eva.mpg.de/lingua/files/wals.html. Oxford: Oxford University Press.

Lyovin, Anatole V. 1997. *An Introduction to the Languages of the World*. New York: Oxford University Press.

Ruhlen, Merritt. 1994. *On the Origin of Languages*. Stanford, CA: Stanford University Press.

Voegelin, C.F., and F.M. Voegelin. 1977. *Classification and Index of the World's Languages*. New York: Elsevier.

## Exercises

The data for exercises 1 to 3 are from *A Guide to the Languages of the World* by M. Ruhlen (Language Universals Project: Stanford University, 1976).

1.  Which tendencies and universals are manifested in the following vowel systems?
    a) Afrikaans (South Africa) ([y] and [ø] are front rounded vowels)

    ```
    i    y         u
         ø    ə    o
         e
    ɛ              ɔ
              a
    ```

    b) Squamish (Washington State)

    ```
    i         u
         ə
         a
    ```

2.  As noted in section 8.2.1, the presence of long and nasal vowel phonemes is governed by implicational universals. Do the vowel systems below comply with the implicational universals that make reference to length and nasality?

a) Maltese Arabic

| | | | |
|---|---|---|---|
| i | u | iː | uː |
| e | o | eː | oː |
| | a | aː | |

b) Awji (North New Guinea)

| | | | | | |
|---|---|---|---|---|---|
| i | | u | ĩ | | ũ |
| e | ə | o | ẽ | ə̃ | õ |
| | a | | | ã | |

3.  Consider the following consonant systems. Do these consonant systems comply with the implicational universals mentioned in this chapter?

a) Tahitian (Tahiti)

| | | |
|---|---|---|
| p | t | ʔ |
| f | | h |
| v | r | |
| m | n | |

b) Palauan (Palau Islands)

| | | | |
|---|---|---|---|
| | t | k | ʔ |
| b | | | |
| | ð | | |
| | s | | |
| m | | ŋ | |
| | l, r | | |

c) Nengone (Loyalty Islands, South Pacific)—Stop and nasal system only

| | | | | | |
|---|---|---|---|---|---|
| pʰ | tʰ | ʈʰ | | kʰ | ʔ |
| b | d | ḍ | | g | |
| m | n | | ɲ | ŋ | |
| m̥ | n̥ | | | ŋ̊ | |

(*Note*: The diacritic [.] indicates a retroflex consonant; [ ̥] marks a voiceless nasal; [ɲ] represents a palatal nasal.)

d) Mixe (South Mexico)

| | | | |
|---|---|---|---|
| p | t | k | ʔ |
| | d | g | |
| | ts | tʃ | |
| | s | x | h |
| v | | ɣ | |
| m | n | | |

4.  Describe the morphological characteristics of each of the following languages in terms of the four-way system of classification outlined in section 8.2.2.
    a) Siberian Yupik
       Angya-ghlla-ng-yug-tuq
       boat  -big   -get -want-3SG
       'He wants to get a big boat.'

    b) Latvian

| las-u | las-ām | rakst-u | rakst-ām |
|---|---|---|---|
| read-1SG.PRES | read-1PL.PRES | write-1SG.PRES | write-1PL.PRES |
| 'I read' | 'we read' | 'I write' | 'we write' |

    c) Japanese
       gakusei-wa          homer-are-na-i
       student-Topic       praise-PASS-NEG-PRES
       'The student is not praised.'

5.  Do a morphological analysis of the following data from Latvian. After you have segmented and identified the morphemes, describe how the data reflects the implicational universals in section 8.2.2.
    a) lidotājs       'aviator (nominative)'
    b) lidotāju       'aviator (accusative)'
    c) lidotājam      'to the aviator (dative)'
    d) lidot          'to fly'
    e) rakstītājs     'writer (nominative)'
    f) rakstītāja     'writer's (genitive)'
    g) rakstīt        'to write'

6.  Note the following data from Malagasy, an Austronesian language spoken on the island of Madagascar. The data are from *Malagasy: Introductory Course*, by C. Garvey (Washington: Center for Applied Linguistics, 1964). Does Malagasy comply with all the word order tendencies mentioned earlier in section 8.2.3?
    a) amin' ny restauranta
       'to the restaurant'
    b) Enti'n ny  labiera ny  mpiasa.
       brings the beer    the waiter
       'The waiter brings the beer.'
    c) Avy   any   Amerika izy.
       come from America he
       'He comes from America.'

# *Nine*

Eung-Do Cook
Darin Flynn

# *Aboriginal languages of Canada*

*He who studies only one Indian language and learns its manifold curious grammatical devices, its wealth of words, its capacity of expression, is speedily convinced of its superiority to all other Indian tongues, and not infrequently to all languages by whomsoever spoken.*

J.W. Powell, *Indian Linguistic Families of America North of Mexico* (1891)

The study of languages spoken by the descendants of the original inhabitants of North America has made a number of significant contributions to the development of linguistics. In practically every book that the student of linguistics reads, the impact of work in this area is evident. It would be no exaggeration to say that the lasting and profound influence of such eminent pioneers of linguistics as Franz Boas, Edward Sapir, and Leonard Bloomfield is due in large part to the seminal work they did on structurally diverse Aboriginal languages in North America, especially in Canada.

The value of current research on North American Aboriginal languages stems primarily from the light that it can shed on the nature of human linguistic competence. Besides refuting the popular misconception that these languages are somehow primitive, this work has also uncovered certain structural and semantic phenomena that are not found in more widely studied languages such as English, French, Mandarin, and so on. Another compelling reason for the study of Aboriginal languages is that it can yield clues (sometimes the only ones available) to help resolve problems in archaeology and anthropology (especially ethnohistory) relating to the origin and migration of the indigenous peoples of the Americas. It is also important to recognize that Aboriginal languages in North America are in a grave state of decline, so that an urgency underlies their study, whether theoretical or historical.

## 9.1 Ethnolinguistic overview

How many Aboriginal languages are there? How are they related genetically? How are they distributed? Although definitive answers cannot yet be given to any of these questions, the current tentative consensus is briefly outlined in the next two sections prior to a comment on the decline of Aboriginal languages in Canada. A discussion of the structural characteristics of Canadian aboriginal languages then follows.

## 9.1.1  Genetic classification

John Wesley Powell's work of 1891, which represents the first attempt at a comprehensive genetic classification of the indigenous languages of North America, recognizes fifty-eight families. Although this classification was preceded by and indebted to many other classifications, it is considered one of the most valuable works in Native American linguistics. Powell's classification of hundreds of different languages into fewer than sixty families was a remarkable achievement, but really only a first step toward a final genetic classification.

In the years following Powell's work, many linguists came to assume that all of the indigenous languages of North America ultimately originated from a small number of mother languages. Consequently, they began trying to place the known language families into larger **stocks** and still larger **phyla**. The best-known classification from this perspective was proposed by Edward Sapir in 1929. In this far-reaching analysis, which owes a great deal to earlier work by Alfred Kroeber and Ronald Dixon, among others, all language families of Aboriginal America were grouped into stocks that, in turn, were organized into six superstocks or phyla. Although not adequately substantiated in all details, this proposal stimulated a great deal of research aimed at the further classification of Aboriginal languages.

A more realistic classification was proposed in 1964. Following Sapir's scheme, 221 languages were grouped into 42 families and 31 isolates, which were then classified into 9 phyla. A great deal more has been learned since this proposal was made, and some aspects of this work are now out of date. Certain languages that were earlier treated as isolates have since been proven to be related. For example, Yurok and Wiyot of California, originally considered isolates, have not only been found to be related to each other, but have been placed in the Algonquian family (as claimed by Sapir as early as 1913). Similarly, studies of Tlingit prove it to be not an isolate but distantly related to Athabaskan languages and Eyak.

On the other hand, there is also strong evidence that what were formerly considered dialects of one language should be treated as separate languages. For example, the Klallam language has recently been recognized as distinct from Straits Salish. Similarly, Dogrib, Bear Lake, and Hare of the Athabaskan family were once believed to be dialects of the same language, but their status has since been reconsidered. The identity of Dogrib as a separate language is now well established and the possibility that Bear Lake and Hare are separate languages is under consideration. Several of the proposed phyla also remain in question; in fact, many linguists have chosen to retreat from such large-scale classification until the histories of the individual families are better understood. (A more up-to-date "Consensus Classification" appeared in the latest Vol. 17 of the Smithsonian's *Handbook of North American Indians*; see Recommended reading at the end of this chapter.)

### Language Matters  **The Amerind Hypothesis**

A new and daring classification has been widely entertained in popular media and in interdisciplinary research. Highly controversial, this classification recognizes the Eskimo-Aleut family and Na-Dené—a stock consisting of the Athabaskan family, Tlingit, Eyak, and perhaps Haida—but places all other indigenous languages of the Americas into a single large group, labelled **Amerind**. Both the methodology and the data underlying this proposal have been subjected to severe criticism, and the Amerind hypothesis is not currently accepted by most specialists in the field.

## 9.1.2  Canada's languages

Canada's Aboriginal peoples fall into three distinct political groupings: First Nations, Inuit, and Métis. Although there is no agreement on the details of genetic classification, there is some consensus that Canada's First Nations represent no less than nine language families and isolates, that the Inuit represent a separate language family, and that the Métis represent a unique mixed language.

The map in figure 9.1 shows the geographic distribution of the widely accepted Aboriginal language families and isolates of Canada discussed in this chapter. Of course, the political border between Canada and the United States is not a linguistic boundary; the traditional homeland of many Aboriginal groups includes portions of both countries.

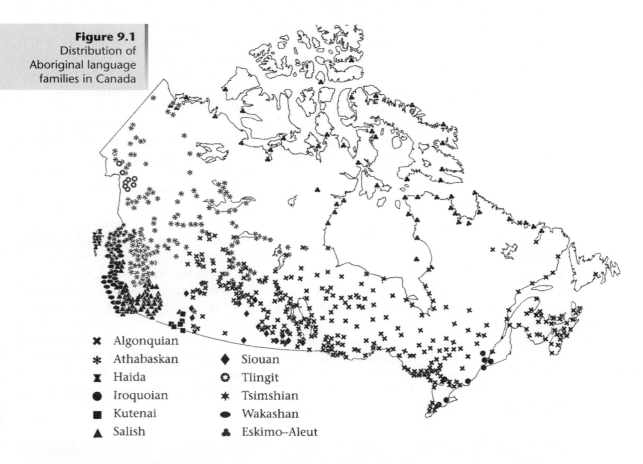

**Figure 9.1**
Distribution of Aboriginal language families in Canada

| | |
|---|---|
| ✖ Algonquian | |
| ✴ Athabaskan | ◆ Siouan |
| ⚊ Haida | ✪ Tlingit |
| ● Iroquoian | ✳ Tsimshian |
| ■ Kutenai | ⬬ Wakashan |
| ▲ Salish | ♣ Eskimo–Aleut |

Languages and affiliations are introduced in descending order of size (in Canada) as follows. Slashes (/) indicate alternative names for languages or dialects. Although some of the names provided may appear exotic, they are in fact the ones preferred by First Nations to identify themselves. Note, too, that there are no exact figures on speaker populations. Figures suggested here are informed current estimates but only approximate, based loosely on Foster (1982), Kinkade (1991), Krauss (1997), Cook (1998), Grime (2000), Mithun (2001), Statistics

Canada's 2001 Census, our own surveys, and personal inquiries to specialists of individual languages or language families and to organizations such as the Saskatchewan Indian Cultural Centre, the Yinka Dene Language Institute (especially Bill Poser), and Aboriginal Languages of Manitoba (especially Carol Beaulieu). The symbol < means 'fewer than'.

## Algonquian

Canada's most widely spoken Aboriginal languages, Cree and Ojibwe, belong to the Algonquian family (see table 9.1). Dialects of both languages are spoken in British Columbia, Alberta, Saskatchewan, Manitoba, Ontario, and Quebec. Cree is also represented in Labrador by the Innu dialects. Malecite-Passamaquoddy and Mi'kmaq are spoken further east, in the Maritime Provinces. (Here and elsewhere, speaker populations outside Canada are provided to give an idea of the overall size of the various Aboriginal linguistic communities. Of the Algonquian languages, only Ojibwe is widely spoken outside Canada.)

| Table 9.1  The Algonquian languages of Canada | | |
|---|---|---|
| Language | Estimated number of speakers in Canada | Estimated number of speakers in the United States |
| Cree (Dialects: Plains, Swampy, Woods, Moose, At(t)ikamek(w), Montagnais and Naskapi Innu) | 80 000 | 1 000 |
| Ojibwe/Anishinaabemowin (Dialects: Odawa, Saulteau(x), Ojibwa/Chippewa, Algonquin, Severn/Oji-Cree) | 45 000 | 5 000 |
| Mi'kmaq/Micmac | 7 000 | 1 200 |
| Blackfoot | 3 000 | 500 |
| Malecite-Passamaquoddy | 750 | 850 |
| Potawatomi/Neshnabémwen | < 50 | 100 |
| Munsee Delaware | < 8 | – |
| Western Abenaki | < 5 | – |

## Eskimo-Aleut

The Inuktitut language (of the Eskimo-Aleut family) is spoken by about two-thirds of the 44 000 Inuit who largely populate Canada's Arctic, from the northwestern part of the Northwest Territories (Inuvialuit) to northern Labrador (see table 9.2). Of those with Inuktitut as mother tongue, almost a third live in northern Quebec (Nunavik) and almost two-thirds live in Nunavut, Canada's newest and largest territory. A syllabary for writing Inuktitut is now in wide use, especially in Nunavut (it is adapted from the Cree syllabary; see chapter 15, section 15.4.4).

| Table 9.2 | The Eskimo-Aleut family in Canada | |
|---|---|---|
| Inuktitut | Estimated number of speakers in Canada | Estimated number of speakers outside Canada |
| Eastern Canadian dialects | 24 000 | Greenland/Denmark (Kalaallisut): 46 000 |
| Western Canadian dialects | 4 000 | Alaska (Inupiaq): 3 000 |

## Athabaskan-Eyak-Tlingit

This family exhibits the greatest internal diversity, with seventeen distinct languages in this country alone (see table 9.3). They are spoken in British Columbia, the Yukon, the Northwest Territories, Alberta, Saskatchewan, and Manitoba. All except Tlingit belong to the Athabaskan subfamily, which is more closely related to Eyak. The last remaining speaker of Eyak died in 2008.

| Table 9.3 | The Tlingit and Athabaskan languages of Canada | |
|---|---|---|
| Language | Estimated number of speakers in Canada | Estimated number of speakers in the United States |
| Tlingit | < 100 | < 400 |
| *Athabaskan:* | | |
| Dëne Sųɬiné/Chipewyan | 15 000 | – |
| Slave(y), including Hare | 3 850 | – |
| Dogrib | 1 900 | – |
| Tŝinlhqot'ín/Chilcotin | 1 200 | – |
| Dakelh/Carrier | 1 250 | – |
| Tutchone (Northern, Southern) | 450 | – |
| Kaska | 400 | – |
| Gwich'in/Kutchin | 350 | 300 |
| Beaver | 200 | – |
| Witsuwit'en-Babine/Nedut'en | 185 | – |
| Sekani | 50 | – |
| Tsúut'ína/Sarcee | < 40 | – |
| Tahltan | < 40 | – |
| Upper Tanana | 10 | 105 |
| Hän | < 5 | 12 |
| Tagish | 2 | – |

## Siouan-Catawban

The Siouan-Catawban language family is represented by three Dakotan languages in Canada: (1) Stoney or Nakoda, spoken exclusively in Alberta; (2) 'Sioux', a now-disfavoured cover term for three dialects spoken in Saskatchewan and southwestern Manitoba: Yankton-Nakota/Dakota or Ihaŋktoŋwaŋ Daƙoťa, Santee-Dakota or Isaŋƭi Daƙoťa, and Teton Lakota or ťitoŋwaŋ Laƙoťa; and (3) Assiniboine-Nakoda (Hohe Naƙoda), spoken in Saskatchewan (see table 9.4). (Separate figures are not available for Yankton and Santee; these are commonly grouped together as 'Dakota'.)

| **Table 9.4** | The Siouan-Catawban family in Canada | |
|---|---|---|
| Dakota/Sioux | Estimated number of speakers in Canada | Estimated number of speakers in the United States |
| Stoney (Nakoda) | 1 500 | – |
| 'Sioux': – Yankton and Santee (Dakota) | < 400 | 15 000 |
| – Teton (Lakota) | < 10 | 6 000 |
| Assiniboine (Nakota) | 34 | Assiniboin: 75 |

## Salish

The Salish family has ten languages centred in British Columbia, but its total speaker population is estimated at fewer than 2000 (see table 9.5).

| **Table 9.5** | The Salish languages of Canada | |
|---|---|---|
| Language | Estimated number of speakers in Canada | Estimated number of speakers in the United States |
| Okanagan/Nsilxcín | 500 | 200 |
| Nlaka'pmx/Thompson | 400 | – |
| Comox-Sliammon | 400 | – |
| Secwepemctsín/Shuswap | 300 | – |
| Lillooet/St'át'imcets | 200 | – |
| Halkomelem (Halq'eméylem, Hul'q'umin'um', hən'q'əmin'əm') | 125 | – |
| Nuxalk/Bella Coola | 20 | – |
| Northern Straits: Saanich/SENĆOŦEN | 20 | – |
| Squamish/Sƙwx̱wú7mesh | 15 | – |
| Sechelt/Shashishalhem | 10 | – |

## Tsimshianic

Tsimshianic languages are located in northwestern British Columbia (see table 9.6). This family is believed to be distantly related to a dozen other language families of the American Pacific Coast, under a proposed phylum called Penutian.

| Table 9.6 | The Tsimshianic languages of Canada | |
|---|---|---|
| Language | Estimated number of speakers in Canada | Estimated number of speakers in the United States |
| Nass-Gitksan | Gitksan/Gitsenimx̱: 900 | – |
| | Nisga'a: 500 | 200 |
| Tsimshian | Sm'algya̱x/Coast Tsimshian: 430 | 70 |
| | Klemtu/South Tsimshian: 1 | – |

## Iroquoian

Another major group of Aboriginal languages represented in Canada is the Iroquoian family, which is found in southwestern Quebec and southern Ontario, as well as in adjoining parts of the United States (see table 9.7).

| Table 9.7 | The Iroquoian languages of Canada | |
|---|---|---|
| Language | Estimated number of speakers in Canada | Estimated number of speakers in the United States |
| Mohawk | < 2 000 | 2 000 |
| Oneida | 150 | < 15 |
| Cayuga | 50 | 10 |
| Onondaga | < 50 | < 15 |
| Seneca | < 25 | 100 |
| Tuscarora | < 7 | 30 |

## Wakashan

The Wakashan family, which is spoken principally on Vancouver Island and the adjacent British Columbia coast, consists of five languages in Canada (see table 9.8). (A sixth Wakashan language, Makah, has about 20 speakers in Washington State, opposite Vancouver Island.)

| Table 9.8 | The Wakashan languages of Canada |
|---|---|
| Language | Estimated number of speakers |
| Nuu-chah-nulth/Nootka | 200 |
| Kwakw'ala/Kwakiutl | 200 |
| Haisla-Henaksiala | 200 |
| Heiltsuk-Oowekyala | Heiltsuk: 200 |
| | Oowekyala: 2 |
| Ditidaht/Nitinat | <10 |

## Isolates

Two language isolates are spoken in Canada: Haida, spoken in the Queen Charlotte Islands off the northern coast of British Columbia, and Ktunaxa, spoken in the Canadian Rockies in southeastern British Columbia (see table 9.9).

| **Table 9.9** | Language isolates of Canada | |
| --- | --- | --- |
| **Language** | **Estimated number of speakers in Canada** | **Estimated number of speakers in the United States** |
| Haida | 35 | 15 |
| Ktunaxa/Kootenay-Kinbasket | 6 | < 6 |

## Contact languages

Contact languages resist genetic classification in terms of language families or isolates, because they do not descend from a single parent language. Michif is a fascinating example of a contact language unique to Canada's Métis, who are (mostly) descendants from Cree or Ojibwe women and French-Canadian fur trappers. This language uses Plains Cree words and grammar for its verbs, and French words and grammar for its nouns. Still, Michif is not mutually intelligible with either Cree or French. There are five hundred or so speakers of Michif in the Canadian Prairies, and another couple of hundred in North Dakota and Montana in the United States. Crucially, many of these speakers do not know Cree or French. Here is an example of a Michif sentence (words in italics derive from Cree; the others derive from French).

(1)   *eːgwanɪ-gi*    liː     savaːz  *kiːpaːʃamwak* la    vjãd
     they       the     Natives      dried    the     meat

Historically, Canada also had its share of trade jargons or pidgins, characterized by rudimentary grammars and limited vocabularies (see chapter 14). For example, at one time or another Inuktitut was mixed with Basque, French, and Montagnais in Labrador-Eskimo Pidgin; with Cree and Montagnais in Hudson Strait Pidgin Inuktitut; with English in Inuktitut-English Pidgin (which was used until the mid-twentieth century); and with Athabaskan languages in Loucheux Jargon.

Chinook Jargon, which originated as a lingua franca in the Pacific Northwest, drew many basic words from Canada's Nuu-chah-nulth (Nootka) and from Canadian French. Its use peaked in the nineteenth century with an estimated 100 000 speakers representing more than 100 mother tongues. There are now probably no more than a dozen speakers of Chinook Jargon in Canada, mostly in British Columbia.

A form of communication using the hands, Plains Sign Talk, was more commonly used as a lingua franca in the Plains area; its use also appears to have peaked in the nineteenth century in Alberta, Saskatchewan, and Manitoba. It is still known by a few Cree, Blackfoot, and Dakota—some deaf, and others hearing, who use it to accompany their oral narratives.

**Language Matters Confusing Signs**

The Plains sign for 'big belly' involves moving the right hand outward and down, fingers pointing left. The sign for 'waterfall' is similar but with fingers pointing forward. Eighteenth-century Cree and French apparently mixed these signs and began referring to the 'Falls Indians', whom they encountered on the Canadian Prairies, as 'Big-bellied Indians'. The Algonquian-speaking Gros Ventres—'Big Bellies' in French— now reside in Montana.

# 9.1.3 Decline of Aboriginal languages

Epidemics (especially smallpox), famines, and innumerable wars reduced the Aboriginal population of North America from over five million at the time of Columbus (the late fifteenth century) to fewer than half a million at the beginning of the twentieth century. Fortunately, Aboriginal peoples are now recovering rapidly from these historical disasters; Canada's Aboriginal population grew from 120 000 in 1925 to a million today.

Nonetheless, many Canadian Aboriginal languages became extinct when their last speakers died, including Laurentian (Iroquoian, Quebec) in the late 1500s; Beothuk (isolate, Newfoundland) in 1829; Nicola (Athabaskan, British Columbia) in the late 1800s; Huron-Wendat (Iroquoian, Quebec) and Tsetsaut/Ts'ets'aut (Athabaskan, British Columbia) in the early 1900s; and Pentlatch (Salish, British Columbia) around 1940. Note that Beothuk appears to have been an isolate; as such, it represents an eleventh language lineage in Canada.

Of the languages that remain, many face imminent extinction. For instance, less than a dozen (elderly) speakers remain for Munsee Delaware (Algonquian), Western Abenaki (Algonquian), Hän (Athabaskan), Tagish (Athabaskan), Squamish (Salish), Sechelt (Salish), Tuscarora (Iroquoian), Ditidaht (Wakashan), Ktunaxa (isolate), and Chinook Jargon. Dialects, too, are disappearing, such as the Ts'ooke and Songish dialects of Northern Straits Salish. Klallam, a closely related Salish language, has no more Canadian speakers; only three remain in Washington State. This state of affairs resulted in part from deliberate action: Aboriginal language use was generally forbidden in church and government-run residential schools to which Aboriginal children were sent from the 1880s to the 1970s.

Other Aboriginal languages with more speakers are nonetheless rapidly becoming obsolete under the influence of English and French, which have become the languages of the nursery and the living-room in most of Canada due in part to the influence of mass media. Recently, however, many Aboriginal communities have sought to counteract the loss of their ancestral languages. With the help of government agencies, museums, and universities, they have launched programs to retain and promote their languages and cultures. As a result of this Renaissance movement, some languages (such as Tsilhqot'in, Ktunaxa, and Secwepemctsín) have seen the establishment of an orthography for the first time, and others have become part of school curricula or even a medium of instruction in lower grades. The long-term effect of this effort on the survival of Aboriginal languages remains to be seen. In the meantime, linguists can assist Aboriginal communities who wish to preserve their languages by becoming involved in the development of sociolinguistic surveys, of curriculum material, and of resource materials such as dictionaries, grammars, and texts.

To end on a positive note: it is remarkable that in spite of the difficulties confronting them, several of Canada's Aboriginal languages—notably Cree, Ojibwe, Inuktitut, and Dëne Suɬiné—remain relatively healthy. For instance, over 90 percent of Quebec's 5 000 Attikamekw speak their dialect of Cree as mother tongue. Two-thirds of the 15 000 Innu in Quebec and Labrador speak their own dialect of Cree as mother tongue, and about a third of them are monolingual in it. Dëne Suɬiné continues to be acquired by children as their first language in many northern Saskatchewan communities, including Fond du Lac, Black Lake, and La Loche. The number of Aboriginal youth learning their heritage tongue as a second language also continues to grow, which may significantly improve the long-term viability of languages otherwise considered endangered or near-extinct.

# 9.2 Structural features

Since there are so many apparently unrelated languages in Canada, it is not surprising to find a great deal of typological variation. Although it is impossible to present even a synopsis of the structural characteristics of these languages, a small selection of what the reader might consider strikingly different and interesting will be given.

## 9.2.1 Phonology

The Algonquian languages (such as Cree and Blackfoot) and the Athabaskan languages (such as Tsúut'ína and Dëne Suɬiné) have long been in contact in the Prairie provinces of Canada. However, the phonological differences between these two language families are striking because Algonquian has one of the simplest phonemic inventories in the world, while Athabaskan has one of the most complex.

Cree vowels may be either short or long, except for /eː/, which is always long. The Cree consonantal system is also simple and straightforward, with no aspiration or glottalization. Consonant clusters are rare, and the most common syllable types are CV, CVC, and V. The vocalic and consonant systems of Cree are given in table 9.10.

**Table 9.10**   Vowel and consonant phonemes in Cree

| Vowel phonemes | | Consonant phonemes | | | | |
|---|---|---|---|---|---|---|
| | | | *Bilabial* | *Alveolar* | *Velar* | *Glottal* |
| i, iː | o, oː | Obstruents | p | t | k | |
| | | | | ts | | |
| eː | a, aː | | | s | | h |
| | | Sonorants | m | n | | |
| | | | | j | w | |

In Dëne Su̜łiné, on the other hand, there are five tense vowels, each of which may be either oral or nasal, as well as a lax vowel, which has no nasal counterpart. The Dëne Su̜łiné consonant system has four times more phonemes than does Cree. It is characterized by a large and symmetrical class of obstruents, particularly affricates, as shown in table 9.11. Another characteristic of Dëne Su̜łiné phonology is the presence of tone, which, along with nasality, makes for many more syllable types in Dëne Su̜łiné than in Cree.

| Table 9.11 | Vowel and consonant phonemes in Dëne Su̜łiné |
|---|---|

**Vowel phonemes**

| *Oral* | | | *Nasal* | |
|---|---|---|---|---|
| i | u | | ĩ | ũ |
| e | ə | o | ẽ | õ |
| | a | | ã | |

**Consonant phonemes**

| | *Labial* | *Interdental* | *Alveolar* | *Alveolar* |
|---|---|---|---|---|
| Plain | p | tθ | t | ts |
| Aspirated | | tθ$^h$ | t$^h$ | ts$^h$ |
| Glottalized | | tθ' | t' | ts' |
| | | ð | | z |
| | | θ | | s |
| | m | | n | r |

| | *Lateral* | *Alveopalatal* | *Velar* | *Labiovelar* | *Glottal* |
|---|---|---|---|---|---|
| Plain | tɬ | tʃ | k | (k$^w$) | |
| Aspirated | tɬ$^h$ | tʃ$^h$ | k$^h$ | (k$^{wh}$) | |
| Glottalized | tɬ' | tʃ' | k' | (k$^w$') | ʔ |
| | l | j | ɣ | w | |
| | ɬ | ʃ | x | (x$^w$) | h |

Note: ɬ is a voiceless, alveolar lateral fricative.

Putting aside the elements in parentheses (whose phonemic status is questionable), there are thirty-five consonantal phonemes in Dëne Su̜łiné, most of which are obstruents. Several sets of stops, affricates, and fricatives constitute the core system. There are two very conspicuous phonological characteristics: a three-way contrast (plain versus aspirated versus glottalized) involving six sets of stops and affricates, and a large inventory of affricates in four series (interdental, alveolar, lateral, and alveopalatal). Particularly worthy of note here are the interdental and lateral affricates, which are seldom found in other language families, as well as the paucity of bilabial stops. The syllable structure is either CV or CVC.

The examples in table 9.12 illustrate CV and CVC syllable types as well as a contrast between oral and nasal vowels and between high tone (marked by the diacritic ´) and low tone.

| Table 9.12 | Vowel and tone contrasts in Dëne Sułiné | | | |
|---|---|---|---|---|
| Low tone/high tone | ɬu | 'fish' | ɬú | 'white fish' |
| | kʰũe | 'house' | kʰũé | 'town' |
| | teskʰoθ | 'I cough' | teskʰóθ | 'I am wide' |
| Oral/nasal | ti | 'prairie chicken' | tĩ(ɣĩ) | 'four' |
| | tsʰá | 'beaver' | tsʰá̃ | 'excrement' |
| | si | 'I' | sĩ | (emphatic particle) |

In Dëne Sułiné, consonant clusters are avoided in syllable margins, and every syllable has a vowel; as already noted, syllables are maximally CVC. Some consonant clusters are allowed in Cree syllables, e.g., *amisk* 'beaver', *ospwaːkan* 'pipe'. Much more complex clusters are tolerated in other Canadian Aboriginal languages. In particular, Blackfoot (Algonquian) allows words like *niʔtsssksksínitaksini* 'one minute', and Oowekyala (Wakashan) and Nuxalk (Salish) are notorious for allowing all-obstruent utterances, as in (2) and (3).

(2) tɬxχspstɬkts (Oowekyala)
    'This (here with me, not visible) will be a nice thwart.'

(3) ts'ktskʷts' (Nuxalk)
    'He arrived.'

## 9.2.2 Morphology

Equally interesting characteristics of North American Aboriginal languages are seen in their morphology, whose complexity has fascinated linguists for a long time. We can illustrate some of these intricacies with the help of several Aboriginal languages spoken in Canada.

### Polysynthesis

The term *polysynthetic* (see chapter 8, section 8.2.2) is often used to underscore the morphological complexities that are easily observable in many Aboriginal languages. **Polysynthetic languages** are characterized by morphologically complex words whose component morphemes often express meanings that would be expressed by separate words in such languages as English and Mandarin. In the Inuktitut language, for instance, a typical word consisting of a root followed by one or more suffixes can be the equivalent of an entire sentence in English. The following utterances are each considered to consist of a single word. (There is allomorphic variation involving the morpheme *gik/rik* meaning 'good'.)

(4) *a.* Iglu-gik-tuq.
     house-good-he-has.3sɢ
     'He has a good house.'

*b.* Qayaq-rik-tuq.
   kayak-good-he-has.3sG
   'He has a good kayak.'

The following words further illustrate polysynthesis in Slave, an Athabaskan language, and Blackfoot, an Algonquian language.

(5) Ts'e-    kʰu-   nĩ-   wa (Slave)
    preverb  them  you  wake
    'You woke them.'

(6) Máːt-  jáːk-  waːxkaji-  waːtsiksi (Blackfoot)
    not    will  go home  he
    'He is not going home.'

## Person and number

Most English speakers are familiar with a three-way contrast involving person (first person—speaker; second person—addressee; third person—other party) and a two-way contrast involving number (unmarked singular versus marked plural). In many Canadian Aboriginal languages, however, a much more elaborate system of contrasts is encountered. As noted in the chapter on morphology, for instance, the Inuit language has three subcategories of number—singular (one), dual (two), and plural (three or more). The following two sets of examples illustrate how these subcategories are marked in nouns and verbs. (In the transcription employed here, the symbol *y* represents a phoneme with the allophones [j] and [ʒ].)

(7) iglu        'an igloo (house)'    niriyu-q    'he ate'
    iglu-k     'igloos (two)'       niriyu-k    'they (two) ate'
    iglu-t     'igloos (three or more)'  niriyu-t    'they (three or more) ate'

The Algonquian languages have an especially elaborate system of person and number marking, as the verb paradigm from Cree in table 9.13 illustrates.

| Table 9.13 | Person and number marking in Cree | |
|---|---|---|
| **pimisin 'to lie down'** | | |
| 1st singular | ni-pimisin-in | 'I lie down' |
| 2nd singular | ki-pimisin-in | 'you lie down' |
| 3rd singular (proximate) | pimisin | 'he or she lies down' |
| 4th singular (obviative) | pimisin-ijiwa | 'the other lies down' |
| 1st plural (inclusive) | ki-pimisin-inaw | 'we (you and I) lie down' |
| 1st plural (exclusive) | ni-pimisin-inaːn | 'we (I and other) lie down' |
| 2nd plural | ki-pimisin-inaːwaːw | 'you (pl) lie down' |
| 3rd plural | pimisin-wak | 'they lie down' |

These examples exhibit a contrast in the first person plural between the so-called **inclusive** and **exclusive**. This contrast is found not only in Algonquian, but also in Iroquoian, Siouan, and Wakashan. The inclusive indicates that the addressee is to be included in the interpretation of the morpheme corresponding to English *we*. Thus, *ki-pimisin-inaw*, the inclusive first person plural form, means either 'you and I lie down' or 'you, I, and someone else lie down'. In contrast, the exclusive form (*ni-pimisin-ina:n*) indicates that the addressee is to be excluded. In English, the phrase 'we lie down' is potentially ambiguous because the grammatical distinctions observed in Cree are not made.

The grammatical distinction between **proximate** and **obviative** (sometimes called third person and fourth person, respectively) is made in all Algonquian languages, as well as in the isolate Ktunaxa. It is difficult to describe, but an example may help illustrate its function. Suppose we are talking about two people (two 'third persons') and that the sentence *He lay down* is used. In English it is unclear which of the two people lay down. Cree speakers avoid this ambiguity by choosing one 'third person' as the focus of the conversation and marking this choice grammatically. One of the ways that this choice can be signalled is by using the focused person's name as subject of a proximate form of the verb. Subsequent references to that person can then be made by means of a proximate verb form. Thus, when a Cree speaker uses the proximate form *pimisin* to express the meaning 'he lay down', listeners know that he or she is talking about the person chosen as the focus of the conversation. Reference to any other person requires use of the obviative form *pimisin-ijiwa*.

## Gender

Several Iroquoian languages (Mohawk, Oneida, and Onondaga) divide third-person pronominals into **masculine**, **feminine**, and **neuter**, in the manner of English (*he*, *she*, *it*) and other Indo-European languages.

(8) Wa<u>ha</u>hnekí:ra?. (Mohawk)
    '<u>He</u> drank it.'

Wa?<u>e</u>hnekí:ra?. (Mohawk)
    '<u>She</u> drank it.' (This can also be used for unspecified sex: 'someone drank it'.)

Wa?<u>ka</u>hnekí:ra?. (Mohawk)
    '<u>It</u> drank it.' (This can also be used for some female persons: 'she drank it'.)

In contrast, grammatical gender in Cree and other Algonquian languages distinguishes between **animate** and **inanimate**. This contrast can be seen in the two different forms of the plural suffix: *-ak* for animate nouns and *-a* for inanimate ones (see table 9.14).

| Table 9.14 | Animate and inanimate nouns in Cree | | | |
|---|---|---|---|---|
| | **Singular** | | **Plural** | |
| Animate | si:si:p | 'duck' | si:si:p-ak | 'ducks' |
| | na:pe:w | 'man' | na:pe:w-ak | 'men' |
| | ospwa:kan | 'pipe' | ospwa:kan-ak | 'pipes' |
| Inanimate | mi:nis | 'berry' | mi:nis-a | 'berries' |
| | astotin | 'cap' | astotin-a | 'caps' |
| | a:tsimo:win | 'story' | a:tsimo:win-a | 'stories' |

Assignment of Cree words to a noun class sometimes seems to lack any natural motivation. The word *ospwa:kan* 'pipe', for instance, belongs to the animate class even though it does not denote a living thing. This practice is somewhat reminiscent of what is found in the gender classification system of English, which can place a few inanimate words (such as those referring to ships and countries) in the feminine class.

## 9.2.3  Syntax

Canada's Aboriginal languages show great diversity in word order (see chapter 8). For example, Wakashan languages such as Oowekyala have a strict VSO order. Salish languages and Ktunaxa are also verb-initial. By contrast, Siouan languages such as Dakota are rigidly SOV. Athabaskan languages are also verb-final.

(9) Daduqʷla wism-aχi   w'ats'-iaχi. (Oowekyala)
    saw       man-the/a dog-the/a
    'The/a man saw the/a dog.'

(10) Tʰatʰaŋka pʰeʒi jutapi (Dakota)        K'òt'íníʔí mitʃàdikòdí ìɣálà (Tsúut'ína)
     oxen       grass eat                   man       beaver       kill
     'oxen eat grass'                        'The man killed a beaver.'

On the other hand, the word order in many other Canadian languages is not fixed. This is the case in Eskimo-Aleut Inuktitut, in Iroquoian languages such as Mohawk, in Algonquian languages such as Cree, and in Michif. (All six orderings in each of (11) and (12) are grammatical and the literal meaning does not change.)

(11) 'The children killed the ducks' (Cree)

| | | |
|---|---|---|
| SVO | Awa:sisak nipahe:wak si:si:pa | 'children killed ducks' |
| SOV | Awa:sisak si:si:pa nipahe:wak | 'children ducks killed' |
| VSO | Nipahe:wak awa:sisak si:si:pa | 'killed children ducks' |
| VOS | Nipahe:wak si:si:pa awa:sisak | 'killed ducks children' |
| OVS | Si:si:pa nipahe:wak awa:sisak | 'ducks killed children' |
| OSV | Si:si:pa awa:sisak nipahe:wak | 'ducks children killed' |

(12) 'Sak likes her dress' (Mohawk)

| | | |
|---|---|---|
| SVO | Sak ra-nuhweʔ-s ako-atyaʔtawi | 'Sak likes her-dress' |
| SOV | Sak ako-atyaʔtawi ra-nuhweʔ-s | 'Sak her-dress likes' |
| VSO | Ra-nuhweʔ-s Sak ako-atyaʔtawi | 'likes Sak her-dress' |
| VOS | Ra-nuhweʔ-s ako-atyaʔtawi ne Sak | 'likes her-dress Sak' |
| OVS | Ako-atyaʔtawi ra-nuhweʔ-s ne Sak | 'her-dress likes Sak' |
| OSV | Ako-atyaʔtawi Sak ra-nuhweʔ-s | 'her-dress Sak likes' |

Also of interest is the oft-repeated claim that many of Canada's Aboriginal languages—Salishan, Wakashan, Iroquoian, and Inuktitut—lack a distinction between 'noun' and 'verb'. This claim is controversial, but most linguists agree that the noun/verb distinction is weak in the syntax of these languages. For example, in Nuu-chah-nulth (Tseshaht dialect) *qu:ʔas* 'man' not only has the noun-like use in (13a), but also the verb-like use in (13b). (Verbs come at the beginning of the sentence in Nuu-chah-nulth.)

(13)  *a.* Noun-like use of *quːʔas*     *b.* Verb-like use of *quːʔas*
           Mamuːk-ma quːʔas-ʔi          Quːʔas-ma mamuːk-ʔi
           work-3SG     man-the        man-3SG   work-the
           'The man is working.'       'The working one is a man.'

# Summing up

This chapter outlines genetic classifications, geographic distributions, and speaker populations of Canada's Aboriginal languages, and presents a selection of phonological and grammatical characteristics of these languages. Even this brief discussion should illustrate just how much languages can differ from each other. Although it has sometimes been claimed that languages may differ in unpredictable ways, it should be remembered that there are striking similarities that underlie surface differences and that these differences can be described in terms of universal categories and processes (phonemes, morphemes, inflection, derivation, phrase structure, and so on). For this reason, the structural diversity of Canadian Aboriginal languages offers the linguist opportunities to reaffirm familiar principles, as well as to discover new insights into the nature of human language.

## Recommended reading

Campbell, Lyle. 1997. *American Indian Languages: The Historical Linguistics of Native America*. Oxford: Oxford University Press.

Foster, Michael K. 1982. "Canada's Indigenous Languages: Past and Present." *Language and Society* 7:3–16. Ottawa: Commissioner of Official Languages.

Goddard, Ives, ed. 1996. *Languages,* Vol. 17 of the *Handbook of North American Indians*. Washington, DC: Smithsonian Institution.

Mithun, Marianne. 2001. *The Languages of Native North America*. Cambridge, UK: Cambridge University Press.

Voegelin, C.F., and F.M. Voegelin. 1965. "Classification of American Indian Languages." Languages of the World, Native America Fascicle 2, section 1.6, *Anthropological Linguistics* 7:121–50.

CHAPTER
# *Ten*

William O'Grady
Sook Whan Cho

# *First language acquisition*

*Human brains are so constructed that one
brain responds in much the same way to a
given trigger as does another brain, all things
being equal. This is why a baby can learn any
language; it responds to triggers in the same
way as any other baby.*

D. HOFSTADTER

Nothing is more important to a child's development than the acquisition of language. Most
children acquire language quickly and effortlessly, giving the impression that the entire
process is simple and straightforward. However, the true extent of children's achievement
becomes evident when we compare their success with the difficulties encountered by adults
who try to learn a second language (see chapter 11). Understanding how children the world
over are able to master the complexities of human language in the space of a few short years has
become one of the major goals of contemporary linguistic research.

This chapter provides a brief overview of the progress that has been made in this area.
We will begin by considering the research strategies used by linguists and psychologists
in the study of linguistic development. We will then describe some of the major findings
concerning children's acquisition of the various parts of their language—phonology, vocabulary, morphology, syntax, and semantics. The chapter concludes with a brief examination of
the contribution of the linguistic environment to language acquisition, the relationship
between the emergence of language and cognitive development, and the possible existence
of inborn linguistic knowledge.

## 10.1 The study of language acquisition

Although we commonly refer to the emergence of language in children as 'language acquisition', the end result of this process is actually a *grammar*—the mental system that allows
people to speak and understand a language. There are at least two reasons for believing that
the development of linguistic skills must involve the acquisition of a grammar.

First, as noted in chapter 1, mature language users are able to produce and understand an
unlimited number of novel sentences. This can only happen if, as children, they have
acquired the grammar for their language. Simple memorization of a fixed inventory of words
and sentences would not equip learners to deal with previously unheard utterances—a basic
requisite of normal language use.

A second indication that children acquire grammatical rules comes from their speech errors, which often provide valuable clues about how the acquisition process works. Even run-of-the-mill errors such as *doed*, *runned*, and *goed* can be informative. Since we know that children don't hear adults produce words like these, such errors tell us that they have formulated a general rule that forms the past tense by adding -*ed* to the verb stem.

Because language acquisition involves the emergence of a grammar, its study is closely tied to the type of linguistic analysis with which we have been concerned in preceding chapters. Indeed, linguists and psychologists studying language acquisition must often look to the study of phonology, morphology, and syntax for help in identifying and describing the grammatical system that children acquire during the first years of life.

## 10.1.1 Methods

The majority of research on the acquisition of language focuses on children's early utterances, the order in which they emerge, and the kinds of errors they contain. Two complementary methods of data collection are used—naturalistic observation and experimentation.

### Two approaches

In the **naturalistic approach**, investigators observe and record children's spontaneous utterances. One type of naturalistic investigation is the so-called **diary study**, in which a researcher (often a parent) keeps daily notes on a child's linguistic progress. Here's a short example, drawn from a diary tracking child's early vocabulary development.

| Date | Child's word | Adult word | Comment |
|------|-------------|-----------|---------|
| June 9, 2003 | krakuh | cracker | said several times to refer to Japanese crackers; used a few days later to refer to Graham crackers |
| June 24, 2003 | G | MG | said on several occasions while pointing at the MG symbol on her father's shirt; used on July 24 to refer to an actual MG roadster |

### Language Matters **Darwin the Linguist**

One of the first language diarists was Charles Darwin, the founder of the theory of natural selection, who kept a detailed record of the development of his son. Among the observations in "A Biographical Sketch on an Infant" (1876) is the following anecdote: "At exactly the age of a year, he invented a word for food, namely *mum*. . . . And now instead of beginning to cry when he was hungry, he used the word in a demonstrative manner or as a verb, implying 'Give me food'."

In *The Descent of Man*, Darwin wrote (chapter 3) that language "has justly been considered as one of the chief distinctions between man and the lower animals."

A more systematic way to collect naturalistic data involves regular taping sessions, often at biweekly intervals, to gather samples (usually an hour at a time) of the child interacting with his or her caregivers. Detailed transcripts are then made for subsequent analysis. A great deal of data of this type is available through CHILDES (the Child Language Data Exchange System), which can be accessed online at http://childes.psy.cmu.edu/. Here is a small excerpt from a CHILDES transcript, containing a fragment of a conversation between Adam (aged 2 years, 4 months) and his mother:

> ADAM: read book.
> MOT: papa bear.
> MOT: yes.
> ADAM: bunny rabbit.
> MOT: did you see bunny rabbit?
> ADAM: bunny rabbit rabbit running.
> MOT: bunny rabbit running?

The CHILDES data base includes thousands of hours of data from more than twenty languages.

Naturalistic studies tend to be **longitudinal** in that they examine language development in a particular child or group over an extended period of time (sometimes as long as several years). As the name suggests, longitudinal studies take a long time to conduct, but they have the advantage of permitting researchers to observe development as an ongoing process in individual children.

Naturalistic data collection provides a great deal of information about how the language acquisition process unfolds, but it also has its shortcomings. The most serious of these is that particular structures and phenomena may occur rarely in children's everyday speech, making it difficult to gather enough information from natural speech samples to test hypotheses or draw firm conclusions. This problem is further compounded by the fact that speech samples from individual children capture only a small portion of their utterances at any given point in development. (Because of the amount of time required to transcribe and analyze recordings, researchers typically have to be content with hour-long samples taken at weekly or biweekly intervals.)

In **experimental** studies, researchers typically make use of specially designed tasks to elicit linguistic activity relevant to the phenomenon that they wish to study. The child's performance is then used to formulate hypotheses about the type of grammatical system acquired at that point in time.

Experimental **research** is typically **cross-sectional** in that it investigates and compares the linguistic knowledge of different children (or groups of children) at a particular point in development. A typical cross-sectional study might involve conducting a single experiment with a group of two year olds, a group of four year olds, and a group of six year olds, taking each of these groups to be representative of a particular stage or 'cross-section' of the developmental process.

## Types of experimental studies

Experimental studies usually employ tasks that test children's comprehension, production, or imitation skills. One widely used method for testing comprehension calls for children to judge the truth of statements that are made about particular pictures or situations presented to them by the experimenter. Figure 10.1 offers an example of one such task.

**Figure 10.1**
"Is every ball on a box?"

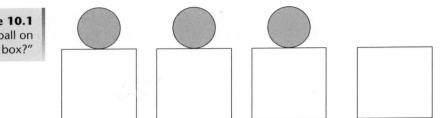

In this particular case, by the way, many preschool children respond by saying no, justifying their answer by noting that one of the boxes doesn't have a ball on it!

A second method for testing comprehension involves supplying children with an appropriate set of toys and then asking them to act out the meaning of a sentence—perhaps a passive structure such as *The truck was bumped by the car*. Children's responses can provide valuable clues about the type of grammatical rules being used to interpret sentences at various stages of development.

In a typical production task, the experimenter presents the child with a situation that calls for a particular type of statement or question. In order to determine whether three-year-old children use inversion when asking *yes-no* questions, for instance, a researcher might design a game in which the child asks a puppet for his opinion about various pictures, as in the example in Figure 10.2.

**Figure 10.2**
"Ask the puppet if the dog is smiling."

If all goes well, the child will respond by asking a question, which in turn creates an opportunity to use the inversion operation that places the auxiliary verb to the left of the subject, as in *Is the dog smiling?* (see chapter 5).

Although production tasks can be useful for assessing certain types of linguistic knowledge, there are many structures (such as passives) that are hard to elicit, even from adults, because they are used only in special contexts. Moreover, because children's ability to comprehend language is often more advanced than their ability to produce sentences of their own, production tasks can provide an overly conservative view of linguistic development unless they are accompanied by other types of tests.

Experiments that have children imitate model sentences can also provide important clues about grammatical development. Although imitation might appear to be easy, it has been found that children's ability to repeat a particular structure provides a good indication of how well they have mastered it. For instance, a child who has not yet acquired auxiliary verbs will repeat the sentence *Mickey is laughing* as *Mickey laughing*.

The principal advantage of the experimental approach is that it allows researchers to collect data of a very specific sort about particular phenomena or structures. Experimentation is not without its pitfalls, however. In addition to the difficulty of designing a good experiment, there is always the possibility that children's performance will be affected by extraneous factors, such as inattention, shyness, or a failure to understand what is expected of them. Nonetheless, by using experimental techniques together with naturalistic observation, linguists and psychologists have made significant progress toward understanding the language acquisition process. This chapter is devoted to a survey of this progress, beginning with the development of speech sounds.

# 10.2 Phonological development

Children seem to be born with a perceptual system that is especially designed for listening to speech. Newborns respond differently to human voices than to other sounds, they show a preference for the language of their parents over other languages by the time they are two days old, and they can recognize their mother's voice within a matter of weeks.

From around one month of age, children exhibit the ability to distinguish among certain speech sounds. In one experiment, infants were presented with a series of identical [ba] syllables. These were followed by an occurrence of the syllable [pa]. A change in the children's sucking rate (measured by a specially designed pacifier) indicated that they perceived the difference between the two syllables, and that they were therefore able to distinguish between [p] and [b].

## 10.2.1 Babbling

The ability to produce speech sounds begins to emerge around six months of age, with the onset of babbling. Babbling provides children with the opportunity to experiment with and begin to gain control over their vocal apparatus—an important prerequisite for later speech. Children who are unable to babble for medical reasons (because of the need for a breathing tube in their throat, for example) can subsequently acquire normal pronunciation, but their speech development is significantly delayed.

### Language Matters **Hearing It All**

Infants are even able to distinguish between sounds in unfamiliar languages. In one experiment, six- to eight-month-old infants who were being raised in English-speaking homes could hear contrasts among unfamiliar consonants in Hindi and Nthlakampx (an Aboriginal language spoken on parts of Canada's West Coast). By the time they were ten to twelve months old, though, this ability had begun to diminish.

Despite obvious differences among the languages to which they are exposed, children from different linguistic communities exhibit significant similarities in their babbling. The tendencies in table 10.1 are based on data from fifteen different languages, including English, Thai, Japanese, Arabic, Hindi, and Mayan. (We focus here on consonant sounds, for which the data is somewhat more reliable than for vowels.)

| **Table 10.1**  Cross-linguistic similarities in babbling | |
|---|---|
| **Frequently found consonants** | **Infrequently found consonants** |
| p  b  m<br>t  d  n<br>k  g<br>s  h  w  j | f  v  θ  ð<br>ʃ  ʒ  tʃ  dʒ<br>l  r  ŋ |

Such cross-linguistic similarities suggest that early babbling is at least partly independent of the particular language to which children are exposed. In fact, even deaf children babble, although their articulatory activity is somewhat less varied than that of hearing children.

## 10.2.2 Developmental order

Babbling increases in frequency until the age of about twelve months, at which time children start to produce their first understandable words. Babbling may overlap with the production of real words for several weeks before dying out. By the time children have acquired fifty words or so, they begin to adopt fairly regular patterns of pronunciation.

Although there is a good deal of variation from child to child in terms of the order in which speech sounds are mastered in production and perception, the following general tendencies seem to exist.

- As a group, vowels are generally acquired before consonants (by age three).
- Stops tend to be acquired before other consonants.
- In terms of place of articulation, labials are often acquired first, followed (with some variation) by alveolars, velars, and alveopalatals. Interdentals (such as [θ] and [ð]) are acquired last.
- New phonemic contrasts manifest themselves first in word-initial position. Thus, the /p/-/b/ contrast, for instance, is manifested in pairs such as *pat-bat* before *mop-mob*.

By age two, a typical English-speaking child has the inventory of consonant phonemes shown in table 10.2.

| **Table 10.2**  Typical consonant inventory at age two | | | | |
|---|---|---|---|---|
| **Stops** | | | **Fricatives** | **Other** |
| p  b  m | | | f | w |
| t  d  n | | | s | |
| k  g | | | | |

By age four, this inventory is considerably larger and typically includes the sounds shown in table 10.3.

| **Table 10.3**   Typical consonant inventory at age four | | | |
|---|---|---|---|
| **Stops** | **Fricatives** | **Affricates** | **Other** |
| p   b   m | f   v | tʃ   dʒ | w   j |
| t   d   n | s   z | | l   r |
| k   g   ŋ | ʃ | | |

Still to be acquired at this age are the interdental fricatives [θ] and [ð] and the voiced alveopalatal fricative [ʒ].

In general, the relative order in which sounds are acquired reflects their distribution in languages of the world (see chapter 8). The sounds that are acquired early are generally found most widely in the world's languages whereas the sounds that are acquired late tend to be less common across languages.

## 10.2.3 Early phonetic processes

Children's ability to perceive the phonemic contrasts of their language develops well in advance of their ability to produce them. So even children who are unable to produce the difference between words like *mouse* and *mouth*, *cart* and *card*, or *jug* and *duck* may nonetheless be able to point to pictures of the correct objects in a comprehension task. Moreover, as the following experimenter's report vividly illustrates, children even seem to know that their pronunciations are sometimes not yet 'right'.

> *One of us spoke to a child who called his inflated plastic fish a fis. In imitation of the child's pronunciation, the observer said: "This is your fis?" "No," said the child, "my fis." He continued to reject the adult's imitation until he was told, "That is your fish." "Yes," he said, "my fis."*

The child's reaction to the adult's initial pronunciation of *fish* shows that he could perceive the difference between /s/ and /ʃ/ and that he had correctly represented the word as /fɪʃ/ in his lexicon even though he could not yet produce it himself.

What precisely is responsible for the special character of the sound patterns in children's early speech? The key seems to lie in the operation of a limited number of universal phonetic processes.

### Syllable deletion

Because syllables bearing primary or secondary stress are more noticeable than their unstressed counterparts, they tend to be more salient to children in the early stages of the language acquisition process. As a result, stressed syllables are more likely to be retained in children's pronunciation than are unstressed syllables (see table 10.4).

| Table 10.4 | Differences in the retention of stressed and unstressed syllables |
|---|---|
| **Word** | **Child's pronunciation** |
| hip po pó ta mus | [pɑs] |
| spa ghé tti | [gɛ] |
| hé li còp ter | [ɛlkɑt] |
| kan ga róo | [wu] |
| té le phòne | [fow] |

However, unstressed syllables in final position tend to be retained, probably because the ends of words are easier to notice and remember (see table 10.5).

| Table 10.5 | Retention of unstressed syllables in final position |
|---|---|
| **Word** | **Child's pronunciation** |
| po tá to | [tejdo] |
| ba ná na | [nænə] |
| to má to | [mejdo] |
| él e phant | [ɛlfən] |

## Syllable simplification

Another frequent process in children's speech involves the systematic deletion of certain sounds in order to simplify syllable structure. In the data in table 10.6, typical of the speech of two- and three-year-old children, consonant clusters are reduced by deleting one or more segments.

| Table 10.6 | Reduction of consonant clusters |
|---|---|

[s] + stop (strategy: delete [s])
stop → [tɑp]
small → [mɑ]
desk → [dɛk]

stop + liquid (strategy: delete liquid)
try → [taj]
crumb → [gʌm]
bring → [bɪŋ]

fricative + liquid (strategy: delete liquid)
from → [fʌm]
sleep → [sip]

nasal + voiceless stop (strategy: delete nasal)
bump → [bʌp]
tent → [dɛt]

Yet another common deletion process in early child language involves the elimination of final consonants, as in the following examples.

(1) dog    [dɑ]
     bus    [bʌ]
     boot   [bu]

Both the reduction of consonant clusters and the deletion of final consonants have the effect of simplifying syllable structure, bringing it closer to the CV template that is universally favoured by children and that is the most widely found pattern in human language in general.

## Substitution

One of the most widespread phonetic processes in early language involves substitution—the systematic replacement of one sound by an alternative that the child finds easier to articulate (see table 10.7). Common substitution processes include **stopping**, the replacement of a fricative by a corresponding stop; **fronting**, the moving forward of a sound's place of articulation; **gliding**, the replacement of a liquid by a glide; and **denasalization**, the replacement of a nasal stop by a non-nasal counterpart.

| **Table 10.7** | Substitution in early speech | |
|---|---|---|
| **Process** | **Example** | **Change** |
| Stopping (continuant → stop) | sing → [tɪŋ] | s → t |
| | sea → [ti] | s → t |
| | zebra → [dibrə] | z → d |
| | thing → [tɪŋ] | θ → t |
| | this → [dɪt] | ð → d, s → t |
| | shoes → [tud] | ʃ → t, z → d |
| Fronting | ship → [sɪp] | ʃ → s |
| | jump → [dzʌmp] | dʒ → dz |
| | chalk → [tsɑ:k] | tʃ → ts |
| | go → [dow] | g → d |
| Gliding | lion → [jajn̩] | l → j |
| | laughing → [jæfɪŋ] | l → j |
| | look → [wʊk] | l → w |
| | rock → [wɑk] | r → w |
| | story → [stowi] | r → w |
| Denasalization | spoon → [bud] | n → d |
| | jam → [dæb] | m → b |
| | room → [wub] | m → b |

## Assimilation

Still another widespread phonetic process in child language is assimilation—the modification of one or more features of a segment under the influence of neighbouring sounds. In the following examples, initial consonants have been voiced in anticipation of the following vowel.

(2)  tell    [dɛl]
     pig     [bɪg]
     push    [bʊs]
     soup    [zup]

Assimilation is also observed in children's tendency to maintain the same place of articulation for all of the consonants or vowels in a word. This can lead to the pronunciation of *doggy* as [gɑgi] (with two velar stops). Other examples include [fɛlf] for *self* (with identical initial and final consonants), [bibi] for *baby* (with identical vowels in both syllables), [kæklin] for *Cathleen* (with identical velar stops), and [næns] for *dance* (with identical nasal consonants).

## 10.3 Vocabulary development

By age eighteen months or so, the average child has a vocabulary of fifty words or more. Common items include the words listed in table 10.8.

| **Table 10.8**    Common items in the first fifty words |
| --- |
| **Entities** |
| Words referring to<br>    people: *daddy, mommy, baby*<br>    food/drink: *juice, milk, cookie, water, toast, apple, cake*<br>    animals: *dog, cat, duck, horse*<br>    clothes: *shoes, hat*<br>    toys: *ball, blocks*<br>    vehicles: *car, boat, truck*<br>    other: *bottle, key, book* |
| **Properties** |
| *hot, allgone, more, dirty, cold, here, there* |
| **Actions** |
| *up, sit, see, eat, go, down* |
| **Personal-social** |
| *hi, bye, no, yes, please, thank-you* |

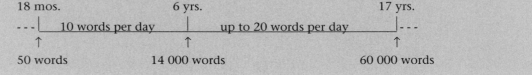

## Language Matters **Moving Along**

Every child develops at his or her own pace, of course, but to the extent that we can depict a 'typical' profile for vocabulary development, it would look something like this. Note the relatively slow start (just 50 words in 18 months), followed by a rapid acceleration that is sustained over a multiyear period.

As table 10.8 shows, nounlike words make up the single largest class in the child's early vocabulary, with verb- and adjectivelike words being the next most frequent category types. Among the most frequent words are expressions for displeasure or rejection (such as *no*) and various types of social interaction (such as *please* and *bye*). Over the next months this vocabulary grows rapidly, sometimes by as much as ten or twelve words a day. By age six, most children have mastered about thirteen or fourteen thousand words.

Children seem to differ somewhat in the types of words that they focus on, especially in the early stages of language acquisition. One of these differences is reflected in the number of nouns in early vocabulary. Whereas some children have a relatively high proportion of such words (75 percent or more) by age two, other learners exhibit a much lower percentage of nouns (50 percent or less). Making up for the smaller number of nouns is a larger vocabulary of socially useful expressions such as *bye, go-away, stop-it, thank-you, I-want-it*, and so on. (Hyphens are used here to indicate that these expressions are not yet segmented into their component words.)

## 10.3.1 Strategies for acquiring word meaning

Children seem to draw on certain strategies when trying to determine the meaning of a new word. This is perhaps easiest to illustrate in the case of noun-type meanings, for which the following strategies appear to be employed.

(3)  Three strategies for learning the meanings of new words.

*The Whole Object Assumption*
A new word refers to a whole object.

*The Type Assumption*
A new word refers to a type of thing, not just to a particular thing.

*The Basic Level Assumption*
A new word refers to objects that are alike in basic ways (appearance, behaviour, etc).

To see how these strategies work, imagine that a mother and her eighteen-month-old daughter are driving through the countryside and they encounter a sheep munching on the grass. The mother points to the animal and says "sheep." What does the child think that the word means? Does it mean 'white'? Or does it mean 'woolly'? Does it refer to the animal? Or to parts of the animal? Or does it refer to the fact that a particular animal is munching on grass?

The Whole Object Assumption allows the child to infer that the word *sheep* refers to the animal itself, not to its parts, not to its whiteness, and not to its wooliness. The Type Assumption allows her to infer that *sheep* refers to a type of animal, not to just one particular sheep. And the Basic Level Assumption leads her to guess that *sheep* is used to refer just to white, four-legged, woolly animals, and not animals in general.

## ✗ Contextual clues   NOT INCLUDED.

Another major factor in vocabulary development is the child's ability to make use of contextual clues to draw inferences about the category and meaning of new words. For instance, from early in the language acquisition process, children can use the presence or absence of determiners to distinguish between names and ordinary nouns. Two-year-old children who are told that a new doll is a *dax* will apply this label to similar-looking dolls as well. However, if they are told that the new doll is *Dax*, they assume that it refers just to the doll they have actually been shown. Like adults, these children treat *dax* as an ordinary noun when it is preceded by *a*, but as a name when there is no determiner.

In another experiment, three- and four-year-old children were asked to act out the meaning of sentences such as 'Make it so there is *tiv* to drink in this glass (of water)'. The only clues about the interpretation of the nonsense word *tiv* came from the meaning of the rest of the sentence and from the child's understanding of the types of changes that can be made to a glass of water. Not only did more than half the children respond by either adding or removing water, but some even remembered what *tiv* 'meant' two weeks later!

## 10.3.2 Meaning errors ✓

The meanings that children associate with their early words sometimes correspond closely to the meanings employed by adults. In many cases, however, the match is less than perfect. The two most typical semantic errors involve overextension and underextension.

### Overextensions

In cases of **overextension**, the meaning of the child's word is more general or inclusive than that of the corresponding adult form. The word *dog*, for example, is frequently overextended

---

### Language Matters **Fast Mapping**

How many times does a child have to hear a new word in order to learn it? In one study, eighteen-month-old children were able to learn pairs of new words after just three exposures. In a study of somewhat older children (two to five year olds), a single encounter with a new word led to impressive success: 81 percent of the children could identify the word's referent the next time they heard it. The rapid learning of new words is called *fast mapping*.

Sources: C. Dollaghan, "Child Meets Word," *Journal of Speech and Hearing Research* 28 (1985):449–54.
   C. Houston-Price, K. Plunkett, and P. Harris, "Word-learning Wizardry at 1;6," *Journal of Child Language* 32 (2005):175–90.

to include horses, cows, and other four-legged animals. Similarly, *ball* is sometimes used for any round object, including a balloon, an Easter egg, a small stone, and so on. As many as one-third of children's words may be overextended at the fifty-word stage of vocabulary development (see table 10.9).

| Table 10.9 | Additional examples of overextension | |
|---|---|---|
| **Word** | **First referent** | **Subsequent extensions** |
| tick tock | watch | clocks, gas-meter, fire hose on a spool, scale with round dial |
| fly | fly | specks of dirt, dust, small insects, child's toes, crumbs of bread |
| quack | duck | all birds and insects, flies, coins (with an eagle on the face) |
| candy | candy | cherries, anything sweet |
| apple | apples | balls, tomatoes, cherries, onions, biscuits |
| turtle | turtles | fish, seals |
| cookie | cookies | crackers, any dessert |
| kitty | cats | rabbits, any small furry animal |
| box | boxes | elevators |
| belt | belts | watch strap |

The evidence collected to date suggests that perceptual properties are the single most important factors in children's first hypotheses about word meanings. As a result, children often overextend a word to include a set of perceptually similar objects that they know to have diverse functions. For example, one child used the word *moon* for the moon, grapefruit halves, and a crescent-shaped car light. Another child used the word *money* for a set of objects ranging from pennies to buttons and beads. If you reconsider the examples of overextension given in table 10.9, you will see that they too can be explained in terms of perceptual similarities.

There is reason to believe that many overextensions may be deliberate attempts to compensate for vocabulary limitations. One indication of this is that particular overextensions often disappear as soon as children learn the right word for the objects that they have been mislabelling. For example, two-year-old Allen was using the word *dog* for dogs, cats, sheep, and other four-legged mammals, but he stopped doing so as soon as he learned the words *cat* and *sheep*. If he thought that *dog* meant 'animal', he could still have sometimes referred to cats and sheep as *dogs* (just as adults sometimes refer to them as animals). The fact that he didn't suggests that he never thought *dog* meant 'animal'; he had just been 'borrowing' it until the right word came along.

A further indication that many overextensions are designed to compensate for vocabulary limitations comes from the fact that children seem to overextend more in their production than in their comprehension. This is not the result that one would expect if children thought that *dog* meant 'animal'.

**Figure 10.3**
A sample over-extension test

Even children who sometimes use *dog* to refer to cows or horses typically point to the right animal when asked to show the dog to the experimenter.

## Underextensions

Another possible type of word-meaning error in early language involves **underextension**, the use of lexical items in an overly restrictive fashion. Thus, *kitty* might be used to refer to the family pet, but not to any other cats. Or the word *dog* might be used for collies, spaniels, and beagles, but not for Chihuahuas.

Underextension errors often reflect children's propensity to focus on prototypical or core members of a category. As noted in section 6.1.3 of chapter 6, the potential referents of many words differ in terms of how well they exemplify the properties associated with a particular concept. For example, among the potential referents of the word *dog*, collies and spaniels have more of the properties associated with the concept 'dog' (long hair, relative size, type of bark, and so on) than do Chihuahuas. While the preference for a prototype can be overruled by factors such as the presence of a non-typical category member in the child's everyday experience (e.g., a Chihuahua as a family pet), the internal structure of concepts can have an important influence on semantic development.

## Verb meanings

Meaning errors also occur with verbs. For example, some preschool children believe that *fill* means 'pour' rather than 'make full'. So, when asked to decide which of the two series of pictures in figure 10.4 (on the next page) is an example of filling, they choose the second series—even though the glass remains empty!

Not surprisingly, there is a tendency for children who make this sort of mistake to use *fill* in the wrong syntactic patterns as well.

(4)  And fill the little sugars up in the bowl . . . (Mark, at age 4 yrs., 7 mos.)
I didn't fill water up to drink it. (E, at age 4 yrs., 1 mo.)
Can I fill some salt into the [salt shaker]? (E, at age 5 yrs.)

These errors disappear as children come to realize that *fill* means 'make full' rather than 'pour into'.

**Figure 10.4**
Sample pictures used to test children's understanding of *fill*. Some children believe that the action depicted in the bottom series of pictures involves filling, even though the glass remains empty.

Source: Jess Gropen, Steven Pinker, Michelle Hollander, and Richard Goldberg, "Syntax and Semantics in the Acquisition of Locative Verbs," *Journal of Child Language*, 18 (1991):115–51. Reprinted with the permission of Cambridge University Press.

## Dimensional terms

Terms describing size and dimensions are acquired in a relatively fixed order, depending on their generality (see table 10.10). The first adjectives of this type to be acquired, *big* and *small*, are the most general in that they can be used for talking about any aspect of size (height, area, volume, and so on). In contrast, the second group of adjectives to emerge—*tall*, *long*, *short*, *high*, and *low*—can only be used for a single dimension (height-length). The remaining modifiers (*thick-thin*, *wide-narrow*, and *deep-shallow*) are still more restricted in their use since they describe the secondary or less extended dimension of an object. For instance, the dimension of a stick that we describe in terms of width or thickness is almost always less extended than the dimension that we describe in terms of height or length, which tends also to be perceptually more salient.

| **Table 10.10** | Order of acquisition for dimensional adjectives | |
|---|---|---|
| **Step** | **Words** | **What they describe** |
| 1 | *big-small* | any aspect of size |
| 2 | *tall-short, long-short, high-low* | a single dimension |
| 3 | *thick-thin, wide-narrow, deep-shallow* | a secondary dimension |

The difficulty of dimensional adjectives for children is also evident in experimental tasks. In one experiment children aged three to five were shown pairs of objects—sometimes a big one and a tall one and sometimes a big one and a long one (see figure 10.5). Younger children did well when asked to choose 'the big one'. However, when asked to choose 'the tall one' or 'the long one', they often picked the big one instead. This suggests that they are initially more sensitive to overall size than to a single dimension like height or length.

**Figure 10.5**
'big'–'tall' versus
'big'–'long'

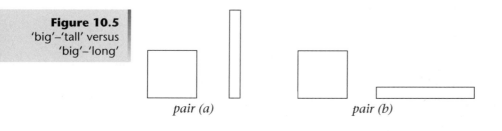

*pair (a)*                    *pair (b)*

## 10.4 Morphological development

As is the case with the sound pattern of language and with vocabulary, the details of morphological structure emerge over a period of several years. Initially, the words produced by English-speaking children seem to lack any internal morphological structure: affixes are systematically absent and most words consist of a single root morpheme.

### 10.4.1 Overgeneralization

Because English has many examples of irregular inflection (*men* as the plural of *man*, *ran* as the past of *run*), children sometimes begin by simply memorizing inflected words on a case-by-case basis without regard for general patterns or rules. As a result, they may initially use irregular forms such as *men* and *ran* correctly. However, when they subsequently observe the generality of *-s* as a plural marker and *-ed* as a past tense marker (usually around age two and a half), they sometimes use these suffixes for the irregular forms—producing words such as *mans* and *runned*. (Errors that result from the overly broad application of a rule are called **overgeneralizations** or **overregularizations**.) Even occasional mixed forms such as *felled*, a blend of *fell* and *falled*, may occur during this period (see table 10.11).

| **Table 10.11** | The development of affixes |
| --- | --- |
| Stage 1: | Case-by-case learning (plural *boys, men*, etc.; past tense *walked, ran*, etc.) |
| Stage 2: | Overuse of general rule (plural *mans*; past tense *runned*) |
| Stage 3: | Mastery of exceptions to the general rule (plural *men*; past tense *ran*) |

---

**Language Matters How Many Times Does It Take to Get It Right?**

How many times does a child have to hear the adult form of an irregular verb before all overregularizations are eliminated? Several hundred times, according to one estimate. That's why children are often relatively quick at figuring out the right past tense form for frequently heard irregular verbs like *go* and *see*, but take much longer to master less common verbs such as *sink* or *win*.

Source: Michael Maratsos, "More Overregularizations After All: New Data and Discussion on Marcus, Pinker, Ullman, Hollander, Rosen and Xu," *Journal of Child Language* 27 (2000):183–212.

---

One of the best indications that children have mastered an inflectional rule comes from their ability to apply it to forms they have not heard before. In a classic experiment, children were shown a picture of a strange creature and told, "This is a wug." A second picture was then presented and the children were told "Now there's another wug. There are two of them. Now there are two . . . ?" (see figure 10.6). Even four- and five-year-old children did well with the plural forms of '*wug* words', demonstrating that the general rules for inflection have been learned by that time, despite the occurrence of occasional errors.

**Figure 10.6**
The 'wug test'

This is a wug.

Now, there's another wug.
There are two of them.
Now, there are two . . .?

Source: Jean Berko, "The Child's Learning of English Morphology," *Word* 14 (1958):150–77. Reprinted courtesy of Jean Berko Gleason.

Although inflectional overgeneralization is very noticeable in young children's speech and can last into the school years, it doesn't affect all irregular verbs all the time. In fact, preschool children seem to overregularize verbs less than 25 percent of the time at any point in development. This suggests that the overgeneralization errors observed in early speech reflect lapses in accessing the appropriate irregular form from the lexicon rather than the failure to learn irregular forms per se.

## 10.4.2 A developmental sequence

An important result of child language research during the 1970s was the discovery that the development of bound morphemes and functional categories (such as determiners and auxiliaries) takes place in an orderly fashion that is quite similar across children. In a pioneering study of three children between the ages of twenty and thirty-six months, the developmental sequence in table 10.12 was found to be typical.

| **Table 10.12** | Typical developmental sequence for non-lexical morphemes |
| --- | --- |
| 1. *-ing* | 5. past tense *-ed* |
| 2. plural *-s* | 6. third person singular *-s* |
| 3. possessive *-'s* | 7. auxiliary *be* |
| 4. *the, a* | |

An interesting feature of this developmental sequence is that it seems to be at least partly independent of the frequency with which the various morphemes occur in adult speech (see table 10.13). For example, the determiners *the* and *a* are the most frequent morphemes in the children's environment even though they are acquired relatively late.

| **Table 10.13** | Typical relative frequency of morphemes in parental speech |
| --- | --- |
| 1. *the, a* | 5. possessive *-'s* |
| 2. *-ing* | 6. third person singular *-s* |
| 3. plural *-s* | 7. past tense *-ed* |
| 4. auxiliary *be* | |

This shows that frequency by itself cannot explain developmental order, although it may have some role to play in conjunction with other factors. (It's also clear that pronunciation by itself is not decisive either, since the three -*s* morphemes are acquired at different times.) What, then, determines the order of acquisition of non-lexical categories and bound morphemes?

## Some determining factors

Research on a variety of languages suggests that several factors are involved.

1.  ***Frequent occurrence, especially in utterance-final position*** Children show a greater tendency to notice and remember elements that occur at the end of the utterance than those found in any other position.

2.  ***Syllabicity*** Children seem to take greater notice of morphemes such as *-ing*, which can constitute syllables on their own, than the plural or possessive suffix *-'s*, whose principal allomorphs (/s/ and /z/) are single consonants.

3.  ***Absence of homophony*** Whereas the word *the* functions only as a determiner in English, the suffix *-s* can be used to mark any one of three things: plural number in

nouns, third person singular in verbs, or possession. The resulting complication in the relationship between form and meaning may impede acquisition.

4. ***Few or no exceptions in the way it is used*** Whereas all singular nouns form the possessive with *-'s*, not all verbs use *-ed* to mark the past tense (*saw, read, drove*). Such exceptions hinder the language acquisition process.

5. ***Allomorphic invariance*** Whereas the affix *-ing* has the same form for all verbs, the past tense ending *-ed* has three major allomorphs—/t/ for verbs such as *chase*, /d/ for forms such as *crave* and /əd/ for verbs such as *recite*. This type of allomorphic variation, which also occurs with the plural, possessive, and third person singular affixes in English, slows morphological development.

6. ***Clearly discernible semantic function*** Whereas morphemes such as plural *-s* express easily identifiable meanings, some morphemes (such as the third person singular *-s*) make no obvious contribution to the meaning of the sentence. Acquisition of this latter type of morpheme is relatively slow.

## 10.4.3 Word formation processes

The major word formation processes in English—derivation and compounding—both emerge early in the acquisition of English. The first derivational suffixes to show up in children's speech are the ones that are most common in the adult language (see table 10.14).

| Table 10.14 | Suffixes in the speech of a child prior to age four | |
|---|---|---|
| **Ending** | **Meaning** | **Example** |
| *-er* | 'doer'* | walk<u>er</u> |
| *-ie* | 'diminutive' | dogg<u>ie</u> |
| *-ing* | 'activity' | Runn<u>ing</u> is fun. |
| *-ness* | 'state' | happi<u>ness</u> |

Note: *-er* also has an 'instrument' meaning, as in *cutter* 'something used for cutting', but this is less frequent in children's early speech.

Children as young as three demonstrate an ability to use derivation to make up names for agents and instruments when presented with questions such as the following.

> *"I've got a picture here of someone who crushes things. What could we call someone who crushes things? Someone who crushes things is called a . . . "*

> *"I've got a picture here of something that cuts things. What could we call something that cuts things? Something that cuts things is called a . . . "*

Children exhibit a propensity for forming compounds, especially of the N-N type, both in experimental settings where they are asked to make up words (e.g., "What would you call a boy who rips paper?") and in their own spontaneous speech. Some of the compounds found in the speech of three and four year olds do not follow the usual pattern for English compounds

---

**Language Matters  It Takes a While**

The full derivational system continues to develop well into the school years. Even grade 4 students have some difficulty using suffixes to recognize the category of unfamiliar words, as when they are asked which of four words best fits in a sentence such as the following:

*You can ___ the effect by turning off the lights.*

| | |
|---|---|
| intensify | intensification |
| intensity | intensive |

They have even more trouble when the possible words are made up rather than real:

*I wish Dr. Who would just ____ and get it over with.*

| | |
|---|---|
| transumpation | transumpative |
| transumpate | transumpatic |

Source: A. Tyler and W. Nagy, "The Acquisition of English Derivational Morphology," *Journal of Memory and Language* 28 (1989):649–67.

---

(e.g., *open man* for 'someone who opens things' and *cutter grass* for 'grass cutter'), but these disappear by age five. Other early compounds have the right structure, but are inappropriate because English already has words with the intended meaning (see table 10.15).

| **Table 10.15** | Some innovative compounds |
|---|---|
| **Child's word** | **Intended meaning** |
| *car-smoke* | 'exhaust' |
| *cup-egg* | 'boiled egg' |
| *firetruck-man* | 'fire fighter' |
| *plant-man* | 'gardener' |
| *store-man* | 'clerk' |

Children's creativity with compounds points to a preference for building words from other words, perhaps because this places less demand on memory than does learning an entirely new word for each concept.

Even the subtlest properties of word formation seem to be acquired in the preschool years. One such property, first discussed in section 4.3.1 of chapter 4, involves the fact that an inflectional suffix such as the plural cannot occur inside compounds (compare *dogs catcher* with *dog catcher*). In one study, children as young as three years of age produced compounds that obeyed this constraint. Thus, when asked a question such as "What do you call someone who eats cookies?" they responded by saying *cookie eater* rather than *cookies eater*.

# 10.5 Syntactic development

Like phonological and morphological development, the emergence of syntactic structure takes place in an orderly manner and reveals much about the nature of the language acquisition process. We will briefly survey some of the milestones in this developmental process here.

## 10.5.1 The one-word stage

As noted earlier, children begin to produce one-word utterances between the ages of twelve and eighteen months. A basic property of these one-word utterances is that they can be used to express the type of meaning that is associated with an entire sentence in adult speech. Thus, a child might use the word *dada* to assert 'I see Daddy', *more* to mean 'Give me more candy', and *up* to mean 'I want up'. Such utterances are called **holophrases** (literally 'whole sentences').

In forming holophrastic utterances, children seem to choose the most informative word that applies to the situation at hand. A child who wanted a candy, for example, would say *candy* rather than *want* since *candy* is more informative in this situation. Similarly, a child who notices a new doll would be more likely to say *doll* than *see*, thereby referring to the most novel feature of the situation he or she is trying to describe.

Table 10.16 lists some of the semantic relations that children commonly express during the one-word stage.

| Table 10.16 | Semantic relations in children's one-word utterances | |
|---|---|---|
| **Semantic relation** | **Utterance** | **Situation** |
| Agent of an action | *dada* | as father enters the room |
| Action or state | *down* | as child sits down |
| Theme | *door* | as father closes the door |
| Location | *here* | as child points |
| Recipient | *mama* | as child gives mother something |
| Recurrence | *again* | as child watches lighting of a match |

Comprehension appears to be considerably in advance of production in the one-word stage, and children are able to understand many multiword utterances during this period. In one experiment, for instance, learners in the one-word stage preferred to look at a depiction of Big Bird hugging Cookie Monster, rather than the reverse situation, when they heard the sentence *Big Bird is hugging Cookie Monster*.

## 10.5.2 The two-word stage

Within a few months of their first one-word utterances, children begin to produce two-word 'mini-sentences'. Table 10.17 provides a sampling of these utterances and the types of meaning

| Table 10.17 | Some patterns in children's two-word speech | |
|---|---|---|
| **Utterance** | **Intended meaning** | **Semantic relation** |
| *Baby chair* | 'The baby is sitting on the chair.' | agent-location |
| *Doggy bark* | 'The dog is barking.' | agent-action |
| *Ken water* | 'Ken is drinking water.' | agent-theme |
| *Hit doggy* | 'I hit the doggy.' | action-theme |
| *Daddy hat* | 'Daddy's hat' | possessor-possessed |

they are commonly used to express. (Although these examples are from English, similar patterns are found in the early development of all languages.)

It is unclear whether children have acquired syntactic categories such as noun, verb, and adjective at this point in their development. This is because the markers that help distinguish among syntactic categories in adult English (e.g., inflection such as the past tense suffix and functional categories such as determiners and auxiliary verbs) are absent during this period. To complicate matters still further, the relative shortness of the utterances produced during the two-word stage means that the positional differences associated with category distinctions in adult speech are often not manifested. Thus, words such as *busy* (an adjective in adult speech) and *push* (a verb) may appear in identical patterns.

(5)  Mommy busy.
     Mommy push.

While this does not show that children lack syntactic categories, it makes it difficult to demonstrate that they possess them. For this reason, researchers are split over whether to describe children's utterances in terms of the semantic relations that they express (as illustrated in table 10.17) or in terms of the syntactic categories of adult speech.

A notable feature of children's two-word utterances is that they almost always exhibit the appropriate word order. This suggests a very early sensitivity to this feature of sentence structure, but there is reason to believe that children do not initially have a general word order rule. Rather, they may have a separate rule for each verb (e.g., 'Put the subject in front of *push*'; 'Put the subject in front of *read*'; and so on). In one experiment, for instance, children aged two to four were taught made-up verbs (such as *tam*, *gop*, and *dack*) for novel actions involving puppet characters. Each verb was presented in one of the following orders:

(6)  *subject-verb-object order*: Elmo tammed the apple.
     *subject-object-verb order*: Elmo the apple gopped.
     *verb-subject-object order*: Dacked apple the Elmo.

The two- and three-year-old children were willing to learn word order patterns not found in English and would often employ the subject-object-verb and verb-subject-object order for new verbs if that was what they had been exposed to. In contrast, the four year olds used the subject-verb-object order regardless of what the experimenter had said, which suggests that they had acquired a general word order rule for English that they automatically extended to new verbs.

## 10.5.3 The telegraphic stage

After a period of several months, during which their speech is largely limited to one- and two-word utterances, children begin to produce longer and more complex grammatical structures. As illustrated in example (7), a defining feature of these patterns is the frequent absence of bound morphemes and non-lexical categories.

(7)  Chair broken.
     Daddy like book.
     What her name?
     Man ride bus today.
     Car make noise.
     Me wanna show Mommy.
     I good boy.

Such speech is often dubbed **telegraphic**, thanks to its resemblance to the clipped style of language found in the now defunct telegram (a pre-email form of communication that required paying by the word).

Although it is certainly true that many important morphemes are missing from children's early speech, these items do not go entirely unnoticed. As noted in section 10.1.3, for instance, children as young as seventeen months can infer from the presence or absence of a determiner whether a novel word refers to a type of object (e.g., a doll) or to a particular object. Eighteen month olds listen longer to a passage containing an *is* + *V-ing* pattern (e.g., *she is playing*) than to one containing ungrammatical *she can playing*. And infants as young as eleven months of age are surprised when *a* or *the* is replaced by a nonsense syllable, or when it is used in the wrong place, as in *book the*.

The telegraphic stage is characterized by the emergence of quite elaborate types of phrase structure. As the examples in (7) help show, children can form phrases consisting of a head and a complement (*like book, ride bus, show mommy*), phrases that include a modifier (such as *today* and *good*), and even full-fledged sentences.

| **Table 10.18** | The development of phrase structure | |
|---|---|---|
| **Stage** | **Approx. age** | **Developments** |
| Holophrastic | 1–1.5 yrs. | single word utterances; no structure |
| Two-word | 1.5–2 yrs. | early word combinations; presence of syntactic categories unclear |
| Telegraphic | 2–2.5 yrs. | emergence of phrase structure, especially head-complement and subject-VP patterns |

Language development from this point onward is rapid. As the examples in table 10.19 on page 357 illustrate, in a matter of just a few months children move from relatively primitive two- and three-word utterances at the beginning of the telegraphic stage to a broad range of morphologically and syntactically intricate sentence types.

## 10.5.4 Later development

In the months following the telegraphic stage, children continue to acquire the complex grammar that underlies adult linguistic competence, including the Move operations outlined in chapter 5.

### Inversion

In the very early stages of language acquisition, children signal *yes-no* questions by means of rising intonation alone. (Recall that auxiliary verbs are a relatively late development.)

(8) See hole?
    I ride train?
    Ball go?
    Sit chair?

Even after individual auxiliary verbs appear in statements in child language, there is often a delay of a few months before they appear at the beginning of the sentence in *yes-no*

| Table 10.19 | Sample utterances from a child's speech over a 12-month period |
|---|---|
| **Age** | **Sample utterances** |
| 28 mos. | Play checkers.<br>Big drum.<br>I got horn.<br>A bunny-rabbit walk. |
| 30 mos. | Write a piece of paper.<br>What that egg doing?<br>I lost a shoe.<br>No, I don't want to sit seat. |
| 32 mos. | Let me get down with the boots on.<br>Don't be afraid of horses.<br>How tiger be so healthy and fly like kite?<br>Joshua throw like penguin. |
| 34 mos. | Look at that train Ursula brought.<br>I simply don't want put in chair.<br>Don't have paper.<br>Do you want little bit, Cromer?<br>I can't wear it tomorrow. |
| 36 mos. | I going come in fourteen minutes.<br>I going wear that to wedding.<br>I see what happens.<br>I have to save them now.<br>Those are not strong mens.<br>They are going sleep in wintertime.<br>You dress me up like a baby elephant. |
| 38 mos. | So it can't be cleaned?<br>I broke my racing car.<br>Do you know the lights went off?<br>What happened to the bridge?<br>Can I put my head in the mailbox so the mailman can know where<br>    I are and put me in the mailbox? |

Source: Steven Pinker, *The Language Instinct* (New York: Morrow, 1994), pp. 269–70. Copyright © 1994 by Steven Pinker. Reprinted by permission of HarperCollins Publishers.

questions. In one study, for example, a young boy began using the auxiliary verb *can* at age two years, five months, but he did not use it in inversion patterns until six months later.

An interesting—but infrequent—error in children's early use of Inversion in both *yes-no* and *wh* questions is exemplified in (9).

(9) *Can* he *can* look?
What *shall* we *shall* have?
*Did* you *did* came home?

In these sentences, the auxiliary verb occurs twice—once to the left of the subject (in the position that it occupies after Inversion) and once to the right (in the position it occupies in deep structure). It has been suggested that this pattern reflects an error in the application of the Inversion transformation in that a copy of the moved auxiliary is left behind in its original position.

## Wh questions

*Wh* questions emerge gradually between the ages of two and four. The first *wh* words to be acquired are typically *what* and *where*, followed by *who, how,* and *why; when, which,* and *whose* are relatively late acquisitions.

(10) Where that?
What me think?
Why you smiling?
Why not me drink it?

With the acquisition of auxiliary verbs, Inversion becomes possible. Interestingly, some children appear to find it easier to carry out the Inversion operation in *yes-no* questions, where it is the only Move operation, than in *wh* questions, where *Wh* Movement must also apply. (For some reason, this is especially true in the case of *why* questions.) The following examples from children's speech all show the effects of applying *Wh* Movement without Inversion.

(11) What I did yesterday?
Where I should sleep?
Why that boy is looking at us?
Why she doesn't like bananas?
Why unicorns are pretend?

## 10.5.5 The interpretation of sentence structure

As noted in chapter 6, the interpretation of sentences draws heavily on various features of syntactic structure. In this section we will briefly consider some aspects of the acquisition of two interpretive phenomena that rely on information about syntactic structure.

## Passives

Children learning English are able to associate thematic roles with particular structural positions at a very early point in the acquisition process. By the time their average utterance length is two words, they are able to respond correctly about 75 percent of the time to comprehension tests involving simple active sentences such as (12), in which *the truck* is the agent and *the car* is the theme.

(12) The truck bumped the car.

However, children find it much harder to interpret certain other types of sentences correctly. This is especially true for passive sentences such as the one in (13), which contains no semantic clues about which NP is agent and which one is theme. (Note that it makes just as much sense for the car to bump the truck as it does for the truck to bump the car. Such sentences are said to be 'reversible'.)

(13)  The car was bumped by the truck.

Although children produce passive sentences in their own speech from around age three, they have continuing difficulty responding appropriately to passive constructions in comprehension tests (see table 10.20).

| Table 10.20 | Accurate interpretation of reversible passive constructions |
| --- | --- |
| **Group** | **Percentage correct** |
| Nursery School | 20 |
| Kindergarten | 35 |
| Grade 1 | 48 |
| Grade 2 | 63 |
| Grade 3 | 88 |

Why should this be so? One possibility is that children expect the first NP in a sentence to bear the agent role and the second NP to bear the theme role. This is sometimes called the **Canonical Sentence Strategy** (see figure 10.7).

**Figure 10.7**
The Canonical Sentence Strategy

NP  …  V  …  NP  is interpreted as:
*agent – action – theme*

The Canonical Sentence Strategy works for active, transitive sentences, but not for passive sentences, where the first NP is the theme and the second NP is the agent.

(14)  Active sentence:   The truck bumped the car.
　　　　　　　　　　　　*agent*　　　　　　*theme -*

　　　Passive sentence:   The car was bumped by the truck.
　　　　　　　　　　　　　*theme*　　　　　　　　*agent*

Children employing this strategy treat the first NP in passive sentences as the agent and the second NP as the theme, so they think the car bumps the truck.

As the data in table 10.20 show, this strategy is applied much less consistently by first graders, who have evidently begun to realize that there is no simple correlation between linear position and thematic roles. A year or so later, children's scores start to rise dramatically, indicating that they have come to recognize the special properties of the passive construction.

## Pronominals and reflexives

In chapter 6, we saw that a reflexive pronoun (*myself, himself, herself,* and so on) must have a 'higher' (i.e., c-commanding) antecedent in the minimal clause containing it.

(15)  *a.* Reflexive pronoun with a higher antecedent in the same clause
　　　　　 I hurt *myself* with the stapler.

　　　 *b.* Reflexive pronoun without a higher antecedent in the same clause
　　　　　 *You hurt *myself* with the stapler.

In contrast, a pronominal (*me*, *him*, *her*) cannot have a higher antecedent in the same minimal clause.

(16) *a.* Pronominal with a higher antecedent in the same clause
  *I hurt *me* with the stapler.

  *b.* Pronominal without a higher antecedent in the same clause
  You hurt *me* with the stapler.

Despite the abstractness of these principles, children appear not to have trouble distinguishing between pronominals and reflexive pronouns in their own speech. In one study of the use of *me* and *myself* in speech transcripts from three children aged two to five, researchers found a few errors of the following type.

(17) *Sample pronoun errors:*
  Mistake involving *me*: I see *me*. (Adam, age 34 mos., looking through a telescope)

  Mistake involving *myself*: Don't you drop me . . . you hurt *myself*. (Abe, age 34 mos.)

Overall though, the children misused *me* only about 5 percent of the time and made mistakes on *myself* less than 1 percent of the time. We will return to this point in section 10.6.4.

## 10.6 What makes language acquisition possible?

In the preceding sections, we have seen that the language acquisition process extends over a period of several years. It is relatively easy to describe what takes place during these years, but it is much more difficult to explain *how* it happens. The sections that follow focus on some of the factors that may contribute to an eventual understanding of how the language acquisition process works.

## 10.6.1 The role of adult speech

Popular opinion holds that children learn language simply by imitating the speech of those around them. This cannot be right, however. Not only do children tend not to repeat the speech of others, but they are typically unable to imitate structures that they have not yet learned. For instance, a child who has not yet acquired the Inversion operation will imitate sentence (18a) by producing (18b).

(18) *a. Model sentence*: Why can't kitty stand up?
  *b. Child's imitation*: Why kitty can't stand up?

A child's own grammar, not the model provided by adult speech, determines what she or he will say at any given point of development.

Of course, language learners must be sensitive in some way to the language in their environment. After all, children who are exposed to English learn to speak English, those exposed to Cree learn Cree, and so forth. It seems, though, that the relationship between input (the language children hear) and acquisition is subtler and more complicated than one might think.

### Caregiver speech

A good deal of work has been devoted to the search for a possible relationship between language acquisition and the type of speech that is typically addressed to young language learners. Such speech is often called **motherese** or **caregiver speech**. Table 10.21 summarizes the principal features of the caregiver speech used by middle-class English-speaking mothers with their children.

| Table 10.21 Some features of English caregiver speech |
|---|
| **Phonetic** |
| Slow, carefully articulated speech<br>Higher pitch<br>Exaggerated intonation and stress<br>Longer pauses |
| **Lexical and semantic** |
| More restricted vocabulary<br>Concrete reference to the here and now |
| **Syntactic** |
| Few incomplete sentences<br>Short sentences<br>More imperatives and questions |
| **Conversational** |
| More repetitions<br>Few utterances per conversational turn |

Caregiver speech could be helpful to children in various ways. For example, exposure to slow, carefully articulated speech may make it easier for children to pick out words and to learn their pronunciation. (Remember that sentences consist of a continuous stream of speech sounds; there are no pauses between words.) Moreover, the acquisition of meaning may be facilitated by the fact that maternal speech tends to concentrate on the here and now, especially the child's surroundings, activities, and needs. The examples in table 10.22 help illustrate this.

| Table 10.22 Some examples of maternal speech | |
|---|---|
| **Mother's utterance** | **Context** |
| *That's right, pick up the blocks.* | the child is picking up a box of building blocks |
| *That's a puppy.* | the child is looking at a young dog |
| *The puppy's in the basket.* | the child is examining a puppy in a basket |

Exposure to language of this type may well make it easier to match morphemes, words, and phrases with meanings—a major part of the language acquisition process.

Although potentially *helpful*, caregiver speech may not actually be *necessary* to the language acquisition process. In Western Samoa, for instance, speech to children is not simplified in the way it often is in North America, and mothers do not try to reformulate their children's unintelligible speech or make any special attempt to understand it. Yet Samoan children have no trouble learning Samoan. Evidently, the speech style typical of middle-class mothers in North America is not essential for language acquisition.

Moreover, even in cultures where it is common, caregiver speech seems to have very selective effects on child language. For instance, the number of *yes-no* questions in maternal speech seems to be correlated with the rate at which auxiliary verbs develop—apparently because auxiliaries occur in the salient sentence-initial position in *yes-no* questions (*Can Jennifer go?*). At the same time, though, many other features of maternal speech seem *not* to affect child language. As we saw earlier (in section 10.3.1), for example, the relative frequency of bound morphemes and non-lexical categories in maternal speech apparently does not determine their order of acquisition.

In and of itself, then, caregiver speech cannot explain how language acquisition occurs. However, research into this subject may contribute to this goal in less direct ways by helping determine the types of linguistic experience that are most valuable to children. This in turn could help linguists identify the types of mechanisms and strategies involved in language acquisition.

## 10.6.2 The role of feedback

It is sometimes suggested that parents help their children learn language by correcting their 'mistakes'. However, studies of actual interactions between parents and children point in a quite different direction. In general, parents tend to be more concerned with the truth of children's utterances than with their grammaticality—one transcript of a parent-child conversation includes *That's right* as a response to the grammatical monstrosity *Mama isn't boy, he's a girl!*

Moreover, even when adults do attempt to correct children's grammatical errors, their efforts often have little effect. The following exchange between a child and his father is typical in this regard.

(19) *Child*:   Want other one spoon, daddy.
  *Father*:   You mean, you want the other spoon.
  *Child*:   Yes, I want other one spoon, please Daddy.
  *Father*:   Can you say "the other spoon"?
  *Child*:   other . . . one . . . spoon.
  *Father*:   Say "other."
  *Child*:   other.
  *Father*:   "spoon."
  *Child*:   spoon.
  *Father*:   "other spoon."
  *Child*:   other . . . spoon. Now give me other one spoon?

Interestingly, however, some research suggests that subtler forms of feedback may have a role to play in the language acquisition process.

### Recasts

Adults often respond to a child's utterance by repeating it, making adjustments to its form and/or content. (Responses of this sort are called **recasts**.)

(20) *Child*:  Daddy here.
     *Mother*:  Yes, Daddy is here.
     *Child*:  Him go.
     *Mother*:  Yes, he is going.
     *Child*:  Boy chasing dog.
     *Mother*:  Yes, the boy is chasing the dog.
     *Child*:  The dog is barking.
     *Mother*:  Yes, he is barking at the kitty.

Recasts provide children with potentially useful information—adding a missing verb (*is* in the first example), changing the form of a pronoun (*him* to *he* in the second example), and so on. On the other hand, parents sometimes modify their children's grammatical utterances too (as in the final example), so recasts also have the potential to be misleading.

It is not yet clear what role recasts play in language learning, and studies to date have yielded conflicting results. For instance, a study of the acquisition of *the* and *a* by three children revealed no link between the frequency of recasts and the rate at which their use of determiners increased—no matter how many recasts children heard, it didn't seem to speed up their learning.

On the other hand, a quite different result emerged from an experiment in which four and five year olds were taught made-up verbs that have irregular past tense forms—for example, *pell* (with *pold* as its past tense). When the children first learned what the verbs meant (they were linked to various funny actions, such as hitting someone with a beanbag attached to a string), they heard only the '-*ing*' forms ('This is called *pelling*'). They therefore had no idea what the past tense forms should be. Just hearing an adult use *pold* to refer to a past pelling action had little or no effect, but being allowed to make 'mistakes' such as *pelled* and then hearing an adult recast the sentence using *pold* had a major impact. In fact, a single recast was often enough to permit learning of the irregular form, which suggests that certain types of feedback have a role to play in the language acquisition process after all.

## 10.6.3 The role of cognitive development

Because there are dramatic changes in both linguistic and non-linguistic abilities during the first years of life, it is tempting to think that the two are somehow linked. Yet, there is considerable evidence to suggest that language acquisition is to a large extent independent of other types of cognitive development. One such piece of evidence comes from the study of individuals whose general cognitive development is deficient but whose language is highly developed. For example, Rick, a severely retarded fifteen year old, performed so poorly on a variety of non-linguistic tasks that his general cognitive level was estimated to be that of a preschool child. Yet, as the following examples illustrate, his speech manifests considerable syntactic and morphological sophistication—with appropriate use of affixes, non-lexical categories, and word order.

(21) She must've got me up and thrown me out of bed.
    She keeps both of the ribbons on her hair.
    If they get in trouble, they'd have a pillow fight.
    She's the one that walks back and forth to school.
    I wanna hear one more just for a change.

> ## Language Matters  **A Linguistic Savant**
>
> A particularly celebrated case of a dissociation between language and cognitive development involves Christopher. Now an adult, Christopher can read, write, and communicate in about twenty languages (including English, Danish, Dutch, Finnish, French, German, Modern Greek, Hindi, Italian, Norwegian, Polish, Portuguese, Russian, Spanish, Swedish, Turkish, and Welsh). He learned some of these languages as a child (based on minimal exposure) and taught himself others as an adolescent and adult, often with amazing speed, as the following account of his encounter with Dutch illustrates.
>
> > In March . . . , shortly before he was due to appear on Dutch television, it was suggested that he might spend a couple of days improving his rather rudimentary Dutch with the aid of a grammar and dictionary. He did so to such good effect that he was able to converse in Dutch—with facility if not total fluency—both before and during the programme (p. 18).
>
> Christopher has a non-verbal IQ (depending on the test) of between 56 and 76, and a mental age of 9.2. He has trouble with addition (he can handle simple cases such as 12 + 13, but not 'carrying over' as in 14 + 19); he is very bad at drawing; and he can't figure out how tic-tac-toe works. He is unable to care for himself and lives in a home for adults with special needs.
>
> Source: Neil Smith and Ianthi-Maria Tsimpli, *The Mind of a Savant* (Oxford: Blackwell, 1995). Reproduced by permission of Blackwell Publishing.

On the other hand, there are also documented cases of people whose IQ is within the normal range but who nonetheless have great difficulty with inflection for the past tense and plural, as illustrated by the examples in (22). (There is reason to believe that this particular disorder is inherited.)

(22)  The boys eat four cookie.
       It's a flying finches, they are.
       The neighbours phone the ambulance because the man fall of the tree.

Case studies such as these suggest that certain aspects of language (in particular, morphology and syntax) are independent of non-linguistic types of cognitive development. This in turn implies that the mental mechanisms responsible for the acquisition of those parts of the grammar are relatively autonomous and that their operation neither follows from nor guarantees general cognitive development.

## 10.6.4  The role of inborn knowledge

There can be no doubt that there is something special about the human mind that equips it to acquire language. The only real question has to do with precisely what that special thing is.

A very influential view among linguists is that children are born with prior knowledge of the type of categories, operations, and principles that are found in the grammar of any human language. They therefore know, for example, that the words in the language they are acquiring will belong to a small set of syntactic categories (N, V, and so on) and that they can be combined in particular ways to create larger phrases (NP, VP, IP, etc.). The set of inborn categories, operations, and principles common to all human languages makes up Universal Grammar (UG), first mentioned in chapter 5.

The view that certain grammatical knowledge is inborn is known as **nativism**. Although nativism has roots in philosophy that date back thousands of years, its popularity in linguistics is due largely to the influence of Noam Chomsky, a linguist at the Massachusetts Institute of Technology. Chomsky's basic claim is that the grammars for human language are too complex and abstract to be learned on the basis of the type of experience to which children have access. Therefore, he argues, significant components of the grammar must be inborn. To illustrate this, we must consider a relatively complex example involving the notion of c-command introduced in chapter 6 (section 6.3.3).

## Principle A

The interpretation of pronouns such as *himself* and *him* is regulated by the following two principles.

(23) *Principle A*
A reflexive pronoun must have an antecedent that c-commands it in the same minimal IP.

*Principle B*
A pronominal must not have an antecedent that c-commands it in the same minimal IP.

These principles have played an important role in the study of language acquisition, and three arguments have been put forward in support of the claim that they are inborn.

First, the notion of c-command is quite abstract. It is not the type of concept that we would expect young children to discover simply by listening to sentences. Since we also know that no one teaches them about c-command, it makes sense to think that this notion is inborn and therefore does not have to be discovered or taught.

Second, the c-command relation seems to be universally relevant to pronoun interpretation. Thus, there appears to be no language in which the equivalent of English *himself* can refer to the boy rather than the boy's father in sentences such as the following (see chapter 6 for discussion).

(24) The boy's father overestimates himself.

The universality of this restriction would be explained if Principles A and B were innate and hence part of the inborn linguistic knowledge of all human beings.

Third, as we saw earlier in this chapter, Principles A and B seem to be available to children from a very early stage in their development—even three year olds appear to have mastered the distinction between reflexives and pronominals in their own speech (although they do sometimes make mistakes in comprehension). Given the complexity of these principles, this provides additional evidence for the claim that they are inborn.

## Parameters

Of course, not every feature of a language's grammar can be inborn. Its vocabulary and morphology must be learned, and so must at least part of its syntax. In the case of phrase structure, for example, UG stipulates that an X' constituent can include a head and its complements, but it does not specify the relative order of these elements. This differs from language to language, so that a child acquiring English must learn that heads precede their complements, whereas a child acquiring Japanese must learn the reverse order. UG includes a parameter for word order that offers a choice between head-initial and head-final order. (We ignore the positioning of specifiers for the purposes of the illustration in table 10.23.)

| **Table 10.23**   The word order parameter | |
| --- | --- |
| **Stipulated by UG** | **Resulting options** |
| X' consists of X and a complement | X–Complement order [head-initial] Complement–X order [head-final] |

There are also phonological parameters: for example, languages can differ from each other in terms of whether they allow two or more consonants in the onset of a syllable—English does (e.g., *gleam, sprint*), whereas Japanese does not.

Thus, part of the language acquisition process involves **parameter setting**—that is, determining which of the options permitted by a particular parameter is appropriate for the language being learned.

## 10.6.5 Is there a critical period?

One of the most intriguing issues in the study of language acquisition has to do with the possibility that normal linguistic development is possible only if children are exposed to language during a particular time frame or **critical period**. Evidence for the existence of such a period comes from the study of individuals who do not experience language during the early part of their lives.

One such individual is the much-discussed Genie, who was kept in a small room with virtually no opportunity to hear human speech from around age two to age thirteen. After many years of therapy and care, Genie's non-linguistic cognitive functioning was described as 'relatively normal' and her lexical and semantic abilities as 'good'. In terms of syntax and morphology, however, many problems remained, as evidenced in the sample utterances in table 10.24.

| **Table 10.24**   Some of Genie's utterances | |
| --- | --- |
| **Utterance** | **Meaning** |
| *Applesauce buy store* | 'Buy applesauce at the store.' |
| *Man motorcycle have* | 'The man has a motorcycle.' |
| *Want go ride Miss F. car* | 'I want to go for a ride in Miss F.'s car.' |
| *Genie have full stomach* | 'I have a full stomach.' |
| *Mama have baby grow up* | 'Mama has a baby who grew up.' |

As these examples show, Genie makes word order errors (the first two examples) and her speech does not contain non-lexical categories or affixes.

Another revealing case study involved Chelsea, a deaf child who was misdiagnosed as retarded and emotionally disturbed. Chelsea grew up without language and was not exposed to speech until the age of thirty-one, when she was finally fitted with hearing aids. After intensive therapy, she is able to hold a job and to live independently. However, her vocabulary consists of only 2000 words and her sentences are badly formed, as the following examples help show.

(25)   The woman is bus the going.
       Combing hair the boy.
       Orange Tim car in.
       The girl is gone the ice cream shopping buying the man.

Based on case studies such as these, it is now widely believed that the ability to acquire a first language in an effortless and ultimately successful way begins to decline from age six and is severely compromised by the onset of puberty.

# Summing up

This chapter has been concerned with the problem of how children acquire the **grammar** of their first language. Research in this area deals with two major issues: the nature of the developmental sequence leading to the emergence of mature linguistic competence in the areas of phonology, vocabulary, morphology, and syntax, and the factors that make it possible for children to acquire a complex grammar. A number of factors may contribute to the child's acquisition of language, including the properties of **caregiver speech**, **recasts**, and inborn linguistic knowledge (**Universal Grammar**). We look to future research for deeper insights into the precise role of these and other factors.

## Recommended reading

Bloom, Paul. 2002. *How Children Learn the Meanings of Words*. Cambridge, MA: MIT Press.

Clark, Eve. 1993. *The Lexicon in Acquisition*. New York: Cambridge University Press.

Clark, Eve. 2002. *First Language Acquisition*. New York: Cambridge University Press.

Gallaway, Clare, and Brian Richards. 1994. *Input and Interaction in Language Acquisition*. New York: Cambridge University Press.

Lust, Barbara. 2006. *Child Language: Acquisition and Growth*. Cambridge, UK: Cambridge University Press.

O'Grady, William. 2005. *How Children Learn Language*. Cambridge, UK: Cambridge University Press.

Piattelli-Palmarini, Massimo, ed. 1980. *Language and Learning: The Debate between Jean Piaget and Noam Chomsky*. Cambridge, MA: Harvard University Press.

Vihman, Marilyn. 1996. *Phonological Development: The Origins of Language in the Child*. Cambridge, MA: Blackwell.

## Exercises

1. One piece of evidence that children acquire a grammar is their production of over-regularized past tense forms such as *doed*, *leaved*, and *goed*. Based on this model, what type of evidence should we look for in order to show that children have acquired the rule that creates 'comparative' forms such as *bigger*, *richer*, and *taller*? (Hint: Think about adjectives that have irregular comparative forms in the adult language.)

2. In one naturalistic study, a search for passive structures in a sample of 18 000 utterances from sixty children yielded only nineteen examples produced by twelve of the children.
   a) Does this mean that the other forty-eight children had not yet learned the passive structure?
   b) How are the disadvantages of the naturalistic method exemplified here?

3. The following transcriptions represent the pronunciation of a two-year-old child. Indicate which phonetic processes have applied in each case.

   | | | | | | | |
   |---|---|---|---|---|---|---|
   | a) | skin | [kɪd] | h) | tent | [dɛt] |
   | b) | spoon | [bun] | i) | teddy | [dɛdi] |
   | c) | zoo | [du] | j) | brush | [bʌt] |
   | d) | John | [dɑn] | k) | bump | [bʌp] |
   | e) | bath | [bæt] | l) | play | [pwej] |
   | f) | other | [ʌdə] | m) | breakfast | [brɛkpəst] |
   | g) | Smith | [mɪt] | | | |

4. Drawing on the phonetic processes posited for the preceding exercise, predict one or more plausible immature pronunciations for each of the following words.
   a) show          e) juice
   b) please        f) thumb
   c) spit          g) zoo
   d) under         h) ring

5. Consider the following examples of overextensions, all of which have actually been observed in children's speech. What is the apparent basis for each of these overextensions?

   | | Word | First Referent | Overextensions |
   |---|---|---|---|
   | a) | sch | sound of a train | music, noise of wheels, sound of rain |
   | b) | bow-wow | dog | sheep, rabbit fur, puppet |
   | c) | baby | baby | people in pictures |
   | d) | sizo | scissors | nail file, knife, screwdriver, spoon |
   | e) | policeman | policeman | mailman, sailor, doctor |
   | f) | strawberry | strawberry | grapes, raspberry |
   | g) | fireworks | fireworks | matches, light, cigarette |
   | h) | Batman | Batman logo on a T-shirt | any logo on a T-shirt |

6. Since children have a tendency to focus on the prototypical members of categories in the acquisition of words, how might you expect children to underextend the following words? What members of the category might you expect children not to include?
   a) bird
   b) pet
   c) toy

**7.** The allomorphic variation associated with the 3rd person singular verbal ending -*s* is identical to that found with plural -*s*.

    a)  Make up a test parallel to the '*wug* test' discussed in section 10.4.1.

    b)  If possible, give your test to children between the ages of three and seven. Are your results similar to the ones discussed in the chapter?

**8.** Based on the discussion in section 10.4.2 about the developmental sequence of morpheme acquisition, consider the acquisition in other languages of the morphemes corresponding to those listed in table 10.12. Would you predict that these morphemes would be acquired in exactly the same order as their English equivalents? Why or why not?

**9.** Considering children's tendency to overgeneralize morphological rules, what might we expect a young child to use in the place of the following adult words? Justify your choice in each case.

    a)  fish (plural)

    b)  went

    c)  mice

    d)  ate

    e)  has

    f)  geese

    g)  brought

    h)  hit (past tense)

    i)  himself

    j)  women

**10.** Each of the following utterances is from the speech of a child in the two-word stage. Identify the semantic relation expressed by each of these utterances.

| *Intended meaning* | *Child's utterance* |
| --- | --- |
| a) Jimmy is swimming. | Jimmy swim. |
| b) Ken's book | Ken book |
| c) Daddy is at his office. | Daddy office |
| d) You push the baby. | push baby |
| e) Mommy is reading. | Mommy read |

**11.** Consider the following data from Jordie, a two-and-a-half-year-old child, in light of the list of morphemes in table 10.12.

| *Intended meaning* | *Jordie's utterance* |
| --- | --- |
| a) Where's my blanket? | Where my blanket? |
| b) Does it go right here, Mommy? | Go right here, Mommy? |
| c) It's running over. | Running over. |
| d) Here, it goes here. | Here, go here. |
| e) No, that's mine. | No, that mine. |
| f) Dinosaurs say gronk. | Dinosaur say gronk. |
| g) There's more. | There more. |

    **i)**  Which of the morphemes in table 10.12 are missing in Jordie's sentences but present in the equivalent adult utterance?

    **ii)**  List the morphemes that are present in both the adult interpretations and in Jordie's speech.

**12.** Now consider the following utterances from a child named Krista.

| *Intended meaning* | *Krista's utterance* |
|---|---|
| a) My name is Krista. | Mine name Krista. |
| b) My last name is Pegit. | Last name Pegit. |
| c) The tape is right there. | Tape right there. |
| d) Daddy's book | Daddy book. |
| e) I've got a book. | I'm got a book |
| f) Read me a story. | Read me story. |
| g) I'll do it. | I'm do it. |
| h) He went outside. | He went outside. |
| i) Open the gate, please. | Open a gate, please. |
| j) Gramma's house. | Gramma's house. |
| k) Smell the flowers. | Smell flowers. |
| l) Shoes on. | Shoes on. |
| m) The wee boy fell down. | Wee boy fell down. |
| n) That's my ball. | That's mines ball. |

  **i)** Which morphemes are missing in Krista's speech, but present in the adult interpretations?

  **ii)** Krista uses the past tense twice in the above utterances. Do you think this is evidence that she has acquired the past tense morpheme? Why or why not?

  **iii)** Comment on Krista's difficulty with possessive pronouns.

  **iv)** Do you think she has acquired possessive -'s? Why or why not?

**13.** The following utterances were produced spontaneously by Holly, age three years.

a) I learned about loving moms.
b) Put him in the bathtub.
c) We eated gummy snakes.
d) Thank you for giving these books us.
e) I don't know.
f) He bited my finger. (When corrected, she said: He bitted my finger.)
g) I runned in the water.
h) I rided on a elephant.

  **i)** Has Holly acquired the past tense morpheme? How do you know?

  **ii)** What is the evidence in Holly's speech that she has learned phrases that consist of a head, a complement, and/or a specifier?

  **iii)** What is the evidence that she has acquired the category noun? the category verb?

**14.** It has been reported that hearing children growing up in homes with non-speaking deaf parents cannot learn spoken language from radio or even television (see p. 278 of *The Language Instinct* by S. Pinker [New York: Morrow, 1994]).

  **i)** Can you think of any reasons for this?

  **ii)** What are the implications of these findings for our understanding of the type of experience that is required for language acquisition?

# *Eleven*

John Archibald

# *Second language acquisition*

*When we talk about acquisition in SLA research, we are not talking about acquisition in the sense that one acquires polo ponies, Lladró figurines, or CBS, but rather in the sense that one acquires vicious habits, a taste for Brie, or a potbelly.*

KEVIN R. GREGG

The field of **second language acquisition** (SLA) research investigates how people attain proficiency in a language that is not their mother tongue. Whether we are looking at someone learning to read Greek in university, or someone becoming fluent in a fifth language in their forties, or a child acquiring a new language after moving to a new country, we refer to it as second language acquisition. The interesting phenomenon of children simultaneously acquiring two languages is generally investigated in the field known as **bilingualism** (which may be thought of as a subdiscipline of SLA research). In this chapter, we will primarily be concerned with second language acquisition in adults.

Over the years, the study of second language acquisition has been undertaken from a variety of different perspectives. In the 1950s and 1960s the primary objective was pedagogic. Researchers were interested in trying to improve the way in which second languages were taught. Therefore, they were interested in discovering how those languages were learned. From the 1970s on, the focus shifted from the teacher to the learner and the field of L2 instruction became somewhat separate.

The reason for this has something to do with what was going on in linguistics, psychology, and first language acquisition research. All three of these areas shifted focus from the external to the internal in the 1960s. Linguistics became concerned with the mental grammar of the speaker, not just the description of the linguistic structures of a given language. Psychology shifted from behaviourism (which denied the importance of mental representations) to cognitive psychology, and research on first language acquisition focused on children's internal grammars. These fields are also crucial to the study of SLA. Linguistics gives us a sophisticated and accurate description of what people are trying to learn (the second language), and what they already know (the first language). Psychology can provide us with a learning theory to account for how people acquire knowledge. Finally, the field of first language acquisition (which has been around longer than the field of second language acquisition) offers various findings that can be productively applied to SLA. For example, we know that children who are acquiring their first language (L1) have grammars that are systematic and that their utterances are not just bad imitations of the adult target. As we will see, second language learners, too, are developing a grammar that is systematic even if it is not nativelike.

# 11.1 The study of second language acquisition

In the case of first language acquisition, we may ascribe the difference between child and adult grammars to either cognitive or biological immaturity in the child. In the case of second language learning by adults, however, we cannot say that the learners are either cognitively or biologically immature. Rather, they are subject to an influence that is absent from the child's situation: the first language itself. Let us diagram the situation as shown in figure 11.1.

| **Figure 11.1**<br>Influences on an inter-<br>language grammar | L1 → Interlanguage Grammar ← L2 |

This diagram illustrates the fact that second language learners have a systematic **interlanguage** (IL) grammar—so called because it is a system of mental representations influenced by both the first and the second language and has features of each.

| **Table 11.1**   Phonological transfer | | |
|---|---|---|
| **English target** | **French speaker** | **German speaker** |
| have [hæv] | [æv] | [hæf] |

The form in table 11.1 produced by the French speakers reflects the fact that French lacks the phoneme /h/ while the pronunciation associated with German speakers can be traced to the fact that German includes a rule of Syllable Final Obstruent Devoicing (which changes the [v] to a [f]). The term **transfer** is used to describe the process whereby a feature or rule from a learner's first language is carried over to the IL grammar. Other examples can be seen in table 11.2.

| **Table 11.2**   More phonological transfer | | | |
|---|---|---|---|
| **L1** | **L2** | **Example** | **Comment** |
| Spanish | English | I espeak Espanish. | Spanish does not allow s + consonant sequences word-initially. |
| English | French | [ty] (you) → [tu] | English does not have the front, rounded vowel [y]. The English speaker substitutes the [u] sound. |
| Quebec French | English | Over dere. | The [ð] sound is replaced by [d]. |
| European French | English | Over zere. | The [ð] sound is replaced by [z]. |
| English | Spanish | [paɾa] 'for' → [para] | As English does not have the tapped [ɾ], an [r] is substituted. |

## 11.1.1 The role of the first language

One of the most easily recognizable traits of a second language learner's speech is that it bears a certain resemblance to the first language. Thus, someone whose first language is French is likely to sound different from someone whose first language is German when they both speak English. Consider in this regard the typical pronunciation of the English word *have* by speakers of French and German shown in table 11.1.

## 11.1.2 The nature of an interlanguage

The first language is not the only influence on the interlanguage grammar, since some properties of the IL can be traced to aspects of the L2. In the case of a German speaker who is learning English, for example, the IL grammar will contain some features of both German and English. Consider how a German speaker learning Canadian English might pronounce the word *eyes*. As illustrated in table 11.3, the learner first applies the rule of Syllable Final Obstruent Devoicing (transferred from German), changing /ajz/ to [ajs]. But the learner also has acquired some knowledge of the target language—in this case, the rule of Canadian Vowel Raising (discussed in chapter 3)—that states that [aj] becomes [ʌj] before a voiceless consonant in the same syllable. Thanks to application of the Syllable Final Obstruent Devoicing Rule, the input form now ends in a voiceless consonant ([s]), which triggers Canadian Raising.

| **Table 11.3** | One possible pronunciation of the English word *eyes* by a German-speaking learner | |
|---|---|---|
| **Target form** | **Result of Final Obstruent Devoicing** | **Result of Canadian Vowel Raising** |
| /ajz/ | [ajs] | [ʌjs] |

This example serves to show us something about the nature of an interlanguage: it contains features of both the L1 and the L2. The speech of second language learners can exhibit non-nativelike characteristics in any linguistic domain, as shown in table 11.4 on page 374. When the interlanguage grammar stops changing, it is said to have **fossilized**.

## 11.1.3 The final state

So far we have been talking about the characteristics of the intermediate grammar. But a discussion of what an IL grammar looks like must consider the **target**, that is, what is to be acquired. The field of SLA, then, must address the issue of actual proficiency or **communicative competence**. Although knowledge of a language's grammar allows us to distinguish between grammatical and ungrammatical sentences, successful communication requires much more than this. The learner must also be able to use the language

**Table 11.4**   Types of errors found in the acquisition of English

| L1 | Example | Error type | Comment |
|---|---|---|---|
| Spanish | My wife is <u>embarrassed</u>. (meaning 'pregnant') | lexical | Spanish *embarazada* = 'pregnant' |
| Various | I live in a two bedroom department. | lexical | Sometimes the wrong word can be chosen. |
| Various | I <u>didn't took</u> the car. | morphological | English doesn't mark the past tense on both auxiliary and main verbs. |
| Various | She <u>get ups</u> late. | morphological | The speaker adds the agreement marker to the particle, not the verb. |
| French | He <u>drinks frequently</u> beer. | syntactic | French places the main verb before the adverb. |
| Various | There's the man that I saw <u>him</u>. | syntactic | Some languages (e.g., Arabic, Turkish) allow pronouns in this position in a relative clause. |

in a way that is appropriate to the situation or context. As figure 11.2 helps illustrate, both grammatical accuracy and communicative ability are part of communicative competence.

Let us now briefly consider each of the major subparts of the model.

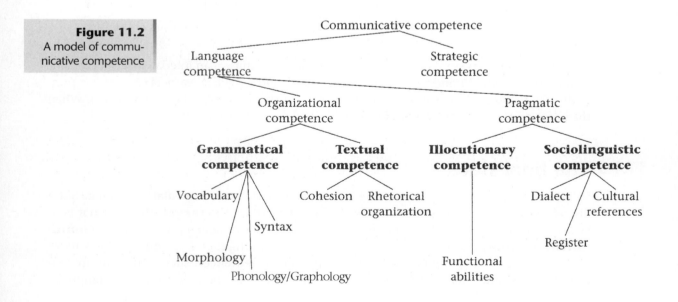

**Figure 11.2**
A model of communicative competence

> ### Language Matters  **Even Though They Are Natural, L2 Mistakes Can be Embarrassing**
>
> "It's those tiny details that do you in: a vowel here, a consonant there. Who would think it would make such a difference? Like the time I thought I was telling my roommate that the sink was plugged again. I said *kinor*. I meant *kiyor*... big deal. But Ruthie had no idea what I was trying to say. I ask you, how hard can it be to figure out that I meant *sink* and not *violin*? Oh, and there was the time her friends came calling, and asked if she was *yeshna* (there). I thought they were asking if she was *yeshena* (sleeping). I said *yes* and closed the door. They thought I was nuts. Fortunately, she woke up and explained that I was only Canadian."
>
> Janet McDonald

## Grammatical competence

**Grammatical competence** has to do with knowledge of the core components of the grammar: phonetics, phonology, morphology, syntax, and semantics. We will address some of these areas in detail in section 11.2.

## Textual competence

Textual competence involves knowledge of well-formedness above the sentence level, including the rules that string sentences together to make a well-formed text in the spoken or written language. As the following examples help show, a text is not just a sequence of grammatical utterances.

(1) MGs can be very temperamental. MGs won't start if they are wet. When they work, MGs are fun to drive. They do not work often.

(2) Like most roadsters, MGs can be very temperamental. For example, they won't start if they are wet. However, on the rare days when they work, they are fun to drive.

The difference between the two texts does not involve the grammaticality of individual sentences, but rather relates to differences in the use of linking words such as *like*, *for example*, and *however*. To be proficient, second language learners have to acquire the ability to organize and link sentences in this way.

## Sociolinguistic competence

As we will see in chapter 14, language use can vary according to the context. For example, we use a different style of language in informal situations than we do in formal ones. This can affect phonology, syntax, and lexical choice, as can be seen in the following two utterances.

(3) I assume we will be working late again this evening? What a shame!

(4) We gotta work late again? Dammit!

In order to be communicatively competent, second language learners need to be able to produce and comprehend a variety of social dialects.

## Illocutionary competence

The meaning of an utterance is not always directly reflected in its surface structure. For example, when uttering the sentence *Have you ever considered professional help?*, a speaker could have in mind a variety of intended meanings. He might mean 'I can't help you, but maybe somebody else could' or 'I think you are a truly disturbed individual; seek help.' The speaker's intent in producing an utterance is referred to as **illocutionary force**. **Illocutionary competence**, then, refers to the ability to comprehend a speaker's intent, and to produce a variety of sentence types to convey a particular intent in various circumstances (e.g., *Are you cold?*, *Could I close the window?*, *Why on earth is the window open?*). This, too, is something that second language learners need to acquire.

In sum, communicative competence is a model of proficiency that allows us to measure second language knowledge and ability, to construct second language proficiency tests, and to design balanced second language courses.

## 11.1.4 Variation in performance

An important goal of L2 research is to integrate the study of competence (linguistic knowledge) and **performance** (actual language use in particular situations). One of the characteristics of the output of second language learners is that it is quite variable. For example, a learner might well produce the following sentence:

(5) I **didn't** like **th**at movie so I told her I **no** want to go **d**ere.

In this (hypothetical) example, the learner is inconsistent, getting one of the two negatives right and correctly pronouncing one of the interdental fricatives. The question that intrigues researchers has to do with what causes this sort of variation. We usually think of knowledge as fairly stable within an individual. So, for example, if you make a mistake while speaking in your native language, you tend not to question your competence in that language, but rather to assume that you made some kind of performance error. So how do we account for learners who behave as if they know how to negate a verb or pronounce [ð] on some occasions, but not others? Do they have the knowledge or don't they?

It is difficult to answer this question, in part because of considerations involving error frequency. If a second language learner gets something wrong 10 percent of the time, is it the same (in terms of competence) as getting it wrong 60 percent of the time? We would probably say that a non-native speaker who gets the English past tense correct 10 percent of the time does not know it, and that someone who gets it right 90 percent of the time does. But what of someone who gets it right somewhere between those two scores? This is a complex research question. The (admittedly simplistic) view adopted in this chapter is that variation falls into the realm of linguistic performance.

Linguistic performance clearly involves the interaction of a number of cognitive systems and has much in common with other skills. A crucial notion for the study of how skills develop involves the distinction between controlled and automatic processing. When acquiring a new skill (e.g., playing golf) we begin by having to devote a lot of conscious or controlled processing to the activity: feet apart, head down, elbow straight, white shoes, etc. Once we become proficient, we 'just' hit the ball; the activity has become automatic.

We need to shift processing from controlled to automatic because, as humans, we have a fixed processing capacity. We can't consciously process everything at once. Shifting some material into automatic processing frees up space for more controlled processing. Consider an example from reading. When we first learn how to read, we devote much of our cognitive processing to determining what the written symbols stand for. When we are focusing on decoding the letters, we do not have the processing capacity to deal with things like reading for prejudice or bias. After a time, though, letter recognition happens automatically in our first language and learners can devote more of their cognitive capacity to higher-level skills.

That native speakers do this kind of thing automatically can be seen by the difficulty we have in proofreading. It is hard to suppress the information we're getting from the context since the mind tries to make sense of what it's reading. Conversely, when we are forced by exceptional circumstances to devote a lot of energy to decoding the print (e.g., a bad photocopy or fax), our higher-level processing slows down; we can't focus as much on the message when we are focusing on the form.

All this is relevant to second language acquisition in that it can help explain the variable performance of L2 learners. When learners are focusing on the form of the L2 utterance, they may be able to produce it accurately. However, when there are extra demands, such as trying to communicate a complex thought or carry on a conversation in a noisy room, errors may occur. This suggests that the learner has a mental representation of the form in question (say a negated verb or a [ð]) but can have difficulty implementing or accessing it under certain conditions.

## 11.2 Interlanguage grammars

Let us turn now to a discussion of the specifics of what is acquired when learning the phonology, morphology, and syntax of a second language. The general question we are trying to answer here is *What is the structure of an interlanguage?* Second language learners are acquiring grammars, and those grammars involve mental representations. Therefore we can investigate the nature of those representations within the various subdomains of linguistic theory. We begin with phonology.

---

### Language Matters **There Are Subtleties In Learning New Lexical Items**

"I suppose hearing a language is a different way of feeling the words. I don't suppose there are synonyms really. I wonder if *moon* means exactly the same thing as *luna*? I don't suppose it does; there's a slight difference. There should be—in every word. So that to learn any language is to find out different ways of viewing, of sensing the universe, the world, or ourselves."

Jorge Luis Borges

The Royal Society of Arts, 5 October 1983

## 11.2.1 L2 phonology

Let us consider what is to be acquired in the domain of phonology. Broadly speaking, we can distinguish between segmental and prosodic phonology. Segmental phonology has to do with the characteristics of phonological segments, like consonants and vowels. Prosodic phonology, on the other hand, has to do with phonological phenomena that affect more than a single segment (e.g., syllables and stress).

### Segmental phonology

As we saw in chapter 3, languages vary in their segmental inventory in that they choose a subset of the sounds found in human languages. There is thus a good chance that a second language learner will have to learn to produce and perceive some new sounds when acquiring a second language.

One of the most obvious characteristics of adult second language speech is that it is 'accented' as the result of phonological and phonetic transfer from the native language. This is why native speakers of English can usually distinguish French-accented English from German-accented English. Consider the examples in table 11.5.

| **Table 11.5**    French- and German-accented English | | |
| --- | --- | --- |
| **English target** | **Quebec French speaker** | **German speaker** |
| [ðə] 'the' | [də] | [zə] |

As both French and German lack the interdental fricative [ð], native speakers of those languages substitute a sound from their L1 wherever English has that sound. Generally, the learners substitute a sound that shares some features with the target sound. In table 11.5, the French speaker substituted a voiced alveolar (coronal) stop, while the German speaker substituted a voiced alveolar (coronal) fricative for the English voiced, interdental (coronal) fricative. Particularly at a beginning level of proficiency, L2 learners pronounce words using their L1 phonological system.

A similar phenomenon can be seen in the phonology of loan words. When a language borrows a word from another language, it makes the word fit into its own phonological system. For example, as we saw in chapter 3, when English borrowed the word *pterodactyl* from Greek, it reduced the onset cluster [pt], which is well formed in Greek but not English. However, no such change was made in the word *helicopter* (with the same Greek root *pter* 'wing') since it already complied with the phonological pattern of English.

### Markedness

One question that has received a lot of attention in SLA research is why some sounds are harder to acquire in a second language than others. Perhaps some sounds are simpler than others. Or perhaps some sound systems are easier for speakers of a certain language to acquire. Would it be easier for a Japanese speaker to acquire English or Vietnamese? As might be expected, these are not simple issues. We cannot talk about the ease or difficulty of entire languages, but we may have something to say about individual sounds.

When linguists try to deal with the notions of ease or simplicity, they make use of the notion of *markedness*. Structures that are simple and/or especially common in human language are said to be **unmarked**, while structures that are complex or less common are said to be **marked**. So, we might say that a sound that is found in relatively few of the world's languages (e.g., [θ]) is marked, while a sound that occurs in many of the world's languages (e.g., [t]) is unmarked.

Markedness is commonly approached from the perspective of language typology, which is concerned with the comparative study of similarities and differences among languages. As noted in chapter 8, researchers have discovered certain implicational universals of the form 'if a language has *x*, it will also have *y*'. For example, if a language has nasal vowels (e.g., [ã]), then it will also have oral vowels (e.g., [a]). Crucial to the understanding of implicational universals is the fact that the implication is unidirectional. Thus a language that has oral vowels does not necessarily have nasal vowels. This allows us to identify [a] as less marked than [ã], in accordance with the following generalization.

(6)  *X* is more marked than *y* if the presence of *x* implies the presence of *y*, *but not vice versa*.

It is interesting to ask whether IL grammars obey such implicational universals and whether this can tell us something about the question of ease and difficulty of learning.

The **Markedness Differential Hypothesis** investigates second language acquisition by comparing the relative markedness of structures in the L1 and the L2. Remember the earlier example of Syllable Final Obstruent Devoicing in German, which explains why a word like *hund* 'dog' is pronounced with a [t] at the end. German speakers learning English typically transfer Syllable Final Obstruent Devoicing into their IL (producing [hæt] for [hæd] 'had') and must learn to make the contrast between [t] and [d] at the ends of words. We might be tempted to think that the principle underlying this phenomenon is something like 'it's hard to learn to make contrasts that your L1 doesn't make'. But when we look at another set of data we see that this is not the case.

French makes a contrast between [ʃ] and [ʒ] in places where English does not, as table 11.6 indicates. If it were invariably difficult for second language learners to make contrasts that are not found in their L1, we would expect English speakers to have difficulty learning to produce [ʒ] at the beginning of words. But they don't. English speakers seem able to learn to pronounce French words like *jaune* 'yellow' and *jeudi* 'Thursday' without trouble.

| **Table 11.6**   The [ʃ]/[ʒ] contrast in English and French | | |
| --- | --- | --- |
| | **English [ʃ]/[ʒ]** | **French [ʃ]/[ʒ]** |
| Initial | <u>s</u>ure [ʃ]/* [ʒ][1] | <u>ch</u>ant ([ʃ])/<u>g</u>ens ([ʒ]) <br> 'song'        'people' |
| Medial | a<u>ss</u>ure ([ʃ])/a<u>z</u>ure ([ʒ]) | bou<u>ch</u>er ([ʃ])/bou<u>g</u>er ([ʒ]) <br> 'to fill up'   'to budge' |
| Final | lea<u>sh</u> ([ʃ])/lie<u>ge</u> ([ʒ]) | ha<u>ch</u>e ([ʃ])/a<u>ge</u> ([ʒ]) <br> 'h'            'age'' |

The notion of markedness can be used to explain why German speakers have difficulty making a new contrast in English, while English speakers don't have difficulty making a new contrast in French. The typological situation is as follows:

- There are languages that have a voicing contrast initially, medially, and finally (e.g., English).
- There are languages that have a voicing contrast initially and medially, but not finally (e.g., German).
- There are languages that have a voicing contrast initially, but not medially or finally (e.g., Sardinian).

These generalizations allow us to formulate the following implicational universal.

(7)  The presence of a voicing contrast in final position implies the presence of a voicing contrast in medial position, which in turn implies the presence of a voicing contrast in initial position.

We can represent this universal graphically as follows:

(8)  initial > medial > final

        C     B     A

The presence of A implies the presence of B and C (but not vice versa), and the presence of B implies the presence of C (but not vice versa). Therefore A is the most marked and C is the least marked. This markedness differential explains the differing degrees of difficulty exhibited by the German and English L2 learners. The German speakers learning English are attempting to acquire a contrast in a universally more marked position (final) whereas the English speakers learning French are attempting to acquire a contrast in a universally unmarked position (initial).[2]

Another way of looking at the acquisition of new sounds is not in terms of ease or difficulty of acquisition but rather in terms of *rate* of acquisition. The **Similarity Differential Rate Hypothesis** (SDRH) makes the claim that the rates of acquisition for dissimilar phenomena are faster than for similar phenomena. In other words, all other things being equal, learners will learn something that is unlike their first language structure *faster* than something that is similar to (and hence could be confused with) a first language structure. The data shown in figure 11.3 describe the acquisition of English [r] (in word-initial position) and English velarised [ɫ] (in word-final position) by a native speaker of Haitian creole, which has a uvular [ʁ] and only a clear alveolar [l]. Note that there is virtually no acquisition of the velarised [ɫ] and little change in rate, whereas the rate of change for [r] is much more dramatic. The dissimilar [r] is acquired at a faster rate than the similar [ɫ].

Of course, the question of how to determine whether two features are similar or dissimilar is not always straightforward. To really test this hypothesis, we would need to look at perceptual, phonetic, phonological, and even orthographic factors that could affect this judgment. Here we will just accept that the two *l*s are more similar than the two *r*s.

## Acquiring new features

One question that often comes up in the field of second language phonology is whether or not you can learn material that is not found in your first language. Some have argued that if a phonological feature is lacking in the L1 then acquiring L2 contrasts based on that

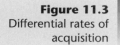

**Figure 11.3**
Differential rates of acquisition

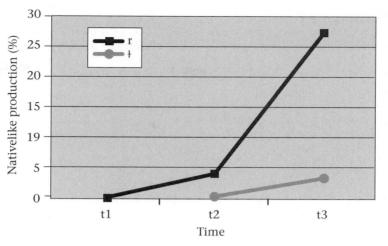

Source: Adapted from "A Longitudinal Study of the Interlanguage Phonology of a Haitian Immigrant Learning English as a Second Language," Applied Project, by M. DeGaytan (Tempe: Arizona State University, 1997).

feature will be impossible. A comparison was made between the relative success of Chinese learners of the English /l/ versus /r/ contrast and the comparative lack of success of Japanese learners attempting to acquire the same contrast. Both Chinese and Japanese lack the /l, r/ contrast but, it was argued, Chinese had the appropriate phonological *feature* in the L1 phonological inventory (we will not go into the details of which feature that is) whereas Japanese lacked it. However, it appears that this is too strong a stance. In some cases, L2 learners *can* acquire contrasts based on features absent from their L1. We will give two brief examples.

First, Japanese learners of Russian can acquire the Russian /r/ (even though they have difficulty with English /r/). They're still lacking the feature in their L1 but they are able to acquire the liquid contrast. Second, it has been shown that English learners of Japanese can acquire long (or geminate) consonants, even though English does not have a phonemic distinction between long and short consonants.

In addition to the segmental inventory, second language learners also have to acquire the prosodic phonology of the target language. For example, they have to acquire the principles of syllabification and stress assignment. We will now look at each in turn.

## Language Matters  **Foreign Accent Syndrome**

There have been several documented cases of what has become known as *Foreign Accent Syndrome.* Patients have been known to suddenly acquire what sounds like a non-native accent. So, a British English speaker may start to sound as if she has a Spanish accent. Or an American English speaker may acquire a British accent. The cases all result from underlying brain damage (from a stroke or some sort of cerebral trauma) but it appears that there is no one brain area that causes this syndrome. In 2006, the *Journal of Neurolinguistics* (vol. 19, no. 5) devoted an entire issue to this subject.

## L2 syllabification

We saw in chapter 3 that syllables have the hierarchical structure shown in figure 11.4.

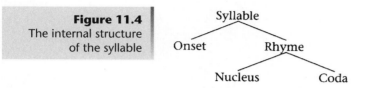

**Figure 11.4**
The internal structure of the syllable

The languages of the world vary according to such things as whether syllabic nodes can branch. Some languages (e.g., Japanese) do not allow branching onsets or codas. Ignoring some complexities, let us assume that all syllables in these languages must be CV or CVC. More complex syllables such as CCVCC are not allowed. A common phenomenon in second language learning involves modifying an L2 word so that it fits the L1 syllable structure. Consider the following words spoken by someone whose L1 is Arabic:

(9) *English target*      *Non-native speaker's version*
    plant           pilanti
    Fred            Fired
    translate     tiransilet

Arabic does not allow branching onsets or codas, so an English word like *plant* cannot be mapped onto a single Arabic syllable. A characteristic of Arabic is that illicit consonant clusters are broken up by an epenthetic [i].[3] With this in mind, let us look at the steps that an Arabic speaker would go through in syllabifying 'plant'.

Step 1   *Initial syllabification:* Assign vowels to a nucleus (N) and the nucleus to a rhyme (R).

Step 2   Assign allowable onset (O) consonants (in Arabic, one).

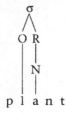

Step 3   Assign allowable coda (Co) consonants (in Arabic, one).

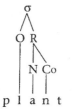

Step 4   Insert an epenthetic [i] to the right of an unsyllabified consonant.

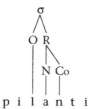

Step 5   Assign vowels to a nucleus and the nucleus to a rhyme.

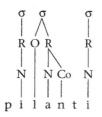

Step 6   Assign allowable onset consonants (in Arabic, one).

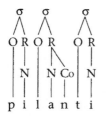

As this example helps show, we can explain why Arabic speakers pronounce English words in the way that they do by investigating the principles of syllabification in the L1. Especially at the beginning levels of proficiency, the structure of the IL is influenced by the structure of the L1.

One study looked at the acquisition of Swedish by Chinese speakers. The researchers were interested in the different types of repair strategies that are available to a learner whose L1 does not allow coda clusters (Chinese allows at most one consonant in the coda while

Swedish can have as many as five consonants at the end of a word). There are two possible repair strategies: epenthesis and deletion. Consider example (10) from English:

(10) *Target word*    *Deleted form*    *Epenthesized form*
    *when*    [wɛ]    [wɛnə]
    *wet*    [wɛ]    [wɛtə]
    *went*    [wɛ]    [wɛntə]

As example (10) illustrates, the *deleted* forms are much more difficult to comprehend for the listener than are the *epenthesized* forms. This study demonstrated that as a learner's proficiency increases, they make more epenthesis repairs than deletion repairs because the epenthesized version is easier for listeners to understand.

## Stress assignment

L2 learners also have to acquire the stress patterns of the language they are trying to learn. Consider an example from Polish, a language in which word-level stress is always assigned to the penultimate syllable. The L1 principle transfers and results in one of the characteristics of a Polish accent in English: the tendency to place stress on the penultimate syllable of English words. The following examples illustrate a non-native stress pattern in which the second-to-last syllable is always stressed.

(11) *English target*    *Non-native form*
    astónish    astónish
    maintáin    máintain
    cábinet    cabínet

## 11.2.2 L2 syntax

L2 learners also have to acquire the syntax of their new language. In this section, we will look at two facets of syntactic structure: the null subject parameter and verb movement.

## Null subjects

As we saw in chapter 5, Universal Grammar includes universal principles (that account for what all natural languages have in common) as well as parameters (that account for cross-linguistic variation). Parameters are like linguistic switches (often binary) that can be set to a particular value as a result of the linguistic input. One of the first parameters to be proposed was the Null Subject (or pronoun-drop) Parameter. Essentially, this parameter is designed to account for the contrast between languages like French and English, which require overt subjects (e.g., *He speaks French/*Speaks French*), and languages like Spanish and Italian, which allow subjects to be omitted (e.g., Spanish *El habla español/Habla español* '[S/he] speaks Spanish').

(12) *The Null Subject Parameter*
The subject of a clause with a verb marked for tense [may/may not] be null.

Languages that allow null subjects tend to have other grammatical traits associated with them. For one, they tend to allow declarative sentences with the word order Verb + Subject as well as Subject + Verb, as in the following examples from Spanish.

(13)  *a.*  Juan llegó.
          John arrived.

       *b.*  Llegó Juan
          arrived John.

Secondly, they tend to allow sentences like the following, in which a complementizer (here *que* 'that') is immediately followed by the trace of a moved *wh* word.

(14)  Quién  dijo usted   que *t*  llegó?
       who    said you    that   arrived?
       'Who did you say that arrived?'

As the following example shows, such sentences are unacceptable in English.

(15)  *Who did you say [CP that [IP *t* arrived]]?
       (deep structure = *you did say that who arrived*)

In other words, languages like English ([–null subject]) do not allow *that*-trace sequences, whereas languages like Spanish ([+null subject]) do.

Studies on L2 learners of English show that Spanish speakers are more likely to judge subjectless English sentences to be grammatical than are French speakers. This is consistent with the assumption that L1 parameter settings are transferred into the IL grammar, at least in the early stages. Learning a second language can be seen as involving the resetting of parameters that have different values in the L1 and the L2.

Moreover, when Spanish subjects are given a task that requires them to change a declarative sentence into a question, they are more likely to produce a sentence that contains a *that*-trace sequence than are French subjects. For example, if Spanish subjects are given a sentence like *Joshua believed that his father would be late* and have to form a question asking about the underlined element, they are more likely than French subjects to produce a sentence like *Who did Joshua believe that t would be late?* This points toward the possibility that the admissibility of null subjects and the acceptability of *that*-trace sequences are somehow both related to the Null Subject Parameter (i.e., speakers of null subject languages are more likely to permit *that*-trace sequences).

However, there are complications. Remember that the study just described had the Spanish and French speakers form new sentences. Another study had both French and Spanish subjects judge the grammaticality of English sentences with a *that*-trace violation. Both groups were quite able to reject those sentences as ungrammatical. For some reason, there is a stronger L1 influence when learners have to form new sentences themselves.

## Verb movement

French and English differ in the setting of the Verb Movement Parameter.

(16)  *The Verb Movement Parameter*
       A Verb marked for tense [raises/does not raise] to I.

We saw in chapter 5 that the transformation of verb movement takes a verb from within the VP and moves it to I (see figure 11.5 on page 386). Simplifying slightly, let us say that English does not allow verb movement but French does. Thus, in French the verb raises to I past a preverbal adverb, but in English it does not. This difference can be seen in the following sentences, in which movement of the verb over the adverb separating it from the I position gives a bad result in English but a good result in French.

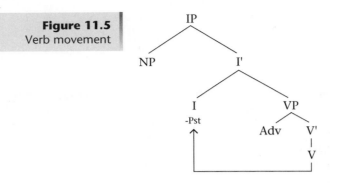

**Figure 11.5**
Verb movement

(17) *a.* *Marie watches often *t* television.
     *b.* Marie regarde souvent *t* la télévision.

Studies have shown that French speakers learning English initially assume that English allows verb raising. In order to learn English they have to reset the value of their verb-raising parameter.

## Markedness and the Subset Principle

Another interesting facet of a parameter-setting approach to SLA has to do with whether adult L2 learners can reset their parameters, and whether the notion of directionality of difficulty captured by the Markedness Differential Hypothesis (see section 11.2.1) can be captured in a parameter-setting model. The Null Subject Parameter can be used to address these questions. To understand how, we must first consider how a parameter-setting model instantiates the notion of markedness.

If we consider the two settings of the null subject parameter (+/−), we can see that the different values generate different grammars, as shown in the following sentences from English and Spanish.

(18) [−null subject]:    I      speak      Spanish.
     [+null subject]:    Yo     hablo      español.
                        Hablo español.

As you can see, the [+null subject] setting generates more grammatical utterances than the [−null subject] setting does. Therefore the [−] setting is said to be a subset of the [+] setting. Graphically, this can be represented as shown in figure 11.6.

The **Subset Principle** stipulates that for first language learners, the initial or default setting will be the subset value (i.e., [−null subject] in the case of the Null Subject Parameter).[4] When attempting to reset from subset to superset or from superset to subset, second language learners need access to different types of evidence. Imagine a learner of English (who has the [–] setting) trying to learn Spanish. The learner's initial assumption will be the L1 parameter setting, which leads to the expectation that all sentences will have overt subjects. When faced with Spanish input, the learner will be exposed to grammatical utterances in the L2 that do not have overt subjects (e.g., *Hablo español* '[I] speak Spanish'), which indicates that the L1 setting is incorrect and needs to be reset. Data like this, which involves grammatical utterances to which one is actually exposed, is referred to as **positive evidence**.

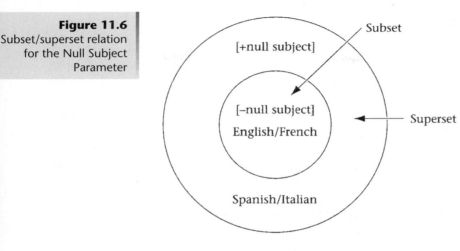

**Figure 11.6**
Subset/superset relation
for the Null Subject
Parameter

Now imagine a learner whose L1 is Spanish ([+]) who is trying to learn English ([−]). The learner's initial assumption will be that English should be [+null subject], like the L1. The learner's IL grammar will allow both sentences with overt subjects and sentences without. Crucially, there will be no positive evidence in the English input directed at this learner to show that the L1 parameter setting is wrong. The learner will hear sentences with overt subjects, which are sanctioned by the current IL grammar, but there will be no direct indication that sentences with null subjects are not allowed. There is no pressure to reset the parameter. In this case, the learner will have to rely on **negative evidence** (i.e., observations about what is missing or ungrammatical in the data) to reset the parameter. In particular, the learner would either have to be explicitly told what is ungrammatical (**direct** negative evidence), or infer that it is ungrammatical on the basis of the fact that no one else ever says it (**indirect** negative evidence).

Given that direct positive evidence is available in one case (English → Spanish), and negative evidence is required in the other (Spanish → English), we might predict that it is harder for Spanish speakers to learn the English value of the Null Subject Parameter than vice versa. In fact, the prediction is borne out. Studies have shown that it is easier for English speakers to reset to the Spanish value of the Null Subject Parameter than it is for Spanish subjects to reset to the English setting.

Let us now consider how an approach based on typological universals would treat the same phenomenon. The presence of null subjects implies the presence of overt subjects, but not vice versa.

(19) overt subjects > null subjects

Null subjects would therefore be thought of as more marked, and, consequently, more difficult to acquire. The Markedness Differential Hypothesis predicts that structures that are more marked typologically will cause difficulty in SLA. The Subset Principle, on the other hand, predicts that structures that are more marked will not cause difficulty because there will be clear evidence that the L1 setting is wrong. Although only the Subset Principle seems to make the correct prediction in the case of the null subjects, further research is necessary in order to see which approach is better able to handle a wider range of data.

## 11.2.3 L2 morphology

The study of second language morphology has a slightly different flavour than the study of either L2 phonology or L2 syntax. L2 phonology has been studied for a long time, though the analyses have changed to reflect changes in linguistic theory. L2 syntax is a much younger field, and much of it has been informed by current linguistic theory. By contrast, L2 morphology has been studied more or less in a theoretical vacuum. In the 1970s, a number of studies collected data on the accuracy of second language learners on a variety of morphemes. This research drew on previous studies in the field of first language acquisition that had attempted to determine the order of acquisition of morphemes in L1 development. The developmental sequence in table 11.7 was found.

| Table 11.7 | Developmental order for first language acquisition |
|---|---|
| 1. *–ing* | The present participle affix (e.g., she is work*ing*) |
| 2. Plural *–s* | (e.g., bottle*s*) |
| 3. Irregular past | (e.g., she *taught* French) |
| 4. Possessive *–s* | (e.g., a child*'s* toy) |
| 5. Copula *be* | (e.g., I *am* happy) |
| 6. Articles | (e.g., *a, the*) |
| 7. Regular past | (e.g., she walk*ed* quickly) |
| 8. 3rd person *–s* | (e.g., she walk*s* quickly) |
| 9. Auxiliary *be* | (e.g., she *is* working) |

Research on second language acquisition focused on whether the developmental sequence in L2 learning was the same as for L1 learning. The order in table 11.8 was found.

| Table 11.8 | Developmental order for second language acquisition | |
|---|---|---|
| 1. *-ing* | 4. Auxiliary *be* | 7. Regular past |
| 2. Copula *be* | 5. Plural *-s* | 8. 3rd person *-s* |
| 3. Articles | 6. Irregular past | 9. Possessive *-s* |

There are many similarities but there are also some differences. For example, note that auxiliary and copula *be* are acquired at a relatively earlier point in L2 than in L1, and that the possessive morpheme *-'s* is acquired later in L2 than in L1. To attempt to explain these patterns, we need to look a little more closely at the structures that implement inflectional morphology. In the syntax chapter we saw that in English, main verbs do not raise to I, but that the copula verb *be* does raise to I if no modal is present (see chapter 5, section 5.4.2). We note the three patterns shown in (20).

(20)   *a.*  If no modal is present: the auxiliary verb moves from inside the VP to I.

       He is [$_{VP}$ probably *t* eating].

    *b.*  If a modal is present: the auxiliary verb does not raise.

       He should [$_{VP}$ probably be eating] vs. *He should be [$_{VP}$ probably *t* eating].

*c.* Main verbs do not raise.

He [$_{VP}$ probably likes eating] vs. *He likes [$_{VP}$ probably *t* eating].

Children acquire *be* as a main verb before they acquire *be* as an auxiliary verb. So, they produce sentences that have only a copula verb (e.g., *He is hungry*) before they produce sentences that include an auxiliary plus a main verb (e.g., *He is working*) as shown in figure 11.7.

**Figure 11.7**
Copula versus auxiliary *be*

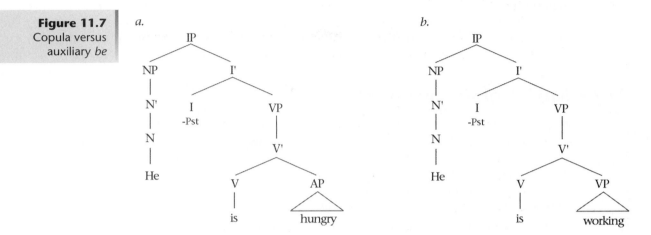

The structure in *b* has an extra level of complexity in that it has a complex verb phrase (one VP within another). In contrast to child L1 learners, adult L2 learners appear to be able to use both the simple copula and auxiliary verbs quite early on. Differences in the L1 and L2 acquisition of 'be' seem to arise from the complexity of the structure.

Remember that children acquire the three *-s* morphemes in the order plural, possessive, third person in their first language. Phonetically, these morphemes have the same realization, so we can't say that the order reflects phonological complexity. The order might be explained by noting that plural is a word-level phenomenon (e.g., *dogs*), possessive is a phrase-level phenomenon (e.g., [*the king of England*]*'s* horse, not *the [*king*]*'s of England horse*), and third-person marking involves a relation between the verb and a phrase (the subject) elsewhere in the sentence (e.g., [*That man*] *usually watches* TV). Like the pattern noted for the development of copula and auxiliary *be*, children seem to be acquiring structures in order of complexity, as shown in figure 11.8.

**Figure 11.8**
Three types of /s/ affix

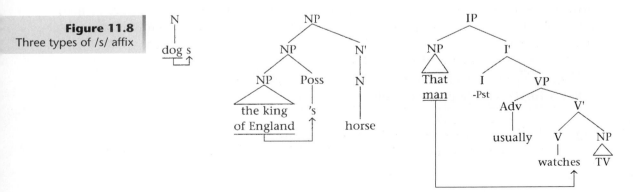

In contrast, adults acquire the plural quite early, but then seem to get both the possessive and the third person marking quite late—perhaps for reasons involving processing. (When concentrating on getting the words right, we do not always have the processing capacity to produce well-formed higher-level structures.) Interestingly, the adults do not seem to find interphrasal morphology (like third-person marking) more difficult than phrasal morphology (like possessives). This may be because the adults have already acquired the grammar for their first language and that grammar most likely has both phrase-level and interphrasal morphological phenomena. In contrast, children could conceivably be building a sentence's structure from the bottom up (words → phrases → sentences).

In summary, we note that the order of acquisition data are intriguing in both first and second language acquisition, even though we await a conclusive explanation of the facts.

## 11.2.4 Morphology and syntax

We conclude this section with a discussion of a recent theoretical approach that looks at the interaction of morphology and syntax in second language learners in an attempt to answer one of the questions we have already posed in this chapter: "If someone leaves something out, does it really mean they don't have a representation for it?" To answer this question, we will consider what second language learners know about tense. It is well known that non-native speakers often make mistakes with the tense of a sentence.

(21) You know, I *call* Bill this morning and nobody *answer*. And I *start* to worry . . . He either *stay* in Eliotville, because he said he *call* me last night, and he never did.

On the surface, we might be tempted to say that this learner lacks knowledge of finiteness due to the lack of overt past-tense marking. Two theoretical positions have been put forward. The first is the **Impaired Representation Hypothesis**, which argues that the learners have some sort of underlying representation deficiency (i.e., problems with the representation of tense). The second is the **Missing Surface Inflection Hypothesis**, which argues that the learners have the correct underlying functional categories but have difficulty mapping surface inflection onto those categories.

How can we decide between these two hypotheses? We will use the data from a longitudinal case study to build our argument for the Missing Surface Inflection Hypothesis. The subject, known as Patty in the literature, is a native Chinese speaker who first acquired English as an adult. An example of her English is given in example (21) above. At the time of the first recording, she had been in the United States for about ten years. She was recorded three times over the next nine years. During that period, she was virtually immersed in English, and yet, as shown in table 11.9, she often does not mark her past tense forms in finite obligatory contexts. Note that she supplies the past

| **Table 11.9**    Patty's past-tense marking in obligatory contexts | | |
|---|---|---|
| **Recording #** | **Suppliance/contexts** | **%** |
| 1 | 24/69 | 34.78 |
| 2 | 191/548 | 34.85 |
| 3 | 46/136 | 33.82 |

tense marking in about 34 percent of the contexts where native speakers must supply the tense marking. Although Patty is clearly not placing the proper inflectional morphology on her finite verbs, we will argue that she does have knowledge of the tense feature that is targetlike.

In section 5 of chapter 5, the notion of case was introduced. We saw that the subject of a finite clause in English receives nominative case (see also the Companion Website at **www.pearsoned.ca/ogrady**, chapter 11). Note now that the subjects of non-finite clauses do not receive nominative case. Compare the pronouns in the sentences in (22).

(22) *a.* I believe that he   is a liar.
             NOM   [finite]

    *b.* I believe him to be a liar.
        ACC   [non-finite]

In (22a) the second verb (*is*) is finite and so the pronoun has nominative case, whereas in (22b) the second verb is infinitival (*to be*) and the preceding pronoun does not have nominative case. Note that *him* is not the object of the verb *believe*—you don't believe him; in fact, you think he's a liar. The point is that there is a connection between finiteness and nominative case marking.

Let us return to our two hypotheses about Patty. The Impaired Representation Hypothesis argues that Patty lacks a fundamental category (finiteness) because she does not mark tense on her verbs, and therefore predicts that we should not expect her to have a connection between finiteness and nominative case marking. The Missing Surface Inflection Hypothesis suggests that she *has* the underlying category of tense and finiteness but lacks the overt morphological marking, and therefore predicts that Patty will demonstrate a connection between finiteness and case marking. So, what does she do? The data in table 11.10 clearly show that Patty correctly assigns nominative case to all the pronominal subjects of her finite clauses.

| **Table 11.10** | Patty's use of nominative case on pronominal subjects | |
| --- | --- | --- |
| **Recording #** | **Nominative subject pronouns/Finite past contexts** | **%** |
| 1 | 49/49 | 100 |
| 2 | 378/378 | 100 |
| 3 | 76/76 | 100 |

Furthermore, she does not *incorrectly* mark pronouns in other contexts, as the sentences in (23) demonstrate.

(23) It's best for *me* to stay in Shanghai.
    It is possibility for *me* to get out.
    That doesn't have anything to do with *me* leaving home.

This argument suggests that Patty does have a mental representation of finiteness that governs her grammatical knowledge with respect to case assignment, even though she has fossilized with respect to the morphological expression of tense on verbs.

## 11.3 Factors affecting SLA

So far, we've looked at some of the characteristics of an IL grammar. Now let's turn to a variety of factors that can influence second language acquisition. It is clear that there is much more variation in the grammars of people learning second languages than in the grammars of people learning first languages. This brings us to the question of what factors might help to account for that variation.

### 11.3.1 Age

One of the obvious ways that language learners vary is in their age. People start learning second languages at different points in their lives. Could the age of onset of L2 learning cause different levels of final proficiency?

This is a question usually considered under what is known as the *critical period hypothesis* (see chapter 10, section 10.6.5). We know that biologically-based critical periods exist in other species. For example, some birds can learn the song of their species only if exposed to it during a particular window of opportunity. If they only hear the song too early or too late, then learning will not take place. (See chapter 16 at **www.pearsoned.ca/ogrady** for further discussion.)

Is second language learning like this? Is there an optimal time (or critical period) to acquire a second language? The answer appears to be 'yes and no'. Proficiency in a language is a remarkably complex thing (see the discussion of communicative competence in section 11.1.4). Usually, discussion of a possible critical period focuses on the area of phonological competence. Although people who begin SLA as adults tend to retain non-nativelike phonology in the target language, it is much more difficult to predict knowledge or ability in any of the other areas of communicative competence (syntax, cohesion, sociolinguistics, etc.) based upon age of acquisition.

In fact, even L2 phonology is not so straightforward as it might first appear to be. We can predict with fair certainty that people who start learning their L2 before the age of seven will have nativelike L2 speech and that people who start learning after fourteen or fifteen will probably have non-nativelike speech. But the results for people who start learning between the ages of seven and fourteen are much more varied. Some end up with accents, and some do not.

There is no current evidence of anything biological that prevents adults from acquiring proficiency in a second language. Factors that have been considered in the past (like brain lateralization; see chapter 13) are now thought to be of little predictive value in determining L2 ability. There is recent research that demonstrates that people who start learning their second language as adults *are* able to reach a final state that is indistinguishable from native speakers. In one study in the syntactic domain, it has been shown that near-native speakers perform like native speakers when it comes to speed and accuracy in grammaticality judgment tasks (of sentences such as "*Who did Mary meet the man after she saw *t*?").

Similarly, studies have shown that there are some people (admittedly a minority, but they do exist) who can start learning their second language as adults and perform within the range of native speakers when it comes to their pronunciation. When native speaker judges listen to tapes of both native and non-native speakers (not knowing which is which) and give a global accent rating, there are always some native speakers who do not get a perfect rating and some non-native speakers who can score more highly than these subjects. Currently, the critical period debate in SLA research is usually couched in terms of the question "Do adults have access to Universal Grammar?" Rather than looking for changes in the brain that coincide with aging, researchers now look to see whether IL grammars are governed by the same constraints as primary languages (e.g., English, Cree, and Swahili).

If adults are engaged in the same kind of developmental process as children, then we would expect their IL grammars to be describable in terms of the same principles and parameters of UG that we use to describe primary languages. Conversely, if adults are acquiring their second languages using qualitatively different learning mechanisms than are used to acquire an L1 (e.g., if they use general problem-solving abilities), then we might expect them to adopt hypotheses that are not sanctioned by Universal Grammar. Something like this may in fact happen in the acquisition of gender in French.

Children learning French as a first language seem to have very little trouble learning gender as they learn the words themselves (e.g., *le livre*, 'the book', is masculine; *la table*, 'the table', is feminine) and so on. On the other hand, adults whose first language does not have gender often have great difficulty learning French gender. They seem to set up complex (but incorrect) rules for predicting the gender of a given noun. For example, they may assume that words naming parts of the body (or some other semantic category) are of one gender, or that words that end with a certain sound sequence are of another. Rules like this sometimes allow non-native speakers to guess the gender correctly, but they still perform significantly differently from native speakers. This is an example of how adults' greater capacity to formulate general rules can sometimes lead them down the wrong path.

## 11.3.2 Individual differences

Learners vary in ways other than age. Broadly speaking, the researcher asks the question, "If learners have a particular quality $x$, does this make them better at second language acquisition?" For example, we might look at the effect of inhibition, left-handedness, or some other individual trait on L2 ability. As intuitively appealing as this avenue is, it is one that must be taken carefully. In particular, there are three points on which we must be explicit:

1. how we define and measure $x$;
2. what it means to be *better*;
3. what aspect of communicative competence we are referring to.

Consider in this regard a trait like empathy. It has been argued that people who are empathetic are better language learners. This is an intuitively appealing notion. People who are empathetic can imagine what it feels like to be in someone else's shoes and they can look at things from another perspective. And second language learning certainly involves looking at things from a different perspective. But in SLA research, we need to find a more precise way to evaluate this hypothesis.

There are tests that claim to measure a person's empathy, but is this notion really a well-defined construct? Is one simply empathetic or not, or are there degrees of empathy? If there are degrees, do we see a correlation between degree of empathy and degree of success? And what does it mean for empathetic learners to be better language learners than people who aren't empathetic? Do they make fewer errors? Less serious errors? Should we expect people with greater empathy to be better at everything in the L2? Or maybe just at phonology and sociolinguistic competence? On what basis could we make a prediction? These are not simple issues. We raise them not to argue that research in individual variation is misguided, but to show some of the complex areas that need to be addressed before we can hope to establish a causal connection between a particular personality trait and success at second language learning.

We can distinguish between two kinds of factors in terms of which individuals can vary: affective factors and cognitive factors. First we will look at the role of affect.

## Affective factors

Affective factors have to do with the emotional side of learning a second language. Clearly there can be a great deal at stake emotionally when learning a second language, and it is possible that emotions affect how successful a second language learner is. Affective factors that have been studied include empathy, anxiety, inhibition, and risk-taking. In this section we will look at one such factor: motivation.

Learners can vary with respect to the amount or type of motivation they have to learn a second language. If someone is highly motivated to learn, will that person do better at learning? In order to answer this question, we need to say a bit more about what it means to be motivated.

Traditionally, two types of motivation have been proposed: **instrumental** and **integrative**. Instrumental motivation involves wanting to learn the L2 for a specific goal or reason. For example, someone might need to pass a language requirement in order to get a graduate degree, or a job with a government agency. Integrative motivation, on the other hand, involves wanting to learn the L2 in order to learn more about a particular culture or fit into it better. For instance, someone might want to learn Japanese in order to learn more about a fascinating culture.

Studies have shown that the degree of integrative motivation correlates with the degree of success in language learning. That is to say, subjects who score highly on tests of integrative motivation do better on certain language tests than comparable subjects who score poorly on the same tests. However, subjects with instrumental rather than integrative motivation can also do well if their level of motivation is high. One study found that subjects who were offered a cash reward if they obtained a certain score on a language test performed much the same as subjects with high integrative motivation. All this seems to suggest that degree of motivation is a better predictor of future learning success than is type of motivation.

## Cognitive factors

Although affective factors have something to do with the emotional side of learning, cognitive factors involve the mechanics of how an individual learns something. Different people seem to learn via different cognitive styles and different learning strategies. We will first address cognitive style.

As individuals, we tend to tackle mental tasks using a particular 'cognitive style'. In contrast with an affective factor like motivation, which may vary from domain to domain (e.g., someone might be more motivated to learn French cooking than to learn the French language), cognitive style is a stable trait across domains.

## Language Matters **Exceptional Language Learning Ability**

Daniel Paul Tammet (born January 31, 1979, in London, England) is a British autistic savant who is gifted with a facility for mathematics problems, sequence memory, and natural language learning. He was born with congenital childhood epilepsy. He can't drive a car, wire a plug, or tell right from left, but he holds the European record for memorizing and recounting *pi* to 22 514 digits in just over five hours.

Tammet can speak several languages, including English, French, Finnish, German, Spanish, Lithuanian, Romanian, Estonian, Icelandic, Welsh, and Esperanto. He particularly likes Estonian because it is rich in vowels and he is creating a new language called Mänti. Mänti has many features related to Finnish and Estonian, both of which are Finno-Ugric languages. Some sources credit Tammet with creating the Uusisuom and Lapsi languages as well.

Tammet is capable of learning new languages very quickly. To prove this for a television documentary, he was challenged to learn Icelandic, a language viewed as one of the world's most difficult, in one week. Seven days later he appeared on Icelandic television conversing in Icelandic, with his Icelandic language instructor saying it was "incredible."

Source: Adapted from Wikipedia.

The study of cognitive style often focuses on a contrast between field dependence and field independence. Learners who are **field independent** are not distracted by irrelevant background information when trying to learn something. These are people who can see the trees without being distracted by the forest. On the other hand, learners who are **field dependent** tend to see the forest but may miss the characteristics of individual trees. Of course, this is not to say that, overall, one trait is good and the other is bad. Field-dependent learners probably are able to synthesize the overall picture better than field-independent learners, but field-independent learners are probably better able to pick out relevant facts.

In terms of second language acquisition, it seems that field-independent learners do better on language tests that focus on analytic tasks such as providing the correct grammatical form in a given sentence:

(24) Yesterday, we ___ the kids to the zoo. (take)

In contrast, field-dependent learners tend to do better on tasks that involve synthesizing their knowledge. For example, they may demonstrate broader communicative competence in that they are more concerned with getting the message across than with the grammatical accuracy of the sentences they use to form their message.

Ultimately, the proficient L2 learner needs to be concerned with both **accuracy** and **fluency**. Broadly speaking, accuracy has to do with whether the learner has the correct representation of a particular linguistic structure (i.e., it involves *knowledge*). Fluency, on the other hand, has to do with the rapid retrieval or processing of those representations (i.e., it involves *skills*). Someone who is not fluent may well have accurate representations but take considerable time and energy to retrieve them. Different learners, though, are probably going to have a natural affinity to emphasize either accuracy or fluency, depending perhaps on their individual cognitive style.

While cognitive styles appear to be relatively stable traits in an individual, there are elements of learning that we have some control over. Each of us has certain **learning strategies** that we can employ to try to fill gaps in our linguistic knowledge. These strategies can be contrasted with **communication strategies**, which are designed to keep communication happening in spite of gaps in knowledge—as when someone uses paraphrase to describe an object for which he or she has no vocabulary item (e.g., *Could you pass me the thing you use for hitting nails?*). In contrast, a learning strategy is used to discover something new about the L2.

Many different learning strategies have been proposed. For example, using the strategy of directed attention, learners may decide in advance to focus on particular aspects of a task and to ignore others. So, when reading a text or listening to a lecture, they might decide to focus only on the main points. Another strategy involves repetition: to retain a lexical item or to improve the pronunciation of a sequence of sounds, the learner may repeat a word or phrase over and over. A third strategy makes use of clarification requests (to the teacher, a peer, or the others in a conversation) about something that is not understood (e.g., How come *stood* does not rhyme with *food*? What's a *liege*?). Under this view, learners have a variety of strategies at their disposal and have to discover which ones work best for them.

This brings us to the interesting question of second language learning in classrooms and the effect that instruction has on L2 learning. Is it really possible to teach someone a second language? Or can you just create an environment in which second language learning can take place? We turn now to the research that has looked specifically at L2 classrooms.

## 11.4 The L2 classroom

It has been flippantly said that people have been successfully acquiring second languages for thousands of years, but when teachers get involved, the success rate plummets. This comment is probably more a reflection of people's unfortunate experience in certain types of language classrooms (that may have been dull or even physically threatening, depending on the century) than it is a statement about general pedagogic utility. However, the fact remains that language classrooms can be sheltered environments where students can benefit from being given the opportunity to learn and practise without being subject to the penalties for failure that can be imposed outside the classroom. For more discussion of L2 pedagogy, go to **www.pearsoned.ca/ogrady**.

We should acknowledge at this point that there is really no such thing as *the* second language classroom. In reality, all classrooms are different because they have different people in them (both students and teachers). Nevertheless, there are three relevant characteristics of a second language classroom that we wish to explore:

1. modified input;
2. modified interaction;
3. focus on form.

## 11.4.1 Modified input

In chapter 10 it was noted that adults do not talk to children in the same way that they talk to other adults. Just as the input directed to children has certain simplifying characteristics, so speech directed at non-native speakers tends to be simplified compared to the speech directed at native speakers. In all communicative situations—whether dealing with a child or an adult, a non-native speaker or a native speaker—we seem to make a rapid assessment of the level of proficiency or background knowledge of the listener, and adjust the input accordingly.

The input aimed at non-native speakers is referred to as **foreigner talk**. The subset of this speech that takes place in classrooms is known as **teacher talk**. Teacher talk (or teacher language) tends not to be as evenly matched to the proficiency of the listener as foreigner talk is, for the simple reason that teachers are usually addressing a class rather than an individual. As a result, some learners may find the modified speech too hard or too easy.

The pedagogic goal of teacher talk is crystal clear: make sure the students know what is being talked about by providing **comprehensible input**. Perhaps surprisingly, this idea has generated an extraordinary amount of conflict in the field of SLA research. Although it seems to be useful to provide learners with comprehensible input, teachers must guard against simplifying too much, which might give the appearance of patronizing the learners or talking to them as if they were stupid rather than on the way to becoming bilingual.

## 11.4.2 Modified interaction

Second language classrooms also differ from the outside world in terms of the kind of interactions that go on there. However, the difference appears to be mainly one of degree, not quality. Inside a classroom, the teacher may engage in the following kinds of strategies:

- more comprehension checks, e.g., Do you understand?; OK?
- more prompting, e.g., Who knows where Moose Jaw is?
- more expansions, e.g., *Student*: Me red sweater.
  *Teacher*: Yes, you're wearing a red sweater, aren't you?

One type of interaction that has received a lot of attention is the **recast**. A recast is a reformulation of a learner's ill-formed utterance that corrects the mistakes.

*Student*: He has car.
*Teacher*: Yes, he has a car.

Studies have shown that recasts can be helpful for second language learners. Teachers use this type of interaction when they don't want to interrupt the flow of communication in the classroom (which can happen when grammatical errors are explicitly corrected). In general, students with higher levels of proficiency appear to benefit more from recasts. Students with lower levels of proficiency benefit more from explicit correction.

Such modified interaction appears to be one of the characteristics that differentiates classrooms from other communicative settings. While all these devices (e.g., comprehension checks) occur in non-classroom discourse as well, they appear to occur more frequently in second language classrooms. Assuming that the teacher realizes that the purpose of the classroom is to prepare the student to understand input and interaction outside of the classroom as well, modified interaction is beneficial.

## 11.4.3 Focus on form

The final characteristic of the second language classroom to be discussed here involves focus on form. The term *focus on form* encompasses two distinct practices that tend to occur in most L2 classrooms: instruction about the language and explicit correction.

Most second language classes present the students with some sort of information about the language—noting, for example, that "English has two different types of 'th' sound (i.e., voiced and voiceless)" or that "French has nasal vowels". Instruction of this type is designed to improve the form (or accuracy) of the student's L2. In all likelihood, other activities that happen in the class will focus on giving the student a chance to improve fluency or particular sociolinguistic skills.

Error correction is also designed to improve the form of the student's L2. Regardless of the methodology used, in most classes today there is some focus on form and some error correction. The interesting research question is whether either of these practices can be shown to have a positive effect on the learner. Do students who get corrected do better than students who don't?

The question may not be as straightforward as it appears. Remember that it has frequently been argued in first language acquisition research that attempts at error correction are relatively infrequent and don't really affect children's grammars. Could it be different for adult second language learners? The learning environment is different in that adult learners (unlike children) are usually exposed to a fair amount of error correction. But does that make a difference? Not surprisingly, this question is difficult to answer. Some studies have argued that second language learners who receive correction develop at about the same pace as those who do not. Other studies have shown certain increases in accuracy as the result of correction.

These results may not be as contradictory as they seem, though. The areas where correction seems to be most useful involve the use of lexical items. However, feedback concerning certain structural phenomena may not be as effective. For example, the previously mentioned study of French speakers learning about the lack of verb movement in English (see section 11.2.2) found that while there were short-term improvements in the learners who were explicitly taught the relevant facts, there were no significant long-term effects. When the learners were tested a year later, they had reverted to their pre-instructional performance.

This doesn't necessarily mean either that students should not be corrected or that there should be no focus on form in the second language classroom. If a balance is struck between classroom activities that focus on form and those that focus on meaningful communication, then there is certainly no evidence that feedback causes any problems. Indeed, to the contrary, there is evidence that students in classes that focus primarily on communication but also include some instruction on form are significantly more accurate than students who are exposed only to instruction that focuses on communication.

Most of the studies to date have considered focus on form within a pedagogical framework (i.e., how does it affect the learner or the classroom), but there are more recent studies that are couched within a cognitive framework. Under this approach, the following questions could be asked:

1. *The noticing issue*: Do learners have the cognitive resources to notice the gap between their interlanguage (IL) utterances and the target language (TL) utterances around them?

   This is a very complex question that involves the details of how memory (working, short-term, and long-term) works. Learners need the coordinated working and long-term memory resources to enable the cognitive comparison of the IL and TL sentences. This sort of comparison eventually leads to knowledge restructuring. Studies suggest that learners do have the cognitive resources to engage in this type of comparison, especially if they are comparing TL utterances that have occurred recently in the discourse.

> ## Language Matters **It Can Be Comforting to Hear Your Native Language**
>
> A seven-year-old Siberian Tiger named Boris moved from a zoo near Montreal to a zoo in Edmonton. At first, zookeepers found him shy and aloof. Then one zookeeper began to speak to him in French. Immediately, the tiger came over to her and seemed much friendlier. So, it's not just humans who get used to a particular language!

2. *The interruption issue*: Is pedagogical intervention that does not interrupt the learner's own processing for language learning even possible?

   Focus on form should be carried out in response to the learner's needs. If (a) the primary focus of the lesson is on meaning, (b) the focus-on-form targets arise incidentally, and (c) the learner shifts attention briefly, then the focus-on-form activity will be relatively unobtrusive. Indeed, rather than being an unwanted interruption, focus-on-form may allow the learner to pay selective attention to a structure for a short period of time, which would be beneficial.

3. *The timing issue*: If so, then precisely 'when', in cognitive terms, should the pedagogical intervention occur?

   Learners appear to benefit from being prepared in advance for some focus-on-form activities. If they know what is coming, it helps them to notice the relevant features in the input. One of the most promising types of intervention is an immediate recast. A corrective recast involves the repetition of an error plus a recast, as shown below:

   *Student*: I think that the worm will go under the soil.
   *Teacher*: I <u>think</u> that the worm <u>will</u> go under the soil? . . . I <u>thought</u> that the worm <u>would</u> go under the soil.

   In sum, adult students usually expect error correction, and teachers are accustomed to providing it. Assuming that the class is not devoted entirely to instruction that focuses on form (with no opportunity for meaningful practice), error correction doesn't seem to cause any harm. In a class with activities that focus on both form and fluency, the students tend to emerge with greater accuracy. Certain types of classroom activities seem to be able to engage the cognitive abilities of adult second language learners and allow them to continue to advance their L2 proficiency.

## 11.4.4 Bilingual education

We will conclude this chapter with a discussion of two types of bilingual education program: minority language maintenance programs and French **immersion** programs. Both are designed to produce bilingual children, but there are important differences. French immersion programs involve children from a majority language (English) being immersed in a minority language (French). As English-speaking children in Canada, they are in no danger of losing their first language since it is so dominant in the culture. Their situation is clearly different from that of children who speak a minority language (e.g., Greek or Italian) and who are submersed in the majority language (English). Not only are these children in some danger of losing their first language, but the sink-or-swim approach can also have strongly negative consequences on their future in school. For these reasons, it should be emphasized that even if we argue for the benefits of immersing English-speaking children in French classrooms, it does not follow that we should submerse speakers of other languages in English classrooms.

Let us look in more detail at some of the issues surrounding bilingual education. We begin with minority language maintenance programs.

## Minority language maintenance programs

Minority language maintenance programs, which are also known as 'heritage language programs' or 'L1 maintenance programs', have been introduced around the world to try to address the fact that minority language children often have difficulty in majority language schools. Even with separate classes of instruction, they tend to have more than their share of problems later in school (including a higher-than-expected drop-out rate). One reason for this becomes evident when one thinks of the challenge these children face. Up until the age of five, they are exposed to a language at home (say, Greek or Cree). Then at age five they are put into an English-speaking school in a class of primarily native English speakers. Typically, they do not understand everything that the teacher is saying, and they do not have the opportunity to develop the basic cognitive skills necessary for functioning in school. These children may thus suffer a setback from which they will never recover.

This poor beginning can lead to minority language students being placed in classes not designed for students intending to pursue post-secondary education, which in turn can lead to an exit from the educational system. To try to change this recurring pattern, a number of bilingual education programs have been set up in places like Canada, Finland, England, and the United States. In all of these programs the children of minority language background receive their initial instruction in the minority language. Over the years of their elementary education, instruction in the majority language is gradually introduced so that by grades three to six, the children receive about half of their instruction in the majority language as well.

The question raised in evaluating these programs (and indeed, the question that led policy-makers to adopt the competing sink-or-swim approach to minority language education) is "What is the effect on the children's English?" Obviously, knowledge of English in places like Canada and the United States is essential. But is submersion in English the only way to acquire proficiency in English? It would seem that the answer is no, since children can become bilingual with relative ease. In virtually all of the bilingual education programs studied, the subjects ended up performing as well as their monolingual L1 and L2 peers by the end of grade six. So, for example, a child who received all instruction in Cree for the first couple of years of schooling and was getting 50 percent English and 50 percent Cree instruction by the end of grade six would be performing in Cree like a monolingual Cree speaker and in English like a monolingual English speaker.

Thus, receiving instruction in the L1 does not have negative consequences on the L2. On the contrary, it seems to have significant positive effects on success in school, on linguistic proficiency, and even on the family situation of the students. The students can understand the teacher (which helps them at school), and they can understand their parents and grandparents (which helps them at home).

## French immersion programs

French immersion programs in Canada involve immersing a majority language student in a minority language class. While any second language can be involved, we will refer to these as French immersion programs. In 1977, there were 37 835 students enrolled in Immersion programs across the country. In 2005 there were 301 000. Clearly, French immersion programs have maintained their popularity in Canada, even though there are many other second language programs such as bilingual education schools available to students who wish to learn languages other than French. French immersion differs from traditional French instruction (also known as Core French) and from submersion programs. It is different from a Core French course in that French is the medium of communication, not the subject of the course. It is teaching *in* French, not teaching *of* French. In a Core French course, French is just another subject (say, 40 minutes a day). In French immersion, all of the instruction is in French, even when the content is geography or music.

French immersion is different from submersion programs in that no student in the class is a native speaker of the medium of instruction. Native speakers of French do not enroll in French immersion classes, so all the students are starting from approximately the same place. Contrast this with a native Cree speaker who is thrown into an English-only class with a large number of native speakers of English.

Probably the two biggest questions that get asked about immersion programs are: (1) What effect does such a program have on the students' English? and (2) How good is their French? The answer to the first question is remarkably similar to the answer provided by the heritage language programs. Children can become bilingual, and instruction in one language does not necessarily mean a diminished capacity for the other language. Often, though, children in French immersion programs exhibit a delay in productive skills (talking and writing) in English in the early years. However, by grade six, on average they are outperforming their monolingual English peers. Boldly stated, children in French immersion learn English.

So how good is their French? Concerns are often expressed that the children who come out of French immersion programs end up speaking a kind of mixed language (which has been called *Frenglish*, or *Franglais*). It is true that immersion students tend to make mistakes in things like French gender, the *tu/vous* distinction (where *vous* is used as an honorific second person singular pronoun), and polite conditionals such as *Je voudrais un crayon* 'I would like a pencil' versus the somewhat less polite simple present form *Je veux un crayon* 'I want a pencil'. Overall, however, their receptive skills (reading and listening) end up virtually nativelike and their productive skills, while not nativelike, are at an advanced level.

In sum, the positive features of French immersion programs can be stated as follows. Children who emerge from French immersion suffer no negative effects on their English, do well in school, outperform their monolingual counterparts in a number of ways, and know a heck of a lot of French.

## Dual language programs

Across Canada and around the world there are also an increasing number of programs known as **dual language programs**. In these programs, students from two linguistic backgrounds are formally instructed in both languages. For example, a dual language program might consist of students who are either native speakers of English or native speakers of Spanish, with all students receiving instruction in both languages. It is felt that these sorts of programs work well at validating the minority languages, and at letting all students understand how difficult it can be to learn a second language. In addition, students are exposed to a number of native speakers of the new language rather than just having the teacher as a model.

# *Summing up*

This chapter has dealt with a number of issues in the field of second language acquisition. We investigated the notion of an **interlanguage grammar** and the influence of both the source and target languages on this grammar in terms of **transfer** and **developmental errors**. Proficiency in a second language requires both knowledge and ability, something captured in a model of **communicative competence**. A learner must acquire knowledge in all linguistic domains (phonetics, phonology, morphology, syntax, and semantics) as well as the ability to use that knowledge in a variety of social contexts.

What is easy or difficult to acquire in a second language has been investigated from a variety of perspectives. We focused on **Universal Grammar** (the **Subset Principle**) and **typological universals** (the **Markedness Differential Hypothesis**). However, it is not just universals that influence second language learning; the specific characteristics of an individual can also affect the process. Affective factors and cognitive factors both influence second language learning. So too do factors such as modified input, modified interaction, focus on form and bilingual education.

The field of second language acquisition is remarkably diverse, in part because of what is involved in L2 learning. Someone who is attempting to learn an additional language must develop new mental representations, and develop facility at accessing those representations in a variety of circumstances. The field of SLA research must therefore draw on philosophy (theories of mind), psychology (theories of learning, theories of performance), linguistics (theories of linguistic structure), and pedagogy (theories of instruction). This is probably the main reason why we have not established anything like a comprehensive theory of how second languages are learned. But bit by bit, piece by piece, we're starting to put together some pieces of the puzzle.

## Notes

1   The asterisk indicates that this sound is not allowed in initial position (except in a few words that have been borrowed from French—e.g., *genre*, *gendarmes*, and so forth).

2   Note that English phonology in general respects the implicational universal given in (7), as can be seen in pairs such as *sip/zip*. The lack of contrast of [ʃ]/[ʒ] in initial position is an accidental gap. Even with this gap, however, it seems that English speakers respect the universal when learning the phonology of a second language. The voicing contrast is easier to acquire in the universally unmarked position.

3   This might happen in a native Arabic word if two morphemes are put together and, as a result, two consonants occur adjacent to each other.

4   As we will see, linguists infer the initial setting of a parameter on the basis of the kind of input or evidence available to the language learner. It is a separate question to determine whether children's early grammars actually have the [+] or [−] setting of the Null Subject parameter. For example, children's early sentences in English often lack overt subjects, which might lead us to believe that the grammars have the [+] setting. However, the early

sentences of English-speaking children do not contain the other structures associated with the [+null subject] parameter setting: *that*-trace patterns and VS order in declaratives. Given the complexity of this issue, we will assume the relationship shown in figure 11.7 when discussing second language learners.

## Recommended reading

Archibald, J., ed. 2000. *Second Language Acquisition and Linguistic Theory*. Oxford: Blackwell.

Cummins, J., and M. Swain. 1986. *Bilingual Education*. London: Longman.

Flynn, S., G. Martohardjono, and W. O'Neil, eds. 1998. *The Generative Study of Second Language Acquisition*. Mahweh, NJ: Lawrence Erlbaum.

Hawkins, Roger. 2001. *Second Language Syntax: A Generative Introduction*. Oxford: Blackwell.

Leather, J., and A. James. 2002. *New Sounds 2000*. Klagenfurt, Austria: University of Klagenfurt Press.

Long, M., and D. Larsen-Freeman. 1991. *Second Language Acquisition Research*. London: Longman.

Sharwood Smith, M. 1994. *Second Language Learning: Theoretical Foundations*. London: Longman.

White, L. 2003. *Second Language Acquisition and Universal Grammar*. Cambridge, UK: Cambridge University Press.

## Exercises

1. Some dialects of Arabic break up clusters by inserting an epenthetic vowel to the *left* of an unsyllabified consonant (unlike the dialect discussed in this chapter). How would a speaker of this dialect pronounce the words *plant*, *transport*, and *translate*? Draw the necessary syllable structures.

2. The following is a sample of non-native writing. The assignment was to write about whether you prefer to live in the city or the country. Look through the sample and 'correct' the errors. Do you have any idea what the student's first language might be? Compare your corrected copy with that of someone else in the class and see if you agree on the corrections.

> *Are you among the number of people who have to choose their place to live? Whenever they have to move from another country, they even change the profession, they want to have a house outside the big city, or they can't find a place in Downtown.*
>
> *Its possible to move as well as you are supported by some essential condition of life I've mention in the following lines.*
>
> *Most of people are living in the Big city to have many of the opportunities that offer the Downtown lifestyle, jobs, studies, activities or whatever but nowadays for instance in TO [Toronto] its really difficult to find a place to live because the percentage of vacancy is slightly under 0% so many people are constrained to move on the suburb, by this way some of these get along this phenomene because they want to avoid the noise, the smog of the city and even they try to find their own place to live with garden and everything, actually to invest money to owe their house which is better than to rent*

*an apartment in downtown, therefore they have to consider the transportation problem to reach the city even to have a car or use the public transportation.*

*to have your own house outside the city required a great initial capital that you have to draft from any bank or you dispose in your account but afterwhat the house become your possession with the years and couple of more will increase the house value, although it is expensive furthermore it should be a great benefit for the owner even though he decided to rent the unoccupied room into the house.*

*Moreless the frienship beetween the person in the subrub is closer they are ore contact with each other and maybe can meet themselves doing yardwork or other kind of activities belong to the suburb lifestyle.*

*But in another (illegible) it should be difficult for the people who haven't ever lived in the suburb to move from th big city because they have to adapt their habits but they can fin amonst a great number of things that they use to have in the city. Otherwise during the last 15 years the business activites has developing around the city quickly in the North America also the supermarket company, manufacture and so on offered the job opportunity to the people outside the big aglomeration in that way it was created some apartments vacaint in the city.*

*For me I don't even care where I have to live but I will observe which part could be the less expensive as well as transportation to reach my job but I will be sure that I'd like to live outside the downtown.*

3. Given what you know about implicational universals, do you think it would be easier for an English speaker to acquire French nasal vowels (e.g., *gant* [gã], 'glove') or for French speakers to acquire English oral vowels?

4. What explanation would you give for a native speaker of French who produced the English sentence *I drink frequently coffee*? How could you explain the fact that when the same speaker produces the sentence *He is frequently late*, it is grammatical? Do any other English verbs have the same properties as *be*? For more help, see chapter 5, section 5.4.1.

5. Which of the following sentences would you classify as positive evidence and which as negative evidence for the learner?

   a) *Non-Native Speaker (NNS):* He study a lot.
      *Native Speaker (NS):* He *studies* a lot.
   b) *NS:* What kind of books do you like to read?
      *NNS:* Mysteries.
   c) *NNS:* I was born in Munich.
      *NS:* Pardon me?
   d) *NNS:* I goed to Montreal on the weekend.
      *NS:* Remember that *go* has an irregular past.

6. Discuss why second language learners, regardless of their first language, might produce forms such as *goed, sheeps,* and *coulds* given that they never hear these forms in input from native speakers of English. Give some other forms analogous to the above that might be generated.

7. What factors can you think of that might influence fossilization? In other words, do you think that some people are more likely to fossilize than others? Do you think it can be reversed? How?

8. Acquiring a second language involves both knowing something about the language, and being able to do something with the language. Do you think that knowledge and skills are related? Can you see any trade-off between accuracy and fluency?

9. Why do you think that non-native speakers of English would be more at risk of leaving the education system than native speakers?

10. Respond to the following statement:

    *It's the school system's job to make sure that non-native speakers of English learn English. They need English in order to be able to succeed in this country. We want them to succeed. If we encourage them to speak their own language, then ghettoes will form and they'll never learn English. And if we want them to learn English, then obviously they need to be exposed to more English. What good is it knowing how to speak another language in North America? What they need is English, English and more English.*

# Twelve

Gary Libben

# Psycholinguistics: the study of language processing

*Leaving one still with the intolerable wrestle*
*With words and meanings*

T.S. Eliot

We engage in language processing most every day of our lives. This processing takes place when we watch television, listen to the radio, read a passing billboard while driving, or discuss the weather. Usually these language activities are carried out with great ease and in a completely subconscious manner. We might sometimes be aware that we are searching for a word, composing a sentence, or straining to understand someone else, but we are never aware of the actual mechanisms and operations involved in producing and understanding language.

**Psycholinguistics** is the study of these language-processing mechanisms. Psycholinguists study how word meaning, sentence meaning, and discourse meaning are computed and represented in the mind. They study how complex words and sentences are composed in speech and how they are broken down into their constituents in the acts of listening and reading. In short, psycholinguists seek to understand *how language is done*.

This chapter introduces the field of psycholinguistics by first discussing some methods used by psycholinguists to probe language representation and processing in the mind. This is followed by a summary of recent research on language processing in the domains of phonetics, phonology, morphology, and syntax. Finally, we will discuss how these various aspects of linguistic processing work together to make the everyday acts of speaking, listening, and reading appear so simple and effortless.

## 12.1 Methods of psycholinguistic research

The key fact that guides psycholinguistic methodology is that language users are unaware of the details of language processing. Simply paying attention to what you are doing will not provide reliable insights into how you access words or build sentences. Perhaps the reason for this is that, in normal use, language processing must occur very quickly. By shielding mental linguistic operations from the conscious mind, it is possible that the language-processing system is maximizing its ability to operate with speed and efficiency.

In order to get a sense of just how subconscious language processing is, you might try the following exercise: give a friend a page of text to read silently and sit opposite him or her. Carefully observe your friend's eyes as they move across the text. You will notice that the eyes do not move smoothly from left to right but rather proceed in a series of jerks called **saccades**. Like most of us, your friend probably has the subjective impression that his or her eyes are moving very evenly across the page. But that subjective impression is incorrect. It seems that we are simply not constructed to be able to monitor many of our automatic activities, including language processing.

A substantial additional challenge for the psycholinguistic researcher comes from the fact that most of language processing does not involve observable physical events such as eye movement, but rather involves mental events that cannot be observed directly. Research in this field therefore requires that mental language-processing events be inferred from observable behaviour. Consequently, a large part of psycholinguistic research is concerned with the development of new (and often very clever) techniques to uncover how language processing is accomplished. Some of these techniques are presented in the following sections.

## 12.1.1 Slips of the tongue

Some of the earliest and most influential studies of language processing examined the spontaneous slips of the tongue produced during speech. Slips of the tongue are also known as **Spoonerisms** after Reverend William A. Spooner, who was head of New College Oxford between 1903 and 1924. Reverend Spooner was famous for producing a great many, often humorous, speech errors. Some of his more well-known mistakes are presented below.

(1) What he intended:     You have missed all my history lectures.
    What he said:         You have hissed all my mystery lectures.

(2) What he intended:     Noble sons of toil
    What he said:         Noble tons of soil

(3) What he intended:     You have wasted the whole term.
    What he said:         You have tasted the whole worm.

(4) What he intended:     The dear old Queen
    What he said:         The queer old dean

Beginning in the 1960s, Victoria Fromkin began to study these and other naturally occurring slips of the tongue and noted that they can be very revealing of the manner in which sentences are created in speech. For instance, as can be seen in the examples above, the characteristic pattern in Reverend Spooner's errors is a tendency to exchange the initial consonants of words in the utterance. When these segment exchanges create new words (as opposed to non-words as in *fire and brimstone* → *bire and frimstone*), the result is often humorous. But here's the important psycholinguistic point: in order for these exchanges to occur, the sentence would have to be planned out before the person begins to say it. Otherwise, how would it be possible in example (1) for the first segment of the sixth word *history* to be transported backwards so that it becomes the first segment of the third word (*missed* → *hissed*)?

Another important observation that Fromkin made was that speech errors also often involve 'mixing and matching' morphemes within words. Consider the following slips of the tongue.

(5) Intended:        rules of word formation
    Produced:       words of rule formation

(6) Intended:        I'd forgotten about that.
    Produced:       I'd forgot aboutten that.

(7) Intended:        easily enough
    Produced:       easy enoughly

All these errors involve morphemes being exchanged within a sentence. As is the case for sound exchange errors, these slips of the tongue provide evidence that a sentence must be planned out before speech begins. They also provide evidence that the morpheme, rather than the word, is the fundamental building block of English sentence production. Note how in example (5) the inflectional suffix -*s* remains in its original place, while the nouns *rule* and *word* reverse positions. In examples (6) and (7), it is the suffixes that move while the stems remain in their original positions. These examples all suggest that morphological components of words can function independently during sentence planning (and of course also in sentence mis-planning).

As can be seen from these examples, slips of the tongue can offer a fascinating window to the mechanisms involved in language production and to the role that linguistic units such as phonemes and morphemes play in that production. But because slips of the tongue are naturally occurring events, the researcher has no control over when and where they will occur and must simply wait for them to happen. In this way, the analysis of slips of the tongue is a **field technique** and differs from the **experimental paradigms** discussed in the following sections. In these experimental paradigms, the researcher takes an active role in controlling the circumstances under which language is processed, the stimuli to which the experimental participants are exposed, and the ways in which participants may respond to these stimuli.

## 12.1.2 Experimental methods: words in the mind

One of the most intense areas of psycholinguistic research has been the investigation of how words are organized in the mind. We are all in possession of a vocabulary that forms the backbone of our ability to communicate in a language. In many ways, this vocabulary must be used

### Language Matters **Early Interpretation of Speech Errors**

Sigmund Freud (1856–1939) allowed his patients to speak as freely as possible, recorded their utterances, and sought to find meaning in unintentional speech errors, which he called *Fehlleistungen* ('faulty actions'). In his 1901 book *The Psychopathology of Everyday Life*, Freud discusses numerous speech errors, which he analyzed as revealing unconscious desires, memories, or conflicts.

#### Early experimentation
Although primarily interested in memory, Hermann Ebbinghaus (1850–1909) may be considered to be the first to have conducted psycholinguistic experiments. In 1885 he reported his use of nonsense syllables (e.g., *bim, lup*) as the basis of investigations into human learning, retention, and recall.

the way a normal dictionary is used. It is consulted to determine what words mean, how they are spelled, and what they sound like. But the dictionary in our minds, our mental lexicon, must also be substantially different from a desktop dictionary. It must be much more flexible, accommodating the new words that we learn with ease. It must be organized so that words can be looked up extremely quickly—word recognition takes less than one-third of a second and the average adult reads at a rate of about 250 words per minute. It must allow us to access entries in terms of a wide variety of characteristics. 'Tip-of-the-tongue' phenomena, in which we are temporarily unable to access a word, are particularly revealing with respect to how flexible access to the mental lexicon can be—we have all experienced episodes in which we eventually retrieve words on the basis of their meaning, sound, spelling, first letter, or even what they rhyme with.

Many psycholinguists conceive of the mental lexicon as a collection of individual units as in figure 12.1. In this figure, the lexicon is shown as a space in which entries of different types are stored and linked together. The main questions that are asked about the mental lexicon are: (1) How are entries linked? (2) How are entries accessed? (3) What information is contained in an entry?

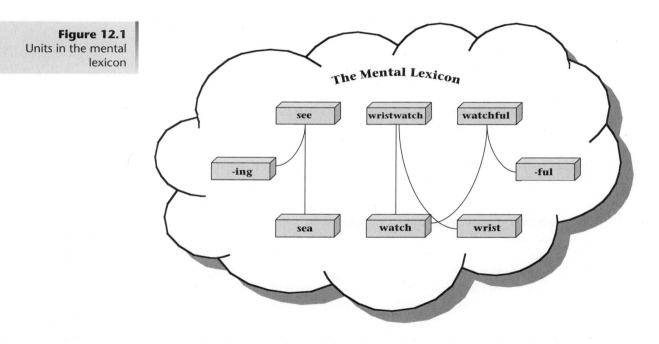

**Figure 12.1**
Units in the mental lexicon

Although these questions are simple and straightforward, there is no way to answer them directly because the human mental lexicon cannot be observed. So the psycholinguist must use special experimental methods to understand how words are organized, accessed, and represented in the mind. We will briefly discuss the two most common of these methods—**lexical decision** and **priming**.

## Lexical decision

In the lexical decision paradigm, the experimental participant (in this example, a native speaker of English) is seated in front of a computer screen. A word appears in the middle of the screen and the participant must judge as quickly as possible whether or not the word is a real English word and press a button labelled 'yes' or a button labelled 'no' (see figure 12.2).

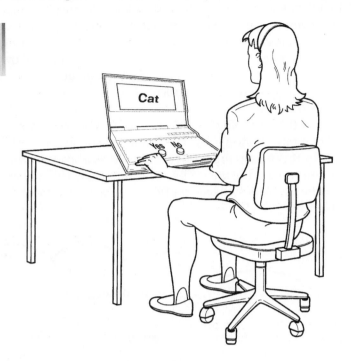

**Figure 12.2**
A lexical decision experiment

This task is very easy for participants to carry out. They typically see and judge hundreds of words in a single fifteen-minute session. In most lexical decision experiments there are two **dependent variables**, that is, things that are being measured: the time that it takes for a participant to respond (**response latency**) and whether or not the participant's judgment is correct (**response accuracy**). A response is judged as correct if a participant responds 'yes' to a real word such as *glove* or *sadness* and 'no' to a non-word such as *blove* or *sadding*.

Lexical decision experiments usually involve comparing participants' performance on one set of stimuli (e.g., nouns) to their performance on another set of stimuli (e.g., verbs). The key to the importance of the experimental paradigm is that, in order for a participant to respond 'no' to a stimulus such as *blove* or 'yes' to a real word such as *glove*, the participant's mental lexicon must be accessed. The lexical decision task can therefore be used to measure the speed and accuracy with which words in the mental lexicon are accessed. It has been found in many experiments that participants take about half a second (500 milliseconds) to press the 'yes' button for frequently used words such as *free*, but almost three-quarters of a second to press the 'yes' button for less common words such as *fret*. This finding has been called the **frequency effect**. Assuming that longer response times reflect processing that is more difficult or complex, this finding suggests that our mental dictionaries are organized so that words that we typically need more often (the frequent words) are more easily and quickly available to us.

Another way in which the lexical decision task can be used to explore language representation and processing is to investigate the speed and accuracy with which participants press the 'no' button for different types of stimuli. It has been found, for example, that pronounceable non-words such as *plib* show slower 'no' response times than unpronounceable non-words such as *nlib*. Thus participants' lexical decisions seem to take into account the phonotactic constraints of the language. It has also been found that non-words that sound like real words (e.g., *blud*, *phocks*) take longer to reject than stimuli that are non-words both visually and phonologically. Again this tells us that aspects of phonology are automatically activated during word reading (note that in the lexical decision task, the participant never has to pronounce the word aloud).

## The priming paradigm

The priming paradigm very often involves the lexical decision task and can be considered an extension of it. Recall that in lexical decision tasks different categories of stimuli (e.g., concrete versus abstract words) are compared in terms of participants' response latency and accuracy. Priming experiments typically involve the same procedure as the lexical decision task except that the word to be judged (now called the **target**) is preceded by another stimulus (called the **prime**). What is measured is the extent to which the prime influences the participant's lexical decision performance on the target stimulus.

The priming paradigm is an excellent technique for probing how words are related in the mind. One of the first experiments using this paradigm showed that response time is faster when a target is preceded by a semantically related prime (e.g., *cat-dog*) as compared to when it is preceded by an unrelated prime (e.g., *bat-dog*). Results of this sort lead us to the view that words are related in the mind in terms of networks. On the basis of evidence from these priming experiments, psycholinguists reason that when a word such as *cat* is seen, its representation is activated in the mind and that activation spreads to other words in the lexical network that are semantically related (e.g., *dog*). Now, because the mental representation for *dog* has already been activated through the prime, it is in a sense 'warmed up' so that when the participant later sees it on the screen as the target, response time is faster than it otherwise would have been. This is called the **priming effect** (as shown in figure 12.3).

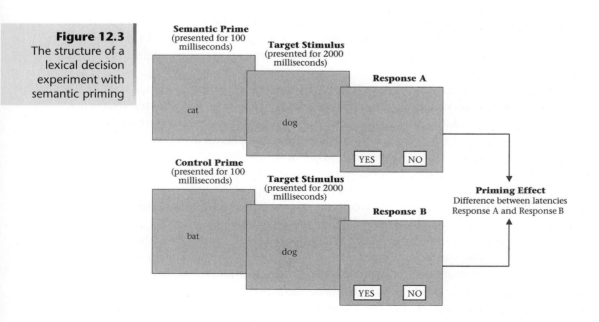

**Figure 12.3**
The structure of a lexical decision experiment with semantic priming

**Semantic Prime** (presented for 100 milliseconds)

**Target Stimulus** (presented for 2000 milliseconds)

**Response A**

cat

dog

YES    NO

**Control Prime** (presented for 100 milliseconds)

**Target Stimulus** (presented for 2000 milliseconds)

**Response B**

bat

dog

YES    NO

**Priming Effect**
Difference between latencies Response A and Response B

In recent years, the priming paradigm has been used to explore many aspects of the representation of words in the mind, and researchers have explored many types of priming in addition to the semantic priming above. For example, priming effects have been found for orthographically related words (e.g., *couch-touch*), phonologically related words (e.g., *light-bite*), and between word roots and complex forms (e.g., *legal-illegality*). This last finding, which suggests that words are represented in the mind in terms of their constituent morphemes, will be discussed further in section 12.2.2.

# 12.1.3 Experimental methods: sentence processing

The lexical decision and priming paradigms discussed so far offer interesting insights into how words are processed, but are of limited use in exploring the processing of sentences. The main reason for this is that the types of questions asked about sentence processing tend to be different from those asked about the mental lexicon. The vast majority of the sentences that we hear are unique events. Therefore, sentence processing must be fundamentally a process that relies on a particular type of computation (as opposed to a particular type of storage, in the case of words). It is presumed that in sentence processing (i.e., in reading or listening) a sentence is understood through the analysis of the meanings of its words and through the analysis of its syntactic structure. Psycholinguists refer to this type of unconscious automatic analysis as **parsing**. Much of the research on sentence processing is concerned with the principles and steps in parsing, its speed, and the manner and conditions under which it can break down.

In this section, we review two groups of experimental paradigms that have been used extensively to study sentence processing. These are timed-reading experiments and eye-movement experiments.

## Timed-reading experiments

Timed-reading experiments begin with the assumption that the more difficult sentence processing is, the longer it should take. Therefore, by timing how long it takes participants to read particular sentence types or parts of sentences, we can study the determinants of sentence-processing difficulty.

One of the more common and revealing timed-reading experimental paradigms is the bar-pressing paradigm in which participants are seated in front of a computer screen and read a sentence one word at a time. The participant begins by seeing the first word of the sentence in the middle of the screen. When the participant presses a bar on the keyboard, the first word disappears and the second word of the sentence appears in its place. This process continues until all the words in the sentence have been read.

The dependent variable in these experiments is the amount of time it takes participants to press the bar after seeing a particular word (i.e., the amount of time they need to process that word).

Bar-pressing experiments can be very revealing about the manner in which sentence processing occurs. Participants do not show equal bar-pressing times across a sentence, but rather a pattern that reflects the syntactic structure of the sentence. An example of such a pattern is shown in figure 12.4, which displays bar-pressing times for the sentence *The Chinese, who used to produce kites, used them in order to carry ropes across the rivers.*

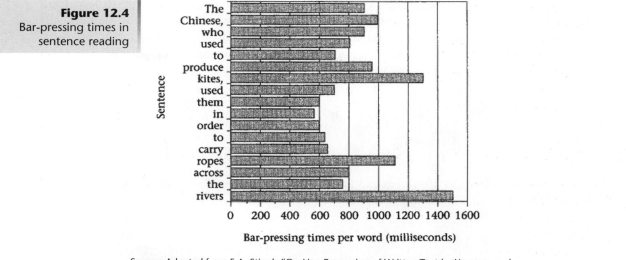

**Figure 12.4**
Bar-pressing times in sentence reading

Source: Adapted from E.A. Stine's "On-Line Processing of Written Text by Younger and Older Children," *Psychology and Aging* 5 (1990):68–78, figure 1, p. 73. Copyright © (1990) by the American Psychological Association. Adapted with permission.

As can be seen in figure 12.4, participants show longer bar-pressing times for processing content words such as nouns and verbs and relatively less time for function words such as determiners, conjunctions, and prepositions. What is particularly interesting is how participants pause at the end of clause boundaries. This increased processing time is interpreted as reflecting the extra amount of time required to integrate preceding information into a complete clause structure. Thus, the greatest bar-pressing time is required for *rivers*, the final noun in the sentence.

## Eye movements

We have already noted that sentence reading involves a series of jerky eye movements called saccades. A number of events occur during these jerky movements. When the eyes are at rest they take a 'snapshot' of two or three words. These snapshots usually last from 200 to 250 milliseconds. While the snapshot is being taken, the language-processing system calculates where to jump to next. During a jump to the next fixation location (usually about eight letters to the right), the reader is essentially blind.

The details of eye movements in sentence reading are studied with sophisticated laboratory procedures in which a participant is often seated in front of a computer screen on which text is displayed. Eye movements are tracked by a device that illuminates the participant's eyes with low-intensity infrared light and records the reflection. The eye-position data are linked to the position of text on the screen so that it is possible to determine how the eyes move from one text position to another.

This technique has revealed that fixation times are typically longer for less frequent words and that the points of fixation are typically centred on content words, such as nouns and verbs, rather than on function words, such as determiners and conjunctions. Difficult sentence structures create longer fixation times as well as many more **regressive saccades**. Regressive saccades are backward jumps in a sentence and are usually associated with mis-parsing or miscomprehension. On average, backward saccades make up 10 to 15 percent of the saccades in sentence reading. But syntactically complex sentences and semantically anomalous sentences (e.g., *The pizza was too hot to drink*) create many more regressive saccades. It has also been found that poor readers jump back and forth through sentences much more often than good readers do.

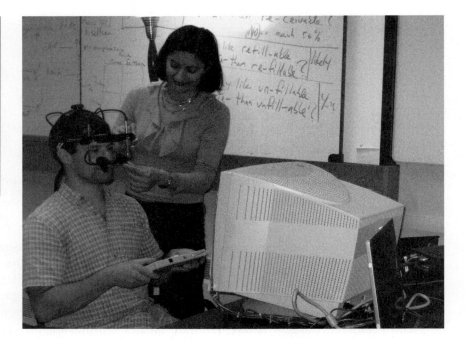

**Figure 12.5**
Head-mounted eye-trackers. Modern eye-trackers can be worn on a lightweight headband. Two cameras positioned below the eyes record eye movements. A camera mounted in the centre of the headband records movements of the head.

## 12.1.4 Brain activity: event-related potentials

Perhaps the most exciting new technique to be used in psycholinguistic research is the study of **event-related potentials** (**ERPs**) produced by the brain during language processing. As a research technique, the ERP paradigm has the same basic advantage as eye-movement studies. The participant simply sits in front of a computer screen and reads. This is a relatively natural language-processing activity that, unlike lexical decision or bar pressing, is similar to what participants do in normal language-processing situations.

ERP experiments measure electrical activity in the brain. Electrodes are placed on a participant's scalp and recordings are made of voltage fluctuations resulting from the brain's electrical activity. The difference between ERP recordings and the more familiar EEG (electro encephalogram) recordings is that, in the EEG, all the electrical activity of the brain is recorded. This electrical activity results from a very large number of background brain activities that are always going on. The advantage of the ERP approach is that it uses a computer to calculate what part of the electrical brain activity is related to a stimulus event (in our case, words or sentences on a screen). This is done by a process of averaging. The computer records the instant at which a stimulus is presented and compares the voltage fluctuation immediately following the stimulus presentation to the random background 'noise' of the ongoing EEG. By repeating this process many times with stimuli of a particular type, random voltage fluctuations are averaged out and the electrical potentials related to that stimulus type can be extracted. The resulting wave forms are the event-related potentials.

The ERP pattern is typically presented as a line graph in which time is shown from left to right and voltage is shown on the vertical axis with negative values on top and positive values on the bottom. An example of an ERP graph is provided in figure 12.6.

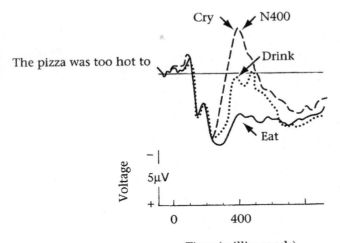

**Figure 12.6**
ERPs elicited by sentence-final words that are congruent, incongruent, and very incongruent with the sentence context

Source: Marta Kutas and Cyma Van Petten's article in M.A. Gernsbacher, ed., *Handbook of Psycholinguistics* (New York: Academic Press, 1994), p. 103.

Figure 12.6 also displays one of the most interesting psycholinguistic findings using ERPs. It turns out that in the processing of implausible sentences, the brain displays a characteristic ERP sign of surprise. Consider the following sentences:

(8)  *a.* The pizza was too hot to eat.
     *b.* The pizza was too hot to drink.
     *c.* The pizza was too hot to cry.

The sentences in (8) are arranged in order of semantic plausibility. In the first case, the last word fits in perfectly well with the sentence and would typically be expected by the reader.

As can be seen in figure 12.6, the ERP for this sentence shows a positive voltage associated with the last word. In the case of (8b), however, in which the last word does not make sense (people do not drink pizza), the ERP is much more negative. As is shown in the horizontal axis, this negative spike occurs 400 milliseconds after the onset of the word. For this reason, this signal of semantic anomaly is called the N400 (negative spike at 400 milliseconds after stimulus presentation). Note how the N400 is even stronger in the case of sentence (8c), which is even less congruent with the sentence context ('drink' is at least associated with food).

The N400 effect can be obtained not only at the ends of sentences but also in any sentence position. This fact suggests that sentence processing is immediate and online. When reading a sentence, we do not wait until the entire string is complete, but rather are constantly building interpretations of the sentence as it unfolds. Whenever what we see or hear contradicts our expectations based on our ongoing interpretative processes, a N400 ERP spike is observed.

> ### Language Matters  Simple Experiments Can Be Very Revealing
>
> One of the most revealing psycholinguistic experiments requires no laboratory and no special equipment. In fact, you can try it with a friend: simply tell your friend that in this experiment you will say a word out loud and his or her task (as a participant in the experiment) is to try as hard as possible to not understand the word. You can give fair warning by counting down 3, 2, 1, and then saying the word (e.g., *water*). Of course, as long as the participant can actually hear the word, it is impossible to not understand it. This is probably the fundamental truth of language processing: it is automatic and obligatory.

The N400 was the first stable language-related ERP wave to be extensively documented. More recently, a number of other ERP signature waves have been isolated. The P600 wave and the ELAN (early left anterior negativity) have been claimed to be markers of syntactic anomaly (in contrast to the semantic anomaly marked by the N400 wave). We should expect that as research in this domain becomes more fine-grained, new ERP patterns associated with language processing will be revealed.

## 12.1.5 Language corpora and databases in psycholinguistic research

Recent technological advances have enabled the creation of databases of many millions of words. These new databases and language corpora make it possible for psycholinguists to incorporate many more variables concerning language use into their experimental analyses. Thus, in addition to the word frequency variable, for example, researchers are able to analyze factors such as how early in life a particular word is typically acquired (age of acquisition), the number of different syntactic contexts in which it can occur, the number of complex words that have that word as a morphological constituent (morphological family size), and the semantic properties of words that it has as neighbours in both speech and writing. This capability has greatly increased the sophistication of both the design and statistical analysis of recent psycholinguistic investigations. Finally, projects such as the English Lexicon Project have created databases of words that can be used as stimuli in psycholinguistic experiments and also databases of lexical decision response times that have been obtained over multiple experiments using those words (see http://elexicon.wustl.edu/).

## 12.2 Language processing and linguistics

In the preceding sections, we discussed some of the methods that psycholinguists use to investigate how language is processed. One of the most important results of such psycholinguistic investigations has been that many of the concepts and principles used by linguists to describe and understand the structure of language in terms of phonetics, phonology, morphology, and syntax have been found to also play an important role in the understanding of how language is produced and comprehended during activities such as speaking, listening, reading, and writing. In this section we will focus on these points of contact between

find that although you now know the correct analysis for the sentence, you misread it the second time just as you did the first time. This suggests that the parsing system is in fact a module that operates automatically and independently.

## Sentence ambiguity

Another important clue to how syntactic processing is accomplished comes from the study of ambiguity. Consider the sentence in (11).

(11)  They all rose.

In fact the last word in (11) is ambiguous. The word *rose* can either be related to *stand* or related to *flower*. However, the sentence context leads us clearly to favour the *stand* version of the word. Does the sentence context therefore inhibit activation of the other meaning of *rose*? This question was investigated in a lexical decision experiment in which the sentence in (11) served as the prime. After seeing the sentence, participants were presented with either the word *flower* or *stand*. The researchers found that the sentence facilitated lexical decision response times to both words. That is, both meanings for the word *rose* in the sentence were activated, even though the sentence clearly presented a bias in favour of one reading over the other.

Even more revealing was a follow-up priming experiment which was identical to the one just described except that there was a pause of several hundred milliseconds between the prime and the target. When the pause was present, the priming effect disappeared for the meaning that was unrelated to the sentence context (i.e., *flower*). This suggests that, in fact, sentence processing proceeds in two stages. In the first stage, all possible representations and structures are computed. In the second stage, one of these structures is selected and all others are abandoned. Of course all this happens very quickly and subconsciously so that we as native speakers of a language are never aware that for a sentence such as (12), we compute two possible interpretations.

(12)  The tuna can hit the boat.

In reading this sentence, you ended up imagining either

- *a.* tuna meat that is packed in a small round can, *or*
- *b.* a large fish swimming toward a boat

The point of the psycholinguistic experiments just described is this: No matter which interpretation you arrived at (*a* or *b*), you probably considered both of them, chose one, discarded the other, and forgot about the whole thing in less than a second.

## 12.3 Putting it all together: psycholinguistic modelling

Up to this point, our discussion of psycholinguistic research has been restricted to examining characteristics of phonetic, phonological, morphological, and syntactic processing and the relation between the concepts used in theoretical linguistics and in psycholinguistics. It is important to note, however, that psycholinguistic research seeks not only to discover which types of representations play a role in language processing, but also how these representations and processes fit together to make activities such as speaking, listening, reading, and writing possible.

Psycholinguistic researchers present their ideas about *how language is done* in terms of models. A psycholinguistic model incorporates the results of experiments into a proposal about how processing takes place. In other words, it is a statement of what happens when.

Suppose, for example, we wished to present the finding discussed in section 12.2.3 that a sentence such as *They all rose* will prime both the words *flower* and *stand*. The model might look like figure 12.11.

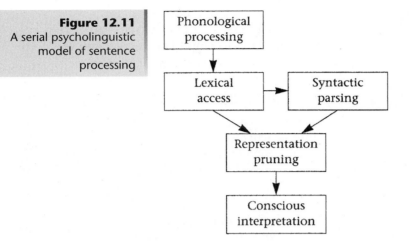

**Figure 12.11**
A serial psycholinguistic model of sentence processing

For our present purposes, it is not important whether this model is actually correct. The purpose of the model is simply to illustrate how psycholinguistic statements can be represented. This model, which looks very much like a computer flow chart, 'says' that when processing a sentence such as *They all rose,* we first perform phonological analysis. This is followed by lexical access, in which all words with matching phonological representations are accessed (including the two words *rose*). Information from lexical access 'feeds' the syntactic parsing module, and information from both the lexical access module and the parsing module are fed to the representation pruning module (the module that discards multiple representations). Finally, the model states that an interpretation becomes conscious only in the final stage of analysis and that there is only one-way information flow to conscious interpretation (in other words, the conscious mind cannot 'peek' at how things are going).

You will note that in creating this model, we have taken two kinds of shortcuts. First, we have created a novel name (i.e., pruning) to describe an operation that has been deduced from the results of psycholinguistic experimentation. Second, our model uses the box notation as a shorthand for a constellation of processes. Thus, it is understood that as the model becomes more elaborated, each one of the boxes in figure 12.11 would be expanded into a flow chart of its own.

As you inspect the model in figure 12.11 you should find that it is really very inadequate. It is missing much important detail, it seems to characterize only one aspect of sentence processing, and it avoids any mention of how meaning is accessed or how sentence interpretation actually takes place. In other words, to be a model of any real value, it would have to be much more elaborate.

Indeed, the types of psycholinguistic models that have been proposed in recent years are very elaborate. This is a good thing. We want models to be as detailed and comprehensive as possible, to take a great deal of experimentation into account and, perhaps most importantly, to show how linguistic and non-linguistic operations work together in the processing of language.

## 12.3.1 The use of metaphors in psycholinguistic modelling

Perhaps the most important characteristic of the model presented in figure 12.11 is the fact that it obviously could not reflect what really happens in the mind of a language user. It is exceedingly unlikely that our minds possess boxes and arrows (or their equivalents). This model, like all psycholinguistic models, employs metaphors for language representations and language processing. The value of these metaphors is that they allow researchers to make specific claims about how language processing works, which can then be tested. For example, through its architecture, the model in figure 12.11 claims that phonological processing precedes lexical access, which in turn precedes syntactic processing. This claim can then be tested in an experiment that investigates whether all phonological processing is complete before syntactic processing begins.

We see then that psycholinguistic models have dual functions. They summarize specific research findings and generate specific hypotheses. They also have the very important function of embodying general perspectives on how language processing works. This is again accomplished through the use of metaphors. These metaphors have the effect of shaping how we conceive of language in the mind and what kinds of questions are asked by psycholinguistic researchers. Finally, these metaphors provide the means by which major families of models can be contrasted in order to test which most accurately describes language processing. In the following sections, we review three of the most important current issues in psycholinguistic modelling: serial versus parallel processing models; single-route versus multiple-route models; and finally, symbolic versus connectionist models.

### Serial versus parallel processing models

Let us return to figure 12.11. By employing the metaphor of a computer program that operates sequentially, the **serial processing model** in figure 12.11 not only makes a claim about sentence processing, but also claims that language processing proceeds in a step-by-step manner. In contrast, a **parallel processing model** claims that phonological, lexical, and syntactic processes are carried out simultaneously. Figure 12.12 represents an example of a parallel processing model. Here information does not flow in a sequential manner. Rather, all modules operate simultaneously and share information. The model in figure 12.12 claims, therefore, that when we hear a sentence, we begin phonological, lexical, and syntactic processes at the same time. As each type of processing proceeds, it informs the other.

**Figure 12.12**
A parallel psycholinguistic model of sentence processing

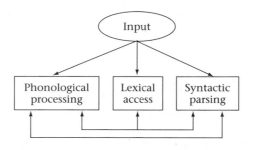

In recent research, serial and parallel processing models have been central in our ability to understand the extent to which bottom-up and top-down processing interact. Serial models correctly characterize those aspects of language processing that are modular and are driven by strict bottom-up procedures, such as phonetic perception. Parallel processing models, on the other hand, are more effective than serial models at characterizing complex processes such as sentence comprehension.

## Single-route versus multiple-route models

Put most directly, **single-route models** claim that a particular type of language processing is accomplished in one manner only. **Multiple-route models**, on the other hand, claim that a language-processing task is accomplished through (usually two) competing mechanisms. Consider, for example, the task of reading English words. Here there are three possibilities: (1) we read a word by looking it up in our mental lexicon based on its visual characteristics; (2) we convert a visual input into phonological representations first and this phonological representation becomes the basis for comprehension; and (3) we do both at the same time. Options (1) and (2) represent single-route models in the sense that they claim that reading is accomplished in one way. Option (3), which is represented in figure 12.13, represents a multiple-route model in that it claims that both mechanisms are employed. Usually such multiple-route models employ the additional metaphor of a horse race by claiming that for some words (e.g., very frequent short words) the direct route is faster but for others (e.g., rare words) the phonological conversion route is faster and 'wins the horse race'.

**Figure 12.13**
A multiple-route model of word reading

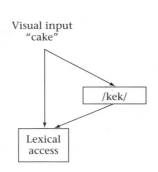

In recent psycholinguistic investigations, the multiple-route approach has been very influential in modelling whether multimorphemic words are decomposed into their constituent morphemes during word recognition or are accessed as whole words. It has been found that although both procedures are active all the time, the whole-word recognition route wins the race for frequent bimorphemic words such as *blackboard*. However, in the case of less frequent words such as *breadboard* or novel multimorphemic forms such as *blueboard*, the morphological decomposition route is the one that provides the basis for comprehension.

## Symbolic versus connectionist models

The final modelling contrast that we review in this section is the contrast between symbolic and connectionist models. These types of models represent fundamentally different views about the nature of mental representations. **Symbolic models** (which include all the ones we have discussed so far) claim that models of linguistic knowledge must make reference to rules and representations consisting of symbols, such as phonemes, words, syntactic category labels, and so forth. **Connectionist models**, on the other hand, claim that the mind can be best modelled by reference to large associations of very simple units (often called **nodes**) that more closely approximate the kinds of processing units (i.e., neurons) that we know the brain to be composed of. Connectionist models typically do not contain direct representations for language units such as words, but rather represent these as an association of nodes. This difference is exemplified in figure 12.14.

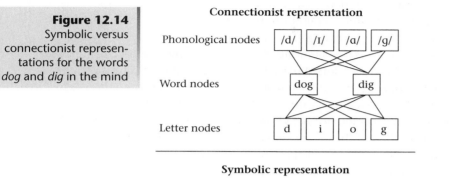

**Figure 12.14**
Symbolic versus connectionist representations for the words *dog* and *dig* in the mind

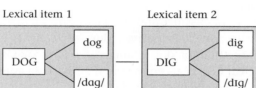

In one sense, the two kinds of representations in figure 12.14 represent exactly the same information—namely, the graphemic and phonological makeup of the words *dog* and *dig*. In another sense, however, they are very different. The connectionist representation shows words as having 'reality' only in the sense that they are bundles of associations between phonological and graphemic nodes. (In some connectionist approaches, the word nodes would not exist at all.) In the symbolic representation, on the other hand, words do indeed have discrete representations in the mind and each representation contains information regarding the word's sound and spelling.

## 12.3.2 Which model is right?

Almost certainly, none of the models that we have discussed is correct. All models represent a researcher's claim about the most current version of the truth. Because psycholinguistics is a very young field, we can expect that any 'current version of the truth' will be very far from the real truth (if there is one). Perhaps this is the reason that psycholinguistic models are so important. They give us the vocabulary with which to ask major questions about mental processing. For example, do our representations consist of symbols corresponding to phonemes, words, and phrases, or are mental representations distributed over a large number of nodes? Does the mind settle into a best way to perform a task, or are all processes horse races between alternative ways to solve a problem? Do mental operations proceed in a step-by-step manner?

These are all big questions and big issues. Language research is at the centre of them. The more we investigate the details of language processing, the more we realize that it offers our best clues to the secrets of human cognition and the more we appreciate how well guarded those secrets are. In the past quarter-century of psycholinguistic research we have learned a great deal about language representation and processing. In the first part of this chapter, we concentrated on the research techniques that have made these advances possible. In this final section of the chapter, we have focused on the yet unresolved major issues.

Although we do not yet know which models are right or which hybrids will be most effective in our evolving understanding of human cognition, the research we have reviewed in this chapter points to a view of language processing that is characterized by massive storage of language forms and by extensive connections among these forms. Language processing also seems to involve automatic and obligatory computational procedures that break down complex language structures into their phonological, morphological, and syntactic constituents during language comprehension, and build them up again during production. We are thus able to conclude that the language system is paradoxically fast and automatic, but not necessarily efficient. The reason for this is probably that the language-processing system is designed to exploit all the linguistic resources of the human brain—its massive storage ability, its apparently unlimited capacity for associations among representations and, finally, its ability to carry out complex computation within modular subsystems. So, whereas theoretical characterizations of language structure strive, quite appropriately, for elegance and simplicity, the language-processing system might strive for exactly the opposite, namely extensive redundancy. The exact manner in which different and perhaps redundant methods of 'doing language' might co-exist in a single human brain has been the subject of a great deal of recent research and debate among psycholinguists and constitutes the next big research challenge in the field.

# Summing up

**Psycholinguistics** is the study of language processing. The field is defined both by an area of subject matter and a particular methodology. Psycholinguists study how people perform the functions of language comprehension and production. They seek to discover the nature of the mental representations that serve these functions and the nature of the cognitive operations and computations that are employed when we understand and produce language.

Because language processing involves computations and representations that cannot be observed and measured directly, psycholinguists have devised special experimental techniques to investigate language processing. Some of these techniques, such as **lexical decision** and **priming**, measure a participant's response time and response accuracy to linguistic stimuli. Other techniques measure eye movement while participants are reading silently and yet others measure electrical activity in the brain during language processing.

Language processing involves many processing modules that are specialized for a particular language-processing task and interact with other modules in restricted ways. Thus, language processing involves a constant interplay between bottom-up and top-down processing. We process phonetic features, phonemes, and words all at the same time. We construct syllable representations, morphological representations, and syntactic representations in a spontaneous and obligatory manner. As conscious beings we are aware of the results of our processing but not of the processing itself.

In general, psycholinguistic studies have revealed that many of the concepts employed in the analysis of sound structure, word structure, and sentence structure also play a role in language processing. However, an account of language processing also requires that we understand how these linguistic concepts interact with other aspects of human processing to enable language production and comprehension.

Psycholinguists typically present their views of how language production and comprehension are achieved in terms of processing models. These models are at the heart of research in psycholinguistics and allow researchers to express the significance of particular research findings, to predict the outcomes of future experiments, and to debate the fundamental characteristics of human cognition.

## Recommended reading

Berko-Gleason, Jean, and Nan Bernstein Ratner. 1998. *Psycholinguistics*. Philadelphia: Harcourt Brace.
Carroll, David. 2007. *Psychology of Language*. Belmont, CA: Wadsworth Publishing.
Field, J. 2004. *Psycholinguistics: The Key Concepts*. London: Routledge.
Gaskell, G. 2007. *Oxford Handbook of Psycholinguistics*. Oxford: Oxford University Press.

## Exercises

1.  How do psycholinguistic investigations of language differ from theoretical linguistic investigations?

2.  Consider the following slips of the tongue. What does each reveal about the process of language production?
    a) They *laked* across the *swim*.
    b) The spy was *gound* and *bagged*.
    c) I will *zee* you in the *bark*.

3.  Imagine that you read that a psycholinguist has reported an experiment in which a priming effect was found for morphological roots on suffixed past tense forms in a lexical decision task.
    a) State the dependent variable in the experiment (i.e., the thing that is observed and measured).
    b) Give an example of a prime stimulus.
    c) Give an example of a target stimulus.

4.  Complete the following sentences by filling in the blanks. In each case, what type of top-down processing and bottom-up processing guided your decision?
    a) The children _____ running in the park.
    b) All _____ movies I like have happy endings.
    c) He tends to see everything as _____ and white.

5.  Recall that according to the cohort model a word is recognized from beginning to end, one phoneme at a time. According to the cohort model, how many phonemes of each

of the following words would have to be processed before a hearer would be sure which word had been spoken?

a) giraffe

b) splat

c) computerize

6. Write the sentences in examples (9) and (10) of this chapter on separate index cards. Take a few other cards and write a normal sentence on each of them. Now, have some friends try to read aloud the sentences on the cards. Do they show evidence that the sentences are more difficult to process?

7. What is a processing model? Try to describe the process of reading single words in terms of a processing model that contains specific modules.

8. Imagine yourself as a psycholinguist trying to devise experiments to investigate how people do language. What experiments would you make up to address the following questions? Be as specific as possible about how you would interpret the question and about what you would do to try to find an answer through psycholinguistic experimentation.

a) Are semantically abstract words easier to process than semantically concrete ones?

b) Are simple clauses more difficult to understand than conjoined clauses?

c) Do people read words from beginning to end?

d) Do people with different levels of education process language in fundamentally different ways?

e) Does the way you parse a sentence depend on what language you speak?

# *Thirteen*

Gary Libben

# *Brain and language*

*The goal of neurology is to understand humanity.*

WILDER PENFIELD

In this chapter we will be concerned with the branch of neuroscience that has as its goal the understanding of how language is represented and processed in the brain. This field of study is called **neurolinguistics**. Although the study of the relationship between brain and language is still in its infancy, much has already been learned about which parts of the brain are involved in various aspects of language production and comprehension. The field of neurolinguistics has also done much to deepen the way we think about the nature of linguistic competence.

The chapter provides a brief survey of brain structure and the methods that are currently available to study the brain. This is followed by a discussion of the different types of language disturbance that result from brain damage and a discussion of how phonology, morphology, syntax, and semantics may be represented in the brain. The chapter concludes by reviewing the current answers to the important neurolinguistic question: Where is language?

## 13.1 The human brain

Contained within your skull is about 1400 grams of pinkish-white matter. It may be the most complex 1400 grams in the galaxy. For most of human history, however, the role of the brain as the centre of mental life remained completely unknown. Even the Greek philosopher Aristotle believed that its primary function was to cool the blood.

We now know much more about the structure and functioning of the brain. But in many ways we are still quite like Aristotle, finding it hard to believe that this wrinkled mass of nerve cells could be the stuff that dreams, fears, and knowledge are made of. Nevertheless, it is, and the task of brain science (or **neuroscience**) is to understand how the breadth and depth of human experience is coded in brain matter.

The brain is composed of nerve cells or **neurons** that are the basic information-processing units of the nervous system. The human brain contains about 10 billion neurons that are organized into networks of almost unimaginable complexity. This complexity results from the fact that each neuron can be directly linked with up to ten thousand other neurons. But the brain is not simply a mass of interconnected neurons. It is composed of structures that seem to play specific roles in the integrated functioning of the brain. The following sections provide a brief overview of these structures.

## 13.1.1 The cerebral cortex

The brain encompasses all the neurological structures above the spinal cord and appears to have evolved from the bottom up. The lower brain structures are shared by almost all animals. These structures are responsible for the maintenance of functions such as respiration, heart rate, and muscle coordination that are essential to the survival of all animals. As we move farther away from the spinal cord, however, we begin to find structures that have developed differently in different species. At the highest level of the brain, the **cerebral cortex**, the differences are most pronounced. Reptiles and amphibians have no cortex at all, and the progression from lower to higher mammals is marked by dramatic increases in the proportion of cortex to total amount of brain tissue. The human brain has the greatest proportion of cortex to brain mass of all animals.

In humans, the cortex is a grey wrinkled mass that sits like a cap over the rest of the brain. The wrinkled appearance results from the cortex being folded in upon itself. This folding allows a great amount of cortical matter to be compressed into the limited space provided by the human skull (in much the same way as the folding of a handkerchief allows it to fit into a jacket pocket). It has been estimated that up to 65 percent of the cortex is hidden within its folds.

It is the human cortex that accounts for our distinctness in the animal world and it is within the human cortex that the secrets of language representation and processing are to be found. The remainder of our discussion of brain structure, therefore, will focus on the features of the cerebral cortex.

## 13.1.2 The cerebral hemispheres

The most important orientation points in mapping the cortex are the folds on its surface. The folds of the cortex have two parts: **sulci** (pronounced /sʌlsaj/; singular: **sulcus**), which are areas where the cortex is folded in, and **gyri** (singular: **gyrus**), which are areas where the cortex is folded out toward the surface.

Figure 13.1 shows a human brain as seen from above, illustrating the many sulci and gyri of the cortex. A very prominent feature is the deep sulcus (in this case called a **fissure** because of its size) that extends from the front of the brain to the back. This fissure, which is known as the **longitudinal fissure**, separates the left and right **cerebral hemispheres**. In many ways, the cerebral hemispheres can be considered to be separate brains and indeed are often referred to as the left brain and the right brain. There are two main reasons for this.

First, the hemispheres are almost completely anatomically separate. The main connection between them is a bundle of nerve fibres known as the **corpus callosum**, whose primary function is to allow the two hemispheres to communicate with one another.

The other reason for considering the hemispheres to be separate brains is that they show considerable functional distinctness. In terms of muscle movement and sensation, each hemisphere is responsible for half the body—oddly enough, the opposite half. Thus the left hemisphere controls the right side of the body and the right hemisphere controls the left side of the body. These **contralateral** (contra = opposite; lateral = side) responsibilities of the cerebral hemispheres account for the fact that people who suffer damage to one hemisphere of the brain (as a result of a stroke or accident) will exhibit paralysis on the opposite side of the body.

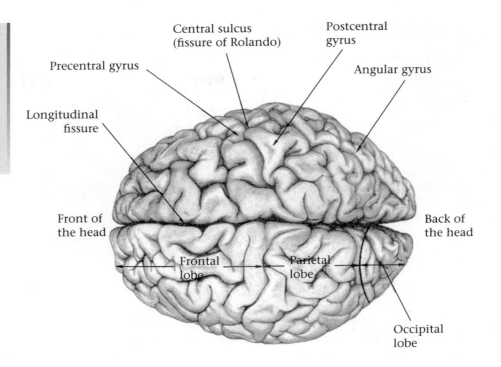

**Figure 13.1**
The cerebral hemispheres seen from above the head. Note the many fissures and gyri of the cortex and the prominence of the longitudinal fissure that separates the left and right hemispheres.

The hemispheres also show functional distinctness with respect to higher cognitive functions. In general, the left hemisphere seems to excel in analytic tasks such as arithmetic, whereas the right hemisphere excels in tasks that require an overall appreciation of complex patterns such as the recognition of familiar faces and melodies.

Despite the fact that the hemispheres show such specialization, we should be cautious about making sweeping generalizations about left brain versus right brain abilities or strategies. In all probability, complex mental activities involve the coordinated functioning of both hemispheres. The representation of language in the brain provides a useful example of this.

Most right-handed individuals have language represented in the left cerebral hemisphere and are therefore said to be left **lateralized** for language. But not every aspect of language is represented in the left hemisphere of right-handers. Adults who have had their left cerebral hemispheres surgically removed lose most, but not all, of their linguistic competence. They typically lose the ability to speak and process complex syntactic patterns but retain some language comprehension ability. Clearly, it must be the right hemisphere that is responsible for whatever language-processing ability remains (see figure 13.2 on page 436).

It has also been reported that right-handed patients who suffer damage to the right cerebral hemisphere exhibit difficulty in understanding jokes and metaphors in everyday conversation. These patients are able to provide only a literal or concrete interpretation of figurative sentences such as *He was wearing a loud tie*. They frequently misunderstand people because they cannot use loudness and intonation as cues to whether a speaker is angry, excited, or merely joking. Thus, the right hemisphere has a distinct role to play in normal language use.

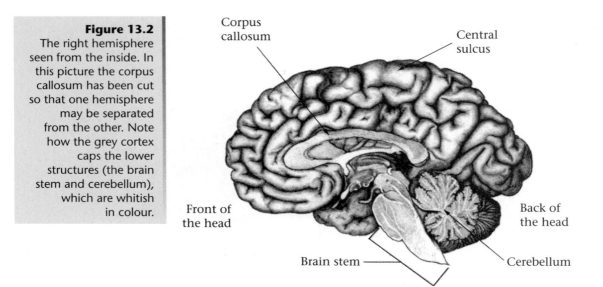

**Figure 13.2**
The right hemisphere seen from the inside. In this picture the corpus callosum has been cut so that one hemisphere may be separated from the other. Note how the grey cortex caps the lower structures (the brain stem and cerebellum), which are whitish in colour.

Corpus callosum

Central sulcus

Front of the head

Back of the head

Brain stem

Cerebellum

Finally, consideration of language representation in the brains of left-handers makes matters even more complex. Contrary to what might be expected, few left-handers have a mirror image representation for language (that is, language localization in the right hemisphere). Rather, they tend to show significant language representation in both hemispheres. Thus, left-handers are generally less lateralized for language.

To sum up, although the left and right hemispheres have different abilities and different responsibilities, complex skills such as language do not always fall neatly into one hemisphere or the other. Research into why this is the case constitutes an important part of neuroscience. This research promises to reveal much about the cerebral hemispheres and about the individual representations and processes that comprise language.

## 13.1.3 The lobes of the cortex

We have seen that the cerebral hemispheres make distinct contributions to the overall functioning of the brain. In addition, each hemisphere contains substructures that appear to have distinct responsibilities. The substructures of the cortex in each hemisphere are called **lobes**. Like the hemispheres, the lobes of the cortex can be located with reference to prominent fissures, sulci, and gyri, which are useful as orientation points in much the same way that rivers and mountain ranges are useful in finding particular locations on a map. As can be seen in figure 13.3, the **central sulcus** (also called the fissure of Rolando) extends from the top of the cortex to another groove known as the **lateral fissure** (also called the Sylvian fissure). These two features are important in the delineation of the cerebral lobes. The **frontal lobe** lies in front of the central sulcus and the **parietal lobe** lies behind it. The **temporal lobe** is the area beneath the lateral fissure. The fourth lobe, the **occipital lobe**, is not clearly marked by an infolding of the cortex, but can be identified as the area to the rear of the **angular gyrus** (which has been found to play an important role in reading).

Figure 13.3 shows the left hemisphere of the brain. It indicates the location of each lobe and its specialized functions. Assuming that this is the brain of a right-hander, it is also possible to identify those areas of the cortex that have a particular role to play in language processing, as we will see.

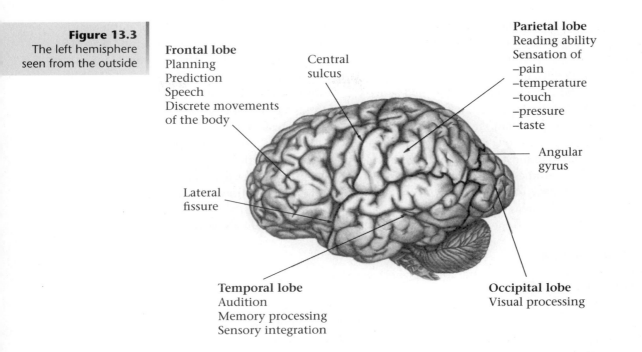

**Frontal lobe**
Planning
Prediction
Speech
Discrete movements
of the body

Central
sulcus

**Parietal lobe**
Reading ability
Sensation of
–pain
–temperature
–touch
–pressure
–taste

Angular
gyrus

Lateral
fissure

**Temporal lobe**
Audition
Memory processing
Sensory integration

**Occipital lobe**
Visual processing

## 13.2 Investigating the brain

Imagine that you could open the top of a living human being's skull and observe the brain
while the individual is engaged in activities such as reading, writing, watching a hockey game,
or having a heated argument. What would you see? The answer is—nothing! To the outside
observer, the working brain shows no evidence of its activity. This is clearly a problem for the
field of neurolinguistics, which requires the use of special investigative techniques to uncover
the secrets of where and how language is processed in the brain. In addition, these special
techniques must meet the ethical requirements of research on human subjects. While other
neuroscientists are able to do much of their research using animal subjects, this option is not
available to neurolinguists.

Imposing as they may be, the problems of investigating the processing of language in the
brain are not insurmountable. Recent decades have seen a number of technological advances
that have greatly facilitated the investigation of the question: What is going on in the brain
when people are engaged in language behaviour? In the following sections, we discuss some
of the techniques of neurolinguistic investigation.

## 13.2.1 Autopsy studies

Until recently the only way to study the brain was through **autopsy studies**. This technique
was most often carried out with patients who were admitted to hospitals displaying a neurological disorder. Careful observations were made of a patient's behaviour, and subsequent to his or
her death, the brain was examined to determine which areas were damaged. By comparing the
area of brain damage and the type of disorder the patient displayed while alive, neurologists
could develop theories about the role of the damaged brain parts in normal brain functioning.

A famous example of this type of analysis comes from the work of Paul Broca, a nineteenth-century French neurologist. In 1860, Broca observed a patient who had been hospitalized for more than twenty years in Paris. For most of his hospitalization, the patient was almost completely unable to speak, but appeared to understand everything that was said to him. Toward the end of his life (he died at age fifty-seven), he also developed a paralysis of the right arm and leg. Immediately after the patient's death (as a result of an unrelated infection), Broca examined the brain. It showed severe damage (called a **lesion**) in the lower rear area of the left frontal lobe. Broca concluded that because the patient was unable to speak, this part of the frontal lobe must normally be responsible for speech production. Since that time, many other autopsy studies have supported Broca's conclusions. This lower rear portion of the left frontal lobe is now called **Broca's area** (see figure 13.4, which shows this and other language-processing areas of the left hemisphere). As will be discussed in section 13.3.1, the impairment of the ability to speak as a result of brain damage is called **Broca's aphasia**.

**Figure 13.4**
Language processes in the left hemisphere. Damage to Broca's area is usually associated with non-fluent speech and difficulty processing complex syntactic patterns. Damage to Wernicke's area (see section 13.3.2) is usually associated with comprehension disturbances. Damage to the area around the angular gyrus results in reading impairment.

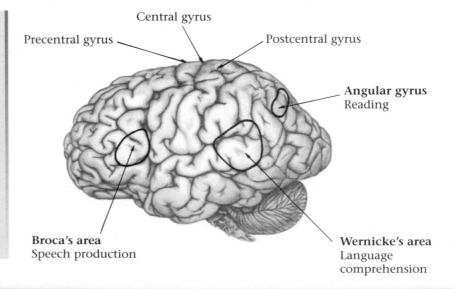

Central gyrus
Precentral gyrus
Postcentral gyrus
Angular gyrus
Reading
Broca's area
Speech production
Wernicke's area
Language comprehension

---

**Language Matters  Phrenology: A Discredited Theory of the Brain, Mind, and Skull**

Franz Joseph Gall was born in 1758 in southwestern Germany. After moving to Vienna, he founded the field of Phrenology, which can be considered to have three basic claims:

(1) The mind can be divided into discrete mental 'organs'.
(2) Particular development in any area results in expanded brain size in that location.
(3) This expansion presses on the skull, and produces bumps that can then be identified and interpreted by the trained phrenologist.

Although it is extremely unlikely that Gall's original mental organs (e.g., combativeness, hope) are correct, the more general idea of mental organs remains a key part of current neuropsychological debate.

We now consider the science behind (2) and (3) to have been almost entirely wrong. But, interestingly, Gall was reported to be extraordinarily good at assessing the abilities and traits of complete strangers (allegedly using his method of feeling the skull). In his time, Gall gained both fame and notoriety. He was forced to leave Vienna and he eventually settled in France, where his work was also discredited within scientific circles.

## 13.2.2 Images of the living brain

Autopsy analysis has been and continues to be an important tool in the understanding of the brain. But an autopsy can be carried out only after the patient's death. Therefore, whatever information it reveals about the nature and extent of the patient's brain damage can no longer be of any use in his or her treatment. One of the earliest techniques used to understand how the living brain processes language was pioneered in Canada by the Montreal neurosurgeon Wilder Penfield. This technique was developed to map the brain of a person who was about to undergo neurosurgery. Prior to the surgical procedure, a portion of the skull was removed and the surface of the brain was stimulated with electrodes carrying small electrical charges in order to map which areas of the individual's brain were involved in particular functions. This would allow the physicians to better assess how surgery might affect the post-operative abilities of the patient and assist the patient and family in weighing the risk-benefit ratio of the planned intervention. Such pre-operative procedures greatly assisted early attempts to produce a functional map of the human cerebral cortex. Interestingly, it was also found that direct electrical stimulation of the brain resulted in temporary loss, rather than enhancement, of function.

Since Penfield's pioneering work in the 1950s, the sophistication of pre-operative techniques has increased greatly. It is now possible to insert electrodes deep into the living brain and isolate the function of a very small number of neurons (i.e., fewer than a thousand at a time). But this, of course, remains a very invasive technique that would only be carried out on patients whose neurological impairment may require brain surgery. Next we review a few other techniques that are, comparatively speaking, much less invasive.

**Computerized Axial Tomography** (also called **CT scanning**) is a technique that uses a narrow beam of X-rays to create brain images that take the form of a series of brain slices. CT scans have offered neuroscientists their first opportunity to look inside a living brain. However, like autopsy, CT scanning provides a static image of the brain. It is most useful in identifying brain lesions and tumours. In order to study the brain in action, however, other techniques are required that are sensitive to dynamic activity.

One such dynamic technique is **Positron Emission Tomography** (also called PET). This technique capitalizes on one of the brain's many interesting properties—it is extremely hungry for glucose and oxygen. Although the brain accounts for only about 2 percent of total body weight, it consumes about 20 percent of the oxygen the body uses while at rest. This oxygen is, of course, carried to the brain by the blood.

In the PET technique, positron-emitting isotopes, which function as radioactive tracers, are injected into the arteries in combination with glucose. The rate at which the radioactive glucose is used by specific regions of the brain is recorded while the subject is engaged in various sorts of cognitive activities. These recordings are used to produce maps of areas of high brain activity associated with particular cognitive functions. Examples of such PET maps are represented in figure 13.5 on p. 440.

Although PET is much less invasive than electrical stimulation of the brain, which requires prior removal of portions of the skull, it is hardly a technique that most people would volunteer for, because of the perceived risks associated with the injection of the radioactive tracer. The two techniques that we will review next also make use of changes in blood flow within the brain in order to associate cognitive function with specific brain regions, but they do so without injection.

**Figure 13.5**
PET scans show how blood flow to the brain shifts to different locations, depending on which task is being performed.

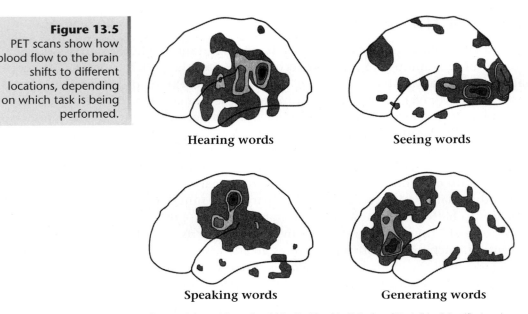

Hearing words

Seeing words

Speaking words

Generating words

Source: Adapted from Gerald D. Fischbach's "Mind and Brain" in *Scientific American* (September 1992). Reprinted by permission of Professor Marcus E. Raichle.

At present, **functional magnetic resonance imaging** (fMRI) is the preferred means of gaining information about the functional anatomy of the brain. The technique also monitors increases in blood flow to specific areas of the brain. It does so by making use of the fact that blood is rich in iron. Although iron comprises only 0.004 percent of the human body, 65 percent of it is found within the hemoglobin of red blood cells. The fMRI technique uses powerful magnetic fields to track this iron, and hence blood flow within the brain. FMRI installations are currently very expensive and therefore not available at all research centres. Nevertheless, the technique has already yielded dramatic evidence of brain activity during language-processing tasks.

A final extremely promising technique for the study of how language is processed in the brain is **magnetoencephalography**, or MEG. The MEG technique records very subtle changes in the magnetic fields generated within the brain. Although MEG also requires a very expensive apparatus, it has advantages over all the other techniques discussed so far. In contrast to PET, it is non-invasive, and, like fMRI, it provides detailed information on which parts of the brain are involved in a language-processing activity. Its key advantage is that it also provides time resolution that is greatly superior to that of fMRI. Using the MEG technique, researchers are able to gain a millisecond-by-millisecond record of how the brain responds to a stimulus event, such as the presentation of a single word. In this way, MEG combines the time-resolution advantages of event-related potentials (ERP) (discussed in chapter 12) and the spatial resolution advantages of fMRI.

Modern brain-imaging techniques such as fMRI and MEG have greatly increased our knowledge of where language processing takes place in the brain. It has been found, for example, that when subjects speak, much blood flows to the left hemisphere of the cortex and to Broca's area in particular. When subjects read, much blood flows to the occipital lobe (because it is responsible for visual processing), to the angular gyrus (which has a special role to play in reading), and to other areas of the left hemisphere. These observations support the view that the left hemisphere is primarily responsible for language and that there are specific language areas within the left hemisphere.

Finally, functional brain imaging studies are playing an important role in increasing our understanding of the differences that might exist between language processing in one's mother tongue and language processing in a second language. Second language processing has been shown to involve a wider variety of cortical sites. This supports the view that the less automatic nature of language use in a second language requires the involvement of diverse mental processes in addition to those specifically dedicated to language.

## 13.2.3 Learning from hemispheric connections and disconnections

In the techniques that have been described, information about language representation in the brain is gained through an investigation of the brain itself. In this section, we review an alternative approach—one that examines behaviour that can be associated with a particular brain hemisphere.

### Dichotic listening studies

**Dichotic listening** studies have been extremely important in the accumulation of the knowledge we possess about the specialization of the cerebral hemispheres. The technique capitalizes on the property of the brain that we discussed in section 13.1.2—namely, that each hemisphere is primarily wired to the opposite side of the body (including the head). So, most of the input to your right ear goes to the left hemisphere of your brain. Now, if the left cerebral hemisphere is indeed specialized for language processing in right-handers, these individuals should process language better through the right ear.

If you are right-handed, you will most probably be able to verify this by observing the difference between holding a telephone receiver to your right ear and holding it to your left ear during a conversation. When the receiver is held to the right ear, it will appear that the speech is louder and clearer. This phenomenon is known as the **right ear advantage (REA)**. In the laboratory technique, stereo earphones are used and different types of stimuli are presented to each ear. In general, the right ear shows an advantage for words, numbers, and Morse code, whereas the left ear shows an advantage for the perception of melodies and environmental sounds such as bird songs.

### Split brain studies

If the left hemisphere is wired to the right ear, why is it possible to understand speech presented to the left ear? There are two reasons for this. The first is that the auditory pathways to the brain are not completely crossed—there are also secondary links between each hemisphere and the ear on the same side of the body. The second is that after the right hemisphere receives information from the left ear, that information can be transferred to the left hemisphere via the corpus callosum—the bundle of fibres that connects the two hemispheres.

Evidence concerning the crucial role that the corpus callosum plays in normal brain functioning comes from the study of patients who have had this pathway surgically severed.[1] Studies that have investigated the effects of this surgery on cognition—so-called **split brain experiments**—have provided dramatic illustrations of what happens when the hemispheres cannot communicate with one another.

It appears from the behaviour of split brain patients that although the right hemisphere does show some language understanding, it is mute. In one of the many split brain experiments, a patient is blindfolded and an object (e.g., a key) is placed in one hand. When the key is held in the right hand, the patient can easily name it, because the right hand is connected to the left hemisphere that can compute speech output. However, when the key is placed in the left hand, the patient cannot say what it is. The right hemisphere, which receives information from the left hand, knows what is there, but it can neither put this into words nor transfer the information across the severed corpus callosum to the left brain.

Split brain experiments have presented new and important knowledge about the functioning of the brain. In terms of overall investigative methodology, however, they are not quite as exotic as they seem. In fact, the logic of split brain experiments is identical to the logic employed by Broca in 1860. In both cases the researcher endeavours to learn how the normal brain works by examining which functions are lost as a result of the brain damage. In the case of split brain studies, the damage is surgically induced. In the case of Broca's aphasia, disease caused an 'experiment in nature'. In section 13.3, we return to these experiments in nature and examine what they reveal about language representation in the brain.

## 13.3 Aphasia

The term *aphasia* refers to the loss of language ability as a result of damage to the brain. The most common cause of aphasia is **stroke** (also called a **cerebrovascular accident**). A stroke occurs when the normal flow of blood to the brain is disrupted, preventing neurons from receiving oxygen and nutrients. Aphasia can also be caused by blows to the head, brain infection, brain tumours, and brain hemorrhage. Currently, aphasia affects more than 1 million people in North America. The syndrome is equally common in men and women, and is most likely to occur in persons over the age of fifty.

In general, the amount and type of aphasic disturbance that a patient will exhibit depends on how much the brain is damaged and where it is damaged. Most individuals who suffer aphasic impairment experience a mixture of deficits in speaking, listening, reading, and writing. However, some other forms of aphasia are much more specific. In these more specific forms, particular skills are lost and others remain intact. The study of these specific aphasias can tell us much about the building blocks of language in the brain. Sections 13.3.1 and 13.3.2 discuss the two most important specific aphasias.

## 13.3.1 Non-fluent aphasia

**Non-fluent aphasia** (also called **motor aphasia**) results from damage to parts of the brain in front of the central sulcus. Recall that an important part of the frontal lobe is concerned with motor activity and that the bottom rear portion of the frontal lobe (Broca's area) is responsible for the articulation of speech (see figure 13.4). Not surprisingly, therefore, non-fluent patients show slow, effortful speech production (hence the term *non-fluent*). The most severe form of non-fluent aphasia is **global aphasia**. In this type of aphasia, the patient is completely mute. Of the less severe forms, **Broca's aphasia** is the most important.

## Language Matters **Brain Size Is Not the Whole Story**

Although humans have relatively large brains (only those of elephants are bigger), an even more important factor may be the amount of cortex (related to the amount of folding into gyri and sulci) and the proportion of uncommitted cortex—areas not assigned a specific function. As shown in the diagram below, humans have a great deal of uncommitted cerebral cortex. Human intelligence is made possible by the richness of associations within that cortex.

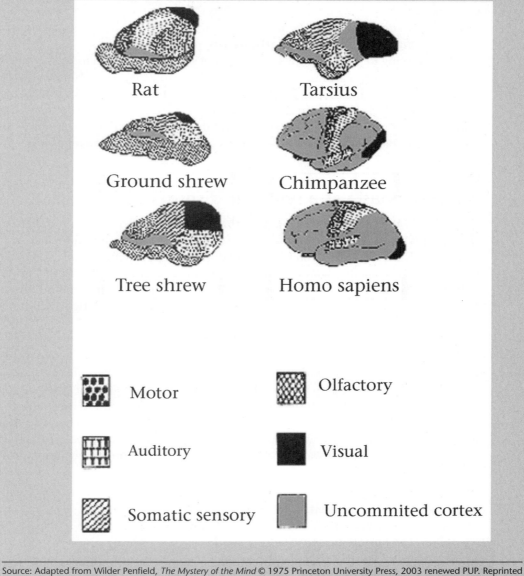

Rat

Tarsius

Ground shrew

Chimpanzee

Tree shrew

Homo sapiens

Motor

Olfactory

Auditory

Visual

Somatic sensory

Uncommited cortex

Source: Adapted from Wilder Penfield, *The Mystery of the Mind* © 1975 Princeton University Press, 2003 renewed PUP. Reprinted by permission of Princeton University Press.

The speech of Broca's aphasics is very halting. Patients have great difficulty in accurately producing the needed phonemes to say a word. For example, a patient who wishes to produce the sentence in (1a) would be likely to produce the utterance in (1b).

(1) *a.* It's hard to eat with a spoon.
    *b.* . . . har eat . . . wɪt . . . pun

The ellipsis dots (...) between the words in (1b) indicate periods of silence in the production of the utterance. Sentences produced at this slow rate tend to also lack normal sentence intonation. This is a common characteristic of the speech of Broca's aphasics and is called **dysprosody**. Note how the patient simplifies the consonant clusters in the words *hard* and *spoon* and changes the /θ/ to /t/ in the word *with*. The speech errors that result from these sorts of phonemic errors are called **phonemic paraphasias**.

It is tempting to think that the impairment of speech production in Broca's aphasia is caused by the fact that Broca's area is adjacent to the motor strip that controls movement of the facial muscles. The problem with this hypothesis is that damage to Broca's area usually produces only mild weakness of the muscles on the opposite side of the face and no permanent damage. Yet, for some reason, even people who can still control the muscles used in speech cannot use language properly after damage to Broca's area. This suggests that Broca's area has a language-specific responsibility.

## Broca's aphasia as a syntactic disorder

Returning to the utterance in (1b), note that the patient also omits a number of words that would normally be used in this utterance. The words that are omitted include *it, is, to, a*—the sort of words that we too would be likely to omit if we were writing a telegram (e.g., *I will meet you in the airport lounge* → *Meet you in airport lounge*). These 'little words' are often called **function words** and their omission in the speech of Broca's aphasics has been referred to as **telegraphic speech**. (We will return to the problem of determining which items belong to the set of function words in section 13.5.)

One possible account of the speech of Broca's aphasics is that it results from an economy of effort. Speech production is very effortful for these patients so they use as few words as possible because, like telegram writers, they are 'paying' by the word. But there are other characteristics of their linguistic abilities that point to a deeper cause—the disturbance of syntactic competence.

In addition to omitting function words, Broca's aphasics tend to omit inflectional affixes such as *-ing*, *-ed*, and *-en* in words such as *running, chased,* and *broken*. They also show difficulty judging the grammaticality of sentences. For example, given sentences such as the ones in (2), Broca's aphasics will not always be able to determine which ones are grammatical and which ones are not.

(2) *a.* The boy ate it up.
    *b.* *The boy ate up it.
    *c.* *Boy ate it up.
    *d.* The boy ate up the cake.

Finally, a close examination of the comprehension of Broca's aphasics offers further support for the view that there is a syntactic component to the disorder.

(3) *a.* The mouse was chased by the cat.
    *b.* The dog was chased by the cat.
    *c.* The cat was chased by the mouse.

Broca's aphasics tend to interpret sentences such as (3a) correctly. In a sentence such as this, knowledge about the behaviour of cats and mice helps the patient to guess correctly at the meaning of the sentence. For sentences such as (3b), however, in which knowledge of the world is not a reliable guide to comprehension, patients are unsure about the meaning. Finally, Broca's aphasics tend to interpret a sentence such as (3c) as though it had the same meaning as (3a). When we read a sentence like (3c), we recognize it as describing an unlikely event, but our interpretation is driven by the syntax of the sentence, not by our knowledge of the world. Many Broca's aphasics appear not to have this ability.

These sorts of observations have led many neurolinguists to reconsider the traditional view that Broca's aphasia is simply a production deficit. The possibility that Broca's aphasia also involves some central disturbance of syntactic competence is intriguing and may lead to a deeper understanding of how syntactic knowledge is represented in the brain. We will return to this question in section 13.4.

A final point about Broca's aphasia is of a less technical nature but is of great importance to the understanding of the syndrome as a whole. Most Broca's aphasics are acutely aware of their language deficit and are typically very frustrated by it. It is as though they have complete understanding of what they should say, but to their constant dismay, find themselves unable to say it. This plight of Broca's aphasics is consistent with our understanding of the role of the frontal lobe, which is usually the site of lesions in the syndrome. Broca's area of the frontal lobe plays an extremely important role in language; however, it does not seem to be involved in the semantic relationships between words and the relationship between units of language and units of thought. The neurological basis of these meaning relationships remains almost entirely unknown. From the analysis of non-fluent aphasia in general and Broca's aphasia in particular, however, we suspect that these semantic relationships are the responsibility of areas of the brain that lie behind the central sulcus—in the temporal and parietal lobes of the brain (see figure 13.3). This suspicion is supported by the type of language deficits associated with damage to the temporal-parietal lobes.

## 13.3.2 Fluent aphasia

The type of aphasia that results from damage to parts of the left cortex behind the central sulcus is referred to as **fluent aphasia** (or **sensory aphasia**). This type of aphasia stands in sharp contrast to non-fluent aphasia. Fluent aphasics have no difficulty producing language, but have a great deal of difficulty selecting, organizing, and monitoring their language production.

The most important type of fluent aphasia is called **Wernicke's aphasia**. The syndrome is named after the German physiologist Carl Wernicke, who, in 1874, published a now famous report of a kind of aphasia that was almost the complete opposite of Broca's aphasia. It was determined from autopsy data that this type of aphasia was associated with a lesion in the temporal lobe just below the most posterior (rear) portion of the lateral fissure. In severe cases, the lesion could also extend upward into the lower portion of the parietal lobe. This area of the brain is now known as Wernicke's area (see figure 13.4).

In contrast to Broca's aphasics, Wernicke's aphasics are generally unaware of their deficit. Their speech typically sounds very good: there are no long pauses; sentence intonation is normal; function words are used appropriately; word order is usually syntactically correct. The problem is that the patient rarely makes any sense. The following is a conversation between an examiner (E) and a Wernicke's patient (P).

(4) *E:* How are you today, Mrs. A?
    *P:* Yes.
    *E:* Have I ever tested you before?
    *P:* No. I mean I haven't.
    *E:* Can you tell me what your name is?
    *P:* No, I don't I . . . right I'm right now here.
    *E:* What is your address?
    *P:* I cud /kʌd/ if I can help these this like you know . . . to make it.
    We are seeing for him. That is my father.

The patient in this conversation produces a number of errors. But note that most of these errors are different from the kinds of errors made by Broca's aphasics. While the patient is able to produce some well-formed structures (e.g., *no, I don't*), these structures appear intermittently amidst various unrelated fragments. Not only are these constructions unrelated to each other, they are also unrelated to the examiner's questions. It appears that the patient has no understanding of the questions being asked.

This patient displays a significant but not severe form of Wernicke's aphasia. Her speech appears to result from a semi-random selection of words and short phrases. In very severe cases of this syndrome, phonemes are also randomly selected and the result is speech that has the intonational characteristics of English but actually contains very few real words of the language. This is termed **jargonaphasia**.

The type of deficit found in Wernicke's aphasia leads us to a greater understanding and a deeper consideration of the nature of language comprehension. Wernicke's aphasia is primarily a comprehension deficit. But as we have seen, when comprehension breaks down, most of what we call language ability breaks down with it. Patients cannot express themselves because they cannot understand what they have just said and use that understanding in the planning of what to say next. In a very real sense, these patients have lost contact with themselves (and therefore with the rest of the world). Wernicke's patients cannot have coherent trains of thought—the brain damage does not allow the parts of the train to be connected.[2]

In summary, our discussion of fluent and non-fluent aphasia has demonstrated how normal language use is a marriage of content and form. In the case of non-fluent aphasia, form is compromised but the content of language remains relatively intact. In contrast, fluent aphasia is characterized by a rapid flow of form with little content.

# 13.4 Acquired dyslexia and dysgraphia

Reading and writing involve a complex array of perceptual and motor skills. In this section we will consider impairments of reading and writing that are caused by damage to the brain. The impairment of reading ability is called **acquired dyslexia** (or **acquired alexia**). The impairment of writing ability is called **acquired dysgraphia** (or **acquired agraphia**). In both cases the term *acquired* indicates that the patient possessed normal reading and/or writing ability prior to brain damage and distinguishes the syndromes from developmental dyslexia and developmental dysgraphia, which deal with disturbances of reading and writing development in children.

## 13.4.1 Reading and writing disturbances in aphasia

Acquired dyslexia and dysgraphia typically accompany the aphasic syndromes that we considered in section 13.3. Most Broca's aphasics show writing disturbances that are comparable to their speaking deficits. In other words, a patient who cannot pronounce the word *spoon* will also not be able to write it correctly. The resulting error in writing (e.g., *poon*) is called a **paragraphia**. In spontaneous writing, Broca's aphasics also tend to omit function words and inflectional affixes. Finally, while the silent reading of Broca's aphasics is very good, their reading aloud shows the same telegraphic style as their spontaneous speech. These observations reinforce the view that the deficit in Broca's aphasia is much more than a speech articulation deficit. It is a production deficit at a very deep level of language planning.

Wernicke's aphasics also show reading and writing deficits that match their deficits in speaking and listening. The writing of Wernicke's aphasics is formally very good. They typically retain good spelling and handwriting. However, like their speaking, what they write makes little sense. Reading comprehension is also severely impaired in Wernicke's aphasia. Patients can see the letters and words, but cannot make any sense of them. Again the conclusion to be drawn is that Wernicke's aphasia, like Broca's aphasia, involves a central disturbance of language competence—the knowledge that underlies language functioning. In such cases of central language disturbance, whatever impairment the patient has in listening and speaking will be matched in reading and writing.

## 13.4.2 Acquired dyslexia as the dominant language deficit

In addition to the reading and writing deficits that accompany aphasia, there are many cases in which the disruption of reading and writing ability is the dominant symptom. This typically follows damage in and around the angular gyrus of the parietal lobe. An analysis of these types of disabilities has led to some very interesting theories about the nature of reading (at least in English).

Before we proceed to discuss two contrasting types of acquired dyslexia, it might be worthwhile to reflect on the abilities involved in the reading of words. Up to this point in the chapter you have read over five thousand words. Some of these words (such as the function words) are very familiar to you and you probably recognized them as wholes. But others, such as *angular gyrus*, are words that you probably read for the first time. How then could you know how to pronounce them? Many theorists believe that readers maintain a set of spelling-to-sound rules that enables them to read new words aloud. These rules are important in the development of reading ability and in the addition of new words to our reading vocabulary.

**Phonological dyslexia** is a type of acquired dyslexia in which the patient seems to have lost the ability to use spelling-to-sound rules. Phonological dyslexics can only read words that they have seen before. Asked to read a word such as *blug* aloud, they either say nothing or produce a known word that is visually similar to the target (e.g., *blue* or *bug*).

**Surface dyslexia** is the opposite of phonological dyslexia. Surface dyslexics seem unable to recognize words as wholes. Instead, they must process all words through a set of spelling-to-sound rules. This is shown by the kinds of errors they make. Surface dyslexics do not have difficulty reading words such as *bat* that are regularly spelled. However, they read irregularly spelled words such as *yacht* by applying regular rules and thus producing /jatʃt/.

The most interesting aspect of surface dyslexics' reading ability is that they understand what they produce, not what they see. For example, a surface dyslexic would be likely to read the word *worm* as /worm/ (and not /wərm/). When asked what the word means, the patient would answer: the opposite of *cold*.

Data from acquired dyslexia allow researchers to build models that specify the components of normal reading ability and their relationship to each other. Clearly, this type of analysis plays a very important role in the development of our understanding of language, the mind, and the brain.

# 13.5 Linguistic theory and aphasia

Looking at aphasia in terms of linguistic theory gives us a new perspective on language in the brain. Linguistic theory has been traditionally concerned with the structure of language, not with how it is used in listening, speaking, reading, and writing. In contrast, the traditional way of looking at aphasia has been in terms of what the patient can and cannot do. The involvement of theoretical linguists in the study of aphasia has caused a minor revolution in the field. Aphasia researchers have begun to think about the deficit in terms of the loss of semantic features, phonological rules, and perhaps syntactic tree structures. Theoretical linguists have also found that the study of aphasia offers an important area for testing theoretical distinctions such as the one between derivational suffixes and inflectional suffixes. In this section, we will look at some of the areas in which the marriage of theoretical linguistics and neurolinguistics has been most fruitful. This fruitfulness has usually meant an increase in the sophistication of the questions that are asked about aphasia. It has also meant the discovery of new and often bizarre aphasic phenomena.

## 13.5.1 Features, rules, and underlying forms

In the area of phonology, we have found that the phonemic paraphasias of Broca's aphasics usually differ from the target phoneme by only one distinctive feature (recall example (1) in section 13.3.1: *with* → /wɪt/) and can therefore be easily described by phonological rules. Observations such as these lead us to believe that phonological features and rules might be good tools to characterize how language is represented and produced.

In the area of morphology, the study of aphasia has offered empirical support for the theoretical distinction between inflection and derivation. As we have discussed, Broca's aphasics show a sensitivity to this distinction in their omission of affixes in speech. Inflectional affixes are commonly dropped, but derivational affixes are usually retained. Perhaps most interesting is the tendency of some aphasics to produce underlying forms of morphemes in reading and repetition. Asked to repeat the word *illegal*, for example, some aphasics will produce *inlegal*, using the underlying form of the negative prefix rather than the allomorph that should occur before a base beginning with /l/. Again, errors such as these point to the possibility that phonological processes such as nasal assimilation and the notion of underlying form are not only an elegant way to represent linguistic competence but are also relevant to the processing of language in the brain.

The study of aphasia also stands to shed light on the nature of semantic representations. Most of the work in this area has concentrated on the many subvarieties of acquired dyslexia. In a syndrome known as **deep dyslexia**, patients produce reading errors that are systematically related to the word that they are asked to read (in the sense that they share some semantic features but not others). Given the word *mother*, for example, a deep dyslexic may read *father*.

The detailed study of semantic deficits associated with brain damage has also led to some very surprising discoveries. Most aphasics and dyslexics find abstract words much more difficult to process than concrete words. But there have been reports of concrete word dyslexia in which the patient shows exactly the opposite problem (having difficulty with concrete words such as *table*). There has even been a report of a patient who shows a selective inability to read words that refer to fruits and vegetables.

## 13.5.2 Agrammatism

In section 13.3.1, we observed that many theorists now believe that Broca's aphasia involves a central syntactic deficit. The syndrome that is characterized by telegraphic speech has been given the name **agrammatism**—to indicate that grammatical ability has been lost. Agrammatism is the aphasic disturbance that has been most studied by linguists. As was discussed in section 13.3.1, it is characterized by the omission of function words such as *it*, *is*, *to*, and *a*, by the omission of inflectional affixes, and by comprehension deficits in cases where the correct interpretation of a sentence is dependent on syntax alone.

In recent years, many linguists have become involved in the problems of characterizing the agrammatic deficit. These problems have raised both specific questions such as: What exactly is a function word? and general questions such as: Is it possible to lose syntax? The involvement of linguists has also generated cross-linguistic studies of agrammatism that provide interesting insights into the interaction between characteristics of the syndrome and characteristics of particular languages.

## 13.5.3 Function words

Intuitively, function words are grammatical words that can be distinguished from content words such as nouns, verbs, and adjectives. In terms of formal syntax, however, they are quite heterogeneous. They include pronouns, auxiliaries, determiners, and prepositions—items that do not fall into any single syntactic category. Much of the recent work in this area by linguists has concentrated on working out what exactly the so-called function words have in common. Some researchers have suggested that they form a phonological group—they are all words that do not normally take stress. Others have pointed to the fact that function words do not normally take affixes and therefore form a morphological group. Still others have suggested that syntactic theory should be modified so that all the words that are lost in agrammatism fall under the heading functional category (this would involve changing the status of prepositions, which are currently treated as lexical categories—see chapter 5).

Whatever the outcome of this debate, it is clear that neurolinguistic evidence has presented a new set of challenges to the field of formal linguistics. One of these challenges is to build bridges between normal and pathological linguistic competence by finding units of analysis that are appropriate to both.

## 13.5.4 **The loss of syntactic competence**

Another, much more general, challenge is to define what it means to possess syntactic competence such that we can speak of its loss. This challenge has forced researchers to address the question: What is the essence of syntactic knowledge? Is it the hierarchical arrangement of elements? Is it the representation of abstract entities such as +Q features and traces?

Some researchers have suggested that agrammatism involves the loss of the ability to deal with the details of syntactic structure, especially when there has been movement. They claim that agrammatics rely on word order rather than structure to interpret sentences and that they employ a default strategy that treats the first NP as the agent. This strategy works reasonably well for simple sentences in which the first NP can be assigned the thematic role of agent and the second NP can be assigned the role of theme as in sentence (5a). It results in miscomprehension, however, for sentences such as (5b) and (5c), where the first NP does not have the role of agent.

(5)  *a.* The girl kissed the boy.
　　 *b.* The girl was kissed.
　　 *c.* It was the girl that the boy kissed.

Other researchers have argued that agrammatism does not involve the loss of syntactic competence, but rather an alteration of that competence. They have claimed that agrammatics have hierarchical syntactic structures but can no longer represent the traces that indicate an NP's position in deep structure. As a result, they are unable to recognize that the subject NP in (5b) bears the theme role since they do not realize that it is the complement of the verb in deep structure (see section 6.6.3 in chapter 6).

## 13.5.5 **Agrammatism in other languages**

Data from other languages has suggested that the original characterization of agrammatism as a syndrome in which function words and inflectional affixes are lost may not reflect the true nature of this phenomenon.

In English, affixes are typically attached to a base that is itself a free form. The past form of the verb *watch*, for example, is created by the addition of *-ed*; the third person singular is created by the addition of *-s*. However, not all languages work this way. In Semitic languages, such as Hebrew, the base is typically a string of three consonants, which is unpronounceable in its uninflected form. Inflections are produced by inserting vowels into this triconsonantal 'skeleton'. For example, the Hebrew root for the verb *to write* is /ktv/. The masculine third person present form of the verb is /kɔtɛv/ and the masculine third person past form is /katav/. If Hebrew agrammatics simply 'lose' inflectional affixes the way they do in English, they should not be able to produce any verbs. As it turns out, Hebrew agrammatics do produce verbs, but instead of dropping inflectional forms, they choose randomly among them. This sort of evidence has provided a convincing argument against the view that agrammatic language results from a simple economy of effort. Rather, it seems that it is a linguistic deficit that involves the mis-selection of linguistic forms. It is only in languages such as English, where the base is also a legal free form, that the agrammatism is characterized by affix omission.

# 13.5.6 Language in the brain: what's where?

We have seen that, in an important sense, normal language use involves the integrated functioning of the entire cortex. Even right-handers who are strongly left lateralized for language show some language deficit in cases of damage to the right hemisphere. Finally, virtually all forms of aphasia are accompanied by word-finding difficulties. This observation suggests that the storage and retrieval of word forms may be diffusely represented in the brain.

Recent evidence has suggested that lexical knowledge is centred in the temporal lobes. Yet, as was originally discussed by Sigmund Freud in his 1891 book *On Aphasia* (Freud studied aphasia before turning to his better-known work on psychoanalysis), knowledge of a word can be characterized as a rich set of associations. Some of these are actually part of the word— for example, what it looks like, what it sounds like, how it is pronounced, and how it is written. But other aspects are not necessarily linguistic—for example, what the referent of the word feels, or sounds, or smells, or looks like. Given these considerations, it is hardly surprising that the representation of a word in the brain may best be considered to be a network rather than a single entity.

In the past decade, an interesting view of how words are represented in the brain has been put forward using the concept of a **cell assembly**. This concept, first developed by Donald Hebb at McGill University in the 1940s, claims that neurons that are repeatedly activated together come to be associated. Individual words in the brain could each be represented as cell assemblies of this sort, and differ in their brain location in accordance with the nature of the associations that form a particular word's assembly (or network). Figure 13.6 shows a suggestion for how action-related words (e.g., *run, jump*) could differ from vision-related words (e.g., *barn, tree*). As shown in this figure, action words are represented more anteriorly and vision words are represented more posteriorly. Of course, many, but not all, action words are verbs and many, but not all, vision words are nouns. Thus, this difference may coincide with a general verb versus noun difference in how words are represented in the brain.

**Figure 13.6**
A view of how words could be represented in the brain

Vision-related words          Action-related words

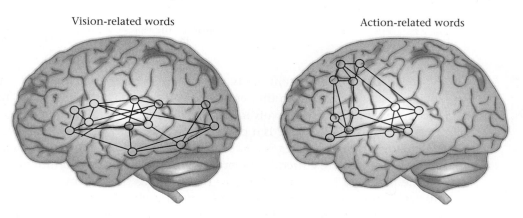

Source: Adapted from the work of F. Pulvermüller, Used by permission of Friedemann Pulvermüller

There seems to be good evidence that the verb-noun distinction does correspond to differences in brain location. There is less consensus, however, for the reason why. It could be that, because verbs are typically associated with actions, they are represented more anteriorly (near the motor strip). On the other hand, it could be purely related to their grammatical category. Recently, some scholars have made this claim and supported it with evidence of a double dissociation between nouns and verbs. As can be seen in figure 13.7, they report one patient, with an anterior lesion, who had difficulty with verbs and another patient, with a lesion extending more posteriorly, who had more difficulty with nouns.

Patient RC has damage to the frontal area of the brain. The patient has particular difficulty producing verbs. Patient JR has damage that extends posteriorly to the angular gyrus. This patient has particular difficulty producing nouns.

**Figure 13.7**
A verb-noun double dissociation

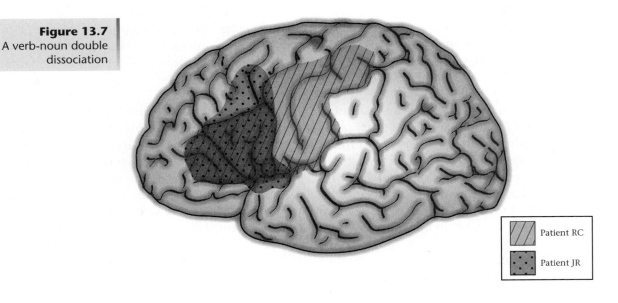

Patient RC

Patient JR

Source: Shapiro, K., and A. Caramazza, "The Representation of Grammatical Categories in the Brain," *Trends in Cognitive Sciences* 7 (2003):201–6 (drawing on p. 204).

The issue of *why* certain areas of the brain are associated with certain aspects of language is not restricted to the representation of words. We have seen, for example, that Broca's area is particularly involved in syntactic processing. Is this because there is a special place for syntax in the brain? Is it perhaps that syntactic processing represents very complex sequencing, and Broca's area is related to the planning of complex motor sequences? These are questions that are currently under intense debate among neurolinguists.

The nature of the debate can serve to remind us that, ultimately, the goal of neurolinguistics is to understand, in neurological terms, what language is. Knowing *where* certain functions are performed in the brain is only the first step. What we really want to understand is how those functions are performed by the brain and why, in the development of our species, particular locations (perhaps because of their cell organization or patterns of neuronal connections) have advantages over others for particular language representations and tasks.

# Summing up

This chapter is concerned with how language is represented and processed in the human brain. **Dichotic listening** studies and **split brain** studies have shown that the **left hemisphere** of the brain carries most of the responsibility for language processing in right-handed individuals. Neuroscientists have also used **autopsy studies**, **computerized axial tomography**, **positron emission tomography**, **functional magnetic resonance imaging**, and **magnetoencephalography** to determine the relationship between particular areas of the left hemisphere and specific language functions. It has been found that **Broca's area** is primarily responsible for speech production, **Wernicke's area** is primarily responsible for language comprehension, and the area surrounding the **angular gyrus** plays an important role in reading. Most of our knowledge concerning language representation in the brain comes from the study of **aphasia**—language disturbance resulting from damage to the brain. Neurolinguists, trained in both linguistics and neuroscience, carefully examine the manner in which linguistic competence is affected by brain damage. Their goal is to increase our understanding of how linguistic knowledge is coded in brain matter and how this knowledge is used in the processes of language comprehension and production.

## Notes

[1] The callosumectomy is a rare surgical procedure used to treat severe forms of epilepsy. It prevents epileptic seizures from spreading to both hemispheres.

[2] It is interesting to note that Wernicke patients have difficulty planning and executing many types of sequenced behaviour, such as purchasing groceries, getting home by bus, or washing laundry.

## Recommended reading

Caplan, D. 1987. *Neurolinguistics and Linguistic Aphasiology.* New York: Cambridge University Press.

Caplan, D. 1993. *Language: Structure, Processing, and Disorders.* Cambridge, MA: MIT Press.

Coltheart, M., J. Patterson, and J.C. Marshall, eds. 1980. *Deep Dyslexia.* London: Routledge & Kegan Paul.

Patterson, K.E., J.C. Marshall, and M. Coltheart, eds. 1986. *Surface Dyslexia.* Hillsdale, NJ: Lawrence Erlbaum.

Rosenbek, J.C., L.L. Lapointe, and R.T. Wertz. 1989. *Aphasia: A Clinical Approach.* Boston: College-Hill Press.

Segalowitz, S. 1983. *Two Sides of the Brain.* Englewood Cliffs, NJ: Prentice-Hall.

Stemmer, B., and Whitaker, H.A., eds. 1988. *Handbook of Neurolinguistics.* San Diego, CA: Academic Press.

## Exercises

1. What distinguishes the human brain from a non-human brain?

2. In what ways can the cerebral hemispheres be considered to be two separate brains?

3. Below is an unlabelled diagram of the left hemisphere. Choose four contrasting colours and colour each lobe of the cortex. Use arrows to point to the central sulcus, the lateral fissure, and the angular gyrus. Finally, use a pencil to indicate areas of lesion that would result in Broca's aphasia, Wernicke's aphasia, and acquired dyslexia. Label these lesions.

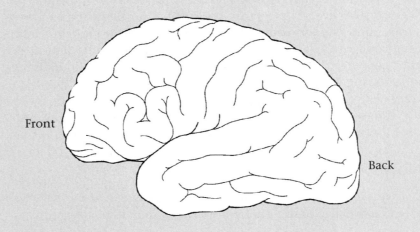

Front                                                           Back

4. What are the relative advantages and disadvantages of the various techniques used to investigate the brain? Consider ethics, cost, intrusiveness, and type of information yielded.

5. What do dichotic listening tests tell us about the specialization of the cerebral hemispheres? Can you think of types of stimuli that would be interesting to present dichotically?

6. Do you think it is possible to learn how the normal brain functions by studying brain-damaged patients? What can the study of aphasia tell us about normal language competence?

7. Contrast the differences in behaviour between fluent and non-fluent aphasics. What could explain these differences?

8. Describe the differences between phonological and surface dyslexia.

9. Many researchers have claimed that agrammatism involves a loss of syntactic knowledge. Imagine a type of aphasia that involves a loss of *phonological* knowledge. How would patients with this type of aphasia behave?

# *Fourteen*

Gerard Van Herk

# CHAPTER Fourteen

# *Language in social contexts*

*They talks with grammar.*

A NOVA SCOTIAN DESCRIBING OTHER NOVA SCOTIANS

**S**ociolinguistics is the study of the relationship between society and language. Language is central to how we deal with other people, and the way we use language says a lot about us. Details of word choice, syntax, and pronunciation reveal us to be members of a particular **speech community**, a group of people who share social conventions, or **sociolinguistic norms**, about language use. When I speak English, most people can tell I'm North American (I pronounce *schedule* with a [sk] sound), Canadian (I rhyme *shone* with *gone,* not *bone*), and probably from Quebec (I drink *soft drinks* and keep my socks in a *bureau*). And language also tells people with shared norms something about their place in the speech community: I'm probably under eighty (I pronounce *whale* and *wail* the same), but I'm definitely not young (I almost never end sentences with a questionlike rising intonation). When I speak French, most people can tell I'm probably from Quebec (I pronounce *tu* with a [ts] sound), from the southwest (by the way I say *garage*), and definitely English (I have English [r] and I say *so* a lot). Of course, members of my speech community don't have to wait for a sentence about whales, schedules, and beverages to place me. Dozens of features mark my speech. Some are **salient** (noticeable) and recognized within the community as having a particular social meaning; they're also called sociolinguistic **markers**. Other features, such as vowel height or the choice between *used to* and *would,* are 'below the radar', but can be shown by large-scale study to be associated with particular social characteristics; these features are called sociolinguistic **indicators**. A speech community's norms affect both markers and indicators. Because these norms are shared by all members of a speech community, sociolinguists study the language of the community, not the speech (or perceptions of the speech) of a single speaker.

These broad definitions let us speak of speech communities of very different sizes. English Montreal is a speech community—its members share norms about what to call soft drinks and whether *marry* and *merry* are pronounced the same (they're not). But in a sense, 'all speakers of English' are a (very big) speech community—we share norms about putting adjectives before nouns, for example, and we can usually more or less understand each other. This criterion—**mutual intelligibility**—is what linguists usually use to determine whether people are speaking 'the same language' or not. If people from two different places—say, Birmingham, Alabama, and Birmingham, England—can understand each other, then they're speaking the same language, and the systematic differences in their speech reflect different **dialects**, or subsets of the same language.

## Language Matters **One Commercial for Two Languages**

The Indic languages Urdu and Hindi are considered separate languages because they're spoken in different countries—Urdu in Pakistan, Hindi in India. But they're mutually intelligible, so speakers of either language can understand Bollywood films on Sunday afternoon television here in Canada. One barrier to communication is that the languages have different writing systems (Arabic for Urdu, Devangari for Hindi). Clever Canadian advertisers get around that problem by using neither system. Instead, words in commercials are often phonetically spelled using the Latin alphabet.

In practice, mutual intelligibility is not always used to decide whether two different ways of speaking should be considered different languages or dialects of the same language. Speakers of Swedish and Norwegian, for example, can understand each other. Swedish and Norwegian are considered two different languages because they're found in two different countries. As the linguist Max Weinreich once said, "A language is a dialect with an army and a navy." The Chinese situation is the opposite—Cantonese and Mandarin are *not* mutually intelligible, but their speakers consider them 'dialects' because they are spoken in the same country, and words of similar meaning in each language are written using the same characters.

Another aspect of the naming issue is that many non-linguists reserve the term *language* for what linguists might call the **standard** variety—the language taught in school, used in formal writing, and often heard from newscasters and other media figures who wish to project authority (or at least competence). All other varieties of the language—those we call **non-standard**—get called 'dialects'. There are almost always value judgments attached to this practice. The standard is seen as good, pure, clear, and rule-governed—a 'real language'— whereas 'dialects' are broken, chaotic, limited, or impermanent. Many sociolinguists avoid the naming problem by using the value-neutral term **variety** for any subset of a language: the standard variety, as well as regional, class, or ethnic varieties. Others reclaim the term *dialect*, and speak of the standard dialect, as well as regional dialects, sociolects, or ethnolects. They'll often say, "Everybody has a dialect."

Two other naming problems related to dialects need to be cleared up. Non-linguists often call non-standard varieties **slang**. To linguists, 'slang' refers only to *words*—either words new to the language, or old words or phrases with new meanings. Slang is usually associated with younger speakers—in fact, a good indicator that a slang term is finished is when middle-aged university professors start using it. Most slang is 'faddish' or short-lived—you don't hear a lot of people saying *groovy* or *the bee's knees* anymore, and *crib* and *dope* and *wack* are starting to sound pretty dated. Some slang terms hang on, however, and become part of the standard language—*mob*, *freshman*, and *glib* all started out as slang. Unlike slang, a dialect is usually distinct in multiple linguistic domains—lexicon, morphology, syntax, and phonology/phonetics.

A second term sometimes used for dialects is **accent**, which linguists use to refer only to pronunciation. Although dialects usually include accent differences, dialect and accent boundaries don't have to match. For example, many people speak Standard English (in terms of grammar and lexicon), but with an accent reflecting their ethnicity, class, and/or region—think of Martin Luther King, Jr., or CBC editorialist Rex Murphy. The reverse situation (standard accent, non-standard grammatical features) is much less common. Try imitating Prince Charles saying, "Ain't no woman like the one I got."

To really study how language and society affect each other, we need to consider the social characteristics of the person speaking—such things as region, gender, or class. We also consider the social relationships between participants in a conversation, and the treatment of language by societies. Each of these objects of study requires its own methods and approaches.

# 14.1 Language variation and social distinctions

It's sometimes said that in any society, social distinctions will develop, and where there are social distinctions, we can expect to find them reflected in linguistic distinctions. The branch of linguistics that tries to measure and explain that connection is known as variation theory, or **variationist sociolinguistics**.

Central to the practice of variationist sociolinguistics is the concept of **structured variation**. In any language variety, there are many linguistic features that can be produced in more than one way. For example, many varieties of English have more than one way to pronounce the sounds represented by '*th*' spellings in *thin, that, brother*, or *path*. In this case, '*th*' is what we call the **variable**—the thing with several possible realizations. Do people say *brother*, or *brudder*, or *bruvver*, or *bro'er*? Each possible realization (interdental fricative, dental stop, labiodental fricative, nothing, etc.) is called a **variant**. The variant that is likely to surface depends on **linguistic factors** like position in the word, voicing, and the like. So far, this is similar to concepts introduced in the phonology chapter: the variable is something like a phoneme, or underlying representation; the variants are like allophones, or surface realizations; and the linguistic factors include what phonologists would call phonetic environments.

But then sociolinguists complicate the analysis, in an attempt to model the complicated situation of language in everyday use. In phonology, rules are usually assumed to apply *every time* a particular environment is found. In other words, they're **categorical**. In sociolinguistic analyses, the 'rules', or **constraints**, are usually **probabilistic**—more or less likely to apply. So interdentals might be more *likely* to be pronounced as stops at the beginning of the word, or when they're voiced, or even with particular lexical items like *this* or *that*, but each linguistic factor explains only part of the variation. At its most complex, sociolinguistic research considers all these factors together, and with the help of computer programs, calculates how much each factor contributes to the likely outcome (see figure 14.1 on page 458).

In our '*th*' example—and in much variationist work—the focus is on linguistic factors affecting variation. In fact, variationist sociolinguistics is sometimes described as 'too much linguistics and not enough socio'. The 'socio' component shows up in two different ways. First, variationist research is usually conducted among speakers of non-standard varieties; this research has made important contributions to our understanding that non-standard varieties are, like the standard, governed by subtle and complex linguistic rules. In fact, a well-known early paper by William Labov, a pioneer of sociolinguistics, is entitled "The Logic of Non-Standard English." Second, variationist work also concerns itself with **social factors** that influence variation in a structured way. In the case of '*th*', the choice of variant might be affected by the speaker's age, sex, or degree of education. We assume some variation within individual speakers (**intra-speaker variation**), especially in terms of style shifting, but most of this work looks at how speech varies according to speakers' social characteristics. In other words, researchers are looking at **inter-speaker variation**. Conceivably, any speaker characteristic could have linguistic consequences; in practice, research has shown several social factors are particularly important. In the following sections, we look at those factors one by one.

**Figure 14.1**
Method: variationist
sociolinguistics

*As in other branches of linguistics, the needs of researchers determine how the research proceeds.*

1. **Find the speech community.** We may investigate our local community, or we may have a specific community in mind, one that can contribute to our knowledge of a particular issue (ethnicity, isolation, etc.). We then find **informants** (also known as **consultants**), people from the speech community who are willing to be recorded. Sometimes these informants are a random sample; sometimes, one informant leads us to another, and so on (a 'snowball sample').

2. **Collect data.** Investigating variation in language use usually calls for large amounts of fairly natural language. This can come from existing material (such as letters), but often we use **sociolinguistic interviews**, with questions that encourage informants to forget that someone from a university is recording their every word. Time-tested questions include *Were you ever in a situation where you thought, 'This is it, I'm going to die'?* and *Did you ever get blamed for something you didn't do?* And, of course, there are particular questions that work well in each community. Sometimes, we elicit more formal speech by having informants read written passages or word lists.

3. **Analyze the data you collect.** Some variables, such as vowel height, are **gradient**, with a full range of values possible. These are plotted through acoustic analysis, with separate vowel plots developed for each segment of the community (or even each informant). Others, such as the choice between fricative or stop for *th* or between *going to* and *will* for future marking, are **discrete**, with easily distinguishable separate variants. These are usually coded for variant and a range of social or linguistic factors.

Consider an example from the Ottawa Intensifier Project's work on online subcultures. We looked at intensifiers—the words people use before adjectives to mean *very*. We found nearly ten thousand sentences with adjectives, and coded each one for the variant used (*very*, *really*, *way*, *so*, *totally*, etc.), location of adjective in the sentence, type of adjective (physical property, human characteristic, etc.), gender of the informant (where known), and subculture (hip-hop fan, country fan, nerd, etc.). Each sentence ended up looking something like this:

> ravmc          *That's a really kickass song.*

The coding string on the left means that the variant used was *really,* the adjective occurred in *attributive* position (before a noun) and was a *value* judgment, and the sentence was written by a *male country* fan. When we examined which variants went with which factors, we found strong patterns of variation depending on gender and subculture (e.g., tween girls are definitely leading a change towards the use of *so*). We also found shared linguistic factors, no matter who was using a variant (e.g., hardly anyone used *so* when the adjective was before a noun, as in *That was a so cool movie*).

## 14.2 Place

Geographical location is probably the most-studied social factor affecting variation. If it's true that we talk *like* who we talk *with*, it makes good sense that we will share linguistic features with our neighbours. **Dialectology**, the study of regional differences in language, is the oldest major branch of sociolinguistics (see figure 14.2). Early linguistics had a major historical focus, and linguists turned to the study of traditional rural dialects, because they preserved older speech features and thus held many clues to earlier stages of the language, especially with respect to sound changes. From there, the field branched out to study other areas of the grammar, especially the lexicon. The goals of the discipline have helped to determine its traditional methods and approaches—in particular, the focus on isolated rural dialects and speakers who are **NORMs** (non-mobile older rural males), and are believed to have retained the most traditional speech.

| | |
|---|---|
| **Figure 14.2**<br>Method: dialect geography | *The goals of dialect geography and dialectology have been to show where particular speech features are found and to discover the boundaries between dialect regions. But dialect geography has also tried to find the most traditional speech in each region, based on the assumption that regional dialects are most distinct when they haven't been influenced by their neighbours, or by mainstream language. These goals tend to lead to specific methods.* |

1. **Find the speakers in a region with the least outside influence.** Traditionally, these have been rural older men who have spent their whole lives in the same area, sometimes known as NORMs (non-mobile older rural males).

2. **With each speaker, run through a (very long!) questionnaire of lexical features known to show regional differentiation.** You probably know a few of these already—do you say *running shoes, tennis shoes,* or *sneakers? Hoagies, grinders, subs,* or *hero sandwiches? Soda, pop,* or *soft drink?*

3. **Record each speaker's responses.** In the days before tape recorders, fieldworkers would write these responses down, and make notes on pronunciation.

4. **Tabulate the results from lots of questionnaires.** Map out each variant. If you can, draw boundaries between different areas. For example, you might find a boundary between *sneaker* users and *running shoe* users somewhere in Quebec or the Maritimes. These boundary lines are called **isoglosses**.

5. **Use your accumulated data to propose dialect areas and boundaries.** If you find a lot of isoglosses in the same place (an **isogloss bundle**), it seems likely that you've found a boundary between dialect areas.

Dialect studies in the early and mid-twentieth century collected huge amounts of data, more than could be analyzed with the technology of the time. Dialectologists are still analyzing that earlier material today, using advanced computer modelling.

In Europe, where much early dialect study was done, countries long settled by speakers of the same language have had the time to develop distinct regional varieties. These varieties reflect settlement patterns that are often more than a thousand years old. For example, the major dialect areas of England still pretty much match the areas settled by different groups—Angles, Saxons, and Jutes—about fifteen hundred years ago. Natural barriers, such as mountain ranges, have helped limit inter-dialect contact, and encouraged dialects to develop along their own distinct paths. The same basic combination of factors—origins of the early settlers and limits on inter-variety contact—also explain dialect differences in North American English. Newfoundland, England's oldest North American colony, was settled by fishermen from southwestern England (the 'West Country') and, later, Irish seamen. The New England area of the United States was settled largely by people from East Anglia. People who settled along the coast farther south came largely from the south of England, while the later arrivals, who moved into the inland Appalachian area, came largely from the north of England and northern Ireland. Each group brought the speech patterns of their home areas with them. Presumably some mixing took place; perhaps some of the uncommon or distinct features of settler dialects were worn down over time, a process known as **dialect levelling**. The English of New Zealand, which was formed much more recently and is thus easier to study, sheds some light on how levelling works. Researchers there describe a three-stage process: the original settler generations kept their home dialects, the next generation chose somewhat randomly from all the linguistic options available, and the third generation levelled out the diversity in favour of the most frequent variant in most cases. Probably something similar happened in North America, centuries before dialectologists and tape recorders were around to document it.

By the time of the American Revolution (1776–83), three major dialect areas had developed in the eastern United States: a Northern variety in New England and the Hudson Valley, the Midland dialect of Pennsylvania, and the Southern dialect. These varieties were already becoming distinct from British English and from each other.

About fifty thousand Americans who remained loyal to Britain moved to the northern colonies after the Revolutionary War, greatly increasing the English-speaking populations of what would later become the provinces of Nova Scotia, Prince Edward Island, New Brunswick, Quebec, and Ontario. These Loyalists brought their American dialects with them, in particular the Midland dialect (especially to Ontario), with a strong contribution of New England speech to the Maritimes. A second wave, the 'late Loyalists', arrived in southern Ontario and Quebec over the next generation or two. The language mix was further enriched by Scots Gaelic speakers (especially in Cape Breton and the Ottawa Valley), by Irish English and Gaelic speakers (especially in Quebec and southern Ontario), and generally by settlers from across the British Isles.

## Language Matters **The *r*-ful Truth About American English**

A good example of colonial-era variation is '*r*-lessness' (which makes modern British English *far* sound like *fah* to most Canadians). By 1776, this feature was already widespread in the south of England, and this was reflected in North American patterns. New England and the coastal South were settled by people from the south of England who maintained social and economic ties with England, and these areas were *r*-less (and, to some extent, still are). Other North American dialects were (and still are) '*r*-ful'.

As waves of English-speaking settlers moved westward, they took their dialects with them. The dialect of central Canada spread across the Prairies; the three major American dialects spread west, blurring and merging as they went, so that dialect maps of North America show a 'fanning out' from the east, and a general mixed dialect in the westernmost areas of the United States (see figure 14.3). Contemporary dialectology looks at a broader range of speakers, including younger speakers and more women, and tracks ongoing changes in dialects. Even in the middle of great change, the dialect distinctions laid down more than three hundred years ago remain strong.

**Figure 14.3**
North American English: dialects and development

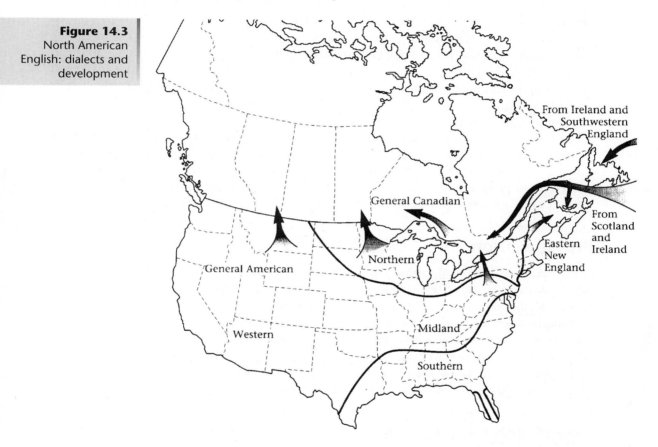

Source: C. Von Baeyer, *The Ancestry of Canadian English,* 1977, Public Service Commission of Canada. Reproduced with the permission of the Public Service Commission of Canada, 2008.

## 14.2.1 Canadian English

Because much of the linguistic input to Canadian English came from the United States, and because Canadians have lived with the cultural and economic effect of their larger neighbour for a long time, it's not surprising that Canadian English in many ways resembles that of parts of the United States. But, as with other cultural traits, Canadians measure their linguistic distinctness in terms of how different they are from Americans. You may remember a popular beer commercial in which a guy named Joe pointed out some things that are distinctly Canadian, including the word for big living-room furniture and the pronunciation of *about*.

## Canadian lexical features

Some Canadian words reflect Canadian legal or political realities, either inherited from Britain (*constable, Crown prosecutor*) or distinct to Canada (*riding* to mean a political district, *acclamation* to mean being elected unopposed). Other words reflect a more immediate reality: we keep our heads warm with a *tuque*, and we fuel ourselves by taking our coffee *double-double*. Unlike Americans, many of us wear *running shoes*, not *tennis shoes* (although some Maritimers, like many Americans, wear *sneakers*). Some of us still wipe away the remains of our double-double with a *serviette*, rather than a *napkin*. We get water from a *tap*, not a *faucet*; we roll up the *blinds*, not the *shades*, and we sit on a . . . *chesterfield*? Perhaps we used to; nowadays, most Canadians, especially younger ones, use the term *couch* or *sofa*. On the whole, however, we are more likely to recognize and use American terms rather than British. Do you call cookies *biscuits*, or wear a *cardigan*? I thought not. Exercises 1 and 9 at the end of the chapter will test your knowledge of some other British-American lexical differences.

Lexical constraints also affect some observed differences in Canadian and American syntax or pronunciation. In most cases, these reflect Canadian retention of British forms. Many Canadians say *She's in hospital* where Americans would say *in the hospital*. Most Canadians pronounce *shone* to rhyme with *gone*—in fact, most Canadians are surprised to find out that Americans rhyme it with *bone*. Canadians all know that the last letter of the alphabet is *Zed*, not *Zee*. And pronouncing *route* like *rout* is still more American than Canadian. For a few words, Canadians seem split down the middle between British and American pronunciations.

## Pronunciation

Only one across-the-board pronunciation feature distinguishes Canadian English from most American dialects, and linguists know it, appropriately enough, as *Canadian Raising* (even though it's found in many other places). Canadians have different pronunciations for the /aw/ diphthong in *lout* and that in *loud*. In *lout* (and in all words where the diphthong comes before a voiceless sound), the nucleus of the diphthong is raised (thus 'Raising') to something like a schwa or the 'wedge' vowel of *cut*. Americans hear this as [u], thus the stereotype of Canadians saying *oot and aboot* for *out and about*. The same process happens with /aj/—*tight* and *tide* have different diphthongs for most Canadians—but this is less likely to be noticed.

## Morphology and syntax

If Canadian English is supposed to reflect a blend of British and American features, it's hardly a surprise that we can find few specifically Canadian forms when it comes to word or sentence structure. There are very few differences between even British and American Englishes in this respect, at least in the standard varieties. British English speakers are more likely to say *She has just gone* or *She has already gone*, while Americans prefer *She just left* or *She already left*. Britons find *I've done it yesterday* more acceptable than Americans do. And many Britons can use *shall* or *whilst* without sounding affected. Presumably Canadians are in between, perhaps closer to Americans. Any national syntactic differences that remain to be discovered are probably in terms of frequency of use of forms, not absolute use or avoidance.

Of course, none of the above statements about American-ness or the shortage of distinguishing features apply to the English of Newfoundland, which reflects its distinct history, as we shall see (will see?) in section 14.4. And even in mainland Canada, we can find subtle regional differences. Many traditional English speakers in the Maritimes have a fairly monophthongal and 'backed' pronunciation of /aj/, rather similar to the one you'd find in coastal Virginia. And from about Sudbury west, you'll often hear long and monophthongal versions of /e/ and /o/—stereotyped in the [goː] and [eː] in Bob and Doug Mackenzie's *How's it goin', eh?* Lexical differences can reflect settlement patterns, as when Western Canadian restaurants call an all-you-can-eat meal a *smorg* (short for the Swedish-derived *smorgasbord*), and the *Canadian Oxford Dictionary* notes names for schoolyard games that are extremely local, sometimes restricted to a single neighbourhood in Toronto.

Contemporary sociolinguists are developing different ways to think of space. We borrow ideas from cultural geographers to distinguish between physical distance and social perceptions of distance. Some places seem 'closer' because we can easily travel there thanks to highways, or the routes followed by airlines, buses, or ferries. For example, a sound change affecting cities in the American Midwest seems to be creeping down Interstate 55 to St. Louis. And some linguistic innovations seem to spread first from big city to big city, 'jumping over' intervening small towns, and only later diffuse into the surrounding regions. In addition, what we think of as space differences often have more to do with who lives where, even though Canadian cities are far less ethnically segregated than their American counterparts. Gottingen Street, Outremont, Regent Park, the Glebe, Gerrard Street, the Downtown East Side . . . if you recognize these place names, your first associations probably have more to do with the ethnicity or socioeconomic status of their residents than with their actual physical location. In this way, space reinforces other social distinctions—you speak like who you speak to, and you tend to speak to people like you!

## 14.3 Time

All spoken languages change. Elsewhere in this book, you've explored the linguistic processes involved. Sociolinguists are interested in the relationship between change over time and the variation found in a community at a single point in time. Think of big changes, like the Great Vowel Shift of earlier English. Presumably, people in England didn't all go to bed one night pronouncing their words one way, and wake up the next morning with a completely different vowel system. At some point, either everybody used both the old and the new pronunciation, or some people always used the old way and some always used the new, or some combination of those two happened. In other words, change over time results in variation in each time period. Add to that the reasonable assumption that people's basic grammar doesn't change that much during their lifetime, and you get a powerful insight: you can 'see' change happening by looking at the differences between old and young speakers. This idea, called the **apparent time hypothesis**, has opened up whole new areas of research—as one major sociolinguistic article puts it, we can use the present (variation) to explain the past (change). This is particularly true if we use the tools of variation, sound recordings and measurement tools, and probabilities.

Consider *whale* and *wail*. Over a *very* long period of time, English speakers have moved toward pronouncing them the same. What were once two separate phonemes have **merged**. We can see this change happening by looking at findings by Canadian sociolinguist Jack Chambers. As the graph in figure 14.4 on page 464 shows, older speakers have lower rates of merger, while younger speakers almost always merge the two sounds.

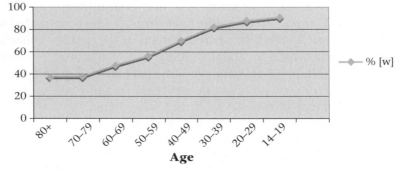

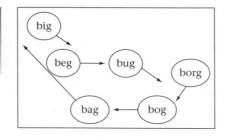

**Figure 14.4**
Percentage of speakers with [w], not [hʍ], in words like *which* and *whine* in central Canada, by age

Source: "Patterns of Variation Including Change" by J.K. Chambers, in *The Handbook of Language Variation and Change*, ed. J.K. Chambers, Peter Trudgill, and Natalie Schilling-Estes, © Blackwell Publishers 2002. Reprinted by permission of Blackwell Publishing.

Changes like this are easy to see when they involve an entire segment—two formerly separate sounds merge, or an alternative pronunciation dies out, or is born. A lot of sound change is subtler than that, though, especially when we look at vowels. Vowels may shift in the vowel space, sometimes so slightly that the change is only evident through acoustic analysis. Modern technology has let us track some big changes that are happening in North American vowel pronunciations. One dramatic shift, affecting about 40 million speakers in the U.S. Midwest, is known as the Northern Cities Shift (see figure 14.5). Younger speakers in cities like Detroit, Chicago, or Buffalo are involved in a complex vowel shift. Their pronunciation of *hot*, for example, sounds to Canadians like *hat*, while their *Ann* sounds like *Ian*. Recently, sociolinguists have identified a Canadian Shift, which is almost the opposite—young urban Canadians have a lower or 'back-er' pronunciation for some vowels, so that the vowel of *bet* moves toward *bat*, and the vowel of *bat* becomes something like *bought*. Vowels in Canada and in the U.S. Midwest have actually 'moved' far enough that speakers of each dialect hear the wrong word when they speak to each other. Canadians actually hear *bet* when Americans say *bat*. And American linguists snicker when Canadian linguists talk about the letter '*s*'. What's interesting about these shifts is that they show the interaction between time and place. The sound shifts show change over time, but they are restricted to pre-existing dialect areas.

**Figure 14.5**
The vowel movements of the U.S. Northern Cities Shift

The findings of apparent-time studies can sometimes be confirmed by **real-time** studies. In Montreal, speakers first interviewed by sociolinguists in the 1970s have been revisited and re-interviewed several times now. For some of their variant linguistic features, apparent-time findings are confirmed; for others, researchers have found some change even in individual speakers. We can also work farther into the past. Older recordings of speakers of

Quebec French and African American English (AAE) show that many contemporary features have a long history. Work on documents written by people with limited literacy shows the same thing. For example, the contemporary AAE term *mother wit,* meaning 'common sense', is found in letters from the 1790s.

# 14.4 Isolation

As mentioned in the discussion of dialectology, speech communities that are isolated in some way seem to preserve older ways of speaking, just as they might also preserve traditional music or farming methods. The isolation involved can be **physical**, isolated from *everybody*; **linguistic**, isolated from speakers of the same or a similar language; or **social**, isolated by conventions or attitudes. Canadian sociolinguists are lucky to have all three types of isolated speech communities available to them. These communities can act as a sort of linguistic 'time machine' for us—as long as we're cautious enough to remember that even isolated speech communities change over time, perhaps in ways very different from mainstream speech.

## 14.4.1 Physical isolation: the case of Newfoundland English

Newfoundland was settled very early by North American standards; its settlers came largely from two clearly defined areas (southwestern England and southeastern Ireland); most immigration occurred before the mid-1800s; and the island is a long way from other heavily populated areas. This combination of historical factors creates an almost 'perfect storm' for dialectologists, with Newfoundland English retaining many distinct speech features that have disappeared or diminished elsewhere. Equally interesting, individual communities in Newfoundland were often isolated from each other, and were settled by people from only one of the two input populations, so that Newfoundland English is not only distinct compared to other North American varieties, but also highly regionally variable within Newfoundland itself.

Several features of the dialect are widely known outside Newfoundland. Many of us have heard mainlanders—comedians, for example—who believe they can 'sound like a Newfoundlander' by adding the word *bye* to the end of every sentence. When the pronunciation of a single word becomes a stereotype of a speech community, linguists call it a **shibboleth**. Many varieties of English have their own shibboleths: Jamaicans say *mon* for *man*. Pittsburghers say *dahntahn* for *downtown*. Canadians say *oot and aboot*. Many Newfoundlanders do, in fact, use *boy* as a marker of solidarity in casual speech (in the same way that many Jamaicans, among others, use *man*). And many Newfoundlanders maintain the older southwestern British merger of /aj/ and /oj/, so that *boy* and *bye* are pronounced the same. But the two words are *not* pronounced in the way mainlanders pronounce *bye*. For Newfoundlanders, the first sound of the diphthong is a mid-central vowel somewhere between schwa and the wedge vowel. Other pronunciation features associated with some varieties of traditional Newfoundland English are the stopping of interdentals (*dat* for *that*), word-initial *h*-deletion (*'Olyrood* for *Holyrood*), word-final consonant cluster deletion (*pos'* for *post*), and raising or tensing of front lax vowels, represented in popular writing by spelling *yes* as *yis*.

Newfoundland English also retains some of the distinct morphology and syntax brought over by the original settlers. Location can be marked with phrase-final prepositions, as in the often-quoted *Stay where you're* **to** *till I comes where you're* **at**. Object pronouns can use subject forms, as in *They see **we***. The plural *–s* suffix is sometimes absent, as in *two **pound***, and the verbal *–s* suffix is found with a range of subjects: *I **goes***, *you **goes***, *all the people **goes***. This salient feature has surfaced recently on Newfoundland t-shirts (see figure 14.6). Many Newfoundlanders also use the **after perfect** aspect, saying *I'm **after** doing it* for *I have just done it*. This presumably Gaelic-influenced feature has spread from the Irish-settled areas of the island into the general population.

The *Dictionary of Newfoundland English* lists thousands of distinct Newfoundland lexical items. Many are regionally restricted, near-obsolete, or associated with particular industries. Some nautical terms have spread into broader use, such as *gaff* to mean *steal*. Others describe specifically Newfoundland phenomena: *slob ice* is loose chunks of ice floating on the surface of the water; *toutons* are fried dough chunks; and *scruncheons* are glorious bits of crisp-fried pork fat, used as a garnish.

Newfoundland English has retained so many older features that linguists are now beginning to use it in comparative work. Scholars of Irish and southwestern Englishes look to Newfoundland English for evidence of earlier stages of those varieties. And the historical and linguistic parallels with Caribbean creoles and African American English may shed light on how those varieties developed.

## 14.4.2 Linguistic isolation: the case of Quebec French

Quebec French is so distinct, and so filled with interesting variation, that it is actually one of the language varieties most studied by sociolinguists. In fact, several major theoretical concepts in sociolinguistics (beyond the scope of an introductory text) have been developed through work on this variety.

Like Newfoundland English, Quebec French is a good example of how isolated language varieties retain older features of a language, while undergoing their own internally motivated processes of language change. Until 1763, the linguistic history of New France was remarkably similar to that of Newfoundland—early settlement from specific regions of Europe (especially northwestern France) to an area far away, and a sudden cessation of immigration. For more than two centuries, however, French in North America has been isolated linguistically, rather than physically. The metaphor of an island of French surrounded by a sea of English is often heard, and English influence is sometimes invoked to explain why the French spoken in Quebec (and elsewhere in Canada) is different from the European standard variety. Certainly some English words have been borrowed into Quebec French. A restaurant might give you a *bill* (rather than a *facture*) for your order of *bines* ('beans') and *toast* (rather than *feves* or *haricots* and *roties*). On the other hand, Quebecers park in a *terrain de stationnement*, whereas in France they use the English loan word *parking*. And people in both Quebec and France look forward to *le weekend*. Other distinct Quebec French forms reflect retention of older forms (*archaïsmes*), such as *flambe* for 'flame' (rather than the European *flamme*), or *doutance* (rather than *doute*) for 'suspicion'. In some cases, words have developed distinct meanings in Quebec French. These include *traversier*, which means 'ferry' in Quebec and 'crossing' in France; *ma blonde*, which means 'my girlfriend' in Quebec and 'my blonde' in France; and *dépanneur*, which means 'repairman' in France but 'convenience store' in Quebec (in both French and English).

Some syntactic differences observed in Canadian French, although sometimes attributed to contact with English, seem to represent either processes that started centuries ago or internally motivated changes. For example, recently unearthed early recordings by folklorists show that the loss of *ne* in casual speech, as when people say *Je sais pas* instead of *Je ne sais pas* for 'I don't know', was widespread even in speakers born as early as 1846. And research on the use of the subjunctive mood in Gatineau seems to show the form strengthening its association with a few verbs and linguistic contexts, rather than undergoing across-the-board English-induced decline. Other features of Quebec French morphosyntax include the use of *Je vas* (instead of *vais*) for 'I go', and the replacement of the standard form *nous* ('we') with *on* (originally 'one', as in 'one never knows'), as shown in table 14.1. Quebecers are also more likely to refer to a single person as *tu* ('you', originally informal) rather than the more formal *vous*. These last few changes all work together to produce a more regular verb-marking system.

**Table 14.1**  Present tense verb forms for *go* in standard and spoken Quebec French

| Meaning | Standard (European) French | Spoken Quebec French |
|---|---|---|
| 'I go' | *Je vais* | *Je* **vas** (pronounced *va*) |
| 'You (sg) go' | Usually *vous allez* | **Tu vas** |
| 'S/he goes' | *Elle/il va* | *Elle/il va* |
| 'We go' | *Nous allons* | **On va** |
| 'You (pl) go' | *Vous allez* | *Vous allez* |
| 'They go' | *Elles/ils vont* | *Elles/ils vont* |

As a Quebecer visiting Paris for the first time, I quickly realized how many phonetic features of my French were distinctive. I diphthongized (and lowered) my /ɛ/, so that I said [pajr] where they said [pɛːr] (*pére*, 'father'). I also diphthongized many nasalized vowels, so that I said [prãjs] where they said [prãs] (*prince*, 'prince'). My short high vowels, [i] and [u], were lax in word-final closed syllables (syllables ending with a consonant). So I said [vɪt] where they said [vit] (*vite*, 'quickly'). Most noticeable of all, I assibilated my /t/ and /d/ before high front vowels and glides, so that I said [tˢydᶻi] where they said [tydi] (*tu dis*, 'you say'). Well, actually, most of them said *vous dites*, and considered my use of *tu* a bit presumptuous. They also wondered how *ma blonde* could have dark hair.

Linguistic isolates are actually more common than you might think. Around the world, languages and language varieties, cut off from their sources, have kept older features and developed along their own paths. In the Dominican Republic, the African American community of Samaná has spoken English since 1824, surrounded by Spanish speakers. Western Louisiana preserves Acadian French. Mennonite communities in North America speak an earlier form of German. And in Turkey, the descendants of Jews who fled the Spanish Inquisition five centuries ago still speak a form of medieval Spanish. We also see a less severe and shorter-lived version of linguistic isolation in immigrant neighbourhoods, whose members often find when revisiting their original homelands that language has moved on without them.

## 14.4.3 Social isolation: the case of African Nova Scotian English

After the American Revolution and again after the War of 1812, groups of African Americans who had fought for the British settled in the Maritime provinces. Some moved on, to found Freetown in Sierra Leone. Some integrated into the surrounding white communities. Several communities remained separate, however. The best known of these is Preston, near Dartmouth, which to this day is populated almost entirely by descendants of those original African American settlers. The community remained separated from the surrounding communities by limited road and transportation services and by racial segregation (some Nova Scotia schools remained segregated until 1964). When older Preston residents were interviewed in the early 1990s, many retained distinct speech features that their ancestors had brought to Canada with them. These included features widespread in African American English (AAE) in the United States, such as copula deletion (*He gonna go*). Even more interesting, they used features of older English not generally found in contemporary American English, black or white, such as verbal –*s* marking (*I goes*). Comparisons of AAE in the social isolate of Preston, the linguistic isolate of Samaná, and in seventy-year-old recordings from the United States showed that similar forms were used by all three groups. The linguistic factors affecting the choice of forms were similar, suggesting that the language of these communities was living evidence of the AAE of earlier centuries.

Less extreme cases of social isolation are often found, and many speech communities prove resistant to change. The sociolinguist Lesley Milroy has proposed the notion of **social networks** to explain why this happens. **Dense** and **multiplex** social networks—where a small group of people interact with each other often and in multiple ways—are much less likely to change. If your neighbours are also your friends, and your co-workers, and your co-worshippers, and your in-laws, and your children and theirs go to school together and play together, the intensity and frequency of your contacts with them will reinforce your traditional way of speaking. In this model, change is brought into the community by people with looser ties, those who work or go to school or hang out elsewhere.

## 14.5 Contact

The other side of isolation, of course, is linguistic **contact**—with speakers of other varieties or of other languages. We've already considered the possibility of **dialect levelling**, where similar dialects that come into contact with each other tend to keep their shared features and get rid of the things that are different (usually by adopting the variant found in the socially or numerically dominant language). A whole range of other phenomena can happen when speakers of different *languages* meet and move toward bilingualism.

## 14.5.1 Code switching and borrowing

**Code switching** is a common phenomenon when people who share more than one language get together and use two (or more) languages (or 'codes') to communicate. Not surprisingly, bilinguals sometimes decide that only one of their languages is appropriate for a particular situation. An example of this **situational code-switching** would be the use of English in a workplace or to talk about work-related topics, and the use of one's native language among friends and family. Some communities are famous for switching back and forth constantly during a single conversation, and the mix that results sometimes gets its own name, usually intended to be derogatory. Spanish-English switching in the United States is often called *Spanglish*, while Canadian French-English switching is *Franglais*.

Monolinguals often assume that this kind of switching happens because speakers are not competent in one of their languages—a sort of deficit hypothesis—or because a concept just can't be expressed in one of the languages—a sort of **lexical gap** explanation. Analysis of recorded multilingual speech doesn't support these ideas, however. Speakers who code-switch most often are usually very fluent in both of their languages, and there are linguistic rules about where in a sentence a switch can happen. The switching becomes a linguistic resource in many communities, used by speakers to signal a bicultural identity or to evoke attributes associated with one of the languages, such as sophistication or identification with local values. Some neighbourhoods in northern Toronto boast particularly skilled code switchers—young people born in Russia, brought up in Israel, and now living in Canada. They're *triple* switchers, moving effortlessly between Russian, Hebrew, and English.

Sometimes switches involve long stretches of each language, as in *Sometimes I'll start a sentence in Spanish y termino en Español*. (Some researchers reserve the term *code switching* for only this type of switch.) More often, a single language will dominate (sometimes called the **matrix language**), and individual words from another language will be inserted, often being changed to obey the rules of the matrix language. (Some researchers call these **nonce borrowings**, 'one-offs' that don't really involve a change of language.) If particularly useful nonce borrowings happen often enough, eventually they get picked up by monolingual speakers of the matrix language. Then they're just called **borrowings** (although they're rarely given back). Presumably, borrowings result from other contact situations as well—speakers of one language use terms from another language to describe new things and activities associated with that new language. Once a word is truly borrowed, it loses its associations with the original language, and is adapted to the pronunciation and morphosyntax of the borrowers. So the Spanish *el legarto* ('the lizard') becomes *alligator*, and when we say *the alligator* we don't know that we're actually saying *the the lizard*. Some types of words are far more likely to be borrowed than others—nouns are especially common, followed by verbs and the occasional adjective or adverb. Function words tend not to be borrowed—they occur too often in our first language to be displaced, and we rarely run into a concept that requires a new pronoun or preposition.

Sometimes, grammatical structures can be borrowed along with individual words. For example, the Acadian French of the Maritime provinces nonce-borrows many verbs from English and adapts them to French morphology, as in *J'ai parké* for 'I parked'. Verb + preposition combinations, however, also keep some of their English structure, as in *J'ai hangé around*, 'I hung around'. In communities where both verbs and prepositions are borrowed, even all-French sentences can end up with English-like word order not found elsewhere in French, as in *le gars que j'ai donné la job à*, 'The guy that I gave the job to'.

## 14.5.2 Contact languages: mixed languages, lingua franca, pidgins, and creoles

Occasionally, in heavy switching communities, you can get sentences where virtually all the content words (nouns, verbs) are borrowed and adapted, while all the function words are from the matrix language. I once heard a co-worker say, "*Tu peux pas parker ton truck dans le spot du station wagon du boss*" ('You can't park your truck in the spot reserved for the boss's station wagon'). If that sort of process became the norm in a language-contact situation, you might eventually end up with a **mixed language**. Mixed languages are not common, and researchers who work on language contact argue (often fiercely) over whether they really exist, and what they tell us about language. One strong candidate for mixed language status is **Michif**, still spoken in and near Manitoba among the Métis, people of mixed Cree and French ancestry. In Michif, most nouns and the words associated with them are derived from French, while most verbs and the words associated with them are derived from Cree (see table 14.2).

| **Table 14.2** | French-origin noun morphology and Cree-origin verb morphology in Michif | | | |
|---|---|---|---|---|
| PAR LA QUEUE | apoci-pit-ew | kihtwam | LE LOUP | ase-kiwe-pahta-w |
| *by the tail* | *inside-out-pull-he/him* | *again* | *the wolf* | *back-go-home-run-he* |
| 'He pulled him inside out by the tail, and the wolf ran home again.' | | | | |

Source: *Mixed Languages: 15 Case Studies of Language Intertwining*, ed. Peter Bakker and Maarten Mous. (Amsterdam IFOTT, 1994). Copyright © Professor Peter Bakker and Professor Maarten Mous.

Non-linguists sometimes assume that creole languages are mixed languages. Linguists, however, use the creole label for the outcome of a very different situation of language contact. When people who speak different languages need to interact on a regular basis, they will often come to choose one particular language to communicate between groups. A language used this way is called a **lingua franca**, named after the language used centuries ago in the Mediterranean by traders from different language backgrounds. A lingua franca can be the native language of one of the interacting groups, or a 'neutral'

## Language Matters **Few Words, No Variants, Many Meanings**

In pidgins, words will usually not take different forms to mark grammatical distinctions. Compare the (invented!) sentences below:

| **Me** - **see** - three - **man** - yesiday | One - **man** - **see** - **me** - bai |
|---|---|
| 'I saw three men (yesterday).' | 'One man will see me (later).' |

*Me*, *see*, and *man* would have different forms in the two sentences in English; here, the distinctions of pronoun case, verb tense, and noun plurality are determined by sentence position, numerals, and adverbials (*yesiday* from *yesterday*, *bai* from *by and by*).

language that is not the home language of one of the groups involved. A neutral language may have social advantages in that it doesn't favour any one group. For example, in post-colonial situations, the former colonial language may act as a lingua franca, despite its historical connotations, just because the different language groups in the country want a linguistically level playing field.

Some contact situations lead to the formation of a **pidgin**, a language stripped down to its essentials. Such a heavily simplified language is capable of conveying the basic information needed for many cross-linguistic purposes. Linguistically, pidgin languages consist of a small set of content words and very little grammatical complexity.

Socially, pidgins tend to develop in two different contact situations. Each situation involves one or more groups having limited access to the **lexifier language**, the language that supplies the basic wordstock for the pidgin. Trade is one such situation. Australian Pidgin English or Chinese Pidgin Portuguese are trade pidgins that developed from European lexifier languages. In the Pacific Northwest, North American natives developed the trade language Chinook Jargon. The other common pidgin formation situation is when people from many language backgrounds are brought together to work on large plantations as slaves or indentured workers. Tok Pisin, a language of the South Pacific that is now a full creole (see below), originally developed this way.

If a pidgin operates as a lingua franca, as in trade situations, it may persist in its simplified form for a long time. In plantation situations, though, the children of the original pidgin speakers may learn the pidgin as a first language, and it may become the native language of the new community. When this happens, the pidgin becomes a full-fledged language known as a **creole**. Creoles greatly expand the number of lexical items and grammatical rules found in the original pidgin. And worldwide, creoles share many grammatical characteristics, despite developing in different situations from different lexifier languages.

Several theories have developed to account for the similarities between creoles. One argument is that creoles the world over have developed from a single template language, which acted as a sort of structural frame into which the actual words of different lexifier languages were slotted. This frame might have been a **proto-pidgin**, perhaps spread by sailors and slavers, or a stripped-down version of one or another West African language. This scenario is called the **relexification hypothesis**.

Another widely held viewpoint is that the similarities in creoles happen when they become the first languages of children, in that all children have access to an innate biological program (a sort of language acquisition device) that leads them to restructure the very basic input of each pidgin in the same way. This is known as the **language bioprogram hypothesis**. Because pidgins and creoles have tended to develop without documentation, it is unlikely that either hypothesis will garner conclusive proof. Observations of the development of Tok Pisin into a full-fledged creole (and the official language of Papua New Guinea) in recent years confirm that major changes occur when a language gets native speakers, consistent with some version of the bioprogram.

Barbadian (creole) English, or **Bajan**, is often assumed to show little variation. In Barbados, however, as elsewhere, we find a range of creole features. A few are shown in table 14.3.

| **Table 14.3** | Some features of Barbadian (Creole) English |
| --- | --- |
| **Linguistic feature** | **Example** |
| 1. Completive *done* | It ***done*** set there since last year. |
| 2. Present tense *–s* absence | He ***send*** somebody. |
| 3. Unmarked past tense | Two day before she ***pass*** away, I ***tell*** her to start crying now. |
| 4. Copula (*be* verb) absence | ***She lucky*** that I ain't throw it on her. |
| 5. *Ain't* | It ***ain't*** concern you. |
| 6. Unmarked possessives | You know some ***people*** cake, you cut it here, you find a lump. |
| 7. Object forms as subjects | ***Them*** ain't want to hear you. |
| 8. Subject forms as objects | I ain't mind **she**. |

Source: From Gerard Van Herk, "Barbadian Lects: Beyond Meso," in *Contact Englishes of the Eastern Caribbean*, ed. Michael Aceto and Jeffrey P. Williams (Amsterdam: John Benjamins, 2003). With kind permission by John Benjamins Publishing Company, Amsterdam/Philadelphia.

Often, creoles co-exist with a local version of their original lexifier languages. This leads to a range of language varieties between the most creole-like, called the **basilect**, and the least creole-like, the **acrolect**. Intermediate stages are called **mesolects**. This range is known as the **creole continuum**. We often assume that the basilect represents something close to the original creole variety, with mesolects reflecting a wearing away of those deep creole features under the influence of the acrolect—a sort of 'bottom-up' explanation. This scenario is supported by evidence that basilectal features 'drop out' as we move up the continuum, sometimes being replaced by a form that looks like the standard but continues to behave like the original basilectal feature. For example, mesolectal past tense markers *did* and *had* may be affected by the same linguistic factors (remember them?) as the basilectal marker *bin*. In other cases, however, there seems to be a break in the middle, as when bare forms like *she see him* represent a single event at the basilectal end, but a recurring or habitual one in the high mesolect. In those situations, a combination of 'top-down' and 'bottom-up' explanations may be needed.

## 14.6 Distinctions within a community: class, ethnicity, and gender

So far, we've looked at social factors that apply to pretty well everyone in a community. The kind of change, isolation, and contact we've been discussing affect entire regional groups. Now, we'll look at what language variation tells us about distinctions within regional communities. These distinctions include class, ethnicity, and gender, among others, as well as the interactions between them.

### 14.6.1 Class

**Class**, or socioeconomic status (SES), is a classic social distinction in studies of industrialized societies, and has played a role in sociolinguistic studies from the beginning. We sociolinguists haven't always had an easy time determining just which social class level to assign to the people we interview. Sometimes, we resort to complex weighting scales, involving income, amount of education, type of housing, and prestige associated with one's occupation. Over time, there seems to have been a tendency to settle on occupational prestige as the major indicator of class.

A finding across many speech communities has been that certain linguistic variants are more closely associated with the upper classes, and that these variants carry the most **prestige**. For example, in most varieties of English, *these things* is a more prestigious utterance than *dem tings*. It involves two higher-prestige forms, one phonological (interdental fricatives rather than dental or alveolar stops), the other syntactic or lexical (demonstrative *these* instead of *them*). Upper classes often adopt prestige norms imported from outside the speech community, as when North Americans adopt British speech features, or Quebecers use the French of France as their model.

Classic sociolinguistic studies, such as William Labov's study of New York's Lower East Side, analyzed people's language in situations that encouraged different degrees of attention to speech, from naturalistic interviews to formal word-list reading (see figure 14.7). They found a strong relationship between class and careful speech styles (those involving a lot of attention to speech). No matter what the task, higher-class speakers used more prestige variants. And no matter what the class, careful style correlated with prestige variants. In other words, as Labov put it, a careful

**Figure 14.7**
Rates of standard pronunciation of /r/ (as in *car*) across social classes and formality of tasks in New York City. Note how the *second*-highest class becomes extremely standard in the most formal task.

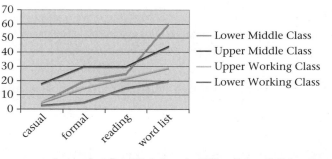

— Lower Middle Class
— Upper Middle Class
— Upper Working Class
— Lower Working Class

Source: *Sociolinguistic Patterns* by William Labov. © University of Pennsylvania Press 1972. Reprinted with permission of the University of Pennsylvania Press.

---

**Language Matters Going Up**

The famous **fourth floor study**, again by Labov in New York, demonstrated that prestige is not an automatic function of a person's income, but relates to context and expectations. The researcher asked employees in three different department stores for directions to a department located on the store's fourth floor, and tabulated how many of their answers involved pronunciation of the [r] in each word ('*r*-ful-ness' being the prestige form). Labov found that even though all the employees earned similar (low) wages, those who worked in the higher-prestige stores used more of the higher-prestige variant. Labov hypothesized that store employees 'borrowed' prestige from their customers, and that this was reflected in their unconscious language choices.

---

pipefitter spoke like a casual salesman, at least in the use of linguistic variables that had social meaning in his speech community. Generally, people of all classes showed the same rate of increase in the use of prestige forms in careful speech. The exception was members of the second-highest class, who sharply increased their use of prestige forms when paying a great deal of attention to speech—in other words, they overcompensated, or in Labov's terminology, they showed (social) **hypercorrection**. This tendency among the second-highest class has shown up in studies in many different communities; it is generally attributed to **linguistic insecurity** among a social group attempting to move up the class ladder.

The concepts of prestige or status seem to transfer across cultures better than the narrower term *class*. In societies where movement between status groups is very difficult, such as in the **caste** system of traditional India, rigid rules have developed (see table 14.4). Members of different castes will often have categorical rules governing word choice. This may sound extreme, but Canadian English is not that different in this respect. How many of us can say *You shall do as I say,* or *whilst,* or describe something as *rather thrilling*, without sounding like we're desperately striving for the social heights?

| **Table 14.4** | Caste differences in Bangalore Kannada | |
|---|---|---|
| | **Brahmin** | **Non-Brahmin** |
| 'it is' | ide | ayti |
| 'inside' | -alli | -aga |
| 'sit' | kut- | kunt- |

Source: *Sociolinguistics: An Introduction to Language and Society.* © Peter Trudgill, 1974, 1983, 1995, 2000.

We'll return to issues of class and prestige when we talk about standard languages and prescriptivism in section 14.8.

## 14.6.2 Ethnicity: the case of African American English

If linguistic distinctions reflect a society's social distinctions, it's no surprise that we find racial or ethnic differences in language. In North America, the ethnic variety (or **ethnolect**) that has received the most attention by far from sociolinguists is African American English (AAE).

This is at least partly to make up for an earlier deficit—AAE was often ignored or marginalized in discussions of North American English until the civil rights movement picked up steam in the 1960s. This shortage of serious study allowed an unearned veneer of respectability to settle over suggestions that the distinct features of AAE resulted from lazy articulation or cultural deprivation, or showed that the language was somehow 'incomplete' or a 'restricted code' not suited to abstract thought. When sociolinguists studied urban AAE in New York, Detroit, and Washington in the late 1960s, they discovered in city after city a linguistic system with remarkably similar structures, governed by similar linguistic constraints, as shown in table 14.5. In this table, you'll see that varieties of English align with each other in complex ways. AAE and NE (Newfoundland English) both express habitual actions with *be*; AAE and Caribbean creoles both use zero copula forms, and *done* in perfect constructions; and almost everybody uses unmarked forms for some past tense verbs (especially *come*, *run*, and *give*). Even varieties that share forms may have different frequencies of use, or different rules for when to use them. It's this complexity that keeps sociolinguists busy sorting out the origins and internal systems of different varieties.

Notice, too, that NE, AAE, and creoles can all use verb forms to express distinctions that Standard English can't (Standard speakers need to use adverbs like 'usually' or 'just'). In other words, in these respects, these non-standard varieties are *more* complex and precise than the standard language, contrary to common linguistic prejudice.

**Table 14.5** Comparing varieties of English

| Function | Standard | Non-standard | NE | AAE | Caribbean creoles |
|---|---|---|---|---|---|
| *Recent perfect* | I've just eaten. | I **done** ate. | I'm **after** eating. | I **done** ate. | I **done** eat. |
| *Copula* | He's coming. He's a fool. | **He's** coming. He's a fool. | **He's** coming. He's a fool. | **He** coming. He's a fool. | **He** coming. He's a fool. |
| *Habitual* | She always, sometimes, often, usually sings. | She always, sometimes, often, usually sings. | She **bees singing**. She **does be** singing. | She **be singing**. She **steady** singing. | She **does/da** sing. She **does be** singing. |
| *Past* | She came. She saw it. | She **come**. She **seen** it. | She **come**. She **seen** it. | She **come**. She **seen** it. | She **come**. She **see** it. |

Note: Speakers of a non-standard variety may also use the standard form, to varying degrees. This table represents their least standard uses.

The 1980s saw a growth of interest in tracing the origins of the distinctive features of AAE. As with pidgins and creoles, the lack of historical documentation of the variety limited the data available to researchers, and perhaps encouraged speculation. Over the past two decades, however, a remarkable number of sources of information on earlier AAE have been discovered. These include the isolated communities mentioned above, writings by travellers of past centuries, the dialogue of old plays, old letters by semiliterate authors, and recordings made in the 1930s and 1940s of elderly ex-slaves. Researchers disagree, often strongly, about what the data from these sources tell us about where AAE came from. Some argue that contemporary AAE features like copula deletion (e.g., *he bad*) show that AAE was once a creole, or something like it; others argue that the AAE of isolated communities shows features (and linguistic factors affecting them) that more closely resemble the earlier English dialects preserved in places like Newfoundland (e.g., *people goes*). Information from both positions converges, though, in showing that AAE has always been a complete, highly structured language variety; the features of AAE today have not appeared overnight.

Contemporary AAE continues to provide avenues of research for sociolinguists. For one thing, new grammatical features seem to be developing, including the use of past perfects with simple past meaning (e.g., *had went* for *went*). And research is moving past the previous focus on the grammatical consistency of the variety to look at regional diversity in AAE's sound system. Sociolinguists are also beginning to pay back a variety that has supplied the data for so much study, by developing teaching materials that help AAE speakers to bridge the dialect gap in the school system.

Ethnicity and language also intersect in how we talk *about* ethnicity. In particular, the preferred names for ethnic groups, sometimes called **ethnonyms**, change over time, reflecting the status of a group in wider society and the degree of power a group is able to exercise over the naming process. In North America, African slaves and their generations of descendants have been called, roughly in chronological order, *African, colored, negro, Negro, Black*, and *African American*. The diminishing acceptability in our culture of **ethnic slurs** like *darky* and *nigger* also reflects changing attitudes toward ethnic naming practices, at least overtly. Terms for ethnic varieties can also change—AAE has also been known at various times as Negro Dialect, Non-standard Negro Vernacular, Black Street Speech, African American Vernacular English, or Ebonics.

## 14.6.3 Gender

Sociolinguists generally find differences in language use that reflect socially assigned sex roles, or **gender roles**. One frequent finding is that when language variation in a community is stable (no change is occurring), women use more of the standard forms associated with 'official' (**overt**) prestige, and switch to prestige forms when paying more attention to their speech. British sociolinguist Peter Trudgill found that not only do men use more non-standard forms than women, but they also claim to use even more of them than they actually do. Trudgill explained this by proposing the idea of **covert prestige**—a sort of linguistic 'street credibility' that men aim for to prove their masculinity. The second gender difference that often surfaces is that when change *does* occur, women use more of the incoming forms than men. This is especially true with **change from above**, changes that are noticeable in the community and work from the upper classes down. Some sociolinguists suggest that women use overt prestige forms and adopt changes from above because of **linguistic insecurity**. But these differences may also reflect gender expectations that limit women's ability to demonstrate toughness, or the fact that women more often do the jobs that require standard speech, such as teacher or receptionist. And women may lead change simply because of their role as child caregivers. If women adopt a new form, it *becomes* a change because children grow up hearing it from women. If men adopt a new form, nobody listens to them.

Researchers have also noted gender differences in **discourse**, the way conversations are structured, especially in same-sex conversations. They often observe that women are more likely to use language to build and maintain relationships (a **rapport** style), while men are more likely to use language to communicate factual information (a **report** style). Overall, women do more work to keep conversations going (*M-hm . . . really? Oh my God!*), ask questions to engage others, organize turn-taking, maintain a single topic for longer, and demonstrate sympathy with others by sharing their problems and experiences with them. Men interrupt more often, ask questions to get information, change topics, and avoid disclosing their problems. These differences lead to the facetious observation, "It's pointless to share your problems with a man, because he'll try to fix them." Some researchers see gender differences in language as reflecting women's lack of power in society; some see them as reflecting different cultures of conversation.

Popular culture expresses this difference by suggesting that men and women are from different (but presumably equal) planets. But in fact, we share not only a planet, but also a speech community. The saying "You talk like who you talk with," which helped us explain the linguistic effects of region, class, and ethnicity, breaks down when it comes to gender. Although many of us speak fairly often with the opposite sex, gender differences in language persist, which suggests that we might use language to perform gender more often than we use it to perform region or class. Men use male-associated language to 'be a man'—more precisely, to be a stereotypical heterosexual man. For example, men in our culture have deeper voices than women. This is partly because male vocal cords are longer. But research in Britain has shown that men's voices are even deeper than longer vocal cords would predict, and suggests that the rest of the difference is social. In other words, men who buy into their gender role overdo it. The markedness of gender-stereotyped language is easy to see by looking at people who opt out. Some recent Canadian research suggests that people who describe themselves as avoiding traditional sex roles also avoid the poles of traditional male or female pronunciations. Work on the speech of men perceived by listeners as gay finds that listeners base their judgments on the use of phonetic features that are also associated with female speech. This also suggests that it is more practical to think of gendered language as a continuum, rather than either/or.

As we saw for ethnicity above, gender and language also intersect when we talk *about* gender . . . or when we assume we're talking about gender. Given the sentence *The nurse wished the professor would stop complaining*, most people will conjure up an image of a female nurse and a male professor, because we associate those occupations with those genders. Our language continues to reflect these sexist assumptions: many people speak of *male nurses* (while female nurses are just *nurses*), and *actors* and *actresses*, where the form for men is the unmarked one. Nowadays, we see a move toward a single inclusive form for both men and women: *actor* for everyone, *chair* rather than *chairman*, and *flight attendant* rather than *stewardess*. Some traditional grammarians still insist on *he* as the pronoun of choice when the sex of the person involved is not specified, as with *someone* or *anyone*: *If anyone wants a good mark, **he** should study*. Replacing *he* with *he or she* is an inclusive option in formal speech, but in informal speech *they* is much more common.

## Situation-specific factors

Study after study has shown that factors like gender and region affect language use. But ticking off these factors on a sociolinguistic checklist doesn't mean that we've explained a community's language use.

In many situations, completely different aspects of social reality may be reflected in language use. In Ontario, speakers with **restricted** use of French (for example, only in school, rather than with friends or family) may lack control of some non-standard, collo-quial features. In rural Guyana, language use varies according to whether people work in plantation fields or not. Some speakers use particular variants to show their **identification** with local values, as when young men in the fishing community of Martha's Vineyard use traditional pronunciations to distance themselves from the tourist economy. Recently, some scholars have adopted the term **community of practice** to explain some language varia-tion—people who come together to engage in some shared activity are likely to develop shared language practices. Penelope Eckert investigated language use in a Detroit-area high school, and found that it reflected membership in one of two groups—*jocks* (who identify with the official system of the institution) and *burnouts* (who don't). My own work on online youth subcultures shows that people can adapt their language to reflect participation in groups like hip-hop fans, tweens, and nerds.

A second issue to keep in mind is that all of these social categories *intersect*. It's the combination of social forces that is played out in language use. Eckert's jocks and burnouts were not identical to middle- and working-class groups, but membership in these groups reinforced students' streaming toward those classes. And being a jock or burnout meant different things for men and women. A gender effect was also clear with online subcultures. For example, male and female hip-hop fans showed strong differences in language use, whereas nerds rejected the most gender-specific terms.

# 14.7 Social interaction and language

We humans aren't sociolinguistic robots, programmed to speak a certain way because of our region, gender, ethnicity, age, and the like. Instead, we reveal (or perform) our social roles in extended language interaction, or discourse. And society also has rules, or conventions, about how discourse should proceed. **Discourse analysis** lets linguists look at the structure of a conversation and what it reveals about the roles of the participants. Some methods of analyzing discourse (speech act theory, pragmatics) are covered in other chapters. Here, we look at two other methods.

## 14.7.1 Ethnography of communication

Ethnography of communication is a way to analyze discourse by using the same sort of methods that anthropologists might use to study other aspects of a culture, such as religious practices. Within **speech situations** (circumstances involving the use of speech), cultures have developed conventions governing interactions, or **speech events**. Ethnography of communication analysis pulls apart speech events into their component parts. Eight basic components have been identified; the acronym SPEAKING may help you remember them, as illustrated in table 14.6.

Table 14.6 demonstrates how the components of this appallingly bad joke can be identified. In a real conversation, we can expect each component to affect the language that is used, and the structure of discourse. You may be familiar with a game popular in improvisational comedy or theatre, where actors begin a scene, somebody shouts *freeze!* and one of these components is changed—for example, a conversation between two theologians (*participants*) is suddenly performed in the style of a *Star Trek* episode (*genre*).

**Table 14.6**   Components of a speech event

**Sample speech event:** A piece of rope walks into a bar and asks for a drink. The bartender says, "We don't serve pieces of rope." The rope goes outside, ties itself up, and frays its ends. It returns to the bar and asks again. The bartender says, "Aren't you the same piece of rope I just refused to serve?" The rope says, "I'm a frayed knot."

|   | Component | Explanation | Analysis of sample |
|---|-----------|-------------|---------------------|
| **S** | setting, scene | place, time, social occasion | a bar |
| **P** | participants | who was there, including audience | bartender, a piece of rope |
| **E** | ends | purpose of event and goals of participants | rope: to get a drink bartender: to refuse |
| **A** | act sequences | content of interaction and related forms | request for a drink and refusal, question of rope's identity |
| **K** | key | emotional tone, mood | hopeful, later annoyed |
| **I** | instrumentalities | mode (spoken, written), type (dialect, style) | spoken, casual speech |
| **N** | norms | conventions of interaction | request addressed, refusal acknowledged, question answered |
| **G** | genres | category/name of event | conversation (and bad pun) |

We can laugh at the adaptations made by the actors, because we share with them an understanding of the often unspoken rules that govern discourse. In other words, we (and they) have **communicative competence**.

Instrumentalities—the 'how' of discourse—help show that the language of interaction is more than the sum of its participants and their social characteristics. For most of us, communicative competence includes control of **style**, or how formal our speech is. We use formal style when we are looking for (overt) prestige, and when we pay attention to our speech; we use informal style in more relaxed situations, and/or when overt prestige is not our goal. The related term **register** also describes a type of speech, but it is more closely associated with a specific speech situation, so we can speak of a *legal register* or *ritual language register*. Sometimes the boundary between register and genre is fuzzy; people often speak of *recipe register*, although we can also think of *recipe* as a genre—it's a widely recognized category of event with its own name. Both style and register are associated with particular phonological, lexical, or syntactic properties. The same sentiment is expressed by the formal *I shall never surrender* and the informal *I ain't never quittin'!* And recipe register is full of imperatives (*Place chicken legs in bag containing spiced flour*) and zero object constructions (*Shake vigorously*), where the shaking refers to the chicken.

A register associated with a particular occupation or activity often develops its own special vocabulary items, known as **jargon**. Jargon can involve special terms, as when linguists refer to *fricatives* or *mediopassives*, or specialized meanings for existing words, as when we give particular linguistic meanings to the words *register* or *style*. Jargon makes communication more effective for in-group members—we don't need to keep saying *those sounds where our phonation is all hissy*. But jargon also excludes non-members, or creates barriers to participation, as you may have noticed through the course of this book.

Act sequences and norms also tell us something about the conventions of conversation. One way to investigate these things is through **ethnomethodology**, also called **conversation analysis**. This method lets us search large collections of recorded natural speech to discover patterns in the distribution of utterances. One very common structure is the **adjacency pair**, a sort of minimal act sequence in which a specific type of utterance by one speaker is followed by a specific type by someone else. An obvious example is *question-answer*, but other recurring examples include *compliment-acceptance*, or *offer-refusal*. Sometimes the first part permits more than one response: in a store, an offer (*Can I help you?*) can trigger either acceptance (*Yes, I'm looking for an Arcade Fire t-shirt*) or refusal (*No, just browsing*). Sometimes one utterance type can be interpreted as another. For example, in cultures where direct requests are discouraged, an overt compliment (*What a nice hat!*) will be interpreted as a request (*May I have it?*). In other cultures, the same compliment may be interpreted as an attribution of wealth (*You must be rich to afford such a hat*) leading up to a request for money, thus requiring a denial (*This old thing? I've had it forever*).

Conversation analysis also deals with who speaks when. It includes identification of conversational **openings** (*How are you?*) and **closings** (*Well, gotta get back to work*). As well, it studies **turn-taking**. At the end of a conversational 'turn', the speaker may try to determine who should speak next (for example, by asking a question), or 'open the floor' to any participant who has something to contribute. If nobody takes over, the original speaker may continue. Sometimes, the turn boundary cues are subtler, including intonation or the use of discourse markers (*so . . .* or *but . . .* ). Cross-culturally, differences in turn-taking cues may cause confusion. Linguists have identified communities with a **high involvement style**, such as Eastern European Jews in New York or radio talk show callers in Jamaica. Here, turns will often overlap (one speaker will start before another finishes). In other communities, including among the Cree, a longer pause is required to signal the end of a turn. A speaker who hadn't developed communicative competence in these communities might be seen by Jamaicans as unwilling to participate, and by the Cree as monopolizing the conversation.

## 14.7.2 Solidarity and power

Even when participants in a conversation share norms, the conversation may be somewhat unbalanced, depending on the **status** of the speakers. Participants may express closeness or intimacy, or shared status (**solidarity**); or, they may maintain a difference and signal the relative social standing of each participant (the **power** relationship). One clear example of this is found in **forms of address**—what the participants call each other. Participants can express solidarity and shared status through reciprocal naming, as when friends call each other by their first names. Where there is a perceived power difference, as with age differences or work relationships, we often see non-reciprocal naming. A teacher or boss may call students or employees by their first names, while students or employees may use title and last name: *Professor Rivero, Mr. Kadonoff*. If you've worked in factories, you've probably observed a gradient form of address: a fellow worker named Vijay Kumar is *Vijay*, a foreman of the same name is *Mr. Vijay*, while the 'big boss' would be *Mr. Kumar*.

Many languages can express power relationships through a different form of address—the choice of pronoun meaning *you*. Generally, the **T form** is used reciprocally among family and close friends, while the **V form** is used reciprocally among people of roughly equal status, but who are not close. When participants are of unequal status, the powerful use the T forms to address the less powerful, while the less powerful use V forms to address the powerful. (The T and V terminology comes from the French pronouns *tu* and *vous*.) Societies can differ on where to draw the line between people who need T-ing or V-ing; Quebec French speakers will use *tu* more readily than European French speakers. This distinction carries so much significance that languages sometimes have a verb meaning 'using the T form'. In German, it's *dützen*; in French, it's *tutoyer*. People will sometimes formally admit somebody into their friendship circle by saying, "You may *tutoyer* me."

## Language Matters **Solidarity and Childbirth**

The choice of T and V forms can be used to create solidarity. Here's an example from an Ottawa-area French speaker:

> *J'emploi le vous formel avec mes supérieurs ou avec des personnes en position d'autorité. Je l'utilise aussi avec mes clients (je suis infirmière). Le seul moment ou je me permet de déroger à cette règle est quand ma cliente est en train d'accoucher et qu'elle est en période de transition (à partir de 7 ou 8 cm). Une fois l'accouchement terminé et le placenta expulsé, je retourne au vouvoiement.*

> 'I use formal *vous* with my superiors or with people in positions of authority. I also use it with my clients (I'm a nurse). The only time I let myself break this rule is when my client is in labour and she's dilated (from 7 or 8 cm onward). Once childbirth is over and the placenta is expelled, I return to using *vous*.'

In some societies, we find **diglossia**—distinctly different varieties act as social registers. The high (H) variety is used in formal situations, official proclamations, and the like; the low (L) variety among friends. In effect, entire languages or language varieties act like V and T forms. Examples include Paraguay (Spanish and Guaraní), Morocco (Standard Arabic and Moroccan Arabic, or *darija*), Switzerland (Standard German and *Schwyzerdütsch*), and Javanese, as table 14.7 shows.

Another way in which power imbalances reveal themselves in interaction is through linguistic **accommodation**, where speakers modify their language patterns to make them

| **Table 14.7** | Dialect of the Prijajis (Javanese) | | | | | | | |
|---|---|---|---|---|---|---|---|---|
| Level | *are* | *you* | *going* | *to eat* | *rice* | *and* | *cassava* | *now* |
| **High** | menapa | pandjenengan | baḍé | ḍahar | sekul | kalijan | kaspé | semanika |
| **Low** | apa | sampéjan | arep | neda | sega | lan | kaspé | saiki |

more like those of the people they're talking to. In a classic study, a Welsh travel agent was wired for sound and recorded through her business day. She adapted her speech to include more local, working-class features when speaking to working-class customers. We often find asymmetrical accommodation, where the less powerful participant in a conversation is forced to accommodate to the more powerful, but not vice versa. For example, speakers of Standard English will often claim they can't understand speakers of regional or ethnic dialects, and expect dialect speakers to do all the accommodating.

## 14.8 How societies deal with language

So far, we've been taking language as our object of study, and looking at how social forces can shape it. But society and language also interact at a strictly social level. In other words, society can treat language the same way it treats clothing, the arts, or business—as a thing to be debated and regulated. In this section, we look briefly at how societies approach language as a social object.

Most speech communities feature more than one language variety. As we've seen in our discussions of English, sometimes one variety is called the **standard**, and is claimed to be more 'correct' than others. Some countries (notably France and Italy) have formal academies responsible for maintaining the purity of language. English has never had a formal academy, but for centuries our linguistic insecurity has been fed by newspaper columnists, authors of dictionaries and grammars, and other self-proclaimed defenders of the language. The standard language industry probably had its heyday between about 1750 and 1900, when a growing middle class trying to move up the linguistic ladder provided a ready market for ever-stricter rules about correct language use. This is the time period that gives us such inappropriate analogies with mathematics as *Two negatives make a positive*. (As the linguist Steven Pinker has pointed out, that should mean it's all right to use *three* negatives, as in *I can't never get no satisfaction*.) The demand for **prescriptive** grammars (the ones that tell us what to do) remains strong today, judging by the success of books like *Eats, Shoots & Leaves*. In Quebec, a weekly television show tests contestants' knowledge of Standard French.

The standard is difficult, if not impossible, to define objectively. We can agree that some forms, like *ain't*, are probably not part of the standard—at least not anymore. Others, like *There's dozens of ways*, are on the boundary. The standard is slightly easier to pin down on social grounds. It's the language of the upper-socioeconomic classes and of educated people, the language of literature or printed documents, the variety taught in schools and used by broadcasters; in North American English, it's the accent of the American Midwest and mainland Canada. In effect, the standard is the language of powerful people. By this definition, however, any idea of 'correctness' disappears. We're left with a sociolect. What's interesting to sociolinguists is the *idea* of a standard: the widely held belief that some ways of speaking are not just different, but actually inherently correct. (Presumably, this is less of an issue for researchers in other disciplines—astronomers don't worry about whether Neptune is 'better' than Mercury.) This belief in the correctness of the standard lets language serve as a barrier to education and employment for speakers of other varieties.

**Attitudes** toward language have been implicitly involved in much of our discussion so far. The idea of a standard language legitimizes the marginalization of other varieties. People often describe non-standard varieties as lazy, illogical, or sloppy, although they may not feel comfortable saying the same things about the people who speak them. On the whole, though, it's not always easy to determine attitudes toward languages. Researchers in Michigan have encouraged speakers to use maps to rate regional varieties in categories such as 'pleasantness' or 'correctness'. As you might expect, respondents considered Michigan speech to be the most correct. The speech of the U.S. South was seen as extremely incorrect, but pleasant. Language attitudes can also be revealed by deconstructing media images. What accents do you hear from characters who are supposed to be stupid? Criminal? Wise? Pretentious?

Attempts to find objective evidence supporting popular linguistic attitudes and prejudices sometimes result in odd **language myths**. It's easy to be puzzled by the once-popular idea that African American English resulted from its speakers having large lips, or by Korean parents who have their children undergo tongue surgery (called a frenulotomy) in the belief that more flexible tongues will lead to accent-less English. Other language myths are more widespread, especially the idea that some language varieties have tiny vocabularies, or are not capable of expressing complex or abstract ideas. Although these notions may reassure people who wish to dismiss those language varieties, they have no basis in fact. The opposite notion is also popular—that certain languages have massive vocabularies for particular items. This is sometimes known as The Great Eskimo Vocabulary Hoax (also the title of a book on the subject), after its most commonly expressed example. Inuit and Yupik languages have roughly the same number of words for snow as English does.

Of course, languages do sometimes find themselves at a loss for words. This is particularly true when a language moves into new domains, typically when a community language becomes a language of power. Different language groups have dealt with this in different ways.

## Language Matters **The Matched Guise Test**

The **matched guise test**, first developed in Canada, tries to get past people's professed viewpoints to gauge their deeply held language attitudes. In the test, subjects are played a range of recordings of people speaking, and asked to rate the speakers according to traits like social class, intelligence, and friendliness. What the subjects don't know is that they're actually listening to the same speaker or speakers several times, using different accents or speaking different languages. Because the only thing that differs between tapes is the accent or language, any differences in ratings are taken to reflect differences in attitudes toward the language varieties involved. Early experiments showed that both English and French speakers rated French recordings lower in intelligence. In the years since, matched guise studies have fairly consistently shown a solidarity/prestige split. Standard speakers are seen as more competent, smarter, even taller! Non-standard speakers are seen as warmer and friendlier. Matched guise studies in the United States have shown that human resources personnel are likely to assign lower-status jobs to speakers of African American English, as well as to speakers with Hispanic or Asian accents.

A real world application of the matched guise test is found in California, where the linguist John Baugh and his associates have spent years collecting information for housing-discrimination cases. They phone landlords and ask about advertised apartments, using identical sentences but adopting African American, Hispanic, or standard American accents. If apartments are available to standard speakers, but are either unavailable or more expensive when non-standard speakers call, discrimination is assumed.

Some languages borrow words. When English became the language of British government and the law hundreds of years ago, it borrowed many of the terms needed from French (*attorney*, *governor general*). When the creole language Tok Pisin became the official language of Papua New Guinea, it borrowed legal terms from English (the Tok Pisin term for *public solicitor* is *pablik salisita*). In other situations, governments establish bodies to oversee **language planning**, which often includes coming up with homegrown solutions to lexical gaps. In Quebec, the *Office de la Langue Française* (OLF) works to develop French-based terms for new or imported concepts (e.g., for lesser-known foodstuffs imported from other countries). The OLF is also responsible for other aspects of language planning, including the implementation of government legislation on language.

Government involvement in language planning often includes the declaration of an **official language** for a particular region or country as a result of legislation. When a language is made an official language, it often affects the political and economic power of the ethnic group that speaks that language. In some cases, official language designations are a response by a majority group to a perceived increase in status or power of a minority group. A good example of this situation is the attempt by 'English-only' groups to have English declared the official language of the United States. Currently, about half of the United States has some sort of law giving English official status. French and English are the official languages of Canada (at the federal level) and New Brunswick; most other provinces conduct official business in either English or French. The Northwest Territories have *eleven* official languages: Chipewyan, Cree, English, French, Gwich'in, Inuinnaqtun, Inuktitut, Inuvialuktun, North Slavey, South Slavey, and Tlicho, although services in all eleven are not available everywhere. According to the 2001 Census, about 6.8 million Canadians have a mother tongue different from the majority language of their province: 1 million French

---

## Language Matters **Language Planning in Tanzania**

The objectives of Tanzania's Institute of Kiswahili Research are a good example of the activities of language planning groups that work to expand the role and usefulness of official languages in post-colonial situations:

- To undertake research in various aspects of Kiswahili morphology, syntax, phonology, sociolinguistics and dialectology.
- To undertake research in Kiswahili lexicography and compile general and subject dictionaries.
- To compile terminologies and coin new terms for different academic and/or specialized fields.
- To co-ordinate and provide translation services to government offices, parastatal organizations, industries, institutions and individuals in and outside the country.
- To carry out research in oral and written literature, theatre arts, folklore and the cultures of the Tanzanian and East African societies.
- To co-operate with other institutions in the development of Kiswahili language and provide consultancy services in different aspects of Kiswahili language and literature.
- To publish teaching material on/in Kiswahili for schools, colleges and universities.
- To see to it that Kiswahili acquires a strong foundation for becoming a medium of instruction for primary, secondary, and tertiary levels of education.

Source: www.udsm.ac.tz/ikr/aboutikr.html

speakers outside Quebec; about 0.5 million English speakers in Quebec; and 5.2 million speakers of other languages across Canada. In other words, nearly a quarter of all Canadians are surrounded by a language other than the one they grew up with.

Language planning policies often have their greatest impact in regulating the language of schooling, which in turn places differential barriers on access to education. Proponents of minority language education or bilingual education argue that teaching subject matter such as science or geography in students' first language levels the playing field by removing the linguistic barrier to learning. Linguistic minority groups have often fought for education in their home languages to help preserve their community's linguistic vitality. These minority language education programs are sometimes interpreted by majority language groups as resistance to assimilation, leading to backlash. In California, the Oakland school district's attempt to recognize the legitimacy of AAE in the learning process was harshly criticized. American Spanish-English bilingual programs have led to restrictive legislation. Currently, Arizona forbids bilingual education, while other jurisdictions restrict funding. In the past, home languages have been **banned** in schools, with harsh punishments for their use. Gaelic was banned in Welsh schools, and Aboriginal languages such as Cree or Blackfoot were banned at residential schools in Canada.

In many cases, minority languages are in danger of dying out. Immigrant languages continue to be spoken elsewhere, so their decline here leads to decreased diversity, but not to **language death**. The situation is different for Canada's Aboriginal languages, some of which now have fewer than one hundred speakers, and for minority languages around the world. Major efforts are being made to support endangered languages through the development of dictionaries, reading materials, and school systems, but the past history of endangered languages is not encouraging. Languages usually come 'back from the brink' only when major political and social will is involved. One such example is Hebrew, which has been built up to become the official language of Israel.

# Summing up

**Sociolinguistics** is the study of language in its social contexts. **Linguistic variation** between **speech communities** reflects social factors such as **region, change over time, isolation,** and **language contact**. Contact situations lead to **bilingualism, code switching**, and **borrowing**, as well as to such contact-driven languages as **mixed languages, lingua francas, pidgins**, and **creoles**. Within speech communities, language reflects important social distinctions, including **class, ethnicity**, and **gender**, as well as the interactions between these factors and locally relevant norms.

**Discourse analysis** looks at language in interactions, using such methods as **ethnography of communication** and **ethnomethodology**. Individual speakers adapt their use of **style, register**, and **jargon** to each interaction, as well as to reflect **solidarity** and **power** relationships between speakers. Often, the language of a high-status group will become known as the **standard** language; this variety will be described as more 'correct' than other varieties, based largely on **attitudes** toward the variety. Attitudes can restrict the social mobility of non-standard speakers. **Language planning** involves attempts by a society to regulate language use through choice of **official language** and language of education, or even by **banning** languages.

Through analysis of language variation, forty years of sociolinguistic research confirms that variation is highly patterned, and affected by a range of linguistic and social factors. This patterning helps reveal the social patterning of language and sociolinguistic competence of speakers, who use language to situate themselves with respect to other speakers and the norms of their society.

## Recommended reading

Chambers, J.K. 1995. *Sociolinguistic Theory*. Oxford: Blackwell.

Chambers, J.K., P. Trudgill, and N. Schilling-Estes. 2002. *The Handbook of Language Variation and Change*. Oxford: Blackwell.

Lippi-Green, R. 1997. *English with an Accent*. London: Routledge.

Meyerhoff, M. 2006. *Introducing Sociolinguistics*. London: Routledge.

Milroy, L., and M. Gordon. 2002. *Sociolinguistics: Method and Interpretation*. Oxford: Blackwell.

Wolfram, W., and N. Schilling-Estes. 1998. *American English*. Oxford: Blackwell.

## Exercises

1. The following short story uses a lot of British English words (underlined). 'Translate' it into North American English.

> As I left the <u>lift</u>, the <u>caretaker</u> stopped me. "I was just about to <u>knock you up</u>," he said. "The <u>estate agents</u> just <u>rang</u>, and they'd like to show your <u>flat</u>. You'll have to <u>sort out</u> all that <u>rubbish</u>."
>
> The flat looked like a <u>dustbin</u>. <u>Sweets</u>, <u>draughts</u>, <u>drawing pins</u>, and <u>biros</u> covered the table. <u>Dungarees</u>, <u>trousers</u>, <u>vests</u>, and <u>pants</u> were all over the <u>cupboard</u>. Where had that <u>nappy</u> come from? Or those <u>tights</u>? The kitchen was even worse. <u>Courgettes</u>, bits of <u>aubergine</u>, <u>biscuit</u> crumbs, and empty <u>crisp packets</u> littered the floor. <u>Treacle</u> was everywhere.
>
> It was too much. I took the lot down to the <u>pavement</u>, tossed it in my <u>boot</u>, and left it behind a <u>hoarding</u> next to the old <u>cinema</u>. I doused it in <u>petrol</u> and lit a match.

2. This exercise will be more fun if you're surrounded by people from a lot of different places. Survey five people (or more). Find out where they're from, and what they call:
   a) a sweetened fizzy drink
   b) a long padded piece of furniture, usually with arms, that seats several people
   c) rubber-soled shoes that you'd wear in the gym
   d) a schoolyard game played by throwing a ball against a wall and naming one person to catch it
   e) a sandwich, usually filled with cold meat or cheese, served on a long bun
   f) the covered area in front of the front door of a house, usually up a couple of steps
   g) undeveloped, usually forested area, where you might go camping or hunting
   h) a winter vehicle with a motorized track

3. Pidgin sentences often resemble the highly simplified language we sometimes use with people who don't speak our language (when we're not busy shouting or waving our credit cards). This has led some scholars to speculate that such **foreigner talk** is involved in pidgin formation. Try to reduce the following paragraph to its simplest:

   *Why do you keep talking to us? I don't want to buy your jewellery. I already told that man over there that I am going to buy jewellery from him. Please go away and do not talk to me.*

   Compare your results with others; they will probably be surprisingly similar.

4. Choose any speech situation (interview, telephone conversation, online chat, classroom lecture, TV show) and analyze it using the components discussed in the section on ethnography of communication (SPEAKING).

5. Work from the list of words given below. Ask at least five people:
   a) How do you pronounce this word?
   b) Do you know of any other pronunciations for this word? What are they?
   c) Who uses these other pronunciations?

   Tabulate your responses.

   Word list: *herb, lever, lieutenant, news, student, missile, despicable, leisure, marry, merry.*

6. You may have seen cartoons where someone has a devil and an angel on her shoulders, representing her negative and positive influences. Spend a week with a 'sociolinguistic angel' on your shoulder. Keep yourself actively aware of language variation that you hear or read by continually thinking, "Is this something I haven't heard before? Is this something that not everyone would say? How might this be said by somebody of a different age, ethnicity, gender, or social class?" If you actively listen, you'll be amazed at how much difference you hear.

7. Choose a paragraph of text at random (perhaps from this book). Try to rewrite it as one of the following:
   a) an explanation for a close friend or family member
   b) a rewrite for a textbook for non-native speakers of English
   c) a ballad
   d) a summary spoken by an overly excited nine year old
   e) a summary spoken by Paris Hilton

8. Decide which of the following sentences are incorrect, according to prescriptive rules.

   *Anyone who has finished their work should stay in their seat.*

   *Whom do you want to speak to?*

   *Who do you want to speak to?*

   *Hopefully, it will be warm tomorrow.*

   *There's dozens of ways to make cookies.*

   *The professor gave the paper to Anton and I.*

*Please prepare a report for Jean-Claude and myself.*

*Between you and I, I think this is a waste of time.*

*The union leader, along with all of her followers, want to talk to you.*

How many 'errors' did you spot?

9. It's commonly believed that variation in Canadian pronunciation reflects an ongoing move from British to American forms, and this may eventually prove to be the case. For most of the words involved, however, variation here reflects a continuation of the variable systems that crossed the Atlantic with early settlers. In the list below, which form do you use?

|  | *British (Standard) English* | *American (Standard) English* |
|---|---|---|
| *lever* | [livər] | [lɛvər] |
| *lieutenant* | [lɛftɛnənt] | [lutɛnənt] |
| *herb* | [hə(r)b] | [ərb] |

# Fifteen

Michael Dobrovolsky
William O'Grady

# Writing and language

*Letters continue to fall like precise rain along my way.*

PABLO NERUDA

Speaking and writing are different in both origin and practice. Our ability to use language is as old as humankind, and reflects the biological and cognitive modifications that have occurred during the evolution of our species. **Writing**, the symbolic representation of language by graphic signs or symbols, is a comparatively recent cultural development, having occurred within the past five thousand years and only in certain parts of the world.[1] Most of the world's languages have no tradition of writing, and many lack a writing system even today.

A further indication of the contrast between speech and writing comes from the fact that spoken language is acquired without specific formal instruction, whereas writing must be taught and learned through deliberate effort. Even in literate societies, there are individuals who cannot read or write. While spoken language comes naturally to human beings, writing does not.

## 15.1 Types of writing

As different as they are, speech and writing share one major characteristic: just as spoken language shows an arbitrary link between sound and meaning, so written language exhibits an arbitrary link between symbol and sound.

All writing can be grouped into two basic types, called logographic and phonographic, depending on the technique that it uses to represent language.

### 15.1.1 Logographic writing

The term **logographic** (from Greek *logos* 'word') refers to a type of writing in which symbols represent morphemes or even entire words.

#### Logograms

Logographic writing is the oldest type of genuine writing. Ancient Mesopotamian cuneiform inscriptions, Egyptian hieroglyphics, and primordial Chinese characters were all highly logographic in their early stages. In fact, all writing systems maintain some logographic writing. Conventional abbreviations such as &, %, $, and the like are logographic, as are the symbols for numerals. To a certain extent, logographic writing can be read independently of its language of origin. For example, the Arabic numbers 1, 2, 7, 10, and so on can be read in any language.

## 15.1.2 Phonographic writing

No writing system is purely logographic, however. Nor can it be, since using a separate symbol to write each word in a language is simply too cumbersome—there are just too many words. Throughout human history, writing systems have always evolved signs that represent some aspect of pronunciation. In **phonographic writing** (from Greek *phōnē* 'sound'), symbols represent syllables or segments. There are two principal types of phonographic writing systems—syllabic and alphabetic.

### Syllabic writing

As the name suggests, **syllabic writing** employs signs to represent syllables (a set of syllabic signs is called a **syllabary**). Languages with relatively simple syllabic structures such as CV or CVC (Japanese and Cree, for example) are well suited to this type of writing, since they contain a relatively limited number of syllable types. In Japanese, for example, the word *kakimashita* '(s/he) wrote' can be written with the five syllabic signs か, き, ま, し, and た: かきました.

### Alphabetic writing

**Alphabetic writing** represents consonant and vowel segments. Unlike the International Phonetic Alphabet, which is devised expressly to represent details of pronunciation, ordinary alphabets generally ignore non-phonemic phenomena. Thus, the spelling of the English words *pan* and *nap* represents the phonemes /p/, /n/, and /æ/, but ignores consonant aspiration, vowel nasalization, and other subphonemic variation. As we will see in section 15.4 of this chapter, some spelling systems also capture certain morphophonemic alternations.

Writing systems emerged and spread around the earth over a long period of time. Though we can trace the spread of some systems over a wide area, writing may have emerged independently in several different places. The next sections trace the development of some writing systems from their pictorial origins.

## 15.2 The early history of writing

It is surprising that we cannot say with certainty how a comparatively recent cultural phenomenon like writing originated. We do know that writing developed in stages, the earliest of which involves direct representation of objects. This is sometimes called *pre-writing*.

## 15.2.1 Pre-writing

Figures and scenes depicted on cave walls and rock faces in the Americas, Africa, and Europe twelve thousand years ago, and perhaps even earlier, may have been forerunners of writing.

Some of these petroglyphs (scenes painted on stone) may represent a type of pre-literate stage that did not evolve into a full-fledged writing system.

These drawings depict a wide range of human and animal activity, and may even have been intended for purposes of linguistic communication. Some illustrations were doubtless a form of religious magic to guarantee a successful hunt or other benefits. Perhaps some were for purely esthetic purposes. Still others, such as those depicting the phases of the moon, may have been part of some form of record keeping. Figure 15.1a shows a pair of elk from a rock wall drawing in Sweden dating from the Old Stone Age (Paleolithic) period, perhaps as far back as 20 000 BC. Figure 15.1b shows an incised eagle bone from Le Placard, France that dates back some thirteen to fifteen thousand years. The incisions, which vary subtly, have been analyzed as a record of lunar phases. Pictorial records thus link the origins of writing with the history of representative art.

**Figure 15.1**
*a.* Paleolithic drawing, Sweden; *b.* Le Placard eagle bone

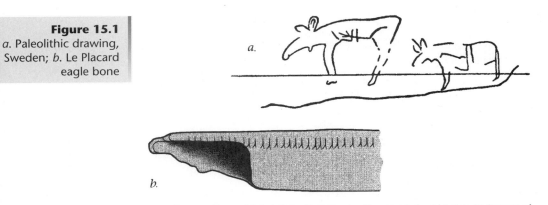

Sources: Figure 15.1a is from Hans Jensen, *Sign, Symbol, and Script: An Account of Man's Efforts to Write*, 3rd ed., rev. and enl. Trans. G. Unwin (London: George Allen and Unwin, 1970), p. 33; figure 15.1b is from A. Marshack, *The Roots of Civilization* (New York: McGraw-Hill, 1972). © A. Marshack 1972.

An even more direct connection links the origin of writing with record keeping. It has been suggested that the idea of writing had its origin in small clay tokens and counters that were used in record keeping and business transactions in the ancient Middle East. These small, fire-baked pieces of clay were apparently used for thousands of years before writing emerged (see figure 15.2). Counters representing cattle and other goods were stored on shelves or in baskets. Eventually, people began to make an impression of the tokens on soft clay tablets rather than storing and shipping the tokens themselves. This may have led to the idea that other objects and events in the world could be represented symbolically in graphic form.

**Figure 15.2**
Ancient Mesopotamian tokens

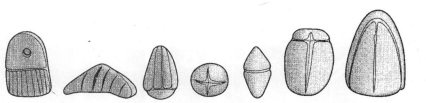

Source: Reprinted with the permission of the Musée du Louvre, Department of Oriental Antiquities.

## 15.2.2 Pictograms

Whatever their purpose, there is no doubt that pictures were among the precursors of the written word. Early writing systems all evolved from pictorial representations called **pictograms** or picture writing. Each pictogram was an image of the object or concept that it represented, and, as far as we know, offered no clues to pronunciation. Pictorial representations of this sort have been found among people throughout the ancient and modern world. Figure 15.3 is an example of Aboriginal picture writing taken from a record kept by a Dakota named Lonedog; these pictures served as a kind of memory aid and not as a detailed record of events.

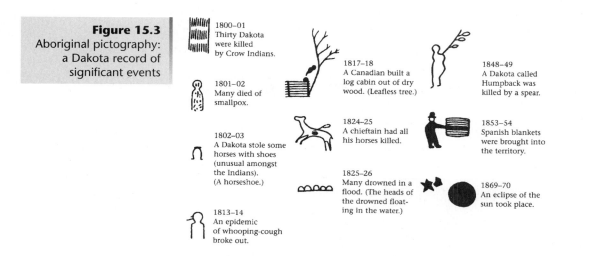

**Figure 15.3**
Aboriginal pictography: a Dakota record of significant events

1800–01
Thirty Dakota were killed by Crow Indians.

1801–02
Many died of smallpox.

1802–03
A Dakota stole some horses with shoes (unusual amongst the Indians). (A horseshoe.)

1813–14
An epidemic of whooping-cough broke out.

1817–18
A Canadian built a log cabin out of dry wood. (Leafless tree.)

1824–25
A chieftain had all his horses killed.

1825–26
Many drowned in a flood. (The heads of the drowned floating in the water.)

1848–49
A Dakota called Humpback was killed by a spear.

1853–54
Spanish blankets were brought into the territory.

1869–70
An eclipse of the sun took place.

Source: Hans Jensen, *Sign, Symbol, and Script: An Account of Man's Efforts to Write*, 3rd ed., rev. and enl. Trans. G. Unwin (London: George Allen and Unwin, 1970), p. 43.

Like any other product of culture, pictography requires a knowledge of the conventions used by the author. Lonedog's record, for example, lists thirty Dakotas killed, but there are only twenty-four short vertical lines. To interpret the record correctly, it is necessary to know that the frame around the short lines consists of six additional joined lines.

Pictograms are still used today, often reflecting the function of this form of pre-writing as a memory aid. Signs indicating roadside services or information in parks are all pictographic in nature, as are the standardized set of symbols developed by the Canadian Olympic Association to indicate sporting events (see figure 15.4).

**Figure 15.4**
Contemporary pictograms: Canadian Olympic signs for sporting events

Source: Courtesy of the Canadian Olympic Committee, TM Canadian Olympic Committee 2007.

A contemporary and very sophisticated development of pictographic writing, **Blissymbolics** (originally called semantography), was developed by Charles K. Bliss. It makes use of a number of recombineable symbols that represent basic units of meaning, as the example in figure 15.5 illustrates. Though Blissymbolics was intended as a means of international, cross-linguistic communication by its inventor, its primary use today is as a means of communication for non-speaking individuals. The Blissymbolics Communication Institute of Toronto sets the standard for the training and application of Blissymbols for this specialized purpose.

**Figure 15.5**
Blissymbolics

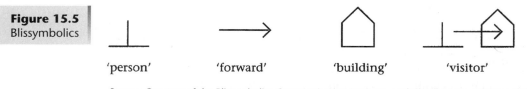

'person'          'forward'          'building'          'visitor'

Source: Courtesy of the Blissymbolics Communication Institute, exclusive licensee, 1982, and derived from the symbols described in the work *Semantography*, original copyright C.K. Bliss, 1949.

As we consider developments that emerge from pictographic representation, it is important to remember that pictograms are not writing in any sense of the word. They do not represent linguistic elements such as segments, syllables, morphemes, or words. They are not written in a sequence that matches the language's word order. And they typically lend themselves to more than one interpretation, often providing only limited clues about their intended meaning.

## 15.3 The evolution of writing

The earliest known pictographic writing came from Sumeria, from where it spread to surrounding areas about five thousand years ago. Over time, inherently ambiguous pictograms came to be used to represent abstract notions as their use was extended to include related concepts. For example, in figure 15.6 the pictogram for 'fire' was also used for 'inflammation', the pictogram for 'hand' was employed to signify 'fist' as well as a particular unit of measurement, and the symbol for 'foot' came to stand for 'go', 'move', and 'go away'.

**Figure 15.6**
Sumerian logograms

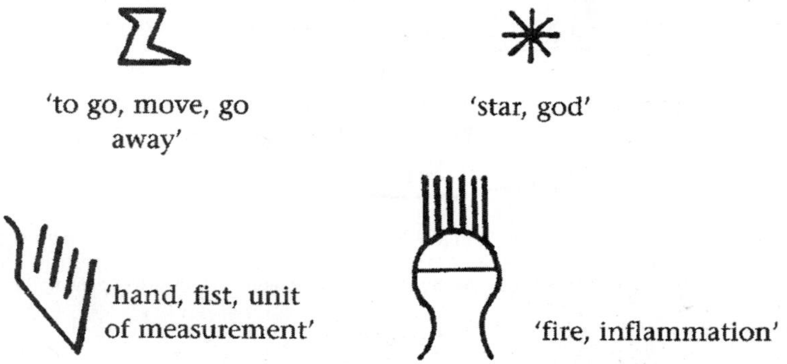

'to go, move, go
away'

'star, god'

'hand, fist, unit
of measurement'

'fire, inflammation'

Source: Adapted from (1) Hans Jensen, *Sign, Symbol, and Script: An Account of Man's Efforts to Write*, 3rd ed., rev. and enl. Trans. G. Unwin (London: George Allen and Unwin, 1970) and from (2) René Labat, *Manuel d'Epigraphie Akkadienne*, 5th ed. (Paris: P. Geuthner, 1976).

Sumerian writing also combined signs to express abstract meanings. For example, a head with fire coming out of the crown indicated 'anger' as shown in figure 15.7.

**Figure 15.7**
The Sumerian logogram
for 'anger'

Source: René Labat, *Manuel d'Epigraphie Akkadienne,* 5th ed.
(Paris: P. Geuthner, 1976).

Although its evolution was gradual, we can state with some certainty that Sumerian writing was logographic because, from a fairly early stage, it was written in a consistent linear order that appears to reflect the order of words in speech. We cannot say with certainty at what date pictures began to be read as words, but once this practice took hold, the stage was set for the evolution to phonographic writing.

## 15.3.1 Rebuses and the emergence of writing

Phonographic writing made its appearance around 3000 BC with the first use of Sumerian symbols to represent sound rather than just meaning. This major development in the history of writing was made possible by the use of the **rebus principle**, which allows a sign to be used for any word that was pronounced like the word whose meaning it originally represented. In the inscription of an economic transaction in figure 15.8, for example, the symbol in the upper left-hand corner, which was originally used to represent the word *gi* 'reed', here represents a homophonous word with the meaning 'reimburse'.

**Figure 15.8**
Sumerian rebus
inscription (c. 3000 BC)

Source: From A.A. Viaman, "Uber die protosumerische Schrift," *Acta Antigua Academiae Scientiarum Hungaricae* 22 (1974):18, as reproduced in John DeFrancis, *Visible Speech: The Diverse Oneness of Writing Systems* (Honolulu: University of Hawaii Press, 1989), p. 76.

Thanks to the rebus principle, concepts that could not be directly depicted by a pictogram/logogram could be represented in writing. Thus, the sign for the word *ti* 'arrow', ➤—, was also used for the word *ti* 'life'.

## 15.3.2 Towards syllabic writing

Once the breakthrough towards phonographic writing had been made, it did not take long (in historical terms) before syllabic writing began to emerge. Within about five hundred to six hundred years, signs that clearly represent not just homophonous words, but parts of words—specifically, syllables—had become well established in Sumerian writing. For example, the word *kir* was represented by the syllabic signs for *ki* and *ir*, written in sequence. (By allowing the function of the symbols to overlap in this way, they avoided the need for a special sign for *r*.) Figure 15.9 illustrates this with the help of Sumerian cuneiform signs that are discussed in more detail in the following section.

**Figure 15.9**
Overlapped Sumerian
syllabic signs

ki   +   ir   =   kir

Source: From Hans Jensen, *Sign, Symbol and Script: An Account of Man's Efforts to Write*, 3rd ed., rev. and enl. Trans. G. Unwin (London: George Allen and Unwin, 1970), p. 95.

Sumerian writing never developed into a pure syllabary. Logographic elements were interspersed with syllabic ones, and many syllabic signs were used to represent syllables with other pronunciations as well.

### Cuneiform

Over the centuries, Sumerian writing was simplified and eventually came to be produced with the use of a wedge-shaped stylus that was pressed into soft clay tablets. This form of writing, initiated in the fourth millennium BC, has come to be known as **cuneiform** (from Latin *cuneus* 'wedge'). In time, a change in writing practices led the cuneiform signs to be modified so that they ended up bearing even less resemblance to their pictographic origins than before. Figure 15.10 illustrates this development for two words.

**Figure 15.10**
Changes in cuneiform
writing

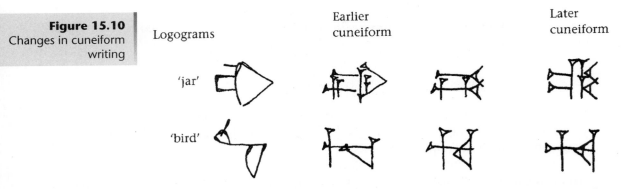

| Logograms | Earlier cuneiform | | Later cuneiform |

'jar'

'bird'

Source: Wayne M. Senner, "Theories and Myths on the Origins of Writing: A Historical Overview," in W. M. Senner (ed.), *The Origins of Writing* (Lincoln: University of Nebraska Press, 1989). Reprinted by permission of the University of Nebraska Press. Copyright © 1989 The University of Nebraska Press.

The cuneiform system was borrowed by the Elamites and Akkadians in the third millennium BC, a little later by the Persians, and in the second millennium BC by the Hittites far to the north in the ancient region of Anatolia (modern Asian Turkey).

Cuneiform writing persisted until about the first few centuries of the Christian era in some areas, and then disappeared from use, not to be rediscovered until the nineteenth century. It was first deciphered from Old Persian texts, a breakthrough that led to the deciphering of Akkadian, Sumerian, and Hittite, among other languages that employed it. This script was used for thousands of years but then was generally replaced by systems of writing employed by the Semitic peoples of the Eastern Mediterranean.

## 15.3.3 Another Middle Eastern writing system: hieroglyphic

At about the time Sumerian pictography was flourishing, a similar system of pictorial communication was in use in Egypt. The Egyptian signs have become known as **hieroglyphs** (meaning 'sacred inscriptions' in Greek). The earliest texts display about five hundred such symbols. Like Sumerian pictograms, the hieroglyphic signs at first represented objects, but later they became logographic as they began to be associated with words.

Egyptian hieroglyphs developed into a mixed system of both word writing and phonographic writing. For example, the sign for the heart and trachea was ⵛ; this represented the word itself: *nfr*. (Only the consonants of words represented by hieroglyphs are known with certainty. The Egyptians did not represent vowels—these can only be partially reconstructed from transcriptions in Greek and other languages that were made much later.) Eventually, this sign came to be disassociated from the word it represented, and was used to transcribe other words that consisted of or included the same sounds, such as the word for 'good', which also contained the consonants *nfr*.

Hieroglyphic symbols eventually came to be used to represent individual consonant phonemes by application of what is called the **acrophonic principle** (from Greek *acros* 'extreme'): sounds are represented by pictures of objects whose pronunciation begins with the sound to be represented. In this way, the first consonant of a word-sign came to be what the sign stood for. For example, the hieroglyph for 'horned viper'

is read logographically as *f-t*. Thanks to the acrophonic principle, this sign is also used to represent the phoneme /f/ in spellings such as *fen* 'pleasant'.

As we will see in section 15.3.4, the acrophonic principle was crucial to the development of true alphabets. In Egyptian writing, however, it was only part of a system that mixed logographic and phonographic elements.

Figure 15.11 provides some additional examples of hieroglyphs. (Throughout this chapter, a macron indicates a long vowel.) Hieroglyphs were used with decreasing frequency until Christian times. By the second century AD, Egyptian began to be written with Greek letters, and by the third century AD, hieroglyphs had been replaced by the Greek alphabet.

**Figure 15.11**
Egyptian hieroglyphs
(c. 1500 BC)

zaa-j
son-my

n_dtjj-j
savior-my

Source: Adapted from Hans Jensen, *Sign, Symbol, and Script: An Account of Man's Efforts to Write*, 3rd ed., rev. and enl. Trans. G. Unwin (London: George Allen and Unwin, 1970), p. 66.

## 15.3.4 The emergence of alphabets

Alphabetic writing emerged slowly from mixed writing systems over a long period in the Middle East. Building on this tradition, the Semitic peoples of ancient Phoenicia (modern Lebanon) devised a writing system of twenty-two consonantal signs as early as 1000 BC. This system was written horizontally, right to left, as had been common in earlier scripts. It ultimately led to the development of many alphabetic writing systems, including both the Greek and Latin alphabets.

The pictorial (and eventually logographic) origins of the Phoenician alphabet are evident in some of its symbols. Figure 15.12 illustrates the development of logograms for a stylized ox's head, a throwing stick, and a wavy flow of water into alphabetic symbols.

**Figure 15.12**
Pictorial and logographic origins of some signs in the Phoenician alphabet

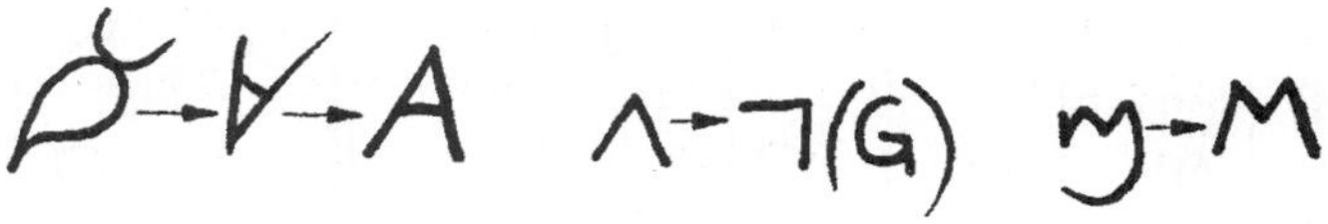

ʔāleph          gīmel          mēm

Source: Adapted from Geoffrey Samson, *Writing Systems, A Linguistic Introduction*. Copyright © 1985 Geoffrey Sampson. All rights reserved. Used with the permission of Stanford University Press, www.sup.org.

These symbols eventually came to be used to represent the consonant phonemes of words by application of the acrophonic principle (see section 15.3.3). In this way, *ʔāleph* was used to represent a glottal stop; *gīmel*, a /g/; and *mēm*, an /m/. Some of the symbols of the Phoenician alphabet had developed from Egyptian hieroglyphics, and, as in hieroglyphic writing, vowels were not represented (see figure 15.11).

The Phoenicians were a trading people, and their alphabetic writing spread to adjacent countries and beyond. Eventually, the Greeks acquired and adapted the Phoenician alphabet.

## The Greek alphabet

The Greeks developed the Phoenician writing system into a full alphabet: each sign represented one phoneme and all phonemes were recorded by a sign. The Greeks were aware that some of the Phoenician symbols represented consonant sounds that were not found in Greek. Some of these symbols were adapted to represent Greek vowels, and other unneeded consonant signs were eventually dropped. Figure 15.13 illustrates the evolution of the Classical Greek and ultimately the Latin alphabet from the original Phoenician consonantal signs.

**Figure 15.13**
Evolution of the Greek
and Latin alphabets

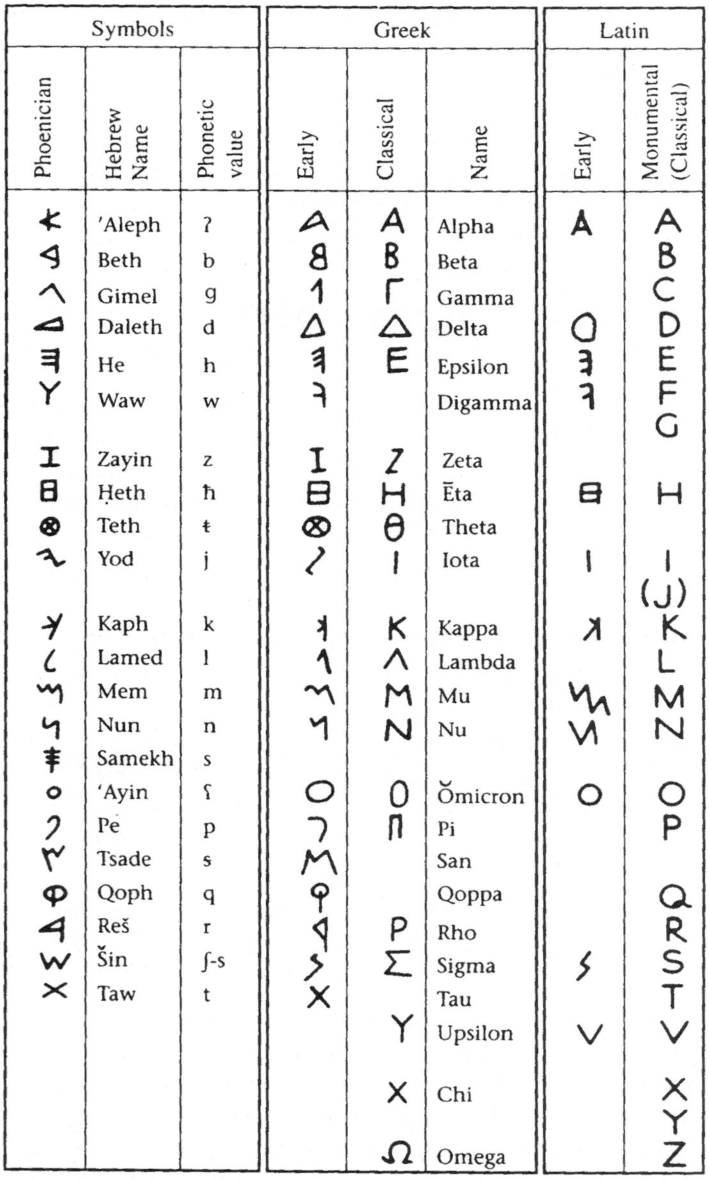

| Symbols | | | Greek | | | Latin | |
|---|---|---|---|---|---|---|---|
| Phoenician | Hebrew Name | Phonetic value | Early | Classical | Name | Early | Monumental (Classical) |
| | 'Aleph | ʔ | | A | Alpha | A | A |
| | Beth | b | | B | Beta | | B |
| | Gimel | g | | Γ | Gamma | | C |
| | Daleth | d | | Δ | Delta | | D |
| | He | h | | E | Epsilon | | E |
| | Waw | w | | | Digamma | | F |
| | | | | | | | G |
| | Zayin | z | I | Z | Zeta | | |
| | Ḥeth | ħ | | H | Ēta | | H |
| | Teth | ṭ | | Θ | Theta | | |
| | Yod | j | | ι | Iota | I | I (J) |
| | Kaph | k | | K | Kappa | | K |
| | Lamed | l | | Λ | Lambda | | L |
| | Mem | m | | M | Mu | | M |
| | Nun | n | | N | Nu | | N |
| | Samekh | s | | | | | |
| | 'Ayin | ʕ | O | 0 | Ŏmicron | O | O |
| | Pe | p | | Π | Pi | | P |
| | Tsade | s | | | San | | |
| | Qoph | q | | | Qoppa | | Q |
| | Reš | r | | P | Rho | | R |
| | Šin | ʃ-s | | Σ | Sigma | | S |
| | Taw | t | | | Tau | | T |
| | | | | Υ | Upsilon | V | V |
| | | | | X | Chi | | X |
| | | | | Ω | Omega | | Y Z |

Source: From *The Encyclopedia Americana*, 1968 Edition, s.v. "Alphabet" by David Diringer. Copyright 1968 by Grolier Incorporated. Reprinted with permission.

As we have seen, Phoenician *ʔāleph* represented a glottal stop. Since Greek had no such phoneme, the *ʔāleph* was employed to represent the vowel /a/ in Greek. Phoenician (*h*) was used to represent the Greek vowel /e/, and other signs were added to the system by the Greeks, including Φ for /f/, X for /x/, ψ for /ps/, and Ω for /ō/.

The Semitic names for the letters (*aleph, beth, gimel, daleth,* and so on) were maintained by the Greeks (as *alpha, beta, gamma, delta,* and so on), but the possible pictorial origins had been lost and the names carried no other meaning.[2] The writing system itself gained its name from the first two letters of the series: alphabet.

## The Roman alphabet

When Greek colonists occupied southern Italy in the eighth and seventh centuries BC, they took their alphabet with them. It was in turn taken up and modified by the Etruscan inhabitants of central Italy, a non-Latin-speaking people who were a political and cultural power before the rise of Rome. It is believed that the Romans acquired their alphabet through the Etruscans. As the Romans grew in power and influence during the following centuries, first as masters of Italy and later of Europe, the Roman alphabet spread throughout their empire.

Under the Romans, the Greek/Etruscan alphabet was again modified, this time with some symbols influenced by the Etruscans. The *G* in Greek writing developed into both *C* for the phoneme /k/ and *G* for /g/. The oldest inscriptions also retained *K* for /k/ in some words, but it was generally replaced by *C*. Similarly, *Q* was retained before /u/. Roman script also employed Greek *U* (= V), *X, Y,* and *Z,* and moved *Z* to the end of the alphabet. The symbols Φ, Θ, ψ, and Ω were among those discarded, and *H* was converted back to a consonant symbol.

Some subsequent changes were made in the alphabet as it was adapted by various peoples of the Roman Empire. In English, for example, *W* was created from two juxtaposed *V*s. Spanish employs a tilde (˜) over *n* (ñ) to signify a palatal nasal, as in *año* /aɲo/ 'year', and French uses a cedilla under *c* (ç) to indicate the dental fricative /s/, as in the spelling of *français* [frãsɛ] 'French'.

Many alphabetic systems other than those of Greece and Rome flourished in Europe and the Middle East. You can find a brief discussion of these systems at our Companion Website at **www.pearsoned.ca/ogrady,** chapter 15.

# 15.4 Some non-European writing systems

This section focuses on the nature and development of writing systems that originated outside the Middle East. While some of these systems emerged in response to external influences, others seem to have been entirely independent innovations. We will focus here on the writing systems of China, Japan, and Korea, as well as on a script developed for use with Cree in Western Canada. For a discussion of writing systems found in other parts of the world, including the Americas, Africa, and India, go to the website at **www.pearsoned.ca/ogrady**.

## 15.4.1 Chinese writing

The Chinese system of writing developed out of pictograms that eventually came to represent morphemes (most of which are also words). The oldest inscriptions are the oracle texts, written on animal bones and tortoise shells and dating back to about 1200 BC. These include many recognizable images, such as ☉ 'sun' and ☽ 'moon'.

A change towards more **symbolic signs** began at an early date as more abstract notions were symbolized, such as ‿ 'above' and ⌒ 'below'. Symbols were also combined to extend meanings metaphorically. For example, the sign for 'to tend (animals)' 牧 is composed of 牛 'cow' and 攴 'hand and whip'. 'To follow' 从 is two men in sequence, and so on. In time, the characters became more abstract. Figure 15.14 shows the historical development of the symbol for 'dog'.

**Figure 15.14**
Historical development of the Chinese symbol for 'dog'

Source: Jerry Norman, *Chinese* (Cambridge, UK: Cambridge University Press, 1988), p. 59.
Reprinted with the permission of Cambridge University Press.

Calligraphy is an ancient and respected art in China, and Chinese writing exists in a number of styles. The script is usually written from left to right along a horizontal axis, although newspapers and older texts begin in the right-hand margin and are read downwards.

The units of contemporary Chinese writing are called **characters**. Many monosyllabic words are presented in true logographic fashion by a character consisting of a single symbol. For example, the Mandarin words [ʃow] 'hand' and [ma] 'horse' are written 手 and 馬, respectively. However, the overwhelming majority of characters (one estimate is 99 percent) consist of two parts.

The main component of a multi-element character, called the **phonetic determinative**, provides information about the pronunciation of the corresponding morpheme. Although about four thousand different phonetic determinatives are used in Chinese writing, they represent pronunciation very imperfectly. Tone, which is contrastive in Chinese (see chapter 2), is not represented at all, and many phonetic determinatives indicate only part of the morpheme's pronunciation. For instance, one determinative (see table 15.1) is used for a wide variety of words ending in *ao* without regard for whether the initial consonant is *j, n, r,* or some other element. Furthermore, due to sound changes over the last centuries, about one-third of all phonetic determinatives provide little or no useful information about current pronunciation. Finally, because Chinese has many homophones, even the most informative phonetic determinatives can be used for many different words.

Chinese characters also include a semantic component, called the **radical** or key, which provides clues about the morpheme's meaning. There are about two hundred different radicals in contemporary Chinese writing. Table 15.1 provides examples of some of the characters that can be formed by combining phonetic determinatives with radicals. Notice that only the phonetic determinative in column A indicates the precise pronunciation (ignoring tone) of the four characters in which it appears. The other determinatives supply helpful, but incomplete, phonetic information. For instance, the determinative *yāo* (column C) has a pronunciation that rhymes with that of the four morphemes it helps to represent.

The usefulness of the information supplied by the radicals also varies. The characters in row 1 represent morphemes whose meaning is at best indirectly associated with that of the radical ('person'), but the radicals in rows 2, 3, and 4 are much more informative. For example, the characters in row 2 all denote actions involving the hand, while those in row 3 refer to things made of wood and those in row 4 all have something to do with liquids.

---

**Table 15.1**    Some Chinese characters

|  |  | Phonetic determinatives | | | |
|---|---|---|---|---|---|
|  |  | A | B | C | D |
|  | Semantic radical | 敖 *(áo)* | 参 *(cān)* | 堯 *(yáo)* | 甫 *(fǔ)* |
| 1 | 亻 'person' | 傲 *(ào: 'proud')* | 傪 *(cān: 'good')* | 僥 *(jiǎo: 'lucky')* | 俌 *(fǔ: 'help')* |
| 2 | 扌 'hand' | 摮 *(ào: 'shake')* | 摻 *(shān: 'seize')* | 撓 *(náo: 'scratch')* | 捕 *(bǔ: 'catch')* |
| 3 | 木 'wood' | 橾 *(áo: 'barge')* | 椮 *(shēn: 'beam')* | 橈 *(náo: 'oar')* | 楠 *(fú: 'trellis')* |
| 4 | 氵 'water' | 滶 *(ào: 'stream')* | 渗 *(shèn: 'leak')* | 澆 *(jiāo: 'sprinkle')* | 浦 *(pǔ: 'creek')* |

Source: John DeFrancis, *Visible Speech: The Diverse Oneness of Writing Systems* (Honolulu: University of Hawaii Press, 1989), p. 107 © 1989 John DeFrancis. Reprinted with permission of University of Hawaii Press.

Although neither phonetic determinatives alone nor semantic radicals alone suffice to identify the morphemes that they are used to represent, they are more than adequate when used in conjunction with each other. Despite these complexities—one authority has described the system as "outsized, haphazard, inefficient, and only partially reliable"—Chinese writing provides its users with an effective way to represent the words and morphemes of the language. Moreover, the lack of efficiency is offset by the fact that the same literary script can be understood by speakers of different Chinese languages. Although a speaker of Mandarin and a speaker of Cantonese may pronounce the word for 'fire' differently—/xwǒ/ and /fɔ̀/, respectively—both can read it from the same character ( 火 ), since Chinese writing does not directly represent a word's phonemic segments.

In recent times, the government of the People's Republic of China has introduced simplified characters (some newly invented) in an attempt to promote literacy. At the same time, a system of writing Mandarin with a modified Latin alphabet, called **pinyin**, has also been introduced. Pinyin is used as a subsidiary system for writing such things as street signs, addresses, and brand names as well as for teaching children how to pronounce characters. It is also sometimes used for computer-related activities, including email.

## 15.4.2 Japanese writing

The writing system of modern Japanese is arguably the most complicated in the entire world. Its use requires knowledge of three distinct scripts, including a pair of syllabaries—**hiragana** and **katakana**—which were created by modifying Chinese characters. Although Japanese can be written exclusively with either syllabary, normal writing involves use of Chinese characters (called **kanji** in Japanese) in addition to hiragana and katakana. Kanji symbols are typically used to represent all or part of a word's root while affixes are represented by hiragana symbols. The phrase *the man's car*, for example, can be written as in figure 15.15, with the roots 'man' and 'car' represented by kanji, and the possessive morpheme *no* written in hiragana.

**Figure 15.15**
A phrase written in a mixture of kanji and hiragana

hito no

人 の

man Gen
kanji hiragana

kuruma de

車 で

car Loc
kanji hiragana

The katakana syllabary, whose symbols are less rounded than their hiragana counterparts (see figure 15.16), is used to write onomatopoeic words as well as words borrowed into Japanese from other languages.

Finally, it should be noted that the Roman alphabet, which the Japanese call *romaji*, is also making inroads. It is not unusual to see all four writing systems used together, especially in advertising (see figure 15.17 on page 503).

Learning to read Japanese is a formidable task, in part because of the way the various scripts are intermingled and in part because of complexities in the use of kanji symbols, which can have more than one pronunciation depending on whether they are used to represent a

**Figure 15.16**
Hiragana and katakana syllabaries and their phonetic values (The conventions for representing voicing, vowel length, and gemination are not indicated here.)

Katakana chart

| COLUMN / LINE | A | I | U | E | O |
|---|---|---|---|---|---|
| SINGLE VOWEL | ア A | イ I | ウ U | エ E | オ O |
| K | カ KA | キ KI | ク KU | ケ KE | コ KO |
| S | サ SA | シ SHI | ス SU | セ SE | ソ SO |
| T | タ TA | チ CHI | ツ TSU | テ TE | ト TO |
| N | ナ NA | ニ NI | ヌ NU | ネ NE | ノ NO |
| H | ハ HA | ヒ HI | フ FU | ヘ HE | ホ HO |
| M | マ MA | ミ MI | ム MU | メ ME | モ MO |
| Y | ヤ YA | | ユ YU | | ヨ YO |
| R | ラ RA | リ RI | ル RU | レ RE | ロ RO |
| W | ワ WA | | | | ヲ O |
| N (in a coda) | ン N | | | | |

Hiragana chart

| COLUMN / LINE | A | I | U | E | O |
|---|---|---|---|---|---|
| SINGLE VOWEL | あ A | い I | う U | え E | お O |
| K | か KA | き KI | く KU | け KE | こ KO |
| S | さ SA | し SHI | す SU | せ SE | そ SO |
| T | た TA | ち CHI | つ TSU | て TE | と TO |
| N | な NA | に NI | ぬ NU | ね NE | の NO |
| H | は HA | ひ HI | ふ FU | へ HE | ほ HO |
| M | ま MA | み MI | む MU | め ME | も MO |
| Y | や YA | | ゆ YU | | よ YO |
| R | ら RA | り RI | る RU | れ RE | ろ RO |
| W | わ WA | | | | を O |
| N (in a coda) | ん N | | | | |

Source: Adapted from Len Walsh's *Read Japanese Today* (Tokyo: Charles E. Tuttle, 1971). Reprinted by permission of the publisher.

**Figure 15.17**
Kanji, hiragana, katakana, and romaji in a Japanese advertisement

word of Chinese or Japanese origin. For example, Japanese has two morphemes with the meaning 'mountain'—/san/, which is of Chinese origin, and the native Japanese /yama/; both are written with the kanji character 山 .

## 15.4.3 Korean writing

Korean was once written with Chinese characters, which had been introduced in the first centuries AD. However, Korean suffixes could not be easily represented by Chinese writing. Various devices were used to alleviate this problem, but inadequacies persisted. Finally, King Sejong (1419–52) commissioned an alphabetic script called **hangul**. After some modifications over the centuries, it became the standard Korean writing system. An especially interesting feature of hangul is that symbols are grouped together into syllable-sized clusters (see figure 15.18).

**Figure 15.18**
Korean hangul

Hangul symbols

| ㅂ | ㅜ | ㄹ | ㄱ | ㅗ | ㅣ |
|---|---|---|---|---|---|
| /p/ | /u/ | /l/ | /k/ | /o/ | /i/ |

Grouped symbols

불              고기

'fire' /pul/      'meat' /koki/

Written form

불고기

'barbecued meat' *pulkoki*

Like Japanese, Korean also makes use of Chinese characters (called **hanja**), although in a more restricted way. Slightly more than half the vocabulary of contemporary Korean is of Chinese origin and many words of this type are written with the help of Chinese characters in newspapers and in scientific articles. However, this practice has been reduced somewhat in recent years in South Korea and it has been eliminated entirely in North Korea.

## 15.4.4 **Cree writing**

Professional linguists have often played a role in the development of Aboriginal American scripts, as have missionaries. The syllabic script of the Cree was the creation of a missionary, James Evans, in the nineteenth century. It was employed for religious literature, and by 1861, the entire Bible appeared in the Cree syllabary. Today, in somewhat modified form, this script is used by Cree speakers across Canada.

Cree morphemes are made up of syllables that combine one of ten initial consonants with one of seven vowels; in some cases, there is also a postvocalic consonant. The Cree writing system provides a separate symbol for each V and CV syllable. As in syllabaries in general, the symbols representing the CV syllables bear no resemblance to those representing syllables consisting of a single vowel; there is no connection, for instance, between the symbols for the syllable /ki/ **P** and the syllable /i/ **Δ**. However, the Cree system is not wholly syllabic since consonants that occur at the end of a syllable must be represented by a separate symbol.

A striking feature of the Cree syllabary is its phonetic symbolism. Vowels are indicated by the direction in which a syllabic symbol faces. Symbols that face 'south' (downward on the printed page) contain /eː/; those facing 'north' (upward) contain /i/ or /iː/; those pointing 'east' (rightward) have /o/ or /oː/, and those looking to the 'west' (leftward) contain /a/ or /aː/. Vowel length is indicated by a superposed dot, as in **ʔ** = /siː/.

Plains Cree, a variety of Cree spoken in Western Canada, is written with the symbols in figure 15.19 (other dialects use slightly different ones).

| **Figure 15.19** Cree syllabary | | | | | | | |
|---|---|---|---|---|---|---|---|
| Δ | *i, ī* | ▽ | *ē* | ▷ | *o, ō* | ◁ | *a* |
| Λ | *pi, pī* | V | *pē* | > | *po, pō* | < | *pa* |
| ∩ | *ti, tī* | U | *tē* | ⊃ | *to, tō* | Ċ | *ta* |
| ⌐ | *ci, cī* | ⌐ | *cē* | ⌐ | *co, cō* | ⌐ | *ca* |
| P | *ki, kī* | ٩ | *kē* | d | *ko, kō* | ᑫ | *ka* |
| ⌐ | *mi, mī* | ⌐ | *mē* | ⌐ | *mo, mō* | L | *ma* |
| σ | *ni, nī* | o | *nē* | ๑ | *no, nō* | ä | *na* |
| ʔ | *si, sī* | ↖ | *sē* | ↗ | *so, sō* | ↖ | *sa* |
| ↗ | *yi, yī* | ↖ | *yē* | ↙ | *yo, yō* | ↘ | *ya* |

Finals

ᐟ *p* ᐠ *t* − *c* ↘ *k* ⊂ *m* ᐢ *s* ⊃ *n* • *y* o *w* ᐧ *h* × *hk* ɬ *l* ɾ *r*

Source: David H. Pentland, *Nēhiyawasinahikēwin: A Standard Orthography for the Cree Language*, rev. ed. (Calgary: Dept. of Linguistics, U. of Calgary, 1978). Copyright © 1978 by David H. Pentland.

The examples in figure 15.20 illustrate the use of the Cree syllabary.

| **Figure 15.20** Three words in Cree syllabary | | | | | |
|---|---|---|---|---|---|
| ȯ Λ | | σ Λ | | ʔ Λ | |
| nīpi | 'leaf' | nipi | 'water' | sīpi | 'river' |

## 15.5 English orthography

The set of conventions for representing language in written form is called an **orthography**. English employs an alphabetic orthography in which symbols are used to represent individual consonants and vowels rather than syllables or words. In this section, we will consider the nature and history of English orthography. Section 15.6 examines the relationship between writing and reading.

### 15.5.1 Irregularities

A frequently expressed complaint about English orthography is that it does not establish a one-to-one relationship between symbols and phonological segments. Table 15.2 lists some well-known examples of this.

| **Table 15.2** Some problems with English orthography | |
|---|---|
| **Problem** | **Examples** |
| Some letters do not represent any segments in a particular word. | through, sign, give, palm |
| A group of two or more letters can be used to represent a single segment. | think /θ/, ship /ʃ/, philosophy /f/ |
| A single letter can represent a group of two or more segments. | saxophone /ks/, exile /gz/ |
| The same letter can represent different segments in different words. | *o* in on /ɑ/, bone /ow/, son /ʌ/, one /wʌ/ |
| The same segment can be represented by different letters in different words. | /u/ in rude, loop, soup, new, sue, to, two |

---

### Language Matters **The Drive for Spelling Reform**

George Bernard Shaw (1856–1950), writer and literary critic, was a strong advocate of spelling reform. The following is an excerpt from a much longer poem that he penned to illustrate the inconsistencies of the sound-letter correspondences in English orthography.

> *Beware of heard, a dreadful word*
> *That looks like beard and sounds like bird.*
> *And dead; it's said like bed, not bead;*
> *For goodness sake, don't call it deed!*
> *Watch out for meat and great and threat*
> *(They rhyme with suite and straight and debt).*

You can find out more about movements for spelling reform at www.barnsdle.demon.co.uk/spell/.

## Historical factors

The relationship between symbol and segment in English orthography has not always been so indirect. In fact, the spelling system used throughout England during the Old English period provided a regular set of direct symbol-segment correspondences. The foundation for today's system, it lacked the symbols *j*, *v*, and *w*, but made use of four symbols that are not part of our current alphabet (see table 15.3).

| Table 15.3 | Old English symbols not found in Modern English spelling | |
|---|---|---|
| **Symbol** | **Name** | **Segment(s) it represented** |
| æ | ash | [æ] |
| ð | eth | [θ] and [ð] |
| þ | thorn | [θ] and [ð] |
| ƿ | wynn | [w] |

The relationship between symbol and segment in English orthography was significantly disturbed in the Middle English period, as the phonological pattern of the language began to change. To see an example of this, we need only consider the Great Vowel Shift, which dramatically altered the pronunciation of long vowels—converting /iː/ into /aj/, /eː/ into /i/, /aː/ into /e/, and so on (see chapter 7). Because Old English orthography used the same symbol for long and short vowels, complications arose when the former vowels changed. Thus, the letter *i*, which had formerly been used only to represent the phonetically similar /iː/ and /i/, ended up representing the very dissimilar /aj/ (the descendant of /iː/) and /ɪ/ (the descendant of /i/). The end result can be seen in the spelling of *hide* and *hid*, *write* and *written*, *ride* and *ridden*, *wide* and *width*, and many other words.

Additional complications arose following the invasion of England by French-speaking Normans in the eleventh century. The use of English in official documents declined and regional orthographies developed in the absence of a national standard. To make matters worse, scribes who were trained primarily to write French and Latin introduced a number of conventions from those languages into English spelling. Among those that have survived are the use of *ch* rather than *c* for /tʃ/ (*cheese*, *chin*, etc.), *th* rather than *þ* (thorn) and *ð* (eth) for /θ/ and /ð/ (*thin*, *this*), and *c* rather than *s* for /s/ (*grace*, *ice*, *mice*).

Toward the end of the fifteenth century, yet another trend developed—the practice of spelling words in a manner that reflected their etymological origin. Enduring examples of this influence are found in the spelling of the words *debt*, *doubt*, *receipt*, and *salmon* (formerly spelled *dette*, *doute*, *receite*, and *samon*), all of which were given a 'silent' consonant to make them look more like the Latin words from which they descended.

By the 1500s English orthography had become increasingly irregular and idiosyncratic, with many different spellings in use for the same word. The word *pity*, for example, could be spelled *pity*, *pyty*, *pitie*, *pytie*, *pittie*, and *pyttye*. As printing presses came into greater use and books became more widely available, the need to reform and regularize English orthography became apparent. In the late 1500s and early 1600s, a number of individuals (most notably Richard Mulcaster and Edmond Coote) formulated and published spelling rules, which were gradually adopted by printers and other literate speakers of English. While these rules retained many of the practices discussed above, they at least

---

**Language Matters  How Do You Spell 'Shakespeare'?**

During William Shakespeare's time (1564–1616), English spelling was still in a state of flux, which may explain why there were so many spellings for his name—Shakespeare, Shakespere, Shakespear, Shakspear, among others. Shakespeare himself wrote his name in different ways, and wavered on the spelling of many words in his plays, as well—he used three different spellings for 'more', three for '-ness', and five for 'sheriff', to mention a few examples.

---

had the effect of stabilizing English spelling. By the 1700s, English orthography was more or less fixed.

The vast majority of the spelling conventions introduced during this period are still in use today. One of the most famous, proposed by Mulcaster in 1582, involves the use of 'silent' *e* at the end of words to indicate a preceding long (tense) vowel, as in *name*, *same*, and *mate*. Even here, though, there are complications and exceptions. In an earlier period, word-final *e* had represented [ə]. Following the loss of this sound in this position in the fourteenth century, final *e* was used quite haphazardly and was often added to words that would otherwise end in a single consonant. The *e* in the modern spelling of *have*, *done*, and *gone*, which contain lax vowels, reflects this practice and has survived even though it does not comply with Mulcaster's rule.

## 15.5.2 Obstacles to reform

Over the years, there have been numerous proposals for the reform of English orthography, including those put forward by Benjamin Franklin, George Bernard Shaw, and Noah Webster. However, far-reaching reforms are unlikely for a variety of reasons. For one thing, they would require a long and difficult period of transition. As the following tongue-in-check suggestion by Mark Twain illustrates, reform would not be painless even if it took place over a period of many years.

> For example, in Year 1 that useless letter 'c' would be dropped to be replased either by 'k' or 's', and likewise 'x' would no longer be part of the alphabet. The only kase in which 'c' would be retained would be the 'ch' formation, which will be dealt with later. Year 2 might reform 'w' spelling, so that 'which' and 'one' would take the same konsonant, wile Year 3 might well abolish 'y' replasing it with 'i' and Iear 4 might fiks the 'g–j' anomali wonse and for all.
>
> Jenerally, then, the improvement would kontinue iear bai iear with Iear 5 doing awai with useless double konsonants, and Iears 6–12 or so modifaiing vowlz and the rimeining voist and unvoist konsonants. Bai Iear 15 or sou, it wud fainali be posibl tu meik ius ov thi ridandant leterz 'c', 'y' and 'x'—bai now jast a memori in the maindz of ould doderers—tu replais 'ch', 'sh' and 'th' rispektivli.
>
> Fainali, xen, after sam 20 iers ov orxogrephkl riform, we wud hev a lojikl, kohirnt speling in ius xrewawt xe Ingliy spiking world . . .

People who knew only the reformed spelling system proposed in this letter would have difficulty reading books written in traditional orthography. Those who wished to read any of the millions of books or articles currently in print would therefore have to either learn the traditional spelling system or have the documents that interested them converted into the new orthography.

A second factor militating against serious orthographic reform has to do with the dialectal variation found within English. Because English is spoken in more parts of the world than any other language, it has many different dialects. Any attempt to establish an orthography based on a principle of one segment, one symbol would result in serious regional differences in spelling. For instance, speakers of Boston English would write *far* as *fa* since they do not pronounce syllable-final /r/. Speakers of some dialects of Newfoundland English would write both *tin* and *thin* as *tin* and *day* and *they* as *day* since they have no /t/-/θ/ or /d/-/ð/ distinction. Moreover, while most Canadians would have identical spellings for *cot* and *caught* (since these words are homophonous in their speech), speakers of English in many other parts of the world pronounce them differently and would therefore spell them differently as well.

## Other considerations

Even if considerations relating to practicality and dialectal variation did not rule out major reforms to our orthography, there might still be reasons for retaining at least some of the current spelling conventions.

One advantage of the contemporary system is that it often indicates derivational relationships among words. For instance, if the words *music* and *musician* or *sign* and *signature* were spelled phonetically, it would be difficult to perceive the relationship between them since the root is pronounced differently in each case.

(1)  music    [mjuzɪk]        musician    [mjuzɪʃ-ən]
     sign     [sajn]          signature   [sɪgn-ɪtʃər]

There are many other such cases where English orthography ignores differences in pronunciation so that a morpheme can have the same or nearly the same spelling in different words (see table 15.4).

| **Table 15.4** | Some cases in which English orthography provides a single spelling for roots with different pronunciations |
|---|---|
| electric – electricity | [k] and [s] represented as *c* |
| insert – insertion | [t] and [ʃ] as *t* |
| right – righteous | [t] and [tʃ] as *t* |
| bomb – bombard | Ø and [b] as *b* |
| damn – damnation | Ø and [n] as *n* |
| impress – impression | [s] and [ʃ] as *ss* |
| allege – allegation | [ɛ] and [ə] as *e*; [dʒ] and [g] as *g* |
| resign – resignation | [aj] and [ɪ] as *i*; Ø and [g] as *g* |
| chaste – chastity | [ej] and [æ] as *a* |
| produce – productive | [u] and [ʌ] as *u* |
| please – pleasant | [i] and [ɛ] as *ea* |

Examples such as these show that English orthography does not simply represent phonemic contrasts. Often, it provides a single representation for the variants of a morpheme, even if this means ignoring morphologically conditioned alternations among phonemes. (For this reason, some linguists have concluded that English orthography is a type of *morphophonemic* spelling system; see chapter 4, section 4.6 for a discussion of morphophonemic alternations.) Once this fact is taken into account, it is possible to see the usefulness of orthographic conventions that allow *c* to stand for either /k/ (*electric*) or /s/ (*electricity*) and *t* to represent /t/ (*insert*) or /ʃ/ (*insertion*).

Morphological considerations are reflected in English orthography in other ways as well. Consider in this regard the spelling of the following words.

(2) mess     lapse
     crass     dense
     kiss     house
     gloss     mouse

Although these words all end in the phoneme /s/, this segment cannot be represented as a simple *s*. Instead, the *s* is either doubled to *ss* (when preceded by a lax vowel, as in the first column) or followed by an *e* (all other cases, as exemplified in the second column). This reflects a general rule of English orthography, which reserves word-final *s* for inflectional suffixes (particularly, the plural and the third person singular). Thus, *s* is permitted in the word *laps* (the plural of *lap*) but not in *lapse*.

Another example of morphological influence is found in the rule that prohibits a final *ll* in polysyllabic words—*plentiful, excel, repel,* and so on. As the following examples show, this rule is systematically suspended in two morphological patterns: compounds (the first column) and derivations consisting of a prefix and its base (the second column).

(3) baseball     unwell
     spoonbill     resell
     landfill     recall

Yet another morphologically constrained rule of English orthography converts postconsonantal *y* to *i* in front of a suffix.

(4) carry     carri-ed
     merry     merri-ly
     marry     marri-age
     candy     candi-es
     beauty     beauti-ful

The existence of conventions and practices such as these demonstrates that English orthography is much more than a system for phonemic transcription. Its intricacies can be understood only through the careful study of the history and structure of the linguistic system that it is used to represent.

## 15.6 Writing and reading

The three types of writing described earlier in this chapter each represent different types of linguistic units—morphemes and words in the case of logographic systems, syllables in the case of syllabaries, and consonants and vowels in the case of alphabets. Because of these differences, each orthography places different demands on readers. We know that different parts of the brain are used for reading logographic writing systems and phonographic orthographies such as syllabaries and alphabets. Because phonological structure is largely irrelevant to logographic writing, people suffering from Broca's aphasia (see chapter 13) typically do not lose the ability to write and read logograms. However, the use of syllabaries and alphabets can be severely disrupted by this type of brain disorder. There are reports of Japanese patients suffering from Broca's aphasia who are unable to use hiragana or katakana (the Japanese syllabaries), but retain mastery of kanji (the logographic writing system).

Further information about the relationship between language and writing systems comes from the study of the congenitally deaf. Because they have never heard speech, these individuals have little or no understanding of the phonological units that alphabets represent. Significantly, they have a great deal of difficulty learning to read English.

The type of linguistic unit represented by an orthography also has an effect on how children with normal hearing learn to read. Each system has its own advantages and disadvantages. Children learning Chinese characters, for instance, have little difficulty understanding what each symbol represents, but it takes them many years to learn enough symbols to be able to write and read all the items in their vocabulary. (Knowledge of several thousand separate symbols is required just to read a newspaper.) Even educated people typically know only a few thousand characters and must use dictionaries for new or unfamiliar words.

This problem does not arise in syllabic and alphabetic orthographies. Because languages have far fewer syllables and phonemes than morphemes or words, the entire inventory of symbols can be learned in a year or two and then used productively to write and read new words. This is the major advantage of sound-based orthographies over word-based writing systems.

There is reason to think that children find syllabaries easier to master than alphabets. Children learning syllabaries (such as Japanese hiragana) are reported to have fewer reading problems than children learning alphabetic orthographies. Although at least some difficulties encountered by children learning to read English may be due to the complexity of English spelling conventions, Italian and German children learning to use their relatively regular alphabetic orthographies also have reading problems, although apparently to a less severe extent.

The advantage of syllabaries over alphabets for young readers apparently stems from the fact that children have less difficulty identifying syllables than phonemes. One study revealed that 46 percent of four year olds and 90 percent of six year olds can segment words into syllables. In contrast, virtually no four year olds and only about two-thirds of all six year olds can segment words into phoneme-sized units. Since learning to read involves an

## Language Matters **Processing the Words**

A common source of problems in reading, writing, and spelling is dyslexia, a learning disability of neurological origin that may affect 10 to 15 percent of the population to some degree. Research suggests that dyslexics process certain types of information in different parts of the brain than do non-dyslexics and that they have particular trouble discriminating among the sounds within words. Even a small processing problem can disrupt the relationship between symbols on the page and the corresponding words, creating an unrecognizable jumble of letters.

Hav ingdys lexiac anmake it hardtodo wellins chool.
Eaxly trexxmxnt xs impxrtant

You can find about more about dyslexia from the International Dyslexia Association website at www.interdys.org.

understanding of the type of unit represented by written symbols, it is not surprising that syllabaries are generally easier for young children to learn.

Of course, it must be remembered that syllabaries may have disadvantages of other sorts. While syllabic writing is feasible for languages such as Japanese that have a relatively small number of syllable types, it would be quite impractical in English where there are dozens of different syllable structures. Ultimately, an orthography must be judged in terms of its success in representing language for the purpose of reading and writing. There is no doubt that an alphabetic orthography is superior to a syllabary for representing the phonological structure of English.

# Summing up

The development of writing has been one of humanity's greatest intellectual achievements. From **pictograms** and **logograms**, the graphic representation of language has developed into **syllabic writing** and the **alphabet**. This was achieved through the discovery of the relationship between graphic symbols and sounds.

Many of the large number of writing systems found throughout the modern world owe their origin directly or indirectly to the Semitic writing systems of the eastern Mediterranean. As the idea of writing spread, new forms of the signs were independently invented and sound-symbol correspondences were altered to accommodate individual languages. Some writing systems derived from the Graeco-Phoenician tradition are today scarcely recognizable as such, since so little remains of the original symbols. In cases where the entire system was invented, perhaps only the idea of writing is traceable to the early traditions.

In all cases, the historical line of development is clear. There seems to be no evidence of a culture that has developed an alphabet and then followed this with the development of a logographic script or a syllabary. But this cultural line of development does not imply that earlier forms of writing are inferior to alphabetic writing. In the case of languages such as Japanese or Cree, the syllabic writing system is as well suited to the phonological structure of the language as an alphabetic script would be.

## Notes

1  Scholars are still not in agreement on this question. Some claim a single common origin in the Middle East for all writing systems. Others state that certain systems, for example, Mayan writing, must have emerged independently. For a further discussion of Mayan writing, go to **www.pearsoned.ca/ogrady**.

2  Ancient Greek was represented by reversing the direction of writing at the end of each line. If the first line of a text was written right-to-left, the next line continued left-to-right, then right-to-left, and so on. This practice was typical of many old writing systems and is known as **boustrophedon** (Greek for 'as the ox turns'), since it was said to resemble the pattern made by plowing a field.

## Recommended reading

Collier, Mark, and Bill Manley. 1998. *How to Read Egyptian Hieroglyphs*. Berkeley: University of California Press.

Cummings, D.W. 1988. *American English Spelling*. Baltimore: The Johns Hopkins University Press.

DeFrancis, John. 1989. *Visible Speech: The Diverse Oneness of Writing Systems*. Honolulu: University of Hawaii Press.

Gelb, I. 1952. *A Study of Writing*. Chicago: University of Chicago Press.

Gibson, E., and H. Levin. 1975. *The Psychology of Reading*. Cambridge, MA: MIT Press.

Gleitman, L., and P. Rozin. 1977. "The Structure and Acquisition of Reading I: Relations Between Orthographies and the Structures of Language." In *Toward a Psychology of Reading*. Edited by A. Reber and D. Scarborough, 1–53. Hillsdale, NJ: Lawrence Erlbaum.

Jensen, H. 1970. *Sign, Symbol and Script*. G. Unwin, trans. London: George Allen and Unwin.

Sampson, G. 1985. *Writing Systems: A Linguistic Introduction*. Stanford, CA: Stanford University Press.

Schmandt-Besserat, Denise. 1989. "Two Precursors of Writing: Plain and Complex Tokens." In *The Origins of Writing*. Edited by W.M. Senner, 27–42. Lincoln: University of Nebraska Press.

Senner, W.M. (ed.). 1989. *The Origins of Writing*. Lincoln: University of Nebraska Press.

Wallace, Rex. 1989. "The Origins and Development of the Latin Alphabet." In *The Origins of Writing*. Edited by W.M. Senner, 121–36. Lincoln: University of Nebraska Press.

## Exercises

1. Suppose you are the user of a pictographic writing system that can already represent concrete objects in a satisfactory way. Using the pictographic symbols of your system, propose ideographic extensions of these symbols to represent the following meanings.

   a) hunt            f) cook
   b) cold            g) tired
   c) fast            h) wet
   d) white           i) angry
   e) strength        j) weakness

2. Construct a syllabary for English that can be used to spell the following words. What problems do you encounter?

   | | | |
   |---|---|---|
   | foe | law | shoe |
   | slaw | slow | slowly |
   | lee | day | daily |
   | sue | pull | shop |
   | ship | loop | food |
   | lock | shock | unlock |
   | locked | shocked | pulled |
   | shops | locker | shod |
   | float | splint | schlock |

**3.** How does English orthography capture the morphophonemic alternations in the following words? Begin your analysis with a phonemic transcription of the forms.

| | | |
|---|---|---|
| a) hymn | hymnal | |
| b) part | partial | |
| c) recite | recitation | |
| d) reduce | reduction | |
| e) design | designation | |
| f) critical | criticize | criticism |
| g) analog | analogous | analogy |

**4.** After discussing the forms in exercise 3, consider the following forms. Does the spelling system treat all cases of allomorphic variation the same way?

| | |
|---|---|
| a) invade | invasion |
| b) concede | concession |
| c) assume | assumption |
| d) profound | profundity |

**5.** Briefly outline the advantages and disadvantages of the three major types of writing that have evolved throughout history.

# Glossary

**Ablative** The case form characteristically used to mark a noun indicating the point away from which there is movement.

**Ablaut** A vowel alternation that marks a grammatical contrast (e.g., *mouse/mice*).

**Absolute universals** Patterns or traits that occur in all languages.

**Absolutive** In some languages, the case associated with both the direct object of a transitive verb and the subject of an intransitive verb.

**Abstract case** Case that need not be expressed as inflection.

**Accent** Phonetic qualities of a language variety which identifies it to speakers of other varieties as different from their own.

**Accidental gaps** Non-occurring but possible forms of a language (e.g., in English, *blork*).

**Accommodation** The modification of speech patterns to match those of other participants in a discourse.

**Accuracy** Second language speech in which the structures are nativelike.

**Accusative** The case form characteristically used to mark a direct object.

**Acoustic phonetics** An approach to phonetics that is concerned with measuring and analyzing the physical properties of sound waves produced when we speak.

**Acquired agraphia** *See* Acquired dysgraphia.

**Acquired alexia** *See* Acquired dyslexia.

**Acquired dysgraphia** The impairment of writing ability in patients who previously possessed normal writing ability (also called acquired agraphia).

**Acquired dyslexia** The impairment of reading ability in patients who previously possessed normal reading ability (also called acquired alexia).

**Acrolect** The variety most closely approximating the one that is considered standard in a creole speech community.

**Acronym** A word that is formed by taking the initial letters of some or all of the words in a phrase or title and pronouncing them as a word (e.g., *NATO* for *North Atlantic Treaty Organization*).

**Acrophonic principle** The representation of sounds by pictures of objects whose pronunciation begins with the sound to be represented (e.g., the sound [b] might be represented by a picture of a bird).

**Active sentence** A sentence in which the NP with the agent role is the subject (e.g., *Helen painted the room*).

**Adjacency pair** An ordered pair of utterances spoken by two different participants in a conversation.

**Adjective (A)** A lexical category that designates a property or attribute of an entity, can often take comparative and superlative endings in English, and functions as the head of an adjective phrase (e.g., *red, obese, hearty*).

**Adstratum influence** The mutual influence of two equally dominant languages on each other (e.g., the influence of English and French on each other in Montreal).

**Adverb (Adv)** A lexical category that typically denotes a property of the actions, sensations, and states designated by verbs (e.g., *quickly, fearfully*).

**Affix** A morpheme that does not belong to a lexical category and is always bound (e.g., *-ing, un-*).

**Affixation** The process that attaches an affix to a base.

**Affricates** Non-continuant consonants that show a slow release of the closure (e.g., [tʃ, dʒ]).

**Affrication** A process in which palatalized stops become affricates.

**After perfect aspect** The use of the word *after* to indicate perfect aspect (e.g., I'm after eating).

**Agent** The thematic role associated with the doer of an action (e.g., *Marilyn* in *Marilyn fed the dolphin*).

**Agglutinating languages** Languages in which words typically contain several morphemes, of which usually only one is a lexical category. The others are clearly identifiable affixes, each of which typically encodes a single grammatical contrast.

**Agrammatism** An aphasic disturbance characterized by the omission of function words and inflectional affixes and by syntactic comprehension deficits.

**Agreement** The result of one category being inflected to mark properties of another (e.g., the verb is marked for the person and/or the number of the subject).

**Allomorphs** Variants of a morpheme (e.g., [-s], [-z], and [-əz] are allomorphs of the English plural morpheme).

**Allophones** Variants of a phoneme, usually in complementary distribution and phonetically similar (e.g., voiced and voiceless *l* in English).

**Alphabetic writing** A type of writing in which symbols represent consonant and/or vowel segments.

**Alveolar ridge** The small ridge that protrudes from just behind the upper front teeth.

**Alveopalatal (area)** The area just behind the alveolar ridge where the roof of the mouth rises sharply (also called **palatoalveolar**).

**Amelioration** The process in which the meaning of a word becomes more favourable (e.g., *pretty* used to mean 'tricky, sly, cunning').

**Amerind** A controversial hypothesis that claims that the languages of North America can be classified into only three families.

**Analogy** A source of language change that involves the generalization of a regularity, on the basis of the inference that if elements are alike in some respects, they should be alike in others as well (e.g., *bring* becoming *brung* by analogy with *ring/rung*).

**Analytic languages** *See* **Isolating languages.**

**Anaphoric reference** Use of a pronominal form to refer to a preceding full noun phrase or verb phrase in discourse.

**Angular gyrus** An area of the brain that plays an important role in reading.

**Animate** A noun class category in some languages (e.g., both *duck* and *pipe* are animate nouns in Cree).

**Antecedent** The element that determines the interpretation of a pronoun (e.g., *Jeremy* in *Jeremy looked at himself in the mirror*).

**Anterior** A place feature that characterizes sounds articulated in front of the alveopalatal region.

**Antonyms** Words or phrases that are opposites with respect to some component of their meaning (e.g., *big* and *small*).

**Aphasia** A language deficit caused by damage to the brain.

**Apocope** The deletion of a word-final vowel (e.g., *name* used to be pronounced with a word-final schwa).

**Apparent time hypothesis** The hypothesis that change over time can be revealed by comparing the speech of older and younger speakers at a single time.

**Areal classification** An approach to language classification that identifies characteristics shared by languages that are in geographical contact.

**Articulatory phonetics** An approach to phonetics that studies the physiological mechanisms of speech production.

**Articulatory simplification** A process that facilitates acquisition (e.g., by deleting a consonant in a complex cluster or inserting a vowel to break up a cluster).

**Arytenoids** Two small cartilages in the larynx that are attached to the vocal folds, enabling the vocal folds to be drawn together or apart.

**Aspiration** The lag in the onset of vocalic voicing, accompanied by the release of air, that is heard after the release of certain stops in English (e.g., the first sound of *top* is aspirated).

**Assimilation** The influence of one segment on another, resulting in a sound becoming more like a nearby sound in terms of one or more of its phonetic characteristics (e.g., in English, vowels become nasal if followed by a nasal consonant).

**Association line** A line linking a symbol that represents a sound segment with a symbol that represents a tone or feature.

**Attitude** Beliefs and feelings that an individual may have about a particular language variety.

**Autopsy studies** Studies based on a post-mortem examination.

**Auxiliary verb (Aux)** Verbs such as *will*, *can*, *may*, *be* and *have* that must always occur with another verb in complete sentences.

**Back** A dorsal feature that characterizes sounds articulated behind the palatal region in the oral cavity.

**Back (of the tongue)** The part of the tongue that is hindmost but still lies in the mouth.

**Back vowel** A vowel that is made with tongue positioned in the back of the oral cavity (e.g., the vowel sounds in *hoot* and *board*).

**Backformation** A word formation process that creates a new word by removing a real or supposed affix from another word in the language (e.g., *edit* came from *editor* through the removal of *-or*).

**Bajan** Barbadian (creole) English.

**Banned language** A language that is prohibited by authorities in a particular domain of use.

**Base** The form to which an affix is added (e.g., *book* is the base for the affix *-s* in *books*, *modernize* is the base for the affix *-ed* in *modernized*).

**Basilect** The variety that shows the greatest number of differences from the standard language in a creole speech community.

**Bilingualism** The state of possessing knowledge of two languages.

**Binary** Phonological features that have both plus (+) and minus (-) values.

**Blade (of the tongue)** The area of the tongue just behind the tip.

**Blend** A word that is created from parts of two already existing items (e.g., *brunch* from *breakfast* and *lunch*).

**Blissymbolics** A contemporary development of pictographic writing that uses a number of recombineable symbols representing basic units of meaning; primarily used for non-speaking individuals.

**Body (of the tongue)** The main mass of the tongue.

**Borrowing** A source of language change that involves adopting aspects of one language into another.

**Bottom-up processing** A type of processing in which the activation of higher mental representations (e.g., words) occurs through the activation of simpler constituent representations (e.g., phonemes).

**Bound morpheme** A morpheme that must be attached to another element (e.g., the past tense marker *-ed*).

**Boustrophedon** The practice of reversing the direction of writing at the end of each line, which was typical of many old writing systems.

**Breathy voice** *See* **murmur**.

**Broca's aphasia** A non-fluent aphasia in which speech is very halting, there are numerous phonemic errors, and there is a lack of intonation.

**Broca's area** The area in the lower rear portion of the left frontal lobe that plays an important role in language production.

**C-command** A syntactic notion that is involved in pronoun interpretation and is formulated as: $NP_a$ c-commands $NP_b$, if the first category above $NP_a$ contains $NP_b$.

**Call** In avian communication, short bursts of sound or simple patterns of notes, typically used as warnings or other group-related signals.

**Canadian Raising** The phonological phenomenon of using the allophones [ʌj] and [ʌw] before a voiceless stop in words such as *right* and *out*.

**Canonical Sentence Strategy** A processing strategy that leads children to expect the first NP in a sentence to bear the agent role and the second NP to bear the theme role.

**Caregiver speech** The type of speech that is typically addressed to young language learners. (*See also* **Motherese**.)

**Case** A morphological category that encodes information about an element's grammatical role (subject, direct object, and so on) (e.g., the contrast between *he* and *him*).

**Caste** A hereditary social group that is prohibited from having contact with members of other castes.

**Categorical rule** A rule that applies every time its structural description is met.

**Cell assembly** A collection of neurons that are repeatedly activated together.

**Central sulcus** The sulcus that extends from the top of the cerebral cortex to the lateral fissure (also called the fissure of Rolando).

**Cerebral cortex** The grey wrinkled mass that sits like a cap over the rest of the brain and is the seat of cognitive functioning.

**Cerebral hemispheres** The left and right halves of the brain, separated by the longitudinal fissure.

**Cerebrovascular accident** *See* Stroke.

**Change from above** Changes that begin in the speech of members of the upper classes and spread to the lower social classes.

**Characters** The units of contemporary Chinese orthography, many of which consist of two parts, a phonetic **determinative** and a semantic **radical**.

**Class** A group of sounds that shares certain phonetic properties (e.g., all voiced sounds).

**Class 1** A group of affixes that (in English) often trigger changes in the consonant or vowel segments of the base and may affect the assignment of stress.

**Class 2** A group of affixes that tend to be phonologically neutral in English, having no effect on the segmental makeup of the base or on stress assignment.

**Clipping** A word formation process that shortens a polysyllabic word by deleting one or more syllables (e.g., *prof* from *professor*).

**Clitic** A morpheme that is like a word in terms of its meaning and function, but is unable to stand alone as an independent form for phonological reasons (e.g. *'m* in *I'm*).

**Closed syllable** A syllable with a coda (e.g., both syllables in *camping*).

**Closing** A discourse unit conventionally used to end a conversation.

**Coarticulation** One sound influencing the articulation of the other in a sequence of phonetic segments—e.g., in the sequence [pl], the tongue tip will start to move towards the alveolar ridge before the lips separate; more than one articulator is active.

**Coda (Co)** The elements that follow the nucleus in the same syllable (e.g., [rf] in *surfboard*).

**Code switching** The systematic alternation between language systems in discourse.

**Cognates** Words of different languages that have descended from a common source, as shown by systematic phonetic correspondences (e.g., English *father* and German *Vater*).

**Cohort model** A model of spoken word recognition that claims that word recognition proceeds by isolating a target word from a cohort of words that share initial segments.

**Coinage** *See* Word manufacture.

**Communication strategies** Strategies used by L2 learners when they are lacking the necessary linguistic knowledge to say what they want to say (e.g., paraphrasing).

**Communicative competence** A speaker's knowledge of the linguistic and social rules or principles for language production or perception.

**Community of practice** Groups of individuals who come together for a shared purpose (and hence develop shared language practices).

**Comparative method** The reconstruction of properties of a parent language through comparison of its descendant languages.

**Complement** The element or elements for which a head is subcategorized and which provide information about entities and locations whose existence is implied by the meaning of the head (e.g., *the book* in *bought the book*).

**Complement clause** A sentence-like construction that is embedded within a larger structure (e.g., *that his car had been totalled* in *Jerry told Mary that his car had been totalled*).

**Complementary distribution** Variants of a phoneme that never occur in the same phonetic environment are in complementary distribution.

**Complementizer (C)** A functional category that takes an IP complement, forming a

**CP (complementizer phrase)** (e.g., *whether* in *I wonder whether Lorna has left*).

**Complex word** A word that contains two or more morphemes (e.g., *theorize, unemployment*).

**Componential analysis** The representation of a word's intension in terms of smaller semantic components called features.

**Compound** The formation of a word by combining two already existent words.

**Compounding** The combination of lexical categories (N, V, A, or P) to form a larger word (e.g., *fire* + *engine*).

**Comprehensible input** The linguistic input to which the L2 learner is exposed that is slightly beyond his or her competence in the target language (i+1).

**Computational system** Operations that combine words and arrange them in particular ways.

**Computerized Axial Tomography** A technique for observing the living brain that uses a narrow beam of X-rays to create brain images that take the form of a series of brain slices (also called **CT scanning**).

**Concatenative** A term used for the morphological process that builds word structure by assembling morphemes in an additive, linear fashion.

**Conflation pattern** A class of meanings created by combining semantic elements such as manner and motion or direction and motion.

**Conjugation** The set of inflected forms associated with a verb (also called a **verbal paradigm**).

**Conjunction (Con)** A functional category that joins two or more categories of the same type, forming a coordinate structure (e.g., *and* in *a man and his dog*).

**Connectionist model** A psycholinguistic theory built around the claim that the mind can be best modelled by reference to complex associations of simple units that approximate neurons.

**Connotation** The set of associations that a word's use can evoke (e.g., in Canada *winter* evokes ice, snow, bare trees, etc.). (*See also* **Denotation.**)

**Consonant deletion** A phonetic process that deletes a consonant (e.g., the deletion of [θ] in *fifths*).

**Consonant weakening** A process that weakens a consonant, usually between vowels, according to the scale of consonantal strength.

**Consonantal** A major class feature that characterizes sounds produced with a major obstruction in the vocal tract.

**Consonantal strength** The relative placement of a consonant on a scale of consonantal strength.

**Consonants** Sounds that are produced with a narrow or complete closure in the vocal tract.

**Constituent** One or more words that make up a syntactic unit (e.g., *the apple* in *the apple fell onto the floor*). (*See also* **Coordination test, Substitution test,** and **Movement test.**)

**Constraints** Conditions that govern the form of a linguistic element (e.g., [r] is deleted after a vowel).

**Constricted Glottis ([CG])** A laryngeal feature that characterizes sounds made with the glottis closed (in English, only [ʔ]).

**Constructional meaning** The meaning associated with a structural pattern above and beyond the meaning of its component words.

**Consultant** A native speaker of a language or variety who provides data to the linguist (also called an **informant**).

**Contact** The situation when a language or variety comes into contact with another language or variety.

**Continuant** A manner feature that characterizes sounds made with free or nearly free airflow through the oral cavity: vowels, fricatives, glides, and liquids.

**Continuants** Sounds that are produced with a continuous airflow through the mouth.

**Contour tones** Moving pitches on a single segment that signal meaning differences.

**Contradiction** A relationship between sentences wherein the truth of one sentence requires the falsity of another sentence (e.g., *Raymond is married* contradicts *Raymond is a bachelor*).

**Contralateral** The control of the right side of the body by the left side of the brain and vice versa.

**Contrast** Segments are said to contrast when their presence alone may distinguish forms with different meanings from each other (e.g., [s] and [z] in the words *sip* and *zip*).

**Conversation analysis** *See* Ethnomethodology.

**Conversational implicature** Information that is conveyed through inference but is not actually said.

**Conversion** A word formation process that assigns an already existing word to a new syntactic category (also called **zero derivation**) (e.g., *nurse* (V) from *nurse* (N)).

**Cooperative Principle, The** The general overarching guideline thought to underlie conversational interactions: Make your contribution appropriate to the conversation.

**Coordinate structure** A pattern built around a conjunction such as *and*, *or*, or *but* (e.g., *Mary and the white horse*).

**Coordination** The grouping together of two or more categories with the help of a conjunction such as *'and'* or *'or'*.

**Coordination test** A test used to determine if a group of words is a constituent by joining it to another group of words with a conjunction such as *and* or *or*.

**CORONAL** A place feature that characterizes sounds made with the tongue tip or blade raised (e.g., [t d s θ]).

**Corpus callosum** The bundle of nerve fibres that serves as the main connection between the cerebral hemispheres, allowing the two hemispheres to communicate with one another.

**Covert prestige** Prestige that is not part of a society's widely expressed and approved belief system.

**Creativity** The characteristic of human language that allows novelty and innovation in response to new thoughts, experiences, and situations.

**Creole** A variety that arises as the native language of the children of members of a pidgin speech community.

**Creole continuum** The gradient differences among basilects, acrolects, and mesolects.

**Cricoid cartilage** The ring-shaped cartilage in the larynx on which the thyroid cartilage rests.

**Critical period** A particular time frame during which children have to be exposed to language if the acquisition process is to be fully successful.

**Cross-sectional research** Research that investigates and compares children (or groups of children) of distinct ages.

**CT scanning** *See* Computerized Axial Tomography.

**Cuneiform** Writing that was initiated in the fourth millennium BC and was produced by pressing a wedge-shaped stylus into soft clay tablets.

**Cyrillic alphabet** An alphabet that combined adaptations of Glagolitic letters with Greek and Hebrew characters, evolving into the alphabets that are currently used to represent some of the languages spoken in the former Soviet Union and in the Balkans.

**D-structure** *See* Deep structure.

**Dative** The case form characteristically used to mark a recipient.

**Deaffrication** A type of segmental simplification that turns affricates into fricatives by eliminating the stop portion of the affricate (e.g., [dʒ] becoming [ʒ]).

**Declension** *See* Nominal paradigm.

**Deep dyslexia** A type of acquired dyslexia in which the patient produces a word that is semantically related to the word he or she is asked to read (e.g., producing *father* when asked to read *mother*).

**Deep structure** The structure formed by the Merge operation in accordance with the X′ schema and subcategorization properties of the heads.

**Degemination** The weakening of a geminate consonant to a non-geminate consonant (e.g., [tt] becoming [t]).

**Degree word (Deg)** A functional category that serves as the specifier of a preposition or an adjective (e.g., *quite* in *quite tired, very* in *very near the house*).

**Deictics** Forms whose use and interpretation depend on the location of the speaker and/or addressee within a particular setting (e.g., *this/that, here/there*).

**Delayed release** A manner feature that characterizes all and only affricate consonants.

**Deletion** A process that removes a segment from certain phonetic contexts (e.g., the pronunciation of *fifths* as [fifs]).

**Denasalization** A common substitution process in child language acquisition that involves the replacement of a nasal stop by a non-nasal counterpart (e.g., *come* is pronounced [kʌb]).

**Denotation** The set of entities to which a word or expression refers (also called its **referents** or **extension**). *See also* **Connotation**.

**Dense social network** A social network in which a small group of people interact frequently.

**Dentals** Sounds made with the tongue placed against or near the teeth.

**Dependent variable** In an experiment, the behaviour or event that is measured in order to gauge the effect of an independent variable.

**Derivation (morphology)** An affixational process that forms a word with a meaning and/or category distinct from that of its base.

**Derivation (syntax)** The process whereby a syntactic structure is formed by syntactic operations such as Merge and Move.

**Derived (phonology)** Resulting from the application of phonological rules to underlying representations.

**Descriptive** A characteristic of linguistic research that seeks to describe human linguistic ability and knowledge, not to prescribe one system in preference to another. (*See also* **Prescriptive**.)

**Design features** Characteristics of human language that are used to compare animal communication systems with human language.

**Determiner (Det)** A functional category that serves as the specifier of a noun (e.g., *a, the, these*).

**Devoicing** Voicing assimilation in which a sound becomes voiceless because of a nearby voiceless sound (e.g., the *l* in *place* is devoiced because of the voiceless stop preceding it).

**Diacritic** A mark added to a phonetic symbol to alter its value in some way (e.g., a circle under a symbol to indicate voicelessness).

**Dialect** A language variety that is systematically different from another variety of the same language and spoken by a socially identifiable subgroup of some larger speech community.

**Dialect levelling** In a region with many dialects, the process by which certain features are lost and a more homogenous dialect emerges.

**Dialectology** The study of regional differences in language.

**Diaphragm** The large sheet of muscle that separates the chest cavity from the abdomen and helps to maintain the air pressure necessary for speech production.

**Diary study** A type of naturalistic investigation in which a researcher (often a parent) keeps daily notes on a child's linguistic progress.

**Dichotic listening** A technique in which stimuli (either linguistic or non-linguistic) are presented through headphones to the left and right ears to determine the lateralization of various cognitive functions.

**Diglossia** The relationship between multiple varieties spoken by one speech community but with sharply distinct domains of use.

**Diphthong** A vowel that shows a noticeable change in quality during its production (e.g., the vowel sounds in *house* and *ride*).

**Diphthongization** A process in which a monophthong becomes a diphthong (e.g., [i:] became [aj] during the Great English Vowel Shift).

**Direct negative evidence** Language instruction involving correction or focus on form.

**Direct object** The NP complement of a verb (e.g., *a fish* in *Judy caught a fish*).

**Discourse** Any social interaction or expression involving language.

**Discourse analysis** The analysis of how utterances are structured in discourse.

**Discrete sign** A sign that is distinguished from other signs by stepwise differences (e.g., voiced and voiceless sounds, the numbers of a digital clock).

**Discrete variable** A variable whose variants are distinctly separate, with no in-between variants possible.

**Dissimilation** A process whereby one segment becomes less like another segment in its environment (e.g., *anma* 'soul' in Latin became *alma* in Spanish).

**Distinctive feature** A feature that is able to signal a difference in meaning by changing its plus or minus value (e.g., the feature [voice] in the words *peer* and *beer*).

**Distribution** The set of elements with which an item can co-occur.

**DORSAL** A place feature that characterizes sounds made with the body of the tongue.

**Dorsum (of the tongue)** The body and back of the tongue.

**Double-blind test** A type of test used in ape language studies in which the researcher is prevented from seeing the stimulus shown to the ape to avoid cueing certain behaviours.

**Downdrift** The maintenance of a distinction among the pitch registers of an utterance even as the overall pitch of the utterance falls.

**Dressage** A type of interaction between trainer and animal that depends on the animal's interpreting subtle cues given by the trainer.

**Dual language programs** Students receiving instruction in both majority and minority languages; an example would be Spanish speakers being taught English in the same class with English speakers being taught Spanish in an English-dominant environment.

**Duetting** The interchange of calls in a patterned manner between two members of a species.

**Dysprosody** The lack of sentence intonation; a common characteristic of the speech of Broca's aphasics.

**Enclitic** A clitic that attaches to the end of a word.

**Endocentric compound** A compound whose rightmost component (in English) identifies the general class to which the meaning of the entire word belongs (e.g., *dump truck* is a type of truck). (*See also* Exocentric compound.)

**Entailment** A relation between sentences in which the truth of one sentence necessarily implies the truth of another (e.g., *Gary is Bernice's husband* entails the truth of *Bernice is married*).

**Environment** The phonetic context in which a sound occurs.

**Epenthesis** A process that inserts a segment into a particular environment (e.g., the insertion of a schwa in the pronunciation of *athlete* as [æθəlit]).

**Eponym** A word created from a name (e.g., watt).

**Ergative** The case associated with the subject of a transitive verb in some languages.

**Ethnic slur** Socially stigmatized names for ethnic groups.

**Ethnolect** A language variety associated with a particular ethnic group.

**Ethnomethodology** A type of discourse analysis that focuses on the structural relationship between utterances in conversations.

**Ethnonym** The preferred name for a particular ethnic group.

**Euphemisms** Words or phrases used in place of taboo items.

**Event-related potentials (ERPs)** A measurement of electrical activity in the brain that is correlated with the presentation of particular stimulus events.

**Evidentiality** A system of morphological contrasts indicating the type of evidence for the truth of a statement.

**Exclusive** A contrast in some languages that indicates that the addressee is to be excluded in the interpretation of the first person plural morpheme. (*See also* Inclusive.)

**Exocentric compound** A compound whose meaning does not follow from the meaning of its parts (e.g., *redneck,* since its referent is not a type of neck). *See also* **Endocentric Compound**.

**Experimental approach** An approach to investigating language in which researchers make use of specially designed tasks to elicit linguistic activity relevant to a particular phenomenon.

**Experimental paradigm** A method of investigation that involves a particular way of presenting stimuli and a particular way of measuring responses.

**Extension** The set of entities to which a word or expression refers (also called its denotation or referents).

**Feature (phonetic)** The smallest unit of analysis of phonological structure, combinations of which make up segments (e.g., [nasal], [continuant]).

**Feature hierarchy** A hierarchical representation of how features are related to each other.

**Features (semantic)** The semantic components that make up a word's intension.

**Feminine** A term used to signal membership in the feminine gender category.

**Field dependent** A cognitive style in which foreground and background information are integrated.

**Field independent** A cognitive style in which relevant information is perceived clearly against the information background.

**Field technique** A method of study that does not involve manipulation and control of factors in a laboratory, but rather involves observing phenomena as they occur.

**Fissure** A relatively deep sulcus of the cerebral cortex.

**Fixed stress** Stress whose position in a word is predictable.

**Flap** A sound commonly identified with *r* in some languages and produced when the tongue tip strikes the alveolar ridge as it passes across it (e.g., in North American English, the medial consonant in *bitter* and *bidder*).

**Flapping** An assimilation process in which a dental or alveolar stop ([-continuant]) changes to a flap ([+continuant]) in the environment of other continuants.

**Fluency** The ability to produce second language speech that is produced automatically and without noticeable hesitation.

**Fluent aphasia** The aphasia that occurs due to damage to parts of the left cortex behind the central sulcus, resulting in fluent speech but great difficulty in selecting, organizing, and monitoring language production (also called **sensory aphasia**).

**Folk etymology** Reanalysis of a word that is based on an incorrect historical analysis (e.g., *hamburger* being reanalyzed into two morphemes, *ham* and *burger*).

**Foreigner talk** The type of speech that is typically addressed to second language learners, characterized by such properties as simple word order and more common vocabulary items (also called **teacher talk**).

**Forms of address** How an individual is addressed (e.g., *Professor, Bob,* etc.).

**Fossilized** A property of an interlanguage grammar that has reached a plateau and has ceased to change.

**Fourth floor study** The study by William Labov that relied on eliciting the phrase "the fourth floor" in department stores frequented by shoppers of different SES. Labov hypothesized that store employees "borrowed" prestige from their customers and that this was reflected in their unconscious language choices.

**Free form** An element that does not have to occur in a fixed position with respect to neighbouring elements and may even be able to appear in isolation.

**Free morpheme** A morpheme that can be a word by itself (e.g., *fear*).

**Free stress** Stress whose position in a word is not predictable and must be learned on a case-by-case basis.

**Free variation** Sounds are in free variation when they do not contrast, can occur in identical phonetic environments, and are phonetically similar.

**Frequency effect** The common experimental finding that words that occur more commonly in a language are processed more quickly and more accurately.

**Frication** The weakening of a stop to a fricative (e.g., [d] becoming [ð]).

**Fricatives** Consonants produced with a continuous airflow through the mouth, accompanied by a continuous audible noise (e.g., [f], [ʃ]).

**Front vowel** A vowel that is made with the tongue positioned in the front of the oral cavity (e.g., the vowel sounds in *seal* and *bat*).

**Frontal lobe** The lobe of the brain that lies in front of the central sulcus and in which Broca's area is located.

**Fronting** A common substitution process in child language acquisition that involves the moving forward of a sound's place of articulation (e.g., *cheese* pronounced as [tsiz]).

**Full reduplication** A morphological process that duplicates the entire word (e.g., in Turkish, /tʃabuk/ 'quickly'/tʃabuktʃabuk/ 'very quickly').

**Function words** Words such as determiners and conjunctions that are lacking in the speech of Broca's aphasics, resulting in telegraphic speech.

**Functional category** A word-level syntactic category whose members are harder to define and paraphrase than those of lexical categories (e.g., auxiliary verbs, conjunctions, determiners, and degree words) (also called **non-lexical category**).

**Functional magnetic resonance imaging (fMRI)** A brain imaging technique that yields information on areas of high brain activity during the performance of cognitive tasks.

**Fusion** The process by which words develop into affixes over time.

**Fusional languages** Languages in which words typically consist of several morphemes; the morphemes that are affixes often mark several grammatical categories simultaneously (e.g., Russian).

**Fuzzy concepts** Concepts that do not have clear-cut boundaries that distinguish them from other concepts (e.g., the concept 'poor').

**Garden path sentence** A sentence that is difficult to process and interpret because its structure biases sentence parsing toward an incorrect analysis.

**Gender roles** Roles or occupations traditionally performed by only one sex.

**Generative grammar** *See* **Transformational grammar.**

**Genetic classification** The categorization of languages according to the ancestor languages from which they developed.

**Genetic relationships** Relationships among languages that have descended from a common ancestor.

**Genetically related languages** Languages that have descended from a common parent (e.g., German and Italian both descended from Indo-European).

**Genitive** The case form characteristically used to mark a possessor.

**Given information** Knowledge that the speaker assumes is available to the addressee at the time of the utterance, either because it is common knowledge or because it has already been introduced into the discourse (also called **old information**).

**Glagolitic script** A script that was introduced in Slavic-speaking areas in the ninth century AD for the translation of the Bible.

**Glide strengthening** The strengthening of a glide to an affricate (e.g., [j] becoming [dʒ]).

**Glides** Sounds that are produced with an articulation like that of a vowel, but move quickly to another articulation (e.g., [j], [w]).

**Gliding** A common substitution process in child language acquisition which involves the replacement of a liquid by a glide (e.g., *play* is pronounced [pwej]).

**Global aphasia** The most severe form of non-fluent aphasia, in which the patient is completely mute.

**Glottals** Sounds produced by using the vocal folds as the primary articulators (e.g., [h], [ʔ]).

**Glottis** The space between the vocal folds.

**Graded sign** A sign that conveys its meaning by changes in degree (e.g., voice volume, a blush).

**Gradient variable** A variable in which there are many subtle options (e.g., the pronunciation of [E] is lower in dialect x than in dialect y).

**Grammar** The mental system of rules and categories that allows humans to form and interpret the words and sentences of their language.

**Grammatical** The status of a sentence that speakers judge to be a possible sentence of their language.

**Grammatical competence** Competence in the structural aspects of language at or below the sentence level.

**Grammaticalize** To express a grammatical contrast through affixes and/or non-lexical (functional) categories.

**Grammaticalization** The change of a lexical form into a grammatical form (e.g., an affix or member of a functional category).

**Grimm's Law** A set of consonant shifts that took place between Proto-Indo-European and Proto-Germanic.

**Gyrus** An area where the cerebral cortex is folded out.

**Hangul** The alphabetic script used to represent Korean, the symbols of which are grouped to represent the syllables of individual morphemes.

**Hanja** The Korean word for the Chinese characters used in Korean writing.

**Head (of a phrase)** The word around which a phrasal category is built (e.g., V, N, A, P).

**Head (of a word)** The morpheme that determines the category of the entire word (e.g., *bird* in *blackbird*).

**Hieroglyphic** An Egyptian pictorial writing system, which later developed into a mixed writing system.

**High** A dorsal feature that characterizes sounds produced with the tongue body raised.

**High involvement style** A style of turn-taking in a conversation where speaker turns overlap.

**Hiragana** The Japanese syllabary that is used in conjunction with katakana and kanji to write Japanese.

**Historical linguistics** The linguistic discipline that is concerned with the description and the explanation of language change.

**Holophrases** Utterances produced by children in which one word expresses the type of meaning that would be associated with an entire sentence in adult speech (e.g., *up* used to mean 'Pick me up').

**Homographs** Words with the same spelling.

**Homonyms** Words that are both homophones and homographs.

**Homophony** The situation in which a single form has two or more entirely distinct meanings (e.g., *club* 'a social organization', *club* 'a blunt weapon').

**Host** The element to which clitics are attached.

**Hypercorrection** The over- or under-use of a variant as a result of its prestige value.

**Iconic sign** A sign that bears some resemblance to its referent (e.g., a picture of a woman on a washroom door).

**Identification** The use of particular linguistic variants to indicate solidarity with a particular community.

**Illocutionary competence** A speaker's knowledge of how a language functions.

**Illocutionary force** The intended meaning of an utterance.

**Immersion** A method of teaching a second language to children in which students are given most of their courses and school activities in the target language.

**Impaired Representation Hypothesis** The hypothesis that second language learners' grammars are lacking certain grammatical features.

**Implicational universal** A universal of language that specifies that the presence of one trait implies the presence of another (but not vice versa).

**Inanimate** A noun class category in some languages. (*See also* **Animate.**)

**Inclusive** A contrast in some languages which indicates that the addressee is to be included in the interpretation of the first person plural morpheme. (*See also* **Exclusive.**)

**Indexical sign** A sign that fulfills its function by pointing out its referent, typically by being a partial sample of it (e.g., the track of an animal).

**Indicator** A linguistic variable which is not noticeable to the listener.

**Indirect negative evidence** The assumption that non-occurring structures in the linguistic environment are ungrammatical.

**Infix** An affix that occurs within its base.

**Inflection** The modification of a word's form to indicate the grammatical subclass to which it belongs (e.g., the *-s* in *books* marks the plural subclass).

**Inflectional languages** *See* Fusional languages.

**Informant** A native speaker of a language or variety who provides data to the linguist (also called a **consultant**).

**Initialism** An abbreviation created by pronouncing a series of letters (e.g., PEI or USA) as letters rather than as a word.

**Insertion rule** An operation that adds an element to a tree structure.

**Instrumental motivation** The desire to achieve proficiency in a new language for utilitarian reasons, such as job promotion.

**Integrative motivation** The desire to achieve proficiency in a new language in order to participate in the social life of the language community.

**Intension** An expression's inherent sense; the concepts that it evokes.

**Intercostals** The muscles between the ribs that help to maintain the air pressure necessary for speech production.

**Interdentals** Sounds made with the tongue placed between the teeth (e.g., [θ], [ð]).

**Interlanguage** The dynamic grammatical system that an L2 learner is using at a particular period in his or her acquisition of a second language.

**Internal change** A process that substitutes one non-morphemic segment for another to mark a grammatical contrast.

**Internal reconstruction** The reconstruction of a proto-language that relies on the analysis of morphophonemic variation within a single language.

**International Phonetic Alphabet (IPA)** The universal system for transcribing the sounds of speech, which has been developing since 1888.

**Inter-speaker variation** Variation that occurs across individuals (e.g., some speakers have the voiceless labiovelar glide [ʍ] and some do not).

**Intonation** Pitch movement in spoken utterances that is not related to differences in word meaning.

**Intransitive** A verb that does not take a direct object (e.g., *sleep*).

**Intra-speaker variation** Variation that occurs within the speech of an individual (e.g., sometimes I say *often* with the "t" and sometimes without).

**Inversion** A transformation that moves the element in the I position to the C position; formulated as: Move I to C.

**Isogloss** A line drawn on a dialect map to indicate that two regions differ for a particular linguistic feature.

**Isogloss bundle** Several isoglosses clustered along the same point on a map.

**Isolating languages** Languages whose words typically consist of only one morpheme (also called **analytic languages**) (e.g., Mandarin).

**Jargon** The vocabulary associated with a specific register.

**Jargonaphasia** A symptom of severe cases of Wernicke's aphasia in which speech contains very few real words of the language.

**Kanji** The Japanese word for the Chinese characters used to write Japanese.

**Katakana** The Japanese syllabary that is used in conjunction with hiragana and kanji to write Japanese.

**LABIAL** A place feature that characterizes sounds articulated with one or both lips.

**Labials** Sounds made with closure or near closure of the lips (e.g., the initial sounds of *bit* and *pot*).

**Labiodentals** Sounds involving the lower lip and upper teeth (e.g., the initial sounds of *freedom* and *vintage*).

**Labiovelars** Sounds made with the tongue raised near the velum and the lips rounded at the same time (e.g., the initial sound of *wound*).

**Language bioprogram hypothesis** The hypothesis that similarities among creoles reflect universal properties of an innate biological program for language acquisition found in the mental makeup of every human being.

**Language contact** A source of language change that involves the speakers of one language frequently interacting with the speakers of another language.

**Language death** The situation in which there are no more speakers of a particular language.

**Language myth** Unsubstantiated beliefs about a language variety.

**Language planning** Official policy with the goal of increasing or limiting the domain of use of a particular language or languages.

**Laryngeal features** Features that represent voicing states.

**Larynx** The box-like structure located in the throat through which air passes during speech production, commonly known as the voicebox.

**Late closure** A proposed parsing principle that claims that, in sentence comprehension, humans tend to attach incoming material into the phrase or clause currently being parsed.

**Lateral fissure** The fissure that separates the temporal lobe from the frontal and parietal lobes.

**Lateral fricative** A lateral sound made with a narrow enough closure to be classified as a fricative.

**Lateralization** The unilateral control of cognitive functions by either the left or the right side of the brain (e.g., language is lateralized in the left hemisphere in most people).

**Laterals** Sounds made with the sides of the tongue lowered (e.g., varieties of *l*).

**Lax vowel** A vowel that is made with a placement of the tongue that results in relatively less vocal tract constriction (e.g., the vowel sounds in *hit* and *but*).

**Learning strategies** The ways in which language learners process language input and develop linguistic knowledge.

**Length** The auditory property of a sound that enables us to place it on a scale that ranges from short to long.

**Lesion** Severe damage to the brain.

**Lexical ambiguity** The result of homophony or polysemy in that a single form has two or more meanings, either related or not.

**Lexical category** The word-level syntactic categories noun (N), verb (V), adjective (A), and preposition (P).

**Lexical decision** An experimental paradigm in which a person sees or hears a stimulus and must judge as quickly as possible whether or not that stimulus is a word of his or her language.

**Lexical diffusion** Linguistic change that first manifests itself in a few words and then gradually spreads through the vocabulary of the language.

**Lexical gaps** Gaps in the lexicon that result from technological innovation or contact with another culture.

**Lexicalization** The process whereby concepts are encoded in the words of a language (e.g., the concepts of 'motion' and 'manner' are both encoded by the word *roll*).

**Lexicon** A speaker's mental dictionary, which contains information about the syntactic properties, meaning, and phonological representation of a language's words.

**Lexifier language** The language that provides most of the lexical items to a contact variety.

**Lingua franca** A language used for the primary purpose of communicating across speech communities whose members speak different languages; usually the second language of all speakers involved.

**Linguistic competence** Speakers' knowledge of their language, which allows them to produce and understand an unlimited number of utterances, including many that are novel.

**Linguistic factor** Linguistic properties that may be correlated with structured variation (e.g., at the beginning of a word, before a vowel, etc.).

**Linguistic insecurity** The degree to which speakers believe that their own variety is not standard.

**Linguistic isolation** A situation in which a speech community is isolated from other speakers of the same language (e.g., Quebec French is surrounded by English in North America).

**Linguistic typology** An approach to language classification that classifies languages according to their structural characteristics without regard for genetic relationships.

**Linguistic universals** Structural characteristics that occur across the languages of the world.

**Linguistics** The discipline that studies the nature and use of language.

**Lobes** Substructures of the cerebral hemispheres that appear to have distinct responsibilities (e.g., frontal lobe, temporal lobe).

**Logogram** A written symbol representing a morpheme or word.

**Logographic writing** A type of writing in which symbols represent morphemes or even entire words.

**Longitudinal fissure** The fissure that extends from the front of the brain to the back and separates the left and right cerebral hemispheres.

**Longitudinal studies** Studies that examine language development over an extended period of time.

**Loudness** The auditory property of a sound that enables us to place it on a scale that ranges from soft to loud.

**Low** A dorsal feature that characterizes vowels made with the tongue body distinctly lowered from a central position in the oral cavity.

**Macrofamilies** *See* Phyla.

**Magnetoencephalography (MEG)** A technique for studying how language is processed that records subtle changes in the magnetic fields generated within the brain.

**Major class features** Features that represent the classes consonant, obstruent, nasal, liquid, glide, and vowel.

**Majority rules strategy** A secondary strategy used to reconstruct proto-forms which stipulates that the segment found in the majority of cognates should be assumed to be part of the proto-form. (*See also* **Phonetic plausibility strategy**.)

**Manner features** Features that represent manner of articulation.

**Manners of articulation** The various configurations produced by positioning the lips, tongue, velum, and glottis in different ways (e.g., nasal, fricative, liquid).

**Marker** A linguistic variable that is noticeable to the listener.

**Markedness Differential Hypothesis** The hypothesis that L2 elements that are different and more marked than the L1 elements will cause difficulty in learning.

**Markedness theory** A theory that classifies traits or patterns of languages as marked (those that are considered to be more complex and/or universally rarer) and unmarked (those that are considered to be less complex and/or universally more common).

**Masculine** A term used to signal membership in the masculine gender category.

**Matrix** An array of features that represents a segment.

**Matrix clause** The larger clause in which a complement clause occurs.

**Matrix language** The dominant language in a code-switching exchange.

**Maxim of Manner** A principle that is thought to underlie the efficient use of language and is formulated as: Avoid ambiguity and obscurity; be brief and orderly.

**Maxim of Quality** A principle that is thought to underlie the efficient use of language and is formulated as: Try to make your contribution one that is true. (Do not say things that are false or for which you lack adequate evidence.)

**Maxim of Quantity** A principle that is thought to underlie the efficient use of language and is formulated as: Do not make your contribution more or less informative than required.

**Maxim of Relevance** A principle that is thought to underlie the efficient use of language and is formulated as: Be relevant.

**Meaning** The message or content that a sign conveys.

**Mental lexicon** *See* Lexicon.

**Merge** A syntactic operation that combines elements to create phrases and sentences.

**Merger** A change in a phonological system in which two or more phonemes collapse into one, thereby reducing the number of phonemes in that language.

**Mesolect** A variety with characteristics that place it at a mid point along the continuum between the acrolect and the basilect in a creole speech community.

**Metaphor** The understanding of one concept in terms of another (e.g., 'argument' understood in terms of 'war': *She annihilated him in the debate*).

**Metathesis** A process that reorders a sequence of segments (e.g., in child language, pronouncing *ask* as [æks]).

**Michif** The language of the Métis people.

**Mid vowel** A vowel that is made with the tongue neither raised nor lowered (e.g., the vowel sounds in *set* and *Coke*).

**Minimal attachment** A proposed parsing principle that claims that, in sentence comprehension, humans tend to attach incoming material into phrase structure using the fewest nodes possible.

**Minimal pair** Two forms with distinct meanings that differ by only one segment found in the same position in each form.

**Missing Surface Inflection Hypothesis** The hypothesis that second language learners may omit surface morphology at times but that their grammars encode appropriate grammatical features.

**Mixed language** A language with many features from two different source languages (e.g., Michif).

**Modifier** An optional element that describes a property of a head (e.g., *blue* in *that blue car*).

**Morpheme** The smallest unit of language that carries information about meaning or function (e.g., *books* consists of the two morphemes *book* and *s*).

**Morphological parsing** A computational process that activates the morphemes making up an utterance.

**Morphology** The system of categories and rules involved in word formation and interpretation.

**Morphophonemics** Rules that account for alternations among allomorphs (also called **morphophonology**).

**Morphophonology** *See* **Morphophonemics**.

**Motherese** The type of speech that is typically addressed to young children (also called **caregiver speech**).

**Motor aphasia** *See* **Non-fluent aphasia**.

**Move** A syntactic operation that transports an element to a new position within a particular sentence.

**Movement test** A test used to determine if a group of words is a constituent by moving it as a single unit to a different position within the sentence.

**Multiple-route models** A psycholinguistic theory built around the claim that a particular type of language processing is accomplished in two or more manners.

**Multiplex** The quality of a social network that indicates the degree to which social network connections are made on the basis of many different kinds of social relationships.

**Murmur** The glottal state that produces voiced sounds with the vocal folds relaxed enough to allow enough air to escape to produce a simultaneous whispery effect (also called **breathy voice**).

**Mutual intelligibility** The situation where speakers of two different varieties are able to understand one another's speech.

**Nasal** A manner feature that characterizes any sound made with the velum lowered.

**Nasal sounds** Sounds produced by lowering the velum, allowing air to pass through the nasal passages.

**Nasalization** The nasalizing effect that a nasal consonant can have on adjacent vowels.

**Native speaker** One who has acquired a language as a child in a natural setting.

**Nativism** The view that certain grammatical knowledge is inborn.

**Natural class** A class of sounds that shares a feature or features (e.g., voiced stops).

**Naturalistic approach** An approach to investigating child language in which researchers observe and record children's spontaneous verbal behaviour.

**Naturalness** A criterion that guides language reconstruction by determining whether or not changes are natural.

**Near-minimal pair** Two forms with distinct meanings that contrast segments in nearly identical environments.

**Negative evidence** Information as to the ungrammatical nature of utterances.

**Neurolinguistics** The study of how language is represented and processed in the brain.

**Neurons** The basic information-processing units of the nervous system, also called nerve cells.

**Neuroscience** The scientific study of the brain.

**Neuter** A term used to signal membership in the neuter gender category.

**New information** Knowledge that is introduced into the discourse for the first time.

**Node** A simple unit of processing posited in connectionist models of the brain.

**Nominal paradigm** The set of related forms associated with a noun (also called a **declension**).

**Nominative** The case form characteristically used to mark a subject.

**Nonce borrowing** A word from language *x* that is used in language *y* by bilinguals but does not become part of its vocabulary.

**Non-fluent aphasia** Aphasia that results from damage to parts of the brain in front of the central sulcus and is characterized by slow, effortful speech production (also called **motor aphasia**).

**Non-lexical category** *See* **Functional category.**

**Non-standard variety** A variety of language containing forms that are viewed pejoratively in the community; generally considered "incorrect" by prescriptive grammarians.

**Non-terminal (intonation) contour** Rising or level intonation at the end of an utterance, often signalling that the utterance is incomplete.

**NORMs** Non-mobile older rural males.

**Noun (N)** A lexical category that typically names entities, can usually be inflected for number and possession (in English), and

functions as the head of a noun phrase (e.g., *key, Bob, perception*).

**Nucleus (N)** A vocalic element that forms the core of a syllable (e.g., the vowel [æ] is the nucleus of the first syllable of *Patrick*).

**Number** The morphological category that expresses contrasts involving countable quantities (e.g., in English, the two-way distinction between singular and plural).

**Object permanence** A milestone in a child's development characterized by the ability to recognize that objects have an existence independent of one's interaction with them.

**Oblique NP** A noun phrase that combines with a preposition.

**Obstruent** Any non-sonorant consonant: fricatives, affricates, oral stops.

**Obviative** A verb form used in some languages to indicate that the referent of the subject is not the entity previously chosen as the focus of the conversation. (*See also* **Proximate.**)

**Occipital lobe** The area of the brain to the rear of the angular gyrus, in which the visual cortex is located.

**Official language** A language with preferred status bestowed by government legislation.

**Old information** *See* **Given information.**

**Onomatopoeic words** Words that sound like the thing that they name (e.g., *plop, hiss*).

**Onset (O)** Within a syllable, the longest sequence of consonants to the left of each nucleus that does not violate the phonotactic constraints of the language in question (e.g., [st] forms the onset of the second syllable in *hamster*).

**Open syllable** A syllable that is not closed by a consonant.

**Opening** A discourse unit conventionally used to begin a conversation.

**Oral sounds** Sounds produced with the velum raised and the airflow through the nasal passage cut off.

**Orthography** A set of conventions for representing language in written form.

**Overextension** A developmental phenomenon in which the meaning of the child's word is more general or inclusive than that of the corresponding adult form (e.g., *daddy* used to refer to any adult male).

**Overgeneralization** A developmental phenomenon that results from the overly broad application of a rule (e.g., *falled* instead of *fell*) (also called **overregularization**).

**Overregularization** *See* Overgeneralization.

**Overt prestige** Linguistic variables that are obviously associated with prestige (e.g., the use of a word like *salubrious*).

**Palatalization** The effect that front vowels and the palatal guide [j] typically have on velar, alveolar, and dental stops, making their place of articulation more palatal (e.g., the first sound of *keep* is palatalized).

**Palatals** Sounds produced with the tongue on or near the palate (e.g., [j]).

**Palate** The highest part of the roof of the mouth.

**Palatoalveolar** *See* Alveopalatal (area).

**Paragraphia** A writing error associated with a linguistic deficit.

**Parallel processing model** A psycholinguistic theory built around the claim that phonological, lexical, and syntactic processes are carried out simultaneously.

**Parameter** The set of alternatives for a particular phenomenon made available by Universal Grammar to individual languages.

**Parameter setting** The determination of which option permitted by a particular parameter is appropriate for the language being learned.

**Paraphrases** Two sentences that have the same basic meaning (e.g., *A Canadian wrote that book* is a paraphrase of *That book was written by a Canadian*).

**Parietal lobe** The lobe of the brain that lies behind the central sulcus and above the temporal lobe.

**Parsing** The mechanism through which a listener or reader processes linguistic input by assigning categories to lexical elements and hierarchical structure to strings of lexical elements.

**Partial reduplication** A morphological process that duplicates part of the base to which it applies (e.g., in Tagalog, *takbuh* 'run' and *tatakbuh* 'will run').

**Partial suppletion** A morphological process that marks a grammatical contrast by replacing part of a morpheme (e.g., *think/thought*).

**Passive sentence** A sentence in which the NP bearing the theme role is encoded as subject (e.g., *The report was prepared by the committee members*).

**Pejoration** The process in which the meaning of a word becomes less favourable (e.g., *wench* used to mean simply 'girl').

**Performance** Actual language use in particular situations.

**Person** A morphological category that typically distinguishes among the first person (the speaker), the second person (the addressee), and the third person (anyone else) (e.g., in English, the difference between *I, you,* and *she/he/it*).

**Pharyngeals** Sounds made through the modification of airflow in the pharynx by retracting the tongue or constricting the pharynx.

**Pharynx** The area of the throat between the uvula and the larynx.

**Pheremones** Chemicals used by animals specifically for communicative purposes.

**Phone** Any sound used in human language (also called a **speech sound**).

**Phoneme** The phonological unit into which predictable variants of non-contrastive segments are grouped (e.g., in English, [t] and [t^h] belong to the phoneme /t/).

**Phonemic paraphasias** Speech errors that result from phonemic substitutions and omissions (e.g., *spoon* may be pronounced as *poon*).

**Phonemic representation** The representation that consists of the phonemes to which allophones belong; predicable phonetic information is not represented (also called **phonological representation**).

**Phonetic determinative** The part of a Chinese character that provides information about the pronunciation of the corresponding morpheme.

**Phonetic plausibility strategy** The primary strategy used to reconstruct proto-forms, which requires any sound changes posited to be phonetically plausible. (*See also* **Majority rules strategy.**)

**Phonetic representation** The representation that consists of predictable variants of allophones.

**Phonetic sound change** A sound change that results in a new allophone of an already existing phoneme.

**Phonetically conditioned sound change** Sound change that begins as subtle alterations in the sound pattern of a language in particular phonetic environments.

**Phonetics** The branch of linguistics that examines the inventory and structure of the sounds of language.

**Phonographic writing** A type of writing in which symbols represent syllables or segments.

**Phonological change** A sound change that results in the addition, elimination, or rearrangement of phonemes (e.g., splits, mergers).

**Phonological dyslexia** A type of acquired dyslexia in which the patient seems to have lost the ability to use spelling-to-sound rules and can only read words that they have seen before.

**Phonological representation** *See* **Phonemic representation.**

**Phonological rules** Rules that derive phonetic representations from underlying representations, accounting for alternations among allophones.

**Phonology** The component of a grammar made up of the elements and principles that determine how sounds pattern in a language.

**Phonotactics** The set of constraints on how sequences of segments pattern.

**Phrase** A unit of syntactic structure consisting of an obligatory head and an optional specifier and/or complements.

**Phyla** The groups into which purportedly related language stocks are placed (also called **superstocks**).

**Physical isolation** A situation in which speech communities are geographically isolated from other speech communities (e.g., island communities).

**Pictograms** Pictorial representations of objects or events.

**Pidgin** A variety that emerges when speakers of different languages are brought together in a stable situation requiring intergroup communication; it has no native speakers and generally is considered to have a reduced grammatical system relative to a non-pidgin.

**Pinyin** The system of writing Mandarin with a modified Latin alphabet, used for such things as street signs and brand names.

**Pitch** The auditory property of a sound that enables us to place it on a scale that ranges from low to high.

**Place of articulation features** Features that represent place of articulation.

**Places of articulation** The points at which the airstream can be modified to produce different sounds.

**Points of articulation** *See* **Places of articulation.**

**Polysemy** The situation in which a word has two or more related meanings (e.g., *bright* 'intelligent', *bright* 'shining').

**Polysynthetic languages** Languages in which single words can consist of long strings of lexical categories and affixes, often expressing the meaning of an entire sentence in English (e.g., Inuktitut).

**Positive evidence** Grammatical utterances in the learner's linguistic environment.

**Positive politeness** The use of politeness conventions to express regard and consideration for other participants in discourse.

**Positron Emission Tomography (PET)** A brain imaging technique that uses radioactive isotopes to measure changes in brain metabolism associated with particular cognitive and behavioural tasks.

**Post-lexical decomposition** The activation of the constituents of a multimorphemic word through the representation of the whole lexical item.

**Postposition** A P that occurs after its complement. (*See also* **Preposition (P)**.)

**Power** The degree of control that one group or individual may hold over another.

**Pragmatics** Speakers' and addressees' background attitudes and beliefs, their understanding of the context in which a sentence is uttered, and their knowledge of how language can be used for a variety of purposes.

**Prefix** An affix that is attached to the front of its base (e.g., *re-* in *replay*).

**Pre-lexical decomposition** The activation of a word's constituent morphemes during comprehension.

**Preposition (P)** A lexical category that functions as the head of a prepositional phrase and occurs before its complement (e.g., *into, with, for*).

**Prescriptive** A characteristic of certain non-linguistic approaches to grammar in that they seek to prescribe one system in preference to another. (*See also* **Descriptive**.)

**Prestige** The social value attached to a linguistic variant considered to be the one used by the group holding the highest esteem in the community; frequently also believed to be the grammatically "correct" form.

**Presupposition** The assumption or belief implied by the use of a particular word or structure.

**Primary stress** The most prominent stress of a word.

**Prime** In a priming experiment, this is the stimulus that is expected to affect a subject's response accuracy and latency to a subsequent stimulus (called the target).

**Priming** A situation in which the presentation of a stimulus has a positive effect on the ease with which a subsequent related stimulus is processed.

**Priming effect** In a priming experiment, this is the extent to which a priming stimulus facilitates the processing of a target stimulus.

**Principle A** The principle that constrains the interpretation of reflexive pronouns and is formulated as: A reflexive pronoun must have an antecedent that c-commands it in the same minimal IP.

**Principle B** The principle that constrains the interpretation of pronominals and is formulated as: A pronominal must not have an antecedent that c-commands it in the same minimal IP.

**Principle of Compositionality, The** A principle underlying sentence interpretation that is formulated as: The meaning of a sentence is determined by the meaning of its component parts and the manner in which they are arranged in syntactic structure.

**Probabilistic rules** Rules or constraints that are not absolute (e.g., [r] is usually deleted after vowels).

**Proclitic** A clitic that attaches to the beginning of a word.

**Productivity** The relative freedom with which affixes can combine with bases of the appropriate category.

**Progressive assimilation** Assimilation in which a sound influences a following segment (e.g., liquid-glide devoicing in English).

**Pronominal** A pronoun whose interpretation may be, but does not have to be, determined by an antecedent in the same sentence (e.g., *he, her*).

**Pronoun** A word whose interpretation can be determined by another element (an antecedent) (e.g., *him, she, themselves, herself*).

**Prosodic properties** *See* Suprasegmental properties.

**Proto-forms** Forms of a proto-language, written with a preceding asterisk to indicate their hypothetical character.

**Proto-Indo-European (PIE)** The proto-language from which evolved most of the languages of Europe, Persia (Iran), and the northern part of India.

**Proto-language** A language reconstructed through the methods of historical linguistics.

**Proto-pidgin** The reconstructed ancestor language that is the source of all pidgins.

**Prototypes** The best exemplars of a concept (e.g., robins or magpies are prototypes of the concept 'bird').

**Proximate** A verb form used in some languages to indicate that the subject of the verb has been chosen as the focus of the conversation and any further use of which (without an overt subject) indicates a reference to that focused entity. (*See also* **Obviative.**)

**Psycholinguistics** The study of the mental processes and representations involved in language comprehension and production.

**Radical** The part of a Chinese character that provides clues about the morpheme's meaning (also called a **key**).

**Rapport style** A discourse style designed to build and maintain relationships.

**Reading** The interpretation of a particular utterance.

**Real-time studies** Studies that investigate a language over a period of time.

**Reanalysis** A source of language change that involves an attempt to attribute an internal structure to a word that formerly was not broken down into component morphemes (e.g., *ham + burger*).

**Rebus principle** In writing, the use of a sign for any word that is pronounced like the word whose meaning the sign represented initially.

**Recast** A repetition of a child's utterance that includes adjustments to its form and/or content.

**Recursivity** A property of operations that can apply over and over again.

**Reduced** A DORSAL feature that characterizes only schwa.

**Reduced vowel** *See* **Schwa.**

**Redundancy** The use of different modalities to convey the same information.

**Reduplication** A morphological process that duplicates all or part of the base to which it applies. (*See also* **Partial reduplication** and **Full reduplication.**)

**Referents** The set of entities to which a word or expression refers (*see also* **denotation** or **extension**).

**Reflexive pronoun** A pronoun that must have a c-commanding antecedent in the same clause (e.g., *himself, herself*).

**Regional dialect** A dialect spoken in a specific geographical region.

**Register** A set of linguistic structures that is associated with a particular speech situation; it may carry an association with a particular style.

**Register tones** Level tones that signal meaning differences.

**Regressive assimilation** Assimilation in which a sound influences a preceding segment (e.g., nasalization in English).

**Regressive saccades** Eye movements in which the eyes dart backward to a section of text that has been previously read.

**Relative clause** A CP that serves as modifier of a noun.

**Relexification hypothesis** The hypothesis that contact varieties of language are generated by using lexical items from one language and the grammatical system of another.

**Report style** A discourse style designed to communicate factual information.

**Response accuracy** The correctness of a subject's responses to particular stimuli provided in an experiment.

**Response latency** The amount of time taken by a subject in an experiment to respond to a stimulus.

**Restricted use** Social situations in which the use of a particular language is restricted to certain environments (e.g., school).

**Retroflex** The *r* made by either curling the tongue tip back into the mouth or by bunching the tongue upward and back in the mouth.

**Rhotacism** A type of weakening that typically involves the change of [z] to [r].

**Rhyme (R)** The nucleus and the coda of a syllable (e.g., [uts] in the word *boots*).

**Right ear advantage** The phenomenon in which people with language in the left hemisphere hear speech louder and clearer with the right ear.

**Root (of the tongue)** The part of the tongue that is contained in the upper part of the throat.

**Root (of a word)** The morpheme in a word that carries the major component of the word's meaning and belongs to a lexical category (e.g., *collect* in the word *collections*).

**Round** A place feature that characterizes sounds made by protruding the lips (e.g., [ɔ], [w]).

**Rounded (sounds)** Sounds made with the lips protruding (e.g., [ow], [ɔ]).

**S-structure** *See* **Surface structure.**

**Saccades** The quick and uneven movement of the eyes during reading.

**Salient features** Linguistic variables that are easily perceived by a speech community.

**Schwa** The lax vowel that is characterized by briefer duration than any of the other vowels (also called a **reduced vowel**) (e.g., the underlined vowels in *Canada*, *suppose*).

**Second language acquisition (SLA)** The acquisition of proficiency in a language that is not one's first language.

**Secondary stress** The second most prominent stress in a word.

**Segmental change** Sound change that involves the simplification of a complex consonant (e.g., deaffrication).

**Segments** Individual speech sounds.

**Semantic broadening** The process in which the meaning of a word becomes more inclusive than its earlier form (e.g., *barn* used to mean 'a place to store barley').

**Semantic decomposition** *See* **Componential analysis.**

**Semantic narrowing** The process in which the meaning of a word becomes less inclusive than its earlier form (e.g., *meat* used to mean 'any type of food').

**Semantic shift** The process in which a word loses its former meaning, taking on a new, often related, meaning (e.g., *immoral* used to mean 'not customary').

**Semantics** The study of meaning in human language.

**Semiotics** The study of signs.

**Sensory aphasia** *See* **Fluent aphasia.**

**Sequential change** Sound change that involves sequences of segments (e.g., assimilation).

**Serial processing model** A psycholinguistic theory built around the claim that language processing proceeds in a step by step manner.

**Shibboleth** A word whose pronunciation has become a stereotype for a speech community.

**Shift** A change in a phonological system in which a series of phonemes is systematically modified so that their organization with respect to each other is altered (e.g., the Great English Vowel Shift).

**Sibilants** *See* **Stridents.**

**Sign** A unit of communication structure that consists of two parts: a signifier and something signified.

**Signal** A sign that triggers a specific action on the part of the receiver (e.g., traffic lights).

**Signified** The real world object that a sign represents, as well as the sign's conceptual content.

**Signifier** That part of a sign that stimulates at least one sense organ of the receiver of a message.

**Similarity Differential Rate Hypothesis** The hypothesis that claims that the rates of acquisition for dissimilar phenomena in two languages are faster than for similar phenomena.

**Simple vowels** Vowels that do not show a noticeable change in quality during their production (also called **monophthongs**) (e.g., the vowel sounds of *cab* and *get*).

**Simple word** A word that consists of a single morpheme (e.g., *horse*).

**Single-route model** A psycholinguistic theory built around the claim that a particular type of language processing is accomplished in one manner only.

**Situational code-switching** Switching between languages for clearly identifiable reasons such as reporting the speech of another or when the topic of conversation switches from personal to business affairs.

**Slang** Informal or faddish usages of language.

**Social factor** Non-linguistic factors that are correlated with variation (e.g., [r] is dropped more often by working-class speakers).

**Social isolation** A situation in which a speech community is socially isolated from other speech communities (e.g., the case of African Nova Scotian English).

**Social network** The connections among members of a speech community.

**Social network analysis** The analysis of linguistic variation according to the degree to which speakers participate in social networks.

**Sociality** A dialect spoken by a particular social group.

**Sociolinguistic competence** The subcomponent of Communicative Competence that characterizes the knowledge and skills necessary for second language learners to use language appropriately in a specific situation.

**Sociolinguistic interview** An interview designed to elicit the most natural speech possible from the **consultant**.

**Sociolinguistic norms** Conventions for use of language structures in particular social situations.

**Sociolinguistics** The study of the relationship between language structures as they are used in discourse and the social roles and/or situations associated with them.

**Solidarity** The degree of intimacy or similarity that one group or individual may feel for another.

**Song** In avian communication, lengthy elaborate patterns of mostly pitched sounds.

**Sonorant** A major class feature that characterizes all and only the "singables": vowels, glides, liquids, and nasals.

**Sound shift** The systematic modification of a series of phonemes (e.g., Grimm's Law).

**Specifier** A word that helps to make more precise the meaning of the head of the phrase and that occurs immediately beneath XP (e.g., *the* in *the book*).

**Spectrogram** An acoustic recording that graphically shows the frequency, intensity, and time of sounds.

**Speech community** Any group of people who share a set of conventions for language use.

**Speech event** An identifiable type of discourse associated with a particular speech situation.

**Speech situation** Any circumstance that may involve the use of speech.

**Speech sound** *See* Phone.

**Spelling pronunciation** A source of language change whereby a new pronunciation arises that reflects more closely the spelling of the word (e.g., *often* pronounced as [ɑftən] rather than [ɑfən]).

**Split** A situation in which allophones of the same phoneme come to contrast with each other due to the loss of the conditioning environment, resulting in one or more new phonemes.

**Split brain experiments** Studies that investigate the effects of surgically severing the corpus callosum.

**Spoonerisms** A type of speech error, named after Reverend William A. Spooner, in which words or sounds are re-arranged with often humorous results.

**Spread Glottis ([SG])** A laryngeal feature that distinguishes unaspirated from aspirated sounds.

**Standard variety** The variety of language spoken by the most powerful group in a community and generally held to be "correct" by prescriptive grammarians.

**Status** The social position of a person in relation to others.

**Stem** The base to which an inflectional affix is added (e.g., *modification* is the stem for *-s* in the word *modifications*).

**Stimulus-bound communication** Communication that only occurs when it is triggered by exposure to a certain stimulus or for certain specific ends (e.g., the warning call of a bird).

**Stocks** The groups into which purportedly related language families are placed.

**Stopping** A common substitution process in child language acquisition that involves the replacement of a fricative by a corresponding stop (e.g., *zebra* is pronounced [dibrə]).

**Stops** Sounds made with a complete and momentary closure of airflow through the vocal tract (e.g., the initial sounds of *pleasure* and *grab*).

**Stressed vowels** Vowels that are perceived as relatively more prominent due to the combined effects of pitch, loudness, and length.

**Strident** A place feature that characterizes the "noisy" fricatives and affricates (in English, [s z ʃ ʒ tʃ dʒ]) (also called **sibilants**).

**Stroke** A hemorrhage in the brain or the blockage or rupture of an artery causing brain damage (also called a **cerebrovascular accident**).

**Structurally ambiguous** A property of phrases or sentences whose component words can be combined in more than one way (e.g., *fast cars and motorcycles*).

**Structured variation** Language variation that is correlated with other factors (e.g., age, sex, or SES).

**Style** The level of formality associated with a linguistic structure or set of structures classified along a continuum between most informal to most formal.

**Subcategorization** The classification of words in terms of their complement options (e.g., the verb *devour* is subcategorized for a complement NP).

**Subject** The NP occurring immediately under IP (e.g., *Irene* in *Irene is a tailor*).

**Subset Principle, The** The initial or default setting of a parameter will correspond to the most restrictive option (i.e., the option that permits the fewest patterns).

**Substitution** A type of auditorily based change involving the replacement of one segment with another similar segment (e.g., in the history of English [f] replaced [x] in some words).

**Substitution test** A test used to determine if a group of words is a constituent by replacing them with a single word.

**Substratum influence** The influence of a politically or culturally non-dominant language on a dominant language in the area (e.g., the borrowing of words into English from Amerindian languages).

**Suffix** An affix that is attached to the end of its base (e.g., *-ly* in *quickly*).

**Sulcus** An area where the cerebral cortex is folded in.

**Superstratum influence** The influence of a politically or culturally dominant language on another language in the area (e.g., the effects of Norman French on English during the Middle English period).

**Suppletion** A morphological process that marks a grammatical contrast by replacing a morpheme with an entirely different morpheme (e.g., *be/was*).

**Suprasegmental properties** Those properties of sounds that form part of their makeup no matter what their place or manner of articulation: pitch, loudness, and length (also called **prosodic properties**).

**Surface dyslexia** A type of acquired dyslexia in which the patient seems unable to recognize words as wholes, but must process all words through a set of spelling-to-sound rules (e.g., *yacht* would be pronounced /jætʃt/).

**Surface representations** The form of the word that is actually produced by a speaker.

**Surface structure** The structure that results from the application of whatever transformations are appropriate for the sentence in question.

**Syllabary** A set of syllabic signs used for representing a language.

**Syllabic** A major class feature that characterizes vowels.

**Syllabic liquids** Liquids that function as syllabic nuclei (e.g., the *l* in *bottle*).

**Syllabic nasals** Nasals that function as syllabic nuclei (e.g., the *n* in *button*).

**Syllabic writing** A type of writing in which each symbol represents a syllable.

**Syllable** A unit of linguistic structure that consists of a syllabic element and any segments that are associated with it. (*See also* **Onset, Nucleus, Coda.**)

**Symbolic model** A psycholinguistic theory built around the claim that models of linguistic knowledge make reference to rules and representations consisting of symbols, such as phonemes, words, syntactic category labels, and so forth.

**Symbolic sign** A sign that bears an arbitrary relationship to its referent (e.g., a stop sign, non-onomatopoeic words).

**Symptomatic** Spontaneously and involuntarily conveying an internal state or an emotion, as in crying (a symptomatic sign).

**Syncope** The deletion of a word-internal vowel (e.g., the deletion of the schwa in *police*).

**Synonyms** Words or expressions that have the same meanings in some or all contexts (e.g., *buy* and *purchase*).

**Syntactic category** The category into which an element is placed depending on the type of meaning that it expresses, the type of affixes it takes, and the type of structure in which it occurs (includes both lexical and functional categories).

**Syntactic parser** The theoretical construct that accounts for the human ability to assign grammatical categories and hierarchical structure to elements in a stream of language input.

**Syntax** The system of rules and categories that underlies sentence formation in human language.

**Synthetic language** A language that permits at least some multimorphemic words with non-sentential meanings.

**Systematic gaps** Gaps in the occurring syllable structures of a language that result from the exclusion of certain sequences (e.g., *pfordv* in English).

**Systematic phonetic correspondences** Sound correspondences between two or more related languages that are consistent throughout the vocabularies of those languages.

**T form** A form of address used for people who are close friends—from the French word *tu*.

**Taboo** Words or phrases that are considered to be impolite or that refer to topics that are conventionally avoided (e.g., death).

**Target** In a priming experiment, this is the stimulus to which a subject must respond and for which response accuracy and latency are measured.

**Target language** The language that an L2 learner is learning.

**Teacher talk** *See* Foreigner talk.

**Telegraphic speech** Speech lacking functional categories and bound morphemes.

**Telegraphic stage** The stage in child language acquisition in which children's utterances are generally longer than two words but lack bound morphemes and most functional categories.

**Template** The innate blueprint of birdsong that predisposes birds to perform a general song that is extremely simplified.

**Temporal lobe** The lobe of the brain that lies beneath the lateral fissure and in which Wernicke's area is located.

**Tense (feature)** A dorsal feature that captures the tense-lax distinction among vowels.

**Tense (verb)** A morphological category that encodes the time of a situation with reference to the moment of speaking (e.g., in English, the two-way contrast between past and non-past).

**Terminal (intonation) contour** Falling intonation at the end of an utterance, signalling that the utterance is complete.

**Textual competence** The subcomponent of Communicative Competence that characterizes the knowledge and skills necessary for second language learners to produce and comprehend well-formed texts beyond the sentence level.

***That*-trace filter** A constraint that prohibits the occurrence of a complementizer + trace sequence.

**Thematic grid** The part of a word's lexical entry that carries information about the thematic roles it assigns.

**Thematic role** A label (such as agent, theme, goal, etc.) used to categorize the relation between the parts of a sentence and the event that the sentence describes.

**Theme** The thematic role of the entity directly affected by the action designated by the verb (e.g., *the ball* in *Tom caught the ball*).

**Thyroid cartilage** The cartilage that forms the main portion of the larynx, spreading outward like the head of a plow.

**Tiers** Levels on the feature hierarchy that reflect the relation of the nodes and features to each other.

**Tip (of the tongue)** The narrow area at the front of the tongue.

**Token** A single instantiation of a variable.

**Tone** Pitch movement in spoken utterances that is related to differences in word meaning.

**Tone language** A language in which differences in word meaning are signalled by differences in pitch.

**Top-down processing** A type of processing using a set of expectations to guide phonetic processing and word recognition.

**Topic** What a sentence or group of sentences is about.

**Trace** The empty element, marked by the symbol *t*, that is left in syntactic structure after an element has been moved.

**Trachea** The tube below the larynx through which air travels when it leaves the lungs; commonly known as the windpipe.

**Transfer** The process by which the first language (L1) influences the interlanguage grammar.

**Transfer error** An error made by a second language learner that can be traced to the first language.

**Transformation** A type of syntactic rule that can move an element from one position to another.

**Transformational grammar** A widely accepted approach to syntactic analysis in which syntactic phenomena are described with the help of transformations (also called **generative grammar**).

**Transitive** A verb that takes an NP complement (a direct object) (e.g., *hit*).

**Tree structure** A diagram depicting the internal organization of a linguistic unit such as a word, phrase, or sentence.

**Trill** An *r*-like sound that is made by passing air over the raised tongue tip, allowing it to vibrate.

**Truth conditions** The circumstances under which a sentence is true.

**Turn-taking** The change-over between speakers' turns in a conversation.

**Typological plausibility** A criterion that guides language reconstruction by referring to universals or existing properties of language.

**Umlaut** A phonological change in Germanic languages that results in the fronting of a vowel in the root under the influence of a front vowel in a suffix.

**Underextension** A developmental phenomenon in which a child uses a lexical item to denote only a subset of the items that it denotes in adult speech (e.g., *car* used to refer only to moving cars).

**Underlying representations** *See* **phonemic representation**.

**Universal Grammar (UG)** The innate system of categories, operations and principles that are shared by all languages.

**Universal tendencies** Patterns or traits that occur in all or most languages.

**Unmarked traits** Those characteristics of language that are considered to be less complex and/or universally more common in languages.

**Unrounded (sounds)** Sounds made without rounding of the lips.

**Utterance** The minimal unit of speech required to state a proposition.

**Uvula** The small fleshy flap of tissue that hangs down from the velum.

**Uvulars** Sounds made with the tongue near or touching the uvula.

**V form** A form of address used for people who are not close friends—from the French word *vous*.

**Variable** A set of forms, any of which may be used to express the same function or meaning and the use of which cannot be expressed by a categorical rule.

**Variant** One of a set of several possible forms that can be used to express the same function or meaning.

**Variationist sociolinguistics** The branch of linguistics that seeks to explain variation in language.

**Variety** A cover term used to refer to language used by a particular speech community; it merely implies that some set of sociolinguistic norms is present.

**Velars** Sounds made with the tongue touching or near the velum (e.g., [ŋ], [k]).

**Velum** The soft area towards the rear of the roof of the mouth.

**Verb (V)** A lexical category that typically designates actions, sensations, and states, can usually be inflected for tense, and functions as the head of a verb phrase (e.g., *see, feel, remain*).

**Verbal paradigm** The set of inflected forms associated with a verb (also called a **conjugation**).

**Vernacular** The variety used by a speaker in the most informal style; generally hypothesized to be the one that they first acquired.

**Vocal cords** *See* Vocal folds.

**Vocal folds** A set of muscles inside the larynx that may be positioned in various ways to produce different glottal states (also called **vocal cords**).

**Vocal tract** The oral cavity, nasal cavity, and pharynx.

**Voice** A laryngeal feature that distinguishes between voiced and voiceless sounds.

**Voiced** The glottal state in which the vocal folds are brought close together, but not tightly closed, causing air passing through them to vibrate (e.g., [æ], [z], [m] are voiced).

**Voiceless** The glottal state in which the vocal folds are pulled apart, allowing air to pass directly through the glottis (e.g., [t], [s], [f] are voiceless).

**Voicing** A historical process in which a voiceless sound becomes voiced.

**Voicing assimilation** Assimilation in which one segment becomes more like a nearby segment in terms of voicing (e.g., liquid-glide devoicing in English).

**Vowel reduction** A process that reduces a full vowel, typically unstressed, to a schwa.

**Vowels** Sounds that are produced with little obstruction in the vocal tract and that are generally voiced.

**Weakening (phonetic)** A process that weakens a segment according to a particular scale of strength.

**Weakening (semantic)** The process in which the meaning of a word weakens (e.g., *soon* used to mean 'immediately' but now means 'in the near future').

**Wernicke's aphasia** The aphasia that results in fluent but nonsensical speech, sometimes characterized by jargonaphasia.

***Wh* movement** A transformation that moves a *wh* phrase to the beginning of the sentence, formulated as: Move a *wh* phrase to the specifier position under CP.

***Wh* question** A sentence that begins with a *wh*-word (e.g., *Who did you see?*).

**Whisper** The glottal state in which the vocal folds are adjusted so that the front portions are pulled close together, while the back portions are apart.

**Word manufacture** The creation of a word from scratch, sometimes with the help of a computer (also called **coinage**) (e.g., *Kodak*).

**Word-based morphology** Morphology in which most complex words are formed from a base that can itself be a word.

**Words** The smallest free forms found in language.

**Writing** The representation of language by graphic signs or symbols.

**X' schema** The blueprint for the internal structure of phrases.

***Yes-no* question** A question for which the expected response is "yes" or "no."

**Zero derivation** *See* Conversion.

# Sources

## Chapter 1

The discussion of word creation is based on an article by Eve Clark and Herb Clark, "When Nouns Surface As Verbs" in *Language* 55:767–811 (1979). The Walbiri data are based on K. Hale's article "Person Marking in Walbiri" in *A Festschrift for Morris Halle*, edited by S. Anderson and P. Kiparsky (New York: Holt, Rinehart and Winston, 1973). The quote at the end of section 1.3.2 is from the book by Steven Pinker titled *The Language Instinct: How the Human Mind Creates Language* (New York: Morrow, 1994), p. 370. The 1857 speech on the status of Canadian English is cited in Mark Orkin's *Speaking Canadian English* (Toronto: General Publishing Company, 1970). The data on word order preferences is from *Typology and Universals* by William Croft (New York: Cambridge University Press, 1990), p. 46. Derek Bickerton's *Language and Species* (Chicago: University of Chicago Press, 1990) and Steven Pinker's *The Language Instinct: How the Human Mind Creates Language* (New York: Morrow, 1994) provide different views of the emergence of language in the human species.

The exercises for this chapter were prepared by Joyce Hildebrand.

To access this section online, please see the Companion Website at **www.pearsoned.ca/ogrady**, chapter 1.

## Chapter 2

Information on the International Phonetic Alphabet can be obtained from the International Phonetic Association, University College, Gower Street, London, WC1E 6BT, UK (website: www.arts.gla.ac.uk/IPA/ipa.html). The estimate of 600 consonants and 200 vowels comes from Peter Ladefoged in a talk given at the University of Hawaii, April 27, 1999. Sarcee data are taken from E.-D. Cook, "Vowels and Tones in Sarcee" in *Language* 47:164–79; Gaelic data are courtesy of James Galbraith. Bini data are adapted from *A Course in Phonetics,* 4th ed., by P. Ladefoged (Toronto: Harcourt, 2001). For a discussion of glottal states, see Jimmy G. Harris, "The State of the Glottis for Voiceless Plosives" in *Proceedings of the 14th International Congress of Phonetic Sciences,* Vol. 3, pp. 2041–44.

To access this section online, please see the Companion Website at **www.pearsoned.ca/ogrady**, chapter 2.

## Chapter 3

A classic and still valuable presentation of phonemic analysis is found in H.A. Gleason, Jr.'s *An Introduction to Descriptive Linguistics* (Toronto: Holt, Rinehart and Winston, 1961). Syllabification and tone are drawn from numerous sources, all summarized by John Goldsmith in *Autosegmental and Metrical Phonology* (Cambridge, MA: Blackwell, 1990). The Malay data are adapted from M. Kenstowicz and C. Kisseberth, *Generative Phonology* (New York: Academic Press, 1979) with additional examples provided by S.L. Lee (personal communication).

Data sources for problems are as follows: for Inuktitut, B. Harnum (personal communication); for Mokilese, S. Harrison's *Mokilese Reference Grammar* (Honolulu: University of Hawaii Press,

1976); for Tamil, R. Radhakrishnan (personal communication); for Gascon, R.C. Kelly's *A Descriptive Analysis of Gascon* (Amsterdam: Mouton, 1978); for Cree, Y. Carifelle and M. Pepper (personal communication); for Canadian French, D.C. Walker's *The Pronunciation of Canadian French* (Ottawa: University of Ottawa Press, 1984) and A. Teasdale (personal communication); for English fast speech, G. Zhang, *Phonological Representation and Analyses of Fast Speech Phenomena in English*, M.A. thesis, Memorial University of Newfoundland, 1994.

To access this section online, please see the Companion Website at **www.pearsoned.ca/ogrady**, chapter 3.

# Chapter 4

The estimate that the average high school student knows 60 000 "basic" words come from *The Language Instinct* by S. Pinker (New York: Morrow, 1994), p. 150. The introduction to words and morphemes draws on the classic treatments found in L. Bloomfield's *Language* (New York: Holt, Rinehart and Winston, 1933), H.A. Gleason's *An Introduction to Descriptive Linguistics* (New York: Holt, Rinehart and Winston, 1966), and C. F. Hockett's *A Course in Modern Linguistics* (New York: Macmillan, 1958). The discussion of word formation seeks to portray those aspects of recent and current work that represent widely accepted views and are appropriate for presentation in an introductory textbook. Much of this work is summarized in the following books: *Morphology: Word Structure in Generative Grammar* by John Jensen (Amsterdam: John Benjamins Publishing, 1990), *Morphology* by Francis Katamba (London: Macmillan, 1993), and *Morphological Theory* by Andrew Spencer (Cambridge, MA: Blackwell, 1991), and the many references cited therein. For a detailed discussion on non-concatenative morphology, see *A-Morphous Morphology* by S. Anderson (New York: Cambridge University Press, 1992).

The Arabic examples in section 4.1.2 are from p. 17 of the book by Spencer cited above. The tier-based analysis of Arabic word structure is based on work by John McCarthy, including his article "A Prosodic Theory of Nonconcatenative Morphology," in *Linguistic Inquiry* 12: 373–418 (1981). The facts concerning the requirement that *-ant* combine with a base of Latin origin (section 4.2.1) are noted on p. 71 of the book by Katamba cited above.

The examples of conversion given in section 4.5.2 come largely from the discussion in the books by Jensen (cited above, pp. 92–93) and pp. 229–31 of *English Word-Formation* by Laurie Bauer (New York: Cambridge University Press, 1983). The examples of Malay blends come from "Malay Blends—CV or Syllable Templates" by M. Dobrovolsky, unpublished ms., University of Calgary. The data on Slavey onomatopoeia is from "Slavey Expressive Terms" by M. Pepper, *Kansas Working Papers in Linguistics* 10:85–100 (1985).

The definition of stem introduced in section 4.4 is from the article by S. Anderson, "Morphological Theory," in *Linguistics: The Cambridge Survey*, Vol. 1, edited by F. Newmeyer, p. 163 (New York: Cambridge University Press, 1988). The discussion of the difference between regular and irregular inflection draws on information from "Rules of Language" by S. Pinker in *Science* 253:530–35 (August 1991). The data in the section on tense come principally from "Tense, Aspect and Mood" by S. Chung and A. Timberlake in *Language Typology and Syntactic Description,* Vol. 3, edited by T. Shopen (London: Cambridge University Press, 1985), pp. 202–58.

The examples used in the section on morphophonemics were taken from the discussion of this subject written by Michael Dobrovolsky for the third edition of this book.

Exercises 1 to 18 were prepared by Joyce Hildebrand. The data in problem 13 is from *Writing Transformational Grammars* by A. Koutsoudas (New York: McGraw-Hill, 1966).

To access this section online, please see the Companion Website at **www.pearsoned.ca/ ogrady**, chapter 4.

# Chapter 5

Transformational syntax is the most popular of the half-dozen major contemporary syntactic theories. Traditionally, it is the theory taught in introductory linguistics courses, both because it is so widely used and because many of the other approaches that exist today have developed in response to it. The particular system outlined here involves a variety of simplifications to make it appropriate for presentation in an introductory course.

The system of subcategorization employed here is loosely based on the one outlined in *Generalized Phrase Structure Grammar* by G. Gazdar, E. Klein, G. Pullum, and I. Sag (Cambridge, MA: Harvard University Press, 1979), which describes a non-transformational approach to syntax.

The information on inversion in Appalachian English comes from *Appalachian Speech* by Walt Wolfram and Donna Christian (Arlington, VA: Center for Applied Linguistics, 1976).

The discussion of the relational analysis of passive sentences on the website is intended to be neutral between Lexical Functional Grammar as outlined in *The Mental Representation of Grammatical Relations*, edited by Joan Bresnan (Cambridge, MA: MIT Press, 1978) and Relational Grammar as described in "Toward a Universal Characterization of Passivization" by D. Perlmutter and P. Postal in *Studies in Relational Grammar I*, edited by D. Perlmutter (Chicago: University of Chicago Press, 1983); the Chinese and Tzotzil examples cited in **www.pearsoned.ca/ogrady** were taken from this paper. The functional analysis of passives on the website draws on the discussion in *Functional Syntax* by Susumu Kuno (Chicago: University of Chicago Press, 1981) and *Functional Syntax and Universal Grammar* by W. Foley and R. Van Valin (New York: Cambridge University Press, 1980).

The exercises for this chapter were prepared by Joyce Hildebrand.

To access this section online, please see the Companion Website at **www.pearsoned.ca/ ogrady**, chapter 5.

# Chapter 6

Surveys of the nature of word meaning and semantic relations can be found in many introductory books on semantics, including those recommended below. A prominent advocate of componential analysis is Ray Jackendoff, whose book *Semantic Structures* (Cambridge, MA: MIT Press, 1991) reviews earlier ideas and offers new proposals. The discussion of a semantic constraint on double object patterns draws on the proposal put forward by Steven Pinker in *Learnability and Cognition* (Cambridge, MA: MIT Press, 1989). The discussion of fuzzy categories and graded membership in section 6.2 draws from Part 1 of *Women, Fire, and Dangerous Things* by G. Lakoff (Chicago: University of Chicago Press, 1987) and the references cited there. The discussion of metaphor takes as its starting point the book *Metaphors We Live By* by G. Lakoff and Mark Johnson (Chicago: University of Chicago Press, 1982). The four Inuktitut words for *snow* in table 6.7 are from *The Handbook of American Indian Languages* by F. Boas (Washington: Smithsonian Institution, 1911); for a longer list of words for *snow*, see *Dictionnaire français-eskimau du parler de l'Ungava* (Québec: Presses de l'Université Laval, 1970); see also "The Great Eskimo Vocabulary Hoax" by G. Pullum in *Natural Language and Linguistic Theory* 7:275–81 (1989). The discussion of verbs of motion is based on the paper "Lexicalization Patterns: Semantic Structure in Lexical Form" by L. Talmy in *Language Typology and Syntactic Description*, Vol. 3, edited by T. Shopen (New York: Cambridge University Press, 1985), pp. 57–149. Data on Hidatsa assertion morphemes in the same section is from *Hidatsa Syntax* by G.H. Matthews (The Hague: Mouton, 1965).

The treatment of structural ambiguity, thematic role assignment, and pronoun interpretation in this chapter presents slightly simplified versions of views widely held within generative grammar in the early 1990s. For a summary of the last two issues, see *Introduction to Government and Binding Theory*, 2nd ed., by L. Haegeman (Cambridge, MA: Blackwell, 1994). The discussion of constructional meaning is based on *Constructions: A Construction Grammar Approach to Argument Structure* by A. Goldberg (Chicago: University of Chicago Press, 1995).

The data used in the discussion of deixis and in exercise 15 come from "Deixis" by S. Anderson and E. Keenan in *Language Typology and Syntactic Description*, Vol. 3, edited by T. Shopen (New York: Cambridge University Press, 1985), pp. 259–308. The discussion of topicalization draws on the "Major Functions of the Noun Phrase" by A. Andrews in *Language Typology and Syntactic Description*, Vol. 1, edited by T. Shopen (New York: Cambridge University Press, 1985), pp. 62–154. The discussion of the Cooperative Principle and the maxims of conversation is based primarily on "Logic and Conversation" by Paul Grice in *Syntax and Semantics*, Vol. 3, edited by P. Cole and J. Morgan (New York: Academic Press, 1975), pp. 41–58 and the paper "Pragmatic Theory" by L. Horn, in *Linguistics: The Cambridge Survey*, Vol. 1, edited by F. Newmeyer, 113–45 (New York: Cambridge University Press).

The exercises for this chapter were prepared by Joyce Hildebrand.

To access this section online, please see the Companion Website at **www.pearsoned.ca/ ogrady**, chapter 6.

# Chapter 7

The textbooks by Anttila, Campbell, Hock, Labov, and Trask provide much more detailed discussions of most of the major topics in this chapter: Raimo Anttila, *Historical and Comparative Linguistics,* 2nd ed. (Amsterdam: John Benjamins, 1989); Lyle Campbell, *Historical Linguistics: An Introduction* (Cambridge, MA: MIT Press, 1999); Hans Henrich Hock, *Principles of Historical Linguistics,* 2nd ed. (Amsterdam: Mouton de Gruyter, 1992); William Labov, *Principles of Linguistic Change: Internal Factors* (Oxford: Blackwell, 1994); R.L. Trask, *Historical Linguistics* (London: Arnold, 1996). They are also excellent sources for references relating to particular topics. Hock is particularly important for providing detailed discussions of syntactic change and the role of typology in reconstruction.

Overviews of historical linguistics as it applies to the development of English are presented in *A History of the English Language* by N.F. Blake (Houndmills, UK: Macmillan, 1996), in *A Biography of the English Language*, 2nd ed., by C.M. Millward (New York: Holt, Rinehart and Winston, 1996), and in *An Historical Study of English: Function, Form and Change* by Jeremy Smith (New York: Routledge, 1996).

The catalogue of sound changes is adapted from catalogues proposed by Theo Vennemann in the article "Linguistic Typologies in Historical Linguistics" in *Società di linguistica italiana* 23:87–91

(1985) and a book entitled *Preference Laws for Syllable Structure and the Explanation of Sound Change* (Amsterdam: Mouton de Gruyter, 1988). Section 7.2 has also benefited from unpublished material (particularly the manuscript "Linguistic Change") kindly made available by Theo Vennemann (University of Munich) to the author during his stay in Munich from 1980–85.

The data on vowel laxing in Canadian French are from Douglas C. Walker's book *The Pronunciation of Canadian French* (Ottawa: University of Ottawa Press, 1984). The data on word order in Old and Middle English come from the book by Joseph Williams, *Origins of the English Language: A Social and Linguistic History* (New York: Free Press, 1975). The examples of English loan words in Gwich'in (Loucheux) are given in *Dene* 1(1): (1985), published by the Dene Language Terminology Committee, Yellowknife, The Northwest Territories. The discussion of borrowing and semantic change in English draws on materials in the book by Williams.

The table depicting lexical diffusion of the stress change in English nouns derived from verbs is taken from the book by Jean Aitchison, *Language Change: Progress or Decay?* (New York: Universe Books, 1985). Aitchison's remarks are based on the article by M. Chen and W. Wang, "Sound Change: Actuation and Implementation" in *Language* 51:255–81 (1975). The data on the realization of [s] as [h] in Spanish were provided by Herbert Izzo of the University of Calgary.

The Germanic cognates used to illustrate family relationships are based on Leonard Bloomfield's classic work, *Language* (New York: Holt, Rinehart and Winston, 1933). Some of the Romance cognates in this section come from *Proto-Romance Phonology* by Robert A. Hall, Jr. (New York: Elsevier, 1976). The quote from Jones is taken from *A Reader in Nineteenth-Century Historical Indo-European Linguistics,* edited and translated by Winfred P. Lehmann (Bloomington, IN: Indiana University Press, 1967) and the quote from Rask is taken from Holger Pedersen's book *The Discovery of Language: Linguistic Science in the Nineteenth Century* (Bloomington, IN: Indiana University Press, 1959).

Exercise 2 is based on data provided by Dr. George Patterson, whose generosity we hereby acknowledge. The data for exercises 3 and 4 are from F. Columbus's *Introductory Workbook in Historical Phonology* (Cambridge, MA: Slavica, 1974). Exercise 10 is based on data provided by David Bellusci. The data for exercise 18 are drawn from *Source Book for Linguistics* by W. Cowan and J. Rakusan (Philadelphia: John Benjamins, 1987).

To access this section online, please see the Companion Website at **www.pearsoned.ca/ ogrady**, chapter 7.

# Chapter 8

The section on the threat to linguistic diversity was written by William O'Grady. It draws heavily on information in *Vanishing Voices: The Extinction of the World's Languages* by Daniel Nettle and Suzanne Romaine. Additional information can be found at the websites of Ethnologue (www.ethnologue.com) and Terralingua (www.terralingua.org).

The section on linguistic typology draws on data from the book by B. Comrie, *The Languages of the Soviet Union* (London: Cambridge University Press, 1981) and from the book by J. Greenberg, *The Languages of Africa* (Bloomington, IN: Indiana University Press, 1966). Other material for this section comes from *Tone: A Linguistic Survey*, edited by V. Fromkin (New York: Academic Press, 1978); J. Hawkins' article "On Implicational and Distributional Universals of Word Order" in *Journal of Linguistics* 16:193–235 (1980); M. Dryer's article "The Greenbergian Word Order Correlations" in *Language* 68:81–138 (1992); *Patterns of Sounds* by I. Maddieson (Cambridge: Cambridge University Press, 1984); M. Ruhlen's book *A Guide to the Languages of the World* (Language Universals Project: Stanford University, 1976); *The World's Major Languages*, edited by B. Comrie (Oxford: Oxford University Press, 1990), and the four-volume series *Universals of Human Language*, edited by J. Greenberg (Stanford, California: Stanford University Press, 1978).

The discussion of morphological typology draws on information presented in B. Comrie's book, mentioned above. The estimate of the relative frequency of languages in which the subject precedes the direct object is based on information in W. Croft, *Typology and Universals* (New York: Cambridge University Press, 1990). The data on OVS and OSV languages is from "Object-Initial Languages" by D. Derbyshire and G. Pullum, *International Journal of American Linguistics* 47:192–214 (1981). The discussion of consonant systems in section 8.2.4 is based on "Phonetic Universals in Consonant Systems" by B. Lindblom and I. Maddieson in *Language, Speech and Mind: Studies in Honor of Victoria Fromkin*, edited by L. Hyman and C. Li, 62–78 (New York: Routledge & Kegan Paul, 1988).

The section on language families is based on the books by B. Comrie and J. Greenberg mentioned above, the book by M. Ruhlen cited above and another book by Ruhlen titled *A Guide to the World's Languages. Volume 1: Classification* (Stanford: Stanford University Press, 1987), and C.F. and F.M. Voegelin's *Classification and Index of the World's Languages* (New York: Elsevier). Additional data derive from C.D. Buck's book *A Dictionary of Selected Synonyms in the Principal Indo-European Languages* (Chicago: University of Chicago Press, 1949); *The American Heritage Dictionary of Indo-European Roots*, revised and edited by C. Watkins (Boston: Houghton Mifflin Company, 1985); the three-volume *Russisches Etymologisches Wörterbuch* compiled by M. Vasmer (Heidelberg: Carl Winter Universitätsverlag); "Syntactic Reconstruction and Finno-Ugric," an article by L. Campbell in *Historical Linguistics 1987*, edited by H. Andersen and K. Koerner (Amsterdam: John Benjamins, 1990), and the Proto-Baltic Dictionary database developed by the author of this chapter.

To access this section online, please see the Companion Website at **www.pearsoned.ca/ ogrady**, chapter 8.

# Chapter 9

The discussion of the genetic relationships among Aboriginal languages draws on John Wesley Powell's article "Indian Linguistic Families of America North of Mexico" in the *Seventh Annual Report, Bureau of American Ethnology* (1891); Edward Sapir's article, "Central and North American Languages" in *Encyclopedia Britannica*, 14th ed., Vol. 5, pp. 138–41 (1929); C.F. and F.M. Voegelin's work, *Map of North American Indian Languages* (Washington, DC: American Ethnology Society, 1966); the article "Canada's Indigenous Languages: Past and Present" by Michael Foster in *Language and Society,* 7:3–16 (Ottawa: Commissioner of Official Languages, 1982); *Handbook of North American Indians*, Vol. 17: *Languages*, edited by Ives Goddard (Washington, DC: Smithsonian Institution, 1996); and Lyle Campbell's book *American Indian Languages: The Historical Linguistics of Native America* (Oxford: Oxford University Press, 1997). The Sapir article has been reprinted in *Selected Writings of Edward Sapir*, edited by D. Mandelbaum (Berkeley, CA: University of California Press, 1949). The Amerind hypothesis is presented by J. Greenberg in his book *Language in the Americas* (Stanford, CA: Stanford University Press, 1987). For some sample criticism, see Campbell's book cited above. The Dakota classification provided is from D. Parks and R. DeMallie in "Sioux, Assiniboine, and Stoney Dialects: A Classification" in *Anthropological Linguistics* 34:233–55 (1992).

Overall Aboriginal population estimates are from Statistics Canada's *Aboriginal Peoples of Canada: A Demographic Profile* (January 21, 2003, report on the 2001 Census) and from Thornton Russell's "Population History of North American Indians" in *A History of Population in North America*, edited by M. Haines and R. Steckel (New York: Cambridge University Press, 2000). The estimates of speaker populations reported here are based primarily on the following sources: Statistics Canada's 2001 Census (report dated December 10, 2002); Michael Foster's article cited above; D.M. Kinkade's article "The Decline of Native Languages in Canada" in *Endangered Languages*, edited by R.H. Robins and E.M. Uhlenbeck (New York: Berg, 1991), pp. 157–76; E.-D. Cook's article "Aboriginal Languages: A History" in *Language in Canada*, edited by J. Edwards (New York: Cambridge University Press, 1998), pp. 125–43; B.F. Grimes's *Ethnologue, 14th Edition* (SIL International, 2000); Michael Krauss's "The Indigenous Languages of the North: A Report on their Present State," *Northern Minority Languages: Problems of Survival*, edited by H. Shoji and J. Junhunen (Osaka, Japan: Senri Ethnological Studies 44, National Museum of Ethnology, 1997), pp. 1–34; Marianne Mithun's book *The Languages of Native North America* (Cambridge, UK: Cambridge University Press, 2001); the Yukon Native Language Centre at the Yukon College in Whitehorse; the Alaska Native Language Center; and numerous expert consultations.

Michif information is from P. Bakker's *A Language of Our Own: The Genesis of Michif, the Mixed Cree-French Language of the Canadian Métis* (Toronto: Oxford University Press, 1997). The data on Dëne Sųłiné vowels comes from F.K. Li's article "Chipewyan" in *Linguistic Structures of Native America* by H. Hoijer et al. (Viking Fund Publications in Anthropology, No. 6, 1946) and E.-D. Cook's article "Chipewyan Vowels" in *International Journal of American Linguistics* 49:413–27 (1983). The data on Cree are from H.C. Wolfart's "Sketch of Cree, an Algonquian language" in *Handbook of North American Indians*, Vol. 17: *Languages*, edited by Ives Goddard (Washington, DC: Smithsonian Institution, 1996), pp. 390–439, and from C.H. Wolfart and J. Carroll's book *Meet Cree: A Guide to the Cree Language*, 2nd rev. ed. (Edmonton: University of Alberta Press, 1981). Mohawk data are from M.C. Baker, *The Polysynthesis Parameter* (New York: Oxford University Press, 1996).

Organizations such as the Saskatchewan Indian Cultural Centre, the Yinka Dene Language Institute (especially Bill Poser), and Aboriginal Languages of Manitoba (especially Carol Beaulieu) provided helpful data.

To access this section online, please see the Companion Website at **www.pearsoned.ca/ ogrady**, chapter 9.

# Chapter 10

For more information on the misinterpretation of *every*, see "Quantifying Kids" by Bart Geurts in *Language Acquisition* 11:197–218 (2003).

Pioneering work on infant perception is reported in "Developmental Studies of Speech Perception" by P. Eimas in *Infant Perception*, edited by L. Cohen and P. Salapatek (New York: Academic Press, 1975). More recent work is reported by J. Mehler, E. Dupoux, T. Nazzi, and G. Dehaene-Lambertz in "Coping with Linguistic Diversity: The Infant's Viewpoint" and by J. Werker, V. Lloyd, J. Pegg, and Linda Polka in "Putting the Baby in the Bootstraps: Toward a More Complete Understanding of the Role of the Input in Infant Speech Processing," both in *Signal to Syntax*, edited by J. Morgan and K. Demuth (Mahwah, NJ: Erlbaum, 1996). The ability to use phonetic contrasts to distinguish between words is examined in "Perception and Production in Child Phonology: The Testing of Four Hypotheses" by M. Edwards in *Journal of Child Language* 1:205–19 (1974). The cross-linguistic data on babbling are summarized and discussed on pp. 9–11 of *Phonological Acquisition and Change* by J. Locke (San Diego: Academic Press, 1983); see also "Adaptation to Language: Evidence from Babbling and First Words in Four Languages" by B. de Boysson-Bardies and M. Vihman in *Language* 67:297–319 (1991). For a recent discussion of the relevance of babbling to the development of control over the vocal tract, see S. Pinker's *The Language Instinct* (New York: Morrow, 1994), p. 266. Differences between children's production and perception of speech sounds are found in *The Acquisition of Phonology: A Case Study* by N. Smith (New York: Cambridge University Press, 1973); the "*fis* phenomenon" is reported in "Psycholinguistic Research Methods" by J. Berko and R. Brown in *Handbook of Research Methods in Child Development*, edited by P. Mussen (New York: John Wiley and Sons, 1960). David Ingram's *Phonological Disability in Children* (London: Edward Arnold, 1976) contains many useful examples of early phonetic processes. The discussion of syllable deletion draws on information in "A Role for Stress in Early Speech Segmentation" by C. Echols, in *Signal to Syntax*, edited by J. Morgan and K. Demuth (Mahwah, NJ: Erlbaum, 1996) and in "The Acquisition of Prosodic Structure: An Investigation of Current Accounts of Children's Prosodic Development" by M. Kehoe and C. Stoel-Gammon in *Language* 73:13–44 (1997). The data on developmental order for speech sounds comes from chapter 8 of *First Language Acquisition: Method, Description and Explanation* by D. Ingram (New York: Cambridge University Press, 1989).

The sample fifty-word vocabulary in section 10.3 is from p. 149 of the book by Ingram cited above. For a brief survey on work on rate of vocabulary development, see *How Children Learn Language* (pp. 7–8), by William O'Grady (Cambridge, UK: Cambridge University Press, 2005). Differences among children in terms of the types of words in their early vocabulary were first noted by K. Nelson in "Structure and Strategy in Learning to Talk" in *Monographs of the Society for Research in Child Development* 38 (149):1–135 (1973). The "*dax* experiment" on proper and common nouns is reported by N. Katz, E. Baker, and J. Macnamara in their article, "What's in a Name? A Study of How Children Learn Common and Proper Nouns" in *Child Development* 45:469–73 (1974); the "*tiv* experiment" is from "The Child as Word Learner" by S. Carey in *Linguistic Theory and Psychological Reality*, edited by M. Halle, J. Bresnan, and G. Miller (Cambridge, MA: MIT Press, 1978). The discussion of strategies for learning word meaning is based on the proposals outlined in *Categorization and Naming in Children: Problems of Induction* by E. Markman (Cambridge, MA: MIT Press, 1989). The contrast between overextension in production and comprehension is described on pp. 152–53 of the book by Ingram cited above. The report of overextension in the speech of Allen is based on the discussion on p. 92 of *The Lexicon in Acquisition* by Eve Clark (New York: Cambridge University Press, 1993). The experimental study on overextension was carried out by J. Thomson and R. Chapman and reported in "Who is 'Daddy' Revisited: The Status of Two-Year-Olds' Over-extended Words in Use and Comprehension" in *Journal of Child Language* 4:359–75 (1977). The experiment on *pour* and *fill* can be found in "Syntax and Semantics in the Acquisition of Locative Verbs" by J. Gropen, S. Pinker, M. Hollander, and R. Goldberg in *Journal of Child Language* 18:115–51 (1991). The experiment on dimensional terms was carried out by P. Harris and J. Morris and is reported in "The Early Acquisition of Spatial Adjectives: A Cross-linguistic Study" in *Journal of Child Language* 13:335–52 (1986).

The remarks on inflectional overgeneralization are based in part on *Overregularization in Language Acquisition* by G. Marcus, S. Pinker, M. Ullman, M. Hollander, T. Rosen, and F. Xu, *Monographs of the Society for Research in Child Development*, Serial No. 228, Vol. 57, No. 4 (1992).

The pioneering work on the developmental order for English bound morphemes and lexical categories was done by R. Brown and reported in his book *A First Language: The Early Stages* (Cambridge, MA: Harvard University Press, 1973); see also "Universal and Particular in the Acquisition of Language" by D. Slobin in *Language Acquisition: The State of the Art*, edited by E. Wanner and L. Gleitman (New York: Cambridge University Press, 1982). The original "*wug* test" was done by J. Berko and is reported in her article "The Child's Learning of English Morphology" in *Word* 14:150–77 (1958). The work on the development of derivational affixes and compounding in English is based on information reported in the book by Eve Clark recommended below and in the article by E. Clark and B. Hecht, "Learning to Coin Agent and Instrument Nouns" in *Cognition* 12:1–24 (1982). The data on the acquisition of the prohibition against inflection within compounds is from "Level-Ordering in Lexical Development" by P. Gordon in *Cognition* 21:73–93 (1985). Word order errors within compounds are reported in "Coining Complex Compounds in English: Affixes and Word Order in Acquisition" by E. Clark, B. Hecht, and R. Mulford in *Linguistics* 24:7–29 (1986).

The data on four year olds' preference for SVO word order with nonsense verbs is from "Characterizing English-Speaking Children's Understanding of SVO Word Order" by Nameera Akhtar in *Journal of Child Language* 26:339–56 (1999). The early sensitivity to the difference between *is V-ing* and *can V-ing* is documented in "Sensitivity to Discontinuous Dependencies in Language Learners" by Lynn Santelmann and Peter Jusczyk in *Cognition* 69:105–34 (1998). The data on the development of question structures is based on the classic article by E. Klima and U. Bellugi, "Syntactic Regularities in the Speech of Children in *Psycholinguistic Papers*, edited by J. Lyons and R. Wales (Edinburgh: Edinburgh University Press, 1966). The auxiliary copying error in question structures is the subject of an experiment reported by M. Nakayama, "Performance Factors in Subject-Auxiliary Inversion," *Journal of Child Language* 14:113–26 (1987). The developmental order for *Wh* words is documented by L. Bloom, S. Merkin, and J. Wootten, "*Wh* Questions: Linguistic Factors That Contribute to the Sequence of Acquisition," *Child Development* 53:1084–92 (1982). For a discussion of the absence of inversion in *why* questions, see "Language Acquisition Is Language Change" by Stephen Crain, Takuya Goro, and Rosalind Thornton in *Journal of Psycholinguistic Research* 35:31–49 (2006). Other descriptions confirming the main points of this account can be found in chapter 9 of the book by Ingram cited above. The data on the acquisition of passive structures come from a study by E. Turner and R. Rommetveit, reported in their article "The Acquisition of Sentence Voice and Reversibility" in *Child Development* 38:650–60 (1967). The data on children's use of *me* and *myself* comes from "Children's Knowledge of Binding and Coreference: Evidence from Spontaneous Speech" by P. Bloom, A. Barss, J. Nicol, and L. Conway in *Language* 70: 53–71 (1994).

The role of correction in language development is examined in "Derivational Complexity and the Order of Acquisition in Child Speech" by R. Brown and C. Hanlon in *Cognition and the Development of Language*, edited by J. Hayes (New York: John Wiley and Sons, 1970). The data on mothers' reactions to children's ungrammatical and grammatical utterances comes from "Brown and Hanlon Revisited: Mothers' Sensitivity to Ungrammatical Forms" by K. Hirsh-Pasek, R. Treiman, and M. Schneiderman in *Journal of Child Language* 11:81–88 (1984). The relationship between *yes-no* questions in maternal speech and the development of auxiliaries is discussed by E. Newport, H. Gleitman, and L. Gleitman in their article, "Mother, I'd Rather Do It Myself: Some Effects and Noneffects of Maternal Speech Style" in *Talking to Children*, edited by C. Snow and C. Ferguson (New York: Cambridge University Press, 1977); see also the discussion in the book by Gallaway and Richards recommended below. The "other one spoon" example is reported on p. 161 of an article by M. Braine, "The Acquisition of Language in Infant and Child," in *The Learning of Language*, edited by C.E. Reed (New York: Appleton-Century-Crofts, 1971). The recast experiment involving nonsense verbs is from "The Contrast Theory of Negative Evidence" by M. Saxton in *Journal of Child Language* 24:139–61 (1997).

The description of Genie and of Rick is based on "Abnormal Language Acquisition and the Modularity of Language" by S. Curtiss in *Linguistics: The Cambridge Survey*, Vol. 2, edited by F. Newmeyer (New York: Cambridge University Press, 1988), pp. 96–116. Chelsea's case is discussed by S. Curtiss in "The Independence and Task-Specificity of Language" in *Interaction in Human Development*, edited by A. Bornstein and J. Bruner (Hillsdale, NJ: Erlbaum, 1989). Christopher is the subject of a book by N. Smith and I. Tsimpli, *The Mind of a Savant: Language Learning and Modularity* (Cambridge, MA: Blackwell, 1995). The examples of sentences produced by speakers who have problems with inflection are from p. 49 of *The Language Instinct* by S. Pinker, cited above.

Exercises for this chapter were prepared by Joyce Hildebrand.

To access this section online, please see the Companion Website at **www.pearsoned.ca/ ogrady**, chapter 10.

# Chapter 11

The model of Communicative Competence is an adaptation of L. Bachman's, *Fundamental Considerations in Language Testing* (Oxford: Oxford University Press, 1990). The Markedness Differential Hypothesis was developed by F. Eckman in "Markedness and the Contrastive Analysis Hypothesis" in *Language Learning* 27:315–30 (1977). The discussion of the Similarity Differential Rate Hypothesis comes from R. Major, "Further Evidence for the Similarity Differential Rate Hypothesis" in J. Leather and A. James, eds., *New Sounds 97* (Klagenfurt, Austria: University of Klagenfurt).

The data from Arabic syllabification come from E. Broselow, "Prosodic Phonology and the Acquisition of a Second Language" in S. Flynn and W. O'Neil, eds., *Linguistic Theory in Second Language Acquisition* (Dordrecht: Kluwer, 1988). The stress data were reported in J. Archibald, *Language Learnability and L2 Phonology* (Dordrecht: Kluwer, 1993). The Null Subject analysis is drawn from L. White, *Universal Grammar and Second Language Acquisition* (Amsterdam: John Benjamins, 1989). The Verb Movement study can be found in L. White, "Adverb Placement in Second Language Acquisition: Some Effects of Positive and Negative Evidence in the Classroom" in *Second Language Research* 7:133–61 (1991). The data on epenthesis versus deletion strategies come from N. Abrahamsson, "Development and Recoverability of L2 Codas" in *Studies in Second Language Acquisition* 25:313–49 (2003).

The L2 morphology data can be found in H. Zobl and J. Liceras, "Functional Categories and Acquisition Order" in *Language Learning* 44(1):159–80 (1994). The discussion of Patty is taken from D. Lardiere, "Mapping Features to Forms in Second Language Acquisition," in J. Archibald, ed., *Second Language Acquisition and Linguistic Theory* (Oxford: Blackwell, 2000). This issue is also discussed in P. Prévost and L. White, "Missing Surface Inflection or Impairment in Second Language Acquisition? Evidence from Tense and Agreement," in *Second Language Research* 16(2):103–33 (2000). The French gender information is discussed in S. Carroll, "Second-Language Acquisition and the Computational Paradigm," in *Language Learning* 39(4):535–94 (1989). The ultimate attainment results for syntax come from Lydia White and

Fred Genesee, "How Native Is Near-Native? The Issue of Ultimate Attainment in Adult Second Language Acquisition," *Second Language Research* 12:238–65 (1996). The discussion of ultimate attainment in phonology comes from Bongarts et al., "Authenticity of Pronunciation in Naturalistic Second Language Acquisition: The Case of Very Advanced Late Learners of Dutch as a Second Language," *Studia Linguistica* 54(2) (2000). The instrumental/integrative distinction comes from R. Gardner, J.B. Day, and P.D. MacIntyre, "Integrative Motivation, Induced Anxiety and Language Learning in a Controlled Environment," in *Studies in Second Language Acquisition* 14(2):197–214 (1992).

The L2 classroom discussion owes much to R. Allwright and K. Bailey, *Focus on the Language Classroom: An Introduction to Classroom Research for Language Teachers* (Cambridge, UK: Cambridge University Press, 1991). The evidence from focus on form was presented by P. Lightbown and N. Spada, "Focus-on-Form and Corrective Feedback in Communicative Language Teaching: Effects on Second Language Learning," in *Studies in Second Language Acquisition* 12(4):429–48 (1990). The discussion of focus-on-form draws on C. Doughty, "Cognitive Underpinnings of Focus on Form," in *Cognition and Second Language Instruction*, edited by Peter Robinson in the Cambridge Applied Linguistics Series (Cambridge, UK: Cambridge University Press, 2001). Bilingual education and French immersion programs are discussed in J. Cummins and M. Swain, *Bilingual Education* (New York: Longman, 1986). The discussion of the role of recasts comes from H. Nicholas, P.M. Lightbown, and N. Spada, "Recasts as Feedback to Language Learners" in *Language Learning* 51(4):719–58 (2001).

To access this section online, please see the Companion Website at **www.pearsoned.ca/ ogrady**, chapter 11.

# Chapter 12

There are many excellent undergraduate textbooks on psycholinguistics. These include *Psycholinguistics* by Joseph Kess (Philadelphia: John Benjamins, 1992) and *Psycholinguistics* by Jean Berko-Gleason and Nan Bernstein Ratner (Philadelphia: Harcourt Brace, 1998). Another excellent source is the *Handbook of Psycholinguistics,* edited by Morton Ann Gernsbacher (New York: Academic Press, 1994). Some of the "slip of the tongue" material in section 12.1.1 is drawn from Victoria Fromkin's chapter on speech production (pp. 272–300) in the Berko-Gleason and Ratner volume cited above.

The discussion of eye-movement data in psycholinguistics was based on the article by K. Rayner and S. Sereno, "Eye Movements in Reading" in the *Handbook of Psycholinguistics,* edited by M.A. Gernsbacher, as well as in the book by K. Rayner and A. Pollatsek, *The Psychology of Reading* (Englewood Cliffs, NJ: Prentice-Hall, 1989).

The material on event-related potentials is discussed in an excellent review article by Marta Kutas and Cyma Van Petten in the Gernsbacher's *Handbook of Psycholinguistics* cited above (pp. 83–133); see p. 103 for a discussion of figure 12.5. The syllable-processing experiment cited in the syllable section was reported in "Phoneme Monitoring, Syllable Monitoring, and Lexical Access" by J. Segui, U. Frauenfelder, and J. Mehler in the *British Journal of Psychology* 72:471–77 (1981) and is discussed by R.E. Remes in "On the Perception of Speech" in the Gernsbacher *Handbook.*

The word-blending studies are reported in a series of studies conducted by Rebecca Treiman; see "The Structure of Spoken Syllables: Evidence from Novel Word Games" in *Cognition* 15:49–74 (1983). A cross-linguistic study using a forced-choice version of these word games is reported in G.E. Wiebe and B.L. Derwing's paper, "A Forced-Choice Blending Task for Testing

Intra-syllabic Break Points in English, Korean, and Taiwanese," in *The Twenty-First LACUS Forum* (Chapel Hill, NC: LACUS, 1994).

The morphological priming experiments are summarized in an article by William Marslen-Wilson, Lorraine Komisarjevsky Tyler, Rachelle Waksler, and Lianne Older, "Morphology and Meaning in the English Mental Lexicon" in *Psychological Review* 101:3–33 (1994). The experiments on selectional restrictions are reported in Libben's article, "Are Morphological Structures Computed During Word Recognition?" in *Journal of Psycholinguistic Research* 22:535–44 (1993) and in Gary Libben's article, "Computing Hierarchical Morphological Structure: A Case Study," in *Journal of Neurolinguistics* 8:49–55 (1994). The priming experiment employing suffixed ambiguous roots (e.g., *barking*) is reported in Roberto G. de Almeida and Gary Libben's article, "Is There a Morphological Parser?" in *Morphology 2000,* edited by W. Dressler and S. Bendjaballah (Philadelphia: John Benjamins, 2001).

The section on the processing of garden path sentences is taken from Lynn Frazier's article, "Sentence Processing: A Tutorial Review," in *Attention and Performance (XII): The Psychology of Reading,* edited by M. Coltheart (London: Lawrence Erlbaum, 1987), 559–96. These sentence types are also discussed in David Caplan's book, *Language: Structure Processing and Disorders* (Cambridge, MA: MIT Press, 1994).

The study of sentence ambiguity was conducted by M.K. Tannenhaus, G.N. Carlson, and M.S. Seidenberg in "Do Listeners Compute Linguistic Representations?" in *Natural Language Parsing,* edited by D.R. Dowty, L. Karttunen, and A.M. Zwicky (New York: Cambridge University Press, 1985).

To access this section online, please see the Companion Website at **www.pearsoned.ca/ ogrady**, chapter 12.

## Chapter 13

Caplan's 1996 book *Language: Structure, Processing and Disorders* (Cambridge, MA: MIT Press) offers a comprehensive overview of the breakdown of language in aphasia and its relation to normal processing. His 1987 book *Neurolinguistics and Linguistic Aphasiology: An Introduction* is an excellent introduction to the field and provides important historical background. A more practical approach to aphasia and its treatment is to be found in J.C. Rosenbek, L.L. Lapointe, and R.T. Wertz's book *Aphasia: A Clinical Approach* (Austin, TX: PRO-ED). The discussion of the MEG technique was based in the overview chapter by A.C. Papnicolaou, P.G. Simos, and L.F.H. Basile in B. Stemmer and H. Whitaker's *Handbook of Neurolinguistics* (referenced below). The discussion of agrammatism was drawn from the rich literature that includes M.-L. Kean's edited volume *Agrammatism* (New York: Academic Press, 1985) and Yosef Grodzinsky's challenging proposals in *Theoretical Perspectives on Language Deficits* (Cambridge, MA: MIT Press, 1990). An alternative approach to Grodzinsky's is well represented by David Caplan and Nancy Hildebrandt's book, *Disorders of Syntactic Comprehension* (Cambridge, MA: MIT Press, 1988). A very readable and insightful book that offers an experiential perspective on aphasic disturbance is Howard Gardner's *The Shattered Mind* (New York: Knopf, 1975).

The material on acquired dyslexia is drawn from *Deep Dyslexia*, edited by M. Coltheart, J. Patterson, and J.C. Marshall (London: Routledge & Kegan Paul, 1980) and *Surface Dyslexia*, edited by K.E. Patterson, J.C. Marshall, and M. Coltheart (Hillsdale, NJ: Lawrence Erlbaum, 1986) as well as Y. Zotterman's book *Dyslexia: Neuronal, Cognitive, and Linguistic Aspects* (Oxford: Pergamon Press, 1982).

Finally, an excellent overview of recent developments in the field of neurolinguistics as a whole is available in the *Handbook of Neurolinguistics*, edited by B. Stremmer and H. Whitaker (New York: Academic Press, 1998).

To access this section online, please see the Companion Website at **www.pearsoned.ca/ ogrady**, chapter 13.

## Chapter 14

For a very thorough guide to variationist methods, see Sali Tagliamonte, *Analysing Sociolinguistic Variation* (New York: Cambridge University Press, 2006). Some information on American English dialects is from Walt Wolfram and Natalie Schilling-Estes, *American English* (Oxford: Blackwell, 1998). Some Canadian lexical items are from the *Canadian Oxford Dictionary*, edited by Katherine Barber (Don Mills, ON: Oxford, 2004). Much of the North American pronunciation information is from the extremely detailed *Atlas of North American English* by William Labov, Sharon Ash, and Charles Boberg (New York: Mouton de Gruyter, 2006).

Information on the pronunciation of *wh* words—and on most central issues in variation theory—is found in J.K. Chambers, Peter Trudgill, and Natalie Schilling-Estes, eds., *The Handbook of Language Variation and Change* (Oxford: Blackwell, 2002). For more on Newfoundland English, consult the *Dictionary of Newfoundland English,* edited by G.M. Story, W.J. Kirwing, and J.D.A. Widdowson (Toronto: University of Toronto Press, 1990). Information on isolated African American communities can be found in Shana Poplack and Sali Tagliamonte, *African American English in the Diaspora* (Oxford: Blackwell, 2001). Detailed social networks information is found in Lesley Milroy, *Language and Social Networks* (Oxford: Blackwell, 1987). The Barbadian English data is from Gerard Van Herk, "Barbadian Lects: Beyond Meso," in Michael Aceto and Jeffrey P. Williams, *Contact Englishes of the Eastern Caribbean* (Amsterdam: John Benjamins, 2003). A great deal of work on class—including the *r*-lessness studies reported here—can be found in William Labov, *Sociolinguistic Patterns* (Philadelphia: University of Pennsylvania Press, 1972). An accessible description of covert prestige is found in Peter Trudgill, *Sociolinguistics: An Introduction to Language and Society* (Toronto: Penguin, 2000), which was also the source of the caste differences material. The discussion of gendered interaction style information is from Deborah Tannen, *You Just Don't Understand: Women and Men in Conversation* (New York: William Morrow, 1990). The Martha's Vineyard material is from one of the very first sociolinguistic studies, reported in William Labov, "The Social Motivation of a Sound Change," in *Word* 19:273–309 (1963). For ethnography of communication, read John Gumperz and Dell Hymes, *Directions in Sociolinguistics: The Ethnography of Communication* (New York: Holt, Rinehart and Winston, 1972).

The ideas behind T and V pronouns are first detailed in Roger Brown and Albert Gilman, "The Pronouns of Power and Solidarity," in *Style in Language*, edited by T. Sebeok (Cambridge, MA: MIT Press, 1960). The classic work on diglossia is Charles A. Ferguson, "Diglossia," in *Word* 15:325–40 (1959). The accommodating Welsh travel agent is described in Nik Coupland, "Accommodation at Work: Some Phonological Data and Their Implications," *International Journal of the Sociology of Language* 46:49–70 (1984). For language myths and more, read Geoffrey K. Pullum, *The Great Eskimo Vocabulary Hoax and Other Irreverent Essays on the Study of Language* (Chicago: University of Chicago Press, 1991).

To access this section online, please see the Companion Website at **www.pearsoned.ca/ ogrady**, chapter 14.

# Chapter 15

Comprehensive surveys of the development of writing and of the world's writing systems are found in the following books: H. Jensen, *Sign, Symbol and Script*, trans. G. Unwin (London: George Allen and Unwin, 1970), I. Gelb, *A Study of Writing* (Chicago: University of Chicago Press, 1952), and John DeFrancis, *Visible Speech: The Diverse Oneness of Writing Systems* (Honolulu: University of Hawaii Press, 1989). The possibility that pure syllabaries may not exist was called to the authors' attention by Prof. W. Poser of the University of Pennsylvania (personal communication). The idea that writing may have originated in record keeping with clay tokens is taken from Denise Schmandt-Besserat, "Two Precursors of Writing: Plain and Complex Tokens," in *The Origins of Writing*, edited by W.M. Senner (Lincoln: University of Nebraska Press, 1989), pp. 27–42.

The discussion of Arabic writing is based on "The Arabic Alphabet" by James A. Bellamy in the book edited by Senner noted above. John DeFrancis (University of Hawaii), Robert Fisher (York University), and Brian King (University of British Columbia) all provided insightful and helpful comments (especially regarding Chinese writing)—so many, in fact, that we were not able to make use of all of them here. Their views are not necessarily those reflected in the chapter, however. The discussion of Chinese writing is derived from DeFrancis (in the book cited above); the presentation of Japanese writing is also indebted to DeFrancis, as well as to M. Shibatani, *The Languages of Japan* (Cambridge, UK: Cambridge University Press, 1990). For a discussion of Cherokee writing, see "Native American Writing Systems" by W. Walker, in *Language in the USA*, edited by C. Ferguson et al. (New York: Cambridge University Press, 1981). Our presentation of the Cree syllabary is from D.H. Pentland, *Nēhiyawasinahikēwin: A Standard Orthography for the Cree Language*, Revised Ed. (Calgary: Dept. of Linguistics, University of Calgary, 1978). David H. Kelley of the University of Calgary provided corrective and helpful advice on Mayan and other Mesoamerican writing. The examples of Northern Indian pictorial script are from John Marshall, *Mohenjo-Daro and the Indus Civilization* (London: A. Probsthain, 1931).

The discussion of the history of English spelling is based on *A History of English Spelling* by D.G. Scragg (New York: Barnes & Noble, 1974). The examples of spelling rules sensitive to morphological structure come from the book by D.W. Cummings, *American English Spelling* (Baltimore: The Johns Hopkins University Press, 1988). Data on children's ability to segment words into syllables and phonemes comes from I.Y. Liberman, reported in the book by E. Gibson and H. Levin, *The Psychology of Reading* (Cambridge, MA: MIT Press, 1975). John Sören Pettersson of Uppsala University commented extensively and helpfully on an earlier version of this chapter.

To access this section online, please see the Companion Website at **www.pearsoned.ca/ ogrady**, chapter 15.

# Language Index

# Index

*Notes:* Page ranges in **bold** refer to the main discussion of a topic. ERP stands for "event-related potential"; L1, for "first language"'; L2, for "second language."